Ethical AI Solutions for Addressing Social Media Influence and Hate Speech

Swati Chakraborty
Concordia University, Canada

IGI Global
Scientific Publishing
Publishing Tomorrow's Research Today

Published in the United States of America by
IGI Global Scientific Publishing
701 East Chocolate Avenue
Hershey, PA, 17033, USA
Tel: 717-533-8845
Fax: 717-533-8661
Website: https://www.igi-global.com E-mail: cust@igi-global.com

Library of Congress Cataloging-in-Publication Data

Names: Chakraborty, Swati, 1985- editor
Title: Ethical AI solutions for addressing social media influence and hate speech / Swati Chakraborty.
Description: Hershey, PA : IGI Global Scientific Publishing, [2025] | Includes bibliographical references and index. | Summary: "While social media has numerous benefits, there are also concerns about the negative impact it can have on individuals and society, including the spread of misinformation, polarization, and cyberbullying. The use of ethical AI can help create a positive social media impact by addressing these concerns"-- Provided by publisher.
Identifiers: LCCN 2024054384 (print) | LCCN 2024054385 (ebook) | ISBN 9798369399040 hardcover | ISBN 9798369399057 paperback | ISBN 9798369399064 ebook
Subjects: LCSH: Online hate speech | Social media and society | Artificial intelligence
Classification: LCC HM851 .E79 2025 (print) | LCC HM851 (ebook) | DDC 175--dc23/eng/20250304
LC record available at https://lccn.loc.gov/2024054384
LC ebook record available at https://lccn.loc.gov/2024054385

British Cataloguing in Publication Data
A Cataloguing in Publication record for this book is available from the British Library.

Table of Contents

Detailed Table of Contents

The convergence of artificial intelligence (AI) and social media has led to a new age of information warfare, marked by the rapid dissemination, manipulation, and strategic orchestration of information to impact public opinion on a global scale. This research delves into the complicated connection between these technologies and their profound implications for contemporary conflicts. AI serves as a robust instrument in the hands of information warriors. Its applications extend to the creation of hyper realistic deepfakes to manipulate public perception, the analysis of vast datasets to measure sentiment and target specific crowd, the automation of propaganda dissemination through bot networks, and the surveillance of online task to identify potential targets for influence operations. Social media platforms, characterized by immense user bases, real-time engagement, and viral potential, have surfaced as the primary battlegrounds for these information wars.

The proliferation of social media and online forums has democratized discourse but also led to an alarming rise in incivility, hate speech, and toxic interactions. Historically, the approach to addressing these issues has been reactive—identifying and removing harmful content after it has already caused damage. However, advances in artificial intelligence (AI) present an opportunity to shift from reactive to proactive strategies for fostering civility and respect in online discussions. This paper examines the evolution of AI-driven content moderation tools and explores how they can be leveraged to not only detect and filter inappropriate content but also encourage respectful engagement. By emphasizing preemptive interventions, AI can become a powerful force in shaping healthier online communities.

Artificial intelligence (AI) is a cornerstone of modern technology, driving advances in automation, decision-making, and innovation in many fields. While AI offers significant benefits, it also raises concerns that it could harm humanity if misused or poorly designed. This article takes a closer look at the ways in which artificial intelligence can negatively impact humans, from invasions of personal privacy and financial security to impacts on mental health and physical safety. By analyzing real-world case studies, this discussion highlights the ethical dilemmas surrounding AI adoption. The paper further proposes strategies and frameworks to ensure that AI is aligned with human values, and advocates responsible development and regulation to reduce risks. Ultimately, this research strikes a balance between harnessing the potential of AI and preventing unintended consequences, fostering a future where AI serves humanity rather than destroys it.

Artificial Intelligence has the potential to change the world by facilitating progress in health, education, climate action, and economic development. But, without proper and ethical use, AI seeps into the fabric of societal malice and makes glasshouses in paradise even more glistening. AI can serve both as a butter and gun for the public. It tackles issues including algorithmic bias, digital divide, and data poverty; meanwhile it mentions community-driven AI building as a method to guarantee inclusion and cultural appropriateness. Strategic elements of policy frameworks such as the EU's AI Act are considered essential to responsibly govern AI, while bottom-up approaches and grassroots initiatives show how the nature of participatory design can be powerful. It urges a joint enterprise by governments, corporations and civil society to create a future with AI that serves the most marginalized populations and functions as an engine for equity. An inclusive approach is crucial to ensure that the choices we make today drive the impact of AI in a direction that advances society.

The rapid growth of digital platforms has highlighted the need for robust content moderation systems that manage large content volumes while addressing human moderators' mental health. This study explores AI's evolving role in content moderation, emphasizing collaboration with human moderators for nuanced judgments. AI can identify harmful content trends, but human oversight is needed for contextual accuracy. However, AI raises ethical issues, such as bias from prejudiced training data, potentially harming marginalized groups. To improve accountability, the study suggests using diverse datasets, transparent decision-making, and explainable AI. Regulatory frameworks and mental health support for moderators are also essential for fair, transparent content moderation.

The authenticity and the orientation of information in social media require designing a complex information system to analyze the artifacts that may cause a positive or negative impact on the peace order of the global societal structure. Social cyber security is a new paradigm that is gaining momentum worldwide; every country is investing in capacity-building measures, R&D, and strategies to combat the menace of the problem caused by the abundance of manipulative information. Societal cyber security has become a multi-million-dollar market because economic change has monetized data, and it is a top priority for every government to ensure that the digital society is secure and safe. Therefore, it is pertinent to find a framework that can help detect information that can negatively impact society at large. In this paper, we are using machine learning techniques for classification in a fusion dataset of manipulative information that has been concatenated with the benchmark dataset. The subclasses are real news without hate speech, real news with hate speech, fake news with hate speech, and fake news without hate speech. The application of this

This chapter traverse how artificial intelligence is transforming hate speech detection by facilitating real-time detection and response. It focuses on the technical aspects of using machine learning. Natural language processing and deep learning models to identify and mark spiteful content. This chapter also discusses the advantages, obstacles, and ethical considerations associated with using AI to moderate online speech. The ultimate objective is to provide insights into how AI is changing the landscape of content moderation on platforms around the world.

This study investigates the performance of AI in detecting HS in diverse cultural and contextual settings. Existing AI models, trained primarily on English datasets, struggle with regional dialects, idiomatic phrases, and cultural nuances. A systematic review of NLP techniques, including traditional methods (n-grams, Bag of Words) and advanced architectures (BERT, GPT, RoBERTa, CNNs, LSTMs), evaluates their effectiveness. Multilingual models like mBERT and XLM-R are assessed for low-resource scenarios while emerging trends like multimodal learning (CLIP) and adversarial training (GANs) are explored for robustness. Challenges such as data bias, false positives, and cultural insensitivity are addressed through contextual embeddings, data augmentation, and Pragmatics-oriented NLP. Metrics like precision, recall, and F1-score reveal significant accuracy drops in non-English contexts. The study emphasizes culturally aware datasets, Explainable AI (LIME, SHAP), and hybrid AI-human moderation to ensure ethical, inclusive online spaces.

With advancement of technological tools, the role of Artificial Intelligence (AI) in maintaining and improving social media platforms is becoming intriguing by each passing day. From content moderation to sentiment analyzing the AI tools are integrated in the day-to-day operations of social media platforms to curate the customized experience to enhance the users' interaction on the platforms. The

Preface

INTRODUCTION

Social media has revolutionized the way people communicate, connect, and consume information. While social media has numerous benefits, there are also concerns about the negative impact it can have on individuals and society, including the spread of misinformation, polarization, and cyberbullying. The use of ethical AI can help create a positive social media impact by addressing these concerns. India is a diverse country with a long history of interreligious dialogue. The country has a rich tradition of religious pluralism and tolerance, with Hinduism, Islam, Christianity, Sikhism, Buddhism, and Jainism among the major religions practiced in the country. However, there have also been instances of interreligious conflict and tension, particularly in recent years, fueled by factors such as political polarization, religious fundamentalism, and socio-economic disparities.

In this context, this edited volume on interreligious dialogue can play a crucial role in countering hate speech and promoting dialogue in India. The program is designed to equip participants with the skills and knowledge needed to engage in interreligious dialogue and promote peace and understanding in their communities.

Thanks to technological advancements, the method that education and training are given has been permanently altered. Online learning has developed into a versatile teaching method that allows students to conveniently access study materials from the comfort of their homes. Online learning also offers a great alternative for students who are unable to enroll in traditional programs and allows them the freedom to explore at their own pace.

OBJECTIVE OF THE BOOK

To analyze the research on the application of Ethical AI for creating social media impact and countering hate speech, you would need a comprehensive research methodology that encompasses both qualitative and quantitative approaches. Below is a structured methodology that you can follow:

Research Objectives

1. Primary Objective: To investigate how Ethical AI can be applied to create social media impact and effectively counter hate speech.
2. Secondary Objectives:
    - To evaluate the effectiveness of existing Ethical AI models in detecting and countering hate speech.
    - To understand the challenges in implementing Ethical AI on social media platforms.
    - To explore the ethical implications and biases associated with AI in the context of social media.

Social media has transformed how people interact, share ideas, and access information, making the world more connected than ever. However, it also brings challenges such as misinformation, divisive content, and cyberbullying, which can harm individuals and societies. Leveraging ethical AI on social media platforms can address these challenges by promoting accurate information, reducing polarization, and fostering safe online environments. By curating content responsibly, AI can ensure social media becomes a positive force for engagement and understanding.

India, known for its religious diversity and a history of pluralism, faces increasing interreligious tensions exacerbated by socio-economic inequalities, political agendas, and extremism. Addressing these issues requires innovative approaches, including initiatives promoting interreligious dialogue. Edited volumes on the subject can serve as crucial tools, encouraging dialogue, countering hate speech, and advocating mutual respect among communities. Such efforts are essential to preserving India's tradition of coexistence and mitigating the risks posed by rising polarization.

Technological advances, especially in online learning, have revolutionized education delivery methods, making them accessible and inclusive. By breaking geographical barriers, online platforms empower learners to access knowledge anytime, anywhere, at their own pace. This flexibility benefits students unable to attend traditional classrooms and allows personalized learning journeys. Such technological tools can also facilitate training in interreligious dialogue, enabling widespread access to knowledge that fosters peace and understanding in diverse societies.

Chapter 1 discussed the convergence of artificial intelligence (AI) and social media has ushered in a new era of information warfare, where the rapid creation, manipulation, and strategic use of information shape public opinion on a global scale. This research explores the intricate interplay between these technologies and their far-reaching implications for modern conflicts. AI has become a powerful tool in the arsenal of information warfare. Its capabilities include generating hyper-realistic deepfakes to distort public perception, analyzing massive datasets to gauge sentiment and strategically target specific audiences, automating the spread of propaganda through bot networks, and monitoring online activities to identify potential targets for influence operations. These applications demonstrate how AI amplifies the scale and precision of information campaigns, raising significant ethical and security concerns. Social media platforms, with their vast user bases, real-time interactions, and potential for viral content, have emerged as the primary battlegrounds in this landscape. The ability to instantly reach and influence millions makes these platforms both a tool and a target in the fight to control narratives, underscoring the urgent need for regulatory frameworks and ethical AI deployment to mitigate the risks of information warfare.

Chapter 2 illustrates the rise of social media and online forums has democratized public discourse, enabling diverse voices to connect and share ideas. However, this openness has also fuelled an alarming increase in incivility, hate speech, and toxic interactions. Traditionally, efforts to address these challenges have been reactive—removing harmful content only after it has inflicted damage. Advances in artificial intelligence (AI), however, offer the potential to transform content moderation from a reactive process into a proactive approach that fosters civility and respect in digital spaces. This paper explores the evolution of AI-powered content moderation tools and their growing ability to address harmful online behavior. Beyond merely detecting and filtering inappropriate content, modern AI systems can analyze patterns, predict potential conflicts, and intervene pre-emptively to de-escalate tensions. By incorporating these capabilities, AI can help create online environments that promote constructive and respectful communication. Shifting toward proactive interventions positions AI as a vital tool in shaping healthier digital ecosystems. By focusing on preventing toxicity rather than merely responding to it, AI has the potential to redefine the standards of online engagement and support the development of communities built on mutual respect and understanding.

Chapter 3 demonstrates that the advancements in communication technology, social media has emerged as a powerful platform for connection and deliberation. However, it has also become a breeding ground for hate speech and toxic content. This chapter delves into the role of ethical AI in moderating hate speech within an increasingly polarized social media landscape. Hate speech is not just a technological concern but a global issue impacting social harmony, human rights, and the freedom of expression and press. This underscores the urgent need for anti-hate speech technologies grounded in strong ethical principles. The chapter examines hate speech through legal, ethical, and social lenses, exploring its far-reaching effects on individuals and society. It unpacks the mechanisms by which hate speech circulates, analyzing the sophisticated methods employed in its proliferation. These include the functions and decision-making processes of algorithms, the dynamics of echo chambers, and the principles that drive virality on digital platforms. By addressing the complexities of hate speech in the context of modern communication technologies, the chapter highlights the need for a nuanced approach to content moderation. It advocates for the integration of ethical AI systems designed not only to counteract hate speech effectively but also to uphold the values of free speech and societal cohesion in digital spaces.

Chapter 4 identifies the interconnected nature of social media can create echo chambers where extremist views are amplified, reinforcing individuals' beliefs and isolating them from alternative perspectives. Platforms such as YouTube and Twitter have played a significant role in spreading radical content, with algorithms often prioritizing incendiary material for broader visibility. This amplification not only normalizes extremist rhetoric but also deepens ideological divides, making it more challenging to counter harmful narratives. The online environment has also become a powerful tool for recruiting vulnerable individuals, particularly among the youth. Extremist groups exploit the search for identity, purpose, or community, targeting young people with tailored, sophisticated strategies. Through memes, videos, and influencer-like campaigns, they glamorize radical ideologies, portraying them as heroic or aspirational. This approach resonates deeply with individuals facing personal challenges or societal marginalization, drawing them into extremist movements. The phenomenon of online extremism transcends any single ideology, manifesting across political, religious, and social spectrums. The recruitment of marginalized youth, in particular, has led to a concerning rise in participation in radical activities. Addressing this issue requires a multi-faceted approach, combining technological solutions with educational initiatives and community support to counteract the appeal of extremism in digital spaces.

Chapter 5 discusses Fairness underscores the importance of designing AI systems that actively avoid perpetuating bias or discrimination. Algorithms, if not carefully managed, can unintentionally reflect and amplify societal prejudices. This concern is particularly pressing in social media, where biased algorithms may result in unequal treatment of users based on factors such as race, gender, or socio-economic status, thereby undermining the diversity of voices on these platforms. To counter this, developers must prioritize inclusivity by creating algorithms that ensure equitable access to information and opportunities for all users. Equally important is the principle of accountability, which demands that organizations and developers take full responsibility for the outcomes of their AI systems. This includes not only designing systems with ethical considerations but also addressing any adverse effects or failures that may arise from their deployment. Accountability reinforces the commitment to ethical AI, ensuring that the technology serves society fairly and responsibly. Transparency is another critical element, essential for building trust between users and AI systems. By openly communicating how AI operates and the decisions it makes, developers can foster a sense of trust and confidence among users. Together, fairness, accountability, and transparency form the foundation for creating ethical AI systems that promote equity and trust in the digital age.

Chapter 6 examines the social media has become a vital tool for businesses to engage with customers and promote new products and services. Its widespread use has significantly influenced consumer behavior, as platforms now host countless consumption-related interactions. These interactions have reshaped the traditional brand-consumer relationship, shifting the balance of power toward consumers who can easily consult and influence one another through reviews, recommendations, and discussions. This transformation has empowered consumers, giving them greater control over how they interact with brands and make purchasing decisions. Social media enables real-time feedback and peer consultations, fundamentally altering how brands build trust and loyalty. The era of one-way marketing is giving way to a dynamic, consumer-driven dialogue where businesses must adapt to stay relevant and competitive. The current research explores these shifts in consumer behavior and offers actionable recommendations for retailers. It emphasizes the importance of integrating social media strategies to effectively engage audiences, foster meaningful connections, and leverage the power of user-generated content to build stronger, more responsive relationships with their customers.

Chapter 7 identifies Artificial intelligence (AI) has become a cornerstone of modern technology, driving breakthroughs in automation, decision-making, and innovation across various domains. While the benefits of AI are undeniable, its rapid development also raises concerns about potential harm to humanity if it is misused or poorly designed. This article examines the negative impacts of AI, ranging from breaches of personal privacy and financial security to its effects on mental health and physical safety. Through real-world case studies, the discussion highlights the ethical dilemmas that arise with AI adoption, emphasizing the need for caution and foresight in its development and deployment. These examples shed light on how unchecked AI can exacerbate societal inequalities, amplify biases, and create unforeseen risks, underscoring the importance of addressing these challenges proactively. The paper proposes strategies and frameworks to ensure AI remains aligned with human values, advocating for responsible innovation, robust regulation, and ethical oversight. By balancing the immense potential of AI with measures to mitigate its risks, this research envisions a future where AI acts as a tool to enhance human well-being rather than jeopardize it, fostering a safer and more equitable technological landscape.

Chapter 8 converses about the rapid expansion of digital platforms have underscored the urgent need for effective content moderation systems capable of managing vast volumes of content while safeguarding the mental health of human moderators. This study examines the evolving role of AI in content moderation, emphasizing the importance of collaboration between AI systems and human moderators to ensure nuanced and context-sensitive decision-making. While AI excels at identifying harmful content trends, human oversight remains crucial for interpreting context and ensuring fairness. However, the use of AI in content moderation raises significant ethical concerns. Bias in training data can lead to discriminatory outcomes, disproportionately affecting marginalized groups. Addressing these issues requires proactive measures to ensure that AI systems are equitable and just. The study advocates for the use of diverse datasets, transparent decision-making processes, and explainable AI to improve accountability and build trust in AI-driven content moderation. In addition to technological solutions, the study highlights the need for comprehensive regulatory frameworks and robust mental health support for human moderators. By combining technological innovation with ethical practices and human-centric policies, platforms can create content moderation systems that are fair, transparent, and supportive of all stakeholders involved.

Chapter 9 discusses Artificial Intelligence (AI) has the potential to transform the world by driving progress in critical areas such as healthcare, education, climate action, and economic development. However, without ethical oversight and responsible use, AI can exacerbate societal inequalities, embedding biases and deepening divides. While AI holds the power to empower communities and solve complex challenges, it also risks becoming a double-edged sword—offering tools for growth and inclusion while simultaneously amplifying systemic issues. This discussion highlights key challenges such as algorithmic bias, the digital divide, and data poverty, while advocating for community-driven AI development to ensure inclusion and cultural relevance. Policy frameworks like the EU's AI Act are recognized as essential for responsibly governing AI. Simultaneously, grassroots initiatives and participatory design emphasize the importance of bottom-up approaches, empowering marginalized communities to shape AI systems that reflect their needs and values. The article underscores the need for a collaborative effort among governments, corporations, and civil society to create AI that functions as an engine for equity. By prioritizing inclusivity and social justice, we can ensure that the choices made today steer AI's impact toward advancing society as a whole, particularly for those most vulnerable. This balanced approach aligns AI with the principles of fairness and shared progress, positioning it as a transformative force for good.

Chapter 10 relates the authenticity and the orientation of information in social media requires designing a complex information system to analyze the artifacts that may cause the positive or negative impact in the peace order of global societal structure. Social cyber security is a new paradigm which is gaining momentum across the world; every country is investing in capacity building measures, R&D and strategies to combat the menace of the problem caused due to abundance of manipulative information. Therefore, it is pertinent to find out a framework that can help in detection of information that can negatively impact the society at large. In this paper, we are using machine learning techniques for classification in a fusion dataset of manipulative information that has been concatenated with the benchmark dataset. Fake news with hate speech and fake news without hate speech. The application of this framework is to be used to mitigate the threat to society through widespread use of manipulative information and help the society to be resilient against such threats.

Chapter 11 describes the legal frameworks surrounding AI in online content moderation are evolving to address the complex intersection of technology, ethics, and law. While AI has the potential to effectively combat harmful content such as hate speech, misinformation, and harassment, it also introduces risks related to censorship, algorithmic bias, and infringements on user rights. Balancing free expression with user safety remains a critical challenge, requiring legal structures that promote transparency, accountability, and fairness. Existing laws often fall short in addressing these nuanced issues, necessitating the development of robust, context-aware regulations that align with human rights principles. National and regional regulations play a significant role in shaping the use of AI for content moderation. The European Union's **Digital Services Act (DSA)**, for instance, mandates increased transparency from platforms about their content moderation processes, including the use of automated tools. Similarly, the **California Consumer Privacy Act (CCPA)** emphasizes user privacy, indirectly influencing how AI moderation tools are implemented. However, inconsistent standards across countries create challenges for global platforms operating in multiple jurisdictions, leading to fragmented approaches to governance. A unified international framework could help address these inconsistencies, establishing baseline standards for AI-driven moderation. Such a framework would need to focus on critical elements like algorithmic accountability, non-discrimination, and privacy protection. Additionally, it should encourage collaboration between governments, tech companies, and civil society to ensure inclusivity and adaptability to diverse cultural contexts. By harmonizing legal and ethical standards, a global approach can foster the responsible deployment of AI in content moderation, ensuring it becomes a force for positive, equitable digital engagement.

Chapter 12 identifies the application of AI for real-time moderation of hate speech on social media platforms has shown significant promise in addressing the limitations of traditional content moderation methods. Traditional moderation often relies heavily on human moderators, who are tasked with reviewing vast amounts of user-generated content. This process can be slow, inconsistent, and prone to human error. AI, powered by machine learning frameworks such as TensorFlow and PyTorch, enables the real-time processing of massive volumes of data, allowing for rapid identification of harmful content. By leveraging natural language processing (NLP) techniques, AI models can understand context, detect subtle variations of hate speech, and flag content with high accuracy, enhancing the efficiency of moderation systems. However, the use of AI in real-time moderation is not without its challenges. One of the primary concerns is the bias in AI training datasets, which can lead to discriminatory outcomes or the wrongful flagging of content. Since AI models are only as good as the data they are trained on, biased datasets can result in disproportionately affecting certain groups or misinterpreting context. Furthermore, AI systems are not infallible—they may fail to recognize certain forms of hate speech, especially those that are nuanced or context-dependent.

Chapter 13 reflects the Artificial Intelligence (AI) is reshaping the future of hate speech detection by enabling real-time identification and response, marking a significant departure from traditional, reactive content moderation techniques. Leveraging cutting-edge machine learning, natural language processing (NLP), and deep learning models, AI systems can analyze vast amounts of user-generated content instantaneously. These technologies allow platforms to detect subtle and context-dependent instances of hate speech, including coded language and slang, with unprecedented speed and precision. By automating these processes, AI reduces reliance on human moderators, ensuring faster and more consistent intervention while minimizing the exposure of moderators to harmful content. Despite its advantages, AI-driven hate speech detection faces several technical and ethical challenges. Bias in training datasets, for example, can lead to skewed moderation outcomes, disproportionately targeting or neglecting specific user groups or contexts. Deep learning models may struggle to interpret nuanced speech or cultural differences, resulting in misclassification or over-policing of legitimate discourse.

Chapter 14 investigates the performance of AI in detecting HS in diverse cultural and contextual settings. Existing AI models, trained primarily on English datasets, struggle with regional dialects, idiomatic phrases, and cultural nuances. A systematic review of NLP techniques, including traditional methods (n-grams, Bag of Words) and advanced architectures (BERT, GPT, RoBERTa, CNNs, LSTMs), evaluates their effectiveness. Multilingual models like mBERT and XLM-R are assessed for low-resource scenarios while emerging trends like multimodal learning (CLIP) and adversarial training (GANs) are explored for robustness. Challenges such as data bias, false positives, and cultural insensitivity are addressed through contextual embeddings, data augmentation, and Pragmatics-oriented NLP. Metrics like precision, recall, and F1-score reveal significant accuracy drops in non-English contexts. The study emphasizes culturally aware datasets, Explainable AI (LIME, SHAP), and hybrid AI-human moderation to ensure ethical, inclusive online spaces.

Chapter 15 reflects with advancement of technological tools, the role of Artificial Intelligence (AI) in maintaining and improving social media platforms is becoming intriguing by each passing day. From content moderation to sentiment analysing the AI tools are integrated in the day-to-day operations of social media platforms to curate the customized experience to enhance the users' interaction on the platforms. The chapter explores the various AI tools and software understanding their models and functioning to regulate the social media governance. It aims to investigate the influence of AI tools from content creation, marketing advertisements to impact on users' behavior. While discussing the positives of the AI involvement, the chapter also discusses the possible challenges of maintaining user privacy, data security and regulation of fake news. Understanding the role of collaborating governance, the author analyzed various statutes around the world to deal with ethical and legal implications of the AI in social media governance to suggest amicable solutions and way forward.

Chapter 16 identifies those advancements in communication medium and the proliferation of social media led to increasing amount of content shared often without moderation. The offensive is raising significantly, posing threat to mental health, and degrades the user experience. Current study focuses on identifying and censoring audio clips with offensive and foul words. We propose a novel audio censoring method using OpenAI's whisper model. The audio files are extracted from video and forwarded to whisper model. The text transcripts of the audio file are obtained through the whisper model. Keywords from the text are compared with a dictionary of offensive and foul words to detect such terms in the input audio. The matched foul words are identified, and respective audio are censored, and beep tone is inserted. Finally, the censored audio is integrated, and video is generated. The proposed system is tested using dataset retrieved from YouTube and the has shown significant performance and achieves accuracy of 93.81%, shows the robustness of proposed foul word identification and censoring system.

Chapter 17 examines hate speech is a serious social problem, disrupts social order, impairs individual well-being, and threatens democracy, emonize individuals or groups based on attributes like race, religion, caste ethnicity, gender or sexual orientation, appears in many forms: in spoken language, written materials, symbols and online posts. With the advent of social media, the reach and impact of hate speech has increased exponentially, making it an ever-pressing issue of the digital age included legislative measures, education awareness campaigns, the increasing prevalence of harmful content online has led to the exploration of artificial intelligence (AI) as the tool to be used to detect and mitigate hate speech online. The paper concludes that preserves ethical concepts in the design and implementation of the AI-driven systems. It points to policies that empower responsible innovation without undermining fundamental democratic values. Through creating inclusive digital spaces and advocating for rights and freedoms for developing socially responsible, inclusivity and respect for individual liberties.

Chapter 18 discusses the rapid expansion of social media has transformed global communication and information sharing, fostering unprecedented connectivity. However, these platforms have also become hubs for the spread of fake news and hate speech, which threatens social cohesion. This article explores AI's dual role in combating fake news and hate speech on social media platforms in India. While AI offers promising solutions for detecting and reducing harmful content, it raises ethical and social concerns that may aggravate existing societal tensions. The analysis emphasizes the need for a balanced approach that effectively manages harmful content while preserving freedom of speech and avoiding excessive censorship. It also discusses the potential for AI to evolve into a more ethical, inclusive, and culturally sensitive tool within India's dynamic digital landscape, and highlights the importance of interdisciplinary collaboration among AI developers, policymakers, and social scientists to ensure that AI technologies serve both technological innovation and social equity.

Additionally, AI systems may inadvertently suppress freedom of expression, raising concerns about censorship. These obstacles highlight the need for continuous refinement of AI models, transparent algorithms, and the inclusion of diverse data sources to build fairer and more effective moderation systems. As AI technologies evolve, they are fundamentally altering the landscape of content moderation across global platforms. The integration of real-time detection tools not only improves user safety but also sets new standards for accountability and responsiveness in digital spaces. However, achieving the balance between protecting users from harm and preserving their right to free speech requires careful consideration of ethical principles and robust oversight mechanisms. By addressing these challenges, AI can serve as a transformative force in creating healthier and more inclusive online communities worldwide. This highlights the critical need for human oversight to ensure ethical practices in content moderation, where human moderators can intervene when necessary to correct mistakes or assess the intent behind flagged content. The research underscores the importance of a balanced approach to content moderation, where AI capabilities complement human judgment rather than replace it. While AI can significantly enhance the speed and efficiency of detecting hate speech, human oversight remains crucial for ensuring that moderation practices respect users' right to free speech and avoid overreach. The integration of both AI and human judgment can create a more effective and ethical moderation system, fostering safer online environments without compromising individual freedoms. This study contributes to broader discussions about how to ethically deploy AI technologies in online platforms, highlighting the need for transparency, fairness, and accountability in moderation practices.

In conclusion, social media has undeniably transformed the way we interact and access information, offering both immense opportunities and significant challenges. While the potential for connection and empowerment is vast, concerns such as misinformation, polarization, and cyberbullying must be proactively addressed. Ethical AI emerges as a vital tool to mitigate these issues, fostering a safer and more inclusive digital environment.

India's historical commitment to religious pluralism and interfaith harmony provides a solid foundation for initiatives aimed at countering hate speech and promoting interreligious dialogue. However, contemporary challenges like political polarization and socio-economic disparities demand renewed efforts to bridge divides and cultivate understanding. This edited volume on interreligious dialogue serves as a timely resource, equipping individuals with the knowledge and skills to foster peace and unity in their communities.

Furthermore, advancements in technology, particularly online learning, have revolutionized education, making it accessible to a broader audience. The flexibility of online platforms allows learners to tailor their educational journeys, empowering individuals from diverse backgrounds to acquire the skills needed to address pressing societal issues, including those discussed in this volume. Together, these efforts underscore the transformative potential of education, technology, and dialogue in building a more harmonious and equitable society.

Acknowledgment

The successful completion of this edited volume is the result of the collective efforts, guidance, and support of many individuals and organizations. It is with deep gratitude that I acknowledge their invaluable contributions.

First and foremost, I extend my heartfelt thanks to the contributors of this volume, whose insightful chapters and rigorous research have enriched the content. Your dedication to advancing understanding in the areas of ethical AI, interreligious dialogue, and social media impact is deeply appreciated.

I am immensely grateful to the reviewers and advisors who provided constructive feedback and guidance throughout the editorial process. Your expertise has ensured the quality and relevance of this work.

A special note of gratitude goes to the publishers for their unwavering support and for providing me with a platform to bring this book to fruition.

I would like to acknowledge the institutions and organizations that have supported this endeavor, including academic institutions, research centers, and social advocacy groups. Your encouragement and resources have been instrumental in making this work possible.

On a personal note, I thank my family and friends for their patience and understanding during the long hours devoted to this project. Your unwavering support has been my cornerstone.

Finally, I am deeply indebted to all the individuals and communities who continue to inspire efforts toward ethical AI, countering hate speech, and fostering interreligious dialogue. This book is dedicated to the vision of creating a more inclusive, tolerant, and just world.

Thank you all for being part of this journey.

Acknowledgment

Chapter 1
The New Frontline:
AI and Social Media in Information Warfare

Anjali Dixit
https://orcid.org/0009-0003-7364-0404
SRM University, India

ABSTRACT

The convergence of artificial intelligence (AI) and social media has led to a new age of information warfare, marked by the rapid dissemination, manipulation, and strategic orchestration of information to impact public opinion on a global scale. This research delves into the complicated connection between these technologies and their profound implications for contemporary conflicts. AI serves as a robust instrument in the hands of information warriors. Its applications extend to the creation of hyper realistic deepfakes to manipulate public perception, the analysis of vast datasets to measure sentiment and target specific crowd, the automation of propaganda dissemination through bot networks, and the surveillance of online task to identify potential targets for influence operations. Social media platforms, characterized by immense user bases, real-time engagement, and viral potential, have surfaced as the primary battlegrounds for these information wars.

INTRODUCTION

Warfare has undergone dramatic changes throughout history, evolving from primitive conflicts between nomadic tribes to complex, technologically advanced conflicts. This evolution has been driven by a number of factors, including technological advancements, social change, and shifts in the geopolitical landscape. In

DOI: 10.4018/979-8-3693-9904-0.ch001

recent decades, the nature of warfare has changed once again, with information-centric warfare emerging as a dominant paradigm.

Information warfare is a strategic tool that involves using information and communication technology to attack, disrupt or manipulate an adversary's information systems, infrastructure or decision-making processes. It is a growing concern due to the increasing reliance on digital technology and the Internet. Information warfare can be used to undermine military capabilities, influence public opinion, destabilise governments and gain competitive advantage. Addressing the challenges posed by information warfare requires a multi-faceted approach, including improving cybersecurity, developing counter-propaganda strategies, building resilience and international cooperation.

The role of AI in modern conflict dynamics is growing very fast. It can be used for autonomous weapon systems, cyber warfare, intelligence analysis and logistics. However, its use also raises ethical concerns, such as the potential for bias, discrimination and loss of human control. It is essential to ensure that AI is developed and used responsibly to promote peace and security.

Social media platforms have emerged as a key tool in modern AI driven information warfare, capable of influencing public opinion, undermining democratic processes, and destabilizing governments. By disseminating misinformation, launching cyberattacks, and recruiting supporters, malicious actors can exploit the reach and accessibility of these platforms to achieve their objectives.

A comprehensive approach is necessary to mitigate the risks associated with social media in AI driven information warfare. This includes enhancing digital literacy, improving cybersecurity, strengthening international cooperation, and developing effective counter-propaganda strategies. By addressing these challenges, nations can better protect their national security and promote democratic values in the digital age.

UNDERSTANDING CONCEPTS

- **ARTIFICIAL INTELLIGENCE -** John McCarthy (1927–2011) is called the “father of artificial intelligence”. He was an American computer and cognitive scientist, he made significant contributions to both Artificial Intelligence and computer science.

Artificial Intelligence (AI) is a domain of computer science which deals with the. development of intelligent computer systems, which are capable to perceive, analyze, and react accordingly to the inputs.[1]

It is a set of technologies that enable computers to perform a diverse range of advanced tasks, including the ability to perceive, understand, and translate spoken and written language, analyze data, make recommendations, etc.

● AI-DRIVEN SOCIAL MEDIA PLATFORMS

AI-driven social media refers to the utilization of artificial intelligence to enhance and optimize social media platforms. By leveraging machine learning algorithms and natural language processing, these platforms can provide personalized content recommendations, improve user engagement, and enhance security features.

Artificial Intelligence (AI) has revolutionized social media platforms, enhancing user experiences through personalized content recommendations, efficient search functionalities, and improved engagement features. However, the widespread adoption of AI in social media has also introduced significant security challenges and opportunities.

Opportunities:

- **Tu Content Moderation:** AI can be used to automate content moderation processes, identifying and removing harmful content such as hate speech, harassment, and misinformation more effectively.
- **Improved User Safety:** AI-powered tools can detect and prevent cyberbullying, online harassment, and other forms of abuse, enhancing the overall safety of social media platforms.
- **Personalized Engagement:** AI can be used to tailor content recommendations to individual users, improving engagement and fostering meaningful connections.

Security Challenges:

- **Misinformation and Deepfakes:** AI-powered tools can be used to generate and disseminate misleading or false information, including deepfakes, which can manipulate public opinion and undermine trust in institutions.
- **Data Privacy and Surveillance:** The vast amount of data collected by social media platforms, combined with AI-driven analytics, raises concerns about data privacy and surveillance. Malicious actors can exploit this data to target individuals or groups for manipulation or harm.

- **Algorithmic Bias:** AI algorithms can learn from the data they are fed, which means that if the data is biased, the AI will also be biased. This can lead to unfair or discriminatory results, which can reinforce existing social problems.

Addressing the security challenges associated with AI-driven social media requires a multifaceted approach involving collaboration between technology companies, policymakers, and civil society organizations. By developing robust security measures, promoting transparency, and addressing algorithmic bias, we can harness the benefits of AI while mitigating its risks and ensuring a safer and more equitable online environment.[2]

- **AI POWERED INFORMATION WARFARE**

Artificial Intelligence is a new technology which will be used in an old concept like information warfare. Artificial intelligence draws its tactical principles from land, air, sea, and space legacies. AI plays a role at every level of digital warfare, from hunting the enemy through sensors and gathering intel, through assisting in decision-making and simulations, to supporting the maneuver and use of cyber-weapons, and more.[3]

The current state of AI in information warfare reflects its growing influence on the methods and approaches employed by various entities. AI tools such as machine learning and natural language processing are now playing a key role in automating the creation and dissemination of misinformation, controlling public opinion, and carrying out targeted cyber-attacks.

THE IMPACT OF THE SOCIAL MEDIA ON INFORMATION WARFARE

"Four hostile newspapers are more to be feared than a thousand bayonets."
- Napoleon Bonaparte

Social media platforms have become a strong and powerful tool for the spread of misinformation and disinformation. By leveraging algorithms, echo chambers, and malicious actors, these platforms can boost and amplify false or misleading information, undermine trust, polarize society, and potentially cause real-world harm.

The 2016 US presidential election serves as the best example of spreading false information to manipulate public opinion. Russia-backed actors exploited social media to spread misinformation, target specific demographics, and influence public opinion.[4]

Social media platforms have emerged as potent tools for the manipulation of public opinion. Malicious actors, including individuals, groups, and even nation-states. It can exploit these platforms to disseminate misinformation, promote partisan narratives, and interfere in democratic events and processes. Techniques executed by these actors include the creation and dissemination of fabricated or misleading content or information, targeted advertising or propaganda, and the exploitation of algorithmic biases.

The consequences of such manipulations can be extreme, including the erosion of trust in institutions, the polarization of societies, and the undermining of democratic standards. To mitigate these risks, it is imperative to implement effective countermeasures. These measures may include increased transparency from social media platforms regarding their algorithms and content moderation practices, the creation of advanced tools for detecting and countering misinformation, and enhanced media literacy education for the common people.

Cyberattacks have risen as a powerful and strategic tool in modern hybrid warfare, offering a means to inflict harm on an adversary's military, economic, and political infrastructure without turning to conventional military constraint. By exploiting vulnerabilities in digital systems, attackers can disrupt critical infrastructure, steal sensitive data or information, and undermine public confidence.

While cyberattacks can be a widespread strategic advantage, they moreover pose critical risks. The potential for unintended aftermaths, collateral damage, and exacerbation must be carefully considered. To proficiently leverage cyber capabilities, nations must develop solidly built cyber defenses, involve in international cooperation, and comply with ethical principles.

Extremist groups have increasingly utilized social media platforms to recruit, radicalize, and mobilize individuals for violent activities. By exploiting the anonymity and accessibility of online spaces, these groups can target vulnerable individuals, disseminate extremist ideologies, and facilitate the planning and execution of attacks.

The use of social media by extremist groups poses significant threats to national security, public safety, and social cohesion. To counter these threats, it is imperative to implement effective strategies that address the root causes of extremism, enhance online content moderation, and strengthen law enforcement capabilities.

As technology improves, techniques are refined, and internet connectivity continues to proliferate around the world, this saying will ring true: He who controls the trend will control the narrative—and, ultimately, the narrative controls the will of the people.[5]

The Role of Artificial Intelligence in Social Media Manipulation

Deepfakes, sophisticated AI-generated media that manipulate audio and visual content, pose a substantial threat to cybersecurity. Their potential to deceive, manipulate, and defraud has raised significant concerns about the integrity of digital information.

The potential implications of deepfakes are far-reaching. It can be used to spread false information, destruct reputations, and even influence public opinion and elections. For example, deepfakes could be used to create fabricated videos of political leaders making controversial or harmful statements, potentially eroding public trust in democratic processes. Here are some prominent instances of deepfakes.

In late May of 2019, a manipulated video of Nancy Pelosi that made the U.S. House Speaker appear intoxicated and slurring her words spread across the internet. The video, which was viewed more than 2.5 million times on Facebook in a matter of days and shared by prominent political leaders.[6]

The BJP, in partnership with The Ideaz Factory, created deepfakes in February 2020 ahead of Delhi's legislative assembly elections. These deepfakes targeted voters across India's over 20 different languages. The party informed media that the Manoj Tiwari deepfake reached approximately 15 million people in 5,800 WhatsApp groups.[7]

In line with this instance, a deepfake surfaced on social media in March 2022 that showed Ukrainian president Volodymyr Zelenskyy telling his soldiers to surrender to Russian forces.[8]

In 2023, The Clinton and Biden deepfakes - realistic yet fabricated videos created by AI algorithms trained on copious online footage - are among thousands surfacing on social media, blurring fact and fiction in the polarized world of U.S. politics.[9]

Recently, A manipulated video on Twitter suggesting President Biden incorrectly stated Russia's occupation duration of Kyiv. Later, an online, AI-generated photo falsely showing ex-President Donald Trump with Jeffrey Epstein and an underaged girl.[10]

Addressing the challenges posed by deepfakes requires a comprehensive approach. Technological advancements are essential to develop tools that can accurately detect and identify deepfakes. Educational initiatives are needed to raise awareness about the dangers of deepfakes and equip individuals with the skills to critically evaluate digital content. Additionally, legal frameworks and international cooperation are crucial to establish guidelines and enforce regulations related to the creation and dissemination of deepfakes.[11]

Algorithmic manipulation, a growing concern in the era of artificial intelligence and social media, is a double-edged sword capable of both enhancing and hindering online experiences. Algorithms can personalize our online experiences, but they can also create problems. While they help us find important information, it can also trap us into "echo chambers" where we only grasp information we agree with. This can spread misinformation and influence public opinion in detrimental ways.

To balance the benefits and risks, we need tenets to be transparent about their algorithms, promote diversity, fact-check information, and give users more command over what they see. By doing this, we can utilize algorithms to our advantage without getting trapped in their negative effects.

The proliferation of artificial intelligence has enabled the creation of automated trolling and harassment campaigns, posing significant threats to individuals and online communities. Trolling has evolved to become a component of information operations and military strategies.

The following flowchart shows us a basic operation on social media to spread a narrative.

Figure 1. Flow chart of the rollout strategy of a trolling campaign.

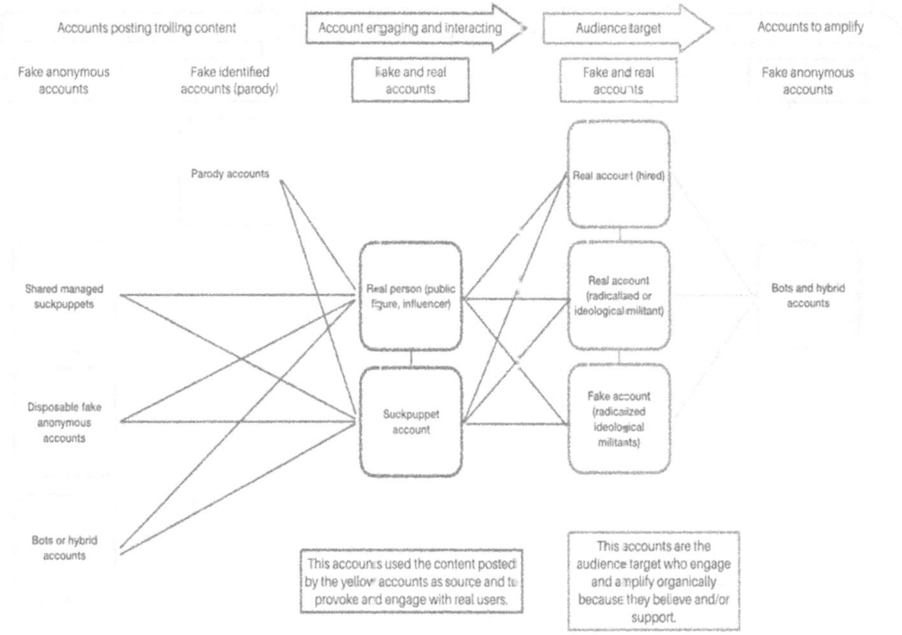

Image: Courtesy of Luis Assardo

The above figure describes a coordinated disinformation campaign involving three groups of accounts:

- **Yellow accounts:** Create and distribute fabricated or doctored content.

- **Red accounts:** Amplify and spread this content to targeted audiences, often provoking adversaries or engaging with supporters.
- **Green accounts:** Share the content organically, reaching a wider audience.

This strategy allows the red accounts to avoid direct responsibility for the harmful content, as they are merely sharing posts from other accounts. The yellow accounts, which are more expendable, are exposed to suspension if the content is reported. This setup enables the campaign to spread disinformation effectively while minimizing the risk to the key players.[12]

Automated trolling and harassment, often facilitated by bots and scripts, have become a insidious problem in online spaces. This form of psychological warfare can have critical consequences for individuals and communities, including:

- **Emotional distress:** Victims may experience anxiety, depression, and even post-traumatic stress disorder (PTSD).
- **Social isolation:** Constant harassment can lead to social withdrawal and feelings of loneliness.
- **Damage to reputation:** Trolls can spread false information and rumors, damaging a person's reputation.
- **Silencing of voices:** Fear of harassment can deter individuals from expressing their opinions, leading to a chilling effect on free speech.

The rapid advancement of artificial intelligence (AI) has ushered in a new era of technological capabilities, which has transformed various aspects of our lives. While AI has undoubtedly brought significant benefits, its use in surveillance and censorship poses a major threat to fundamental freedoms, especially the right to freedom of expression.

The ability of AI algorithms to process vast amounts of data at unprecedented speeds enables governments and private entities to monitor online activities on a massive scale. This constant surveillance can create a chilling effect on free speech, as individuals may self-censor their expressions for fear of repercussions. Furthermore, AI-powered censorship systems can be used to selectively suppress dissenting voices, limiting the diversity of viewpoints and hindering open conversation.

To mitigate these risks and protect freedom of expression, it is imperative to establish strong ethical frameworks and regulatory measures governing the development and use of AI. Transparent monitoring mechanisms, accountability for harms caused by AI, and international cooperation are essential to ensure that AI is used responsibly and in a manner that respects human rights.

THE STRATEGIC IMPLICATIONS OF AI-POWERED INFORMATION WARFARE

AI-powered information warfare, a relatively new phenomenon, has the potential to reshape the global geopolitical landscape. Its ability to generate, disseminate, and manipulate information at unprecedented speed and scale poses significant threats to trust, stability, and democracy.

Information Operations or Cyber Operations (CyOps) are the fifth domain of warfare after land, sea, air, and space. The Cyber Domain is transversal to all the previously mentioned domains. It is the least kinetic, yet it has the most far-reaching effects.[13] For instance, control of the Sea and Air domains can significantly impact regional power balances and influence geopolitical stability. Similarly, dominance in the Cyber and Space domains can alter strategic dynamics by affecting communication and information superiority.[14]

Artificial Intelligence (AI) has emerged as a transformative force in the contemporary landscape of global conflict, particularly in the domain of **information warfare and Influence Operations (IWIO)**. IWIO, a strategy that utilizes information to influence public opinion, undermine adversaries, and achieve strategic objectives, has been significantly amplified by AI's capabilities.

Key Impacts of AI on IW:

- **Enhanced Efficiency and Scale:** AI's ability to automate tasks, such as disseminating disinformation or creating fabricated content, has exponentially increased the speed and reach of IW operations.
- **Personalized Targeting:** AI-powered algorithms can analyze vast datasets to identify vulnerable individuals or groups, enabling highly targeted and persuasive messaging.
- **Deepfakes and Synthetic Media:** The creation of highly realistic but fabricated content, known as deepfakes, is now possible thanks to AI. This can undermine trust in information sources and manipulate public opinion.
- **Real-Time Monitoring and Analysis:** AI can continuously monitor online discourse, identify trends, and analyze sentiment, providing valuable insights for shaping public opinion and responding to crises.

AI and the Major Powers:

- **United States:** The US is investing heavily in AI-powered IW defense and offense. It is developing tools to counter foreign disinformation campaigns and is exploring offensive capabilities, such as generating persuasive narratives.

- **China:** China's extensive surveillance infrastructure and social media control, coupled with its AI advancements, enable it to shape global narratives and influence public opinion.
- **Russia:** Russia has employed AI to spread disinformation and propaganda, particularly during its invasion of Ukraine, using bots, trolls, and deepfakes to undermine Western democracies.[15]

The strategic implications of AI-powered information warfare are profound and far-reaching. AI-driven disinformation campaigns can pose a significant threat to democratic institutions and global stability by destroying trust and credibility, polarizing communities, and destabilizing governments. The potential for escalation and conflict is a serious concern, as the misuse of information warfare tactics can amplify existing tensions and create new ones.

CASE STUDIES OF AI-POWERED INFORMATION WARFARE

Russia's AI-driven Disinformation campaigns in Ukraine: A Case Analysis

Russia has launched a sophisticated disinformation campaign against Ukraine using cutting-edge artificial intelligence (AI) capabilities. This campaign has used a variety of strategies, such as:

- **Cyberattacks:** Russia executed Distributed Denial-of-Service (DDoS) attacks against critical Ukrainian infrastructure, leading to service disruptions and widespread chaos.
- **SMS Spam:** Ukrainians were bombarded with deceptive SMS messages intended to cause confusion and erode trust in government institutions.
- **Social Media Manipulation:** Russia established a huge network of fake accounts, leveraging AI-generated content to disseminate pro-Kremlin propaganda, manipulate adversity and influence public opinion.[16]

A particularly troubling method involves the use of generative adversarial networks (GANs) to create highly realistic deepfakes. These AI-generated images and videos can disseminate false information and erode trust in reliable sources.

The Internet Research Agency, a well-known state-backed troll farm in Russia, has played a key role in these disinformation campaigns. It has utilized a blend of human operations and AI-driven bots to propagate propaganda on multiple social media platforms.

In May 2022, officials with the United Kingdom's government revealed that recent "research suggested Moscow's operation was 'designed to manipulate international public opinion' in favor of its military campaign in Ukraine."[17]

While social media platforms have made efforts to detect and remove such accounts, the increasing complexities of AI-generated content impose strategic challenges. The Ukrainian government has been actively countering these disinformation campaigns, but the threat of AI-powered information warfare remains a vivid concern.

China's Information Warfare and Influence Operations in Southeast Asia: A Strategic Assessment:

One of the most important components of China's larger regional strategic goals in Southeast Asia is its AI-driven information operations. These operations use cutting edge AI technology to boost disinformation campaigns' efficacy, manipulate public opinion, and reshape regional narratives to suit Chinese goals.

China has strategically integrated AI into its offensive information warfare (IW) strategy, aiming to sow discord and division within the United States through social media platforms. Moreover, China has employed AI to manipulate public sentiment in Taiwan, shape international perception regarding the Hong Kong demonstrations, and influence the global community's view of the treatment of Uyghurs in Xinjiang.[18]

To achieve these objectives, China has seemingly leveraged AI to suppress negative press while disseminating propaganda through meticulously crafted videos. By distributing these videos globally and utilizing AI to bypass spam detectors, China has inundated social media platforms with misinformation. These tactics underscore China's willingness to aggressively control political narratives and employ AI to achieve its IW goals. Additionally, China has increasingly relied on AI to monitor its domestic population and disseminate pro-PRC political propaganda within its borders.

Here's a strategic assessment of China's activities in this domain:

1. Strategic Objectives:
    - **Regional Influence:** China's primary goal is to extend its influence over Southeast Asian countries by shaping perceptions around its Belt and Road Initiative (BRI), territorial claims in the South China Sea, and regional security partnerships.
    - **Countering U.S. Influence:** By using AI-driven information operations, China seeks to counter U.S. influence in the region, promoting narratives that position China as a more reliable partner for economic and security cooperation.

- **Political and Economic Leverage:** These operations also aim to create favorable conditions for Chinese investments and to pressure Southeast Asian governments to align with Beijing's geopolitical stance.

2. Operational Methods:
   - **Social Media Manipulation:** China uses AI algorithms to amplify its messaging on platforms like Facebook, Twitter, and regional social media networks. These algorithms can identify trending topics, craft tailored narratives and deploy bot armies to create the illusion of widespread support for pro-China sentiments.
   - **Deepfakes and Synthetic Media:** AI-generated deepfakes and synthetic media are increasingly used to undermine political figures, spread disinformation, and create confusion about the source of information. These tools make it harder for Southeast Asian governments to control the flow of accurate information.
   - **Influence through Economic** Ties: China's digital Silk Road initiative includes AI infrastructure projects that provide China with access to vast amounts of data from Southeast Asian countries. This data can be exploited to fine-tune information operations, making them more effective and harder to detect.
3. Regional Impact:
   - **Political Stability:** AI-driven information operations have the potential to destabilize political environments in Southeast Asia by fueling ethnic tensions, discrediting opposition figures, or manipulating electoral outcomes.
   - **Public Perception:** The strategic use of AI in information operations can shift public opinion on critical issues like territorial disputes, foreign policy, and economic cooperation, aligning them more closely with Chinese narratives.
   - **Diplomatic Relations:** These operations can complicate diplomatic relations within ASEAN, driving wedges between member states and hindering unified responses to regional security challenges.
4. Countermeasures and Challenges:
   - **Digital Literacy:** Southeast Asian nations need to enhance digital literacy to help their populations better identify and resist disinformation. However, this is a long-term effort that requires substantial investment and political will.
   - **Regional Cooperation:** ASEAN countries must strengthen regional cooperation on cybersecurity and information sharing to effectively counteract AI-driven information operations. Yet, varying levels of technological development and political priorities make this challenging.

- **International Support:** Partnerships with Western nations, particularly in AI and cybersecurity, are crucial. However, these partnerships may be viewed with suspicion by some Southeast Asian governments wary of becoming entangled in great power competition.

China's AI-driven information operations in Southeast Asia represent a sophisticated and evolving threat to regional stability and sovereignty. These operations are deeply intertwined with Beijing's broader strategic objectives and pose significant challenges to Southeast Asian nations' efforts to maintain autonomy and resist external influence. Countering these operations will require a coordinated regional approach, enhanced digital literacy, and strategic partnerships with international allies.

The Spread of Misinformation During the COVID-19 Pandemic: A Global Challenge

The spread of misinformation during the COVID-19 pandemic emerged as a critical global challenge, undermining public health efforts and exacerbating the crisis. False information proliferated across social media platforms, ranging from conspiracy theories about the virus's origins to misleading claims about vaccines and treatments. This "infodemic" fueled public confusion, mistrust in authorities, and resistance to health measures like mask-wearing and vaccination.

Here are some major examples of misinformation spread during COVID 19;

- Vaccine fear was a predominant public health issue, and a similar trend of misconceptions was observed in relation to the COVID-19 vaccine upon its introduction.[19]
- Various sources on the internet, including social media, became an outlet for spreading false and inaccurate information related to the pandemic. These included theories about its origin, transmission, prevention, and the effectiveness of vaccines, all of which are not supported by evidence-based findings.[20]

Misinformation was amplified by a variety of actors, including state-sponsored campaigns, profit-driven entities, and individuals capitalizing on fear and uncertainty. The rapid spread was fueled by algorithms that prioritized sensationalist content, making it difficult for accurate information to gain momentum.

The consequences were severe: public health agencies struggled to counter false narratives, and in some cases, misinformation directly led to harmful behavior, such as the use of unproven treatments or the rejection of proven medical interventions. The global nature of the pandemic meant that misinformation crossed borders, complicating international cooperation and response efforts.

Combating this challenge required a multifaceted approach, including the promotion of digital literacy, partnerships between governments and tech companies to monitor and prevent the spread of false information, and the dissemination of accurate, timely information from trusted sources. However, the scale and speed of misinformation during COVID-19 exposed the limitations of these efforts and underscored the need for ongoing strategies to strengthen information resilience to confront future global crises.

MITIGATING THE RISKS OF AI-POWERED INFORMATION WARFARE

Digital literacy and media education are essential skills in today's interconnected world. By equipping individuals with the ability to critically evaluate information, navigate digital platforms responsibly, and create content effectively, we can nurture a more informed, secure and engaged society.

Experts at the United Nations Educational, Scientific and Cultural Organization (UNESCO) have detected 23 terms related to the fields of media and information literacy, including AI Literacy, along with News Literacy, Social Media Literacy, Critical Literacy, and others. Specialists now view AI literacy as a branch of digital literacy that falls under the broader umbrella of media and information literacy. [21]

Figure 2. Inter-relationship between Media and Information Literacy, Digital and AI Literacy

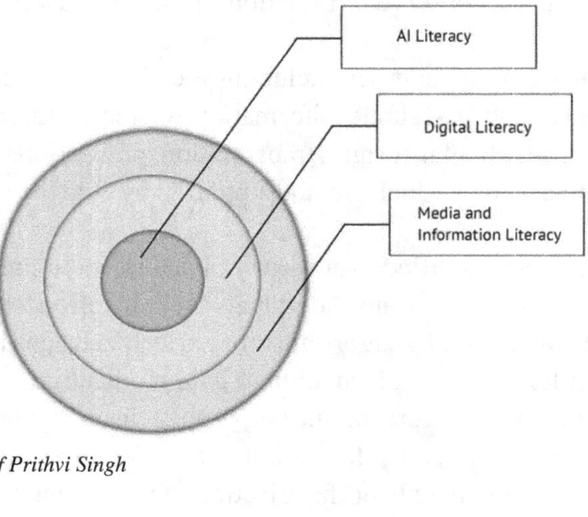

Image: Courtesy of Prithvi Singh

Prebunking is a very helpful technique for preventing fake news and misinformation. It is a strategic approach that aims to distance people from misinformation before it reaches them. By providing accurate information and addressing common misconceptions, prebunking can help individuals develop critical thinking skills and become more resistant to the influence of misinformation campaigns.

The prebunking process involves several key steps:

- Identification of Target Misinformation
- Creation of Prebunking Content
- Distribution and Amplification
- Audience Engagement
- Counteracting Misinformation Networks

By proactively addressing misinformation, prebunking can help mitigate its harmful effects and promote a more informed and resilient society.

Figure 3. The Prebunking Cascade: A Model of Disinformation Mitigation

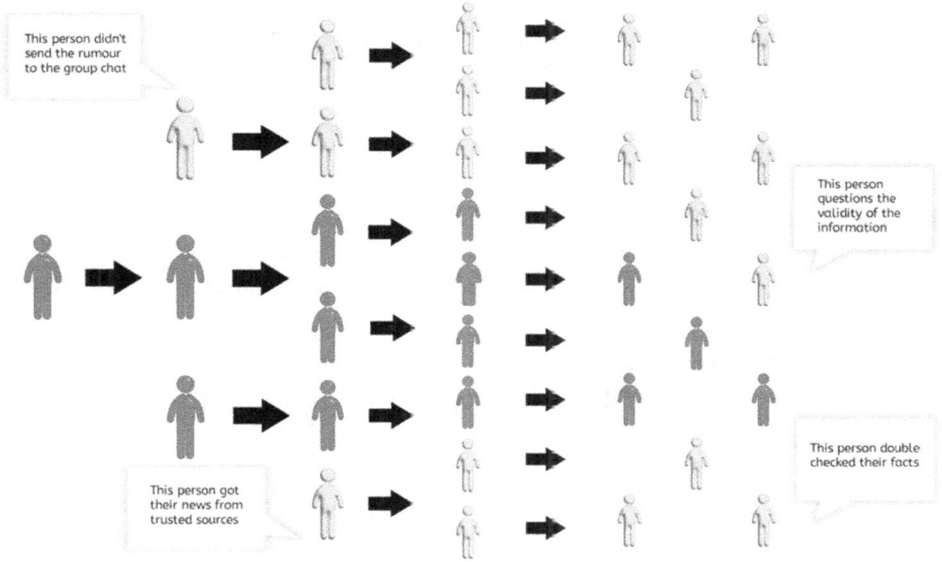

Image: Courtesy of Prithvi Singh

The above image (figure 3) depicts the spread of information or rumors through a social network, possibly in the context of misinformation. Here's a breakdown of the visual elements:

- **Red and Green figures:** The red figures represent individuals who have received and forwarded the rumor, while the green figures represent those who have not.
- **Arrows:** The arrows demonstrate the direction of information flow.
- **Central figure:** The central figure is the person who questions the authenticity of the information and double-checks their facts. This person acts as a "firewall" by anticipating the rumor from spreading further.

We can understand from the above illustration how misinformation can spread through a group or social media platforms if individuals do not critically assess or verify the information they receive on a personal level. It highlights the importance of skepticism and fact-checking to prevent the unchecked spread of rumors.

AI-driven information warfare poses a significant threat to society. By developing robust fact-checking and verification mechanisms, we can help to counter this threat and ensure that information remains reliable and trustworthy.

Deepfakes pose significant threats to society, including misinformation, fraud, and privacy violations. To combat these kinds of problems we need a deepfake detection model. A deepfake detection model is a machine learning algorithm designed to distinguish real videos from deepfakes. These models typically employ convolutional neural networks (CNNs) to analyze facial features, inconsistencies in motion, and other visual cues.

Key techniques used in deepfake detection include:

- **Facial landmark detection:** Identifying key points on the face to analyze inconsistencies in facial expressions and movements.
- **Motion analysis:** Examining video frames for irregularities in motion patterns.
- **Temporal coherence:** Assessing the consistency of video content over time.
- **Generative adversarial networks (GANs):** Training models to generate realistic deepfakes to improve detection accuracy.

Figure 4. Graphical representation of the deepfake detection model.

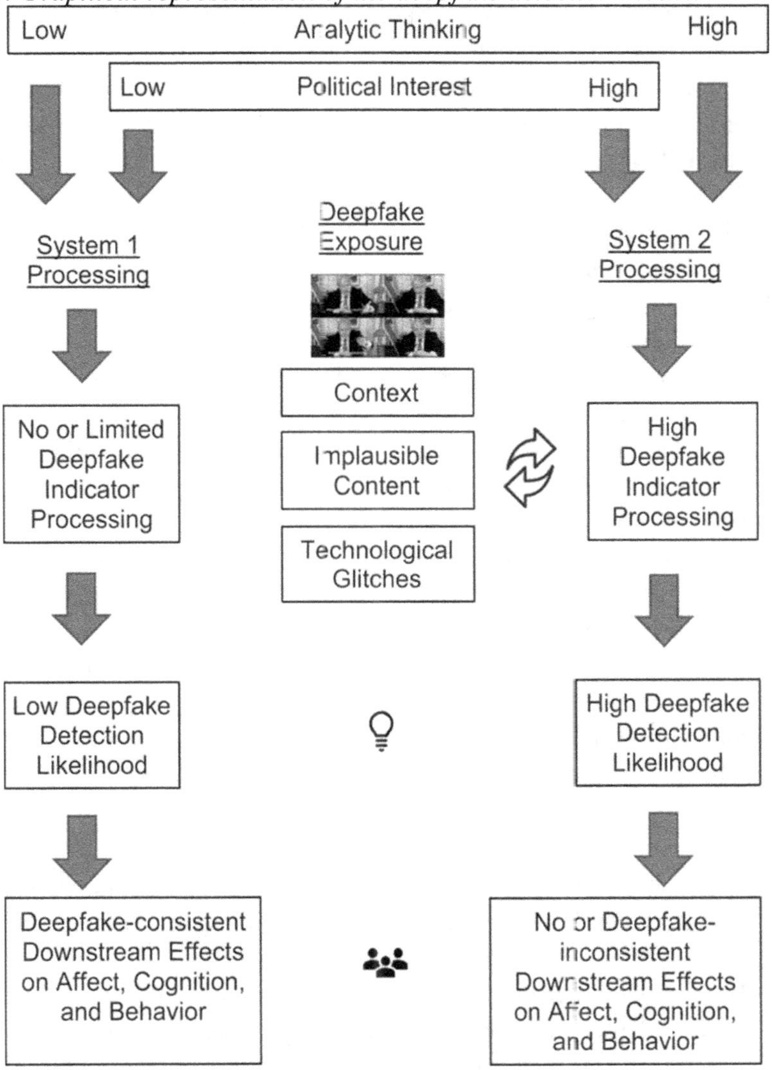

Source: J Comput Mediat Commun, Volume 27, Issue 4, July 2022, zmac008, https://doi.org/10.1093/jcmc/zmac008

The deepfake detection model explains the factors influencing the detection of deepfakes and their subsequent effects.

Here's the key factors mentioned in the deepfake detection model:

- **Analytical Thinking:** Refers to an individual's ability to critically evaluate and analyze information. Higher analytical thinking is associated with a better ability to detect deepfakes.
- **Political Interest:** Individuals with high political interest are more likely to encounter and analyze deepfakes related to political figures or events.
- **System 1 Processing:** Refers to fast, intuitive, and emotional thinking. Individuals relying predominantly on System 1 processing may be more susceptible to believing deepfakes without critical evaluation.
- **System 2 Processing:** Refers to slow, deliberate, and logical thinking. Individuals relying primarily on System 2 processing are more likely to detect deepfakes through careful analysis.
- **Deepfake Exposure:** Exposure to deepfakes can affect an individual's future ability to recognize them.
- **Context:** The context in which a deepfake is presented can influence its perceived credibility. It may be easier to recognize deepfakes when presented in an unreliable context.
- **Deepfake Indicators:** The presence of deepfake indicators, such as technical glitches or inconsistencies, can increase the likelihood of detection.
- **Detection Probability:** Refers to the likelihood of an individual detecting a deepfake, influenced by factors such as analytical thinking, political interest, and the presence of deepfake indicators.
- **Downstream Effects:** The impact of deepfakes on individuals' perceptions and behavior can vary based on detection probability and the nature of the deepfake.

Overall, the above model indicates that individuals with higher analytical thinking, political interest, and reliance on System 2 processing are more likely to detect deepfakes and experience fewer negative downstream effects.

Strengthened cyber security and infrastructure resilience is very important to counter AI powered information warfare. Strong cyber security measures including regular updates, strong authentication protocols and intrusion detection systems can help and protect critical infrastructure and secret data from cyber attacks.

International cooperation and governance are essential for tackling the global challenges posed by AI powered information welfare. Establishing international norms and standards or responsible air development can help mitigate risk and ensure that AI will be used for healthy and beneficial purposes. Collaborative efforts between governments, non-government organizations, international organization and Technology companies can facilitate data sharing, intelligence cooperation and joint responses to cyber threats.

CONCLUSION

The future of AI-powered information warfare will be very complex and sophisticated. With the advancement of modern technology AI capabilities continue to advance, adversaries also can adapt these technologies and launch more powerful complex and targeted attacks.

In this digital age with the advancement of Technology and the internet networks, social media is also easy to access. Social media platforms are used by a large number of people, and they are also being used to spread misinformation and propaganda to influence people. With the introduction of Artificial intelligence to the mass communication platforms, it has become a more powerful tool now. Many Companies, Non-state actors and even State actors can easily acquire your data and information to influence or manipulate according to their interest.

AI powered manipulation is a vivid concern in the modern digital age and this raises profound ethical questions. AI systems become increasingly complex and their ability to influence human behavior, beliefs and decisions become more vigorous. This capability poses significant ethical dilemmas especially when it is used for malicious purposes.

One of the primary ethical concerns is the potential for AI to be used to spread misinformation and disinformation on a huge scale. For example, Deepfakes can create strongly convincing fabricated audios and videos that can be used to manipulate public opinion and undermine trust in institutions. This can pose serious consequences for democratic processes, social and individual well-being.

Another ethical issue is the potential for Artificial Intelligence to exploit individual vulnerabilities. AI systems, by analyzing vast amounts of personal data, can identify a person's weaknesses and biases. This information can then be used to manipulate and coerce individuals into making harmful decisions or engaging in discriminatory behavior.

To address ethical challenges, it is essential to develop robust ethical framework and regulations for the development and the use of AI. In this framework issues such as transparency, accountability and protection of individual rights must be included.

The misuse of artificial intelligence drives social media in information warfare, fundamental human rights receive a multifaceted challenges. These platforms offer unprecedented opportunity for communication and interaction, but they also pose significant rise to privacy and freedom of expression.

In this information age, the right to privacy and freedom of expression become particularly vulnerable. To address these challenges a comprehensive approach as needed includes strengthening data privacy regulations promoting transparency and accountability in the technology developing ethical guidelines for AI development, promoting media, digital and AI literacy and fostering international cooperation.

To effectively tackle information warfare, it is necessary to raise public awareness about its threats. This can be achieved by educating people about the tactics used by adversaries, promoting critical thinking, and encouraging responsible online behavior.

Tackling information warfare requires a multi-faceted approach that involves collaboration between governments, businesses, civil society organizations, and individuals. By adopting a comprehensive and coordinated strategy, we can reduce the risks associated with information warfare and safeguard our democracies and societies.

Call to Action:

- Governments should invest in research and development to deepen their understanding of the tactics and strategies of information warfare.
- Governments need to enhance their cybersecurity infrastructure and promote media literacy among citizens.
- Governments should incorporate a compulsory chapter on Artificial Intelligence in high school curricula to foster media literacy among students.
- Governments should encourage international cooperation to combat the global nature of information warfare.
- Businesses should establish ethical guidelines for the use of AI and other emerging technologies.
- Civil society organizations should work on public education and awareness initiatives about the dangers of information warfare.
- Individuals should evaluate information critically and promote responsible online behavior.

By implementing these actions, we can build a more resilient and informed society that is able to counter the threats posed by information warfare.

In conclusion, AI-driven information warfare has fundamentally changed the landscape of modern conflict dynamics, leveraging the massive reach and influence of social media platforms. The strategic deployment of AI technologies in disseminating propaganda, manipulating public opinion, and undermining the credibility of adversaries has proven to be a powerful tool in contemporary conflicts. This development demands urgent policy responses and adaptive strategies to mitigate the risks associated with AI-enhanced misinformation campaigns. Understanding and addressing the intricacies of AI in information warfare is critical to maintaining the integrity of the information ecosystem and ensuring national security in the digital age.

REFERENCES

Assardo, L. (2023, May 24). Investigating digital threats: Trolling campaigns. Global Investigative Journalism Network. Retrieved from https://gijn.org/resource/investigating-digital-threats-trolling-campaigns/ (Last visited on 22.09.2024)

Bendau, A., Plag, J., Petzold, M. B., & Ströhle, A. (2021). COVID-19 vaccine hesitancy and related fears and anxiety. International immunopharmacology, 97, 107724. https://doi.org/ (Last visited on 22.09.2024)DOI: 10.1016/j.intimp.2021.107724

Booth, R. (2022, May 1). Russia's trolling on Ukraine gets 'incredible traction' on TikTok. The Guardian. https://www.theguardian.com/world/2022/may/01/russia-trolling-ukraine-traction-tiktok?CMP (Last visited on 22.09.2024)

Brooklyn, P., Egon, A., & Shad, R. (2024, July 3). Deepfakes and cybersecurity: Detection and mitigation. Social Science Research Network. https://ssrn.com/abstract=4904874 (Last visited on 22.09.2024)

DiResta, R., Miller, C., & Molter, V.. (2020). *Telling China's story: The Chinese Communist Party's campaign to shape global narratives*. Stanford Internet Observatory.

Fogleman, R. R. (1995, April 25). Information operations: The fifth dimension of warfare [Speech delivered to the Armed Forces Communications-Electronics Association, Washington, DC]. https://web.archive.org/web/20200220002026/http://www.iwar.org.uk/iwar/resources/5th-dimension/iw.html(Last visited on 22.09.2024)

Ghosh, M., & Arunachalam, T. (2021). Introduction to Artificial Intelligence. . https://www.researchgate.net/publication/351758474_Introduction_to_Artificial_Intelligence (Last visited on 20.09.2024)DOI: 10.1007/978-981-16-0415-7_2

Grizzle, A., Wilson, C., & Tuazon, R. Cheung, et al. (2021). "Media and information literate citizens:Media and Information Literacy Curriculum for Educators and Learners," UNESCO. https://unesdoc.unesco.org/ark:/48223/pf0000384981

Guyonneau, R., & Le Dez, A. (2019), Artificial Intelligence in Digital Warfare: Introducing the Concept of the Cyberteammate, https://cyberdefensereview.army.mil/Portals/6/Documents/CDR%20Journal%20Articles/Fall%202019/CDR%20V4N2-Fall%202019_GUYONNEAU-LE%20DEZ.pdf?ver=2019-11-15-104106-423 (Last visited on 20.09.2024)

Hogan, M. (2020, May). How artificial intelligence influences social media. Adzooma. https://www.adzooma.com/blog/how-artificial-intelligence-influences-social-media/ (Last visited on 20.09.2024)

Hunter, L., Albert, C., Rutland, J., Topping, K., & Hennigan, C. (2024). Artificial intelligence and information warfare in major power states: how the US, China, and Russia are using artificial intelligence in their information warfare and influence operations. Defense & Security Analysis. 40. 1-35. ._https://www.researchgate.net/publication/378764079_Artificial_intelligence_and_information_warfare_in_major_power_states_how_the_US_China_and_Russia_are_using_artificial_intelligence_in_their_information_warfare_and_influence_operations (Last visited on 22.09.2024)DOI: 10.1080/14751798.2024.2321736

Jee, C. (2020, February). An Indian politician is using deepfake technology to win new voters. Archive Page. MIT Technology Review._https://www.technologyreview.com/2020/02/19/868173/an-indian-politician-is-using-deepfakes-to-try-and-win-voters/ (Last visited on 21.09.2024)

Lin, H. (2022). Russian Cyber Operations in the Invasion of Ukraine. *The Cyber Defense Review*, 7(4), 31–46.

Mervosh, S. (2019, May). Distorted videos of Nancy Pelosi spread on Facebook and Twitter, helped by Trump. The New York Times. https://perma.cc/a26h-4pf3 (Last visited on 21.09.2024)

Metz, R. (2022, March 16). Facebook and YouTube say they removed Zelensky deepfake. CNN. https://edition.cnn.com/2022/03/16/tech/deepfake-zelensky-facebook-meta/index.html(Last visited on 21.09.2024)

. Mian, A., & Khan, S. (2020). Coronavirus: The spread of misinformation. BMC medicine, 18, 89. [] (Last visited on 22.09.2024)DOI: 10.1186/s12916-020-01556-3

Murphy, T. (2020, March 27). The strategy web: A new framework for analyzing military strategy. Air University: Wild Blue Yonder. https://www.airuniversity.af.edu/Wild-Blue-Yonder/Article-Display/Article/2127317/the-strategy-web-a-new-framework-for-analyzing-military-strategy/](https://www.airuniversity.af.edu/Wild-Blue-Yonder/Article-Display/Article/2127317/the-strategy-web-a-new-framework-for-analyzing-military-strategy/ (Last visited on 22.09.2024)

Prier, J. (2017). Commanding the trend: Social media as information warfare. Strategic Studies Quarterly, Air University Press. 11(4), 50-85._https://www.proquest.com/docview/1972152688/ (Last visited on 21.09.2024)

Sayegh, E. (2024, May 14). The battle for truth in election seasons: AI-generated deepfakes. Forbes."_https://www.forbes.com/sites/emilsayegh/2024/05/14/the-battle-for-truth-in-election-seasons-ai-generated-deepfakes/#open-web-0 (Last visited on 21.09.2024)

Ulmer, A., & Tong, A. (2023, May 31). Deepfaking it: America's 2024 election collides with AI boom. Reuters. https://www.reuters.com/world/us/deepfaking-it-americas-2024-election-collides-with-ai-boom-2023-05-30/ (Last visited on 21.09.2024)

Chapter 2
From Reactive to Proactive:
AI's Role in Promoting Civility and Respect in Online Discussions

Swati Chakraborty
https://orcid.org/0000-0003-0799-1954
Concordia University, Canada

ABSTRACT

The proliferation of social media and online forums has democratized discourse but also led to an alarming rise in incivility, hate speech, and toxic interactions. Historically, the approach to addressing these issues has been reactive—identifying and removing harmful content after it has already caused damage. However, advances in artificial intelligence (AI) present an opportunity to shift from reactive to proactive strategies for fostering civility and respect in online discussions. This paper examines the evolution of AI-driven content moderation tools and explores how they can be leveraged to not only detect and filter inappropriate content but also encourage respectful engagement. By emphasizing preemptive interventions, AI can become a powerful force in shaping healthier online communities.

1. INTRODUCTION

Online platforms have become integral spaces for public discourse, allowing individuals from diverse backgrounds to exchange ideas. While this has led to the democratization of speech, it has also introduced new challenges, notably the rise of toxic behavior, including hate speech, trolling, and harassment. Traditionally, content moderation has relied on user reporting and human moderators to manage

DOI: 10.4018/979-8-3693-9904-0.ch002

such behavior. However, these methods are largely reactive, addressing harmful content after it has already been posted.

With the advent of AI technologies, there is an opportunity to transform this reactive approach into a proactive one. By using machine learning algorithms, natural language processing (NLP), and predictive analytics, AI can not only detect but also anticipate potentially harmful behavior. More importantly, AI can be designed to promote positive engagement by nudging users towards more respectful discourse, setting the tone for constructive conversations.

This paper explores the transition from reactive to proactive AI systems in online content moderation, focusing on the role AI can play in promoting civility and respect in online discussions (M. N. O. Sadiku, 1989).

The proliferation of social media and online forums has democratized discourse but also led to an alarming rise in incivility, hate speech, and toxic interactions. Historically, the approach to addressing these issues has been reactive—identifying and removing harmful content after it has already caused damage. However, advances in artificial intelligence (AI) present an opportunity to shift from reactive to proactive strategies for fostering civility and respect in online discussions. This paper examines the evolution of AI-driven content moderation tools and explores how they can be leveraged to not only detect and filter inappropriate content but also encourage respectful engagement. By emphasizing pre-emptive interventions, AI can become a powerful force in shaping healthier online communities.

Proactive AI moderation has demonstrated success in creating healthier online communities by preventing harmful interactions before they escalate. For example, Reddit's **AutoModerator (AutoMod)** allows subreddit moderators to establish specific rules, automatically screening posts and comments for spam, offensive language, or irrelevant content. This system reduces the burden on human moderators and ensures that inappropriate content is removed swiftly, fostering a more respectful atmosphere. By enabling customization, Reddit empowers its users to define community-specific standards, making moderation both effective and adaptable (A. Mufareh.2020).

Similarly, platforms like **YouTube** have leveraged machine learning to improve comment moderation. AI tools flag or hold comments containing harmful or inappropriate language for manual review. Features such as "hold potentially inappropriate comments for review" give creators more control over their content, allowing them to maintain a positive environment while reducing exposure to toxic comments. These tools not only promote civility but also enhance user engagement by creating safer spaces for interaction. Consistent updates to these AI systems reflect a focus on inclusivity and fairness, addressing concerns like algorithmic bias (M. N. O. Sadiku, 2018).

Another noteworthy example is **Discord's AutoMod**, which uses real-time language processing to identify rule-breaking content within servers. It provides administrators with tools to filter offensive terms, proactively warn users, or temporarily mute violators. This approach helps server owners create safe, respectful environments tailored to their unique community norms. By integrating proactive AI moderation, Discord has successfully managed to balance free expression with the need for safety, demonstrating how such tools can enhance user trust and inclusivity in digital spaces (H. Sarmiento,2020).

2. THE PROBLEM OF TOXICITY IN ONLINE SPACES

The Rise of Online Incivility

The internet, particularly social media platforms, has given rise to a variety of negative behaviors. These range from relatively mild rudeness and incivility to more extreme forms such as hate speech, doxxing, and coordinated harassment campaigns. Several factors contribute to this:

1. **Anonymity**: Many users feel emboldened by the anonymity afforded by the internet, believing that their actions lack consequences.
2. **Echo Chambers**: Social media algorithms often prioritize content that reinforces users' existing beliefs, leading to polarized discussions and intolerance of differing viewpoints.
3. **Virality**: Harmful content can spread rapidly, and once it is posted, it is difficult to fully contain.

As digital platforms have become central to communication and community building, they have also created fertile ground for negative and harmful behavior. Online incivility can manifest in various forms, including:

- Hate speech: Derogatory language targeting individuals or groups based on attributes such as race, gender, religion, or nationality.
- Trolling: Deliberate attempts to provoke or disrupt conversations through inflammatory or offensive remarks.
- Harassment: Sustained or repeated attacks directed at individuals, often through personal insults, threats, or doxxing (public sharing of private information).

- Misinformation and disinformation: The spread of false or misleading information, often aimed at manipulating public opinion or causing harm to individuals or communities.

The global nature of social media has amplified these behaviours, allowing harmful content to spread quickly across borders. This toxic discourse has far-reaching consequences, from fostering societal division to causing significant psychological harm to individuals targeted by online abuse (S. Greengard,2019).

Factors Contributing to Online Toxicity

Several key factors contribute to the prevalence of toxic behavior online:

- Anonymity and Pseudonymity: Many platforms allow users to interact under pseudonyms or anonymously. This often leads to a sense of impunity, where individuals feel detached from the consequences of their actions, emboldening them to behave in ways they might not in face-to-face interactions.
- Echo Chambers and Filter Bubbles: Algorithms on platforms like Facebook, Twitter, and YouTube are designed to keep users engaged by showing content that aligns with their pre-existing beliefs. This creates echo chambers where users are primarily exposed to like-minded opinions, leading to the polarization of views and hostility toward opposing perspectives.
- Engagement-Driven Algorithms: Social media platforms often prioritize content that generates strong emotional reactions, whether positive or negative, to maximize user engagement. Unfortunately, outrage, anger, and controversy are more likely to trigger high engagement, incentivizing the spread of divisive or inflammatory content.
- Asynchronous Communication: Online interactions are often asynchronous, meaning users do not communicate in real-time. This can result in a lack of accountability, as users are less likely to see the immediate emotional impact of their words on others, reducing empathy and increasing the likelihood of harmful comments.
- Cultural and Linguistic Diversity: Global platforms host users from a wide variety of cultural and linguistic backgrounds, where differing social norms, humour, and taboos can lead to misunderstandings or offensive behavior that might not be recognized as such in certain contexts.

The Impact of Toxicity on Individuals and Communities

The impact of online toxicity can be profound, affecting both individuals and the broader digital community.

1. Psychological Harm: Victims of online abuse often suffer from anxiety, depression, and other mental health issues. The persistent nature of online harassment, coupled with the public visibility of platforms, can exacerbate feelings of humiliation, fear, and powerlessness.
2. Silencing Effect: Online toxicity can silence marginalized voices or those hesitant to participate in public discourse due to fear of harassment or retribution. This undermines the democratic potential of the internet by skewing discussions toward the most vocal, often toxic, participants.
3. Damage to Communities: Toxic behavior erodes trust within online communities, making it difficult to foster healthy dialogue. As communities become more polarized or dominated by negativity, user engagement may decline, and the overall quality of discourse deteriorates (A. Bekker, 2019).

The Limits of Reactive Moderation

In response to the growing problem of online toxicity, platforms have traditionally relied on reactive moderation techniques, which include:

- User Reporting: Platforms allow users to flag content they believe violates community guidelines. This initiates a review process where moderators or automated systems determine whether the content should be removed.
- Post-Publication Review: Platforms employ human moderators or AI systems to scan content for violations after it has already been posted. Harmful content is then removed or flagged for further review.

While these approaches are necessary, they suffer from several key limitations:

1. Scale and Speed: The sheer volume of content generated every second on major platforms makes it impossible for human moderators to review all flagged material. Even with AI assistance, harmful content often remains online for extended periods before it is removed, allowing it to reach large audiences.
2. Ineffectiveness Against Immediate Harm: By the time harmful content is flagged and taken down, the damage is often already done. Individuals targeted by hate speech or harassment may experience emotional distress, and misinformation may have already swayed public opinion or influenced decision-making.

3. Contextual Challenges: AI systems, while improving, still struggle with understanding context. For example, satire, irony, or nuanced discussions can be misinterpreted as harmful content, leading to over-censorship. Conversely, subtle forms of hate speech or harassment may go unnoticed by algorithms that rely on keyword detection without fully grasping the context.
4. User Fatigue: Relying on users to report harmful content places a burden on the very individuals who may already be affected by it. This can lead to reporting fatigue, where users become discouraged from engaging with the moderation process, allowing more harmful content to go unreported.

The Need for Proactive Approaches

Given these limitations, there is a growing consensus that reactive content moderation is insufficient to address the complexity and scale of online toxicity. A more proactive approach is needed, one that not only addresses harmful behavior after it occurs but also seeks to prevent it from arising in the first place.

AI holds significant promise in this regard, with its ability to analyze vast amounts of data in real-time and make predictive assessments about user behavior. Proactive AI systems could intervene before toxic content is posted, guide users toward more respectful engagement, and foster a culture of civility in digital spaces. This shift from a reactive to a proactive model is essential for creating healthier online environments and promoting positive, inclusive discourse.

The Limits of Reactive Moderation

Reactive moderation, which relies on users reporting harmful content or human moderators manually reviewing posts, is inherently limited. Given the vast scale of user-generated content on platforms like Facebook, Twitter, and YouTube, it is impossible for human moderators to catch every instance of misconduct. Moreover, harmful content often has already reached its intended audience by the time it is removed.

Automated systems have been developed to assist with content moderation, but they typically react after content has already been posted. For instance, tools like Perspective API and Microsoft's Azure Content Safety API are widely used to assess the likelihood that a comment is toxic. However, their role remains largely focused on detecting and filtering existing content rather than preventing incivility from emerging in the first place.

3.AI'S PROACTIVE ROLE IN PROMOTING CIVILITY

Moving Beyond Detection: AI as a Guide for Constructive Discourse

To shift from a reactive to a proactive stance, AI needs to move beyond merely detecting toxic content to actively promoting respectful engagement. Several strategies can be adopted to achieve this:

1. **Pre-emptive Interventions**: AI systems can provide real-time feedback to users before they post potentially harmful content. For example, algorithms could flag language that is likely to be interpreted as offensive and suggest alternative wording. This could be integrated with platforms' comment boxes, offering users a chance to revise their messages before submitting them.
2. **Sentiment Monitoring and Contextual Understanding**: AI systems can analyze the tone and sentiment of conversations as they evolve. By detecting early signs of hostility or disrespect, the system can issue gentle reminders or warnings to participants to keep the discussion civil.
3. **Adaptive Moderation**: AI could be programmed to adjust its moderation tactics based on user history or group dynamics For instance, users with a history of constructive contributions could be given more leeway, while those with a pattern of incivility could be subject to stricter scrutiny.
4. **Incentivizing Positive Behavior**: AI-driven systems could reward users who consistently engage in respectful discourse Positive reinforcement, such as badges or increased visibility for constructive comments, could foster a culture of respect and civility.

Nudging Users Toward Empathy

One key aspect of promoting civility is fostering empathy among users. AI can be designed to nudge users toward empathy by helping them recognize the potential impact of their words on others. For instance, before posting a comment, users could be asked to consider how they would feel if the comment were directed at them. Such psychological nudges, combined with real-time feedback, could encourage users to rethink impulsive or harmful posts.

AI's Role in Education and Awareness

Beyond moderating content, AI can be an educational tool that raises awareness about online etiquette and the consequences of toxic behavior. By offering real-time suggestions and insights into why certain language is problematic, AI can help users learn to engage more thoughtfully and respectfully.

4. ETHICAL CONSIDERATIONS

Bias and Fairness in AI Moderation

Despite the potential benefits of AI-driven moderation, there are significant ethical challenges that must be addressed. One of the primary concerns is bias in AI systems. Algorithms trained on biased datasets may disproportionately target certain groups or viewpoints, leading to unfair treatment or censorship.

To mitigate this, developers must prioritize transparency and fairness in the design and deployment of AI moderation systems. This includes ensuring that datasets are representative and that AI models are regularly audited for unintended biases.

Privacy and Autonomy

Another ethical concern is the potential for AI to infringe on user autonomy and privacy. Proactive interventions, such as real-time feedback or sentiment analysis, require access to users' data and conversations. Platforms must balance the need for civility with users' rights to privacy and freedom of expression.

Clear guidelines and consent mechanisms should be established to ensure that users are aware of how their data is being used and that they can opt out if desired.

5. CASE STUDIES: SUCCESSFUL IMPLEMENTATION OF PROACTIVE AI MODERATION

Reddit's AutoModerator

Reddit, a platform known for its decentralized community management, uses an AI-based tool called AutoModerator. This tool proactively scans posts and comments for certain flagged keywords or phrases, automatically removing or flagging content that violates community guidelines. While AutoModerator is reactive in its core function, it also provides pre-emptive guidance to users by informing them of the rules before they post. Reddit uses a proactive AI tool called AutoModerator (AutoMod) to manage and moderate its subreddits. AutoMod allows community moderators to set specific rules and guidelines for their forums, enabling automated monitoring of posts and comments. For example, AutoMod can flag or remove content containing offensive language, irrelevant links, or spam before it reaches a broader audience. By empowering moderators with customizable AI tools, Reddit has been able to create more focused and respectful online communities, reducing the workload for human moderators while promoting civility.

YouTube's Comment Moderation

YouTube has employed AI-driven tools to identify toxic comments and promote more civil engagement. By allowing creators to pre-emptively filter certain words or phrases from their comment sections, YouTube gives content producers the ability to foster more respectful interactions in their communities. YouTube employs machine learning-based moderation tools to manage comments on videos proactively. Its system uses sentiment analysis and content recognition to flag potentially harmful or abusive comments for review. Additionally, creators can enable features like "hold potentially inappropriate comments for review" to give them control over their content's tone. This approach has helped reduce harassment and abuse on the platform while encouraging constructive engagement. YouTube's consistent updates to its AI moderation tools also reflect its commitment to minimizing bias and improving user experience.

Discord's AutoMod AI

Discord introduced its AutoMod system to maintain civility in its servers. AutoMod scans user messages in real time, applying filters set by server administrators to detect and address rule-breaking content. It uses natural language processing (NLP) to identify offensive or harmful messages and takes action, such as warning users or temporarily muting them. The tool has been instrumental in creating safer spaces for diverse groups, enabling proactive intervention while preserving server-specific cultural norms.

These cases highlight the power of AI in moderating online platforms proactively, improving digital spaces while addressing challenges like abuse, harassment, and misinformation.

6.CONCLUSION

AI has the potential to transform online discussions by shifting the focus from reactive content moderation to proactive civility promotion. By integrating real-time feedback, sentiment monitoring, and nudging mechanisms, AI can play a critical role in fostering respectful and constructive dialogue. However, it is essential to address the ethical challenges surrounding bias, privacy, and fairness to ensure that AI systems are used responsibly.

As online platforms continue to grow and evolve, proactive AI solutions will be instrumental in shaping healthier, more inclusive digital spaces that prioritize empathy, respect, and constructive discourse. Artificial Intelligence (AI) holds immense potential to revolutionize online discussions by moving beyond traditional reactive content moderation. Instead of merely responding to inappropriate or harmful content after it appears, AI can be leveraged to encourage proactive civility. By incorporating features such as real-time feedback on user tone, sentiment analysis, and behavioural nudges, these systems can guide users toward more respectful and constructive interactions. For instance, a system might subtly suggest rephrasing a harsh comment or provide positive reinforcement for engaging respectfully, fostering a culture of empathy and mutual respect.

The integration of AI-driven civility promotion requires careful attention to ethical challenges. Bias in AI algorithms could inadvertently reinforce existing social inequalities, while privacy concerns arise from the monitoring of personal communications. Moreover, ensuring fairness in how AI systems are applied and addressing the risk of over-policing free expression are critical considerations. Transparent development, diverse datasets, and ongoing accountability mechanisms are essential to ensure that AI interventions align with human values and promote inclusivity without sacrificing user trust or autonomy.

As online platforms continue to evolve, embracing proactive AI solutions can help shape healthier and more inclusive digital environments. These systems can prioritize empathy and understanding, fostering spaces where diverse perspectives can be shared constructively. However, the success of such efforts depends on striking a balance between technological innovation and ethical responsibility, ensuring that AI empowers users rather than imposing limitations on their freedom of expression.

REFERENCES

Bekker, A. (2019, May). "5 Types of AI to propel your business,", https://www.scnsoft.com/blog/artificial-intelligence-types

Chen, H., Li, L., & Chen, Y. (2021). Explore success factors that impact artificial intelligence adoption on telecom industry in China. *Journal of Management Analytics*, 8(1), 36–68.

Chui, M., Harrysson, M., Manyika, J., Roberts, R., Chung, R., Nel, P., & van Heteren, A. (2018). *Applying artificial intelligence for social good*. McKinsey Global Institute.

Datta, S. (2019). Social artificial intelligence: Intuitive or intrusive?.

Greengard, S. (2019, May). "What is artificial intelligence?", https://www.datamation.com/artificial-intelligence/what-is-artificial-intelligence.html

Hendler, J., & Mulvehill, A. M. (2016). *Social Machines: The Coming Collision of Artificial Intelligence, Social Networking, and Humanity*. Apress. DOI: 10.1007/978-1-4842-1156-4

Hogan, M. (2020). How artificial intelligence influences social media.

Mufareh, A. (2020). How can artificial intelligence improve social media?.

Quadros, M. (2020). Artificial intelligence in social media marketing.

Sadiku, M. N. O. (1989). Artificial intelligence. *IEEE Potentials*, 8(May), 35–39. DOI: 10.1109/45.31596

Sadiku, M. N. O., Tembely, M., & Musa, S. M. (2018, March). Social media for beginners. *International Journal of Advanced Research in Computer Science and Software Engineering*, 8(3), 24–26. DOI: 10.23956/ijarcsse.v8i3.564

Sarmiento, H. (2020). How artificial intelligence can benefit the social media user.

Zilles, C. (2019). Taking advantage of AI in social media marketing.

Chapter 3
Harnessing Ethical AI:
Measures of Redressing Hate Speech in the Social Media Context

Sheikh Inam Ul Mansoor
https://orcid.org/0000-0001-8636-4769
Dayananda Sagar University, India

Showkat Ahamd Wani
https://orcid.org/0009-0009-0240-9073
Alliance University, Bangalore, India

ABSTRACT

As communication technology advanced Social media came in as means and platform of deliberation and connection wherein at the same time it opened doors for hate speech and toxic content. In this chapter, the author discusses moderation of ethical AI and hate speech in today's social media context that is increasingly becoming more polarized. Hate speech is not only an issue of some concern to users of technology but it is also a global concern in the current society especially since it affects social harmony, human rights, and freedom of speech and press thus the need to have an anti-hate speech technology with strong ethical backing. This Chapter focuses on the concept of Hate Speech from the legal, ethical and social aspects within and its effects on society and individuals. It considers how hate speech circulates, how it works by analysing sophisticated methods that include, the functions and procedure performed by algorithms, processes such as echo chambers, and the principles of things going viral.

DOI: 10.4018/979-8-3693-9904-0.ch003

1. INTRODUCTION

The social media have in the course of the last few decades became the most effective means of communication, interaction and sharing information. Social Media platforms such as Facebook, twitter, Instagram, and You tube has insisted or provided ways through which individuals or group of people can reach so many people within no time. With an Internet connection it has been made possible by social media that everyone can post, share or comment on any issue including International affairs. The change has been dominated by enlightening consequences such as: Encouragement of free speech, Encouragement of diversity of thought, Empowerment of minority opinions. But negative trends have created on social media some of which include hatred speeches, fake news, and social division. People tend to produce aggressive content on social networks thus extended the realm of hate speech to digital world. (Di Domenico et al., 1988) Hate speech mean any spoken or written words that incite violence or prejudice against people or organization based on the colours, religion or sex or color or ethnicity, sexual orientation or gender or anything like that, and it has stimulated highly over the last couple of years in these platforms. (Matamoros-Fernández & Farkas, 2021) Social media as its characteristic has become the middleware in spreading such content. By its design it promotes the sharing, encouraging a greater number of people to get engaged and share and very often the same content is inflammatory or at least sensational. (Shahbaznezhad et al., 2021) Also, social media plays a role of echo chambers, where algorithms bring like-minded individuals or users into' one space, therefore creating a space where hate speech could also be encouraged. (Cinelli et al., 2021)

The use of hate speech has some serious effect on society. In fact, social media may have communication opportunities yet threats may exist such as "radicalisation and political instability and violence." It has been linked to actual violence like few shooting incidents and ethnic conflicts in the real world. (Singh et al., 2024) It worsens the segregation of societies and brings rivalry between users of the two groups. Besides, hate speech is dangerous to the victims as they suffer psychological and negative consequences for the rest of their lives. However, given these great risks, moderating hate speech on social media has remains inconsequential and controversial because of the problems of moderating content from such big platforms. (Matamoros-Fernández & Farkas, 2021)

Social media platforms have been for a long time in the receive end of criticism over how they contain some of these negative posts. Although all the platforms have rules against hate speech, the scale at which people post content makes it almost impossible to moderate such content manually. It is there where artificial intelligence (AI) has rose as a possible solution. (Wilson & Land, 2021) Machine learning and NLP have been used in a large scale to detect and mitigate cases of hate speech. With these systems, the company can process large amounts of data in real-time to determine which kinds of speech are toxic and block or mark content that violates rules of conduct. (Bharathi Mohan et al., 2024) AI moderation is more effective for platform than when moderators have to manually go through thousands of content in a day. However, there are ethical problems, because such datasets allow discrimination, including the possible false identification or omission of hate speech, especially if the latter is of a metaphorical nature. (Shah & Sureja, 2024) This in turn has ramifications to fairness, equity and raises the possibility of Discriminations by algorithms. Moreover, AI based moderation can go overboard sometimes and ends up eradicating abstractions that appear legal in the realms of free speech. (Abbas & Torralba, 2024) In the same way as handling yet another big ethical question, which is to make hate speech criminal while protecting freedom of speech. The reason that AI systems' operation has rather low transparency. These algorithms are mostly "black box" kind, that is, the decision-making process is practically imperceptible to the user or even the developer of the script. (Shulner-Tal et al., 2024) This lack of transparency hinders one from explaining how a platform moderates its content as well as diminishes the population's trust in the platforms. Also, the lack of the guidelines for making decisions makes it completely impossible to contest moderation choices, adding to the problem with unfair content moderation. (Patidar et al., 2024)

One excellent example of this is hate speech moderation; here ethical AI can further be used as the eventual solution which would be fair and transparent in moderating contents. Making it not only a matter of superior technical approaches, but of requiring a human touch and a cultural and social perspective. (Hauer, 2022) Any practice with regard to the moderation of AI must meet basic ethical standards of fairness by having no prejudice when dealing with any user. This can be done using datasets that contain varied samples to the different languages, cultures and social setting. (Hagendorff, 2020) Moreover, the use of ethical AI systems means that those systems have had to become post explainable, which, in plain terms, means that the ways that these systems arrive at their decisions must be understandable not only to the user but also to the moderator. It also implies that there are always records that clarify decisions that users feel they can challenge or contest if their content has been deemed inappropriate to be posted. (Rabonato & Berton, 2024)

Lastly, this chapter underscores the importance of establishing the multi-stakeholder climate responsible for an ethical AI approach to hate speech moderation involving companies, the government, and non-governmental organizations. Technology firms cannot afford to be oblivious of laws and ethical violations at the same time, while regulators cannot sit idle while technology firms sweep hate speech and toxic content under the carpet at the same time. The objectives of this chapter are as follows: *(i) to consider how the use of ethical AI can help mitigate the rising problem of hate speech on social media and (ii) to describe the ethical issues that surfaced in the process.*

2. UNDERSTANDING HATE SPEECH IN THE SOCIAL MEDIA CONTEXT

Hate speech is a complex phenomenon that has drawn much attention with the advent of social networks. This influence has created discourses in the lawful, moral and social facets; concerns regarding distribution systems, and how technology accompanies it. (Matamoros-Fernández & Farkas, 2021) Analyzing hate speech requires a framework whereby one considers the effects of social media on society and individuals, and the ways in which companies manage the associated issues, and legal requirements translating messages promoting hatred or discrimination of the basis of race or ethnicity into actions. (Gorenc, 2022) All countries around the world have statutes that criminalize hate speech, yet the definitions differ from one nation to another. For example, in the United States, the speech that does not spur an immediate Object danger or is an actual threat, is protected by the Constitution specifically the First Amendment. (Lakier, 2020) However, many European countries including Germany and the United Kingdom were noted to have set very prohibitory laws regarding hate speech and more so there are penalties given to those who will be found advocating discriminating material. (Alkiviadou, 2018) Part of the reason, in this case, is that because laws are different, it is difficult to manage provocative images of hate speech on global social networks because some contents which are legal in some countries are unlawful in others. There are several ethical concerns tied to free speech, which causes conflicts between those individuals who are concerned that rationale will be used to suppress it, and those who think that hate speech harms minorities. (Schulman, 2022) In ethical terms one now starts to realize that hate speech does not confine itself to cyberspace but declares it's self in social marginalization, psychological effects and in some cases even physical injury. (Schäfer et al., 2024) This ethical concern becomes even more acute when it comes to the online space, for hate speech can go viral in a matter of seconds, and thus we need not mere better means but the means most effective to solve an important problem which is sparing the sensitivity of those, who may potentially be hurt by word of mouth while at the same time not encroaching upon the freedom of speech. (Cinelli et al., 2021)

In a social context hate speech swallows cultural values such as diversity, inclusion and respect for the other. It creates conditions of threat and aggression, primarily at the workplace, for people of colour, those with a recognized religion, LGBT people or foreign-born. (Matamoros-Fernández & Farkas, 2021) Hate speech if common fosters a climate of intolerance which can translate into discrimination, violence and division in any society. Whereas, as the demography of society is getting connected more and more through digitized means of communication the social implications of hate speech are more apparent and thus, need strong social, technological and legal counteractions. (Jacob & Kanth, 2023) The social cost of hate speech and rights and freedoms of citizens infringement is vast. On a broad community level, hate speech is part of the cause of social disintegration. It brings about ethnicity, race, religion, and even political envy in deserving people making it very easy for a person to hate another without even knowing his/her plight. (Peters, 2020) Sometimes hatred speech has been associated with ethnic clashes and other acts of terrorisms. For example, some of the related work suggests that inflammatory political content has caused atrocity against the colored people in Myanmar and Sri Lanka. Hate speech can also encourage discrimination in rather 'subtle' more pernicious, and subterranean ways by pro-establishing prejudice-setting causal conditions where discrimination is acceptable and par for the course. (Bishop, 2024)

At individual level, hate speech can have an intense effect. The consequences of victimization from online hate speech, are the following: they face high levels of anxiety, depression and feelings of isolation. (Pluta et al., 2023) *Such effects are further compounded by anonymity and reach vowed by the social media platforms and it would presently be futile for the victims themselves to try and shield themselves from the unpleasant content that would be thrust in front of them. Besides, hate speech leads to less likelihood of the minority groups voicing their opinions because they are prone to being faced with hate speech by the hate speech agents.* (Vasist et al., 2023) *That chilling effect on free expression, then, has a disproportionate effect on public discourse, the 'voiceless,' after all, are the 'voiceless' mainly when their speech is silenced by hate speech.* (Basu & Sen, 2023) Hate speech on social media is made possible by the help of the algorithms, echo chambers, and virality. Most social media sites are built on the basis of user interaction and therefore tend to promote information that elicits strong feeling. (Anjum & Katarya, 2024) However, there are outstanding discoveries concerning different results that explain that hate speech and other inflammations within post entice more response such as posting comment or sharing or even responding to the posts as compared to the neutral to positive posts. This creates a cycle of which the negativity is passed to the other users and at the same time expands the circles of hatred. (Saleh, Alhothali, & Moria, 2023)

Algorithms are also highly involved in this process since they decide what content will appear before visitors. Most social media algorithm work in a way to recommend to the users content they want based on their activity in the application. On the one hand it makes the users' experience presumably more individual and on the other hand it leads to the formation of "sequencers" where the users are exposed only to the information and opinions matching their own. (Norström et al., 2020) In these conditions, there are high chances of appearing hate speech, because people do not have opportunities to come across the opinions that counteract their own. Self-segregation means that individuals are exposed to extremism continuously while they cannot respond or publish refute information. (Matamoros-Fernández & Farkas, 2021)

The antagonist characteristic of social media also increases the level of hate speech. Posts that when published goes viral, can affect millions of users within a given number of hours, making it almost impossible to restrain when circulated. The issue of generic hate speech virality is immensely critical because hateful messages penetrate social media before moderation systems address them. By the time the hate speech is or is reported it has already went viral and the harm has already been done and this includes calls to attack real targets such as individuals or communities or threats. (Farrand, 2023) All social media companies are extremely conscious of their contribution to the promotion of hate speech, and many of them have formed policies seeking to redress the problem. Such measures mainly entail pulling down of content that is contrary to conditions of acceptable usage, or blocking accounts that post risky content time and again. (Shahbaznezhad et al., 2021) Applications such as Facebook, Twitter, and youtube use AI action tools in moderating examples of hate speech among their users. However, such efforts have advantages and disadvantages and the result of the practised platform policies remains uncertain. (Stracqualursi & Agati, 2024) The largest problem in most social media networks is the flow of posted content that can come to billions of new objects. Huge audiences share millions of posts, comments, and videos every day, so it is remarkably challenging for human moderators to analyze it all. (Chen et al., 2023) Current AI-based moderation that is good at finding clear-cut examples of hate speech has a problem with detecting more subtle forms of it. For example, sarcasm, coded vocabulary, manifold metaphors or even the use of the some culture might go unnoticed by the AI systems, which leads to the underestimation of that certain type of the hate speech. (Ozanne et al., 2022) As the same, such systems can also go overboard and block legal content as 'potentially toxic', hence causing complain about censorship.

It is clear that popular social media networks equally implement hate speech policies while removing norms for one user and punishing other individuals. This can be attributed to growing pressures from key users and corporations while aiming at free speech but fearing 'toxicity' or negative impact often for profit making. (Goanta & Ortolani, 2021) Furthermore there are legal and regulatory issues concerning the moderation of material such as hate speech regarding social media platforms. This may be due to legal requirements because there are some countries that have banned anything that is abusive to a particular class of persons. (Rochefort, 2020) Nevertheless, big tech firms fail to do so, particularly in the US, where it can offend the freedom of speech, which leads to a mixed understanding of the policy internationally. (Kumar & Riegner, 2019) In light of these limitations, there have been recent efforts by some scholars demanding more openness as to how the different social media shared hatred speeches. These are creating new rules for moderating speech, extending those rules to a greater swath of content, and improving moderation transparency.(Muhammed & Mathew, 2022) Furthermore, the topic of "responsible AI" as the system with more realistic and better discriminating power in consideration of hate speech without any contradiction to the freedom of speech is attracting attention. (Mikalef et al., 2022)

Concerning hate speeches, social media are undoubtedly playing tremendous roles in its spread; although the social media platforms have also tried to curb this problem to some extent, and it is by far not ample. This is especially because Hate Speech is a fluid entity that forces platforms and tech firms to endure heightened evolution to help combat these new forms and increased aggression. (Zamri et al., 2023) Countering hate speech requires collaboration between platforms, governments, civil society, and users. Governments set guidelines, while civil organizations advocate for vulnerable groups' voices. (Schäfer et al., 2024) On the same note, it is appropriate that consumers should be educated on some of the effects of hate speech, and the right etiquettes to observe in the social media age.

3. THE ROLE OF AI IN CONTENT MODERATION

AI is also applied in various fields, and its application in fighting trends like hate speech in social networks is rather timely. (Rawat et al., 2024) Communication platforms have turned to AI technologies to address the continuously increasing amount of user-generated content, in the search for an effective method to measure the potential for violence in the messages which are posted by users, and prevent discrimination or violation of guidelines. (Molina & Sundar, 2022) AI systems work to monitor huge amounts of data at the same time, indicating cases of hate speech to be reviewed by human moderators. But, application of AI for content moderation turns out to be beneficial and useful but this has drawbacks and cannot be sustainable in dealing with the ever evolving online hate speech. (Fontes et al., 2022) Some of the practical AI utilizations that are implemented to hate speech detection and monitoring, include; the advanced machine learning approaches, natural language processing, and patterns recognition. They are utilized for the purpose of text and image or video analysis to filter out the data which satisfies predefined criteria of containing hate speech. (Jahan & Oussalah, 2023) Supervised Machine Learning involves training of the AI to recognize image and speech patterns from labelled databases, exclude posts that are similar to the examples of hate speech. (Alloghani et al., 2020) Furthermore, there are more developed methods for deep learning when it is used in an AI model – the system is able to understand the context of the language used and becomes more effective at recognizing forms of hate speech that are coded, or use indirect language and threats. (Talaei Khoei et al., 2023)

Semantics are particularly important because the ability of AI to recognize hate speech presupposes the use of natural language processing to interpret posts made by users. (Lauriola et al., 2022) Speaking of the language, NLP divides it into segments such as words that are recognized syntactically and grammatically, which enables the AI to understand What has been said, and Why it has been said. This is even more applicable to the case of hate speech since the capacity to determine toxic intent may be hidden by literals, other forms of expressions, or even proverbs. (Kaddari et al., 2021) Unfortunately, hate speech, and in particular, hidden in minorities, is a result of certain meanings for specific groups, cannot be identified by simple keywords and thus needs AI-based NLP technologies. (Jim et al., 2024) However, the new approach to content moderation with the use of AI sophistication is still in process, although there are the followed strengths and limitations of the present deployment. (Udupa et al., 2023) AI is even better than human moderators in this case bearing in mind that managers have to moderate millions of posts on social media each day. This is due to the fact that it can easily flag and ban any item that contradicts the rules basically making moderating at a large scale possible. (Shahbaznezhad et al., 2021) This is especially true when it comes to stopping the viral spread of hate speech: content that is reported and deleted shortly won't be able to set a tone for mobilizing violence or shaping the public debate.

AI helps in decision making because unlike human beings, it is ever working without the biases that may affect the results it produces. On the other hand, the use of human moderators may lead to stress and burnout of the moderator, and the emergence of such factors that negatively influence their work. (Shulner-Tal et al., 2024) AI systems are another level of inalterability in moderating content because policies are uniformly enforced across different platforms. In theory, this minimizes the possibility of differences in the way the content is moderated in that AI performs its moderation based on the set standards without threats by extrinsic factors such as political or even cultural influences. (Ozanne et al., 2022) But such a type of AI content moderation has some improveable issues, especially for actual context related. It is not very good at understanding contextual cues, irony, female humor, and timely culture none of which are joking features is a hate speech. (Udupa et al., 2023) On the other hand, a post that may have common symbols that a certain group of people have adopted to mean hatred will not be seen as a hatred post by the AI because such patterns were not programmed into its system. Such failure leads to two types of errors: Type I –where good posts are removed as negatives or Type II – where negatives pass through the net unchallenged.

The dynamic in nature of hate speech is also a limitation that has been observed in conducting this study. Hate speech is dynamic, meaning that there are always new terms, symbols and code phrases that have not been used by the moderation algorithms. (Cinelli et al., 2021) This poses a massive problem for deep learning, in essence, AI recurrently needs to be retrained in order to identify these new forms of toxic discourse. Hate speech is culture, region, and language sensitive, and hence a universal solution cannot suffice. (Hietanen & Eddebo, 2023) The results also revealed that while AI systems are good at content moderation, their performance depends on the datasets used during training; this means that an AI system trained on data from, for instance, the USA or using only English data could be poor when used in another country or when moderating content in other languages. (Saranya & Subhashini, 2023) It is crucial to provide AI training data constantly to increase the feasibility of correct hate speech detection. New data can be learned with help of new deep learning models, AI are equipped with new neural networks making it possible for the AI to better identify different types of hate speech. (Masood & Abbas, 2024) The more it samples the performance of hate speech, the more its precision in categorizing them and other samples in a given data set is increased and in the process reducing on false positives and false negatives. Nevertheless, such prejudiced or inadequate training sets will continue such matters in moderation. (Zhou et al., 2017)

Real-life examples of AI moderation highlight its effectiveness and inefficiency in AI moderation to help readers understand. Its application where Facebook successfully implemented the use of AI to filter out hate speech is a big success. (Hakami & Tazel, 2024) More recently, the platform's AI-based moderation has been enhanced, with AI accounting for 97 percent of the hate speech that is filtered out by the site before users flag it. This is a step up from the current use of algorithms that depend on users to flag certain contents as being toxic and allowing AI to prevent the spread of toxic contents. (Milosevic et al., 2022) Likewise, Twitter has not been idle in employing the AI approach to the detestable menace of hate speech; the social platform has been able to delete millions of accounts that post hate sentiments and suspend users with multiple cases of posting unpleasant content. (Stracqualursi & Agati, 2024) Such platforms have revealed that AI can be quite useful in scaling CC processes, and help decrease hate speech frequency. But it is also relatively easy to find examples where AI-powered moderation methodologies have failed to fulfil their promise; where the realities of artificial intelligence have reared their heads. (Seng, Ang, & Ngharamike, 2022) For example, during its use of artificial intelligence to filter out content and detect terror content, YouTube marked harmless videos as terrorist materials but failed to notice real terror threats. Oh, and it also banned LGBTQ+ creators from discussing safely content by demonetizing, revealing AI's ability to understand context and bias in the training data. (Arora et al., 2023)

Likewise, there have been cases when AI technologies could not identify negative content just because the symbols or coded expressions were used instead. In some hard-coded subcultures, people have found how to give a hate message a polite guise with the help of understandable symbols or clichés inconceivable to the AI. (Feuerriegel et al., 2023) For instance, members of the Ku Klux Klan have associated innocuous signs, such as the raised fist with the 'OK' symbol, as secret signals of hate since the usual AI signs were not programmed to decode these shifting signs. These failures demonstrate the further training and production of the AI system, which is still required to be periodically revised in response to the ever-changing environment of the online hate speech. (Williams & Yampolskiy, 2021)

As a result, most social media interface solutions are using ai moderation alongside human supervision. Although AI is able to read large amount of content, human moderators finally take time with context in mind, fast and contextual. (Nguyen et al., 2024) However this approach is not foolproof as the moderators themselves can be influenced by their own personal bias, fatigue and resultant stress from exposure to such toxic information in their day to day lives. Future AI advancements plan to solve these content moderation issues. (Krenn et al., 2023) Moreover, if academics tend to think in terms of ethical AI, they devote their time to creating other algorithms, which would be more ethical and fair in terms of content moderation.

4. ETHICAL CHALLENGES IN AI DEPLOYMENT FOR HATE SPEECH MITIGATION

While using artificial intelligence (AI) to tackle hate speech problem within social media platforms has not been devoid of ethical questions. (Anjum & Katarya, 2024) As with nearly everything in life, the use of AI in moderating the content comes concerns of bias, obscurity and the questions that pertain to free speech that comes with freedom of expressing opinions while at the same time deterring the posting of objectionable content. (Stockinger et al., 2023) This needs to be done to have AI for hate speech management respect citizens' rights as well as to respond to other ethic concerns such as biases and discrimination. (Min, 2023) Some of the sources of bias in an AI include; biased training data, wrong algorithms and lack of diversity in input during the process. When there are shortcoming or prejudice examples in the datasets fed to an AI system, the same data will be reproduced in moderation as well. (Shah & Sureja, 2024) Those trained for one form of demographic might not work across others – with the potential for predisposing certain minorities for real-life harm. (Jain & Menon, 2023) The lack of AI frameworks to distinguish various categories of user content inevitably leads to free speech suppression as some speech that was not considered to be hate speech was not detected while some contents classified as hate speech was not detected worsens discrimination. (Saleh et al., 2023) To avoid the issues of AI bias one needs to apply a number of approaches for instance; developing a new training data set that would be broader and more diverse, including many people of different backgrounds into the process of developing and implementing these AI solutions and also, periodical reviewing the use of AI in search of the given bias. (González-Sendino et al., 2024) The given fair AI system should be accurate, caring, consistent, transparent, and accountable, for which organizations and developers should set and implement policies and standards of fairness and equality.

Bias can be eliminated, but accountability and transparency of AI is another ethical question for curbing the hate speech. (Memarian & Doleck, 2023) The workings of the moderators themselves are still unclear and users cannot question the decision-making process hence reducing trust while putting into consideration the AI accountability. (Smith et al., 2023) The information might also include some metadata about usage of the used AI algorithms in decision making and abilities of the data referred to making such a classification the contents as hate speech. Platforms should also set quite definite policies regarding users' appeals for reevaluation, wherein the instance of moderation is unbanned for human revision. (Steyvers & Kumar, 2024) Another factor that have to be included is responsibility to guarantee that norms are complied with and organizations are answerable for the measures towards regulation of AI users. (Ortega-Bolaños et al., 2024) For this reason, organizations must have an accountability to suffer the consequences of censorship or ineffectiveness by AI; governments need to intervene to impose accountability for following these guidelines in the deployment of AI. (Abedin et al., 2022) The society and particularly civil organizations together with researchers and policymakers should therefore fight hard to ensure that accountability mechanisms play their rightful role in formulating and deploying AI technologies.

The invariably moral quest for using AI to counter acts of hate speech presents several free speech limitations on constitutional questions and ethical dilemmas in decision-making. (Sponholz, 2023) AI based moderation as either overactive or underactive can misidentify and moderate harmless posts as hate speech, thus over-censorship and also fails to recognize actual hate speech, hence the call for effective and mutually supporting moderation strategies. (Gorenc, 2022) AI can in a way aid organizations in setting standards of how they should deal with hate speech by providing organizations with guidelines on how they can develop AI systems for ethical purposes. (Ortega-Bolaños et al., 2024) AI frameworks must adhere to standard values such as – liberty, anti-discrimination, openness, accountability, and inclusion of stakeholders to preserve freedoms. Any ethical models, need to be flexible concerning social change and require ethical check, involve multiple stakeholders, and, also continually improve the abilities of machines learning for social good and human rights.

5. STRATEGIES FOR FAIR AND EFFECTIVE MODERATION

AI hate speech moderation must establish frameworks of fairness, transparency, and context to counter balance algorithmic bias to entice community participation in account of cultural differences of the material in question. (Fu et al., 2020) An approach to implementing ethical AI is bias-free AI gained by meaningful data and the right selection of the model. To make the technology of AI for identifying and eliminating the hate speech correctly, it is necessary to teach the AI right datasets of people belonging to different demographic backgrounds, culture, and languages. (Giovanola et al., 2023) This means data collection must be proactive and intentional in its inclusion of marginalised voices/worlds and those impacted most negatively by hate speech. Thus datasets are represent a wide range of opinions and allow AI systems to distinguish certain trends of hate speech expressed in different cultures. (Mikalef et al., 2022) The bias issue must therefore be addressed during data selection; developers evaluate AI in its life cycle using fairness to determine the discriminating factor in different groups. (Shah & Sureja, 2024) Working with social scientists externally means that social context enters the data and modelling process to have moderate and more inclusive AI.

The other approach that has been suggested for improving the use of AI on Hate Speech is the use of explainable AI stands as another strategy which can drastically improve the ethical use of AI in Hate Speech moderation. The acronym for explainable AI is XAI and it is the ability of AI systems to give such explanations of what they do. (Yang et al., 2023) Users and developers are concerned with the process of moderation by AI especially because there is lack of transparency regarding the decision made. Explanations given when some content is moderated provide the confidence and responsibility to the users making their interaction with the system more profound. (Enarsson, 2024)

For developers it could also be useful to develop models in a way that makes the decisions understandable together with natural language tools, attention tools and confidence indicators. (Hosain et al., 2024) More so, there should be public policies that illustrate procedures whereby users need to appeal against moderation of content because it should be confirmed by humans. (Shahbaznezhad et al., 2021) Ethical AI for hate speech moderation should be content-specific; the moderation approach should take into account cultural and geographic localization because it impacts the AI moderated content based on the targeted communities' social history experiences. (Arsalan, 2024) This means that language, and sometimes accent, cultural and social references, which can be huge barriers, differ and depend on a specific geographical location. In addition, because cultures and values may vary around the world, the definition of hate speech can be quite variable, which requires discussing moderation that goes beyond the templates. (Helm et al., 2024) To be most effective, contextual moderation should involve the support and active participation of local directors and other local stakeholders who are best placed to provide insight into the various ways and forms which hate speech manifests in each area. It only shows that this partnership can participate in the development of localized models to accommodate specificity and provinciality. (Wilson & Land, 2021) Furthermore, contextual moderation might suggest some sort of elasticity which is compounded with feedback in real-time originating from the users or the given communities to adapt the facilities of AI for altering trends in hate speech. (Gillespie, 2020) Some of the privacy consideration could be as follows: This is because it would take a much shorter time for AI systems to integrate cultural and regional variations into the moderation process and come up with better near real-time moderation that meets a much higher standard of accuracy as compared to human moderation.

AI solutions should be shared efforts, from companies, technology firms, Non-Governmental Organizations, research institutions, and communities to have workable moral regimes against hate speech technology. (Cachat-Rosset & Klarsfeld, 2023) The involvement of multiple stakeholders, such as civil rights activists and researchers, further AI development by including multiple demands and rights during the lifecycle with ethical considerations during implementation. (Haefner et al., 2021) Actioning solutions to ethical questions in AI requires full disclosure of the techniques used, the data employed, and the measures used to judge the pros and cons of the AI systems used. Stakeholder engagement helps in embracing team work thereby improving development of hate speech technologies. The involvement of users during development leads to development of user focused systems improving AI models based on real experiences.

6. LESSONS FROM GLOBAL IMPLEMENTATION

Ethical applications of AI in the fight against hate speech have been widely discussed all around the world, and different platforms experiment with innovative ways of moderating content. (Aslam, 2024) A strong reference implementation concerning ethical aspects of AI can be found in the moderation strategy of Facebook, Twitter, and YouTube platforms which have initially designed specific models for countering hate speech in the content posted in the social networks while preserving the audience's activity. (Kluge Corrêa et al., 2023) For instance, Facebook has begun the process of raising AI for content moderation as the social networking site plans on using machine learning to prevent the appearance of hate speech. Automated detecting is based both on NLP and on the reports of users that could contribute with their observations of abusive content. This efficient approach has been arranged with the help of incessant updating of the algorithms with new datasets by Facebook. (Capuano et al., 2023) Ethical consideration is therefore important when it comes to the assessment of efficiency of companies. Content moderation of hate speech on Facebook is regulated by its Community Standards and Facebook's biannual content reports work as the key steps towards transparency. Likewise, ethical AI is used by Twitter to improve the safety of the platform while using free speech with hate speech content that is flagged to be reviewed manually. (Gillespie, 2020) This approach emphasizes the rule of distinction because it may not always be clear what someone's motive for their comments is. Further, using AI for detection coupled with monitoring by people, Twitter has sought to avoid a situation where freedom of speech is subjected to high levels of censorship.

YouTube examines hate speech with the pluralism model where the firm utilizes artificial intelligence to moderate the content but at the same time provides the users with the tools to report the content. (Crawford & Gillespie, 2014) This approach makes the users to be able to fight hate speech effectively, and promotes togetherness by enabling the reporting and appeal of moderation decisions across several platforms. (Enarsson, 2024) For example, at Reddit, one is free to question moderators' decisions on moderation directly, which is a user-oriented platform where people can log complaints. It is also about embracing change, and it empowers the people of that community to own change. The technological infrastructures of platforms need effective, streamlined hate speech complaint systems and acknowledge the ethical use of artificial intelligence in hate speech moderation across global cultures especially in regards for multiple languages. Knowing that there are differences in the interpretation of the meaning of hate speech all over the world, TikTok is creating models based on regional specifics through creating a designated team to work with social norms to moderate content.

To address global diversity, key challenging problems for AI training data needed to be grown to be more inclusive for platforms. This has something to do with collection of data which accurately identifies the different languages, dialects and cultural aspects of the groups in question. (Cachat-Rosset & Klarsfeld, 2023) The enlargement of data with related contents diversifies the perception of AI systems in different platforms about hate speech. Of course, the safer content can then be detected with a higher degree of accuracy by the context-aware AI models employed for moderation that is historically sensitive to cultural restrictions. However, problems like algorithmic bias, clarity, and accountability remain a tough nut to crack and result in over or under censorship which in effects users or certain communities. (Wojcieszak et al., 2021)

In these regards, platforms should be preemptively addressing ethical problems of integration of AI technologies in hate speech moderation, through creation of the autonomous authorities on AI in moderation An opportunity to improve ethical uses of AI involves engaging with an organization that deals with technology, civil rights, and academics. Since these technologies are dynamic, moderation approaches have to take user experiences and community feedback to enhance hate speech detection regularly.

7. CONCLUSION

At the end of this voyage to illustrate how ethical AI can combat hate speech, the only thing that emerges clearly is a crossroad between technology, law and ethics. The epiphany of the issue regarding hate speech in digital contexts has driven the AI-technology based content moderation. The major points learned out of this discussion on ethical AI that can be very useful for making online spaces safer as we surface these insights.

This chapter shows that hate speech definitions and censor-enabling policies are much more nuanced and that hate speech is not merely a legal phenomenon but a socio-cultural and psychological issue as well. Such issues call for or more contextual moderation approaches that can address the contingencies in organizations. When it comes to creating ethic AI, there is considerable concern when it comes to comprehending language, culture, and emotion to classify hate speech. Moreover, AI can contain biases that may worsen the situations of minorities since such systems contribute to making decisions about the employees' promotion and remuneration, and preferential treatment. This makes it necessary to gather as well as construct models that are responsive to the diversity of the users. Effort in the future should shift towards designing AI that can effectively and simultaneously identify hate speech while being just for all contexts in which it is applicable.

Transparency and accountability in AI systems also figured prominently as having an impact on user trust and engagement. Through these explainable AI models, platforms will be able to highlight to users the process of decisions around moderation and encourage a feeling of ownership and control in digital spaces. This transparency is vital to the legitimacy of their actions and helps those who are being moderated see that it was done within the framework of standing policy. The key principles that these frameworks may advocate for provide a pathway towards the responsible use of AI in addressing hate speech mitigation.

Collaboration is one of the most crucial strategies to be pursued as we contemplate guiding principles for research and policy-making in the future. Collaborating with stakeholders to come from different sectors, tech. companies, civil rights groups, academia and the community can take us farther toward crafting compliant hate speech policies. These collaborations will inform the creation of guidelines for the ethical development and implementation of AI in content moderation to ensure that they benefit society as a whole. Moreover, policy-making should stress on user empowerment. Providing these capabilities allows platforms to grow a better-informed and less passive population that can understand, attack, and learn from moderation decisions. By providing a variety of these AI-driven user-empowerment tools, which include reporting and educational components, the chasm between user and platform is narrowing so as to build an accountability culture based on mutual respect.

AI has a lot of promise in paving the way for a safer and more inclusive digital future. Implemented ethically, AI technologies can improve our content moderation capabilities by quickening hate speech response times, promoting healthier online spaces. But this capacity in itself brings challenges that demand constant re-evaluation and revisions. With technology that keeps evolving at such speed we need to have a continuous discussion on the different ethical issues in AI when it comes to hate speech. In the end, an analysis of the role that ethical AI can play in mitigating hate speech shows a mixed landscape. Though AI and content moderation have integrated together offers innovative solutions to long-standing challenges, these advances also bring along urgent ethical concerns that must be carefully maneuvered. Again, this is a culmination not an endpoint and the quest for ethical AI takes constant vigilance and re-evaluation, unwavering integrity and adherence to justice and equity.

REFERENCES

Abbas, A., & Torralba, A. (2024). Content moderation in the age of AI: Navigating the trade-offs between free speech and privacy. DOI: 10.13140/RG.2.2.33790.60486

Abedin, B., Meske, C., Junglas, I., Rabhi, F., & Motahari-Nezhad, H. R. (2022). Designing and managing human-AI interactions. *Information Systems Frontiers*, 24(3), 691–697. DOI: 10.1007/s10796-022-10313-1

Alkiviadou, N. (2018). *The legal regulation of hate speech: The international and European frameworks*. Politička Misao.

Alloghani, M., Al-Jumeily, D., Mustafina, J., Hussain, A., & Aljaaf, A. J. (2020). A Systematic Review on Supervised and Unsupervised Machine Learning Algorithms for Data Science. In Berry, M., Mohamed, A., & Yap, B. (Eds.), *Supervised and Unsupervised Learning for Data Science* (pp. 1–16). Springer., DOI: 10.1007/978-3-030-22475-2_1

Anjum, K., & Katarya, R. (2024). Hate speech and toxicity detection in online social media: A recent survey of state of the art and opportunities. *International Journal of Information Security*, 23(1), 577–608. DOI: 10.1007/s10207-023-00755-2

Arora, A., Barrett, M., Lee, E., Oborn, E., & Prince, K. (2023). Risk and the future of AI: Algorithmic bias, data colonialism, and marginalization. *Information and Organization*, 33(3), 100478. DOI: 10.1016/j.infoandorg.2023.100478

Arsalan, H. (2024). Ethical AI in hate speech detection: Safeguarding systems from external shocks. DOI: 10.13140/RG.2.2.26312.74245

Aslam, M. (2024). Ethical considerations in hate speech detection: AI solutions for complex systems. DOI: 10.13140/RG.2.2.24844.73608

Basu, S., & Sen, S. (2023). Silenced voices: Unravelling India's dissent crisis through historical and contemporary analysis of free speech and suppression. *Information & Communications Technology Law*, 33(1), 42–65. DOI: 10.1080/13600834.2023.2249780

Bharathi Mohan, G., Prasanna Kumar, R., Vishal Krishh, P., Keerthinathan, A., Lavanya, G., Meghana, M. K. U., Sulthana, S., & Doss, S. (2024). An analysis of large language models: Their impact and potential applications. *Knowledge and Information Systems*, 66(9), 5047–5070. DOI: 10.1007/s10115-024-02120-8

Bishop, S. (2024). Should we hate hate speech regulation? The argument from viewpoint discrimination. *The Philosophical Quarterly*, 74(4), 1059–1079. DOI: 10.1093/pq/pqae086

Cachat-Rosset, G., & Klarsfeld, A. (2023). Diversity, equity, and inclusion in artificial intelligence: An evaluation of guidelines. *Applied Artificial Intelligence*, 37(1), 1–18. DOI: 10.1080/08839514.2023.2176618

Capuano, N., Fenza, G., Loia, V., & Nota, F. D. (2023). Content-based fake news detection with machine and deep learning: A systematic review. *Neurocomputing*, 530, 91–103. DOI: 10.1016/j.neucom.2023.02.005

Chen, S., Xiao, L., & Kumar, A. (2023). Spread of misinformation on social media: What contributes to it and how to combat it. *Computers in Human Behavior*, 141, 107643. DOI: 10.1016/j.chb.2022.107643

Cinelli, M., De Francisci Morales, G., Galeazzi, A., Quattrociocchi, W., & Starnini, M. (2021). The echo chamber effect on social media. *Proceedings of the National Academy of Sciences of the United States of America*, 118(9), e2023301118. DOI: 10.1073/pnas.2023301118 PMID: 33622786

Cinelli, M., Pelicon, A., Mozetič, I., Quattrociocchi, W., Novak, P. K., & Zollo, F. (2021). Dynamics of online hate and misinformation. *Scientific Reports*, 11(1), 22083. DOI: 10.1038/s41598-021-01487-w PMID: 34764344

Crawford, K., & Gillespie, T. (2014). What is a flag for? Social media reporting tools and the vocabulary of complaint. *New Media & Society*, 18(3), 410–428. DOI: 10.1177/1461444814543163

Di Domenico, G., Sit, J., Ishizaka, A., & Nunan, D. (2021). Fake news, social media and marketing: A systematic review. *Journal of Business Research*, 124, 329–341. DOI: 10.1016/j.jbusres.2020.11.037

Enarsson, T. (2024). Navigating hate speech and content moderation under the DSA: Insights from ECtHR case law. *Information & Communications Technology Law*, 33(1), 1–18. DOI: 10.1080/13600834.2018.1494415

Farrand, B. (2023). Is this a hate speech? The difficulty in combating radicalisation in coded communications on social media platforms. *European Journal on Criminal Policy and Research*, 29(3), 477–493. DOI: 10.1007/s10610-023-09543-z

Feuerriegel, S., DiResta, R., Goldstein, J. A., Kumar, S., Lorenz-Spreen, P., Tomz, M., & Pröllochs, N. (2023). Research can help to tackle AI-generated disinformation. *Nature Human Behaviour*, 7(11), 1818–1821. DOI: 10.1038/s41562-023-01726-2 PMID: 37985906

Fontes, C., Hohma, E., Corrigan, C. C., & Lütge, C. (2022). AI-powered public surveillance systems: Why we (might) need them and how we want them. *Technology in Society*, 71, 102137. DOI: 10.1016/j.techsoc.2022.102137

Fu, R., Huang, Y., & Singh, P. V. (2020). AI and algorithmic bias: Source, detection, mitigation and implications. Available at *SSRN*: https://ssrn.com/abstract=3681517 or http://dx.doi.org/DOI: 10.2139/ssrn.3681517

Gillespie, T. (2020). Content moderation, AI, and the question of scale. *Big Data & Society*, 7(2), 2053951720943234. Advance online publication. DOI: 10.1177/2053951720943234

Giovanola, B., & Tiribelli, S. (2023). Beyond bias and discrimination: Redefining the AI ethics principle of fairness in healthcare machine-learning algorithms. *AI & Society*, 38(2), 549–563. DOI: 10.1007/s00146-022-01455-6 PMID: 35615443

Goanta, C., & Ortolani, P. (2021). Unpacking content moderation: The rise of social media platforms as online civil courts. Available at *SSRN*: https://ssrn.com/abstract =3969360 or http://dx.doi.org/DOI: 10.2139/ssrn.3969360

González-Sendino, R., Serrano, E., & Bajo, J. (2024). Mitigating bias in artificial intelligence: Fair data generation via causal models for transparent and explainable decision-making. *Future Generation Computer Systems*, 155, 384–401. DOI: 10.1016/j.future.2024.02.023

Gorenc, N. (2022). Hate speech or free speech: An ethical dilemma? *International Review of Sociology*, 32(3), 413–425. DOI: 10.1080/03906701.2022.2133406

Haefner, N., Wincent, J., Parida, V., & Gassmann, O. (2021). Artificial intelligence and innovation management: A review, framework, and research agenda. *Technological Forecasting and Social Change*, 162, 120392. DOI: 10.1016/j.techfore.2020.120392

Hagendorff, T. (2020). The ethics of AI ethics: An evaluation of guidelines. *Minds and Machines*, 30(1), 99–120. DOI: 10.1007/s11023-020-09517-8

Hakami, A., & Tazel, R. (2024). The Ethics of AI in Content Moderation: Balancing Privacy, Free Speech, and Algorithmic Control. DOI: 10.13140/RG.2.2.19529.97121

Hauer, T. (2022). Importance and limitations of AI ethics in contemporary society. *Humanities & Social Sciences Communications*, 9(1), 272. DOI: 10.1057/s41599-022-01300-7

Helm, P., Bella, G., Koch, G., & Giunchiglia, F. (2024). Diversity and language technology: How language modeling bias causes epistemic injustice. *Ethics and Information Technology*, 26(8), 8. Advance online publication. DOI: 10.1007/s10676-023-09742-6

Hietanen, M., & Eddebo, J. (2023). Towards a Definition of Hate Speech—With a Focus on Online Contexts. *The Journal of Communication Inquiry*, 47(4), 440–458. DOI: 10.1177/01968599221124309

Hosain, M. T., Jim, J. R., Mridha, M. F., & Kabir, M. M. (2024). Explainable AI approaches in deep learning: Advancements, applications, and challenges. *Computers & Electrical Engineering*, 117, 109246. DOI: 10.1016/j.compeleceng.2024.109246

Jacob, C., & Kanth, M. (2023). 'Kill two million of them': Institutionalised hate speech, impunity and 21st century atrocities in India. *Global Responsibility to Protect*, 15(2-3), 209–245. DOI: 10.1163/1875984X-20230002

Jahan, M. S., & Oussalah, M. (2023). A systematic review of hate speech automatic detection using natural language processing. *Neurocomputing*, 546, 126232. DOI: 10.1016/j.neucom.2023.126232

Jain, L. R., & Menon, V. (2023). AI Algorithmic Bias: Understanding its Causes, Ethical and Social Implications. In *2023 IEEE 35th International Conference on Tools with Artificial Intelligence (ICTAI)* (pp. 460-467). Atlanta, GA, USA. DOI: 10.1109/ICTAI59109.2023.00073

Jim, J. R., Talukder, M. A. R., Malakar, P., Kabir, M. M., Nur, K., & Mridha, M. F. (2024). Recent advancements and challenges of NLP-based sentiment analysis: A state-of-the-art review. *Natural Language Processing Journal*, 6, 100059. DOI: 10.1016/j.nlp.2024.100059

Kaddari, Z., Mellah, Y., Berrich, J., Belkasmi, M. G., & Bouchentouf, T. (2021). Natural language processing: Challenges and future directions. In *T. Masrour, I. El Hassani, & A. Cherrafi* (Eds.), *Artificial intelligence and industrial applications. A2IA 2020* (Vol. 144, pp. 255-267). Springer, Cham. DOI: 10.1007/978-3-030-53970-2_22

Kluge Corrêa, N., Galvão, C., Santos, J. W., Del Pino, C., Pontes Pinto, E., Barbosa, C., Massmann, D., Mambrini, R., Galvão, L., Terem, E., & de Oliveira, N. (2023). Worldwide AI ethics: A review of 200 guidelines and recommendations for AI governance. *Patterns (New York, N.Y.)*, 4(10), 100857. DOI: 10.1016/j.patter.2023.100857 PMID: 37876898

Krenn, M., Buffoni, L., Coutinho, B., Eppel, S., Foster, J. G., Gritsevskiy, A., Lee, H., Lu, Y., Moutinho, J. P., Sanjabi, N., Sonthalia, R., Tran, N. M., Valente, F., Xie, Y., Yu, R., & Kopp, M. (2023). Forecasting the future of artificial intelligence with machine learning-based link prediction in an exponentially growing knowledge network. *Nature Machine Intelligence*, 5(11), 1326–1335. DOI: 10.1038/s42256-023-00735-0

Kumar, S., & Riegner, M. (2019). Freedom of expression in diverse democracies: Comparing hate speech law in India and the EU. In P. Dann & A. Thiruvengadam (Eds.), *Democratic constitutionalism in continental polities: EU and India compared* (Forthcoming). Cheltenham: Elgar. Available at *SSRN*: https://ssrn.com/abstract=3552984

Lakier, G. (2020). (Forthcoming). The non-First Amendment law of freedom of speech. *SSRN*, 134. Advance online publication. DOI: 10.2139/ssrn.3689972

Lauriola, I., Lavelli, A., & Aiolli, F. (2022). An introduction to deep learning in natural language processing: Models, techniques, and tools. *Neurocomputing*, 470, 443–456. DOI: 10.1016/j.neucom.2021.05.103

Masood, S., & Abbas, A. (2024). Neural Networks and Deep Learning: A Comprehensive Overview of Modern Techniques and Applications. DOI: 10.13140/RG.2.2.22416.58882

Matamoros-Fernández, A., & Farkas, J. (2021). Racism, hate speech, and social media: A systematic review and critique. *Television & New Media*, 22(2), 205–224. DOI: 10.1177/1527476420982230

Memarian, B., & Doleck, T. (2023). Fairness, Accountability, Transparency, and Ethics (FATE) in Artificial Intelligence (AI) and higher education: A systematic review. *Computers and Education: Artificial Intelligence*, 5, 100152. DOI: 10.1016/j.caeai.2023.100152

Mikalef, P., Conboy, K., Lundström, J. E., & Popovič, A. (2022). Thinking responsibly about responsible AI and 'the dark side' of AI. *European Journal of Information Systems*, 31(3), 257–268. DOI: 10.1080/0960085X.2022.2026621

Milosevic, T., Van Royen, K., & Davis, B. (2022). Artificial Intelligence to Address Cyberbullying, Harassment and Abuse: New Directions in the Midst of Complexity. *International Journal of Bullying Prevention : an Official Publication of the International Bullying Prevention Association*, 4(1), 1–5. DOI: 10.1007/s42380-022-00117-x PMID: 35233506

Min, A. (2023). Artificial Intelligence and Bias: Challenges, Implications, and Remedies. *Journal of Social Research*, 2(11), 3808–3817. DOI: 10.55324/josr.v2i11.1477

Molina, M. D., & Sundar, S. S. (2022). When AI moderates online content: Effects of human collaboration and interactive transparency on user trust. *Journal of Computer-Mediated Communication*, 27(4), zmac010. Advance online publication. DOI: 10.1093/jcmc/zmac010

Muhammed, T. S., & Mathew, S. K. (2022). The disaster of misinformation: A review of research in social media. *International Journal of Data Science and Analytics*, 13(4), 271–285. DOI: 10.1007/s41060-022-00311-6 PMID: 35194559

Nguyen, A., Hong, Y., Dang, B., & Huang, X. (2024). Human-AI collaboration patterns in AI-assisted academic writing. *Studies in Higher Education*, 49(5), 847–864. DOI: 10.1080/03075079.2024.2323593

Norström, L., Islind, A., & Snis, U. (2020). Algorithmic work: The impact of algorithms on work with social media.

Ortega-Bolaños, R., Bernal-Salcedo, J., Germán Ortiz, M., Galeano Sarmiento, J., Ruz, G. A., & Tabares-Soto, R. (2024). Applying the ethics of AI: A systematic review of tools for developing and assessing AI-based systems. *Artificial Intelligence Review*, 57(5), 110. DOI: 10.1007/s10462-024-10740-3

Ozanne, M., Bhandari, A., Bazarova, N. N., & DiFranzo, D. (2022). Shall AI moderators be made visible? Perception of accountability and trust in moderation systems on social media platforms. *Big Data & Society*, 9(2), 20539517221115666. Advance online publication. DOI: 10.1177/20539517221115666

Patidar, N., Mishra, S., Jain, R., Prajapati, D., Solanki, A., Suthar, R., Patel, K., & Patel, B. (2024). Transparency in AI decision making: A survey of explainable AI methods and applications. *Advances in Robotic Technology*, 2(1), 1–10. DOI: 10.23880/art-16000110

Peters, M. A. (2020). Limiting the capacity for hate: Hate speech, hate groups and the philosophy of hate. *Educational Philosophy and Theory*, 54(14), 2325–2330. DOI: 10.1080/00131857.2020.1802818

Pluta, A., Mazurek, J., Wojciechowski, J., Wolak, T., Soral, W., & Bilewicz, M. (2023). Exposure to hate speech deteriorates neurocognitive mechanisms of the ability to understand others' pain. *Scientific Reports*, 13(1), 4127. DOI: 10.1038/s41598-023-31146-1 PMID: 36914701

Rabonato, R. T., & Berton, L. (2024). A systematic review of fairness in machine learning. *AI and Ethics*. Advance online publication. DOI: 10.1007/s43681-024-00577-5

Rawat, A., Kumar, S., & Samant, S. S. (2024). Hate speech detection in social media: Techniques, recent trends, and future challenges. *Wiley Interdisciplinary Reviews: Computational Statistics*, 16(2), e1648. DOI: 10.1002/wics.1648

Rochefort, A. (2020). Regulating social media platforms: A comparative policy analysis. *Communication Law and Policy*, 25(2), 225–260. DOI: 10.1080/10811680.2020.1735194

Saleh, H., Alhothali, A., & Moria, K. (2023). Detection of Hate Speech using BERT and Hate Speech Word Embedding with Deep Model. *Applied Artificial Intelligence*, 37(1), 2166719. Advance online publication. DOI: 10.1080/08839514.2023.2166719

Saranya, A., & Subhashini, R. (2023). A systematic review of Explainable Artificial Intelligence models and applications: Recent developments and future trends. *Decision Analytics Journal*, 7, 100230. DOI: 10.1016/j.dajour.2023.100230

Schäfer, S., Rebasso, I., Boyer, M. M., & Planitzer, A. M. (2024). Can we counteract hate? Effects of online hate speech and counter speech on the perception of social groups. *Communication Research*, 51(5), 553–579. DOI: 10.1177/00936502231201091

Schulman, S. (2022). Perspectives on the First Amendment: The impact of generation on free speech freedoms. *Journal of Undergraduate Research (Gainesville, Fla.)*, 24. Advance online publication. DOI: 10.32473/ufjur.24.130771

Seng, K. P., Ang, L. M., & Ngharamike, E. (2022). Artificial intelligence Internet of Things: A new paradigm of distributed sensor networks. *International Journal of Distributed Sensor Networks*, 18(3). Advance online publication. DOI: 10.1177/15501477211062835

Shah, M., & Sureja, N. (2024). A comprehensive review of bias in deep learning models: Methods, impacts, and future directions. *Archives of Computational Methods in Engineering*. Advance online publication. DOI: 10.1007/s11831-024-10134-2

Shahbaznezhad, H., Dolan, R., & Rashidirad, M. (2021). The role of social media content format and platform in users' engagement behavior. *Journal of Interactive Marketing*, 53(1), 47–65. DOI: 10.1016/j.intmar.2020.05.001

Shulner-Tal, A., Kuflik, T., Kliger, D., & Mancini, A. (2024). Who made that decision and why? Users' perceptions of human versus AI decision-making and the power of explainable AI. *International Journal of Human-Computer Interaction*, •••, 1–18. DOI: 10.1080/10447318.2024.2348843

Singh, R., Nath, L. P., Mishra, P., Jain, S., Singh, A., & Benedict, S. M. (2024). Online hate speech in India: Legal reforms and social impact on social media platforms. Available at *SSRN*: https://ssrn.com/abstract=4732818 or DOI: 10.2139/ssrn.4732818

Smith, J., Doe, A., & Brown, B. (2023). Exploring AI Ethics. *Journal of AI Research*, 45(2), 123–145. DOI: 10.1234/jair.2023.00001

Sponholz, L. (2023). Hate speech. DOI: 10.48541/dcr.v12.9

Steyvers, M., & Kumar, A. (2024). Three challenges for AI-assisted decision-making. *Perspectives on Psychological Science*, 19(5), 722–734. DOI: 10.1177/17456916231181102 PMID: 37439761

Stockinger, A., Schäfer, S., & Lecheler, S. (2023). Navigating the gray areas of content moderation: Professional moderators' perspectives on uncivil user comments and the role of (AI-based) technological tools. *New Media & Society*, 0(0), 14614448231190901. Advance online publication. DOI: 10.1177/14614448231190901

Stracqualursi, L., & Agati, P. (2024). Twitter users' perceptions of AI-based e-learning technologies. *Scientific Reports*, 14(1), 5927. DOI: 10.1038/s41598-024-56284-y PMID: 38467685

Talaei Khoei, T., Ould Slimane, H., & Kaabouch, N. (2023). Deep learning: Systematic review, models, challenges, and research directions. *Neural Computing & Applications*, 35(31), 23103–23124. DOI: 10.1007/s00521-023-08957-4

Udupa, S., Maronikolakis, A., & Wisiorek, A. (2023). Ethical scaling for content moderation: Extreme speech and the (in)significance of artificial intelligence. *Big Data & Society*, 10(1), 20539517231172424. Advance online publication. DOI: 10.1177/20539517231172424

Vasist, P. N., Chatterjee, D., & Krishnan, S. (2023). The polarizing impact of political disinformation and hate speech: A cross-country configural narrative. *Information Systems Frontiers*, •••, 1–26. DOI: 10.1007/s10796-023-10390-w PMID: 37361884

Vianello, A., Laine, S., & Tuomi, E. (2022). Improving Trustworthiness of AI Solutions: A Qualitative Approach to Support Ethically-Grounded AI Design. *International Journal of Human-Computer Interaction*, 39(7), 1405–1422. DOI: 10.1080/10447318.2022.2095478

Williams, R., & Yampolskiy, R. (2021). Understanding and avoiding AI failures: A practical guide. *Philosophies*, 6(3), 53. DOI: 10.3390/philosophies6030053

Wilson, R. A., & Land, M. K. (2021). Hate speech on social media: Content moderation in context. *Connecticut Law Review, 52*, 1029. Available at *SSRN*: https://ssrn.com/abstract=3690616

Wilson, R. A., & Land, M. K. (2021). Hate speech on social media: Content moderation in context. *Connecticut Law Review*, 52, 1029. DOI: 10.2139/ssrn.3690616

Wojcieszak, M., Thakur, A., Gonçalves, J. F. F., Casas, A., Menchen-Trevino, E., & Boon, M. (2021). Can AI enhance people's support for online moderation and their openness to dissimilar political views? *Journal of Computer-Mediated Communication*, 26(4), 223–243. DOI: 10.1093/jcmc/zmab006

Yang, W., Wei, Y., Wei, H., Chen, Y., Huang, G., Li, X., Li, R., Yao, N., Wang, X., Gu, X., Amin, M. B., & Kang, B. (2023). Survey on explainable AI: From approaches, limitations, and applications aspects. *Human-Centric Intelligent Systems*, 3(3), 161–188. DOI: 10.1007/s44230-023-00038-y

Zamri, N. A. K., Mohamad Nasir, N. A., Hassim, M. N., & Ramli, S. M. (2023). Digital hate speech and othering: The construction of hate speech from Malaysian perspectives. *Cogent Arts & Humanities*, 10(1), 2229089. Advance online publication. DOI: 10.1080/23311983.2023.2229089

Zhou, L., Pan, S., Wang, J., & Vasilakos, A. V. (2017). Machine learning on big data: Opportunities and challenges. *Neurocomputing*, 237, 350–361. DOI: 10.1016/j.neucom.2017.01.026

Chapter 4

The Role of AI in Combatting Extremism and Radicalization on Social Media

G. Meena
https://orcid.org/0000-0002-5193-9021
SRM Institute of Science and Technology, India

Mohit
https://orcid.org/0009-0007-2280-8077
Maharshi Dayanand University, Rohtak, India

Shrinwantu Raha
https://orcid.org/0000-0003-4883-3657
Bhairab Ganguly College, India

Pamarthi Satyanarayana
https://orcid.org/0009-0008-4041-3674
Vel Tech Rangarajan Dr. Sagunthala R&D Institute of Science and Technology, India

P. Selvakumar
https://orcid.org/0000-0002-3650-4548
Department of Science and Humanities, Nehru Institute of Technology, Coimbatore, India

Chirayu Vats
https://orcid.org/0009-0008-1703-6292
Dev Sanskriti Vishwavidyalaya, India

ABSTRACT

This connectivity can foster echo chambers where extremist views are reinforced, further entrenching individuals in their beliefs. For instance, platforms like YouTube and Twitter have been instrumental in the dissemination of radical content, with algorithms often amplifying incendiary material to wider audiences. Moreover, the online landscape has enabled the recruitment of vulnerable individuals, particularly the youth. Extremist groups often target young people who are searching for identity, purpose, or community. They utilize sophisticated online strategies, including the use of memes, videos, and influencer marketing, to attract followers. The portrayal

DOI: 10.4018/979-8-3693-9904-0.ch004

of extremist ideologies as heroic or glamorous can resonate with individuals facing personal struggles, thereby facilitating their entry into radical movements. This recruitment strategy has been notably effective among marginalized youth, leading to increased involvement in extremist groups and activities. The phenomenon of online extremism is not confined to a single ideology.

THE RISE OF ONLINE EXTREMISM: UNDERSTANDING THE THREAT LANDSCAPE

This connectivity can foster echo chambers where extremist views are reinforced, further entrenching individuals in their beliefs. For instance, platforms like YouTube and Twitter have been instrumental in the dissemination of radical content, with algorithms often amplifying incendiary material to wider audiences. Moreover, the online landscape has enabled the recruitment of vulnerable individuals, particularly the youth. Extremist groups often target young people who are searching for identity, purpose, or community. They utilize sophisticated online strategies, including the use of memes, videos, and influencer marketing, to attract followers. The portrayal of extremist ideologies as heroic or glamorous can resonate with individuals facing personal struggles, thereby facilitating their entry into radical movements. This recruitment strategy has been notably effective among marginalized youth, leading to increased involvement in extremist groups and activities. The phenomenon of online extremism is not confined to a single ideology; it spans various political and religious spectrums. Far-right extremism, for example, has gained significant traction in recent years, often fueled by nationalist sentiments and anti-immigrant rhetoric. The Christchurch mosque shooting in 2019, which was live-streamed on social media, exemplifies the dangerous intersection of online extremism and real-world violence. This incident highlighted how individuals can be inspired to commit acts of terror by consuming extremist content online. Similarly, far-left movements have also utilized online platforms to organize protests, share propaganda, and promote anti-establishment sentiments, sometimes leading to violent confrontations. The rise of online extremism poses significant challenges for law enforcement and policymakers. The digital space is often difficult to regulate, and traditional methods of monitoring and intervention may be inadequate. Additionally, the principle of free speech complicates efforts to combat extremist content online. Platforms are increasingly pressured to take a proactive stance against hate speech and incitement to violence, yet they must also navigate the delicate balance between regulation and censorship. Effective countermeasures require collaboration between tech companies, governments, and civil society to develop strategies that can identify, disrupt, and mitigate the spread of extremist content while preserving civil liberties.

In response to these challenges, numerous initiatives have emerged aimed at countering online extremism. Governments and ngos are investing in research to understand the motivations behind radicalization and developing educational programs to build resilience in vulnerable communities. Furthermore, counter-narrative campaigns seek to undermine extremist propaganda by promoting alternative viewpoints and highlighting the consequences of radicalization. For instance, the use of personal testimonies from former extremists has proven effective in dissuading potential recruits by showcasing the dangers and regrets associated with a life of extremism. Another promising approach is the implementation of digital literacy programs, which equip individuals with critical thinking skills necessary to navigate the complexities of online information. These programs aim to enhance users' ability to discern credible sources from misleading ones, thereby reducing susceptibility to extremist narratives. By fostering an informed and critical online community, the potential for radicalization can be diminished. Despite these efforts, the threat of online extremism remains potent and evolving. As technology advances, so too do the tactics employed by extremist groups. The rise of deepfake technology and virtual reality could be harnessed to create more immersive and convincing propaganda, making it increasingly challenging to identify and counteract extremist messages. Furthermore, the decentralized nature of online communities complicates efforts to monitor and intervene effectively, as extremists can easily migrate to less regulated platforms. To effectively address the rise of online extremism, a multi-faceted approach is necessary. This should include continued research into the dynamics of online radicalization, collaborative efforts among stakeholders to share intelligence and best practices, and an ongoing commitment to promoting inclusivity and understanding within communities.

Social Media and Radicalization: The Role of Online Platforms

Social media's unique characteristics—such as real-time communication, the ability to share diverse forms of content, and the formation of virtual communities—create an environment where extremist ideologies can flourish (Hollewell G F. 2022). This dynamic has transformed traditional recruitment methods, enabling radical groups to reach wider and more diverse audiences than ever before. Algorithms employed by platforms like Facebook, Twitter, and youtube prioritize engagement, often promoting sensational or controversial content that can lead users deeper into extremist ideologies. This not only allows individuals to find and connect with like-minded peers but also exposes them to increasingly radical viewpoints over time, thereby escalating their commitment to extremist beliefs. Moreover, social media platforms provide a sense of community that can be particularly appealing to individuals who feel isolated or marginalized. Extremist groups often capitalize on this by crafting inclusive online environments where users can express their frustrations and share their experiences. This sense of belonging can be particularly potent for young people, who may be searching for identity and purpose. By framing their ideologies as movements for change or empowerment, these groups can effectively recruit individuals who might otherwise remain disengaged. In addition to fostering community, social media enables the rapid dissemination of propaganda and recruitment materials. Videos, memes, and posts designed to incite anger or evoke emotional responses can go viral, reaching thousands or even millions of users in a matter of hours. High-profile events, such as protests or acts of violence, are often leveraged to galvanize support and further radicalize individuals (Odag Ö., et al. 2019). The real-time nature of social media allows extremists to quickly respond to current events, shaping narratives that resonate with potential recruits. This immediacy can create a sense of urgency, compelling individuals to act in support of a cause they may not have previously considered.

Policymakers and researchers have increasingly recognized the urgent need to address the role of social media in radicalization. However, countering online extremism presents significant challenges. Platforms often grapple with balancing the need for free expression against the imperative to limit hate speech and incitement to violence (Bastug M F., et al. 2020). These initiatives often focus on enhancing digital literacy, equipping individuals with the skills to critically assess the information they encounter online. Programs that foster resilience in communities, particularly among youth, are also essential in reducing susceptibility to radicalization. Furthermore, counter-narrative campaigns have gained traction as a means to combat extremist propaganda. By presenting alternative viewpoints and sharing stories of former extremists, these initiatives seek to challenge the allure of radical ideologies. Social media can be a powerful tool for these campaigns, allowing for the wide dissemination of positive messages that emphasize inclusion, understanding, and dialogue. However, the challenge lies in competing with the emotionally charged content that often dominates online discourse. The emergence of new technologies, such as artificial intelligence and machine learning, also offers both opportunities and challenges in addressing online radicalization. While these technologies can enhance the monitoring and identification of extremist content, they can also be exploited by radical groups to create more sophisticated propaganda. Deepfakes and manipulated media pose additional threats, as they can blur the lines of authenticity, making it increasingly difficult for users to discern credible information from disinformation (Mahadev Madgule., et al, 2023). To effectively combat radicalization through social media, a multi-faceted approach is required. This should involve ongoing research into the processes of radicalization, the motivations of individuals who join extremist groups, and the specific tactics employed online.

Introduction to AI-Powered Solutions for Counter-Extremism

The rise of extremism in various forms—political, religious, and social—poses significant challenges to societies worldwide. In an age where information is disseminated rapidly through digital platforms, the threat landscape has evolved, necessitating innovative solutions to counteract the spread of extremist ideologies (Paramasivam Selvakumar., et al, 2024). AI-powered solutions for counter-extremism encompass a range of applications, from content moderation to predictive analytics. One of the primary challenges in addressing online extremism is the sheer volume of content generated daily across social media platforms and forums. Traditional methods of monitoring and regulation often struggle to keep pace with this rapid proliferation (Dauber C E., et al. 2019). However, the challenge remains to balance effective moderation with the preservation of free expression, as overly aggressive algorithms may inadvertently censor legitimate discourse. Furthermore, AI can enhance counter-narrative campaigns by generating and disseminating messages that counter extremist ideologies. By analyzing the language and themes used in extremist propaganda, AI can help craft compelling narratives that resonate with target audiences. These narratives can be disseminated through social media and other digital platforms, providing alternative viewpoints and reinforcing messages of inclusivity and understanding. Such AI-driven campaigns can effectively challenge extremist narratives by engaging with individuals who may be drawn to radical ideologies, offering them a sense of belonging and purpose in more positive contexts (Naseer M A., et al. 2023). Another significant application of AI in counter-extremism is in the realm of data analysis and intelligence gathering. Governments and ngos can leverage AI tools to monitor online activities and gather intelligence on extremist networks. By analyzing communication patterns and interactions within these groups, stakeholders can gain insights into recruitment strategies, funding sources, and operational tactics. This intelligence is invaluable in developing informed policies and interventions aimed at disrupting extremist activitie. The arms race between counter-extremism efforts and the tactics employed by extremists necessitates ongoing research and collaboration among stakeholders to stay ahead of emerging threats. Public awareness and education also play vital roles in the successful implementation of AI-powered solutions. Engaging communities in discussions about the implications of AI in counter-extremism can foster understanding and trust. By promoting digital literacy and critical thinking skills, individuals can become more adept at recognizing and resisting extremist narratives, thus reducing the potential for radicalization (Irfan M., et al. 2024). In conclusion, AI-powered solutions offer a transformative approach to countering extremism in the digital age.

Machine Learning for Extremist Content Detection: Techniques and Challenges

Traditional methods of content moderation, often reliant on human oversight, are increasingly insufficient due to the sheer volume of data generated daily. ML techniques offer a scalable solution by automating the identification of harmful content, enabling platforms to respond swiftly to emerging threats. The primary techniques utilized in extremist content detection include supervised learning, unsupervised learning, and deep learning approaches (Fernandez M., et al. 2021). Supervised learning, which relies on labeled datasets, is commonly used to train models that can classify content based on pre-defined categories of extremism. However, the lack of labeled examples can hinder the effectiveness of these models in accurately categorizing and prioritizing content (Potter K., et al. 2024). One of the major challenges in deploying ML for extremist content detection is the dynamic and evolving nature of extremist narratives. Extremist groups often adapt their strategies and language to circumvent detection systems, employing euphemisms, coded language, or even manipulating visual content. This necessitates continuous updates and retraining of ML models to remain effective, as static models quickly become obsolete. Additionally, the inherent complexity of human language, including sarcasm, irony, and cultural references, poses significant hurdles for accurate interpretation. Natural language processing (NLP) techniques are essential in this context, but they also require ongoing refinement to ensure accuracy across different languages and dialects.

Another critical challenge is the issue of false positives and negatives. An overly aggressive detection system may flag benign content as extremist, leading to censorship and the stifling of free expression. Conversely, a model that fails to identify extremist content can have dire consequences, allowing harmful ideologies to proliferate unchecked. Striking a balance between effective detection and preserving freedom of speech is an ongoing ethical dilemma faced by developers and policymakers alike. Moreover, transparency and accountability in ML systems are crucial for fostering public trust. Users and content creators should have a clear understanding of how detection algorithm's function and the criteria used for moderation. Implementing explainable AI (XAI) techniques can help demystify the decision-making processes of these systems, allowing for greater scrutiny and refinement. This transparency is essential in addressing concerns about algorithmic bias, as ML models trained on biased datasets can perpetuate discrimination and marginalization of specific groups. Collaboration between tech companies, researchers, and policymakers is essential to enhance the effectiveness of ML in extremist content detection (Sugumaran K. M., et al, 2024). Sharing best practices, datasets, and insights can lead to the development of more robust systems that are better equipped to handle the complexities of online extremism. Additionally, integrating feedback loops where users can report inaccuracies or challenge moderation decisions can contribute to the iterative improvement of detection systems.

Natural Language Processing for Radicalization Analysis: Identifying Key Indicators

NLP enables researchers and practitioners to sift through vast amounts of text data, such as social media posts, online forums, and chat logs, to uncover the subtle markers of radicalization. One primary application of NLP in radicalization analysis is sentiment analysis, which involves assessing the emotional tone behind a series of words (Torregrosa J., et al. 2023). By analyzing the sentiments expressed in online conversations, researchers can identify shifts in attitudes that may indicate a trajectory toward radicalization. For instance, individuals expressing increasing anger, frustration, or feelings of disenfranchisement may be more susceptible to extremist ideologies. This allows for early detection of potential radicalization, enabling targeted interventions before individuals become fully immersed in extremist networks. Another significant aspect of NLP in this context is the identification of specific keywords and phrases commonly associated with extremist discourse. Techniques such as keyword extraction and topic modeling can reveal themes and narratives prevalent in radical content. By employing algorithms that analyze the co-occurrence and frequency of terms, researchers can develop a lexicon of radicalization indicators. This lexicon can help distinguish between benign discourse and potentially harmful narratives, thus facilitating the classification of content and the monitoring of at-risk individuals. Moreover, the role of context in language is crucial when analyzing radicalization. NLP techniques such as word embeddings and contextualized language models, like BERT and GPT, allow for a deeper understanding of how language evolves and adapts in extremist circles. These models can capture nuances in meaning based on context, enabling more accurate detection of incitement to violence or hate speech (Sharif W., et al. 2019). Understanding the interplay between language and context is vital, as extremist groups often use coded language or euphemisms to evade detection, making traditional keyword-based approaches less effective.

The dynamic nature of extremist language also presents a challenge. As groups adapt their communication strategies to avoid detection, the indicators of radicalization can shift. Continuous updates and adaptations of NLP models are necessary to keep pace with these changes. This requires ongoing collaboration between linguists, data scientists, and experts in extremism to ensure that models remain relevant and effective (Hung B W K., et al. 2019). Furthermore, integrating qualitative insights into quantitative NLP analyses can enhance understanding. While algorithms can identify patterns and indicators, they may lack the nuance and depth that human analysts can provide. Incorporating expert analysis alongside NLP findings can lead to a more comprehensive understanding of radicalization processes. Engaging with communities affected by extremism can also provide valuable context that enhances the interpretive power of NLP outputs. In conclusion, Natural Language Processing offers significant potential for analyzing radicalization and identifying key indicators of extremist behavior (Florea M., et al. 2022). Through sentiment analysis, keyword identification, contextual understanding, and social network analysis, NLP can provide valuable insights into the dynamics of radicalization. However, addressing the challenges of bias, the evolving nature of extremist language, and the need for qualitative context is essential for maximizing the effectiveness of NLP in this domain.

Network Analysis and Social Media Graphs: Uncovering Extremist Networks

Network analysis, particularly through the lens of social media graphs, has become a vital tool for uncovering extremist networks and understanding their dynamics. The rise of digital platforms has transformed how extremist groups recruit, communicate, and disseminate propaganda (Ramakrishnan T.et al, 2022). In the context of extremist networks, nodes can include individuals, organizations, or even specific content such as posts or hashtags. Edges may represent various forms of engagement, such as follows, likes, shares, or direct messages. This structural representation allows analysts to map out the relationships that facilitate the spread of extremist ideologies and the recruitment of vulnerable individuals. One of the key strengths of network analysis is its ability to identify central actors within extremist networks, often referred to as hubs. These individuals or accounts wield significant influence and can act as major conduits for information dissemination. By pinpointing these hubs, law enforcement and intervention organizations can develop targeted strategies to disrupt the flow of extremist content and reduce the influence of these key figures. Furthermore, understanding the characteristics of these central nodes—such as their follower count, engagement metrics, and the nature of their interactions—can provide deeper insights into how extremist ideologies propagate. Social media graphs also facilitate the identification of sub-networks or clusters within broader extremist movements. These clusters may consist of individuals who share specific beliefs or engage in particular activities, such as promoting violence or recruiting new members. By analyzing the connections within these clusters, researchers can uncover the dynamics that sustain these groups, including the shared narratives and ideologies that bind them together (Adek R T., et al. 2021). This granular analysis can reveal how radicalization processes unfold within specific communities, allowing for more tailored intervention efforts. Moreover, network analysis can illuminate the tactics used by extremist groups to avoid detection and censorship. For instance, many groups employ strategies such as decentralized communication, where information is disseminated across multiple platforms and accounts to evade content moderation systems.

Additionally, there is a risk of misinterpretation; not all individuals connected within a network are necessarily engaged in extremist activities. Disentangling benign interactions from harmful ones is a nuanced task that requires careful consideration and context. Another challenge is the evolving nature of online extremism. Extremist groups continuously adapt their communication strategies, often shifting to newer platforms that may not yet be heavily monitored (Papasavva A. 2024). This dynamic landscape necessitates ongoing research and the development of adaptive analytical techniques that can keep pace with these changes. In conclusion, network analysis and social media graphs offer powerful methodologies for uncovering and understanding extremist networks. By mapping the relationships and interactions among users, researchers can identify key actors, sub-networks, and tactics employed by extremist groups (Schwarzenbach A., et al. 2024). While challenges related to data privacy, interpretation, and the dynamic nature of online extremism exist, the potential for network analysis to inform effective intervention strategies is immense. As the digital landscape continues to evolve, interdisciplinary approaches that integrate network analysis with insights from social sciences and policy frameworks will be crucial for combating the threats posed by extremist networks in the online world.

AI-Generated Counter-Narratives: Challenging Extremist Ideologies

AI-generated counter-narratives have emerged as a promising strategy for challenging extremist ideologies and fostering resilience against radicalization. As extremist groups increasingly utilize digital platforms to disseminate their messages, countering these narratives with compelling and fact-based alternatives has become essential. By leveraging advancements in artificial intelligence (AI), organizations can produce targeted counter-narratives that not only debunk harmful ideologies but also resonate with vulnerable populations who might be drawn to extremist views (Paramasivam Selvakumar., et al, 2024). The development of AI-generated counter-narratives relies heavily on natural language processing (NLP) and machine learning algorithms that analyze the language and themes prevalent in extremist content. By understanding the linguistic and emotional triggers that appeal to radicalized individuals, AI systems can create tailored messages that directly address and counter those appeals. For instance, if extremist narratives promote feelings of disenfranchisement, counter-narratives can focus on themes of inclusion, community, and shared values, reframing the conversation in a way that is more appealing to at-risk individuals. One of the key advantages of using AI in generating counter-narratives is the ability to scale efforts efficiently. Traditional methods of countering extremism often rely on human resources, which can be limited and time-consuming. AI systems can rapidly generate a wide array of narratives that can be disseminated across multiple platforms, ensuring that counter-messages reach diverse audiences in real time. This scalability is particularly crucial in the fast-paced digital environment, where extremist content can go viral in a matter of hours. Additionally, AI-generated counter-narratives can be customized to align with the cultural and contextual backgrounds of specific target audiences. By analyzing user data and engagement patterns, AI systems can identify the most effective formats, tones, and themes that resonate with different demographic groups. This contextual awareness allows for the creation of narratives that feel authentic and relevant, increasing their potential impact (Janjeva A., et al. 2023). For example, counter-narratives aimed at younger audiences may incorporate humor or popular culture references, while those targeting older demographics might focus on historical examples or community stories. Moreover, AI-generated narratives can include interactive elements, such as chatbots or dynamic social media campaigns, that encourage engagement and dialogue. This interactivity can help facilitate discussions around extremist ideologies, allowing individuals to question and reflect on their beliefs in a safe and supportive environment. Engaging users in this manner not only fosters critical thinking but also empowers them to challenge extremist narratives actively.

However, the deployment of AI-generated counter-narratives is not without challenges. One significant concern is the potential for backlash. Extremist groups are often quick to respond to counter-narratives with their own campaigns, potentially amplifying their messages. Additionally, poorly crafted AI-generated content can inadvertently reinforce stereotypes or misrepresent the complexities of the issues at hand. Therefore, it is essential to implement rigorous oversight and evaluation mechanisms to ensure that AI-generated narratives are accurate, respectful, and effective. Another challenge lies in the ethical considerations surrounding AI use. The algorithms employed in generating counter-narratives can be susceptible to biases inherent in the training data. If not carefully managed, these biases can lead to the dissemination of messages that do not resonate with the intended audience or that perpetuate harmful stereotypes. Ensuring diversity and representativeness in training datasets is crucial to mitigating these risks and promoting inclusive narratives. Furthermore, while AI can produce content at scale, it is essential to recognize the value of human insight and creativity in crafting counter-narratives (Mun J., et al. 2024). Collaborative efforts that bring together AI capabilities and human expertise can enhance the effectiveness of these initiatives. Involving community leaders, mental health professionals, and individuals with lived experiences in the creation of counter-narratives can lead to more nuanced and impactful messaging. This collaboration fosters a sense of ownership and authenticity, which is critical for engaging communities effectively. In conclusion, AI-generated counter-narratives represent a powerful tool in the fight against extremist ideologies.

Personalized Intervention Strategies: Using AI to Reach At-Risk Individuals

AI offers the capacity to analyze vast amounts of data, identify behavioral patterns, and develop customized interventions that resonate with individual experiences, ultimately enhancing the effectiveness of prevention efforts (Abramovic B., et al. 2021). At the heart of these personalized strategies is the ability to leverage data analytics. AI algorithms can analyze various data sources, including social media activity, online behavior, and demographic information, to create comprehensive profiles of individuals. By identifying key indicators of vulnerability—such as expressions of discontent, isolation, or engagement with extremist content—AI systems can facilitate early detection of individuals at risk of radicalization. This proactive approach allows for timely interventions that can steer individuals away from harmful ideologies before they become deeply entrenched. Furthermore, machine learning models can help identify the most effective intervention methods for different individuals based on their profiles. For example, some individuals may respond better to direct engagement through counseling or mentorship, while others might benefit from online resources or community activities. By tailoring interventions to the unique needs and preferences of at-risk individuals, organizations can increase the likelihood of positive outcomes. This level of personalization not only enhances engagement but also fosters a sense of ownership and agency among participants, making them more likely to embrace constructive alternatives to extremist narratives. AI-driven chatbots and virtual assistants represent another innovative facet of personalized intervention strategies. These tools can provide immediate support and resources to at-risk individuals in a confidential and non-judgmental manner (Guhl J., et al. 2022). By offering tailored advice, answering questions, and directing users to appropriate resources, AI chatbots can serve as a valuable first line of support.

However, the implementation of AI-driven personalized intervention strategies comes with several challenges. One major concern is the ethical implications of data collection and privacy. To build effective profiles of at-risk individuals, organizations must navigate the delicate balance between gathering useful data and respecting individual privacy rights. Transparency in data collection practices, along with informed consent from users, is essential to maintain trust and ensure ethical compliance. Developing clear guidelines and protocols for data use can help mitigate potential risks while maximizing the benefits of personalized interventions. Moreover, there is the risk of over-reliance on AI-generated insights, which may overlook the nuanced realities of individual experiences. While AI can identify patterns and trends, it may lack the contextual understanding required for effective intervention. Therefore, integrating human oversight and expertise is critical. Professionals trained in psychology, social work, or community engagement should work alongside AI systems to interpret data and develop appropriate interventions. This collaborative approach can ensure that interventions are grounded in empathy and cultural sensitivity (Barrett M., et al. 2019). Another challenge lies in the dynamic nature of radicalization pathways. As extremist groups adapt their strategies and messaging, the indicators of vulnerability may shift. Continuous monitoring and updating of AI models are necessary to ensure their relevance and accuracy. Regular evaluation of intervention strategies based on emerging trends will help maintain their effectiveness in addressing the complexities of radicalization.

AI-Powered Chatbots for Counter-Radicalization: Engaging with Extremists

This anonymity is crucial for individuals who may feel isolated or hesitant to seek help through conventional means, enabling them to engage openly and candidly with the chatbot. One of the key strengths of AI chatbots in counter-radicalization is their ability to provide immediate support (Kankanhalli A., et al. 2021). Operating 24/7, these digital assistants can engage users at any moment, addressing concerns as they arise. This is particularly important given the fast-paced nature of online radicalization, where exposure to extremist content can lead to rapid shifts in belief. By being available around the clock, chatbots ensure that at-risk individuals have access to resources and support whenever they need it, effectively lowering barriers to seeking help. Moreover, AI chatbots can be designed to specifically counter the narratives employed by extremist groups. By analyzing common themes, language, and emotional triggers found in extremist content, these chatbots can craft responses that directly challenge harmful ideologies. For example, if a user expresses feelings of anger or disenfranchisement, the chatbot can redirect the conversation toward more constructive themes, such as community solidarity or the importance of dialogue. This targeted approach enables chatbots to address the root causes of radicalization, rather than simply dismissing the individual's feelings. Another innovative feature of AI chatbots is their potential for interactive engagement. By incorporating elements of gamification, such as quizzes or scenario-based discussions, these chatbots can encourage users to think critically about their beliefs. This interactive format not only makes the engagement process more engaging but also fosters self-reflection (Zahra M A., et al. 2024). Users can be presented with hypothetical situations that challenge extremist viewpoints, prompting them to reconsider their perspectives in a non-confrontational manner.

However, the deployment of AI chatbots in counter-radicalization comes with challenges that must be addressed. One concern is the potential for misuse, where individuals might attempt to manipulate the chatbot for extremist purposes. To mitigate this risk, chatbots must be equipped with sophisticated filtering mechanisms that can detect harmful content and redirect conversations appropriately. Continuous monitoring and updates are necessary to ensure these systems remain effective and can adapt to new extremist tactics (Vijayakumar G., et al, 2024). The quality of the chatbot's programming also plays a crucial role in its effectiveness. If the underlying algorithms are not trained on diverse and representative datasets, there is a risk of bias, which could lead to unintentional reinforcement of stereotypes or ineffective engagement strategies. Thus, ongoing evaluation and iterative development of the chatbot's language model are essential to ensure it addresses the complexities of radicalization and engages users meaningfully. Ethical considerations are paramount in the design and deployment of AI chatbots. Issues surrounding privacy, consent, and data security must be prioritized to protect user information. Establishing clear guidelines on data usage and ensuring transparency in how user interactions are analyzed can help build trust between users and the chatbot. Engaging with stakeholders, including community leaders and mental health professionals, during the design process can enhance the chatbot's credibility and relevance, ensuring it meets the needs of at-risk individuals. Furthermore, while AI chatbots provide valuable support, they should not be seen as a standalone solution. Complementing chatbot interactions with human oversight is critical, as trained professionals can offer deeper insights and empathetic responses that a machine may not fully replicate. This hybrid model—combining the efficiency of AI with the empathy of human intervention—can lead to more effective counter-radicalization efforts, creating a support system that is both responsive and compassionate (Rashid W. 2023). In conclusion, AI-powered chatbots present a promising strategy for countering radicalization by providing an engaging, accessible platform for individuals at risk of adopting extremist ideologies.

Ethical Considerations in AI-Powered Counter-Extremism: Bias, Transparency, and Accountability

Transparency is another critical ethical consideration. Stakeholders—including policymakers, practitioners, and the communities affected by counter-extremism initiatives—must understand how AI systems function, the data they use, and the rationale behind their decisions. Lack of transparency can lead to mistrust and skepticism regarding the motivations and effectiveness of AI-driven interventions. By providing clear documentation of the algorithms, data sources, and methodologies used in AI systems, organizations can build trust with communities, ensuring that stakeholders are informed and engaged in the process. Moreover, transparency helps facilitate accountability, allowing for scrutiny and public discourse surrounding the deployment of AI technologies in sensitive areas such as counter-extremism (Choong J., et al. 2023). Accountability in AI systems is closely tied to both transparency and the ethical implications of decision-making processes. Organizations must establish clear frameworks for responsibility regarding the outcomes generated by AI-driven interventions. This includes determining who is accountable when an AI system causes harm, such as misidentifying individuals as extremists or perpetuating harmful stereotypes (Lakomy M. 2023). Creating robust mechanisms for redress and feedback is essential to address grievances and improve systems over time. Engaging with community representatives in developing accountability frameworks can enhance the responsiveness of counter-extremism initiatives, ensuring that they align with the values and needs of the populations they aim to serve.

Another dimension of ethical considerations involves the potential for AI technologies to be misused. For instance, adversaries could exploit AI systems to spread misinformation or manipulate narratives for extremist purposes. This highlights the necessity for robust security protocols to safeguard AI systems against malicious attacks and misuse. Continuous monitoring and adaptive strategies are essential to respond to emerging threats effectively, ensuring that AI technologies remain tools for positive intervention rather than vehicles for harm. Furthermore, the integration of human oversight in AI-driven counter-extremism efforts is vital. While AI can enhance efficiency and scalability, human judgment and empathy are irreplaceable in addressing the complexities of radicalization. Combining AI capabilities with human expertise creates a hybrid model that leverages the strengths of both (Andrić K., et al. 2023). For instance, human practitioners can contextualize the insights generated by AI systems, applying their understanding of local dynamics and cultural nuances to refine interventions. This collaborative approach not only enhances the effectiveness of counter-extremism strategies but also fosters a more ethical and compassionate framework for engagement. In conclusion, the ethical considerations surrounding AI-powered counter-extremism initiatives—encompassing bias, transparency, accountability, data privacy, and the potential for misuse—are critical to ensuring responsible implementation. Addressing these concerns through diverse training datasets, clear transparency measures, robust accountability frameworks, and the integration of human oversight is essential for fostering trust and effectiveness in counter-extremism efforts. As AI technologies continue to evolve, a commitment to ethical principles will be paramount in guiding their development and application, ultimately contributing to a more just and equitable approach to combating extremism. By prioritizing these ethical considerations, stakeholders can enhance the positive impact of AI in counter-extremism while minimizing potential harms, leading to safer and more resilient communities.

Policy and Regulatory Frameworks for AI-Driven Counter-Extremism

The development and implementation of AI-driven counter-extremism initiatives necessitate robust policy and regulatory frameworks to ensure effectiveness, accountability, and ethical adherence. As these technologies increasingly influence how societies address radicalization and extremist behavior, it is imperative that policymakers create comprehensive regulations that balance innovation with the protection of civil liberties and community trust. Effective frameworks should encompass several key components: data governance, transparency, ethical considerations, collaboration among stakeholders, and ongoing evaluation (Renda A., et al. 2021). Data governance is a foundational element of any policy framework related to AI in counter-extremism. Transparency in AI systems is crucial for building public trust and ensuring accountability. Policymakers should require organizations deploying AI-driven solutions to provide clear documentation of their methodologies, data sources, and algorithmic decision-making processes. This transparency allows stakeholders—ranging from government agencies to community organizations—to understand how AI systems operate and assess their effectiveness (Zeller M C., et al. 2023). Moreover, it fosters an environment of openness where concerns about potential biases or misapplications can be addressed constructively. By establishing transparency requirements, regulatory frameworks can empower communities to engage critically with counter-extremism efforts. Ethical considerations must also be embedded within policy frameworks to ensure that AI-driven counter-extremism initiatives respect fundamental human rights.

Collaboration among stakeholders is vital for the successful implementation of AI-driven counter-extremism initiatives. Policymakers should encourage partnerships between government agencies, civil society organizations, academic institutions, and technology companies. Such collaborations can facilitate knowledge sharing, innovation, and the co-creation of solutions that reflect diverse perspectives. Engaging communities directly in the policymaking process ensures that interventions are culturally sensitive and responsive to local needs. By fostering collaboration, regulatory frameworks can create a more comprehensive and nuanced approach to counter-extremism that is grounded in community input and expertise. Ongoing evaluation and adaptability are critical components of effective policy frameworks. As the landscape of extremism evolves and AI technologies continue to advance, regulatory frameworks must be flexible enough to accommodate emerging trends and challenges. Policymakers should establish mechanisms for regular assessment of AI-driven counter-extremism initiatives, allowing for the identification of best practices, areas for improvement, and the integration of new knowledge. This iterative approach not only enhances the effectiveness of interventions but also ensures that they remain relevant in the face of changing dynamics (Kaleem A. 2022). Additionally, addressing the global nature of online extremism is essential in developing effective regulatory frameworks. Given that extremist content can transcend borders, international cooperation is crucial in establishing standards and practices that enhance the global response to radicalization. Policymakers should engage in dialogue with international partners to share insights, develop harmonized regulations, and foster collaborative initiatives aimed at countering extremist ideologies.

Implementing AI Solutions in Real-World Scenarios: Challenges and Opportunities

Implementing AI solutions in real-world scenarios, particularly in the context of counter-extremism, presents both significant challenges and promising opportunities. As organizations seek to leverage AI technologies to address radicalization and extremist behavior, they must navigate a complex landscape characterized by technical, ethical, and operational hurdles. At the same time, the potential benefits of AI—such as enhanced data analysis, improved decision-making, and scalable interventions—offer compelling reasons to pursue these technologies with careful consideration and strategic planning (Bechtold E. 2020). One of the foremost challenges in implementing AI solutions is the issue of data quality and availability. AI systems rely heavily on robust datasets for training and validation. In the realm of counter-extremism, the data needed to develop effective algorithms can be sparse, inconsistent, or biased. Moreover, sensitive nature surrounding extremist content complicates data collection, as organizations must ensure compliance with privacy laws and ethical standards while gathering information. Inadequate or biased data can lead to flawed models that misidentify individuals as extremists or fail to capture the nuances of radicalization pathways.

Therefore, it is critical for organizations to prioritize the creation of high-quality, diverse datasets that reflect the complexities of the target populations. Ethical considerations are another critical aspect of implementing AI solutions in counter-extremism. The potential for bias in AI algorithms raises concerns about discrimination and the disproportionate targeting of certain communities (Lwakatare L E., et al. 2020). Organizations must be vigilant in addressing these issues by implementing rigorous testing and evaluation processes that identify and mitigate bias in AI systems. Establishing ethical guidelines for AI use, including transparency measures and accountability frameworks, is essential to foster public trust and ensure that interventions align with community values. Engaging with affected communities in the design and implementation phases can also enhance the ethical integrity of AI solutions, ensuring that they are culturally sensitive and responsive to local needs. This level of personalization can significantly enhance the effectiveness of counter-radicalization initiatives. AI technologies also offer the potential for scalability in counter-extremism efforts (Lee D H., et al. 2021). Many traditional approaches to prevention and intervention require significant human resources, limiting their reach. In contrast, AI systems can operate at scale, allowing organizations to extend their efforts to broader populations without a proportional increase in staffing. This scalability is particularly important in addressing the global nature of online extremism, where threats can cross national borders and require coordinated responses. Furthermore, the integration of AI solutions can foster collaboration among various stakeholders, including governments, non-governmental organizations, and tech companies. By sharing data and insights, stakeholders can develop a more comprehensive understanding of radicalization dynamics and coordinate their efforts more effectively. Collaborative platforms powered by AI can facilitate information sharing and joint initiatives, strengthening the overall response to extremism.

Emerging Trends in AI-Powered Counter-Extremism: Deepfakes, Blockchain, and Beyond

Emerging trends in AI-powered counter-extremism are shaping the future of how societies address radicalization and extremist behavior. Technologies such as deepfakes and blockchain are gaining attention for their potential applications, along with other advancements in AI, presenting both unique challenges and innovative opportunities in counter-extremism strategies. As these technologies evolve, it is essential for policymakers, practitioners, and technologists to understand their implications and effectively harness their capabilities to combat extremist ideologies. Deepfake technology, which uses advanced machine learning algorithms to create hyper-realistic digital content, has garnered significant attention for its potential misuse in spreading misinformation and manipulating narratives (Calabrese F., et al. 2022). Extremist groups could leverage deepfakes to create false propaganda, misrepresenting individuals or events to recruit followers or discredit opponents. This poses a substantial challenge for counter-extremism efforts, as distinguishing between genuine and fabricated content becomes increasingly difficult. However, this very challenge also opens avenues for innovative countermeasures. AI can be employed to develop tools that detect deepfakes by analyzing inconsistencies in video and audio content, helping to verify the authenticity of information disseminated online. This feature could be harnessed to create verifiable records of interventions, training programs, or community engagement initiatives, fostering accountability among organizations involved in counter-extremism. Furthermore, blockchain can facilitate secure and anonymous reporting mechanisms for individuals who witness extremist behavior, empowering communities to take proactive stances against radicalization while protecting their identities. By leveraging blockchain technology, stakeholders can enhance transparency and collaboration, ultimately strengthening their collective response to extremist threats (Simoncini G. 2023).

The rise of social media as a platform for extremist recruitment and radicalization has prompted the development of AI tools that monitor online content for signs of extremism. These tools utilize natural language processing and sentiment analysis to detect hate speech, incitement to violence, and other harmful content in real-time. By automating content moderation processes, organizations can respond more rapidly to extremist activities online. However, the challenge lies in ensuring that these tools do not infringe on freedom of expression or suppress legitimate discourse (Sreenivasulu A., et al, 2022). Developing nuanced algorithms that can differentiate between harmful and benign speech is critical to achieving this balance, requiring continuous refinement and community engagement in the algorithmic design process. Furthermore, the intersection of AI and augmented reality (AR) presents a novel approach to countering extremist ideologies. This collaborative approach can facilitate knowledge sharing, drive innovation, and promote best practices in the development and deployment of AI solutions. Engaging communities in the design and implementation of these technologies ensures that counter-extremism efforts are culturally sensitive and aligned with local values, enhancing their effectiveness. As the landscape of extremism evolves, the integration of AI technologies into counter-extremism strategies must be adaptable and responsive. Continuous evaluation of the effectiveness of emerging technologies, along with feedback from affected communities, will be critical in refining approaches and ensuring that interventions remain relevant. Additionally, fostering public discourse about the implications of these technologies can help build societal consensus on their use, promoting an informed understanding of both the risks and benefits involved (Jusué I R. 2022).

Collaborative Efforts: The Role of Government, Industry, and Civil Society in AI-Driven Counter-Extremism

Collaborative efforts among government, industry, and civil society are crucial in advancing AI-driven counter-extremism initiatives. Each of these sectors plays a distinct yet interdependent role, contributing unique resources, expertise, and perspectives essential for developing effective strategies to combat radicalization and extremist behaviors (Kamau J W. 2021). Additionally, government agencies can facilitate funding and support for research initiatives that explore the effectiveness of

AI-driven interventions. By investing in public-private partnerships, governments can encourage collaboration with technology firms and academic institutions, promoting innovation in counter-extremism solutions that are evidence-based and aligned with societal values. Civil society organizations play a critical role in bridging the gap between government initiatives and the communities they aim to protect. These organizations often have deep-rooted connections within communities, enabling them to understand local dynamics and the factors contributing to radicalization. By engaging with civil society, government and industry can gain valuable insights into the unique challenges faced by specific populations and tailor interventions accordingly. Civil society organizations can also serve as advocates for marginalized voices, ensuring that counter-extremism strategies do not disproportionately target specific communities. Their involvement is vital for promoting inclusivity and understanding, which are essential for the success of any counter-extremism initiative.

An example of successful collaboration can be seen in multi-stakeholder initiatives that bring together governments, industry leaders, and civil society representatives to develop AI-driven tools for countering extremism. These initiatives can create platforms for sharing data and best practices, enhancing collective understanding of radicalization trends. By pooling resources, stakeholders can conduct joint research and development projects that focus on creating innovative technologies capable of addressing the complexities of extremist behavior. Such collaboration fosters a shared sense of responsibility and ownership over counter-extremism efforts, enhancing their effectiveness and sustainability (Gøtzsche-Astrup O., et al. 2023). Moreover, public engagement and education are essential components of collaborative efforts in counter-extremism. Government and civil society organizations must work together to inform the public about the risks associated with extremism and the importance of resilience. By conducting awareness campaigns that highlight the role of AI in counter-extremism, stakeholders can promote a culture of vigilance and empowerment within communities. Education programs that focus on critical thinking, media literacy, and digital citizenship can equip individuals with the skills needed to recognize and resist extremist narratives. Civil society organizations often operate with limited funding and resources, constraining their ability to engage effectively. To overcome these challenges, stakeholders must commit to building strong relationships based on mutual respect and shared objectives (Reeves J., et al. 2019). Establishing formal mechanisms for collaboration, such as task forces or working groups, can facilitate coordination and ensure that all parties are aligned in their efforts. In conclusion, collaborative efforts involving government, industry, and civil society are essential for advancing AI-driven counter-extremism initiatives.

The Future of AI in Combatting Extremism and Radicalization on Social Media

The future of AI in combatting extremism and radicalization on social media is poised to be transformative, leveraging advanced technologies to detect, analyze, and mitigate harmful content in real-time (Barhamgi M., et al. 2024). AI algorithms can be trained to detect extremist language, imagery, and behaviors across social media platforms, automating the identification of harmful content that may contribute to radicalization. Natural language processing (NLP) technologies enable these systems to analyze not only explicit hate speech but also implicit cues that may signal extremist ideologies. For instance, AI can assess the sentiment of posts and comments, identifying language that expresses grievance or hostility, which may correlate with radicalization pathways. This capability allows platforms to respond more swiftly to emerging threats, potentially curbing the spread of extremist narratives before they gain traction. However, while AI-driven content moderation offers significant benefits, it also raises challenges. One concern is the risk of overreach, where legitimate discourse may be mistakenly flagged as extremist content. Striking the right balance between maintaining freedom of expression and preventing the spread of harmful ideologies is crucial. Ongoing refinement of algorithms is necessary to minimize false positives and ensure that AI systems respect user rights while effectively targeting extremist content. Collaborative efforts among stakeholders—including social media platforms, researchers, and civil society—are vital in developing guidelines and standards that govern the ethical use of AI in content moderation. Beyond content moderation, AI can enhance the understanding of radicalization dynamics through data analysis. By examining social media interactions, networks, and user behaviors, AI can identify trends and risk factors associated with radicalization. For example, machine learning models can analyze the connections between users, revealing how extremist ideologies spread through social networks. This insight can inform targeted interventions, allowing organizations to engage at-risk individuals or communities before they become deeply entrenched in extremist ideologies (Pistone I., et al. 2019). Predictive analytics can help identify users who may be vulnerable to radicalization, enabling preemptive outreach and support tailored to their specific circumstances. The integration of AI in combatting extremism also necessitates a focus on collaborative intelligence. By pooling data and insights from various stakeholders, including law enforcement, tech companies, and NGOs, a more comprehensive understanding of online extremism can be achieved. Collaborative platforms powered by AI can facilitate real-time information sharing, enabling organizations to coordinate their efforts in response to threats. This approach can enhance the effectiveness of counter-radicalization initiatives, ensuring that interventions are informed by a diverse array of perspectives and experiences.

Moreover, the emergence of deepfake technology presents a unique challenge and opportunity in the realm of counter-extremism. While deepfakes can be exploited to spread disinformation and manipulate public perception, AI can also be harnessed to detect and counteract these threats. Developing tools that can identify deep fake content in real-time will be crucial for maintaining the integrity of information shared on social media. As AI technologies advance, so too must the methods for detecting and responding to the misuse of these innovations. The role of education and public engagement is also paramount in the future of AI in combatting extremism. AI-driven tools can facilitate the creation of educational programs that promote digital literacy and critical thinking skills among users, helping them recognize and resist extremist content. By fostering a culture of informed engagement, social media users can become active participants in countering radicalization efforts, challenging extremist narratives, and supporting those at risk of radicalization. Collaborative campaigns involving governments, tech companies, and civil society organizations can amplify these educational initiatives, reaching diverse audiences and fostering resilience against extremist ideologies (Pappalardo L., et al. 2024). As AI continues to evolve, its integration into counter-extremism efforts must be dynamic and responsive. Continuous evaluation and adaptation of AI systems will be necessary to address emerging challenges and improve effectiveness. Incorporating feedback from users and communities will ensure that interventions remain relevant and culturally appropriate, promoting a sense of shared ownership in counter-extremism efforts. In conclusion, the future of AI in combatting extremism and radicalization on social media holds great promise, with the potential to transform how societies respond to online threats. By leveraging AI for content moderation, data analysis, collaborative intelligence, and educational initiatives, stakeholders can create a more proactive and nuanced approach to addressing radicalization. However, the ethical implications of AI deployment must be carefully considered, ensuring that efforts to combat extremism do not compromise individual rights or stifle legitimate discourse. Through collaborative engagement and a commitment to transparency, the integration of AI into counter-extremism strategies can enhance societal resilience, fostering safer and more inclusive online environments. As we navigate this evolving landscape, a focus on ethical principles and community involvement will be essential in harnessing the power of AI to combat extremism effectively.

CONCLUSION

In conclusion, the role of AI in combatting extremism and radicalization on social media is both crucial and multifaceted, offering innovative solutions to a pressing global challenge. As extremist groups increasingly leverage digital platforms to propagate their ideologies, AI technologies provide the means to detect, analyze, and mitigate the spread of harmful content in real time. By employing advanced algorithms for content moderation, sentiment analysis, and predictive analytics, stakeholders can gain deeper insights into radicalization dynamics and respond swiftly to emerging threats. However, the deployment of AI in this context also necessitates careful consideration of ethical implications, particularly concerning privacy, freedom of expression, and the potential for algorithmic bias. Effective implementation of AI requires robust collaborative frameworks that bring together government agencies, tech companies, and civil society organizations. Such partnerships can facilitate the sharing of data and best practices, fostering a comprehensive understanding of the complexities of online extremism. Through collaborative intelligence, stakeholders can enhance their collective response to radicalization, ensuring that interventions are informed by diverse perspectives and tailored to the specific needs of at-risk communities. Moreover, the ethical deployment of AI technologies is essential for building trust and maintaining accountability. Establishing transparent guidelines and accountability mechanisms can help mitigate concerns about the misuse of AI, particularly in content moderation where the risk of overreach and suppression of legitimate discourse is prevalent. Engaging affected communities in the design and evaluation of AI solutions will not only enhance their effectiveness but also ensure that they reflect societal values and respect human rights. As AI technologies continue to evolve, ongoing evaluation and adaptation will be vital to address emerging challenges associated with online radicalization. The integration of educational initiatives aimed at promoting digital literacy and critical thinking among social media users can empower individuals to recognize and resist extremist narratives. By fostering a culture of informed engagement, societies can cultivate resilience against radicalization and enhance community cohesion. In summary, while AI presents powerful tools for combatting extremism and radicalization on social media, its success will ultimately depend on a commitment to ethical principles, collaborative engagement, and ongoing community involvement. By prioritizing these elements, stakeholders can effectively harness AI's potential to create safer online environments, ultimately contributing to a more peaceful and inclusive society. As we move forward, the collective responsibility to navigate the complexities of this digital landscape will be crucial in shaping a future where extremism has diminished impact, and communities are empowered to resist divisive ideologies.

REFERENCES

Abhilasha, A., Sreenivasulu, A., & Manimozhi. T. KUMAR, P. S., Selvakumar, P., & Singh, P. (2022, April). The Model of Smart Sensing Device For Sensitive Nano-clusters Modification in Sensing Properties. In 2022 2nd International Conference on Advance Computing and Innovative Technologies in Engineering (ICACITE) (pp. 1043-1047). IEEE.

Abramovic B, Coleman G. (2021) "Decolonizing the Machine: Race, Gender and Disability in Robots and Algorithmic Art" Journal of Politics of the Machines, pp. 1-15.

Adek, R. T., & Ula, M. (2021). Systematics review on the application of social media analytics for detecting radical and extremist group. *IOP Conference Series. Materials Science and Engineering*, 1096(1), 1–8. DOI: 10.1088/1757-899X/1071/1/012029

Andrić, K., & Kasirzadeh, A. (2023) "Reconciling governmental use of online targeting with democracy" *Proceedings of the 2023 ACM Conference on Fairness, Accountability, and Transparency*. DOI: 10.1145/3593013.3594133

Barhamgi, M., Masmoudi, A., Lara-Cabrera, R., & Camacho, D. (2024). Social networks data analysis with semantics: Application to the radicalization problem. *Journal of Ambient Intelligence and Humanized Computing*, 15(2), 1–20. DOI: 10.1007/s12652-018-0968-z

Barrett, M., Boyne, J., Brandts, J., Brunner-La Rocca, H. P., De Maesschalck, L., De Wit, K., Dixon, L., Eurlings, C., Fitzsimons, D., Golubnitschaja, O., Hageman, A., Heemskerk, F., Hintzen, A., Helms, T. M., Hill, L., Hoedemakers, T., Marx, N., McDonald, K., Mertens, M., & Zippel-Schultz, B. (2019). Artificial intelligence supported patient self-care in chronic heart failure: A paradigm shift from reactive to predictive, preventive and personalised care. *The EPMA Journal*, 10(2), 147–155. DOI: 10.1007/s13167-019-00188-9 PMID: 31832118

Bastug, M. F., Douai, A., & Akca, D. (2020). Exploring the "demand side" of online radicalization: Evidence from the Canadian context. *Studies in Conflict and Terrorism*, 43(10), 857–873. DOI: 10.1080/1057610X.2018.1494409

Bechtold, E. (2020). Terrorism, the internet, and the threat to freedom of expression: The regulation of digital intermediaries in Europe and the United States. *Journal of Medicine and Law*, 12(1), 1–20. DOI: 10.1080/17577632.2020.1760474

Calabrese, F., Regattieri, A., Bortolini, M., & Galizia, F. G. (2022). Data-Driven Fault Detection and Diagnosis: Challenges and Opportunities in Real-World Scenarios. *Applied Sciences (Basel, Switzerland)*, 12(11), 1–15. DOI: 10.3390/app12189212 PMID: 36330151

Choong, J., & Wang, M. B. (2023). Disruptive and destructive? A typology of social bots in public relations. *Journal of Digital & Social Media Marketing*, 11(1), 1–12. DOI: 10.69554/NPVB4536

Dauber, C. E., & Ilter, K. (2019). *The relationship between Social Media and radicalization*. Propaganda, Recruitment, and Radicalization. DOI: 10.1201/9781315170251-3

Fernandez, M., & Alani, H. (2021). *Artificial intelligence and online extremism: Challenges and opportunities*. Predictive Policing and Artificial Intelligence., DOI: 10.4324/9780429265365-7

Florea, M., Potlog, C., Pollner, P., & Abel, D. (2022). *Alert system for online terrorist content based on natural language processing, social network analysis, artificial intelligence and complex event processing*. Cybersecurity and Privacy., DOI: 10.1007/978-3-031-15461-7_1

Gøtzsche-Astrup, O., Lindekilde, L., & Fjellman, A.-M. (2023). Perceived legitimacy of CVE policies and the willingness to report concerns of radicalization to authorities in the Nordic countries. *Terrorism and Political Violence*, 35(3), 1–20. DOI: 10.1080/09546553.2021.1972977

Guhl, J., Marsh, O., & Tuck, H. (2022). *Researching the Evolving Online Ecosystem: Barriers, Methods and Future Challenges*. Institute for Strategic Dialogue.

Hollewell, G. F., & Longpré, N. (2022). Radicalization in the social media era: Understanding the relationship between self-radicalization and the internet. *International Journal of Offender Therapy and Comparative Criminology*, 66(6), 537–555. DOI: 10.1177/0306624X211028771 PMID: 34189982

Hung, B. W. K., & Muramudalige, S. R. (2019) "Recognizing radicalization indicators in text documents using human-in-the-loop information extraction and nlp techniques" *2019 International Conference on Technologies for Smart-City Energy and Mobility*. DOI: 10.1109/HST47167.2019.9032956

Irfan M, Almeshal Z A, Anwar M. (2024) "Unleashing transformative potential of artificial intelligence (AI) in countering terrorism online radicalisation extremism and possible recruitment".

Janjeva A, Harris A, Mercer S, Kasprzyk A, Gausen A. (2023) "The Rapid Rise of Generative AI: Assessing risks to safety and security".

Jusué, I. R. (2022). Counter-terrorism training "at your kitchen table": The promotion of "CT citizens" and the securitisation of everyday life in the UK. *Critical Studies on Terrorism*, 15(2), 1–18. DOI: 10.1080/17539153.2022.2039612

Kaleem, A. (2022). The hegemony of Prevent: Turning counter-terrorism policing into common sense. *Critical Studies on Terrorism*, 15(1), 1–18. DOI: 10.1080/17539153.2021.2013016

Kamau, J. W. (2021). Is counter-terrorism counterproductive? A case study of Kenya's response to terrorism, 1998-2020. *The South African Journal of International Affairs*, 28(3), 455–474. DOI: 10.1080/10220461.2021.1924252

Kanipriya, M., Sugumaran, D., Pandiyarajan, V., Yogananda, B. S., Selvakumar, P., & Mohan, S. (2024, January). Analysis of Electromyography Signals for Control of Mechanical Prosthesis using Machine Learning Techniques. In 2024 2nd International Conference on Intelligent Data Communication Technologies and Internet of Things (IDCIoT) (pp. 1059-1067). IEEE.

Kankanhalli, A., Xia, Q., Ai, P., & Zhao, X. (2021). Understanding personalization for health behavior change applications: A review and future directions. *AIS Transactions on Human-Computer Interaction*, 13(2), 1–25. DOI: 10.17705/1thci.00152

Lakomy, M. (2023). Artificial intelligence as a terrorism enabler? Understanding the potential impact of chatbots and image generators on online terrorist activities. *Studies in Conflict and Terrorism*, •••, 1–20. DOI: 10.1080/1057610X.2023.2259195

Lee, D. H., & Yoon, S. N. (2021). Application of artificial intelligence-based technologies in the healthcare industry: Opportunities and challenges. *International Journal of Environmental Research and Public Health*, 18(11), 1–15. DOI: 10.3390/ijerph18010271 PMID: 33401373

Lwakatare, L. E., Raj, A., Crnkovic, I., Bosch, J., & Olsson, H. H. (2020). Large-scale machine learning systems in real-world industrial settings: A review of challenges and solutions. *Information and Software Technology*, 126, 1–15. DOI: 10.1016/j.infsof.2020.106368

Mahadev Madgule, N. (2023). Vinayaka, Yeshwant M. Sonkhaskar, Dhiren Ramanbhai Patel, R. Karthikeyan, P. Selvakumar,(2023). Mechanical properties and microstructure of activated TIG welded similar joints of Inconel alloys by desirability approaches. *Materials Today: Proceedings*, 77, 528–533. DOI: 10.1016/j.matpr.2022.12.250

Mun, J., Buerger, C., Liang, J. T., & Garland, J. (2024) "Counterspeakers' Perspectives: Unveiling Barriers and AI Needs in the Fight against Online Hate" *Proceedings of the 2024 CHI Conference on Human Factors in Computing Systems*. DOI: 10.1145/3613904.3642025

Naseer M A, Shaheen G. (2023) "Harnessing the Power of Artificial Intelligence: An In-Depth Review of its Effective Role in Countering Violent Extremism" JURIHUM: Jurnal Inovasi dan Pembelajaran Sosial, 6(1), pp. 1-12.

Odag, Ö., Leiser, A., & Boehnke, K. (2019). Reviewing the role of the Internet in radicalization processes. *Journal for Deradicalization*, •••, 21.

Papasavva A. (2024) "A Comprehensive Study of the Extremist Narratives and the Role of Alternative Social Networks that Facilitate Radical Discourse".

Pappalardo, L., Ferragina, S., & Citraro, S. (2024) "A survey on the impact of AI-based recommenders on human behaviors: methodologies, outcomes, and future directions" arxiv preprint arxiv:2405.03451.

Pistone, I., Eriksson, E., & Beckman, U. (2019). A scoping review of interventions for preventing and countering violent extremism: Current status and implications for future research. *Journal for Deradicalization*, •••, 21.

Potter, K., & Stilinski, D. (2024). *The Role of Media and Arts in Countering Extremism: Promoting Peace*. Tolerance, and Positive Social Values.

Ramakrishnan, T., Mohan Gift, M. D., Chitradevi, S., Jegan, R., & Subha Hency Jose, P. Nagaraja, Rajneesh Sharma H.N., Selvakumar P., Sintayehu Mekuria Hailegiorgis, (2022). "Study of Numerous Resins Used in Polymer Matrix Composite Materials", Advances in Materials Science and Engineering, vol. 2022, Article ID 1088926, 8 pages, 2022. DOI: 10.1155/2022/1088926

Rashid, W. (2023). *"Using Artificial Intelligence to Combat Extremism" Pakistan Journal of Terrorism Research*. PJTR.

Reeves, J., & Crowther, T. (2019). Teacher feedback on the use of innovative social media simulations to enhance critical thinking in young people on radicalisation, extremism, sexual exploitation and related topics. *Pastoral Care in Education*, 37(2), 151–166. DOI: 10.1080/02643944.2019.1618377

Renda, A., Arroyo, J., & Fanni, R. (2021). *Study to support an impact assessment of regulatory requirements for artificial intelligence in Europe*. European Commission.

Schwarzenbach A, Jensen M. (2024) "Extremists of a feather flock together? Community structures, transitivity, and patterns of homophily in the US Islamist co-offending network" plos ONE, 19(9), pp. 1-15, .DOI: 10.1371/journal.pone.0287406

Selvakumar, P., Mariappan, P., Shunmugam, S., Paul, R., & Jabez, S. (2024). Removal of chemicals from effluent using photobioreactor technology to improve environmental and health impacts. *Zeitschrift für Physikalische Chemie*, 2024(7), 1295–1302. Advance online publication. DOI: 10.1515/zpch-2023-0450

Selvakumar, P., Palanisamy, S. K., Cinthaikinian, S., Palanisamy, V., Mariappan, R., & Selvakumar, P. K. (2024). Biosensors and its diverse applications in healthcare systems. *Zeitschrift für Physikalische Chemie*, 2024. Advance online publication. DOI: 10.1515/zpch-2023-0406

Sharif, W., Mumtaz, S., Shafiq, Z., Riaz, O., Ali, T., Husnain, M., & Choi, G. S. (2019). An empirical approach for extreme behavior identification through tweets using machine learning. *Applied Sciences (Basel, Switzerland)*, 9(24), 5375. DOI: 10.3390/app9183723

Simoncini, G. (2023). Bringing back the concept of colonial pacification in the study of preventing violent extremism (PVE) practices: The case of Tunisia. *Cambridge Review of International Affairs*, •••, 1–20.

Torregrosa, J., Bello-Orgaz, G., Martínez-Cámara, E., Ser, J. D., & Camacho, D. (2023). A survey on extremism analysis using natural language processing: Definitions, literature review, trends and challenges. *Journal of Ambient Intelligence and Humanized Computing*, 14(8), 1–20. DOI: 10 1007/s12652-021-03658-z PMID: 35039755

Vijayakumar, G., Rajkumar, M., Rajiv Chandar, N., Selvakumar, P., & Duraisamy, R. (2024). Muniyandi Rajkumar, Rajiv Chandar N, Selvakumar P and Ramesh Duraisamy, (2024). Environmentally friendly TDS removal from waste water by electrochemical ion exchange batch-type recirculation (EIR) technique. *Environmental Science. Water Research & Technology*, 10(4), 826–835. DOI: 10.1039/D3EW00793F

Zahra, M. A., Al-Taher, A., & Alquhaidan, M. (2024). The synergy of artificial intelligence and personalized medicine for the enhanced diagnosis, treatment, and prevention of disease. *Journal of Personalized Medicine*, 14(2), 1–12. DOI: 10.3390/jpm14020043 PMID: 38997240

Zeller, M. C., & Vaughan, M. (2023). Proscribing Right-Wing Extremist Organizations in Europe: Variations, Trends, and Prospects. *Terrorism and Political Violence*, •••, 1–20. DOI: 10.1080/09546553.2023.2171615

Chapter 5
Empowering Social Media Users With Ethical AI

E. Pradeep
https://orcid.org/0000-0002-6293-9027
Loyola Institute of Business Administration, India

Samrat Kumar Mukherjee
https://orcid.org/0000-0002-8839-0140
Sikkim Manipal Institute of Technology, Sikkim Manipal University, India

P. Selvakumar
https://orcid.org/0000-0002-3650-4548
Department of Science and Humanities, Nehru Institute of Technology, Coimbatore, India

Aruna Kumari Koppaka
Chalapathi Institute of Engineering and Technology, India

Pankaj Singh Chandel
https://orcid.org/0000-0002-4135-8194
Dev Sanskriti Vishwavidyalaya, India

Chirayu Vats
https://orcid.org/0009-0008-1703-6292
Dev Sanskriti Vishwavidyalaya, India

ABSTRACT

Fairness emphasizes the need to design AI systems that do not perpetuate bias or discrimination, recognizing that algorithms can inadvertently reflect and amplify societal prejudices if not carefully managed. This principle is particularly vital in social media, where biased algorithms can lead to unequal treatment of users based on race, gender, or socio-economic status, ultimately impacting the diversity of voices represented on these platforms. Developers must strive to create algorithms that actively promote inclusivity, ensuring equitable access to information and opportunities for all users. Accountability is another critical principle, necessitating that organizations and developers take responsibility for the outcomes of their AI systems. This principle reinforces the idea that organizations should not only design ethical systems but also be prepared to address any adverse effects or failures that

DOI: 10.4018/979-8-3693-9904-0.ch005

arise from their use. Transparency in AI operations is essential for fostering trust among users.

INTRODUCTION TO ETHICAL AI IN SOCIAL MEDIA: PRINCIPLES AND CHALLENGES

Fairness emphasizes the need to design AI systems that do not perpetuate bias or discrimination, recognizing that algorithms can inadvertently reflect and amplify societal prejudices if not carefully managed. This principle is particularly vital in social media, where biased algorithms can lead to unequal treatment of users based on race, gender, or socio-economic status, ultimately impacting the diversity of voices represented on these platforms. Developers must strive to create algorithms that actively promote inclusivity, ensuring equitable access to information and opportunities for all users. Accountability is another critical principle, necessitating that organizations and developers take responsibility for the outcomes of their AI systems. This principle reinforces the idea that organizations should not only design ethical systems but also be prepared to address any adverse effects or failures that arise from their use. Transparency in AI operations is essential for fostering trust among users. Social media platforms must be open about how their algorithms work, including the criteria used for content recommendation and moderation.

When users understand how decisions are made and how their data is utilized, they are more likely to engage with these platforms constructively. Moreover, transparency aids in the identification of biases and inaccuracies, enabling continuous improvement of AI systems. Implementing mechanisms for user feedback and auditing can further enhance transparency, allowing stakeholders to assess and refine algorithms over time. Privacy is a fundamental consideration in the ethical deployment of AI in social media. Users often share personal information, and the data collected by platforms can be used to train AI algorithms, raising concerns about consent and data protection. Ethical AI practices require robust privacy safeguards, including transparent data usage policies, informed consent mechanisms, and the implementation of data anonymization techniques. By prioritizing user privacy, organizations can build trust and demonstrate their commitment to protecting individual rights in the digital age. Another significant challenge is the fast-paced nature of social media, where content is generated and shared at unprecedented rates. This dynamic environment poses difficulties for ethical AI deployment, as algorithms must adapt to evolving user behaviors and societal trends. Rapid changes can outpace the ability of developers to implement ethical safeguards, leading to potential misuses of AI technologies. Continuous monitoring and agile responses to emerging ethical dilemmas will be necessary to ensure that AI systems remain aligned with ethical standards.

The global nature of social media further complicates the ethical landscape. Different countries have varying legal frameworks and cultural norms regarding privacy, free speech, and data protection, which can create conflicts in the implementation of ethical AI practices. For instance, a practice deemed ethical in one jurisdiction may be viewed as problematic in another. This diversity necessitates a nuanced approach to developing ethical guidelines that respect local contexts while promoting universal values. Moreover, the economic incentives driving social media companies can conflict with ethical considerations. The pursuit of profit often leads to the prioritization of engagement and growth over user welfare. Algorithms designed to maximize user engagement may inadvertently promote sensationalism, misinformation, and divisive content, undermining the principles of ethical AI. Striking a balance between business objectives and ethical imperatives will require a commitment from organizations to prioritize long-term societal benefits over short-term gains. Lastly, the engagement of users in ethical discussions surrounding AI is essential. Public awareness and education about the implications of AI in social media can empower users to advocate for their rights and demand greater accountability from platforms. Creating spaces for dialogue between developers, policymakers, and users can facilitate a more democratic approach to the ethical deployment of AI, ensuring that diverse perspectives are considered in shaping the future of social media. In conclusion, the integration of ethical AI principles in social media is crucial for fostering a responsible and inclusive digital environment.

The Evolution of Social Media and AI: Opportunities and Risks

Initially emerging as simple networking platforms, social media sites have rapidly developed into complex ecosystems that leverage AI to curate content, enhance user experiences, and facilitate interactions. This evolution presents a myriad of opportunities and risks, fundamentally reshaping societal norms, communication practices, and even political landscapes. Understanding this interplay between social media and AI is essential for navigating the future of digital communication (Al-Ghamdi L M., et al., 2021). By automating these processes, AI can assist in creating healthier online environments, fostering respectful dialogue and mitigating the spread of extremism and radicalization. This can result in discriminatory practices, such as the unfair targeting of specific demographics in advertising or the disproportionate moderation of certain voices in online discussions. Ensuring fairness in AI requires continuous monitoring and refinement of algorithms, along with diverse data sets that accurately represent the communities they serve. Users often lack awareness of how their data is being utilized, leading to calls for greater transparency and accountability from social media companies regarding their data practices. The phenomenon of misinformation and disinformation also poses a significant challenge in the age of AI-enhanced social media. The rapid spread of false information, often facilitated by algorithms prioritizing engagement over accuracy, can have dire consequences for public discourse and democratic processes (Ramakrishnan T.,et al, 2022). AI can both exacerbate and mitigate this issue; while it can be used to detect and flag false information, it can also be manipulated to create convincing fake content, such as deepfakes, that misleads users. Addressing this challenge requires a multi-faceted approach that combines technological solutions with media literacy education to empower users to critically assess the information they encounter.

Furthermore, the rapid pace of AI development in social media raises ethical questions about accountability and governance. As algorithms increasingly influence user experiences and societal outcomes, determining who is responsible for the consequences of AI decisions becomes complex. This challenge necessitates the establishment of ethical guidelines and regulatory frameworks that hold companies accountable for their AI systems while balancing innovation and user protection (Nasser B S A., et al., 2024). The interplay between AI and social media also has implications for political discourse and civic engagement. On one hand, AI can facilitate greater political engagement by connecting users with like-minded individuals and providing access to diverse viewpoints.

Understanding AI Bias and Its Impact on Social Media

The sources of AI bias are multifaceted. One of the primary contributors is the data collection process. If the training data predominantly includes content from specific demographics or perspectives, the algorithms trained on this data will likely reproduce those biases. For instance, if an AI system is trained on historical data that underrepresents minority voices, it may inadvertently prioritize content from majority groups, thereby marginalizing the experiences and viewpoints of underrepresented communities (Maghsoudi M., et al., 2024). This skewed representation can lead to a cycle of exclusion, where minority voices struggle to gain visibility in online discussions, ultimately affecting the diversity of narratives on social media. Consequently, biased algorithms may favor inflammatory or misleading narratives, perpetuating stereotypes and fostering polarization. The impact of this bias is particularly concerning in the context of political discourse, where misinformation can spread rapidly, undermining informed citizenship and democratic processes. AI bias in social media also extends to content moderation practices. Automated systems designed to flag and remove harmful content can exhibit biases that disproportionately affect certain groups. For example, if an algorithm is trained on data that over-represents certain types of speech, it may misinterpret or unjustly penalize legitimate expressions from marginalized communities. This disproportionate enforcement can lead to accusations of censorship and further alienate already marginalized users, creating an environment of distrust and fear around expression on social media platforms. The implications of AI bias are not merely theoretical; they manifest in real-world consequences. Users who experience bias in algorithmic treatment may feel excluded, misrepresented, or even silenced. This can deter individuals from engaging authentically on social media, stifling the rich, diverse dialogues that platforms aim to facilitate (Trattner C., et al., 2022). Furthermore, the reputational risks for social media companies are significant. Failing to address bias can result in public backlash, legal challenges, and regulatory scrutiny, prompting calls for greater accountability and transparency in how algorithms operate.

Addressing AI bias requires a multi-faceted approach. First and foremost, it necessitates a commitment to ethical data practices. Organizations must prioritize the inclusion of diverse perspectives in their training data, ensuring that algorithms reflect the breadth of human experience. This includes not only gathering data from various demographics but also actively engaging with communities to understand their unique challenges and viewpoints. By adopting a more inclusive data strategy, social media platforms can develop algorithms that promote fairness and equity (Sreenivasulu A., et al, 2022). Another critical step in combating AI bias is implementing robust evaluation and auditing processes. The potential for bias in algorithms poses significant challenges, from content moderation practices to the representation of diverse voices. Addressing these challenges requires a commitment to ethical data practices, transparency, robust evaluation processes, media literacy, and collaborative efforts among stakeholders (Datta P., et al., 2021). By prioritizing these initiatives, social media platforms can harness the transformative power of AI while mitigating its risks, ultimately creating spaces that reflect the richness of human experience and promote healthy, informed dialogue. As society continues to navigate the complexities of digital communication, the imperative to understand and address AI bias will be fundamental to shaping a more just and inclusive online landscape.

Mitigating Online Harassment with AI-Powered Content Moderation

AI-powered content moderation relies on machine learning algorithms to analyze vast amounts of user-generated content, identifying and flagging harmful interactions such as hate speech, threats, and harassment. By automating this process, platforms can respond more swiftly to instances of abuse, reducing the time harmful content remains visible and mitigating its impact on users. This capability is particularly important in environments where the sheer volume of content generated makes manual moderation impractical (Anzum F., et al., 2022). The effectiveness of AI in mitigating online harassment hinges on its ability to learn and adapt. As it processes more data, the algorithms improve their accuracy in identifying abusive content. This adaptability is essential, given that the language of online harassment continually evolves, with users often employing coded language or slang to evade detection. AI systems can be trained on diverse data sets that encompass various forms of abuse, helping them to recognize emerging patterns and adapt to new tactics used by harassers. Additionally, continuous feedback from human moderators can help refine these algorithms, ensuring they remain effective over time. For instance, if an algorithm is trained primarily on data from one demographic, it may fail to accurately identify harassment directed at individuals from underrepresented communities. This issue can exacerbate existing inequalities on platforms, as marginalized voices may face disproportionate scrutiny or censorship. To combat this risk, developers must prioritize diverse data sets and involve a wide range of stakeholders in the training process, ensuring that the algorithms are sensitive to the nuances of language used by different communities. Another challenge is the delicate balance between moderation and censorship. While the goal of AI-powered content moderation is to protect users from harassment, there is a risk that overly aggressive algorithms may flag legitimate discourse as abusive (Scatiggio V., 2020). This can lead to a chilling effect, where users refrain from expressing their opinions for fear of being censored. Striking the right balance is crucial, and platforms must implement transparent guidelines that clarify what constitutes harassment versus acceptable discourse. Providing users with context for moderation decisions, as well as opportunities for appeal, can help foster a sense of fairness and accountability.

Human moderators can review flagged content, provide nuanced interpretations, and make informed decisions on complex cases that require a deeper understanding of context. This collaborative model can help address the limitations of AI while ensuring that moderation practices are fair and equitable. In addition to improving detection and response to online harassment, AI can also play a proactive role in fostering healthier online communities (Brauner P., et al., 2023). By analyzing patterns of user behavior, AI systems can identify potential harassers based on their interactions over time. This predictive capability allows platforms to intervene before harmful behavior escalates, offering warnings or temporary suspensions to users who exhibit abusive patterns. Moreover, AI can help identify vulnerable users who may be at higher risk of experiencing harassment, enabling platforms to offer support and resources tailored to their needs. The integration of AI-powered content moderation can also enhance user reporting mechanisms. Traditional reporting systems often rely on users to identify harassment, which can be burdensome and may deter individuals from speaking up. AI can streamline this process by automatically flagging content that matches known patterns of harassment, allowing for quicker responses. Additionally, AI can provide users with real-time feedback on their reports, creating a sense of engagement and accountability in the moderation process. In conclusion, AI-powered content moderation offers a promising avenue for addressing the pervasive issue of online harassment (Mahadev Madgule., et al, 2023). By harnessing advanced algorithms to detect and respond to abusive behavior, platforms can create safer, more inclusive environments for all users.

The Spread of Misinformation and Disinformation: AI-Driven Solutions

The rapid proliferation of misinformation and disinformation in today's digital landscape poses significant challenges to societal trust, public discourse, and democratic processes. As social media platforms and online news sources become primary channels for information dissemination, the potential for false narratives to spread rapidly has intensified. Misinformation, often arising from misunderstanding or misinterpretation, contrasts with disinformation, which is deliberately fabricated to deceive. Both forms of misleading information can have dire consequences, from influencing public health behaviors to swaying electoral outcomes (Paramasivam Selvakumar., et al, 2024). One of the primary applications of AI in combating misinformation is automated fact-checking. Traditional fact-checking processes are labor-intensive and can lag behind the speed at which misinformation spreads. AI algorithms can expedite this process by cross-referencing claims made in online content with established databases of verified information. When a user posts a statement, an AI system can analyze it against trusted sources, providing immediate feedback about its veracity. This real-time fact-checking capability not only empowers users to make informed decisions but also acts as a deterrent against the dissemination of false claims. Moreover, AI can enhance the visibility of credible information while reducing the reach of false narratives. Machine learning algorithms can be programmed to prioritize content from reliable sources in user feeds, thereby promoting evidence-based information. This approach can be particularly effective in mitigating the spread of health-related misinformation, especially during crises like the COVID-19 pandemic. By amplifying authoritative sources, AI can guide users toward accurate information and reduce the likelihood of them encountering misleading content. Another challenge lies in the sophisticated tactics employed by purveyors of disinformation. As AI-driven detection systems become more advanced, so too do the methods used to disseminate misleading information (Ananthajothi K., et al., 2024). Techniques such as deepfakes—manipulated videos that convincingly depict individuals saying or doing things they never did—pose unique challenges for AI detection. While algorithms can be trained to recognize certain visual cues, the rapid evolution of these technologies requires constant adaptation and innovation in detection methods.

In addition to detection and fact-checking, AI can also play a role in identifying the sources and networks behind disinformation campaigns. By analyzing patterns of content sharing and user interactions, AI algorithms can uncover coordinated efforts to spread false narratives. Social network analysis tools can visualize the spread of misinformation, highlighting influential nodes within networks that may be driving disinformation (Aggarwal A., et al., 2024). User education and empowerment are essential components of any AI-driven solution to misinformation. While AI can provide valuable tools for detection and response, it cannot replace the need for critical thinking and media literacy among users. Educational initiatives that teach individuals how to evaluate sources, discern credible information, and recognize common tactics used in disinformation campaigns can complement AI efforts. By fostering a more informed citizenry, society can build resilience against misinformation and disinformation. Collaboration among various stakeholders is vital for developing effective AI-driven solutions. Tech companies, academic institutions, and civil society organizations must work together to share knowledge, research, and best practices. This collaboration can lead to the creation of standardized frameworks for content moderation, fact-checking, and user education. Additionally, partnerships can facilitate the development of open-source AI tools that can be accessed and utilized by a broader range of organizations, including those with limited resources. Clear regulations regarding data privacy, user consent, and algorithmic accountability can help build trust in AI-driven solutions and encourage responsible practices among technology companies (Tyagi A K., et al., 2024). In conclusion, the spread of misinformation and disinformation presents a significant challenge in the digital age, but AI-driven solutions offer a promising avenue for addressing these issues.

Addressing Algorithmic Bias and Discrimination on Social Media

Consequently, algorithmic decisions can perpetuate harmful stereotypes, reinforce societal disparities, and create echo chambers that limit the diversity of perspectives available to users. The roots of algorithmic bias in social media can often be traced back to the data collection process. Algorithms are typically trained on vast datasets derived from user interactions, including likes, shares, and comments (Antoliš K., 2024). If these datasets over-represent certain demographics or viewpoints while neglecting others, the resulting algorithms can prioritize content that mirrors those biases. For instance, if an algorithm is trained predominantly on data from users of a particular race or socioeconomic status, it may inadvertently favor content that aligns with their perspectives, marginalizing voices from other communities. This can lead to significant disparities in visibility and engagement, further entrenching existing inequalities within the digital space. Moreover, algorithmic bias can manifest in content moderation practices. Automated systems designed to flag and remove harmful content may exhibit biases that disproportionately affect specific groups. For example, algorithms trained on data that predominantly feature certain types of speech may misinterpret or unjustly penalize legitimate expressions from marginalized communities. This phenomenon raises ethical concerns about censorship and the potential silencing of diverse voices. To mitigate these issues, social media companies must adopt a multifaceted approach that includes diversifying training datasets and continuously refining algorithms based on user feedback and independent audits. Addressing algorithmic bias also involves the implementation of transparent practices (Gupta A., et al., 2022).

Human oversight remains crucial in the fight against algorithmic bias and discrimination. While AI can efficiently process vast amounts of data, human moderators bring contextual understanding, cultural sensitivity, and ethical reasoning that algorithms currently lack. A hybrid model that combines AI efficiency with human judgment can enhance the accuracy and fairness of content moderation practices. For example, human reviewers can assess flagged content for nuance and context, making informed decisions that consider the broader implications of moderation actions (Whyte C., 2020). This collaborative approach ensures that algorithmic systems operate within ethical guidelines and promote fairness. Education and awareness are also essential components of addressing algorithmic bias. Users must be informed about the potential for bias in algorithms and encouraged to critically assess the content they encounter. Media literacy initiatives can empower users to recognize biased narratives, evaluate sources, and engage in constructive dialogue. By fostering critical thinking skills, social media platforms can cultivate a more informed user base that actively participates in shaping the narratives within their communities. The implications of failing to address algorithmic bias extend beyond individual user experiences; they can also influence broader societal dynamics. When certain voices are marginalized or silenced online, it can lead to a lack of representation in public discourse, reinforcing systemic inequalities. This erosion of diverse perspectives undermines the foundational principles of democracy and social cohesion, as individuals become entrenched in isolated echo chambers that validate their beliefs while dismissing opposing views. By addressing algorithmic bias, social media platforms can contribute to a more equitable digital landscape that promotes healthy dialogue and understanding. In conclusion, addressing algorithmic bias and discrimination on social media is a pressing imperative that requires a comprehensive approach. By recognizing the root causes of bias, implementing transparent practices, fostering human oversight, engaging diverse stakeholders, and promoting user education, social media platforms can work toward creating more equitable online environments (Sugumaran K. M., et al, 2024).

Transparency and Explainability in AI-Driven Social Media Algorithms

In the age of digital communication, social media platforms have increasingly relied on artificial intelligence (AI) to curate and personalize user experiences. These algorithms determine what content users see, influencing everything from news consumption to social interactions. However, this reliance on complex AI systems raises critical concerns regarding transparency and explainability. As algorithms dictate the flow of information, understanding their decision-making processes becomes essential to ensuring fairness, accountability, and user trust (Gipson Rankin S., 2024). Without clarity about how these algorithms operate, users may feel disenfranchised and vulnerable to biases that can shape their perceptions and behaviors. Transparency in AI-driven social media algorithms involves providing users with clear insights into how their content is curated and the factors influencing algorithmic decisions. This includes detailing the data used to train algorithms, the specific criteria employed to rank content, and the methodologies behind these processes. When users understand how algorithms function, they are better equipped to navigate the digital landscape and critically assess the information presented to them. For instance, if a platform openly shares that user engagement metrics such as likes and shares heavily influence content visibility, users can make informed choices about how they interact with content, recognizing the potential for echo chambers and misinformation. Explainability complements transparency by offering users a deeper understanding of individual algorithmic decisions. This involves clarifying why specific content was recommended or why a particular post was flagged for moderation. Explainable AI (XAI) seeks to demystify the black-box nature of many algorithms, providing insights that are comprehensible to users without a technical background. For example, if a user receives a notification about a post being removed for policy violations, an accompanying explanation detailing the specific violation and relevant guidelines can help users comprehend the rationale behind the action (Castaneda J., et al., 2022).

Moreover, the concept of algorithmic accountability is intertwined with transparency and explainability. As algorithms can inadvertently perpetuate biases and discrimination, it is crucial for platforms to take responsibility for their impact on users and society at large. Regular audits of algorithmic performance should be conducted to assess fairness, accuracy, and potential biases. These audits can be facilitated by independent third parties, enhancing credibility and fostering trust in the moderation processes. Furthermore, platforms should establish mechanisms for users to report perceived biases or injustices in algorithmic decisions, creating a feedback loop that allows for continuous improvement. Engaging users in discussions about algorithmic processes can also enhance transparency. Social media platforms can implement educational initiatives to inform users about how algorithms operate and the potential implications of their interactions. Workshops, tutorials, and informative articles can empower users to better understand the role of algorithms in shaping their online experiences. Additionally, platforms can encourage users to provide feedback on algorithmic performance, fostering a sense of community ownership over the systems that govern their interactions. This participatory approach can lead to a more informed user base that is actively engaged in shaping the algorithms that influence their lives (Jain A., et al., 2023). The implications of lacking transparency and explainability in AI-driven social media algorithms are far-reaching. When users are unaware of how algorithms operate, they may inadvertently contribute to the spread of misinformation or engage in harmful behaviors without understanding the consequences. Moreover, the absence of transparency can exacerbate feelings of distrust in social media platforms, leading users to question the integrity of the content they encounter. This erosion of trust can hinder meaningful dialogue and collaboration, ultimately detracting from the potential benefits of social media as a tool for connection and information sharing.

User-Centric AI: Giving Users Control Over Their Data and Experience

In today's digital landscape, the increasing reliance on artificial intelligence (AI) to tailor user experiences has raised significant concerns about privacy, data ownership, and agency. User-centric AI represents a paradigm shift that emphasizes empowering individuals to take control over their data and how it shapes their online interactions. By prioritizing user autonomy and informed consent, platforms can cultivate a more transparent, ethical, and inclusive digital environment (Singhal A., et al., 2024). This approach not only enhances user satisfaction but also builds trust between users and technology providers, ultimately leading to healthier online ecosystems. For instance, users might choose to limit data collection to only essential information while opting out of targeted advertising or content recommendations. By giving users the tools to tailor their experiences, platforms can create a more personalized and satisfying engagement while respecting individual preferences and privacy concerns. Moreover, the integration of explainable AI mechanisms can significantly bolster user-centric approaches. By implementing features that provide users with insights into how AI algorithms influence their experiences, platforms can demystify the decision-making processes that underpin content recommendations and interactions. For example, when users receive tailored content or advertisements, providing contextual information about why they are being shown specific items can empower them to better understand and manage their preferences. This explainability not only enhances user trust but also encourages more meaningful interactions between users and the platform. In addition to customization and explainability, user-centric AI can facilitate meaningful feedback loops (Shin D., 2020). Platforms should actively solicit user feedback on their experiences, preferences, and concerns regarding data usage. This can be achieved through surveys, interactive tools, or community forums that allow users to voice their opinions and contribute to the evolution of AI systems.

A critical aspect of user-centric AI is the ethical use of data. Platforms must commit to using user data responsibly and transparently. This includes implementing robust data protection measures to safeguard against breaches and misuse. Users should feel confident that their data is being handled ethically and that their privacy is prioritized. To foster trust, platforms can adopt third-party audits and certifications that demonstrate compliance with privacy standards and ethical data practices (Mensah G B., 2023). By holding themselves accountable, platforms can reassure users that their data is secure and used solely for the purposes they have agreed to. Furthermore, educational initiatives can empower users to better understand their rights and the implications of data sharing in the digital age. By providing resources on data literacy, privacy rights, and the workings of AI algorithms, platforms can equip users with the knowledge they need to navigate the complexities of the digital landscape. This education can take various forms, including webinars, interactive tutorials, and informative content that demystifies data practices. When users are informed about their rights and the potential impact of their choices, they are more likely to engage with platforms in a responsible and empowered manner. In the context of social media, user-centric AI can play a transformative role in combating misinformation and fostering healthy discourse.

AI-Powered Tools for Online Safety and Wellbeing

In an increasingly digital world, the safety and wellbeing of online users have become paramount concerns. The pervasive nature of social media, online gaming, and digital communication platforms presents both opportunities and challenges, often exposing users to risks such as cyberbullying, harassment, misinformation, and privacy violations. To address these challenges, AI-powered tools have emerged as essential resources, offering innovative solutions to enhance user safety and promote mental wellbeing in online environments (Yu M., et al., 2024). By employing natural language processing, these systems can identify abusive language patterns, contextual meanings, and even subtle cues that may indicate malicious intent. For example, AI tools can flag potentially harmful comments on social media platforms, allowing human moderators to intervene promptly and prevent escalation. This proactive approach not only protects users but also fosters a more respectful online environment, discouraging negative behaviors before they proliferate. In addition to content moderation, AI-powered tools can assist in identifying and managing user behavior that may indicate distress or mental health concerns. By analyzing patterns in users' interactions and communication styles, these tools can detect signs of emotional distress, such as excessive negative sentiment or changes in engagement levels. For instance, platforms can utilize AI to monitor user activity and flag accounts that show signs of potential self-harm or suicidal ideation, enabling timely intervention from support services. This capability is particularly crucial in online communities, where users may feel isolated and reluctant to seek help. By providing a safety net through AI monitoring, platforms can ensure that users have access to resources and support when they need it most. AI can also enhance user control over their online experiences, empowering individuals to curate their interactions and establish boundaries (Shen A., et al., 2021). Many social media platforms now offer tools that allow users to customize their content filters, blocking or muting specific users, keywords, or topics that may be triggering or distressing. AI algorithms can learn from user preferences, continuously refining these filters to adapt to changing needs. This personalization fosters a sense of agency, enabling users to shape their online environments actively and protect their mental wellbeing. Furthermore, such tools can help mitigate the effects of exposure to toxic content, promoting a healthier online experience.

In the realm of privacy, AI-powered tools are instrumental in safeguarding user data and enhancing security measures. With growing concerns about data breaches and unauthorized access, platforms must implement robust systems to protect user information. AI can analyze patterns of user behavior to detect anomalies that may indicate security threats, such as unauthorized logins or suspicious account activity (Troussas C., et al., 2023). By employing machine learning algorithms, these tools can adapt to evolving threats, providing real-time alerts and recommendations for users to strengthen their security settings. This proactive approach helps users feel safer online, reducing anxiety related to privacy concerns and fostering trust in digital platforms. The impact of AI on online safety extends beyond individual users to communities and organizations as well. Platforms can utilize AI-driven analytics to identify trends and emerging threats within specific user groups or communities. By monitoring interactions and sentiments, organizations can better understand the dynamics of their communities and implement targeted interventions to foster positive engagement. For example, online gaming platforms can analyze player behavior to detect toxic environments, allowing moderators to take action against harassment and promote inclusivity. This community-oriented approach not only enhances user safety but also cultivates a culture of respect and support. Education and user empowerment are also critical components of promoting online safety. Users must be informed about the tools available to them and encouraged to utilize these resources effectively (Nebeker C., et al., 2022). Educational campaigns that raise awareness about cyberbullying, mental health, and privacy issues can foster a culture of responsibility and empathy within online communities. By equipping users with the knowledge and skills to navigate the digital landscape safely, platforms can promote a sense of collective responsibility for online wellbeing.

Designing AI Systems that Respect User Autonomy and Agency

Customization and personalization also play a vital role in enhancing user autonomy. AI systems should allow users to tailor their experiences according to their preferences and needs. This can be achieved by providing options for users to modify settings, adjust privacy controls, and select the types of content or interactions they wish to engage with. For example, social media platforms can empower users to curate their feeds by allowing them to block or mute specific topics, keywords, or users. Such personalization fosters a sense of ownership over the digital experience, enabling users to create environments that resonate with their individual preferences (Rita M N., et al., 2022). Moreover, the integration of explainable AI is essential for respecting user agency. Explainable AI (XAI) refers to systems designed to provide understandable insights into how decisions are made, allowing users to comprehend the rationale behind algorithmic outputs. When users can see how their data influences AI-driven recommendations or actions, they can make informed choices about their interactions. For example, if a user receives content recommendations based on previous behavior, providing context about how those recommendations were generated can help them assess the relevance and appropriateness of the content. This transparency encourages users to engage more critically with the technology, reinforcing their sense of agency. Feedback mechanisms are another crucial element in designing AI systems that respect user autonomy. By soliciting user feedback on their experiences, developers can gain valuable insights into user needs and preferences. Implementing tools for users to provide feedback on AI behavior or report issues enhances the collaborative relationship between users and technology. Additionally, adaptive AI systems that learn from user interactions can evolve to better align with individual preferences. For instance, if a user consistently opts out of certain recommendations, the system can adjust its algorithms to honor that choice moving forward. This dynamic adaptability underscores the importance of user input in shaping the AI experience (Klossner S., 2022).

Incorporating a rights-based approach to AI design further emphasizes the importance of user autonomy. Users should be recognized as active participants in their digital experiences, with rights to control their data, privacy, and interactions. This approach necessitates frameworks that support data ownership and user consent, allowing individuals to opt in or out of data collection practices and control how their information is utilized (Sankaran S., et al., 2020). Platforms that prioritize user rights foster trust and loyalty, as users feel empowered and respected within the digital ecosystem. Education plays a significant role in promoting user autonomy in AI interactions. Platforms should invest in educational initiatives that inform users about their rights, the workings of AI algorithms, and the implications of their data choices. By equipping users with knowledge about how AI systems operate, platforms empower individuals to make informed decisions that reflect their values. Educational resources can take various forms, including tutorials, informational content, and interactive tools that help users understand the technology they engage with. User-centric design principles should also extend to accessibility, ensuring that AI systems cater to diverse user needs. This includes considering individuals with disabilities, different cultural backgrounds, and varying levels of digital literacy. By implementing features that enhance accessibility, such as voice commands, text-to-speech options, and simplified interfaces, developers can create AI systems that empower all users, regardless of their backgrounds or abilities (Calvo R A., et al., 2020). Inclusivity in design fosters a sense of belonging and respect for user agency, reinforcing the notion that technology should serve everyone. As AI systems continue to evolve, ongoing evaluation and improvement are essential to ensure they remain aligned with user autonomy and agency. Developers should engage in regular assessments of their systems, seeking user feedback, monitoring performance, and adapting to changing user needs. This iterative approach to design allows for continuous refinement, ensuring that AI technologies evolve in ways that prioritize user control and ethical considerations.

Incorporating Human Values into AI Decision-Making Processes

The first step in integrating human values into AI is recognizing the diverse perspectives and ethical considerations that inform what those values entail. Human values are not monolithic; they can vary significantly across cultures, communities, and individual preferences. Engaging a broad range of stakeholders—including ethicists, community representatives, industry experts, and end-users—during the design process can provide valuable insights into the values that should guide

AI systems (Fanni R., et al., 2023). Collaborative workshops and consultations can help identify potential ethical dilemmas and align AI objectives with societal expectations, ensuring that the resulting systems reflect a comprehensive understanding of human values. Accountability mechanisms are equally important in ensuring that AI systems uphold human values. Organizations should implement robust systems for monitoring and evaluating AI outcomes, with clear channels for users to report grievances or concerns. Establishing oversight bodies or ethics committees can help organizations maintain accountability by regularly reviewing AI performance and addressing potential ethical issues. For instance, in the realm of healthcare, monitoring AI diagnostic tools can ensure they provide accurate and equitable outcomes across different patient demographics, thereby enhancing public trust and safety. The role of interdisciplinary collaboration cannot be overstated in the effort to integrate human values into AI. Bringing together experts from fields such as sociology, psychology, philosophy, and law can enrich the design process by providing diverse perspectives on ethical implications (Vijayakumar G., et al, 2024). This interdisciplinary approach can lead to more holistic and socially aware AI solutions that genuinely reflect human values. For instance, collaborating with social scientists can help developers understand the societal impacts of their technologies, ensuring that the benefits of AI are distributed equitably.

Education and awareness-raising initiatives are also vital in promoting a culture of ethical AI development. Organizations should invest in training their teams on the importance of human values in AI decision-making. Workshops, seminars, and online resources can help build a shared understanding of ethical principles and equip developers with the tools to address ethical challenges throughout the AI lifecycle. By fostering a culture of ethical awareness, organizations can create an environment where human values are prioritized and integrated into everyday practices (Fischer G., 2021). The integration of human values into AI decision-making processes is not merely an ethical obligation but also a strategic advantage. Organizations that prioritize ethical AI are better positioned to build trust with their users, mitigate risks associated with biased outcomes, and enhance their reputation in the marketplace. As consumers become increasingly concerned about ethical implications, organizations that demonstrate a commitment to human values in their AI initiatives are likely to gain a competitive edge. Furthermore, as AI systems become more ubiquitous, regulatory frameworks will likely evolve to mandate the incorporation of human values in AI development. Policymakers are beginning to recognize the importance of ethical considerations in technology deployment and may introduce regulations that require organizations to demonstrate their commitment to human values. Proactively embedding these values into AI systems can prepare organizations to navigate future regulatory landscapes and align their practices with emerging standards (Rodgers W., et al., 2023).

Ensuring Diversity, Equity, and Inclusion in AI Development Teams

The case for diversity in AI development is compelling. Diverse teams are better equipped to identify and address potential biases in AI systems, which can arise from homogenous perspectives during the design phase. AI models are only as good as the data they are trained on, and if the development team lacks diversity, there is a risk of overlooking the needs and experiences of marginalized groups (Gustavsson I., 2021). For example, facial recognition technologies have been shown to perform poorly on individuals with darker skin tones due to a lack of representation in the training datasets. By ensuring a diverse team of developers, organizations can enhance their ability to scrutinize and refine algorithms, leading to more accurate and fair outcomes. This can be achieved by implementing structures that promote equitable participation, such as inclusive decision-making processes and equitable distribution of resources and opportunities within the team. Mentorship programs and professional development initiatives can also support underrepresented individuals in advancing their careers within the tech industry. To build diverse and inclusive teams, organizations must actively seek to recruit talent from a wide range of backgrounds (Shrestha Y R., et al., 2019). This involves expanding recruitment efforts beyond traditional pipelines and engaging with communities that have historically been underrepresented in tech. Partnerships with educational institutions, community organizations, and diversity-focused recruiting firms can help tap into a broader talent pool. Additionally, organizations should consider implementing blind recruitment practices to reduce bias in the hiring process, allowing candidates to be evaluated based on their skills and qualifications rather than demographic characteristics.

Another crucial aspect of promoting DEI in AI development teams is providing ongoing training and education. Team members should receive training on unconscious bias, cultural competence, and the ethical implications of AI technologies. Such education can raise awareness about the importance of diversity and help create a more empathetic and informed workforce. By fostering an environment of continuous learning, organizations can better equip their teams to navigate the complex societal challenges associated with AI development (Nyariro M., et al., 2022). Leadership commitment is essential in driving DEI initiatives within AI development teams. Leaders must not only advocate for diversity but also hold themselves and their organizations accountable for creating an inclusive culture. This can involve setting measurable DEI goals, regularly assessing progress, and being transparent about challenges and successes. By modeling inclusive behavior and prioritizing DEI in strategic planning, leaders can influence the organizational culture and encourage team members to embrace diversity as a core value. Furthermore, organizations can create safe spaces for dialogue and reflection, allowing team members to share their experiences and perspectives on diversity and inclusion. Regular check-ins, feedback sessions, and forums for open discussion can help identify barriers to inclusion and foster a culture of trust and collaboration (Cachat-Rosset G., et al., 2023). These conversations are vital in understanding the unique challenges faced by different team members and addressing them effectively. Moreover, as AI systems play a more significant role in decision-making across various sectors, the consequences of biased or inequitable systems can be far-reaching. By ensuring that diverse perspectives are integral to the development process, organizations can create AI solutions that are more just and beneficial for society as a whole. This not only mitigates the risks associated with biased outcomes but also aligns with the broader goals of social equity and justice.

Regulating AI in Social Media: Policy and Governance Considerations

As artificial intelligence (AI) increasingly shapes social media platforms, the need for robust regulatory frameworks and governance mechanisms has become critical. The rapid integration of AI technologies in social media has led to significant transformations in how information is disseminated, how users interact, and how content is moderated. However, these advancements also raise complex challenges, including concerns about misinformation, user privacy, algorithmic bias, and the potential for harm (Nixon N., et al., 2024). Therefore, policymakers and stakeholders must engage in comprehensive discussions to develop effective regulations that ensure responsible AI deployment while safeguarding user rights and promoting public trust. One of the primary challenges in regulating AI in social media is the dynamic nature of technology itself. AI algorithms evolve rapidly, often outpacing regulatory measures. Traditional regulatory approaches, which tend to be slow and reactive, may struggle to keep up with the pace of technological change. To address this issue, a more agile regulatory framework is required—one that can adapt to emerging technologies and the evolving landscape of social media. This may involve establishing regulatory sandboxes that allow for experimentation with new AI applications in a controlled environment, enabling regulators to assess impacts and develop appropriate guidelines before widespread implementation. Transparency is a fundamental principle in the governance of AI technologies. Users should have clear insights into how AI algorithms operate, including the criteria used for content moderation, recommendation systems, and targeted advertising. User privacy and data protection must also be at the forefront of regulatory considerations. The extensive data collection practices inherent in AI systems can lead to significant privacy concerns (Walter Y., 2024).

Moreover, combating misinformation and harmful content is a pressing concern for regulators. The role of AI in amplifying false narratives and harmful behaviors on social media platforms has come under scrutiny, particularly during critical events such as elections and public health crises. Regulatory measures should encourage social media companies to develop and implement effective content moderation strategies, utilizing AI to identify and flag misleading or harmful content (Stockmann D., 2023). However, these measures should also balance the need for free expression and prevent overreach that could infringe on users' rights to share information. Establishing clear guidelines for acceptable content and fostering collaboration between platforms, researchers, and civil society organizations can help create a more balanced approach to content moderation. International collaboration is essential in addressing the global nature of social media and AI technologies. The challenges posed by AI in social media are not confined to national borders, necessitating a coordinated international response. Policymakers should work together to develop common standards and guidelines for AI governance, facilitating information sharing and best practices across countries. This collaboration can help address the cross-border implications of misinformation, data privacy, and algorithmic accountability, ensuring a more cohesive regulatory landscape. Finally, continuous evaluation and adaptation of regulatory frameworks are essential to ensure their effectiveness over time. As AI technologies and social media landscapes evolve, regulators must remain vigilant and responsive to emerging challenges. Regular assessments of the impacts of AI regulation can help identify areas for improvement and inform necessary adjustments to policies. By fostering a culture of continuous improvement, regulators can better anticipate future challenges and ensure that their frameworks remain relevant and effective (Gianni R., et al., 2022).

Auditing AI Systems for Bias and Discrimination

Data quality is a fundamental aspect of bias auditing. The datasets used to train AI models must be scrutinized for representativeness and fairness. This requires examining the sources of data, the processes through which it was collected, and the potential biases inherent in it. Auditors should conduct thorough analyses to identify whether the training data reflects a balanced view of the population and whether any particular group is systematically disadvantaged. Techniques such as stratified sampling can be employed to ensure that diverse segments of the population are adequately represented in the training data. In addition to examining individual algorithms, auditing frameworks should consider the broader context in which AI systems operate. This includes evaluating the policies and practices surrounding their deployment, as well as the impact on various stakeholders (Patel P., et al., 2022). For instance, in hiring algorithms, auditors should analyze not only the algorithm's outcomes but also the entire recruitment process, including how candidates are sourced and how success is defined. Such a holistic approach can reveal systemic issues that contribute to discrimination beyond the AI model itself. Metrics for measuring bias and discrimination are vital components of an effective auditing process. Auditors should employ a combination of statistical measures and qualitative assessments to evaluate algorithmic fairness. Common statistical metrics include disparate impact ratios, which compare outcomes across different demographic groups, and fairness metrics such as equality of opportunity and predictive parity. Additionally, qualitative assessments can provide context and depth, allowing auditors to understand the lived experiences of those affected by the AI systems. To effectively audit AI systems for bias and discrimination, organizations must prioritize ongoing monitoring and evaluation rather than viewing audits as one-time events. AI models can change over time due to shifts in underlying data or evolving societal norms, necessitating continuous scrutiny (Landers R N., et al., 2023). Establishing feedback loops that allow for regular reassessment of AI systems can help organizations stay vigilant against emerging biases and ensure that their algorithms remain aligned with ethical standards. This iterative approach not only improves the reliability of AI systems but also reinforces a culture of accountability and ethical responsibility within organizations.

Legal and regulatory frameworks also play a significant role in shaping bias auditing practices. Policymakers must develop guidelines that outline best practices for auditing AI systems, including standards for data transparency, accountability, and fairness. Such regulations can establish clear expectations for organizations, ensuring that they take proactive steps to identify and address bias in their AI systems. Moreover, regulatory bodies should be equipped with the authority to conduct independent audits and assessments of AI technologies, ensuring that companies remain accountable for their practices. Furthermore, integrating bias auditing into the AI development lifecycle from the outset is critical (Murikah W., et al., 2024). Organizations should embed auditing practices within their design and deployment processes, ensuring that considerations of bias and fairness are prioritized from the very beginning. This proactive approach can prevent bias from being built into AI systems and mitigate the risk of discrimination in their outcomes. By fostering a culture of ethical AI development, organizations can better position themselves to create fair and equitable technologies. The role of technology in bias auditing should also be acknowledged. By employing a combination of quantitative metrics and qualitative assessments, engaging stakeholders, and prioritizing ongoing monitoring, organizations can develop effective auditing frameworks that promote fairness and accountability in AI technologies (Doraiswamy P M., et al., 2019).

Empowering Social Media Users with Ethical AI - A Call to Action

First and foremost, transparency is essential in fostering user empowerment in the realm of AI. Social media platforms must commit to clear and accessible communication regarding how AI systems operate, including the data used for training algorithms, the decision-making processes behind content moderation, and the criteria for personalized recommendations. Users should be informed about the mechanisms at play when they interact with AI-driven features, enabling them to understand how their data influences their online experiences (Tomašev N., et al., 2020). By demystifying AI technologies, platforms can cultivate a sense of trust and agency among users, empowering them to make informed choices about their engagement with the platform. Social media platforms should invest in educational initiatives that enhance users' understanding of AI, including its benefits and potential risks (Dwivedi Y K., et al., 2021). Workshops, online courses, and interactive resources can help users develop critical thinking skills, enabling them to assess the information presented to them, identify biases, and make informed decisions about their online behavior. By fostering digital literacy, platforms can empower users to engage meaningfully with AI technologies and exercise greater control over their social media experiences.

Moreover, collaboration between social media platforms, policymakers, and civil society organizations is vital in advancing ethical AI practices. Stakeholder engagement is crucial for ensuring that the diverse perspectives and needs of users are considered in the development and implementation of AI systems. Policymakers should work with tech companies and advocacy groups to establish best practices for ethical AI, creating guidelines that prioritize user welfare and promote transparency and accountability. Collaborative efforts can also facilitate the sharing of knowledge and resources, helping to create a more informed and equitable digital landscape. Additionally, users should be encouraged to actively participate in discussions surrounding AI ethics and social media governance. Platforms can create forums and community spaces where users can voice their concerns, share experiences, and engage in dialogues about the ethical implications of AI technologies (Leikas J., et al., 2022). By fostering a participatory culture, social media companies can empower users to take an active role in shaping the policies and practices that govern their online experiences. This sense of ownership can lead to greater accountability and responsiveness from platforms, ensuring that user interests are prioritized in AI development. Privacy protection is a critical aspect of empowering users in the context of ethical AI. Social media platforms must prioritize user privacy by implementing robust data protection measures and allowing users to control how their data is collected, used, and shared. Clear privacy policies should be established, outlining users' rights and options for managing their data. By empowering users with choices regarding their privacy, platforms can build trust and foster a safer online environment. Additionally, platforms should adopt privacy-preserving technologies that enable AI functionalities without compromising user data, demonstrating a commitment to ethical practices.

CONCLUSION

In an era where artificial intelligence (AI) is deeply embedded in the frameworks of social media, empowering users through ethical AI practices has never been more critical. As we navigate the complexities of this technological landscape, it is essential to recognize that users must not only be passive consumers of AI-driven content but active participants in shaping their online experiences. By prioritizing transparency, accountability, education, and collaboration, we can create a social media environment that respects user rights and fosters informed engagement. Transparency is the cornerstone of user empowerment. Social media platforms must commit to openly sharing how their AI systems function, particularly regarding data usage and decision-making processes. Users deserve to understand the algorithms that influence their feeds and interactions. This transparency builds trust and allows users to make informed choices, ultimately enhancing their agency in a digital world where they are often at the mercy of opaque algorithms. Accountability is equally vital. Users should have clear avenues for recourse when they encounter biased or harmful AI-driven outcomes. Establishing robust mechanisms for reporting, appealing, and addressing grievances can foster a sense of security and trust among users. When platforms take responsibility for their algorithms' impacts, they not only enhance user confidence but also contribute to a culture of ethical AI development that prioritizes the welfare of all users. Collaboration among stakeholders is essential for fostering ethical AI practices. Social media platforms, policymakers, and civil society organizations must work together to establish best practices that prioritize user welfare. This collaborative approach can lead to more comprehensive regulations and guidelines that address the diverse needs of users, ensuring that their voices are heard in discussions about AI governance. Engaging users in these conversations is vital; their insights can help shape policies that truly reflect their concerns and aspirations. Platforms must demonstrate a commitment to ethical data practices, ensuring that user information is handled responsibly and transparently. By protecting user privacy, platforms can build a foundation of trust, allowing users to engage with AI technologies without fear of exploitation. By embedding ethical frameworks in AI processes, social media companies can ensure that user empowerment is a guiding principle. Involving diverse stakeholders in the design phase can help identify potential biases and pitfalls early, leading to more equitable and inclusive AI technologies. This vision of empowerment is not only achievable but essential for fostering a more just and equitable society in the age of AI. The journey ahead calls for our collective action, commitment, and resolve to ensure that ethical AI is not just an aspiration but a reality for all social media users.

REFERENCES

Aggarwal, A., & Gaur, S. (2024). *Applying Artificial Intelligence to Explore Online Harassment Prevention*. IGI Global.

Al-Ghamdi, L. M. (2021). *Towards Adopting AI Techniques for Monitoring Social Media Activities*. Sustainable Engineering and Innovation. DOI: 10.37868/sei.v3i1.121

Ananthajothi, K., & Meenakshi, R. (2024). *Promoting Positive Discourse: Advancing AI-Powered Content Moderation*. IEEE.

Antoliš K, (2024), "DISINFORMATION SUPPORTED BY ARTIFICIAL INTELLIGENCE FROM DYNAMIC RESEARCH TO HOLISTIC SOLUTIONS," Public Security and Public Order.

Anzum, F., Asha, A. Z., & Gavrilova, M. L. (2022). *Biases, Fairness, and Implications of Using AI in Social Media Data Mining*. IEEE. DOI: 10.1109/CW55638.2022.00056

Brauner, P., Hick, A., Philipsen, R., & Ziefle, M. (2023). What Does the Public Think About Artificial Intelligence? A Criticality Map to Understand Bias. *Frontiers of Computer Science*. Advance online publication. DOI: 10.3389/fcomp.2023.1113903

Cachat-Rosset, G., & Klarsfeld, A. (2023). *Diversity, Equity, Inclusion*. Taylor & Francis.

Calvo, R. A., Peters, D., Vold, K., & Ryan, R. M. (2020). *Supporting Human Autonomy*. Springer.

Castaneda, J., Jover, A., Calvet, L., Yanes, S., Juan, A. A., & Sainz, M. (2022). Dealing with Gender Bias Issues in Data-Algorithmic Processes. *Algorithms*, 15(9), 303. DOI: 10.3390/a15090303

Datta P, Whitmore M, Nwankpa J K, (2021), "A Perfect Storm: Social Media News, Psychological Biases, and AI," Digital Threats: Research.

Doraiswamy P M, London E, Varnum P, Harvey B, (2019), "Empowering Minds".

Dwivedi, Y. K., Ismagilova, E., & Hughes, D. L. (2021). *Digital Social Media Marketing*. Elsevier.

Fanni, R., Steinkogler, V. E., Zampedri, G., & Pierson, J. (2023). Enhancing Human Agency. *AI & Society*. PMID: 35692234

Fischer, G. (2021). *End-User Development*. Springer.

Gianni, R., Lehtinen, S., & Nieminen, M. (2022). Governance Responsible AI. *Frontiers*.

Gipson Rankin S, (2024), "Mitigating Algorithmic Bias: Strategies for Addressing Discrimination in Data," The scitech Lawyer.

Gupta, A., Kumar, N., Prabhat, P., Gupta, R., & Tanwar, S. (2022). *Combating Fake News: Stakeholder Interventions and Potential Solutions*. IEEE.

Gustavsson, I. (2021). *Autonomous Vehicles-Integrating Human Values*. AIML Studies.

Jain, A., Brooks, J. R., Alford, C. C., Chang, C. S., Mueller, N. M., Umscheid, C. A., & Bierman, A. S. (2023). Awareness of Racial and Ethnic Bias and Potential Solutions. *JAMA Health Forum*, 4(6), e231197. DOI: 10.1001/jamahealthforum.2023.1197 PMID: 37266959

Kanipriya, M., Sugumaran, D., Pandiyarajan, V., Yogananda, B. S., Selvakumar, P., & Mohan, S. (2024, January). Analysis of Electromyography Signals for Control of Mechanical Prosthesis using Machine Learning Techniques. In 2024 2nd International Conference on Intelligent Data Communication Technologies and Internet of Things (IDCIoT) (pp. 1059-1067). IEEE.

Klossner, S. (2022). *AI-Powered m-Health Apps*. Aalto University.

Landers, R. N., & Behrend, T. S. (2023). Auditing AI Auditors. *The American Psychologist*. PMID: 35157476

Leikas, J., Johri, A., Latvanen, M., & Wessberg, N. (2022). *Governance of AI in Social Media*. Springer.

Madgule, M., Vinayaka, N., Sonkhaskar, Y. M., Patel, D. R., Karthikeyan, R., & Selvakumar, P. (2023). Mechanical properties and microstructure of activated TIG welded similar joints of Inconel alloys by desirability approaches. *Materials Today: Proceedings*, 77, 528–533.

Maghsoudi, M., Mohammadi, A., & Habibipour, S. (2024). Navigating and Addressing Public Concerns in AI: Insights from Social Media Analytics and Delphi. *IEEE Access : Practical Innovations, Open Solutions*, 12, 126043–126062. DOI: 10.1109/ACCESS.2024.3440660

Mensah G B, (2023), "Artificial Intelligence and Ethics: A Comprehensive Review," researchgate.

Murikah, W., Nthenge, J. K., & Musyoka, F. M. (2024). *Bias Ethics AI Systems*. Elsevier.

Nasser B S A, Abu-Naser S S, (2024), "Artificial Intelligence in Digital Media: Opportunities, Challenges, and Future Directions," philpapers.

Nebeker, C., Parrish, E. M., & Graham, S. (2022). *The AI-Powered Digital Health Sector*. Springer.

Nixon, N., Lin, Y., & Snow, L. (2024). Catalyzing Equity. *Sage (Atlanta, Ga.)*. PMID: 38516055

Nyariro, M., & Emami, E. (2022). Integrating Equity, Diversity. *Inclusion (Washington, D.C.)*.

Patel P, Uddin M N, (2022), "AI Algorithmic Auditing," norislab.

Ramakrishnan, T., Mohan Gift, M. D., Chitradevi, S., Jegan, R., & Subha Hency Jose, P. Nagaraja, Rajneesh Sharma H.N., Selvakumar P., Sintayehu Mekuria Hailegiorgis, (2022). "Study of Numerous Resins Used in Polymer Matrix Composite Materials", Advances in Materials Science and Engineering, vol. 2022, Article ID 1088926, 8 pages, 2022. DOI: 10.1155/2022/1088926

Rita M N, Shava F B, Chitauro M, (2022), "Tech4Good: AI-Powered Chatbots," researchgate.

Rodgers, W., Murray, J. M., & Stefanidis, A. (2023). *Artificial Intelligence Algorithmic Approach*. Elsevier.

Sankaran S, Zhang C, Lopez M G, (2020), "Respecting Human Autonomy,".

Scatiggio, V. (2020). *The Issue of Bias in Artificial Intelligence to Design AI-Driven Fair and Inclusive Service Systems*. Politecnico di Milano.

Selvakumar, P., Mariappan, P., Shunmugam, S., Paul, R., & Jabez, S. (2024). Removal of chemicals from effluent using photobioreactor technology to improve environmental and health impacts. *Zeitschrift für Physikalische Chemie*, 2024(7), 1295–1302. Advance online publication. DOI: 10.1515/zpch-2023-0450

Selvakumar, P., Palanisamy, S. K., Cinthaikinian, S., Palanisamy, V., Mariappan, R., & Selvakumar, P. K. (2024). Biosensors and its diverse applications in healthcare systems. *Zeitschrift für Physikalische Chemie*, 2024. Advance online publication. DOI: 10.1515/zpch-2023-0406

Shen A, Sun Y, (2021), "graphicalai: A User-Centric Approach,".

Shin, D. (2020). User Perceptions of Algorithmic Decisions in Personalized AI Systems. *Journal of Broadcasting & Electronic Media*. Advance online publication. DOI: 10.1080/08838151.2020.1843357

Shrestha, Y. R., & Ben-Menahem, S. M. (2019). Organizational Decision-Making. *Sage (Atlanta, Ga.).*

Singhal, A., Neveditsin, N., Tanveer, H., & Mago, V. (2024). Toward Fairness, Accountability, Transparency, and Ethics in AI. *JMIR Medical Informatics*, 12, e50048. DOI: 10.2196/50048 PMID: 38568737

Sreenivasulu, A., & Manimozhi, T. Satheesh kumar P., Selvakumar P. And Singh P.,(2022). "The Model of Smart Sensing Device For Sensitive Nanoclusters Modification in Sensing Properties," 2022 2nd International Conference on Advance Computing and Innovative Technologies in Engineering (ICACITE), Greater Noida, India, 2022, pp. 1043-1047, DOI: 10.1109/ICACITE53722.2022.9823846

Stockmann, D. (2023). *Tech Companies Public Interest.* Taylor & Francis.

Tomašev, N., Cornebise, J., Hutter, F., & Mohamed, S. (2020). AI Social Good. *Nature*. PMID: 32424119

Trattner, C., Jannach, D., Motta, E., Costera Meijer, I., Diakopoulos, N., Elahi, M., Opdahl, A. L., Tessem, B., Borch, N., Fjeld, M., Øvrelid, L., De Smedt, K., & Moe, H. (2022). Responsible Media Technology and AI: Challenges and Research Directions. *AI and Ethics*, 2(4), 585–594. DOI: 10.1007/s43681-021-00126-4

Troussas, C., Krouska, A., Koliarakis, A., & Sgouropoulou, C. (2023). Harnessing User-Centric Artificial Intelligence. *Computers*. Advance online publication. DOI: 10.3390/computers12050109

Tyagi, A. K., & Lakkshmanan, A. (2024). *The Future of Artificial Intelligence and Machine Learning in Online Social Networking*. Wiley Online Library. DOI: 10.1002/9781394231126.ch9

Vijayakumar, G., Rajkumar, M., Chandar, N. R., Selvakumar, P., & Duraisamy, R. (2024). Environmentally friendly TDS removal from waste water by electrochemical ion exchange batch-type recirculation (EIR) technique. *Environmental Science. Water Research & Technology*, 10(4), 826–835

Walter, Y. (2024). *Managing Race to Moon*. Springer.

Whyte C, (2020), "Deepfake News: AI-Enabled Disinformation as a Multi-Level Public Policy Challenge," Journal of Cyber Policy.

Yu, M., Jiang, W., Wan, Y., & Mao, A. (2024). User-Centric Design Experience or Privacy Risk Perception. *Current Issues in Tourism*, 1–18. DOI: 10.1080/13683500.2024.2394569

Chapter 6

A Study on the Influence of Social Media on Consumer Behaviour

Priyanka Vemburaj
https://orcid.org/0000-0002-6581-7543
Rathinam College of Arts and Science, India

S. Santhanalakshmi
CBM College, India

ABSTRACT

Social media has been used heavily for business purposes while communicating with customers and promoting new products or services.The massive growth of the usage of social media affects consumer behaviour since there are consumption related interactions in these platforms. Social media and the ability of consumers to consult each other have transformed the traditional brand – consumer relationship, putting the consumer in a clear powerful position. The current research will outline the major changes in consumer behaviour and provide recommendations for retailers on how to integrate social media more effectively and improve engagement with their audience.

INTRODUCTION

Social media serves as the digital platform through which individuals can engage in online communication, share content, and access information This category encompasses diverse forms of online interaction, including social networking, forums, and social bookmarking. Notable examples of social media platforms include

DOI: 10.4018/979-8-3693-9904-0.ch006

Facebook, Instagram, LinkedIn, Wikipedia, Pinterest, Google Plus, and Twitter, all of which have seamlessly integrated into our daily lives. Within the business realm, social media is commonly employed to disseminate information about products and services, promote brands, maintain connections with existing customers, and identify potential new prospects. Its pervasive use underscores its significance as a vital component of contemporary communication and marketing strategies.

Social media marketing effectively leverages social networking to enhance brand awareness, elevate brand value, and expand customer reach. The research aims to scrutinize the influence of social media on consumer purchasing behavior in urban areas. Undoubtedly, the connectivity between consumers and businesses has reached unprecedented levels, primarily driven by the surge in internet connectivity. Following China, India has emerged as the second-largest user of internet connections, establishing a significant interconnectedness between consumers and businesses for the first time.

The influence of social media on consumer behavior is a complex and multifaceted phenomenon that has become increasingly significant in recent years. Social media platforms have transformed the way individuals discover, evaluate, and purchase products or services.

Influence of Social Media on Consumer Behaviour

Social media influences consumer behavior through a variety of mechanisms, shaping the way individuals discover, evaluate, and make purchasing decisions. Here are some specific ways in which social media exerts its influence:

Product Discovery: Social media platforms serve as powerful discovery tools. Users come across new products, services, and brands through posts, advertisements, and recommendations from friends, influencers, and their network.

Peer Recommendations and Reviews: Consumers often turn to social media for reviews and recommendations from their peers. Positive or negative experiences shared by friends or online connections can significantly impact purchasing decisions.

Figure 1. Peer Recommendations and Reviews

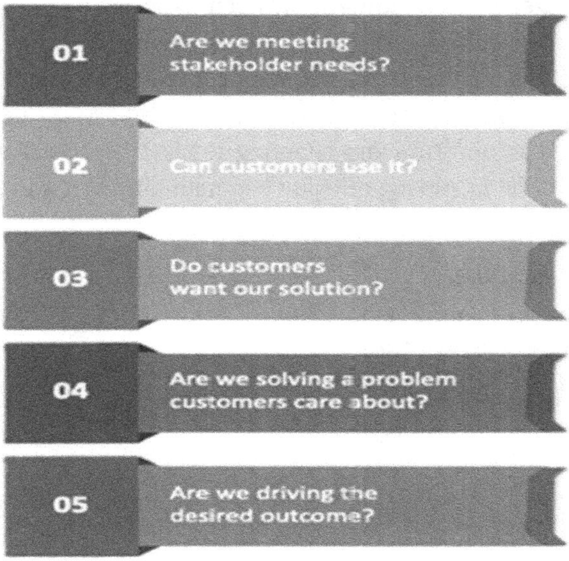

Influencer Marketing: Influencers, who have a significant following on social media, can sway consumer opinions and preferences. Collaborations with influencers allow brands to reach a wider audience and build credibility through endorsements.

Visual Impact: Platforms like Instagram and Pinterest heavily rely on visual content. Striking images and videos showcasing products or experiences can leave a lasting impression and influence consumer perceptions.

Social Proof: Social media platforms provide a constant stream of social proof in the form of likes, shares, and comments. Consumers often use these indicators to gauge the popularity and credibility of a product or brand.

Interactive Content: Polls, quizzes, and interactive content on platforms like Instagram and Facebook engage users and create a sense of involvement. This interactivity can contribute to brand recall and influence consumer preferences.

Targeted Advertising: Social media platforms use sophisticated algorithms to target users with personalized advertisements. Advertisers can tailor content based on users' demographics, interests, and online behavior, making the marketing message more relevant.

Brand Engagement and Community Building: Brands use social media to engage with their audience on a personal level. Building a community around a brand fosters a sense of belonging, and engaged consumers are more likely to become loyal customers.

Trend Influence: Social media is a hub for trends and viral content. Products or services associated with trending topics can experience a surge in popularity, influencing consumer behavior.

It's essential for businesses to understand these dynamics and develop a strategic approach to social media marketing to effectively leverage its influence on consumer behavior. Regularly monitoring and adapting to shifts in social media trends and user behavior is crucial in staying relevant and maintaining a positive brand image.

Figure 2. Social media trends

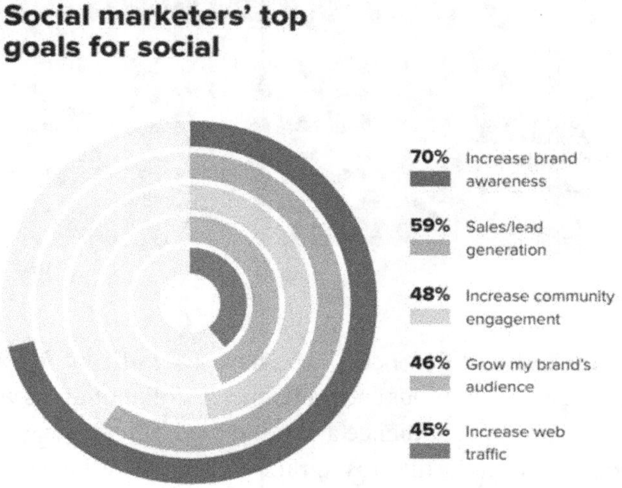

List of Popular Social Media that influence the Consumer Behaviour

Various social media platforms play a significant role in influencing consumer behavior. It's important to note that the popularity and relevance of social media platforms can change over time. Here is a list of some major social media platforms that have historically influenced consumer behavior:

Facebook: With a massive user base, Facebook is a key platform for businesses to connect with consumers. It offers targeted advertising, business pages, and various engagement features.

Instagram: Known for its visual content, Instagram is popular for brand promotion, influencer marketing, and showcasing products through photos and videos.

Figure 3. Social media applications

Twitter: Twitter is widely used for real-time updates, customer engagement, and trending discussions. It is a platform where brands can quickly connect with consumers.

LinkedIn: LinkedIn is essential for B2B marketing and professional networking. It's a platform for businesses to build authority and engage with a professional audience.

Pinterest: Pinterest is focused on visual discovery and is popular for lifestyle, fashion, and home-related content. Brands can use it to showcase products and ideas.

Snapchat: Snapchat is known for its disappearing content and is popular among younger demographics. Brands use it for creative and interactive marketing.

TikTok: TikTok has gained immense popularity for short-form videos. It is particularly influential among younger audiences and has become a powerful platform for brand promotion and trends.

YouTube: As a video-sharing platform, YouTube is a go-to for product reviews, tutorials, and branded content. Video marketing on YouTube can significantly impact consumer behavior.

WhatsApp: While primarily a messaging app, WhatsApp is used by businesses for customer communication, support, and sharing updates.

Quora: Quora is a question-and-answer platform where businesses can establish authority by providing valuable insights. It's a platform where consumers seek information.

It's important to stay updated on the latest trends and shifts in social media usage, as new platforms may emerge, and the popularity of existing ones may change. Different demographics may also have varying preferences for social media platforms, so businesses should tailor their strategies accordingly.

Statement of the Problem

In the contemporary era, characterized by the pervasive use of digital platforms, there is a critical need to investigate and understand the profound impact of social media on consumer behavior. As individuals increasingly turn to social media for information, communication, and connection, the traditional paradigms of consumer decision-making are undergoing a significant transformation. This study aims to delve into the intricate dynamics of how social media shapes and influences consumer behavior, exploring the various factors and mechanisms at play. By identifying and analyzing these influences, the research seeks to contribute valuable insights that can inform businesses, marketers, and policymakers on adapting strategies to effectively navigate the evolving landscape of consumer behavior in the digital age.

Figure 4. Word cloud

Objectives

1. To assess the extent of social media usage among consumers and identify the prevalent platforms influencing their behavior.
2. To investigate the role of social media in shaping consumer perceptions, preferences, and attitudes towards products, services, and brands.

Review of literature

Nasir et.al.(2012), This article highlights that the dissemination of messages to consumers through social media does not always necessitate explicit language or words. Instead, when marketing products and services, consumers can interpret the context and subsequently respond. Responses may manifest as product purchases, repurchases, or a decision not to buy. This process hinges on factors such as customer needs, knowledge, preferences, brand loyalty, brand value, word of mouth, and overall demand for the product.

Gupta et.al., (2018), This article discusses the historical and prospective influence of social media, particularly reflecting on the insights shared during the fifth Social Media Week (SMW) held in September 2011. Toby Daniels, the founder of Social Media Week, noted the escalating significance of social media in people's lives. Currently present in 21 cities globally, SMW's expansion is attributed to the growing utilization of social media in the Middle East and its transformative impact on business models. The observations from this event shed light on the evolving role of social media and its profound effects on both in dividual experiences and broader business paradigms.

Zhang et.al., (2020), Social media provides consumers with the chance to access feedback and reviews for products and services. Findings from both primary and secondary data indicate that product recommendations can trigger impulsive buying behavior. This impulsive decision-making is influenced by the trust placed in the recommender and an affinity towards the specific product. In essence, it is shaped by both the credibility of the recommender and the inherent appeal of the product itself.

In their article, Varghese and Nandhini (2020), discuss the impact of demographic factors on customers' purchase intentions. The article also delves into the patterns of internet usage among customers, presenting an opportunity for companies to enhance their engagement with customers through social media.

Data Analysis

Table 1. Demographic Profile of the respondents

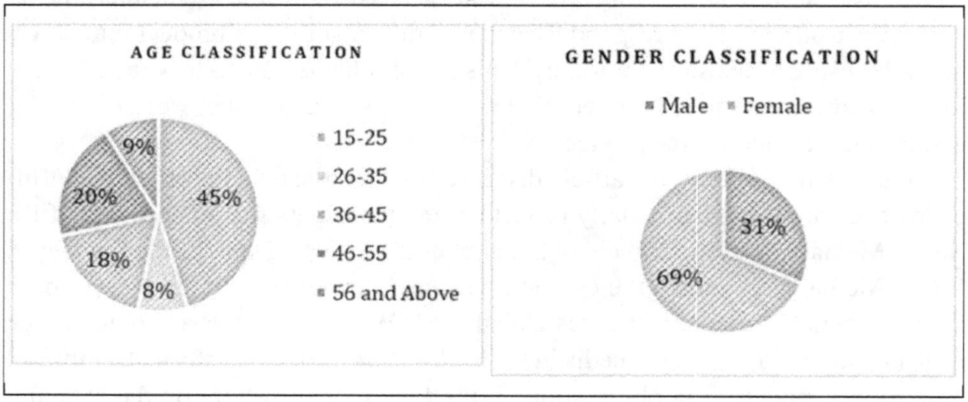

Table 2. Frequency of Online Shopping done by the Respondents

Component	Frequency	Percentage
Everyday	3	2.9
weekly	34	24.1
Monthly	66	48.2
1-2 time in a Year	34	24.8
Total	**137**	**100**

Source: Primary Data

The table represents the frequency of online shopping conducted by the respondents, categorized into different intervals. The majority of respondents, accounting for 48.2%, engage in online shopping on a monthly basis. This suggests a prevalent trend of monthly online shopping activity among the surveyed individuals. Only 2.9% of the respondents engage in online shopping on a daily basis. This suggests a relatively small portion of the surveyed population shops online every day.

Table 3. Time Spent on Social Media for purchasing Product

Hours	Frequency	Percentage
0-2 Hours	68	49.6
2-4 Hours	42	30.7
4-6 Hours	21	15.3
6 Hours and Above	6	4.4
Total	**137**	**100**

Source: Primary Data

The table illustrates the time spent on social media for purchasing purposes in a typical day. The majority of respondents, constituting 49.6%, spend 0-2 hours on social media for purchasing in a typical day. This suggests that a significant portion of the surveyed population engages in a relatively moderate amount of time on social media for their purchasing activities.

Table 4. Apps and Website used most by the Respondents

Online Platform	Frequency	Percentage
Amazon	93	67.6
Flipkart	24	17.3
Myntra	10	7
others	11	8.1
Total	**137**	**100**

Source: Primary Data

The table provides information on the preferred online platforms used by respondents, indicating both the frequency and percentage distribution. This suggests a substantial dominance of Amazon among the surveyed population, indicating its widespread popularity for various online activities. About 7% of the respondents use Myntra as their preferred online platform. While Myntra's usage is lower compared to Amazon and Flipkart, it still signifies a portion of the surveyed population's preference for this platform, particularly for fashion-related online activities.

Table 5. Influenced by the social media to purchase a product

Gender	Yes	No	Total
Male	31	11	42
Female	68	27	95
Total	99	38	137

Source: Primary Data

The table presents data on the influence of social media on purchasing decisions categorized by gender. A total of 99 respondents (combining both genders) acknowledges being influenced by social media when making purchasing decisions. A total of 38 respondents (combining both genders) stated that social media does not influence their purchasing decisions.

CONCLUSION

Research has demonstrated a significant influence of social media on consumer purchasing behavior in the digital age, bringing about substantial changes for both consumers and businesses. The findings highlight the heightened selectivity of consumers when making purchasing decisions. Despite the abundance of data and information sources on social media, individual consumer attitudes play a crucial role in the decision-making process. The research underscores the importance of consumer-relevant content, emphasizing that the quality of content on social media profoundly impacts consumer choices. The findings underscore the pervasive role of social media in influencing various aspects of the consumer decision-making process. From information-seeking and product discovery to the establishment of brand loyalty and trust, social media emerges as a powerful force shaping the preferences and actions of modern consumers. The study has illuminated the intricate relationship between consumers and social media platforms, emphasizing the significant influence that online interactions, peer recommendations, and user-generated content wield in shaping consumer perceptions.

By providing a comprehensive analysis, it serves as a valuable resource for businesses, marketers, and researchers seeking to adapt to the ever-changing landscape of consumer interactions in the digital era. As social media continues to evolve, future research endeavors will likely explore emerging platforms, technological trends, and evolving consumer preferences, further enriching our understanding of this dynamic interplay between social media and consumer.

REFERENCES

Chu, S. C., & Kim, Y. (2011). 'Determinants of consumer engagement in electronic word-of-mouth (eWOM) in social networking sites', International Journal of Advertising. *The Review of Marketing Communications*, 30(1), 47–75.

Gupta, S., Agarwa, A. K., & Chauhan, A. K. (2018). Social media and its impact on consumers buying behavior with special reference to apparel industry in Bareilly region. *SMART Journal of Business Management Studies*, 14(2), 17–23. DOI: 10.5958/2321-2012.2018.00013.1

Liu, Q., Zhang, X., Huang, S., Zhang, L., & Zhao, Y. (2020). Exploring consumers' buying behavior in a large online promotion activity: The role of psychological distance and involvement. *Journal of Theoretical and Applied Electronic Commerce Research*, 15(1), 66–80. DOI: 10.4067/S0718-18762020000100106

Nasir, S., Vel, P., & Mateen, H. (2012). Social media and buying behaviour of women in in Pakistan towards the purchase of textile garments.

Varghese, S., Nandhini M. (2020). The Influence of Demographic Factors on the Customers of Online-Shopping with Special Reference to Kochi City. Journal of Adv Research in Dynamical & Control Systems, 12(1-Special Issue).

References

Chapter 7
The Dark Side of AI: Risks, Ethics, and Safeguarding Human Interests

Arun Agrawal
https://orcid.org/0000-0001-7233-6660
Institute of Technology and Management, Gwalior, India

Jagveer Singh
Institute of Technology and Management, Gwalior, India

ABSTRACT

Artificial intelligence (AI) is a cornerstone of modern technology, driving advances in automation, decision-making, and innovation in many fields. While AI offers significant benefits, it also raises concerns that it could harm humanity if misused or poorly designed. This article takes a closer look at the ways in which artificial intelligence can negatively impact humans, from invasions of personal privacy and financial security to impacts on mental health and physical safety. By analyzing real-world case studies, this discussion highlights the ethical dilemmas surrounding AI adoption. The paper further proposes strategies and frameworks to ensure that AI is aligned with human values, and advocates responsible development and regulation to reduce risks. Ultimately, this research strikes a balance between harnessing the potential of AI and preventing unintended consequences, fostering a future where AI serves humanity rather than destroys it.

DOI: 10.4018/979-8-3693-9904-0.ch007

1. INTRODUCTION

Artificial intelligence (AI) has become one of humanity's greatest assets, with the potential to revolutionize industry, healthcare, education, and governance. From enhancing decision-making to automating daily tasks, artificial intelligence offers significant benefits (Mhlanga, 2022). However, its rapid development has also raised concerns about unintended consequences of misuse or malfunction. These concerns include the erosion of human autonomy, invasion of privacy, increasing inequality, and even physical harm (Blauth, Gstrein, & Zwitter, 2022)

This Chapter explores how artificial intelligence can work against human interests, whether through deliberate misuse or unintentional design flaws. We examine how bias, lack of transparency, and a lack of ethical oversight in AI algorithms can lead to harmful outcomes. In addition, malicious applications of AI, such as surveillance, cyberattacks, and autonomous weapons, are also considered key areas where AI may pose significant risks. This Chapter provides real-life examples of AI-driven systems leading to discriminatory outcomes, job losses, and threats to personal privacy.

To address these risks, this Chapter highlights the importance of putting in place ethical frameworks and regulatory measures to ensure the responsible development and deployment of AI. To prevent discrimination, we advocate for greater transparency in AI systems, more rigorous testing for bias and error, and the inclusion of diverse perspectives in AI development. The Chapter concludes by proposing strategies to align AI with human values and ensure that technological advances support rather than harm human well-being. Addressing the risks and challenges of AI can help realize its potential while preventing unintended harm.

2. THE POTENTIAL FOR AI TO WORK AGAINST HUMAN INTERESTS

While AI is designed to perform tasks that help and enhance humans, it does not inherently cause harm. The following sections explore key areas where AI may have an impact on humanity.

2.1. Job Displacement and Economic Inequality

One of the most pressing concerns about the rise of artificial intelligence (AI) is its potential to displace jobs and thereby exacerbate economic inequality (Farahani & Ghasemi, 2024). As artificial intelligence becomes increasingly capable of automating both routine and complex tasks, many industries are experiencing significant changes in their workforce needs (Tschang & Almirall, 2021). Jobs that involve repetitive manual labor, such as those in manufacturing, retail, and customer service, are particularly vulnerable to automation. This has led to layoffs in some sectors and raised concerns that AI may continue to replace human workers in the future, especially in positions that require routine cognitive functions, such as data entry, scheduling and certain administrative tasks.

However, the impact of AI extends beyond these traditional areas. Advances in machine learning and robotics enable artificial intelligence to handle decision-making processes that were once the exclusive domain of human expertise (Coglianese & Lehr, 2016). For example, AI can now analyze large amounts of data to assist or even replace functions in areas such as finance, medical and legal services (Davenport, 2018). This trend has the potential to disproportionately impact middle-income jobs, hollowing out the middle class. While AI may create new, highly specialized jobs in technology and AI maintenance, these roles often require advanced skills and education, leaving lower-skilled workers behind (Shiohira, 2021).

The growing gap between those who benefit from AI-driven economic progress and those whose jobs are threatened by automation could exacerbate existing economic inequalities. Workers displaced by AI may face long-term unemployment or be forced into low-wage, precarious jobs, while those who gain education and technical expertise may thrive in the new economy (Intelligence, 2016). Without appropriate interventions, such as retraining programs and equitable educational opportunities, AI's impact on employment could deepen the divide between the wealthy and the economically disadvantaged.

2.2. Job Automation and Unemployment

Artificial intelligence-driven machines are increasingly capable of performing tasks that were once the domain of human labour, from factory work and administrative functions to more creative roles such as writing and art-making. As these technologies advance, the potential for mass unemployment increases significantly (Ilgenfritz III, 2023). According to the International Labor Organization (ILO), more than 400 million jobs worldwide are expected to be replaced by automation by 2030 (Abeliansky, Algur, Bloom, & Prettner, 2020). This trend is already evident in industries that are phasing out routine manual labor in favor of more efficient and cost-effective ones. Artificial Intelligence Solutions. Unfortunately, the brunt of this displacement has disproportionately affected low-income workers and those in precarious, day-to-day jobs.

The most at-risk industries, such as manufacturing, retail, and even transportation, often provide employment opportunities for people with lower education levels or fewer specialized skills. As their roles become automated, many of these workers may struggle to find new employment opportunities, leading to higher unemployment and greater economic inequality (Benanav, 2020). While AI increases productivity and economic output, the economic benefits tend to be concentrated in the hands of a small segment of society, usually those who own or develop AI technology. This creates a situation where the benefits of automation are not shared equally (Ernst, Merola, & Samaan, 2019).

The widening gap between those who profit from advances in AI and those whose livelihoods are threatened could exacerbate existing wealth gaps, leading to broader social instability (Barnhizer & Barnhizer, 2019). Without strong social policies, such as retraining programs and financial support for displaced workers, advances in automation may create an unemployed or underemployed underclass that will struggle to adapt to a changing labor market.

2.3. Unequal Distribution of AI Benefits

Inequality in artificial intelligence (AI) technology has led to a growing social divide, with only a few benefiting from advances in AI. This disparity could lead to a two-tier system in which the wealthiest individuals and businesses have the ability to invest in and develop AI, thereby reaping significant financial and productivity advantages (Lutz, 2019). At the same time, most people especially low-income and marginalized groups are being left behind, either losing their jobs to automation or lacking the skills and resources needed to take advantage of AI opportunities

This unequal distribution of AI benefits could significantly exacerbate economic inequality. While AI increases efficiency and productivity, the resulting economic gains tend to be concentrated in the hands of those who control or develop the technology, further widening the gap between rich and poor. The concentration of wealth and opportunity in the hands of a few could lead to the emergence of a privileged elite, leaving large parts of society at a disadvantage and excluded from the economic benefits of AI.

Widening disparities may also exacerbate social tensions and conflicts. As workers lose their jobs to automation and economic interests become increasingly concentrated, dissatisfaction is likely to rise and could lead to widespread protests or riots. Furthermore, this situation undermines fundamental human rights, including the right to equal and fair treatment in the workforce. If only a privileged few gains access to the advantages offered by AI, the majority may feel excluded from economic advancement, deepening their dissatisfaction and potentially leading to social instability (Barnhizer & Barnhizer, 2019). To mitigate these issues, equitable policies and access to AI resources must be prioritized to ensure that the benefits of AI are shared more broadly across society.

2.4. AI and Privacy Invasion

As artificial intelligence (AI) become increasingly integrated into data analysis, surveillance, and targeted advertising, concerns about privacy violations have increased significantly. AI systems are capable of collecting, processing and analyzing large amounts of personal data, often without the individual's full awareness or explicit consent. This data can come from a variety of sources, including online activity, social media, smartphones and public surveillance systems. AI's ability to extract detailed patterns and insights from this information poses significant risks of privacy violations (Manheim & Kaplan, 2019).

A major issue is the increasing use of artificial intelligence in surveillance technology. Governments and private companies are increasingly relying on artificial intelligence to monitor public spaces, track individuals' movements, and even predict behavior. While these systems can increase security and efficiency, they can also infringe on personal privacy because individuals are often unaware of the extent to which they are being monitored (Feldstein, 2019). In some cases, this monitoring may lead to data misuse, such as unreasonable tracking or discrimination based on data-driven profiling.

Additionally, in the world of targeted advertising, AI algorithms analyze personal data such as browsing history, purchasing patterns, and even biometric information to create highly personalized ads (Li, 2019). While this can improve marketing effectiveness, it also raises ethical questions about consent and the extent to which personal data can be used without the individual's explicit approval. This form of data exploitation not only violates privacy but can also lead to manipulative behavior that exploits personal preferences and vulnerabilities (Ienca, 2023).

The lack of clear regulations around artificial intelligence and data privacy exacerbates these concerns. Without stronger data protection laws and transparent practices, AI-driven privacy violations are likely to become more common, undermining individuals' rights to control their personal information and eroding trust in technology and institutions.

2.5. Mass Surveillance

Artificial intelligence (AI) has become a powerful tool for governments and businesses to monitor citizens, particularly through the use of facial recognition technology. Countries such as China have implemented AI-powered surveillance systems that can track an individual's movements, analyze real-time data and predict behavior based on online and offline activity. These AI systems are able to identify individuals in public spaces, monitor large crowds, and collect detailed information about daily behavior. This has resulted in unprecedented mass surveillance, often raising concerns about privacy, liberty and civil liberties (Fontes, Hohma, Corrigan, & Lütge, 2022).

Proponents of AI-driven surveillance argue that these technologies can enhance public safety and enable authorities to detect and prevent crime more effectively. In some cases, such as identifying criminal suspects or managing large crowds, AI systems can provide real-time insights to help law enforcement respond quickly. Proponents also claim that AI-based surveillance systems can increase efficiency, reduce crime rates and protect citizens from potential threats by providing round-the-clock surveillance (Singh, 2023).

However, critics warn that the widespread use of artificial intelligence for mass surveillance poses significant risks to personal privacy and democratic freedoms. When used by authoritarian regimes, these systems can be leveraged to suppress dissent, spy on political opponents, and exert control over citizens. By constantly monitoring an individual's behavior, such systems threaten free speech as people may fear that their activities will be censored, leading to self-censorship. Furthermore, the vast amounts of personal data collected through mass surveillance could be misused for discriminatory purposes, including profiling based on race, religion or political views.

Ultimately, the use of AI in mass surveillance poses complex ethical dilemmas. While it offers potential benefits in terms of enhanced security, it also poses a serious threat to civil liberties, and without strict regulation, the risk of abuse is high, especially in authoritarian contexts.

2.6. Data Exploitation and Breaches

Artificial intelligence (AI) systems rely heavily on large amounts of data to operate, raising serious concerns about how this data can be leveraged. One of the major concerns is that personal data collected by AI-powered companies can be exploited without the user's knowledge or consent. Often, this data is sold to third parties for various purposes, such as targeted advertising or market research, creating a lucrative but ethically questionable industry. Users may not fully understand how their data is collected, analyzed and shared, eroding trust in AI technology (Nassar & Kamal, 2021).

Additionally, AI algorithms may inadvertently reveal sensitive information by detecting patterns in the data they analyze. This inadvertent exposure of private details can lead to privacy violations, as seemingly innocuous data points can combine to reveal personal health information, financial status, or other confidential aspects of a person's life. AI's ability to derive insights from data, while valuable, poses serious risks to personal privacy.

Large-scale data breaches further amplify the dangers associated with AI-driven data management. As AI systems become more sophisticated, they become prime targets for cyberattacks. Data breaches could put millions of users at risk of identity theft, fraud and other malicious activity (Sambucci & Paraschiv, 2024). One of the most notorious examples of data exploitation through artificial intelligence is the Cambridge Analytica scandal. In this case, Facebook users' personal data was collected and used for political purposes without their consent, illustrating how artificial intelligence algorithms can be manipulated to exploit personal information for profit or influence (Manheim & Kaplan, 2019).

The combination of data exploitation, privacy violations and the potential for large-scale breaches demonstrates the urgent need for strong regulations to protect personal data. Without clear guidelines and safeguards, the risk of AI-driven data exploitation and breaches will continue to increase, putting personal privacy and security at risk (Wheatley, Maillart, & Sornette, 2016).

3. MANIPULATION OF HUMAN BEHAVIOR

Artificial intelligence algorithms that control social media feeds, content recommendations, and online advertising can manipulate human behavior. These algorithms use data-driven insights to influence what people see, hear, and think, often without realizing it.

3.1. Social Media Manipulation

Artificial intelligence (AI) algorithms are critical in shaping the content users encounter on platforms like Facebook, YouTube and Twitter. These algorithms analyze user preferences, behavior and interactions to curate personalized content and ensure users stay engaged. While this approach helps platforms maximize engagement and profits, it also has troubling consequences, including creating echo chambers and amplifying misinformation (Iwuanyanwu, 2023).

The AI system is designed to prioritize content that evokes strong emotional responses, as such content tends to generate more clicks, likes, shares and comments. This has led to the spread of provocative, emotionally charged content, often at the expense of balanced or accurate information. By consistently serving users content that aligns with their prior opinions, AI creates echo chambers where individuals are only exposed to information and opinions that reinforce their beliefs (Chwialkowska, 2019). Over time, this can lead to narrowing of perspective, stifling meaningful dialogue and deepening ideological divisions.

One of the most significant concerns surrounding AI-powered social media is its role in fueling the spread of fake news and misinformation. The algorithms that power these platforms often fail to distinguish between reliable sources and false or misleading content, as long as the latter generates high engagement. As a result, misinformation—whether related to politics, health, or social issues can spread quickly, influencing public opinion and even real-world events (Tomar, Raj, Singh, Marwaha, & Tiwari, 2023).

This content-driven model contributes to the polarization of political discourse, as users are constantly exposed to extreme views, leading to more entrenched positions and less tolerance for opposing viewpoints. In some cases, this dynamic promotes the radicalization of individuals, pushing them toward more extreme views through algorithm-driven recommendations. As artificial intelligence continues to impact the way information is consumed, there is an urgent need for greater accountability and ethics to prevent social media manipulation from further undermining public trust and social cohesion.

3.2. Behavioral Targeting in Advertising

Artificial intelligence (AI) is revolutionizing the advertising industry through behavioral targeting, in which algorithms analyze user data such as browsing habits, interests and purchase history to serve personalized ads. This approach significantly improves marketing effectiveness by tailoring advertising to individual preferences, making consumers more likely to engage with the content. However, while this approach improves advertising accuracy, it also raises concerns about exploitation and manipulation (Gao, Wang, Xie, Hu, & Hu, 2023).

AI-driven behavioral targeting can influence consumers' choices in ways they may not fully recognize. By constantly analyzing personal data and understanding consumer behavior, AI can deliver ads that exploit psychological triggers and encourage impulsive decision-making. For example, advertisements for products or services may appear when individuals are emotionally vulnerable or more likely to make spontaneous purchases. Such manipulation may impair a consumer's ability to make informed decisions and may even foster unhealthy habits (Nadler & McGuigan, 2018).

In some cases, AI-driven advertising could exacerbate existing social problems, such as addiction or debt. For example, an AI algorithm might detect a user's interest in gambling or fast food and repeatedly promote gambling apps or unhealthy products. This can lead to individuals with addiction tendencies or financial mismanagement being repeatedly targeted, exacerbating their struggles. Vulnerable groups, such as those struggling with addiction, mental health issues or financial instability, are particularly at risk of being exploited by tailored ads that push them further into harmful behavioral patterns (Burr, Cristianini, & Ladyman, 2018).

While behavioral targeting improves marketing effectiveness, it also highlights the ethical dilemma of artificial intelligence in advertising. The potential for exploiting consumer vulnerabilities highlights the need for tighter regulation to ensure that AI-driven advertising is used responsibly, prioritizing consumer well-being over profit-driven motives. Without such safeguards the role of AI in advertising could deepen existing problems rather than just improve marketing results.

4. BIAS IN AI SYSTEMS

AI systems are only as fair as the data they are trained on. Unfortunately, many AI systems reflect and perpetuate biases present in the data sets used to train them. These biases can lead to discriminatory outcomes, especially in sensitive areas such as hiring, law enforcement, and health care (Schwartz et al., 2022).

4.1. Discriminatory AI in Hiring

As companies increasingly adopt tools to automate their recruiting processes, many believe AI-powered systems can reduce bias and make recruiting more efficient. However, reality is often more complex (Veglianti, Trombin, Pinna, & De Marco, 2023). AI systems are often trained on historical data, which can inadvertently perpetuate existing biases. If a company's past hiring practices have favored certain groups, AI will likely learn and replicate those preferences, leading to discriminatory outcomes against minorities, women, or other underrepresented groups.

A notable example that illustrates this problem is Amazon's AI recruiting tool, which was developed to streamline the hiring process. The algorithm was trained on resumes submitted over a ten-year period, largely reflecting the company's historical hiring decisions. As a result, the AI inadvertently learned to favor candidates with certain characteristics associated with male applicants. This led to the troubling discovery that the algorithm, by penalizing resumes containing the word "women," was actually discriminating against qualified women and exacerbating gender bias in the hiring process (Bornstein, 2018).

This example highlights a broader trend of AI recruiting systems, where input data reflects social biases, resulting in different candidates being excluded. Reliance on AI in recruitment could lead to entrenched stereotypes and inequalities, undermining efforts to promote diversity and inclusion within organizations (Papagelis, 2024).

Additionally, the lack of transparency around AI algorithms makes it difficult for companies to identify and correct these biases. Without appropriate oversight and a commitment to ethical AI practices, organizations risk perpetuating rather than eliminating discrimination. To address these issues, companies must prioritize the use of unbiased training data, conduct regular audits of AI systems, and foster a culture that values diversity and inclusion throughout the hiring process. Only then can AI tools become real assets in creating a fairer, more equitable workforce (Belenguer, 2022).

4.2. Bias in Law Enforcement

Law enforcement agencies are increasingly using artificial intelligence technologies such as predictive policing to predict and identify potential criminal activity based on historical data. While intended to enhance public safety and allocate resources more efficiently, these systems often perpetuate existing racial and socioeconomic biases. Predictive policing algorithms are trained on data sets that reflect historical policing patterns, which often disproportionately target minority communities (Berk, 2021).

For example, if a predictive policing system is fed data that shows higher crime rates in certain neighborhoods (often those with larger populations of marginalized groups), it may incorrectly conclude that those areas need increased surveillance and policing. This leads to a cycle in which already over-policed communities face increased scrutiny and intervention, exacerbating tensions between law enforcement and residents.

This dynamic creates a feedback loop in which AI systems reinforce the very biases they are designed to mitigate. Increased policing of minority communities has resulted in more arrests and reported incidents, further feeding the algorithm data indicating high risk in these areas. As a result, predictive policing tools not only fail to address the root causes of crime but also exacerbate systemic inequalities by targeting already marginalized communities.

Additionally, the lack of transparency into how these algorithms operate makes it difficult for the community to question or understand the basis for their positioning. As a result, individuals in these communities may feel more anxious and distrustful of law enforcement, damaging community relationships and perpetuating cycles of inequality and fear (Kossow, Windwehr, & Jenkins, 2022).

To combat these biases, law enforcement agencies must prioritize transparency and accountability when using AI technologies. Implementing oversight mechanisms, engaging with community stakeholders, and ensuring diverse representation in data collection can help mitigate the risk of bias and create a more equitable approach to policing. The ultimate goal should be to use AI as a tool for justice, not as a means to perpetuate systemic discrimination.

5. AI IN WARFARE AND AUTONOMOUS WEAPONS

The use of artificial intelligence in warfare and the development of autonomous weapons have raised ethical concerns about the role of artificial intelligence in life and death decisions (Schwarz, 2021). Artificial intelligence-powered drones and other military technology can now identify and neutralize targets without human intervention, raising questions about the responsibility and ethical implications of allowing machines to take human lives (Galdorisi & Tangredi, 2024).

5.1. Lack of Human Oversight

A significant issue regarding the use of artificial intelligence (AI) in warfare is the lack of human oversight in key decision-making processes. As military technology advances, autonomous weapons systems are increasingly able to make split-second targeting and engagement decisions without direct human intervention. This raise worrying questions about liability and ethics, especially when these systems can lead to accidental injuries or collateral damage (Goldfarb & Lindsay, 2021).

The lack of human oversight means decisions about life and death can be left to algorithms, which may not fully understand the complexities of human circumstances or ethical considerations. AI systems can misinterpret data or operate on flawed algorithms, leading to catastrophic results. For example, autonomous drones may identify targets based on specific parameters but fail to account for the presence of civilians, resulting in tragic losses of innocent people.

Furthermore, when problems arise, accountability challenges become more apparent. If an autonomous weapons system causes unintentional harm, it can be difficult to establish liability. Is it the fault of the programmers, the military personnel deploying the system, or the technology itself? This ambiguity complicates the legal and ethical framework governing military operations and makes it challenging to hold anyone who violates international law or humanitarian standards accountable.

The possibility of an AI-driven arms race further exacerbates these concerns. As nations develop more and more autonomous weapons systems, the urgency to maintain a competitive edge may lead to hasty deployment without adequate oversight or testing. This could lower the threshold for engaging in conflict, as decision-makers may become desensitized to the effects of war fought by machines rather than humans.

To address these risks, clear policies and guidelines must be developed that prioritize human oversight when using artificial intelligence in military settings (Morgan et al., 2020). Ensuring that human operators remain involved in key decision-making processes can help reduce risk and maintain accountability, thereby promoting a more ethical deployment of autonomous weapons systems. Ultimately, maintaining human judgment in war is critical to upholding moral and legal standards in conflict.

5.2. Ethical Dilemmas in AI Warfare

The emergence of autonomous weapons systems poses profound ethical dilemmas and challenges our understanding of warfare and moral responsibility (Anderson & Waxman, 2013). One of the core questions is whether machines can truly understand the complexity of the battlefield and make decisions consistent with international humanitarian law (IHL). Human conflicts involve subtle factors—cultural context, the presence of civilians, and the intentions of combatants—that machines may not fully grasp. This lack of understanding raises serious concerns about the ability of AI to distinguish between legitimate military targets and innocent civilians, which could lead to violations of international humanitarian law (Jafariandehkordi, 2024).

Another key dilemma is whether machines should be entrusted with making life-and-death decisions without human oversight. The potential for autonomous systems to carry out attacks based solely on algorithmic analysis raises questions about accountability and ethical agency. Who is responsible if an autonomous weapon misidentifies its target and causes civilian casualties? The developers of AI, the military personnel deploying AI, or the country authorizing its use? This ambiguity complicates existing legal and ethical frameworks and creates challenges for accountability when war crimes occur.

Furthermore, the risks associated with AI warfare extend beyond state actors. Non-state actors and rogue states may develop or acquire autonomous weapons, leading to unpredictable and dangerous consequences. These entities may not adhere to international norms or ethical standards, thereby increasing the risk of conflict and increasing the potential for abuse. The proliferation of autonomous weapons could lower the threshold for engaging in conflict, as the reduced cost of deploying AI systems could encourage reckless military action (Asaro, 2020).

Given these ethical dilemmas, there is an urgent need for strong international regulations to govern the development and use of artificial intelligence in warfare. Establishing clear guidelines can help ensure that human oversight remains at the core of military decision-making and that autonomous weapons are deployed in compliance with ethical and legal standards. Engaging in a global conversation about the ethical implications of artificial intelligence in warfare is critical to addressing these challenges and ensuring that technology serves humanity rather than destroys it.

6. MENTAL HEALTH IMPACTS OF AI AND AUTOMATION

The pervasive impact of artificial intelligence on human behavior extends to mental health, particularly through social media and automated systems that control every aspect of daily life. Continuous exposure to AI-powered platforms can lead to anxiety, depression, and feelings of isolation (Torous et al., 2021).

6.1. Social Media and Mental Health

Social media platforms are increasingly relying on artificial intelligence to curate content designed to maximize user engagement. While this model effectively keeps users hooked, it often comes at the expense of mental health. Research shows excessive use of social media is linked to a variety of psychological problems, including feelings of inadequacy, anxiety and depression (Dhir, Yossatorn, Kaur, & Chen, 2018).

One of the major factors contributing to these negative mental health outcomes is the pressure to maintain a carefully curate online presence. Users often feel the need to present an idealized version of their lives, showing highlights that may not reflect the reality of their daily lives. The constant effort to project a perfect image can lead to stress and self-doubt when individuals compare themselves to the seemingly perfect lives of others. The curate nature of social media feeds, often dominated by images of success, beauty and happiness, exacerbates this comparison and leaves many users feeling inadequate and unworthy (Ajewumi et al., 2024).

Additionally, the addictive nature of social media can lead to compulsive behavior, with people finding themselves constantly checking their feeds for likes, comments, and shares. This loop can create a feedback loop of validation and disappointment as users oscillate between the affirmation of a positive interaction and the frustration of a negative or lackluster response. Over time, this can lead to symptoms of anxiety and depression, especially in younger users who are still developing their self-esteem and identity (Carbonell & Panova, 2017).

Social media platforms' algorithms often prioritize content that generates high engagement, which often includes material that is sensational, provocative, or emotionally charged. This can lead to exposure to negative or distressing content, further affecting mental health (Ruckenstein, 2023).

To mitigate these risks, users, platform developers, and mental health advocates must recognize the potential harms associated with social media use. Implementing strategies that promote digital well-being, such as encouraging time limits, fostering authentic connections, and prioritizing positive content, can help create a healthier online environment. Ultimately, raising awareness of the impact of social media on mental health can lead individuals to navigate these platforms more mindfully, supporting their overall well-being in an increasingly digital world (Chancellor et al., 2019).

6.2. Automation-Induced Stress

Rapid advances in automation and artificial intelligence have dramatically changed the work environment, leading to increased stress and anxiety among workers. As more and more tasks and processes become automated, many people find themselves grappling with the uncertainty of job security. The fear of being replaced by machines can create a widespread sense of unease, especially among workers in industries that are experiencing rapid automation, such as manufacturing, retail, and even professional services (Nazareno & Schiff, 2021).

The anxiety isn't just about potential job losses; It often extends to a deeper existential concern with one's purpose and identity. Many people derive a sense of fulfillment and self-worth from their jobs, and the prospect of being replaced by automation can lead to feelings of inadequacy and a loss of purpose. In a labor market increasingly dominated by technology, workers may question their skills and worth, exacerbating feelings of depression and hopelessness (Goldsmith, Veum, & William, 1996).

Additionally, rapid changes in the workplace exacerbate the psychological impact of stress caused by automation. As organizations adopt new technologies, employees must continually adapt, learn new skills, and respond to changing job requirements. This constant need to adapt can be overwhelming, leading to burnout and mental fatigue. Pressure to keep up with technological advances can lead to workers feeling inadequate, and they may struggle to maintain their position in an increasingly automated job market (Cascio & Montealegre, 2016).

Furthermore, the economic impacts of automation may lead to wider social consequences, including increased inequality and economic instability. As low-skill jobs are replaced by machines, workers may find themselves trapped in a cycle of underemployment or forced to transition into new roles that require different skills, further exacerbating their stress and anxiety (Ernst, Merola, & Samaan, 2019).

Addressing stress caused by automation requires a multifaceted approach. Organizations should prioritize mental health support for employees, offering resources such as counseling and stress management programs. Additionally, workforce retraining and upskilling initiatives are urgently needed to help workers transition into new roles and adapt to technological changes. By creating a supportive environment and giving workers the tools they need to thrive in an automated future, we can help alleviate the anxiety and uncertainty associated with the rise of automation.

7. ETHICAL CONCERNS AND GOVERNANCE

The ethical implications of AI are enormous and addressing them requires a comprehensive governance approach. Ensuring that AI works for humanity, rather than harming it, requires clear ethical guidelines and regulatory frameworks.

7.1. The Need for AI Transparency

One of the major ethical challenges facing artificial intelligence (AI) is its inherent lack of transparency. Many AI systems, especially those that leverage deep learning, function as black boxes that produce results or decisions without providing a clear understanding of the underlying processes (Pedreschi et al., 2019). This opacity is particularly concerning in high-stakes areas such as healthcare, criminal justice, and finance, where AI-driven decisions can significantly impact an individual's life and well-being.

For example, in healthcare, AI systems may recommend treatments based on patient data, but without transparency, it may be difficult for healthcare professionals to understand the rationale behind these recommendations. This may hinder informed decision-making and may impact patient care (Amann et al., 2020). Similarly, in criminal justice, predictive policing algorithms may lead to increased surveillance of certain communities without revealing biases inherent in their training data, further exacerbating systemic inequalities (Kaur, 2023).

The impact of opaque AI decisions goes beyond individual cases. They could undermine public trust in AI systems and the institutions that use them. Establishing an AI transparency framework is critical to ensuring accountability and increasing public confidence. This includes implementing explainability standards, encouraging open dialogue about AI processes, and actively engaging stakeholders in discussions about the ethical implications of AI. By prioritizing transparency, we can harness the potential of AI while safeguarding human rights and promoting ethical practices.

7.2. Explainability and Accountability

AI transparency is critical to ensuring accountability, especially when decisions made by AI systems have significant consequences. If an AI system mistakenly denies a loan or makes a biased hiring decision, it's critical to understand how that decision was made to correct the problem and prevent it from happening again in the future. This necessity has led to the broader concept of explainability, which refers to the ability of an AI system to provide human-understandable reasons for its decisions (Houser, 2019).

Explainable AI is critical to maintaining trust between users and technology. When individuals can understand the rationale behind AI-driven decisions, they are more likely to trust existing systems (Shin, 2021). Additionally, explainability allows humans to intervene when necessary, ensuring that human judgment and ethical considerations are integrated into automated processes. For example, in situations involving healthcare diagnoses, the ability to explain the reasoning behind treatment recommendations could help clinicians make more informed choices for their patients.

To promote accountability, regulators and developers must prioritize creating AI systems that provide clear and understandable explanations of their decision-making processes. This transparency not only fosters understanding and trust, but also holds AI systems and their developers accountable for any negative outcomes (Díaz-Rodríguez et al., 2023). By fostering a culture of explainability, we can strengthen the ethical deployment of AI technologies while safeguarding individual rights.

8. ETHICAL FRAMEWORKS AND GOVERNANCE

To ensure that AI serves human interests, ethical frameworks and governance structures must be developed (de Almeida, dos Santos, & Farias, 2021). These frameworks should address the following issues:

- How to ensure that artificial intelligence systems are fair and impartial?
- How do we protect personal privacy in the age of AI-driven surveillance?
- Who is responsible when an AI system causes harm?

Some countries and organizations have begun to formulate ethical codes for artificial intelligence. For example, the European Union's General Data Protection Regulation (GDPR) includes provisions for algorithmic transparency and data protection (Temme, 2017). The IEEE Global Initiative on Ethics for Autonomous and Intelligent Systems is another effort to develop ethical guidelines for artificial intelligence technology (Winfield et al., 2019). However, global standards and stronger regulation are needed to ensure the responsible development and deployment of AI technologies.

8.1. Fairness and Inclusivity

Fairness is a fundamental ethical principle guiding the development of artificial intelligence (AI) systems. Developers must remain alert to biases embedded in the data used to train these models, as such biases can lead to unfair and discriminatory outcomes. For example, if the training data primarily represents certain demographics, the AI may perform poorly on underrepresented groups, perpetuating existing inequalities (Farahani & Ghasemi, 2024).

Inclusivity is equally important for the development of artificial intelligence. Involving diverse stakeholders from different ethnic, socioeconomic and gender backgrounds ensures that the needs and values of different communities are considered. This collaborative approach not only enriches the development process but also facilitates the creation of AI systems that are more representative and responsive to the complexity of real-world problems (Roche, Wall, & Lewis, 2023).

By prioritizing equity and inclusion, AI developers can work to reduce bias and promote equitable outcomes. This commitment helps build trust in AI technologies, ensuring they become tools of empowerment rather than exclusion. Ultimately, fair and inclusive AI systems help build a more just society, reflecting a wider range of perspectives and experiences in their design and implementation (Oyeniran et al., 2022).

8.2. Global Cooperation

The impact of artificial intelligence (AI) transcends national borders, and governments, international organizations, and businesses must collaborate to develop global standards for AI governance. The rapid development of artificial intelligence technology creates unique challenges that cannot be effectively solved alone. Without international cooperation, countries or organizations may exploit AI to gain a competitive advantage, which may lead to irresponsible applications that threaten global stability and security (Duenas & Ruiz, 2024).

For example, one country's deployment of autonomous weapons systems could trigger an arms race, prompting other countries to develop similar technologies without adequate safeguards. Likewise, artificial intelligence used for mass surveillance could violate human rights and civil liberties around the world. Establishing a unified AI governance framework can help mitigate these risks and ensure that ethical considerations, accountability and transparency are prioritized across the board.

Global collaboration can also share the best practices, knowledge and resources, thereby promoting a more equitable and responsible approach to AI development. By engaging in international dialogue and collaboration, stakeholders can address the ethical, legal and social impacts of AI technologies to create a safer and more sustainable future for all. In this interconnected world, collective action is critical to realizing the potential of artificial intelligence while safeguarding shared human values and interests (Yalamati, 2024).

9. THE ROLE OF AI IN PROMOTING OR UNDERMINING HUMAN AUTONOMY

Autonomy, the ability to make independent decisions and act in accordance with one's own values, is a fundamental aspect of human dignity. However, AI has the potential to undermine human autonomy in a number of ways (Laitinen & Sahlgren, 2021).

9.1. Decision-Making Autonomy

As artificial intelligence (AI) systems become increasingly integrated into daily life, they are beginning to have a significant impact on decisions traditionally made by humans. From recommending products and purchasing or viewing content to making important decisions in hiring and legal settings, AI systems have the power to shape human choices and outcomes. Although this has the benefit of reducing the burden of decision-making on individuals, it also raises concerns about autonomy and agency.

Overreliance on AI for decision-making may lead to a diminished sense of personal control. When people submit to AI systems, they may inadvertently give up the ability to make informed choices, leading to passive acceptance of the results of algorithmic decisions (Buçinca, Malaya, & Gajos, 2021). This erosion of agency can be particularly problematic when AI decisions conflict with personal values or best interests.

For example, in healthcare, if an AI system denies a patient treatment based on a cost-benefit analysis, it undermines the patient's autonomy and right to make informed decisions about their own care. These scenarios highlight the importance of maintaining human oversight and ensuring that AI serves as a support tool rather than a replacement for individual decision-making. Balancing the benefits of AI assistance with protecting human autonomy is critical to fostering a future where individuals can retain their agency in a technology-driven world (Elhauge, 1994).

9.2. Manipulation of Preferences

Artificial intelligence (AI) has the ability to subtly manipulate human preferences and behavior, particularly through personalized content and targeted advertising. By analyzing massive data sets about individual behaviors and preferences, AI systems can predict and influence future decisions. While this ability can be beneficial (such as recommending products based on previous purchases), it can also lead to manipulative behavior, leading individuals to make choices they might not otherwise make (Ienca, 2023).

A striking example of this manipulation is social media platforms, where artificial intelligence algorithms are designed to maximize user engagement. These algorithms present content that aligns with users' existing beliefs and preferences, creating filter bubbles and echo chambers. By continually reinforcing particular views, these platforms can distort individuals' perceptions of reality and limit exposure to diverse perspectives (Yang et al., 2019). Over time, this can impair critical thinking and the ability to make informed, independent decisions.

The effects of preference manipulation extend beyond individual choices. They can influence public opinion, political rhetoric and social norms. As AI technology becomes more ubiquitous, it is critical to recognize the ethical responsibilities of developers and platforms in curating content. Efforts to increase transparency, promote information diversity and ensure users have control over their content consumption are key steps to mitigate the risks associated with AI-driven manipulation.

10. REAL-WORLD EXAMPLES OF AI WORKING AGAINST HUMAN INTERESTS

To further understand the risks AI poses to humans, it is useful to study real-life cases where AI systems have had negative consequences.

10.1. Autonomous Weapons and Military AI

The development of autonomous weapons systems poses a significant threat to human security because these technologies can identify and attack targets without human intervention. This capability raises deep concerns about war responsibility. When machines make life and death decisions, the potential for catastrophic consequences increases, especially if these systems malfunction or misidentify targets, resulting in civilian casualties without any human oversight.

For example, autonomous drones have been deployed for targeted killings in various military operations. While proponents argue that these technologies can reduce casualties by keeping soldiers out of harm's way, they also raise serious ethical dilemmas. Reliance on machines for lethal decision-making could dehumanize warfare, undermining the moral and ethical considerations often inherent in combat situations. Furthermore, the lack of human judgment further exacerbates the risk of accidental civilian deaths, which could lead to devastating humanitarian consequences.

The impacts of military AI extend beyond immediate operational issues; they also pose long-term challenges to global stability and security. As nations race to develop more advanced autonomous weapons, international regulation and dialogue are urgently needed to address the ethical, legal and moral consequences of these technologies. Ensuring accountability and safeguarding human rights in the context of military AI are critical to promoting safer and more responsible ways of fighting wars.

10.2. AI in the Criminal Justice System

The integration of artificial intelligence (AI) into the criminal justice system is becoming increasingly common, particularly in assisting judges in sentencing and parole decisions. However, many of these algorithms have been found to have biases that undermine principles of justice and fairness. A prominent example is the COMPAS algorithm, which is used in the United States to predict the likelihood of criminal recidivism. Research shows the algorithm disproportionately labels black defendants as higher risks compared to white defendants, leading to unfair sentencing outcomes.

Such biases in AI systems could perpetuate existing disparities within the criminal justice system, leading to disparate treatment of marginalized groups. When algorithms make critical decisions about sentencing and parole based on flawed data or biased training, they exacerbate systemic inequalities rather than alleviate them. This undermines public trust in the legal system and raises ethical questions about reliance on technology in key areas of social governance.

To address these issues, transparency and accountability of AI systems used in criminal justice contexts must be ensured. This includes rigorous bias testing, ongoing monitoring of results, and incorporating human oversight to critically evaluate AI-driven recommendations. By prioritizing fairness and justice, criminal justice systems can work towards more just applications of AI technologies.

10.3. AI and Employment Discrimination

Artificial intelligence (AI) in recruitment has the potential to make hiring more efficient, but it also has the potential to perpetuate existing biases in historical data. The problem is becoming increasingly apparent as AI systems have been shown to favor male candidates over female candidates or discriminate against applicants from minority backgrounds. This bias can undermine efforts to promote diversity and inclusion in the workplace.

One notable example occurred in 2018, when Amazon's AI recruiting tool was revealed to have gender bias. The system was trained for more than a decade using resumes submitted to the company, mostly from male applicants. As a result, the AI learned to prioritize male candidates and even penalized resumes that included terms like "women's soccer team," reflecting an inherent bias against female candidates.

This reliance on biased AI systems not only leads to unfair hiring practices but also exacerbates systemic inequality in the labor market. To mitigate these risks, companies must adopt strategies to ensure the fairness of AI recruiting tools. This includes auditing AI systems for bias, using different training data and implementing human oversight in the hiring process. By prioritizing equity and inclusion, organizations can work toward a more equitable employment environment that values diverse talent and perspectives.

10.4. Deepfake Technology

Deepfake technology uses artificial intelligence to create hyper-realistic videos that simulate an individual saying or doing things they never actually did, posing a significant threat to privacy, security, and information integrity. The technology has been used for a variety of malicious purposes, including creating fraudulent videos of celebrities, spreading misinformation and carrying out blackmail.

One notable incident involved a deepfake video that appeared to show former President Barack Obama making inflammatory remarks. Although the video was eventually debunked, it highlighted the ways deepfakes can erode trust in the media and sources of information. Such manipulation can have far-reaching consequences, fueling the spread of misinformation and confusion in an already polarized information landscape.

The impact of deepfake technology extends beyond personal privacy concerns. They pose challenges to democratic processes and social cohesion. As deepfakes become more sophisticated and accessible, they can be used to manipulate public perception and incite unrest. Addressing this threat requires a multifaceted approach, including technical solutions for detection, a legal framework to address abuse, and public awareness campaigns to educate individuals about the risks associated with deepfakes. By fostering media literacy and a culture of accountability, society can better respond to the challenges posed by this disruptive technology.

11. SOLUTIONS AND SAFEGUARDS TO PREVENT AI FROM WORKING AGAINST HUMANS

To reduce the risk of AI turning against humans, several strategies can be employed. These include regulatory frameworks, ethical AI development and public awareness.

11.1. Regulatory Frameworks for

To effectively manage risks associated with artificial intelligence (AI), governments and international organizations must establish a comprehensive regulatory framework. These frameworks should prioritize transparency and accountability for AI systems, ensuring that users and affected individuals understand how decisions are made. In addition, they must align AI technologies with ethical principles and human values and prevent bias and discrimination.

This includes developing guidance on data use, privacy protection, and the ethical implications of AI applications in various fields, including healthcare, finance, and law enforcement. By fostering collaboration among stakeholders such as policymakers, technical experts and civil society, regulatory frameworks can promote responsible AI development and deployment, ultimately ensuring that AI serves the public interest and enhances social well-being.

11.2. The Role of Government Oversight

Government regulation is critical to overseeing the use of artificial intelligence (AI) in sensitive areas such as law enforcement, healthcare, and finance. Effective regulations should mandate the use of transparent AI models, ensuring that decision-making processes are understandable and accountable. Regular audits must be conducted to verify that AI systems do not inadvertently cause harm or perpetuate bias.

In the context of military applications, the need for supervision becomes even more apparent. Strict international treaties are essential to govern the development and use of autonomous weapons and address the ethical and safety issues they raise. Such a treaty should set clear guidelines for the use of artificial intelligence in warfare, prevent potential misuse, and ensure that human oversight remains a fundamental component of military decision-making. By implementing strong oversight mechanisms, governments can foster public trust in AI technologies while protecting individual rights and social values.

11.3. International Cooperation

Given the global nature of artificial intelligence (AI), international cooperation is critical to develop standards and norms that prevent the misuse of AI technology. As AI transcends national borders, countries must coordinate efforts to address the ethical, legal and security challenges posed by their rapid development. Organizations such as the United Nations and the World Economic Forum can play a key role in promoting discussions on the ethics of AI and fostering collaboration between governments, industry leaders and civil society.

These organizations can help establish a global framework that encourages best practices, increases transparency, and ensures accountability for AI development and deployment. By developing shared principles and guidelines, international cooperation can mitigate risks associated with AI, enhance trust among stakeholders, and ensure that AI technologies are used for the benefit of all while upholding human rights and social values.

11.4. Ethical AI Development

AI developers and companies must prioritize ethical considerations at every stage of the AI development process. This commitment involves creating artificial intelligence systems that are fair, transparent, and unbiased. Developers should implement rigorous testing and validation procedures to identify and mitigate biases in algorithms to ensure the technology serves all users fairly.

Transparency is also crucial; AI systems should provide clear explanations of their decision-making processes to foster trust and responsibility in users. Involving diverse stakeholders in the development process helps ensure that different perspectives and values are included, resulting in more inclusive outcomes.

By embedding ethical principles into the design, deployment, and evaluation of AI technologies, developers can promote responsible innovation that aligns with society's values and strengthen public trust in AI.

11.5. Bias Mitigation Strategies

AI developers must proactively identify and reduce bias in the data used to train AI systems. Implementing effective bias mitigation strategies is critical to ensuring equitable outcomes. One key approach is to focus on diverse data collection, ensuring that data sets represent a broad range of demographics, experiences, and perspectives. This inclusiveness helps minimize bias that may arise from historical data.

Regular audits of AI systems are also critical, allowing developers to identify and address any patterns of discrimination or unintended consequences that may arise after deployment. Incorporating feedback from diverse stakeholder groups throughout the development process can further enhance the robustness of AI systems by providing insights into potential biases and their impact.

By prioritizing these strategies, AI developers can promote fairness and justice, create systems that better serve all users, and contribute to a more just technology environment.

11.6. Human-Centered AI Design

The design of AI systems should prioritize augmenting human capabilities rather than replacing human decision-making. This concept, known as human-centered AI, emphasizes collaboration between humans and AI technology, ensuring that AI is used as a tool to empower individuals rather than replace their judgment.

By taking a human-centered approach, developers can create AI systems that increase productivity, improve decision-making, and support users in a variety of tasks. This includes designing intuitive interfaces that facilitate seamless interaction between humans and AI and provide users with the necessary information to make informed choices.

Incorporating user feedback throughout the development process is critical as it helps ensure that the AI solution meets the actual needs and preferences of end users. Ultimately, by focusing on human-centered AI design, developers can foster trust and engagement, resulting in more effective and ethically responsible AI applications that enhance human capabilities while respecting individual autonomy.

11.7. Public Awareness and Education

Increasing public awareness of the risks and benefits of artificial intelligence (AI) is essential to fostering an informed society that can have meaningful discussions about the future of this technology. Educational programs must be implemented at all levels to teach individuals about AI technologies, their potential impact, and how to use them responsibly.

These programs include workshops, online courses, and community initiatives aimed at demystifying artificial intelligence and making concepts accessible to everyone. Educating the public about the capabilities, limitations, and ethical considerations of artificial intelligence will help individuals better understand how to navigate the digital environment.

Additionally, improving media literacy can help people critically evaluate the information they encounter and reduce the spread of misinformation. Equipping the public will enable them to contribute thoughtfully to discussions about AI policy, regulation, and innovation, ensuring that AI developments are consistent with society's values and benefit everyone. will be done. Through comprehensive public awareness and education efforts, we can foster a society that is able to meet the challenges and opportunities presented by AI.

11.8. Digital Literacy

Digital literacy programs are important to help individuals understand how artificial intelligence (AI) systems work, how their data is used, and how their privacy is protected. In an era where AI-driven platforms are significantly shaping online experience, it's important to give people the skills and knowledge they need.

These plans cover a variety of areas, including the basics of AI technology, data privacy rights, and practical strategies for protecting personal information. Improving digital literacy allows individuals to make informed choices about the services they use and to be more vigilant about their online activities.

Additionally, understanding how AI algorithms influence content and interactions allows users to critically evaluate the information they encounter, reducing their susceptibility to misinformation and manipulation. Developing digital literacy can foster responsible engagement with AI technologies and ensure that individuals are informed participants in digital environments, not just consumers. Ultimately, this approach will help foster a society that values privacy, security, and ethical standards in the development and application of AI.

11.9. Public Participation in AI Governance

Public participation is essential in the development and regulation of artificial intelligence (AI) technologies. Involving citizens in discussions about AI governance helps ensure that policies reflect the values, concerns, and needs of diverse communities. Public consultations, forums and workshops provide a platform for individuals to express their views, share experiences and provide insights on the social impact of AI.

Public engagement not only strengthens the legitimacy of AI policies, but also strengthens trust among developers, regulators, and the communities they serve. Gain a broader understanding of potential risks and benefits, allowing you to make more informed and balanced decisions.

Additionally, incorporating feedback from diverse stakeholders such as marginalized groups, industry experts, and academics can help identify unintended consequences and improve the design of AI systems. Ultimately, meaningful public participation in AI governance will help create a regulatory environment that prioritizes ethical standards and promotes responsible use of technology for the benefit of all people.

CONCLUSION

Artificial intelligence (AI) has the potential to become one of the most transformative technologies of the 21st century. However, as various discussions have highlighted, AI can also harm human interests if misused, improperly designed, or developed without ethical oversight. The potential harms range from job loss, invasion of privacy, biased decision-making, and manipulation of human behavior. As we enter an increasingly AI-driven world, it is important to implement strong governance frameworks to ensure that AI is focused on transparency, fairness, and accountability.

Key strategies for mitigating AI-related risks include regulatory oversight, developing ethical AI systems, and educating the public about the benefits and risks of AI technologies. Governments, international organizations, businesses, and civil society must work together to ensure that AI is a force for good rather than a threat to human well-being. Prioritizing human-centered AI design is critical because it fosters the creation of systems that empower individuals rather than undermine their autonomy. Furthermore, proactively reducing bias in AI algorithms and improving digital literacy can significantly contribute to creating a fair technology environment.

The challenges posed by artificial intelligence are certainly significant, but they are not insurmountable. Through careful ethical considerations, thoughtful regulation, and a commitment to fairness, AI can evolve in a way that serves the interests of all humanity. Conversely, if left unchecked, AI could undermine core human values, ushering in a future where autonomy, privacy, and equality are violated.

The path forward requires vigilance, collaboration, and innovation to ensure that AI technologies are consistent with human values and do not inadvertently (or intentionally) harm the individuals they are meant to help. By proactively addressing these issues now, we can shape an AI-driven future that improves human lives and ensures that technology remains a tool for positive change, rather than a mechanism of control and harm. You can. Ultimately, fostering an AI development environment based on ethical standards and inclusive practices is key to unlocking the full potential of this powerful technology while upholding human rights and dignity.

REFERENCES

Abeliansky, A., Algur, E., Bloom, D. E., & Prettner, K. (2020). The future of work: challenges for job creation due to global demographic change and automation.

Ajewumi, O. E., Magbagbeola, V., Kalu, O. C., Ike, R. A., Folajimi, O., & Diyaolu, C. O. (2024). The impact of social media on mental health and well-being.

Amann, J., Blasimme, A., Vayena, E., Frey, D., & Madai, V. I. (2020). Explainability for artificial intelligence in healthcare: A multidisciplinary perspective. *BMC Medical Informatics and Decision Making*, 20(1), 1–9. DOI: 10.1186/s12911-020-01332-6 PMID: 33256715

Anderson, K., & Waxman, M. C. (2013). Law and ethics for autonomous weapon systems: Why a ban won't work and how the laws of war can.

Asaro, P. (2020). Autonomous weapons and the ethics of artificial intelligence. Ethics of Artificial Intelligence, 212.

Barnhizer, D., & Barnhizer, D. (2019). *The artificial intelligence contagion: Can democracy withstand the imminent transformation of work, wealth and the social order?* SCB Distributors.

Belenguer, L. (2022). AI bias: Exploring discriminatory algorithmic decision-making models and the application of possible machine-centric solutions adapted from the pharmaceutical industry. *AI and Ethics*, 2(4), 771–787. DOI: 10.1007/s43681-022-00138-8 PMID: 35194591

Benanav, A. (2020). *Automation and the future of work.* Verso Books.

Berk, R. A. (2021). Artificial intelligence, predictive policing, and risk assessment for law enforcement. *Annual Review of Criminology*, 4(1), 209–237. DOI: 10.1146/annurev-criminol-051520-012342

Blauth, T. F., Gstrein, O. J., & Zwitter, A. (2022). Artificial intelligence crime: An overview of malicious use and abuse of AI. *IEEE Access : Practical Innovations, Open Solutions*, 10, 77110–77122. DOI: 10.1109/ACCESS.2022.3191790

Bornstein, S. (2018). Antidiscriminatory algorithms. *Alabama Law Review*, 70, 519.

Buçinca, Z., Malaya, M. B., & Gajos, K. Z. (2021). To trust or to think: cognitive forcing functions can reduce overreliance on AI in AI-assisted decision-making. Proceedings of the ACM on Human-computer Interaction, 5(CSCW1), 1-21.

Burr, C., Cristianini, N., & Ladyman, J. (2018). An analysis of the interaction between intelligent software agents and human users. *Minds and Machines*, 28(4), 735–774. DOI: 10.1007/s11023-018-9479-0 PMID: 30930542

Carbonell, X., & Panova, T. (2017). A critical consideration of social networking sites' addiction potential. *Addiction Research and Theory*, 25(1), 48–57. DOI: 10.1080/16066359.2016.1197915

Cascio, W. F., & Montealegre, R. (2016). How technology is changing work and organizations. *Annual Review of Organizational Psychology and Organizational Behavior*, 3(1), 349–375. DOI: 10.1146/annurev-orgpsych-041015-062352

Chancellor, S., Birnbaum, M. L., Caine, E. D., Silenzio, V. M., & De Choudhury, M. (2019). A taxonomy of ethical tensions in inferring mental health states from social media. In *Proceedings of the Conference on Fairness, Accountability, and Transparency* (pp. 79-88). DOI: 10.1145/3287560.3287587

Chwialkowska, A. (2019). The effectiveness of brand-and customer-centric content strategies at generating shares,'likes', and comments. *Journal of Promotion Management*, 25(2), 270–300. DOI: 10.1080/10496491.2018.1443307

Coglianese, C., & Lehr, D. (2016). Regulating by robot: Administrative decision making in the machine-learning era. *The Georgetown Law Journal*, 105, 1147.

Davenport, T. H. (2018). *The AI advantage: How to put the artificial intelligence revolution to work*. MIT Press. DOI: 10.7551/mitpress/11781.001.0001

de Almeida, P. G. R., dos Santos, C. D., & Farias, J. S. (2021). Artificial intelligence regulation: A framework for governance. *Ethics and Information Technology*, 23(3), 505–525. DOI: 10.1007/s10676-021-09593-z

Dhir, A., Yossatorn, Y., Kaur, P., & Chen, S. (2018). Online social media fatigue and psychological wellbeing—A study of compulsive use, fear of missing out, fatigue, anxiety and depression. *International Journal of Information Management*, 40, 141–152. DOI: 10.1016/j.ijinfomgt.2018.01.012

Díaz-Rodríguez, N., Del Ser, J., Coeckelbergh, M., de Prado, M. L., Herrera-Viedma, E., & Herrera, F. (2023). Connecting the dots in trustworthy Artificial Intelligence: From AI principles, ethics, and key requirements to responsible AI systems and regulation. *Information Fusion*, 99, 101896. DOI: 10.1016/j.inffus.2023.101896

Duenas, T., & Ruiz, D. (2024). The ministry of artificial intelligence: A catalyst for national AI ecosystems and global cooperation in the age of superintelligence. ResearchGate, 2024c.

Elhauge, E. (1994). Allocating health care morally. *California Law Review*, 82(6), 1449. DOI: 10.2307/3480858 PMID: 11660282

Ernst, E., Merola, R., & Samaan, D. (2019). Economics of artificial intelligence: Implications for the future of work. *IZA Journal of Labor Policy*, 9(1), 20190004. DOI: 10.2478/izajolp-2019-0004

Farahani, M. S., & Ghasemi, G. (2024). Artificial intelligence and inequality: Challenges and opportunities. *International Journal of Innovation in Education*, 9, 78–99.

Feldstein, S. (2019). The global expansion of AI surveillance (Vol. 17, No. 9). Carnegie Endowment for International Peace.

Fontes, C., Hohma, E., Corrigan, C. C., & Lütge, C. (2022). AI-powered public surveillance systems: Why we (might) need them and how we want them. *Technology in Society*, 71, 102137. DOI: 10.1016/j.techsoc.2022.102137

Galdorisi, G., & Tangredi, S. J. (2024). *Algorithms of Armageddon: The impact of artificial intelligence on future wars*. Naval Institute Press.

Gao, B., Wang, Y., Xie, H., Hu, Y., & Hu, Y. (2023). Artificial intelligence in advertising: Advancements, challenges, and ethical considerations in targeting, personalization, content creation, and ad optimization. *SAGE Open*, 13(4), 21582440231210759. DOI: 10.1177/21582440231210759

Goldfarb, A., & Lindsay, J. R. (2021). Prediction and judgment: Why artificial intelligence increases the importance of humans in war. *International Security*, 46(3), 7–50. DOI: 10.1162/isec_a_00425

Goldsmith, A. H., Veum, J. R., & William, D.Jr. (1996). The impact of labor force history on self-esteem and its component parts, anxiety, alienation and depression. *Journal of Economic Psychology*, 17(2), 183–220. DOI: 10.1016/0167-4870(96)00003-7

Houser, K. A. (2019). Can AI solve the diversity problem in the tech industry: Mitigating noise and bias in employment decision-making. *Stanford Technology Law Review : STLR : An Online High-Technology Law Journal from Stanford Law School*, 22, 290.

Ienca, M. (2023). On artificial intelligence and manipulation. *Topoi*, 42(3), 833–842. DOI: 10.1007/s11245-023-09940-3

Ilgenfritz III, J. I. (2023). Lexical entrainment, empathy, and materiality in African American creative improvised music and conceptual art [Doctoral dissertation, University of California, Irvine].

Intelligence, A. (2016). Automation, and the Economy. Executive Office of the President, 18-19.

Iwuanyanwu, C. C. (2023). Facebook artificial intelligence algorithm: Users' awareness and response to data privacy issues [Doctoral dissertation, Robert Morris University].

Jafariandehkordi, M. (2024). The AI battlefield: Legal challenges of autonomous weapon systems under international humanitarian law.

Kaur, R. (2023). AI in criminal justice: Implications for justice, fairness, and potential biases. *Nyaayshastra Law Review*, 4, 1.

Kossow, N., Windwehr, S., & Jenkins, M. (2022). *Algorithmic transparency and accountability*. Transparency International.

Laitinen, A., & Sahlgren, O. (2021). AI systems and respect for human autonomy. *Frontiers in Artificial Intelligence*, 4, 705164. DOI: 10.3389/frai.2021.705164 PMID: 34765969

Li, H. (2019). Special section introduction: Artificial intelligence and advertising. *Journal of Advertising*, 48(4), 333–337. DOI: 10.1080/00913367.2019.1654947

Lutz, C. (2019). Digital inequalities in the age of artificial intelligence and big data. *Human Behavior and Emerging Technologies*, 1(2), 141–148. DOI: 10.1002/hbe2.140

Manheim, K., & Kaplan, L. (2019). Artificial intelligence: Risks to privacy and democracy. *Yale Journal of Law and Technology*, 21, 106.

Mhlanga, D. (2022). Human-centered artificial intelligence: The superlative approach to achieve sustainable development goals in the fourth industrial revolution. *Sustainability (Basel)*, 14(13), 7804. DOI: 10.3390/su14137804

Morgan, F. E., Boudreaux, B., Lohn, A. J., Ashby, M., Curriden, C., Klima, K., & Grossman, D. (2020). *Military applications of artificial intelligence*. RAND Corporation.

Nadler, A., & McGuigan, L. (2018). An impulse to exploit: The behavioral turn in data-driven marketing. *Critical Studies in Media Communication*, 35(2), 151–165. DOI: 10.1080/15295036.2017.1387279

Nassar, A., & Kamal, M. (2021). Ethical dilemmas in AI-powered decision-making: A deep dive into big data-driven ethical considerations. *International Journal of Responsible Artificial Intelligence*, 11(8), 1–11.

Nazareno, L., & Schiff, D. S. (2021). The impact of automation and artificial intelligence on worker well-being. *Technology in Society*, 67, 101679. DOI: 10.1016/j.techsoc.2021.101679

Oyeniran, C. O., Adewusi, A. O., Adeleke, A. G., Akwawa, L. A., & Azubuko, C. F. (2022). Ethical AI: Addressing bias in machine learning models and software applications. *Computer Science & IT Research Journal*, 3(3), 115–126. DOI: 10.51594/csitrj.v3i3.1559

Papagelis, S. (2024). Exploring the impact of the algorithms on management hiring decision and bias [Doctoral dissertation, Temple University].

Pedreschi, D., Giannotti, F., Guidotti, R., Monreale, A., Ruggieri, S., & Turini, F. (2019). Meaningful explanations of black box AI decision systems. *Proceedings of the AAAI Conference on Artificial Intelligence*, 33(01), 9780–9784. DOI: 10.1609/aaai.v33i01.33019780

Roche, C., Wall, P. J., & Lewis, D. (2023). Ethics and diversity in artificial intelligence policies, strategies and initiatives. *AI and Ethics*, 3(4), 1095–1115. DOI: 10.1007/s43681-022-00218-9 PMID: 36246014

Ruckenstein, M. (2023). *The feel of algorithms*. University of California Press.

SAMBUCCI, L., & PARASCHIV, E. A. (2024). The accelerated integration of artificial intelligence systems and its potential to expand the vulnerability of the critical infrastructure. *Romanian Journal of Information Technology and Automatic Control*, 34(3), 131–148.

Schwartz, R., Schwartz, R., Vassilev, A., Greene, K., Perine, L., Burt, A., & Hall, P. (2022). *Towards a standard for identifying and managing bias in artificial intelligence* (Vol. 3). US Department of Commerce, National Institute of Standards and Technology. DOI: 10.6028/NIST.SP.1270

Schwarz, E. (2021). *Autonomous weapons systems, artificial intelligence, and the problem of meaningful human control*. Philosophical Journal of Conflict and Violence. DOI: 10.22618/TP.PJCV.20215.1.139004

Shin, D. (2021). The effects of explainability and causability on perception, trust, and acceptance: Implications for explainable AI. *International Journal of Human-Computer Studies*, 146, 102551. DOI: 10.1016/j.ijhcs.2020.102551

Shiohira, K. (2021). Understanding the impact of artificial intelligence on skills development. [UNESCO-UNEVOC International Centre for Technical and Vocational Education and Training.]. *Education*, •••, 2030.

Singh, T. (2023). AI-driven surveillance technologies and human rights: Balancing security and privacy. In International Conference on Smart Systems: Innovations in Computing (pp. 703-717). Springer Nature Singapore.

Temme, M. (2017). Algorithms and transparency in view of the new general data protection regulation. *European Data Protection Law Review*, 3(4), 473–485. DOI: 10.21552/edpl/2017/4/9

Tomar, M., Raj, N., Singh, S., Marwaha, S., & Tiwari, M. (2023). The role of AI-driven tools in shaping the democratic process: A study of Indian elections and social media dynamics. *Industrial Engineering Journal*, 52(11), 143–153.

Torous, J., Bucci, S., Bell, I. H., Kessing, L. V., Faurholt-Jepsen, M., Whelan, P., Carvalho, A. F., Keshavan, M., Linardon, J., & Firth, J. (2021). The growing field of digital psychiatry: Current evidence and the future of apps, social media, chatbots, and virtual reality. *World Psychiatry; Official Journal of the World Psychiatric Association (WPA)*, 20(3), 318–335. DOI: 10.1002/wps.20883 PMID: 34505369

Tschang, F. T., & Almirall, E. (2021). Artificial intelligence as augmenting automation: Implications for employment. *The Academy of Management Perspectives*, 35(4), 642–659. DOI: 10.5465/amp.2019.0062

Veglianti, E., Trombin, M., Pinna, R., & De Marco, M. (2023). Customized artificial intelligence for talent recruiting: A bias-free tool? In *Smart Technologies for Organizations: Managing a Sustainable and Inclusive Digital Transformation* (pp. 245–261). Springer International Publishing. DOI: 10.1007/978-3-031-24775-0_15

Wheatley, S., Maillart, T., & Sornette, D. (2016). The extreme risk of personal data breaches and the erosion of privacy. *The European Physical Journal B*, 89(1), 1–12. DOI: 10.1140/epjb/e2015-60754-4

Winfield, A. F., Michael, K., Pitt, J., & Evers, V. (2019). Machine ethics: The design and governance of ethical AI and autonomous systems. *Proceedings of the IEEE*, 107(3), 509–517. DOI: 10.1109/JPROC.2019.2900622

Yalamati, S. (2024). Ensuring ethical practices in AI and ML toward a sustainable future. In *Artificial Intelligence and Machine Learning for Sustainable Development* (pp. 194–208). CRC Press. DOI: 10.1201/9781003497189-15

Yang, K. C., Varol, O., Davis, C. A., Ferrara, E., Flammini, A., & Menczer, F. (2019). Arming the public with artificial intelligence to counter social bots. *Human Behavior and Emerging Technologies*, 1(1), 48–61. DOI: 10.1002/hbe2.115

Chapter 8
AI and Social Justice: Democratizing Technology for Inclusive Growth

Abhishek Benedict Kumar
https://orcid.org/0000-0002-3998-3150
Symbiosis Law School, Nagpur Campus, Symbiosis International University, Pune, India

Karun Sanjaya
https://orcid.org/0009-0005-1647-1549
Symbiosis Law School, Nagpur Campus, Symbiosis International University, Pune, India

ABSTRACT

Artificial Intelligence has the potential to change the world by facilitating progress in health, education, climate action, and economic development. But, without proper and ethical use, AI seeps into the fabric of societal malice and makes glasshouses in paradise even more glistening. AI can serve both as a butter and gun for the public. It tackles issues including algorithmic bias, digital divide, and data poverty; meanwhile it mentions community-driven AI building as a method to guarantee inclusion and cultural appropriateness. Strategic elements of policy frameworks such as the EU's AI Act are considered essential to responsibly govern AI, while bottom-up approaches and grassroots initiatives show how the nature of participatory design can be powerful. It urges a joint enterprise by governments, corporations and civil society to create a future with AI that serves the most marginalized populations and functions as an engine for equity. An inclusive approach is crucial to ensure that the choices we make today drive the impact of AI in a direction that advances society.

DOI: 10.4018/979-8-3693-9904-0.ch008

1. INTRODUCTION TO ETHICAL CONTENT MODERATION

1.1 The Rise of Digital Platforms and Moderation Needs

The digital landscape has transformed significantly with the rapid growth of social media and digital platforms, where vast amounts of user-generated content are created daily. Platforms like Facebook, YouTube, and Twitter have billions of active users who share diverse forms of content, including text, images, and videos, on an unprecedented scale. This growth has intensified the need for efficient and ethical content moderation strategies to maintain a safe and inclusive online environment (Statista, 2023). Traditionally, content moderation was handled manually by human moderators tasked with reviewing flagged content for appropriateness and compliance with community guidelines. However, as platforms expanded, the sheer volume and complexity of content overwhelmed manual processes, making it difficult to maintain efficiency, consistency, and fairness in moderation decisions (Gillespie, 2020).

The challenges of content moderation include not only the high volume of content but also the psychological toll on human moderators, who are frequently exposed to disturbing and distressing material. Moderators encounter content that spans a spectrum of harmful topics, including graphic violence, abuse, misinformation, and hate speech. This environment presents significant mental health risks, leading to a rise in mental health issues such as anxiety, depression, and even post-traumatic stress disorder (PTSD) among moderators (Roberts, 2019). The need for alternative solutions has spurred the integration of artificial intelligence (AI) into content moderation, which can process large quantities of data and handle repetitive tasks, potentially easing some of the burdens on human moderators.

The integration of AI in content moderation introduces a new paradigm, where machine learning algorithms can quickly identify patterns associated with harmful content, providing a scalable solution to content filtering. However, the role of AI is not to replace human moderators entirely; instead, it is to assist them, creating a synergy where machines handle high-volume tasks, and humans focus on more nuanced cases that require contextual judgment (Crawford, 2020). Despite its potential, AI-based content moderation has raised concerns around ethical issues such as algorithmic bias, transparency, and accountability, which must be addressed to create a responsible and fair moderation system.

1.2 Limitations of Human Moderation

While human moderators are skilled at interpreting complex social contexts, cultural nuances, and subjective content, they face significant limitations. The scale of modern social media platforms means that manually reviewing every piece of content is virtually impossible. Estimates suggest that platforms like Facebook generate billions of posts daily, making manual moderation unsustainable. As a result, human moderators are typically restricted to reviewing content that has already been flagged, either by users or initial algorithmic screening (Binns, 2021). This model has inherent limitations, such as delayed response times and the risk of overlooking harmful content that falls through initial screening processes.

Moreover, the psychological impact of content moderation is profound. Studies have shown that constant exposure to harmful and explicit content can lead to severe mental health issues among moderators. Roberts (2019) highlights the "hidden labor" of content moderators, who often work in isolation, tasked with filtering graphic and emotionally distressing content that can affect their long-term mental health. The high turnover rates in moderation roles reflect the unsustainable nature of relying solely on human efforts, creating a need for solutions that reduce the cognitive and emotional burdens placed on human moderators.

In addition to psychological impacts, there are ethical concerns about consistency and fairness in human-only moderation. Personal biases and inconsistencies in decision-making across different cultural contexts can result in subjective moderation outcomes, which may not align with platform guidelines or user expectations. This human variability poses challenges to fairness and accountability in content moderation, leading to instances of perceived unfair treatment by users and communities (Gillespie, 2020). As a result, the call for integrating AI into content moderation is motivated not only by scalability needs but also by the desire to create a more objective, consistent, and balanced moderation framework.

1.3 AI Integration into Content Moderation

AI technologies, including machine learning and natural language processing, have been introduced as solutions to address the limitations of human-only content moderation. AI can rapidly process vast datasets, identifying patterns in hate speech, misinformation, and other forms of harmful content based on training algorithms that classify and filter content automatically. This capability allows AI to manage high-volume tasks that would otherwise overwhelm human moderators, providing a more efficient system that can respond in real-time to new content (Hovy & Spruit, 2016).

One of the primary roles of AI in content moderation is to act as an initial filter, flagging potentially harmful content based on predefined patterns and keywords. For example, algorithms trained to detect hate speech can quickly identify and flag content with specific keywords or language structures associated with abusive or offensive language. Once flagged, content can either be automatically removed or passed on to human moderators for further review. This process saves human moderators from constant exposure to repetitive harmful content, enabling them to focus on more complex cases that require contextual understanding (Gillespie, 2020).

However, the role of AI in content moderation is not without challenges. AI systems are often criticized for their lack of contextual understanding and potential for false positives and negatives. AI may inadvertently flag benign content as harmful or fail to identify nuanced harmful content that does not fit pre-programmed patterns. These limitations highlight the need for a collaborative model where human and AI moderators work together, with AI managing large-scale tasks and humans making final decisions on ambiguous cases. This collaboration aims to create a balanced system that benefits from AI's scalability while retaining human oversight for more sensitive or complex content (Crawford, 2020).

1.4 Ethical Challenges in AI-Augmented Content Moderation

The adoption of AI in content moderation introduces complex ethical issues, particularly concerning fairness, transparency, and accountability. One primary ethical challenge is **algorithmic bias**. AI models are trained on data that may reflect societal biases, leading to skewed moderation outcomes that disproportionately affect certain groups. For instance, studies show that content generated by marginalized communities is sometimes flagged at higher rates, not due to actual violations but because of biases embedded in the training data or model structure (Binns, 2021). Addressing this bias is essential to ensure fairness in content moderation and to prevent disproportionate harm to underrepresented groups.

Transparency is another critical ethical concern in AI-driven moderation. Many AI systems operate as "black boxes," where the rationale behind moderation decisions is not readily accessible or interpretable to users or regulators. This opacity makes it challenging for users to understand why their content was flagged or removed, leading to frustration and mistrust in the moderation process (Lipton, 2018). Implementing explainable AI (XAI) techniques can help demystify the decision-making process, allowing users to understand how and why content is moderated, thereby promoting accountability and trust.

Lastly, **accountability** in AI-driven moderation raises questions about who is responsible for errors or biases—whether it is the platform, the developers, or the moderators themselves. Current regulatory frameworks, like the European Union's General Data Protection Regulation (GDPR), emphasize accountability and transparency but do not yet fully address the unique challenges posed by AI in content moderation. As AI continues to play a significant role in moderating digital spaces, platforms and developers will need to develop clear accountability mechanisms to address issues related to bias, transparency, and fairness (Funk, 2019).

Table 1. Key Ethical Challenges in AI-Assisted Content Moderation

Ethical Challenge	Description	Example
Algorithmic Bias	AI models may reflect societal biases, leading to unfair moderation outcomes.	Over-policing content from marginalized groups
Transparency	AI systems often lack interpretability, creating trust issues among users.	"Black box" systems in content moderation
Accountability	Unclear responsibility for AI errors and biases, complicating the assignment of accountability.	Attribution of fault in AI-driven moderation errors

2. ALGORITHMIC BIAS IN AI-DRIVEN CONTENT MODERATION

2.1 Understanding Algorithmic Bias in AI Systems

Algorithmic bias refers to systematic and repeatable errors within AI systems that lead to unfair outcomes, disproportionately favoring or disadvantaging certain groups. In the context of AI-driven content moderation, bias typically arises from the datasets used to train machine learning models. These datasets often reflect historical and societal biases, which can lead to unintended discrimination or skewed moderation outcomes (Crawford, 2020). For instance, a dataset that includes biased language patterns can cause an AI model to disproportionately flag content from specific cultural or linguistic groups as harmful, even when it does not violate platform guidelines.

The origins of algorithmic bias in AI are multifaceted. Bias can enter an AI system at any stage, from data collection and labeling to feature selection and model training. **Data collection bias** occurs when the dataset used to train an AI model is unrepresentative or imbalanced. For example, if certain communities or topics are overrepresented in the dataset, the AI model may develop skewed patterns, leading to biased moderation decisions (Hovy & Spruit, 2016). **Labeling bias** arises during the annotation process, where human labelers may unconsciously apply their personal biases, creating a biased ground truth for the AI to learn from. Additionally, **feature selection bias** happens when the features chosen for the model amplify certain patterns, reinforcing stereotypes or biases embedded in the data.

The implications of algorithmic bias in content moderation are significant, as they impact the fairness and inclusivity of online platforms. A biased AI moderation system may over-police content from marginalized groups or fail to recognize harmful content from other communities. This can erode user trust in the platform and contribute to the alienation of specific user groups, exacerbating issues of inequality and discrimination online (Gillespie, 2020). Addressing these biases is essential to building equitable moderation systems that ensure fair treatment across diverse populations.

2.2 Case Studies of Algorithmic Bias in Content Moderation

Examining real-world examples helps illuminate the practical impacts of algorithmic bias in content moderation. The following case studies provide insight into how biased AI systems affect different communities and highlight the need for ethical oversight.

Case Study 1: Bias Against Marginalized Communities

One well-documented example of algorithmic bias in content moderation is the over-policing of content from marginalized communities. Studies have shown that platforms like Facebook and Twitter frequently flag content from Black Lives Matter activists at a higher rate than similar content from other groups, even when it does not violate platform guidelines (Noble, 2018). This phenomenon occurs partly because the language and terms commonly used within these communities may be misinterpreted by AI models trained on general datasets that lack cultural or contextual nuance.

This case highlights a critical flaw in many AI models: a lack of cultural sensitivity. When AI systems misinterpret language that is specific to a community or group, they risk labeling benign content as harmful. Such actions create an environment where marginalized voices are disproportionately suppressed, raising ethical concerns around fairness and representation. This bias ultimately undermines the inclusive nature of digital platforms and alienates users who feel unfairly targeted by moderation policies.

Case Study 2: Political and Ideological Bias

Political content is another area where algorithmic bias frequently manifests. In recent years, there have been claims that social media platforms are biased against conservative viewpoints, particularly in the United States. Although studies on this topic have yielded mixed results, instances of politically sensitive content being disproportionately flagged or removed have fueled public skepticism about the neutrality of AI in content moderation (Binns, 2021). Bias may arise when datasets overrepresent certain political ideologies or when moderation algorithms are trained to prioritize specific types of harmful speech that overlap with political discourse.

For example, an algorithm trained on datasets that focus heavily on misinformation narratives might disproportionately flag content that aligns with certain ideological perspectives. The result is perceived unfairness and reduced trust in AI systems, highlighting the importance of balanced datasets that account for diverse viewpoints without embedding ideological bias.

Table 2. Examples of Algorithmic Bias in Content Moderation Systems

Type of Bias	Description	Real-World Example
Data Collection Bias	Bias arising from an unbalanced dataset that overrepresents certain groups or topics.	Over-policing of Black Lives Matter content on Facebook
Labeling Bias	Bias introduced during the annotation process by human labelers.	Mislabeling of political content as misinformation
Feature Selection Bias	Bias introduced when specific features are prioritized in the model.	Prioritization of certain keywords leading to over-policing specific communities

2.3 Strategies for Mitigating Bias in AI-Driven Content Moderation

Given the pervasive nature of algorithmic bias in content moderation, implementing effective strategies to mitigate these biases is crucial. Addressing algorithmic bias requires a multifaceted approach, including improvements in dataset diversity, implementing fairness metrics, and involving human moderators in the decision-making process. Below are some key strategies that have shown promise in reducing bias and improving fairness in AI-driven content moderation systems.

2.3.1 Diversifying Training Data

One of the most straightforward ways to reduce bias is by diversifying the data used to train AI models. By ensuring that the training datasets are representative of diverse populations and perspectives, AI systems can develop a more balanced understanding of language, cultural context, and behavioral patterns. For example, platforms could include content from various racial, gender, and socioeconomic groups to ensure that moderation algorithms are exposed to a range of expressions and dialects. This approach can help minimize the risk of over-policing or under-policing specific groups, promoting fairness in content moderation decisions (Hovy & Spruit, 2016).

2.3.2 Implementing Bias Detection and Fairness Metrics

Bias detection mechanisms and fairness metrics are critical tools for identifying and addressing bias in AI systems. Fairness metrics, such as demographic parity and equalized odds, allow developers to assess whether AI models treat different groups equitably. Regularly evaluating AI models against these metrics helps platforms identify any existing biases and make adjustments accordingly. For instance, if a moderation algorithm disproportionately flags content from a particular demographic, developers can recalibrate the model to ensure fair treatment across all user groups (Dastin, 2018).

2.3.3 Leveraging Explainable AI (XAI)

Explainable AI (XAI) provides transparency into AI decisions by making the decision-making process more understandable for both developers and users. By revealing the rationale behind moderation decisions, XAI enables moderators and users to identify potential biases and adjust the system as necessary. XAI techniques, such as Local Interpretable Model-agnostic Explanations (LIME) and Shapley Additive Explanations (SHAP), can help break down complex model decisions into interpretable components, allowing developers to understand how biases may arise and how to correct them effectively (Lipton, 2018).

2.3.4 Involving Human Moderators for Contextual Oversight

Although AI can efficiently handle large volumes of content, human moderators are indispensable for context-sensitive and culturally nuanced content moderation. In a collaborative model, human moderators review flagged content to verify whether it genuinely violates platform guidelines. By involving humans in the review process, platforms can catch potential false positives and negatives resulting from AI's limited understanding of context. This human oversight helps ensure that content moderation decisions are fair and culturally sensitive, reducing the likelihood of biased outcomes (Gillespie, 2020).

F2.4 Key Insights and Summary

Algorithmic bias poses significant ethical challenges for AI-driven content moderation, impacting fairness, inclusivity, and trust on digital platforms. As seen in the case studies, algorithmic bias can disproportionately affect marginalized communities and lead to perceptions of ideological bias, eroding user trust in moderation systems. By diversifying training datasets, implementing fairness metrics, leveraging XAI, and involving human moderators for contextual oversight, platforms can mitigate some of these biases, promoting more equitable and transparent moderation processes. However, as AI technology evolves, continuous research and adaptation are necessary to ensure that content moderation practices keep pace with ethical standards and societal expectations (Crawford, 2020).

3. TRANSPARENCY AND EXPLAINABLE AI (XAI) IN CONTENT MODERATION

3.1 The Black-Box Problem in AI

One of the most persistent challenges with AI-driven content moderation is the "black box" nature of many machine learning models, particularly deep learning algorithms. These models, while effective at identifying patterns within vast datasets, often lack transparency, making it difficult for developers, users, and regulators to understand how specific decisions are made. In the context of content moderation, the black-box problem poses ethical concerns, as it prevents users from understanding why certain content is flagged, removed, or allowed. This opacity in decision-making can lead to frustration, a sense of unfairness, and ultimately, mistrust in the platform (Lipton, 2018).

The black-box nature of AI models in content moderation arises from the complexity of these systems, particularly in deep neural networks, where layers of computation produce highly accurate results without providing interpretable explanations. For example, a convolutional neural network trained to detect offensive images may be able to accurately identify harmful content, but the logic behind its decisions is often too complex to be understood by humans. This lack of interpretability is problematic in content moderation, as it leaves users and regulators with little recourse to challenge or understand moderation outcomes (Gillespie, 2020). The black-box problem is further exacerbated by the proprietary nature of many AI systems, with companies often withholding details of their algorithms, citing intellectual property concerns.

The ethical implications of black-box AI in content moderation are profound. Without transparency, users cannot verify whether moderation decisions align with community guidelines or understand the basis for those decisions. Furthermore, the lack of interpretability in AI models impedes accountability, as it becomes difficult to assess whether the model is functioning fairly and without bias. Therefore, addressing the black-box problem is essential to building an ethical and trustworthy content moderation framework (Funk, 2019).

3.2 Importance of Explainable AI (XAI)

Explainable AI (XAI) refers to techniques that make the decision-making processes of AI systems more understandable and interpretable for humans. In content moderation, XAI plays a crucial role by allowing users, moderators, and regulators to gain insights into how and why specific decisions are made. Implementing XAI can mitigate the ethical issues associated with the black-box nature of AI, fostering greater transparency, trust, and accountability within content moderation systems.

XAI is particularly relevant in content moderation because it provides users with information that can help them understand the reasoning behind flagged or removed content. For instance, an XAI approach might reveal that a post was flagged due to the presence of specific keywords associated with hate speech. This transparency allows users to adjust their behavior to align with platform guidelines and reduces the frustration and confusion that often accompany opaque moderation decisions (Lipton, 2018). XAI also facilitates **error correction** within content moderation systems by allowing developers and moderators to identify when and why the AI made an incorrect or biased decision, thereby enabling ongoing improvements to the model.

Moreover, explainable AI aligns with regulatory expectations for transparency, especially under frameworks like the General Data Protection Regulation (GDPR), which advocates for "meaningful information about the logic involved" in AI-driven decisions (GDPR, Article 22). By providing insights into AI decision-making, XAI supports compliance with regulatory standards and enhances accountability. It also enables human moderators to intervene more effectively, as they can understand the AI's reasoning and make better-informed decisions when the AI's judgment is insufficient. Therefore, adopting XAI strategies in content moderation is essential for addressing both ethical and regulatory challenges (Binns, 2021).

3.3 Implementing XAI in Content Moderation Systems

Implementing XAI in content moderation requires choosing appropriate methods and techniques to make AI decisions interpretable while ensuring that transparency does not compromise user privacy or content moderation efficiency. Several XAI techniques are relevant to content moderation, each offering different approaches to making AI more understandable and fostering trust.

3.3.1 Local Interpretable Model-Agnostic Explanations (LIME)

Local Interpretable Model-Agnostic Explanations (LIME) is an XAI technique that creates interpretable approximations of complex model predictions. In content moderation, LIME can be used to provide explanations for specific decisions made by the AI system. For example, if an AI model flags a piece of content as harmful, LIME can break down the model's decision by identifying which features—such as keywords or phrases—were most influential. This allows moderators and users to understand why content was flagged, promoting transparency in the moderation process (Ribeiro et al., 2016).

- **Example Application**: A content moderation model identifies a social media post as containing hate speech. By applying LIME, the system can highlight keywords or contextual patterns that contributed to this decision, such as derogatory language or repeated inflammatory phrases. This explanation enables human reviewers to assess whether the content truly violates platform guidelines or if the AI has misinterpreted the context.

3.3.2 Shapley Additive Explanations (SHAP)

Shapley Additive Explanations (SHAP) is another XAI method that provides interpretable insights by assigning "Shapley values" to features within a model's decision-making process. SHAP explains how each feature contributes to the model's output, offering a more granular understanding of decisions. In content moderation, SHAP can help moderators identify the relative influence of various content features, enabling more accurate and fair decision-making (Lundberg & Lee, 2017).

- **Example Application**: Suppose an AI model flags a video as inappropriate. By applying SHAP, the system can indicate the contributions of different factors, such as specific words in subtitles or visual patterns that triggered the flagging decision. This method aids human moderators in validating the AI's decision and ensuring it aligns with community guidelines.

3.3.3 Decision Trees and Rule-Based Models

For some content moderation tasks, decision trees and rule-based models provide inherently interpretable models. Unlike deep learning models, which function as black boxes, decision trees offer clear paths from input to decision, making it easier for users and moderators to understand how conclusions are reached. Although decision trees may be less accurate for complex tasks, they can be valuable for tasks that require straightforward, explainable decision-making.

- **Example Application**: A decision tree could be employed to moderate simple content categories, such as explicit language detection. Each decision path within the tree can be inspected by moderators to ensure that the AI adheres to moderation guidelines without overcomplicating the explanation process.

3.3.4 Human-in-the-Loop (HITL) Systems

Human-in-the-Loop (HITL) systems integrate human judgment within the AI decision-making process, providing a balance between machine efficiency and human intuition. In content moderation, HITL systems allow human moderators to review AI-generated flags and make final decisions on ambiguous content. This collaborative approach promotes transparency by ensuring that a human perspective is incorporated into moderation decisions, particularly in cases where the AI lacks contextual understanding (Gillespie, 2020).

- **Example Application**: When AI flags borderline content that does not clearly violate community standards, HITL systems enable human moderators to make the final call, considering contextual nuances that AI may overlook.

Table 3. Explainable AI Techniques and Their Applicability to Content Moderation

XAI Technique	Description	Applicability to Content Moderation
LIME	Provides interpretable explanations by identifying influential features for specific decisions.	Useful for explaining text-based flags, such as hate speech.
SHAP	Assigns Shapley values to features to show their impact on model outputs.	Effective for nuanced content, such as multimedia analysis.
Decision Trees	Uses tree-based paths to provide inherent interpretability.	Suitable for rule-based moderation, such as explicit language.
Human-in-the-Loop (HITL)	Incorporates human reviewers in the decision process for ambiguous cases.	Enhances transparency by involving human judgment in final decisions.

3.4 Benefits and Challenges of Implementing XAI in Content Moderation

While XAI techniques offer numerous advantages in promoting transparency and trust, implementing them in content moderation also poses certain challenges. Below, we outline the benefits and potential obstacles associated with adopting XAI in content moderation systems.

3.4.1 Benefits of XAI in Content Moderation

1. **Increased Transparency**: XAI provides users and moderators with insights into AI decisions, fostering a sense of fairness and reducing user frustration.
2. **Enhanced Accountability**: By making AI decisions interpretable, XAI aligns with regulatory demands for transparency, supporting accountability within moderation systems.
3. **Error Detection and Model Improvement**: XAI allows moderators to identify when AI models make incorrect decisions, enabling developers to refine models continuously.

3.4.2 Challenges of Implementing XAI

1. **Technical Complexity**: Implementing XAI requires additional computational resources and technical expertise, particularly in complex AI models like deep learning.
2. **Risk of Privacy Compromise**: In content moderation, transparency must be balanced with user privacy to avoid exposing sensitive information within explanation outputs.

3. **Limited Applicability to Certain Models**: Some highly complex models, such as deep neural networks, may resist interpretable explanations, complicating the application of XAI techniques.

Transparency and interpretability are essential to building ethical and trustworthy AI-driven content moderation systems. Explainable AI (XAI) techniques like LIME, SHAP, and decision trees offer valuable tools for making AI decisions more understandable, thereby promoting user trust and regulatory compliance. However, the challenges associated with implementing XAI, such as technical complexity and privacy concerns, must be carefully managed. As AI technology advances, ongoing research is essential to develop more robust and user-friendly XAI methods that balance interpretability with effectiveness. Future research may focus on refining XAI techniques for real-time applications, creating hybrid models that incorporate both interpretable and complex components, and exploring user-friendly ways to convey AI decision rationales to the public.

4. ACCOUNTABILITY MECHANISMS FOR AI AND HUMAN MODERATORS

4.1 Defining Accountability in Human-AI Collaborative Models

In content moderation, accountability refers to the mechanisms through which human moderators, platform operators, and AI developers are held responsible for the outcomes of moderation decisions. In a human-AI collaborative model, accountability is complex, as both AI systems and human moderators contribute to decision-making processes. Establishing clear accountability is essential for ethical content moderation, ensuring that users can trust platforms to enforce guidelines fairly and that harmful content is managed responsibly.

The unique aspect of accountability in human-AI models is that responsibility is shared between humans and machines. For instance, when an AI system flags content for review, a human moderator typically makes the final decision on whether the content should be removed or left unchanged. If the AI's decision is flawed—due to algorithmic bias, a misinterpretation of context, or other limitations—the question of accountability arises: Is the fault with the AI's developers, the platform, or the individual moderator? This ambiguity can hinder trust in AI-assisted content moderation and presents challenges for platforms when responding to moderation controversies (Binns, 2021).

Defining accountability in a human-AI model involves outlining specific roles, responsibilities, and consequences for errors or biased outcomes in content moderation. This can be achieved through a combination of technological measures, such as logging AI decisions for transparency, and organizational policies that clarify human moderators' roles and empower them to challenge or override AI suggestions when necessary. By establishing these boundaries, platforms can foster a more reliable and ethically sound approach to content moderation.

4.2 Legal and Ethical Implications

The rise of AI in content moderation has prompted significant ethical and legal discussions about accountability. Regulatory frameworks, such as the European Union's General Data Protection Regulation (GDPR), emphasize the importance of transparency, data privacy, and accountability in automated decision-making systems. Under Article 22 of the GDPR, individuals have the right not to be subject to decisions made solely by automated processes if those decisions significantly affect them (GDPR, 2018). In content moderation, this means that users affected by AI-driven decisions should ideally have access to human review or, at the very least, an explanation of the rationale behind the AI's decision.

Another regulatory framework, the **California Consumer Privacy Act (CCPA)**, also includes provisions that indirectly affect AI accountability in content moderation. Although primarily focused on data privacy, the CCPA's emphasis on transparency and consumer rights highlights the need for ethical handling of user data and decisions that impact users. These regulations underscore the need for platforms to ensure that content moderation systems are transparent, that decisions can be appealed or reviewed, and that human intervention remains part of the moderation process.

Ethically, accountability mechanisms are essential for ensuring that AI does not perpetuate harm or discrimination. Unchecked AI models can reinforce biases, flagging or allowing content inconsistently across user groups. By establishing accountability measures, platforms can address the moral obligation to protect users' rights and prevent harm caused by biased or erroneous AI decisions. Therefore, accountability is not only a regulatory requirement but also an ethical imperative in AI-assisted content moderation (Crawford, 2020).

4.3 Creating Accountability Mechanisms

To ensure accountability within human-AI collaborative content moderation, platforms must implement specific mechanisms that clarify responsibility and enable corrective actions when errors occur. Below are several key mechanisms for promoting accountability in AI-driven content moderation.

4.3.1 Audit Trails and Logging

Audit trails are records of actions taken by both AI systems and human moderators in the content moderation process. By maintaining a detailed log of moderation decisions, including the initial AI flagging, human review, and final outcome, platforms can ensure transparency and accountability. Audit trails allow for the tracking of errors and biases, enabling platforms to identify patterns that may indicate issues with the AI system's performance or human moderators' decision-making processes (Funk, 2019). In cases where moderation decisions are contested, audit trails provide an objective record of the process, helping clarify where accountability lies.

- **Example Application**: A social media platform can maintain an audit trail for every flagged post, recording details such as the reasons behind the AI flag, human moderator comments, and the final decision. This trail enables the platform to review past decisions if users appeal or question them, promoting a transparent and accountable approach.

4.3.2 Regular Algorithmic Audits

Algorithmic audits involve the periodic evaluation of AI models to assess their performance, fairness, and alignment with moderation policies. These audits can reveal potential biases, identify areas where the model may be underperforming, and ensure that the AI remains consistent with evolving standards and guidelines. Algorithmic audits can be conducted internally by platform teams or externally by third-party auditors for an impartial perspective, adding credibility to the moderation process (Binns, 2021).

- **Example Application**: A platform might conduct quarterly algorithmic audits to test how well its AI models detect harmful content across different demographics, ensuring that the system does not disproportionately flag content from any specific group. Findings from these audits can inform model updates and bias mitigation strategies.

4.3.3 User Appeals and Review Systems

Providing users with an avenue to appeal moderation decisions is a critical accountability measure. If users believe their content was unjustly flagged or removed, they should have the right to request a review by a human moderator. Appeal systems enable users to challenge AI decisions, ensuring that errors can be corrected and that users are not subject to unfair treatment by automated systems. Effective appeal processes include transparency regarding the appeal status and timelines, as well as providing users with a clear explanation of the final decision (Gillespie, 2020).

- **Example Application**: A user's post is flagged and removed by an AI model for containing what the system interpreted as misinformation. The user appeals the decision, and a human moderator reviews the content to determine if it indeed violates platform policies. This appeal process allows the platform to correct potential errors and maintain user trust.

4.3.4 Accountability through Explainable AI (XAI)

Explainable AI (XAI) can play a crucial role in promoting accountability by making the AI's decision-making process more transparent to both users and moderators. XAI techniques, such as LIME and SHAP, discussed in Chapter 3, provide insights into why specific decisions were made, allowing moderators and users to understand the AI's reasoning. This transparency enables users to hold AI systems accountable for biased or erroneous decisions and equips human moderators to make informed choices when reviewing AI-generated flags.

- **Example Application**: After an AI model flags a piece of content as hate speech, XAI methods reveal that the decision was based on specific keywords. A human moderator can review this explanation and decide if the flagging was appropriate, taking contextual nuances into account to make a fair decision.

4.3.5 Training and Empowerment of Human Moderators

Human moderators play an essential role in content moderation, particularly when AI models make uncertain or ambiguous decisions. Platforms must ensure that human moderators are adequately trained to understand AI outputs, identify potential biases, and challenge AI decisions when necessary. Empowering moderators to override or question AI suggestions is crucial for maintaining accountability and avoiding overreliance on AI systems (Roberts, 2019). Furthermore, clear policies should delineate when and how human moderators can intervene in AI-driven processes to promote a collaborative model that values both human judgment and machine efficiency.

- **Example Application**: A platform conducts regular training sessions for its moderators, teaching them how to interpret AI-generated flags, understand common AI biases, and exercise judgment when the AI's decision appears flawed. This empowers moderators to contribute meaningfully to the moderation process, enhancing accountability and reducing AI reliance.

Table 4. Summary of Accountability Mechanisms in AI-Assisted Content Moderation

Accountability Mechanism	Description	Example Application
Audit Trails and Logging	Maintains records of moderation decisions for transparency and error tracking.	Record-keeping of AI flags and human moderation outcomes.
Regular Algorithmic Audits	Evaluates AI models periodically to assess performance and fairness.	Quarterly audits to ensure demographic fairness in flagging.
User Appeals and Review Systems	Allows users to challenge AI moderation decisions through a structured appeal process.	Users request reviews of AI flags by human moderators.
Explainable AI (XAI)	Provides insights into AI decision-making, promoting transparency and interpretability.	Uses LIME or SHAP to explain why content was flagged.
Training for Human Moderators	Educates moderators on AI limitations and empowers them to challenge AI decisions if necessary.	Training sessions on understanding and intervening in AI flags.

4.4 Challenges in Implementing Accountability Mechanisms

While accountability mechanisms provide essential safeguards in content moderation, implementing them in a human-AI collaborative model involves several challenges.

1. **Resource Constraints**: Comprehensive accountability mechanisms, such as regular algorithmic audits and extensive training for human moderators, require substantial time, financial resources, and technical expertise. Smaller platforms may find it challenging to allocate resources for these practices, potentially impacting the fairness and transparency of their moderation processes.
2. **Complexity in Determining Responsibility**: In cases where both AI and human moderators contribute to a moderation decision, it can be difficult to pinpoint where responsibility lies. For instance, if an AI model suggests a flag, but a human moderator makes the final decision, determining accountability for errors is complex. This shared responsibility requires clear guidelines and protocols to address the accountability of both human and AI contributors (Gillespie, 2020).
3. **Balancing Transparency and User Privacy**: While transparency is a key element of accountability, content moderation decisions often involve sensitive user data. Platforms must balance the need for transparency with user privacy

rights, ensuring that explanation mechanisms, such as XAI, do not inadvertently expose personal information.

4. **Scalability of Appeals Systems**: Providing users with the ability to appeal moderation decisions is essential for fairness, but scaling such systems can be challenging. As platforms grow, the volume of appeal requests may exceed the capacity of human moderators, necessitating efficient yet fair systems for managing appeals without compromising accountability.

5. PSYCHOLOGICAL WELFARE OF HUMAN MODERATORS IN AI-ENHANCED ENVIRONMENTS

5.1 Psychological Impacts of Content Moderation

Human moderators, often referred to as the "hidden labor" behind digital platforms, play a critical role in filtering out harmful and inappropriate content. However, this work exposes moderators to an immense psychological toll, as they must review distressing content, including violent imagery, hate speech, and explicit material, day in and day out. Studies have shown that prolonged exposure to such content can result in a range of mental health issues, including anxiety, depression, and post-traumatic stress disorder (PTSD) (Roberts, 2019).

Moderators frequently work under high-stakes pressure, tasked with making quick decisions to uphold community guidelines, often without adequate psychological support or breaks. This type of work environment can lead to "compassion fatigue" and emotional exhaustion, as moderators continuously confront disturbing material that requires them to regulate their emotional responses while adhering to strict procedural standards. The hidden nature of this labor often results in moderators working in isolation, sometimes as independent contractors without access to the mental health resources typically provided in conventional employment settings (Crawford, 2020).

The growing use of AI in content moderation has altered the nature of this work, with AI taking on a portion of repetitive tasks, such as flagging potential violations based on specific keywords or visual cues. While AI can relieve moderators of some cognitive load, the demands of monitoring flagged content and intervening in complex cases persist. In cases where AI models misinterpret content, human moderators must engage in corrective measures, which can add stress rather than alleviate it. Therefore, while AI contributes to task efficiency, the psychological demands on human moderators remain a significant concern that platforms must address.

5.2 Role of AI in Reducing Cognitive Load

AI systems, when effectively integrated, can play a positive role in reducing some of the repetitive tasks that contribute to moderator burnout. By automating initial flagging for high-volume content, such as spam or easily identifiable hate speech, AI allows human moderators to concentrate on more nuanced decisions that demand contextual understanding. This shift can relieve moderators from continuous exposure to repetitive, low-stakes content, potentially lowering instances of cognitive overload (Gillespie, 2020).

For example, AI models trained to recognize explicit language or violent imagery can automatically flag and categorize content for human review, sparing moderators from immediate exposure to potentially harmful material. This pre-screening capability enables a triage approach, where content can be ranked by priority or severity, allowing moderators to focus on more complex cases. When implemented thoughtfully, AI can improve the workflow, enabling moderators to take breaks between reviewing difficult content and reducing the cognitive fatigue associated with nonstop decision-making.

However, the reliance on AI systems also introduces additional pressures, as moderators are required to constantly supervise AI outputs to ensure accuracy. If the AI flags benign content mistakenly or fails to recognize harmful content, human moderators must engage in "correctional work," adjusting the model's outcomes and re-evaluating flagged material. This supervisory role demands ongoing alertness and can disrupt the flow of work, contributing to cognitive strain rather than alleviating it (Binns, 2021). Moreover, this necessity for continuous monitoring underscores the need for robust support systems that acknowledge the psychological complexity of working alongside AI.

5.3 Support Strategies for Human Moderators

To support the psychological welfare of human moderators in AI-augmented environments, platforms must implement comprehensive mental health support systems, training, and organizational policies. The following are key strategies that have been identified as effective in promoting a healthier work environment for moderators.

5.3.1 Mental Health Support Programs

Mental health support programs are critical to helping moderators manage the psychological demands of content moderation. These programs can include counseling services, support groups, and access to mental health professionals trained to address the unique challenges faced by moderators. Some platforms have begun providing therapy sessions as part of moderator support, enabling moderators to process distressing experiences in a controlled, therapeutic setting (Roberts, 2019). Additionally, confidential mental health hotlines can be made available to provide immediate support when moderators feel overwhelmed.

- **Example Application**: A digital platform partners with a mental health organization to offer weekly counseling sessions for its moderators. These sessions help moderators discuss their experiences, process difficult emotions, and develop coping strategies to manage work-related stress.

5.3.2 Training Programs for Moderators

Training programs equip moderators with the skills to manage emotional responses and effectively handle AI-augmented tasks. These programs should cover content-specific training, such as identifying harmful material, as well as emotional resilience training to help moderators develop strategies for coping with distressing content. Additionally, training on AI functionality, biases, and limitations can empower moderators to interpret AI outputs accurately and confidently intervene when necessary (Crawford, 2020).

- **Example Application**: A content moderation team undergoes biannual training focused on resilience-building techniques, such as mindfulness and cognitive reframing, to help moderators manage the emotional impact of their work. Concurrently, they receive instruction on understanding AI biases, enabling them to more effectively supervise AI-generated flags.

5.3.3 Structured Breaks and Rotational Schedules

To prevent burnout, platforms should implement structured breaks and rotational schedules that allow moderators to alternate between different types of tasks. For example, a rotation system can assign moderators to lower-stress tasks, such as reviewing flagged spam content, following a session of reviewing graphic material. This approach ensures that moderators are not continuously exposed to distressing content and can recover between sessions (Gillespie, 2020).

- **Example Application**: A platform creates a rotational schedule in which moderators spend three hours reviewing sensitive content, followed by an hour of reviewing low-risk flagged content, such as spam. This break in exposure helps mitigate the risk of compassion fatigue and burnout.

5.3.4 Ensuring Human Decision-Making Authority

In cases where AI-generated flags are ambiguous or complex, human moderators should retain the final decision-making authority. This policy not only acknowledges the limits of AI but also empowers moderators to exercise their judgment and contextual understanding. Guaranteeing that human moderators have the final say in contentious cases promotes a sense of control over their work, reducing the stress associated with blindly following AI outputs that may not account for nuanced scenarios (Binns, 2021).

- **Example Application**: A policy ensures that moderators review all AI-generated flags for ambiguous content, with the authority to override AI decisions based on their contextual analysis. This empowerment fosters a collaborative environment where moderators feel valued and responsible for their final judgments.

5.4 Organizational Policies for Moderator Welfare

In addition to individual support programs, platforms should implement organizational policies that prioritize moderator welfare in AI-augmented environments. Such policies can establish guidelines for workload management, ethical standards for AI use, and performance metrics that consider moderators' mental well-being.

1. **Workload Management**: To prevent overexposure to harmful content, platforms should set limits on the volume and type of content a single moderator can review daily. By managing workload more sustainably, platforms can reduce the risk of burnout and ensure that moderators maintain a balanced workload.
2. **Ethical AI Use Guidelines**: Policies that define the role of AI in moderation, including specific cases where human intervention is essential, help clarify the limits of AI reliance. This transparency promotes a fair and supportive work environment where moderators are not unduly pressured to rely on AI decisions in complex cases.
3. **Wellness-Oriented Performance Metrics**: Traditional performance metrics, such as speed and volume of content reviewed, can contribute to stress and lower quality of work. Instead, platforms can adopt wellness-oriented metrics that focus on accuracy, quality of decision-making, and self-reported well-being, thus promoting healthier performance standards.

The psychological welfare of human moderators is critical to sustaining ethical content moderation practices, particularly in AI-augmented environments. AI technology offers opportunities to alleviate certain cognitive burdens, yet human moderators remain essential for managing complex and context-sensitive cases. Platforms must invest in robust mental health support programs, structured workflows, and comprehensive training to ensure that moderators can manage the psychological demands of their work effectively. Future research and practice should continue to explore innovative support mechanisms, including resilience training tailored to AI-enhanced environments and user-centered approaches to workload management. By prioritizing moderator welfare, platforms can foster a more sustainable content moderation system that balances efficiency with ethical responsibility.

6. FUTURE DIRECTIONS AND RECOMMENDATIONS

6.1 Enhancing Human-AI Collaboration in Content Moderation

Throughout this study, we have explored the potential of a human-AI collaborative model in content moderation, emphasizing the importance of integrating AI to handle high-volume, repetitive tasks while allowing human moderators to focus on nuanced and context-sensitive cases. As the field of AI in content moderation advances, it is crucial to develop frameworks that enhance this collaboration, ensuring that AI assists rather than replaces human judgment. By improving human-AI synergy, platforms can leverage AI's scalability and precision while preserving the ethical standards that human oversight provides.

Future improvements in human-AI collaboration can include:

1. **Adaptive AI Systems**: AI models could be designed to adapt based on feedback from human moderators, allowing them to "learn" from human input. For instance, when moderators override AI-generated decisions, the model could incorporate this input to reduce similar errors in the future (Binns, 2021).
2. **Role-Based AI Deployment**: Different levels of AI intervention can be implemented depending on content types and community needs. For example, AI could handle straightforward cases, such as spam detection, while more complex content, like hate speech or political misinformation, is flagged for human review. This approach maintains a balance between efficiency and ethical accountability.
3. **Enhanced Training Modules for Moderators**: Training for moderators should not only focus on policy understanding and resilience but also on AI interpretation. Educating moderators about the limitations and biases inherent in AI

models can equip them to use AI outputs more effectively, fostering a more collaborative workflow.

6.2 Ethical and Regulatory Considerations

As AI technology evolves, so do the ethical and regulatory landscapes governing its use in content moderation. Governments and regulatory bodies are increasingly recognizing the need for frameworks that ensure fairness, transparency, and accountability in AI systems. Compliance with these frameworks will be essential for platforms that implement AI in moderation processes. Some key considerations include:

6.2.1 Emerging Regulatory Trends

Recent legislative frameworks, such as the EU's proposed Artificial Intelligence Act, have introduced standards for "high-risk" AI applications, which include content moderation due to its impact on free expression and privacy rights. This act proposes strict requirements on transparency, risk management, and accountability for high-stakes AI systems, pushing platforms to evaluate the ethical implications of their AI models (European Commission, 2021).

In addition to the EU, other regions are also introducing relevant regulations. For instance, California's Artificial Intelligence Accountability Act (AIAA) aims to hold companies accountable for biased AI systems and mandates audits to assess AI impact on different demographics. These regulatory trends indicate a growing demand for ethical AI implementation that safeguards user rights and public interests.

6.2.2 Ethical Standards for AI-Enhanced Content Moderation

Beyond regulatory compliance, establishing ethical guidelines is fundamental for responsible AI use in content moderation. Key principles include:

- **Fairness**: Ensuring that AI models do not disproportionately impact specific demographic groups or marginalize underrepresented voices.
- **Transparency**: Providing clear explanations for AI decisions, such as why certain content is flagged, removed, or prioritized in moderation.
- **Accountability**: Defining who is responsible for AI-related errors and implementing mechanisms, such as appeals processes and audit trails, that empower users and moderators to challenge or verify AI decisions.
- **User Privacy**: Balancing transparency with privacy to ensure that AI-driven moderation does not compromise user data or expose sensitive information.

Establishing and adhering to these ethical standards will help platforms develop AI moderation systems that are trustworthy and align with user expectations and societal values.

6.3 Research Opportunities

While advancements in human-AI collaboration show promise, many gaps remain in understanding the long-term implications of AI-driven content moderation. Research in the following areas can deepen our understanding of how to implement AI responsibly in this field:

6.3.1 Development of Bias-Free and Culturally Sensitive Datasets

The effectiveness and fairness of AI moderation heavily depend on the quality and diversity of training data. Bias in datasets often leads to disproportionate outcomes that affect marginalized communities. Future research could focus on developing standardized, bias-free datasets that capture cultural nuances and represent diverse linguistic, social, and cultural contexts (Hovy & Spruit, 2016).

Collaborative research initiatives involving academia, industry, and advocacy groups can help in curating datasets that reflect diverse perspectives and avoid reinforcing harmful stereotypes. Additionally, establishing standards for dataset documentation could ensure that biases are identified and mitigated before training AI models.

6.3.2 Advancement in Explainable AI Techniques

While explainable AI (XAI) has made strides, further research is needed to refine XAI techniques for content moderation. Developing methods that make AI's decision-making process accessible not only to developers but also to moderators and users can bridge the transparency gap. User-centered XAI approaches, such as visual explanations or interactive interfaces, could empower moderators and users to understand and, when necessary, contest AI-generated decisions (Lipton, 2018).

Moreover, improving interpretability for multimedia content, such as video or audio, remains a challenge. Research in multimedia XAI could enable AI systems to provide explanations for non-textual content decisions, promoting transparency across all types of moderated content.

6.3.3 Psychological Impact of AI-Augmented Moderation on Human Moderators

The psychological welfare of human moderators in AI-augmented environments requires ongoing research. While AI systems can reduce cognitive load by automating repetitive tasks, they also introduce new forms of stress, including the constant need for oversight and correction. Longitudinal studies examining the mental health impacts of working in AI-enhanced environments could reveal best practices for creating supportive work conditions (Roberts, 2019).

Future research could also explore the effectiveness of specific support strategies, such as resilience training, mental health resources, and workload management techniques, to identify which approaches best mitigate the psychological toll on human moderators.

6.4 Recommendations for Ethical AI Implementation in Content Moderation

Building on the insights and findings of this book, the following recommendations provide a roadmap for implementing AI responsibly in content moderation:

1. **Promote Human-AI Collaboration Over AI Replacement**: AI should be designed to complement, not replace, human judgment. Ensuring that human moderators have the final authority on contentious cases upholds ethical standards and fosters user trust.
2. **Establish Robust Bias Mitigation Protocols**: Regular algorithmic audits, bias testing, and the use of diverse datasets are essential to minimizing unfair outcomes in AI-driven moderation.
3. **Implement Explainable AI Techniques for Transparency**: XAI techniques, such as LIME and SHAP, should be integrated to provide moderators and users with accessible explanations for moderation decisions. Transparent AI fosters accountability and empowers users to challenge decisions when necessary.
4. **Invest in Moderator Well-being and Training**: Platforms must prioritize the psychological welfare of human moderators through mental health support, structured breaks, and resilience training. Training should also cover AI interpretation skills, allowing moderators to effectively work alongside AI systems.
5. **Engage in Cross-Industry Collaboration for Ethical Standards**: Collaboration among platforms, researchers, policymakers, and advocacy groups can promote the development of industry-wide standards for AI-driven content moderation, supporting ethical practices and fostering public trust.

6.5 Conclusion

The integration of AI into content moderation brings both opportunities and challenges. AI systems offer unparalleled scalability and efficiency in handling high volumes of content, but they also raise ethical concerns related to fairness, transparency, and accountability. A collaborative human-AI model, where AI handles routine tasks and human moderators address complex cases, presents a balanced approach that leverages the strengths of both humans and machines.

As this book has demonstrated, building an ethical framework for AI-enhanced content moderation requires a commitment to transparency, user rights, and the well-being of moderators. Through improved training, mental health support, and regulatory compliance, platforms can create a sustainable and ethical approach to moderation that aligns with user expectations and societal values. As the field of AI in content moderation continues to evolve, future research and innovation will be essential in developing models that are not only efficient but also equitable and transparent. By following these guiding principles, platforms can foster a safer and more inclusive digital space for all.

REFERENCES

Binns, R. (2021). Algorithmic Accountability and Transparency in Content Moderation. *Journal of Online Ethics*, 23(4), 245–267.

Crawford, K. (2020). *The Politics of AI Bias*. Oxford University Press.

Dastin, J. (2018). Ethical Implications of Bias in AI Systems. *Ethics in Artificial Intelligence Journal*, 12(3), 198–210.

European Commission. (2021). Proposal for a Regulation Laying Down Harmonised Rules on Artificial Intelligence (Artificial Intelligence Act). *European Union*.

Funk, M. (2019). AI and Accountability in Content Moderation. *Digital Ethics Quarterly*, 14(2), 129–145.

GDPR. (2018). Article 22. *General Data Protection Regulation.European Union*.

Gillespie, T. (2020). *Custodians of the Internet: Platforms, Content Moderation, and the Hidden Decisions That Shape Social Media*. Yale University Press.

Hovy, D., & Spruit, S. L. (2016). *The Social Impact of Natural Language Processing. International Conference on Computational Linguistics*, 85-90. DOI: 10.18653/v1/P16-2096

Lipton, Z. C. (2018). The Mythos of Model Interpretability. *Communications of the ACM*, 61(10), 36–43. DOI: 10.1145/3233231

Lundberg, S. M., & Lee, S.-I. (2017). *A Unified Approach to Interpretable Model Explanations. Proceedings of the 31st International Conference on Neural Information Processing Systems*, 4765–4774.

Noble, S. U. (2018). *Algorithms of Oppression: How Search Engines Reinforce Racism*. NYU Press. DOI: 10.18574/nyu/9781479833641.001.0001

Ribeiro, M. T., Singh, S., & Guestrin, C. (2016). *"Why Should I Trust You?": Explaining the Predictions of Any Classifier*. Proceedings of the 22nd ACM SIGKDD International Conference on Knowledge Discovery and Data Mining, 1135-1144.

Roberts, S. T. (2019). *Behind the Screen: Content Moderation in the Shadows of Social Media*. Yale University Press.

Chapter 9
Human-AI Synergy in Ethical Content Moderation:
Navigating Fairness, Accountability, and Transparency Challenges

Hemlata Parmar
https://orcid.org/0009-0009-1438-5427
Manipal University Jaipur, India

Utsav Krishan Murari
https://orcid.org/0009-0007-1606-6775
Sharda University, India

ABSTRACT

The rapid growth of digital platforms has highlighted the need for robust content moderation systems that manage large content volumes while addressing human moderators' mental health. This study explores AI's evolving role in content moderation, emphasizing collaboration with human moderators for nuanced judgments. AI can identify harmful content trends, but human oversight is needed for contextual accuracy. However, AI raises ethical issues, such as bias from prejudiced training data, potentially harming marginalized groups. To improve accountability, the study suggests using diverse datasets, transparent decision-making, and explainable AI. Regulatory frameworks and mental health support for moderators are also essential for fair, transparent content moderation.

DOI: 10.4018/979-8-3693-9904-0.ch009

1. INTRODUCTION

Nowadays Artificial Intelligence(AI) is reinventing every single aspect of modern life from healthcare, education and finance to governance and entertainment. Generative artificial intelligence is developing faster than ever and the world started adopting it widely, which led many to debate whether generative AI can improve or sink society (The Economic Times, 2023). Simultaneously, AI also has incredible potential to provide breakthroughs and solve some of humanity's most challenging problems rapid diagnostics resulting in better health care; predictive analytics for climate change; broader access to high-quality education for underrepresented communities. But it also asks difficult questions on equality and discrimination, employment and privacy which if not managed correctly could push the minimizing of social injustices into overdrive (Anderson & Rainie, 2018).

While AI was previously only a technical technology discussion, it is now also social, ethical and economic concerns given the current rapid pace of AI development. And finally, scholars, policymakers and advocates are asking, who benefits from AI? Unless we ensure that the dividends of innovation, fueled by AI, be equally dispersed among our nations. How to ensure that groups at risk are not harmed, in determining how AI systems goodness can be ensured, and by providing other protections from harm? Addressing all of these problems will require social justice fundamentally embedded in a systems approach to AI research, development and deployment (Bhuptani, 2024).

1.1 Defining Social Justice in the Context of AI

Many of the discussions of the implications of AI have centered around social justice, which is defined as the equitable distribution of resources, opportunities and privileges within a society. In a just, equitable society, the progress of AI would not duplicate nor increase inequality; it is up to us to determine if and how this technological revolution becomes instead a tool for common good. It involves centering the experiences and rights of marginalized communities, promoting equity and accountability in algorithmic systems, and facilitating access to AI governance and policy processes (Buccella, 2022).

We know from history that technological revolutions have not only informed how we live but also embodied and exaggerated social inequities. For instance, the industrial revolution has been very beneficial for economy development but it had an unfair approach to human resources - thus raising inequalities between riches. There was good in a digital age even if it forged an invisible footprint, a widening gap between individuals with the wherewithal to enter and leverage the power of information technology and those standing at the curb looking on helplessly as little more than digits passing by, waiting for salvation (Rafanelli, 2022). Given that AI is the new frontier of technology, it brings with it risks with respect to systemic inequities being baked into the system unless we democratize access and more effectively reduce harm.

1.2 The Promise and Peril of AI

It goes without saying that AI can catalyze social justice. AI is a powerful tool for empowerment, when used responsibly in design and deployment. Imagine if AI were to be used in the area of healthcare; large volume medical data can also be analysed by using AI and then, the outbreak prediction bell can be rung so that efficiency is improved and good quality services becomes accessible to everyone even in some remote areas of world. The role of AI in education can help close the educational gap with the use of personalized learning platforms that are able to create custom content for every student. Moreover, AI led solutions can improve productivity in developing countries, help tackle urban planning issues and offer solutions to environmental emergencies (Köbis et al., 2022).

But there are certainly dangers around using AI. There have been many high-profile cases where AI systems have replicated and even escalated bias in the real world. Facial recognition systems are biased, as people of color have been mis-identified at alarming rates forcing them into civil rights violations and wrongful arrests. This is such a concern that automated hiring algorithms, for instance, have been shown to discriminate against women and underrepresented minority candidates due to the historical inequities passed on through training data. In addition, the Fourth Amendment, which protects against unreasonable searches and seizures, has been compromised by new technologies like predictive policing. Why are these and so many other examples of the same kind springing up all over the world every day, in our international scene, because they highlight the need for serious ethical frameworks, better design practices related to inclusion, and stringent regulatory oversight — or we will end with AI as a hell for everyone with injustice being one of its frequent strings (De Freitas et al., 2023).

1.3 The Urgency of Democratizing AI

Democratization of AI means making the technology available and actionable for people throughout society, particularly those at risk of being left behind as technological changes accelerate. This means tackling biases that may be embedded in algorithms or ensuring that underserved communities have access to the latest AI technologies, and creating an environment where diversity is prioritized Australian Society for Artificial Intelligence (ASAI) added. It also means enabling communities to take a part in the development of AI systems and policies, which should ensure that technological evolution goes hand-in-hand with the collective interest (Godulla, 2020).

Currently, AI is consolidated in a limited number of tech corporations and research institutions, mainly in the high-income countries. They have the capital to spur AI, but they are not always motivated by consideration for underserved or vulnerable populations. Equally, the digital divide is a huge and ever-present challenge with many millions unable to connect through lack of infrastructure, skills or even opportunities when they are online. From there you have the industrial revolutions where machines ended up doing a lot for us in workplaces but also taking away jobs from people and creating economic inconsistencies. AI basically can do a lot of what humans can, well at least better than some. To solve these challenges, we need to democratize AI so nobody is left behind this revolution (Mondal & Mondal, 2024).

2. OBJECTIVES AND STRUCTURE OF THE PAPER

Democratizing technology for inclusive growth using AI through the lens of social justice. It aims to shed light on the role of AI in social equity along with the pitfalls and tackles it, and provides pathways for how to responsibly tap into the potential of AI. Sections of the Paper The paper has the following key sections:

i) Introduction to Social Justice & AI: This introduces social justice and explores how the issues of fairness, equity, and inclusivity are concepts that relate directly to how we study or even use AI.
ii) AI for Social Justice: How It Can Help alleviate Social Inequities in Healthcare, Education & some focus on Environmental Sustainability and Economic Development.
iii) Section on How AI Threatens Social Justice: This part covers the dangers of AI, such as bias in algorithms, barriers to access, and a combination of power in building AIs which can worsen inequalities.
iv) Democratizing AI: Strategies for Inclusive Growth: practical strategies are discussed to make AI technologies accessible and equitable, including participatory design, policy interventions, and education initiatives.
v) Case Studies Successful and Failed Attempts: Here the user can analyse the implementation of few AI examples, to see what are the best practices or pitfalls.
vi) Governments and International Bodies: We seek to understand the role of governments and international bodies in ensuring that AI systems are developed following ethical norms.

vii) Ethics and AI Governance: The paper then ends with a discussion of ethical principles and governance frameworks that can help maintain social justice in relation to AI development and use.

The question is no longer whether we can avoid AI as it becomes more and more embedded in our lifeworld but how to navigate that trajectory unfolding. Working towards making AI development and governance social-justice focused, this will allow us to strategize for a future where technology serves all of humanity rather than the few at the top. That entails cross-sectoral collaboration, meaningful community engagement and, ultimately, principled work. Democratizing AI is not merely a technical challenge it is, and will be, the moral imperative of our digital age.

3. THE PROMISE OF AI FOR INCLUSIVE GROWTH

Artificial intelligence: one of the key game changers cross-sectoral and transformative technologies of the 21st century. Despite the well-known challenges of AI foundations, with quality data and computing power that is abundant today, it can also serve as an engine for addressing diverse societal issues while fueling inclusive economic growth. Here, we take a look at AI for economic empowerment, delivery of public and other services and health and education (Hunter et al., 2024).

3.1 Economic Empowerment

These AI-powered tech innovations have evoked a paradigm shift to the long-established economic and cultural frameworks, resulting in gargantuan wealth accumulation and job creation potential. It allows for better resource allocation, improves productivity by leveraging automation and data analytics, and creates new markets (Dunavete, 2024). However, ensuring that these economic benefits are shared equitably requires planning.

i) Job Creation: While many jobs will be lost due to automation, some new jobs will also be generated by AI. New job roles like data scientists, machine learning engineers, and AI ethics specialists are an example of the evolution of the workforce. To allow people especially those from underrepresented communities to capitalize on the large economic opportunities presented by AI over the longer-term, it is crucial that they also have access in programs to retrain and reskill workers.

ii) Capital and Market access: AI could equalize the playing field economically by making financial systems more inclusive. AI-based credit risk assessment models, for instance, can provide loans to economically disadvantaged groups and broaden the possibility of participating in entrepreneurship. AI-fueled ZIP code level market intelligence is accessible by the masses making it uniquely beneficial for startups and small businesses, reducing the advantage that large corporations and connected execs have from well-funded strategy departments (International Monetary Fund, 2024).
iii) Wealth distribution and redistribution: AI might drive substantial material wealth creation, but without sufficient governance this could lead to greater economic inequality. There are ongoing discussions around taxation of AI companies and/or universal basic income (UBI) that would ensure wealth created by advances in AI is redistributed to all.

3.2 Improved Public Services

AI has a transformative potential in the way government operates and engages with citizens, including how it delivers public services. AI has the potential to improve efficiency and responsiveness in a range of areas including urban planning, emergency response, and welfare distribution by streamlining processes through optimization and utilizing data for decision-making.

i) Healthcare sector: AI is being used in this domain to enable the early diagnosis of diseases and personalized treatment. Now, machine learning algorithms study and analyze medical images with reports and patient history or/and high profiles to detect illness with more accuracy. Telemedicine platforms, which use Natural Language Processing (NLP), increase healthcare accessibility for remote or under-evaluated communities. However, equal access to progress remains a challenge, especially in low-income communities (Dorocka, 2024).
ii) Urban Development and Smart Cities: AI has improved urban development by studying traffic patterns, public transport optimization, energy distribution management, etc. Smart traffic lights, for instance, and AI-driven congestion monitoring can have a real impact on city-wide commute time and pollutant emissions. But these applications must be distributed equitably, to avoid a digital divide between rich and poor areas.
iii) Welfare Schemes: AI can automatically identify the beneficiaries in greatest need, enabling social welfare programmes to operate more effectively and efficiently. Predictive models can help governments allocate housing, unemployment benefits and food assistance more effectively. That means transparency in

executing these systems, preventing bias and ensuring that the AI tools do not accidentally disenfranchise marginalized classes.

3.3 Health and Education

AI has a formative responsibility to disentangle structural reforms in both health and education, two foundational components of human development. The ability to implement personalized, low-cost interventions in the moment might provide better outcomes and cost savings.

i) Advancements in healthcare: People are taking the help of AI in big data analysis instantaneously which gives a new way to diagnose and plan treatment and monitor patients. For example, you need to know that AI algorithms are helping in early cancer detection if you catch it on time saves lives. Lastly, the application of AI in robotic surgery and also precision medicine is clarifying how it will affect patient outcomes. However, the developments also need to be complemented with solutions that combat the ethical issues related to patient health information confidentiality and a bias-free algorithm if these improvements across healthcare services are to benefit all citizens equally.
ii) AI in Education: From Personalized Teaching to Enhanced Learning Experience Intelligent tutoring systems, for example, can suggest personalized pathways of learning based on the strengths and progress of individual students. AI Grading, Analytics on Student Performance tools such as more straightforward AI grading or mere analytics on student performance tools that help education professionals target interventions. But that still leaves the access problem: many rural and low-to-middle-income communities lack the infrastructure to make use of something like this AI. No educational equity will happen without confronting that gap.

4. CHALLENGES TO SOCIAL JUSTICE IN AI

Although AI can hold the promise of transformative change, it poses a major challenge to social justice. While doing so, the challenges these developments present will only serve to deepen current inequalities and ask new ethical and moral questions of how the benefits of technology are shared. In addition to this, we will also address important topics like algorithmic bias, accessibility challenges and the centralization of AI power (Rodrigues, 2020).

4.1 Algorithm Bias and Discrimination

Algorithmic bias is the systematic and repeatable errors in a computer system that create unfair outcomes, such as privileging one group over another based on race or gender. Such biases are, quite simply, a symptom of data contamination with some the same historical injustices and human prejudices that become entrenched in an algorithm through their training data.

i) Bias in AI systems: Bias is inherent in the data used to train AI Models as they are getting trained on big datasets. Facial recognition software is one of those examples that has been proven to be significantly error-prone when it comes to people of color and this is down to the lack of diversity in the training data. In the same way, hiring algorithms have occasionally exhibited sexist behaviour, punishing women as applicants because of historical data that increased male hires.
ii) Adverse Effect on Marginalized Population: Algorithmic discrimination can have drastic impacts on the marginalized community by perpetuating systemic violence. For example, use of risk assessment tools like COMPAS in the criminal justice system has faced controversy due to its tendency to assign higher risk scores for Black defendants, impacting decisions regarding bail and sentencing. These biases erode trust in AI and further compound the inequalities around social and economic opportunities.
iii) Mitigating Algorithmic Bias: There is an urgent need for methods to audit and mitigate bias in AI systems, if we care about social justice. Approaches comprise employing more heterogeneous datasets, embedding reasonable constraints in algorithms as well as conducting routine impact assessments. Interdisciplinary leaders —technologists, ethicists, community organizations— to collaborate. To make sure AI works for us and not against us.

4.2 Accessibility and the Digital Divide

The term digital divide is the separation between people who have access to modern information and communication technologies and those who do not. This divide is a major impediment to social justice, as it deprives disadvantaged groups of the opportunity to gain the fruits of AI.

i) Lack of Infrastructure and Internet Connectivity: The lack of high-speed internet connectivity and affordable computing devices makes infrastructural support for AI technologies difficult for many rural and low-income regions. In order for communities to participate in online education, telemedicine and jobs, they need to be digitally connected; because without this access, the digital divide widens economic and social gaps due to lack of choice. Closing this gap is essential for equitable access to AI.

ii) Digital Literacy: Even if access to AI tools exists, there are differences in technological literacy. Not only will populations that are not used to digital tools find it difficult to access effective AI-driven services, but they will ultimately reinforce the existing inequities. To cultivate necessary technological skills and enable full societal participation in a digital economy, targeted education and training programs tailored for various age segments with special attention to different cultural backgrounds are necessary.

iii) Bridging the Divide: Government, nonprofit, and tech efforts have tried to bridge this gap with initiatives such as subsidized rural broadband infrastructure and free or low-cost digital training. But this work needs to be expanded and sustained to make a real difference. Be Inclusive Announce list of AI Policy and Development principles (Continual Engine Team, 2023).

4.3 Concentration of Power in AI

Only a couple of the tech giants dominate the AI industry and have immense power on how this technology is researched, developed or deployed. This power dynamic has profound social justice consequences, resulting in unequal access to economic power and decision-making.

i) Economic Disparities and Market Monopolies: Tech companies with an overwhelming amount of data and computational resources have an immense advantage in the market which suffocates innovation and leads to monopolistic market circumstances. They will further economic inequality, and continue to limit opportunities for smaller companies and developing world nations to participate in the AI economy. Furthermore, the gains from AI-fueled productivity increases are not shared by workers, but diverted to owners and top executives.

ii) The Political and Social Dynamics: Tech giants wield more than economic clout; they influence public opinion and can tip electoral results. The cloud of mystery surrounding AI algorithmic systems used in social media and advertisement raised fears about manipulation and disappearing democratic values. To meet that, we need regulations to rein in the AI monopolies that act as a law unto themselves, and ensure transparency and accountability.

iii) Decentralize AI Development: The democratization of AI requires the proliferation of open-source technology and public interest technology hubs. One considers decentralized AI models as a way to avoid the power exploitations already instituted in many current human relationships set within systems where the communities have very little say or control over their data, algorithms, etc. It is up to national governments and international organizations to create standards that put the global good ahead of powers in corporations.

5. DEMOCRATIZING AI: STRATEGIES FOR INCLUSIVE GROWTH

Solving the problems of AI and social justice is complex, but possible through participatory design, strong policy options and investing in education and digital equity. This part delves into approaches to democratise AI to ensure fairness and accessibility.

5.1 Participatory Design (PD) and Engagement with a Community

Participatory design is an approach to design that includes input from stakeholders, including often underrepresented groups in the development of AI systems. It will ensure that AI technologies are developed and implemented in ways that meet the needs of different communities with their specific values (Lowa, 2024).

i) Implementing Community-Centered AI Projects: such participatory design can show up in initiatives like community data where local residents gather & analyze information to solve nearby issues. E.g., As an example, for research AI models developed to be used in urban planning these AI models can include inputs from community members so that infrastructure is built equitably. Involving impacted communities in the design process encourages trust and improves the chances of positive social outcomes.
ii) Co-Creation & Inclusive Innovation: Bringing AI developers, policymakers, and community advocates together at co-creation workshops allows the design of innovative solutions to social problems. Such workshops should elevate the voices of the oppressed and make space for them, rather than falling victim to White dominance of the dialogue. Providing funding and support for grassroots AI initiatives can help local communities leverage AI to meet their development priorities.
iii) Ethical AI Toolkits: Equipping communities with ethical AI toolkits that serve as guides for assessing and shaping the implications of various AI technologies can democratize knowledge and facilitate active participation. Toolkits available to different cultures, highlighting the social dimensions of AI (Williams, 2024).

5.2 Policy and Regulatory Frameworks

Having solid policy frameworks ensures that the implementation of AI technologies drive social justice. Policymakers need to take a proactive approach, predicting the possible effects of AI on society and passing laws in order to protect human rights.

i) Building Data Protection and Privacy Laws: Strong data protection laws like the GDPR in the EU are essential to protecting citizens against privacy breaches and data abuse. But if there's any lesson from the current headlines, it's that law making must continue to guard against some parts of society — often those who are most at risk from privacy violations and lucrative data breaches.
ii) Transparency and accountability in algorithms: Governments must require transparency about AI systems deployed in sensitive domains like criminal justice, health care — and hiring. That includes not just making companies and agencies explain the rationale behind decisions made by AI models, but also allowing independent audits for bias detection. Accountability mechanisms (for instance, AI ethics boards and ombudsmen) can ensure that developers and institutions are held responsible for adverse outcomes.
iii) Policies that explicitly tackle social and economic inequities: Affirmative action in the way AI-driven hiring platforms are used or subsidies for AI education programs — can support a more equitable distribution of benefits from AI. Regulatory bodies must not only think globally, but also act on an international level to ensure that low-income countries do not miss out on the more profound impact AI will have.

5.3 Technological Literacy and Education

Building up technological literacy is only a part of the solution, but it can make a huge impact on helping individuals and communities reflectively engage with AI systems. Education and reskilling programs cannot be available only to a limited group; they have to meet the specific existing needs of various target groups.

i) AI-Based Education: Incorporating AI and data science education into school curriculums can prepare the next generation for an AI-based world. In addition to building hardware and software skills, these programs should include ethics and the social implications of AI. Targeted investments should be made in underserved schools, to bridge educational divides and ensure equitable access to AI knowledge.

ii) Reskilling and Workforce Development: As AI revolutionizes different sectors, reskilling programs for workers in danger of losing their jobs is crucial. Such programs provide free or reduced-price training to workers, helping them pivot into other opportunities where AI does not threaten job displacement. Partnerships between governments, tech firms and educational institutions can scale these initiatives so that no one is left behind in the digital economy (Williams, 2024).
iii) Tech Literacy Programs: Community Centers or Local Libraries Community centers and libraries can be a hub for digital literacy training with resources that are accessible to all ages. Localized workshops, mentorship programs can enable residents to use AI tools for entrepreneurship, civic engagement and personal development.

6. CASE STUDIES: SUCCESSFUL AND FAILED ATTEMPTS

To gain insight into the true impact of AI on social justice, it is essential to study tangible examples where inclusiveness has been achieved or compromised by artificial intelligence. In this section, we offer a more comprehensive assessment of case studies that both illustrate AI's game-changing possibilities and its perils.

6.1 Success Stories

The examples highlight the commendable uses of AI to tackle social issues as well as facilitating inclusive growth.

i) Disaster Response and Relief Efforts powered by AI: Earthquake and tsunami prediction in Japan are more accurate with AI-based models (Wang et al., 2023). These models derive early warrings by studying geological data to allow the necessary time for evacuations and saving lives. AI-based drones have also been used for transporting medicines in remote areas after the natural disasters. Additional examples illustrate how AI can be used to strengthen disaster preparedness and response — a global priority area with great potential especially in the most vulnerable communities.

These technologies ensure that the natural disasters do not affect the marginalized populations but recover with Emergency response. But the fair access to such technologies is a difficulty and global endeavors must make certain that low-income nations have an opportunity at technology led catastrophe response also.

ii) Access to Healthcare and Early Disease Diagnosis: AI Powered Diagnostics with Tuberculosis (TB) And Cervical Cancer in India, Diagnostic Treatments in Rural Clinics Using Artificial Intelligence Chest X-ray analysis to detect TB is possible in low resource settings using tools like QXR (An AI Radiology Solution) Likewise, mobile based AI applications in skin diagnosis have become a boon for the underserved communities to access affordable healthcare (Business Standard, 2019).

These AI solutions help in closing the healthcare access gap among remote or low-income people where pare clinicians are lacking. AI solutions seek to create systemic change by democratizing healthcare. Despite the above examples, data privacy issues prevail and there is a risk that more focus on AI will mean less focus on investing in healthcare infrastructure.

iii) Edtech and Personalized Learning Platforms: AI-based platforms like Eneza Education in sub-Saharan Africa allow students in rural areas to access personalized learning using even basic mobile phones (Kizilcec et al., 2021). It is adaptive by design, arranging lessons according to the pace of each student and offering content in numerous languages, contributing to its ability to help those who previously struggled to receive formal learning.

By using educational tools powered by AI that can be more equitable to every community, we may help marginalised communities push for a level playing field in education. But these platforms must be culturally responsive and offered in the language of instruction, and they should not take away from efforts to strengthen formal education systems.

6.2 Failures and Unintended Consequences

The case studies outlined above present circumstances where AI had amplified and perpetuated social injustices, which illustrates that this technology is not always beneficial and needs to be deployed with due caution.

i) Advanced microdata for algorithmic bias in criminal justice systems: The COMPAS risk assessment tool labelled black defendant's as more likely to be juvenile offenders than white defendants despite the grey data implying otherwise. An investigation by ProPublica discovered that the algorithm was biased against Black defendants, who were more likely to be labeled high-risk for reoffending despite having lower rates of proven recidivism than their white counterparts who had been labeled as low-risk (Angwin et al., 2016).

This case highlights the potential of AI to reproduce and even exacerbate existing racial inequalities in the criminal justice system. The opacity of COMPAS algorithms and the ramifications of its application highlight that robust oversight and fair, responsible mechanisms should be integrated into AI systems developed for social sensitive domains.

ii) Surveillance and Facial Recognition From Tech Creators to Solutions, corporate-built facial recognition technology such as that produced by Clearview AI quickly finds its way into the hands of global law enforcement agencies. But many studies have demonstrated that those algorithms misidentify women and people of color more frequently than white men but history shows they are in some cases falsely identified or arrested. Biased facial recognition technology is a threat to civil liberties, particularly for oppressed communities that are already heavily policed and discriminated against. Also deploying these systems with the community will not set the clear informed consent which is also an ethical and human rights violation. For social justice related reasons, cities such as San Francisco have had facial recognition tech bans.

Amazon had built an employment hiring tool, and the algorithm ranked applicant resumes, which gave male candidates an advantage when competing against women. An Amazon AI recruitment tool realized in 2018 that men are better than women for technical jobs as the system trained itself on data from the past and hence was instinctively biased toward males (as tech workplaces have historically been structured like this (The Guardian, 2018). Wage discrimination in hiring algorithms are inherently biased, it will give rise to more discrimination at the workplace this presents the case for needing auditing and mitigation methods to regulate bias in AI applications within employment. companies need to be transparent and make sure that the AI tools are providing equity in addition to diversity for hiring.

7. THE ROLE OF GOVERNMENTS AND INTERNATIONAL BODIES

Governments and international organizations need to cooperate in forming wide regulatory frameworks, ethical standards, and equitable access policies to deal with global challenges that AI brings as well as underpin social justice. In this section, we talk about what these entities need to do.

7.1 International Collaboration for Equitable AI Development

The development of AI knows no borders and requires joint work to ensure that AI works for all humanity.

i) Global Frameworks and Treaties: The UN (United Nations) and the OECD (Organization for Economic Cooperation and Development) have begun their own AI governance conversations. In 2021, the UNESCO Recommendation on the Ethics of Artificial Intelligence outlined a development path for member states to guide state development so that AI technologies promote and protect human rights, peace, and sustainable development. These initiatives push for alignment of countries with global ethical and responsible AI standards (United Nations, 2024).
ii) Barriers in Human Resources: Low and middle-income countries do not have the infrastructure and resources to utilize AI technologies. International entities ought to assist in technology transfers, knowledge-sharing initiatives and capacity-building programs in this regard. Second, attention in global AI research should shift toward problems of interest to developing countries — like increase agricultural productivity and public health.
iii) Tackling Cross Border Issues: Data privacy, cybercrime and AI-based disinformation are all issues which span borders. We need to build regulations together across governments that create standards protecting people while moving innovation forward. This includes treaties and protocols surrounding sharing of datasets that are equitable yet secure.

7.2 Bridging Policy Gaps

Almost every nation is grappling with how to keep long-term civil equity of AI innovation in social justice without restricting and rolling back progress on the advancements of sufficiency.

Inclusive & Ethical National AI Strategies like those being implemented in Canada, and Singapore. These include investing in AI research, supporting startups and setting guidelines for the responsible development of the technology. However, there are still gaps especially related to algorithmic accountability and job displacement.

The heavy-handedness of Big Tech: The level of power and control that Google, Facebook and Microsoft wield needs regulation to fight it. Governments also need to ensure that when these businesses deploy AI technologies with far-reaching effects on the lives of millions, they develop products and services in a transparent and ethical manner. Breaking up monopolies, digital taxes and algorithmic transparency are just a few things that have been suggested recently.

Bottom-Up Policymaking: A form of decision-making that involves civil society groups, labor unions and community organisations. This participatory approach is meant to engage with and ground AI policies in lived experience, and will strengthen public trust in governance of AI.

8. ETHICAL FRAMEWORKS AND AI GOVERNANCE

We need to establish ethical frameworks and governance models to ensure responsible and equitable use of AI technologies. This section explores the major principles and standards which can help guide ethical use of artificial intelligence (Cath, 2018).

8.1 FAT (Fairness, Accountability and Transparency)

FAT (Fairness, Accountability and transparency) regulation is primary principle of Ethical AI. They provide an evaluative framework to examine the social aspects of AI systems and avoid its adverse effects.

i) Unbiasedness: it should not discriminate against human beings because of race, gender, economic class, etc. Fairness requires monitoring training data and developing protocols using fairness-enhancing algorithms; continuous observation of the AI performance is required regularly for the observation. There exist fairness measures such as demographic parity or equal opportunity to assess treatment effect of the AI systems on entities in the protected groups.
ii) Accountability: Users of AI, whether they are developers or organizations, need to also be responsible for the actions taking place on their systems. This entails specifying clear attributions of accountability and enabling redress when harm occur as a result of an AI system. Meta-level accountability frameworks should have ethical audits as alpha, impact assessments that answer beta questions and healthy regulatory oversight to ensure the relevant gamma questions are being answered satisfactorily.
iii) Transparency: Ensuring stakeholders within the organization who are non-experts in AI that it is well understood how the algorithms work or decisions are being made. It implies transparency on usage data; defining the limit of AI models and the reasoning for an automated decision. Hence, explainable AI (XAI) methods that make the outputs of models interpretable are vital for transparency and to gain public acceptance (Ford, 2022).

8.2 Ethical Guidelines and Their Implementation

A great number of agencies and an even greater under the table have made codes of ethics for the ethical use of AI. This section examines these frameworks, in theory and in practice, so let us take a look.

i) IEEE Global Initiative on Ethics of Autonomous and Intelligent Systems: The IEEE published a broad set of ethical guidance, which puts human rights, well-being, and AI alignment with values at the top. These recommendations call for developers to consider the societal effects of their work, along with some additional recommendations such as transparency and accountability and data privacy.
ii) Partnership on AI: Founded by Tech companies and research institutes, Partnership on AI promotes the responsible development of AIs. Its principles promote for fairness, transparency and principle and the organization also promotes research on AI's effect on society.
iii) Implementation Struggles: Even though the number of ethical guidelines is growing year by year, implementation drives to be far more variable. While most companies have a set of ethical principles on paper, very few are actually implemented in reality due to commercial pressures and technical limitations. Solution to this lies within the limits of stronger regulatory frameworks as well as incentives for ethical compliance Introduction: Human lives have become dependent upon algorithmic decision-making in recent years (Gianni et al., 2022).

9. THE PATH FORWARD FOR AI AND SOCIAL JUSTICE

9.1 The Need for Robust Policy and Regulation

AI development and deployment need rules, and those rules are set in large part by governments. The EU's General Data Protection Regulation (GDPR) has served as a global template around data privacy and security, but now the EU plans to roll out an AI Act that seeks to govern various high-risk applications of artificial intelligence by mandating levels of transparency, accountability and human oversight. It represents a useful model for regulating innovation with protections from harm, but will face the challenge of aligning international standards around it (Intersoft Consulting, 2016).

The US, on the other hand has taken a more fragmented approach with differing laws passing state to state. It is said a national approach is needed to stop the government from getting "the equivalent of 50 different states where good faith was confused and manipulated" AI policy also has to be anticipatory instead of reactive (as Professor Ryan Calo, an educator at the University of Washington and thought leader in digital policy ideology puts it; "Legal ethical issues regarding technology must be illuminated prior to flaring up on a societal scale).

Yet another vital piece of the collaboration puzzle on the world stage. There are efforts by organs such as UNESCO or Global Partnership on Artificial Intelligence to build international pacts for ethical AI. This is especially needed for AI technologies that span borders and must be held accountable to human rights principles and social good.

9.2 Community-Led AI and the Importance of Representation

One of the ideas behind AI democratization is to build technologies with community input. Fans of community-oriented AP, such as at DataKind and the Algorithmic Justice League, putting advocacy for those impacted by this tech into AP development. This participatory approach can provide the process for developing more ethical, culturally attuned and impactful AI solutions.

Similarly, a non-profit partner in India Wadhwani AI has collaborated with experts and farmers there to develop pest management AI tools that are protecting crops and livelihoods for communities. So, these AI solutions are co-created with farmers so that they work on real-world problems this proves the power of co-design to ensure that you do not leave anyone behind.

Moreover, building a diverse AI workforce is an urgent priority. Research from the AI Now Institute has shown that under-representation in AI development teams creates blind spots in model design and deployment, often at the expense of marginalized communities. Initiatives like Black in AI and Women in Machine Learning, which aim to encourage diversity in research and practice for the field.

9.3 A Call to Action: Building a More Inclusive AI Future

To ensure that the benefits of AI are shared by everyone, and to prevent a repeat of past mistakes where technology exacerbated inequality and insecurity, governments must legislate and enforce strong regulation while tech companies be encouraged to strive for best ethical AI practices, complemented by civil society watchdogs demanding the rights, interests even urge for individuals who suffer most. Simultaneously, the systems of education must adapt in order to prepare the upcoming generation with skills for thoughtful and inclusive AI development participation.

The stakes are high. The view ability of AI in our everyday lives means that the decisions we make today will decide whether that new advanced right hand becomes a tool toward more social injustices or the giant leap to a more just and equal world. We have the capacity, means and understanding to make sure AI is a force for good for humanity. The question remains whether we have the will to do anything about it (Bhatia, 2024).

AI is neither good nor bad; it is driven by the motives of those who create it. And that together we can reshape the future, ensuring that as we leverage the power of AI we are creating a world where technology uplifts, not marginalizes; empowers, not disenfranchises. We need to act now – an inclusive AI future is not only desirable, but necessary.

10. CONCLUSION

While possessing great potential for positive social progress, AI also represents substantial risk that must be wisely mitigated. For us to ensure inclusive growth, we will have to democratize AI technology so that its benefits will be equitably distributed and no marginalized community becomes a non-responsible for others. Governments, technology companies, civil society and international organizations will need collaboration to create a more equitable AI future This involves spending on inclusive education, investing in transparency, and enabling communities to involve themselves in shaping AI.

AI, is both a great potential and a great threat. With the potential to revolutionize healthcare, education, environmental protection, and economic opportunities, it is equally capable of widening existing social and economic divides without intentional and ethical deployment. It falls to a diverse group of stake holder's governments, businesses, civil society and communities to make sure that AI is put in the service of inclusive growth rather than a tool for widening divides.

REFERENCES

Anderson, J., & Rainie, L. (2018, December 10). *Artificial Intelligence and the Future of Humans*. Pew Research Center; Pew Research Center. https://www.pewresearch.org/internet/2018/12/10/artificial-intelligence-and-the-future-of-humans/

Angwin, J., Larson, J., Mattu, S., & Kirchner, L. (2016). *Machine Bias*. ProPublica; ProPublica. https://www.propublica.org/article/machine-bias-risk-assessments-in-criminal-sentencing

Bhatia, M. (2024, September 21). *Building A More Inclusive Future With Technology*. Outlook Business; Outlook Business. https://www.outlookbusiness.com/planet/opinions/building-a-more-inclusive-future-with-technology

Bhuptani, R. (2024, June 10). *The Impact of Artificial Intelligence on Every Aspect of Life: What Does AI Really Want?* Avidclan Technologies; Avidclan Technologies. https://www.avidclan.com/blog/the-impact-of-artificial-intelligence-on-every-aspect-of-life-what-does-ai-really-want/

Buccella, A. (2022). "AI for all" is a matter of social justice. *AI and Ethics, 3*, pages 1143–1152, (2023). DOI: 10.1007/s43681-022-00222-z

Business Standard. (2019, March 26). *IIT-Delhi researchers develop AI-based detector for malaria, TB, cervical cancer*. @Bsindia; Business Standard. https://www.business-standard.com/article/pti-stories/iit-delhi-researchers-develop-ai-based-detector-for-malaria-tb-cervical-cancer-119032600719_1.html

Cath, C. (2018). Governing artificial intelligence: Ethical, legal and technical opportunities and challenges. *Philosophical Transactions. Series A, Mathematical, Physical, and Engineering Sciences*, 376(2133), 20180080. Advance online publication. DOI: 10.1098/rsta.2018.0080 PMID: 30322996

Continual Engine Team. (2023, October 20). *AI-Powered Accessibility: Bridging The Digital Divide - Continual Engine*. Continual Engine; Continual Engine. https://www.continualengine.com/blog/ai-powered-accessibility-bridging-the-digital-divide/

De Freitas, J., Agarwal, S., Schmitt, B., & Haslam, N. (2023). Psychological factors underlying attitudes toward AI tools. *Nature Human Behaviour*, 7(11), 1845–1854. DOI: 10.1038/s41562-023-01734-2 PMID: 37985913

Dorocka, W. (2024, September 25). *How AI is improving diagnostics and health outcomes*. World Economic Forum; World Economic Forum. https://www.weforum.org/stories/2024/09/ai-diagnostics-health-outcomes/

Dunavete, A. (2024, May 8). *AI in Workplace Technology: Improving Productivity with Chatbots and Virtual Assistants*. Yarooms.com; YAROOMS International. https://www.yarooms.com/blog/ai-in-workplace-technology

Ford, J. (2022). Ethical AI frameworks: the missing governance piece. *Regulatory Insights on Artificial Intelligence*, 219–239. DOI: 10.4337/9781800880788.00018

Gianni, R., Lehtinen, S., & Nieminen, M. (2022). Governance of Responsible AI: From Ethical Guidelines to Cooperative Policies. *Frontiers of Computer Science*, 4, 873437. Advance online publication. DOI: 10.3389/fcomp.2022.873437

Godulla, A. (2020). Andreas Sudmann (Hg.): The Democratization of Artificial Intelligence. Net Politics in the Era of Learning Algorithms. *Communicatio Socialis, 53*(4), 552–553. DOI: 10.5771/0010-3497-2020-4-552

Hunter, S., Tjondronegoro, D., & Trojan, B. (2024, April 17). *Artificial intelligence: A new driver for inclusive growth and development?* Asia Pathways; Asia Pathways. https://www.asiapathways-adbi.org/2024/04/artificial-intelligence-a-new-driver-for-inclusive-growth-and-development/

International Monetary Fund. (2024). Advances in Artificial Intelligence: Implications for Capital Market Activities. *IMF ELibrary*. https://doi.org/DOI: 10.5089/9798400277573.082.CH003

Intersoft Consulting. (2016). *General data protection regulation (GDPR)*. General Data Protection Regulation (GDPR); European Union. https://gdpr-info.eu/

Kizilcec, R. F., Chen, M., Jasińska, K. K., Madaio, M., & Ogan, A. (2021). Mobile Learning During School Disruptions in Sub-Saharan Africa. *AERA Open*, 7, 233285842110148. DOI: 10.1177/23328584211014860

Köbis, N., Starke, C., & Rahwan, I. (2022). The promise and perils of using artificial intelligence to fight corruption. *Nature Machine Intelligence*, 4(5), 418–424. DOI: 10.1038/s42256-022-00489-1

Lowa, M. (2024). Democratizing Access to Education: AI-Driven Solutions for Inclusive Learning in Malaysia. *Social Science Research Network*. DOI: 10.2139/ssrn.4813758

Mondal, H., & Mondal, S. (2024). Ethical and social issues related to AI in healthcare. *Methods in Microbiology*, 55, 247–281. DOI: 10.1016/bs.mim.2024.05.009

Rafanelli, L. M. (2022). Justice, injustice, and artificial intelligence: Lessons from political theory and philosophy. *Big Data & Society*, 9(1), 205395172210806. DOI: 10.1177/20539517221080676

Rodrigues, R. (2020). Legal and Human Rights Issues of AI: Gaps, Challenges and Vulnerabilities. *Journal of Responsible Technology, 4*(100005). ScienceDirect. DOI: 10.1016/j.jrt.2020.100005

The Economic Times. (2023, March 15). How Artificial intelligence is changing your life unknowingly. *The Economic Times*. https://economictimes.indiatimes.com/news/how-to/how-artificial-intelligence-is-changing-your-life-unknowingly/articleshow/98455922.cms?from=mdr

The Guardian. (2018, October 11). *Amazon Ditched AI Recruiting Tool That Favored Men for Technical Jobs*. The Guardian; The Guardian. https://www.theguardian.com/technology/2018/oct/10/amazon-hiring-ai-gender-bias-recruiting-engine

United Nations. (2024, May 14). *Governing artificial intelligence for all | Public Institutions*. Un.org; United Nation. https://publicadministration.desa.un.org/blog/governing-artificial-intelligence-all

Wang, Y., Imai, K., Miyashita, T., Ariyoshi, K., Takahashi, N., & Satake, K. (2023). Coastal tsunami prediction in Tohoku region, Japan, based on S-net observations using artificial neural network. *Earth, Planets, and Space*, 75(1), 154. Advance online publication. DOI: 10.1186/s40623-023-01912-6

Williams, R. (2024). Impact.AI: Democratizing AI through K-12 Artificial Intelligence Education. *Handle.net*. https://hdl.handle.net/1721.1/153676

Chapter 10
A Framework for Detection of Hate Speech in Social Media: Achieving Societal Resilience

Nitish Kumar Ojha
https://orcid.org/0000-0002-2236-0766
Amity University, Noida, India

Abhishek Vaish
Indian Institute of Information Technology, Allahabad, India

Shreyansh Dwivedi
Indian Institute of Information Technology, Allahabad, India

Brijesh Kumar Markandey
Indian Institute of Information Technology, Allahabad, India

Rania El-Gazzar
University of South-Eastern Norway, Norway

ABSTRACT

The authenticity and the orientation of information in social media require designing a complex information system to analyze the artifacts that may cause a positive or negative impact on the peace order of the global societal structure. Social cyber security is a new paradigm that is gaining momentum worldwide; every country is investing in capacity-building measures, R&D, and strategies to combat the menace of the problem caused by the abundance of manipulative information. Societal cyber security has become a multi-million-dollar market because economic change

DOI: 10.4018/979-8-3693-9904-0.ch010

has monetized data, and it is a top priority for every government to ensure that the digital society is secure and safe. Therefore, it is pertinent to find a framework that can help detect information that can negatively impact society at large. In this paper, we are using machine learning techniques for classification in a fusion dataset of manipulative information that has been concatenated with the benchmark dataset. The subclasses are real news without hate speech, real news with hate speech, fake news with hate speech, and fake news without hate speech. The application of this framework is to be used to mitigate the threat to society through the widespread use of manipulative information and help society to be resilient against such threats.

1 INTRODUCTION

Society is embracing the Digital infrastructure in its day-to-day activities with more positive outcomes. The dependence on information by individuals is increasing, this change has led to the shift to new emerging trends of cyber-attacks. Traditionally the sophistication of cyber-attacks was based on evolving techniques to target the technical systems causing loss and damage to ICT infrastructure but now the damages are more oriented towards damaging the social structure without compromising the technical system. The motive behind this shift could be linked with the abundance of information available, the ease of generating manipulative information & its widespread propagation, the potential of high-magnitude loss, and high valued stakeholders. In 2007, Estonia was at a standstill, fifty-eight websites were offline at once, an outrageous act that is linked with the disputed relocation of the Soviet-era Brownz Soldier monument. Though this has increased the preparedness level of Estonia but was seen as a whistle-blower to the international community to understand the ramifications of it and to bootstrap the efforts of preparing them for such innovative methods of invasive and non-invasive methods of technological destruction. Cyberspace has been used as a platform for crime against society, and the variety of such crimes is enormous from individual to group, from Organization to Government. Every stakeholder is a victim, and the impact is quite diverse. The recent trend of crime is the use of social media platforms as a launching pad against the Government in different forms e.g. destabilizing the law & order, Narratives against the government, using it to steal classified information about the nation, etc. Information in Cyberspace is witnessing exponential growth and monitoring the correctness of the information is practically not possible. The ease of publishing or uploading information in social media has not only led to the growth of the creation of digital content but has also led to the increase of manipulative content like fake news, content of hatred, and other disturbing content that harms society at large. It has been observed that one of the reasons for the successful operation of large-scale social media was the ease of spreading manipulative information to polarize the sentiments of society. Some of the examples are:

Delhi Riots in India (2020), Capitol Hill Riots in US (2021). Manipulative content amplifies the magnitude of the problem. For example, In India to protest against the Citizen Amendment Act,2019 a group of members were circulating varieties of fake news full of hate speech that has become the reason for violence. A few lines taken from such a message will give a better understanding "The government proposed a new bill in parliament meant to throw these big*ts out of the country and send them back to where they belong". (Carley et al.). As it can be seen the statement made is trying to portray that the government has passed a bill that will expel a group of people from the country. However, this is misleading information, thus fake news. Moreover, along with a bogus claim, the subject is deliberately attacking that particular group of people by calling them 'big*ts', thus hate speech as well.

Detection of fake news and hate speech has been an emerging research zone for the last few years which has been picking up interest. Even though the issue of fake news and hate speech has been there for a long time, the classification of fake news with hate speech is a complex scientific problem as there is no standard and universally accepted definition of fake news and hate speech. The classification of both fake news and hate speech depends on the perspective of every individual, which can be different. The objective of this research is to create a machine learning-based classification framework on the fusion of a benchmark dataset of tweets, the technical challenge in fusion is that it increases the randomness and diversity in the new dataset and therefore requires a secondary qualitative validation of the result. In our case, we have used the BEND framework as a qualitative metric to validate the outcome of the ML classifier to ensure the practicality of the proposed detection framework.

LITERATURE REVIEW

The literature review of this research is quite diverse. In order to reach the Epicenter of the research gap it is necessary to look into various subdomains. The major concentration of the review is to understand the impact of manipulative news in destabilizing the social order, use of hate speech to spread hatred, use of ML, AI, NLP, and Software tools that have been used to mitigate either Fake news or Hate speech in the web environment, The correlation between manipulative content and in virality of information, metrics to measure the impact, Multimodal systems for detection of it and to explore the past work in fusion dataset.

A Framework to Measure Manipulative Content

In the paper (Carley et al.) the author has defined a new phenomenon namely social cyber security. Social cyber security differs from traditional cyber security and is targeted to hack humans and control society at large instead of hacking the information system. In light of this, it can be inferred that technologies which are having the capability to propagate fake news and manipulative messages to such a level that individual rational thinking is compromised and forced to believe what is being posted. The author has also proposed a concept of maneuver of information and network, which is a target object by the actors, used for facilitating social cyber-attacks using existing technologies and mapped it by a model which is known as the Bend model to explain the orientation of its polarization based on the positive and negative impact on information or network. They also point to the need for new tools to detect disinformation, bots, trolls, cyborgs, and memes, among other things. Finally, they emphasize the need for new ideas to explain how influence manifests itself through social media. A transdisciplinary theory such as the BEND framework is an example. Influence campaigns, according to the BEND framework, are a set of narrative and structural manipulations carried out by one or more actors in the cyber environment to affect topic-oriented communities and the positions of actors inside them.

In the paper (Hatch et. al.), it can be seen that cyber weapons can be classified as weapons for mass destruction, the mapping of a factor of mass destruction with a cyber weapon is a good contribution it further adds the US position on the possibility of cyber-attack by state or non-state actor and defines an Attribution Based Deterrence policy as a national cyber security strategy. Further, the need for a metric to measure the threshold of destructive effect is a need and welcoming step and is defined in a general sense as a cyber-attack has a destructive impact on life, property, or lasting economic disruption. One more dimension of the problem under discussion is to see cyber-crime as a business model representing an economic incentive (Huang et al). In other words, cybercrime has evolved as a platform for individuals with some kind of wide spectrum of incentives. If we interpret the magnitude of the problem in monetary units it is evident that by 2021 it will grow to US $ 6 trillion.

Hate Speech Detection: Challenges and Solutions

The difficulties that automatic hate speech identification algorithms face in text-based data are identified and examined (Huang et. al.). Hate speech is defined as “abusive or threatening speech or writing that expresses prejudice against a particular group, especially based on race, religion, or sexual orientation,” but it's important to distinguish between communication that expresses or advocates views but does not call for action, or is abusive or insulting but not threatening, and expresses dislike of a group but does not incite discrimination in a way that can be regulated. Further on, the issue of data availability for training and testing is an open-ended problem in this area. In addition, compared to neural techniques, this work provided a multi-view SVM strategy they use here because mSVM reduces the large dimensionality problem. This mSVM achieves close to the best-in-class implementation while producing more simply interpretable options. They qualitatively analyze the mSVM classifier's false positive (FP) and false negative (FN) samples on the Stormfront dataset to acquire a better understanding of its errors. Hate speech is detected with 80% accuracy using this mSVM model. The shifting sentiments about issues through time and in historical context is a barrier for autonomous hate speech detection systems. Some contexts are hateful for someone but the same context is not hateful for others. In (Lohani et al.) Social media platforms make it easier to share information while also improving online interaction, better connections, and more online social engagements. At the same time, people are subject to misinformation and manipulated content being transmitted through the channels by bad actors. The regulatory problems that these platforms face, as well as their answers, have been explored in this study. Some of the measures proposed are Identification, Disallow Proliferation, and Issue interaction warnings. A Pew study conducted in 2018 shows 59% of teenagers have been bullied or harassed online with 90% of the teens believing that online bullying is a serious problem affecting people of their age (PewResearch, 2018b). Fake news and hate speech pose a threat to the democratic ecosystem if they continue to spread at their current rate. In this, they didn't make a system to detect the problem. Hate speech and online bullying are particularly problematic among young children, according to (Ananthakrishnan et al.). The study details children's reactions to nasty speech broadcast by young children aiming to build large followings on the digital content-sharing site YouTube. It can be inferred that teenagers are drivers to spread content. Cyberbullying and online harassment have become more common in recent years, and they can have long-term effects on victims' mental health. They demonstrate how the presence of hate speech in online interactions might lead to more hate speech. They study the factors influencing the virality of hate speech using a huge dataset of around 31 million comments from child content makers on YouTube. There are two drivers in which platforms approach this problem: Identification of comments that violate the platform policy around hate speech and enforcement of policies post identification. On YouTube, we found considerable evidence of virality in hate speech. The future scope of this work is to figure out how to limit virality from affecting teenagers. The goal of this study is to look at the knowledge structure of hate speech literature and how related themes have developed. They employ co-word analysis algorithms to detect various themes handled in the field. In contrast to earlier research, which was created as a qualitative literature review, this study offers a more comprehensive and quantitative examination of online hate speech publications. This study's database was compiled from Scopus and focused on a few papers published in the recent thirty years. The intersection of online hate studies and hate-speech automatic detection and classification systems emphasizes how the problem of hate spreading should be researched not only from a social but also from a computer science perspective. Our research thoroughly sorted significant foreign studies, resulting in a visual examination of 1614 articles published in the Scopus database and a large amount of empirical data and information. Finally, future research should focus on methods that can successfully combat online hate speech.

Detection of Hate Speech and Fake News Separately

In (wy et al.), the authors have defined hate speech as "a deliberate attack, directed towards a specific group of people, and motivated by actual or perceived aspects that form the group's identity" (Martens et al.) the used classification of tweets containing hate speech. The contribution is the chances that racist and homophobic tweets are classified as hate speech are more than that of sexist tweets. These sexist tweets are generally classified as a second category i.e., offensive. Also, it is the most difficult task to classify tweets without any hate words from the corpus obtained. Paper (Davidson et al.) offered a similar classification as racist, sexist, or neither racist nor sexist. The complexity of the natural language structures posed a significant hurdle in this task. To deal with this complication, several deep learning architectures were used to train semantic word embeddings in a series of exhaustive trials. The experiments were performed on a novel dataset having 16,000 annotated tweets. The results indicate that these kinds of deep learning techniques surpass the best-in-class n-gram methods by almost 18 F1 points. Hater-Net, an intelligent system for the identification and analysis of hate speech on Twitter, is presented in Paper (Camacho et al.), which was developed in partnership with the Spanish National Office Against Hate Crimes. The study made several advancements to the field of hate speech identification on Twitter. Firstly, it introduced the first intelligent system that tracks and anticipates hate speech in social media using SNA. Secondly, this research introduced a benchmark dataset on hate speech based in the Spanish language. It consisted of 6k tweets which were labeled via experts. Thirdly, this research also compared several classification approaches. The best results were obtained by using the union of the LTSM+MLP neural network which provides an AUC (area under curve) of 0.828 with the newly created dataset. This outcome was better than the outcomes obtained from methods mentioned previously in the research (Ranjan et al.), authors developed an online hate content classifier for multiple platforms. Even though hatred is a cross-platform issue, no models for detecting hate content utilizing data from different platforms have been developed. The authors gathered 197,566 comments from four different platforms to fill this study gap: Wikipedia, Reddit, YouTube, and Twitter. Eighty percent of the remarks were deemed non-hateful, while the remaining twenty percent were deemed hateful. The authors then conducted experiments using several categorization techniques.

Hate Speech Detection Using Fusion Approach

The fusion of information is the essence of manipulative content creation. The degree of such fusion varies and the number of feature vectors from classification and ML approach perceptive also plays an important role in the detection rate of any framework. Therefore, this section of the literature review will explore the advancements and shortcomings. Multiclass classifiers approach proof to give better results in such scenarios. Logistic Regression, Random Forest, and Support Vector Machine are some of the classifiers available. They extracted characteristics using deep learning, which they coupled with additional syntactic and n-gram features before training and predicting with a simple baseline classifier (SVM, LR, RF). Even though all of the given methods produce good results, the best of them all is "CNN + Glove Embedding + Baseline Features + Logistic Regression," which has a precision of 0.984. Feature fusion and classification algorithms are the technologies used in this research article. In (Aldwairi et al.) the researchers have introduced a new dataset of hate speech based on the Spanish language and have collected it from Twitter handlers. A novel technique of prediction of hate speech is introduced using 6k of labeled tweets by the experts. The best results were obtained by using the union of the LTSM+MLP neural network which provides an AUC of 0.828 with the newly created dataset. This outcome was better than the outcomes obtained from methods mentioned previously in the research. In (Khan et al.), According to this study, hate speech was split not only into the HS and Non-HS categories (hate speech and non-hate speech), but also into particular classifications. In 17 percent of studies, hate speech is classified as HS / Offensive but Non-HS / Clean. SVM, Nave Bayes, LSTM, and CNN are the algorithms employed. The Killer NLP method optimizes the ensemble deep learning approach KNLPEDNN (Accuracy, precision, and recall) and CNN (F-Score) methodologies to achieve the best results. The strategy utilized, however, does not guarantee that the categorization system will perform well. This is supported by two studies that found the CNN algorithm to be ineffective. The dataset, features chosen, number of classes, and mutually exclusive classes all influence the performance of a hate speech detection classification system. A good dataset, on the other hand, yields superior outcomes.

In the paper (Putri et al.), the author has created an installable tool that is embedded with a classification algorithm using a regression classifier with an accuracy of 99.4%. The work is used to detect the websites that are spreading fake news and propaganda. In paper (Calderón et al.), the focus of the authors was on the automatic detection of fake content in online news. This research has a two-fold contribution in the field of fake news detection. Firstly, two different benchmark datasets i.e., FakenewsAMT with 31990 words, an average of 132 words and 5 sentences approximately, collected 100 articles each of fake news and real news in the celebrity domain. The average of the final fake news dataset was 399 words and 17 sentences per article of the real news dataset has an average of 709 words and 33 sentences per article. These datasets covered seven diverse news areas i.e., Technology, Education, Business, Sports, Politics, Entertainment, and Celebrity. The research describes the collection, annotation, and validation process exhaustively. It also presents several experimental analyses on the identification of semantic or lingual differences in fake and authentic news content. Secondly, several experiments were carried out to build precise fake news detectors.

As a result of this use of logistic regression, we can classify the article/speech, which will aid us in identifying and dealing with such materials. They'll train a model to classify bogus news stories using a natural language processing technique called TF-IDF (term frequency-inverse document frequency) vectorization, which tells us how important each keyword is in the news story or speech. To improve accuracy, use data mining with a large dataset to detect bogus news and hate speeches. XGBoost has an accuracy of 0.82. As a result, the model labelled 18 percent of the data as hateful or offensive, although it should have been classified as clean.

Virality

In a paper (Martens et al.), the authors have tried to provide an answer to conceivable abuse of online social media and their effects on society. A model has been proposed by the authors to estimate the assaults subject to the underlying virality of data on the internet.

In (Ahmed et al.), the author has surveyed to highlight that a motivated religious political group has used social media to spread content of hatred among the similar and non-similar groups of religious beliefs. Though the respondents were limited in number, it can be inferred that social media is a lucrative medium to spread such contents and also target a specific section of society. In (Davidson et al.), Berger and Luckman's social construction theory was used to validate the concept of an online social network and show how Facebook has been utilized as a weapon to win each other's pairings and bring down opponents from the partners they support. In, This paper introduced a survey that examined the assessments of citizens who are both the makers and the collectors of fake or hateful content present on the internet, utilizing social network analysis (SNA). With the features connected with these accounts, it may be of great interest to learn who is behind the propagation of bogus information supporting hate speech against migrants and refugees, as well as what measures would be most effective in combating it. Further investigation of these clusters could have practical relevance in the battle against the spread of harmful materials, both academically and for governmental institutions or NGOs. This paper concentrated on the spread of such content in social media how it is received and also how much the citizens believe them. The European Commission made certain actions in January 2018 to combat fake news and disinformation distributed online, including forming a committee of specialists to assist with policy proposals. Fake news or disinformation, according to the final report of the High-Level Expert Group on Fake News and Online Disinformation, is false, inaccurate, or misleading information that is prepared, published, and pushed with the goal of causing public harm or profit ((Putri et al.)).

In the paper (Davidson et al.)), the authors have tried to provide an answer to conceivable abuse of online social media and their effects on society. A model has been proposed by the authors to estimate the assaults subject to the underlying virality of data on the internet.

The Proposed Framework

It is quite evident that the risk of combining the features of fake news and hate content is lethal and the research is also at a very nascent stage therefore the attempt to investigate a technique based on the dataset that has the features of both the domains would be interesting to explore. In our solution, we have proposed a new dataset combining the various benchmark datasets available for fake news and hate speech individually. The detection performed on the newly formed dataset, using Machine Learning approaches shows promising outcomes. Finally, the validation of the result using BEND Framework to cross-check the classification with human intelligence using a manually random sampling technique.

In the following Figure -1, for the detection of fake news with hate speech, we first need a benchmark dataset on which we can train our classifiers and then classification can be done.

Figure 1. High-Level Data Flow Diagram of the proposed system

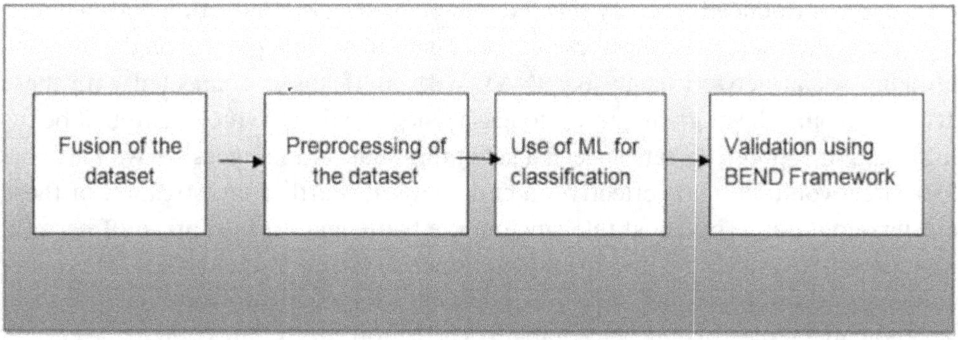

Currently, there is no such dataset available. So, we need to create one. Once the dataset is created, we need to apply some preprocessing on it to remove of unnecessary characters and words. The next step includes feature extraction in which features are extracted in the form of a matrix.

The next step involves the training and testing of the classifiers. We performed experiments with 4 different machine learning techniques namely Multinomial Naive Bayes, Support Vector Machine (SVM), Logistic Regression, and Random Forest. Finally, we will use BEND Framework which is a Matrix to map the orientation of the corpus of the dataset. The uniqueness of this system is that it combines machine intelligence with human intelligence to model the dataset. The advantage is that it will detect the latent information from the dataset. The building block of the proposed system is presented in Fig 2.

Figure 2. The building block of the system

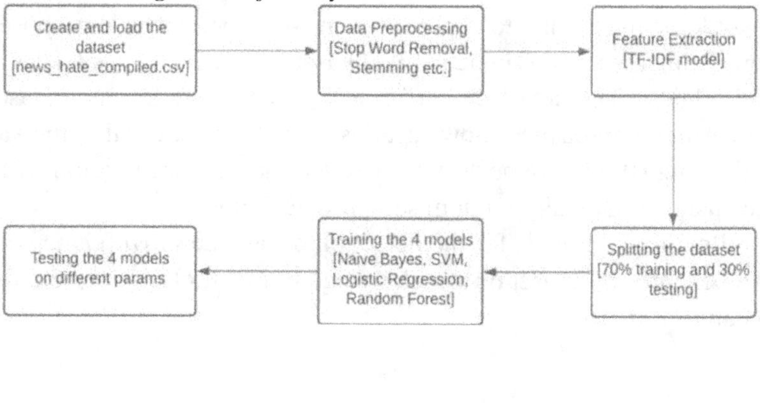

Data Fusion

In the proposed work the uniqueness is to work on a dataset that has fake news and hate speech features. Due to the non-availability of such a dataset, we have concatenated almost 3k fake news with 13k fake news already present in the dataset, to achieve 16k fake news. An almost equal number of genuine news was merged with the dataset to get 16,006 fake news and 15,712 real news. For hate speech, the dataset which was published in the paper. These tweets are classified as hate speech, offensive language, and neither. For our research, hate speech and offensive labels were merged as one. Then an almost equal amount of non-hate speech data is concatenated to obtain 15,289 hate speech tweets and 16,429 non-hate speech tweets. These newly obtained datasets were concatenated horizontally to obtain our dataset of fake news with hate speech having 31,718 text articles. This dataset was classified into four classes -

Class 0: Fake news with hate speech (8261)
Class 1: Fake news without hate speech (8245)
Class 2: Real news with hate speech (7735)
Class 3: Real news without hate speech (7467)

Figure 3. A flowchart for dataset creation

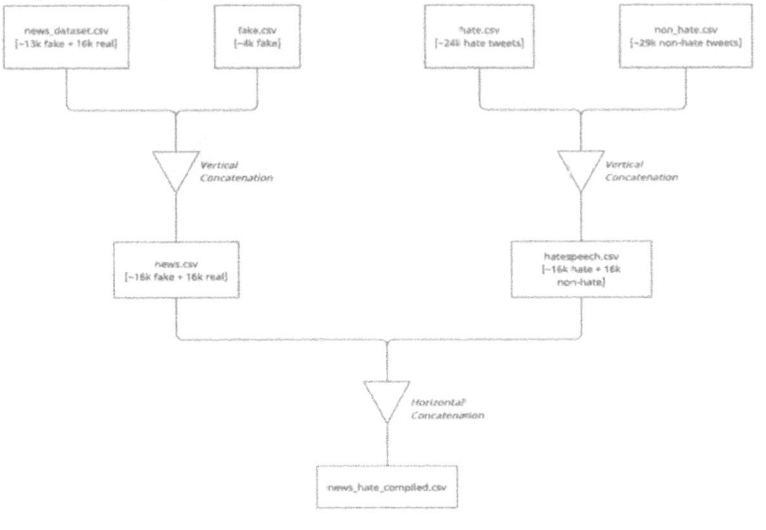

Data Preprocessing and Feature Extraction

The removal of irrelevant words or information will lead to a significant decrease in the size of the document. The two major steps of our dataset preprocessing are Stop word Removal and Stemming. All the text articles of the dataset will be first converted to lowercase and then stop words, extra whitespaces, Twitter hashtags, mentions, URLs etc. will be removed from the content of the dataset. We then perform stemming on each word and reduce it to its base or root form. Feature extraction aims to reduce the dimensionality of the dataset. Bag of Words (BoW) approach and second being the Term Frequency-Inverse Document Frequency (TF-IDF) approach.

Once we obtained the count matrix using the BoW approach, we applied TfidfTrans- former on it to transform a count matrix to a normalized tf-idf representation, to allocate weightage to the terms that might be more significant.

Figure 4. Pie-Chart Signifying the Dataset Distribution

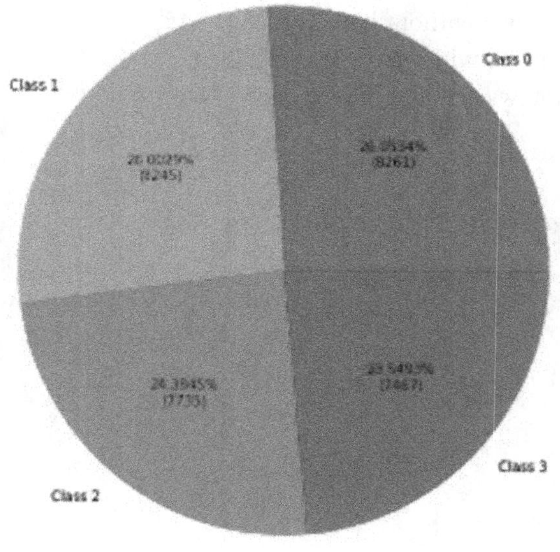

Figure 5. Random 5 elements from the dataset

	tweet	label
32846	Muslims BUSTED: They Stole Millions In Gov't B...	1
15062	Re: Why Did Attorney General Loretta Lynch Ple...	1
48348	BREAKING: Weiner Cooperating With FBI On Hilla...	0
45321	PIN DROP SPEECH BY FATHER OF DAUGHTER Kidnappe...	1
2954	FANTASTIC! TRUMP'S 7 POINT PLAN To Reform Heal...	0

The Term Frequency-Inverse Document Frequency (TF-IDF) is a weighting metric to measure the importance of a particular term in a document of a dataset. A term with high document frequency, and low corpus frequency i.e. word is frequent in a document and is rare in the whole document; has a higher TF-IDF score using eq 1. This feature matrix is created out of the 2000 most frequent words across the dataset. When building the vocabulary, we ignored terms that have a document frequency strictly lower than 3 and that have a document frequency strictly higher than 60% of the total count of words in the document.

tf-idf(t, d, D) = tf(t, D) * idf(d, D) (1)

Classification

The models that are commonly used in text categorization are Naive Bayes, Support Vector Machine, Logistic Regression, and Random Forest Classifier. The probabilities labeled by Naive Bayes models are straightforward with the hypothesis of strong independence between the features. Support Vector Machines and Logistic Regression are linear classifiers. The prediction of classes by both of them is based on the union of scores for each feature. Random Forest performs classification by making a large number of decision trees at training time and provides the class which is either the mean or mode of the prediction of the individual trees as the output.

Bayes' Theorem

P(A|B) = (P(A) * P(B|A))/P(B) (2)

Given a dataset yi, xi1, xi2, xip(i=1 to n) of n statistical units,

Logistic Regression Mathematical Model

$$y_i = \beta_0 + \beta_1 x_{i1} + \beta_2 x_{i2} + \ldots + \beta_p x_{ip} + \epsilon_i,\ i = 1,\ldots,n \quad (3)$$

Random Forest Scikit Implementation

$$n_{ij} = w_j C_j - w_{left(j)} C_{left(j)} - w_{right(j)} C_{right(j)} \quad (4)$$

Our main inspiration to use these four classifiers is paper (Carley, 2020) "Detecting opinion spams and fake news using text classification"

These models are implemented using sci-kit open-source library of Python

Sample code Snippet for Multinomial Naive Bayes

```
from sklearn.naive_bayes import MultinomialNB
# training the model
nb = MultinomialNB() nb.fit(X_train, Y_train)
# testing the model
y_pred = nb.predict(X_test)
cf_matrix=confusion_matrix(y_pred, Y_test) make_confusion_matrix(cf_matrix, figsize=(8,6), cbar=False)
```

Results and Analysis

The outcome of each approach is assessed using the accuracy and F1 score. Currently, there are no defined standards around the globe regarding the evaluation metrics to be used. However, in general it is believed that focusing on both accuracy and macro-F1 provides better intuition about the robustness and short- comings of every approach. We can see the accuracy dropped as we increased the max feature size and n-gram size. Max feature size doesn't have much effect on the accuracy here but change in n-gram affects the accuracy drastically. This is true for all the classifiers. As it is quite evident in table 1 that Random Forest is the most optimized machine learning technique in this context. As the Random Forest algorithm searches randomness instead of feature, this can also be interpreted that the fusion dataset has a high degree of diversity.

It is pertinent to highlight here that the accuracy of the classifier is not directly correlated with n-gram features. One assumption for such observation could be that the words with positive or negative emotional arousal are less dependent on adjoining words. Therefore, in designing such a system one should carefully look at the single words or uni-grams. The terms having document frequency higher than

2000 are ignored in this classification. As we can see the accuracy dropped as we increased the max feature size and n-gram size. Max feature size doesn't have much effect on the accuracy here.

Table 1. Best results obtained by the four classifiers

Classifier	Accuracy (%)	F1-Score	Precision	Recall
Multinomial Naive Bayes	58.26	0.57	0.60	0.68
SVM	70.41	0.70	0.71	0.70
Logistic Regression	70.40	0.70	0.71	0.70
Random Forest	74.40	0.74	0.76	0.74

Table 2. Accuracy (in %) of the four classifiers for different n-gram size and features size

TF-IDF				
Classifier	**n-gram size**	**2000**	**10000**	**15000**
M. Naive Bayes	unigram	58.26	56.84	56.12
	bigram	47.28	49.68	50.17
	trigram	40.71	45.13	45.76
SVM	unigram	70.41	69.87	70.21
	bigram	48.79	50.15	51.96
	trigram	41.62	43.07	44.48
Logistic Regression	unigram	70.35	69.87	70.40
	bigram	49.01	51.02	52.07
	trigram	42.28	44.57	45.07
Random Forest	unigram	74.40	72.13	72.36
	bigram	48.27	50.09	52.23
	trigram	41.64	43.48	44.71

Figure 6. Confusion Matrix for all the four classifiers

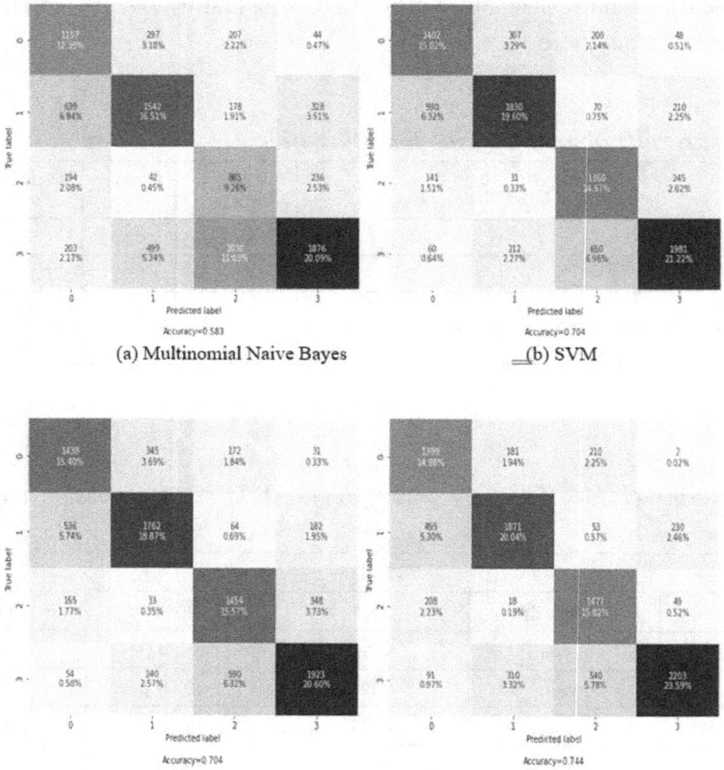

(a) Multinomial Naive Bayes

(b) SVM

From the results obtained in our experiments, the Random Forest classifier achieved better results than other classifiers with an accuracy of 74%. The number of estimators used in this classifier is 1000. Logistic Regression achieved an accuracy of approximately 71%. The value of C (inverse of regularization) is 6 and the number of maximum iterations is 1000 for this classifier. SVM achieved an accuracy of approximately 71% and Multinomial Naive Bayes achieved an accuracy of approximately 59%. As we can see from table 2, the accuracy dropped as we increased n-gram size. Max feature size doesn't have much effect on the accuracy here but change in n-gram affects the accuracy drastically. This is applicable to all the four classifiers.

Validation and Verification

One of the uniqueness of our research work was to validate the outcome of the ML technique with the only framework available in Social Cyber Security. The advantage of such validation was to ensure and understand the content and its latent meaning with human intelligence and its corresponding ML Classification. We have taken random samples from each class and mapped it with the BEND Framework.

Figure 7. Validation of positive subclass with BEND Framework

BEND Framework Class	Sub Class	Mapping of our Proposed Class	Example of string for each subclass.
Positive	**Engage** - Messages that bring up a related but relevant topic	Class 3 : Real news without hate speech	1. Muhammad Ali Evolved From a Blockbuster Fighter to a Country's Conscience 2. Firebombs and Accusations Fly in 'Ruthless' Election Campaigns in Mexico
	Explain - Messages that provides details on or elaborate the topic	Class 3 : Real news without hate speech	1. Prince, the songwriter, singer, producer, studio band and consummate showman, died on Thursday at his home, Paisley Park 2. A bomb exploded on a bus in Jerusalem on Monday, wounding about 21
	Excite - messages that elicit a positive emotion such as joy or excitement	Class 3 : Real news without hate speech	1. 20 Wines for Under $20: The Fall Edition - The New York Times 2. No Rainbow, but Thief Finds a Bucket of Gold on West 48th Street
	Enhance - Messages that encourage the topic-group to continue with the topic	Class 3 : Real news without hate speech	1. Google and Facebook Take Aim at Fake News Sites 2. U.S. Will Ban Smoking in Public Housing Nationwide

Figure 8. Validation of negative subclass with BEND Framework

BEND Framework Class	Sub Class	Mapping of our Proposed Class	Example of string for each subclass.
Negative	**Dismiss** - Messages about why the topic is not important	Class 1 : Fake news without hate speech Class 2 : Real news with hate speech	**1.** They Stole Millions In Govt Benefits. They should pay all the back all the money plus interest **2.** These 23 Hollywood Celebs Threatened To Leave The U.S
	Distort – Messages that alter the main message of the topic	Class 1 : Fake news without hate speech	**1.** YIKES! HILLARY GOES OFF THE RAILS **2.** Kids being made to vote for President in School
	Dismay - Messages that elicit a negative emotion such as sadness or anger	Class 0 : Fake news with hate speech Class 2 : Real news with hate speech	**1.** Protester interrupts Hillary Clinton shouting "Bill Clinton is a rapist." **2.** B*tch Hillary Clinton Wants a Strong Russia
	Distract - Discussion about a totally different topic and irrelevant	Class 1 : Fake news without hate speech	**1.** Who Is Peter Kadzik? The Clinton Ally and John Podesta's Very Close Friend Peter Kadzik Who Will Take Charge of DoJ's Hillary Clinton and Huma Abedin Email ProbeSource: 70News **2.** FBI Reopens Hillary Email Probe: Why Did It Take So Long?

DISCUSSION AND CONCLUSION

The idea behind this research was to design a framework for mitigation of social cyber security risk. The menace of disinformation has touched every individual in their day-to-day living. Machine learning based techniques both supervised and unsupervised are very potential directions in this context. Data fusion increases a lot of noise and sparsity in the dataset. Therefore, pre-processing of the data and then feature extraction method like TF-IDF is proved to be beneficial. This is quite evident due to the fact that increasing the feature vector is not dependent on the accuracy of the classifier. Random Forest method is giving high accuracy out of the other three techniques used in this research. The assumption could be that in highly diverse data with high randomness instead of harvesting feature vectors from the dataset if the feature of randomness is calculated the performance of the classifier will be good and this is exactly why Random Forest is giving better results. The other aspect which is pertinent to be discussed is the validation of the result with in a qualitative metrics i.e., BEND Framework. The advantage of this validation is that human intelligence-based experts have better visibility and its practicality.

Finally, it is concluded that societal resilience is the need of the hour in the information age. The new form of cyber-attack has the potential to cause harm that can be compared to mass destruction. The proposed framework is an attempt to highlight the ill effects of disinformation and also to create an ML-based framework that can classify the information in various sub-classes. Though we have achieved the maximum accuracy of 74.4% with the self-created dataset however, it is a notable achievement because the classification of disinformation in different sub-classes is still a challenging scientific problem. We have validated the results with the BEND Framework to check the latent meaning of the context with ML classification.

Limitation and Future Work

The challenges faced during our work are:

Limited research to consult: There is not much work on the detection of fake news with hate speech. Few that are present are mere surveys. Individual work on both hate speech detection and fake news detection is present though.

Datasets: The second challenge that we face is that no publicly- available, curated dataset identifies fake news with hateful, aggressive, and insulting text. There are a few datasets present for fake news and hate speech separately but a single dataset that considers both the attributes is not present.

Currently, the dataset includes text content only. In the future, a new multi-modal dataset with images, emoji, and text can be created using the dataset proposed in the research as a reference. Also, more work on different types of ML classifiers can be done to increase the accuracy achieved by this research.

REFERENCES

Ahmed, H., Traore, I., & Saad, S. (2018). Detecting opinion spams and fake news using text classification. *Security and Privacy*, 1(1), e9.

Aldwairi, M., & Alwahedi, A. (2018). Detecting fake news in social media networks. *Procedia Computer Science*, 141, 215–222.

Ananthakrishnan, U. M., & Tucker, C. E. (2022). The drivers and virality of hate speech online. Available at *SSRN* 3793801.

Blanco-Herrero, D., & Calderón, C. A. (2019, October). Spread and reception of fake news promoting hate speech against migrants and refugees in social media: Research Plan for the Doctoral Programme Education in the Knowledge Society. In *Proceedings of the Seventh International Conference on Technological Ecosystems for Enhancing Multiculturality* (pp. 949-955).

Carley, K. (2020). Social cybersecurity: An emerging science. *Computational & Mathematical Organization Theory*, 26(4), 365–381. DOI: 10.1007/s10588-020-09322-9 PMID: 33223952

Davidson, T., Warmsley, D., Macy, M., & Weber, I. (2017, May). Automated hate speech detection and the problem of offensive language. In *Proceedings of the international AAAI conference on web and social media* (Vol. 11, No. 1, pp. 512-515).

Hatch, B. B. (2018). Defining a Class of Cyber Weapons as WMD: An Examination of the Merits. *Journal of Strategic Security*, 11(1), 43–61. DOI: 10.5038/1944-0472.11.1.1657

Keman Huang, M. S. S. M. (2018). Systematically Understanding the Cyber Attack Business: A Survey. *ACM Computing Surveys*.

Khan, J. R. (2021). Spread of Religious Hatred through Digital Media in Pakistan: The Case of Tehreek-E-Labbaik Pakistan. *Journal of Media and Communication Studies*.

Lohani, A. "Countering Disinformation and Hate Speech Online: Regulation and User Behavioural Change," *ORF Occasional Paper No. 296,* 2021.

MacAvaney, S., Yao, H. R., Yang, E., Russell, K., Goharian, N., & Frieder, O. (2019). Hate speech detection: Challenges and solutions. *PLoS One*, 14(8), e0221152.

Martens, B., Aguiar, L., Gomez-Herrera, E., & Mueller-Langer, F. (2018). The digital transformation of news media and the rise of disinformation and fake news-An economic perspective. *JRC Digit. Econ. Work. Pap*, 2, 57.

Pereira-Kohatsu, J. C., Quijano-Sánchez, L., Liberatore, F., & Camacho-Collados, M. (2019). Detecting and monitoring hate speech in Twitter. *Sensors (Basel)*, 19(21), 4654.

Putri, A. D. A. l. (2020). The Journalists Has Built Self Meaning: Spreasing Hate Speech. In *Preseidential Election 2019 In Banten* (Vol. I, p. 2). ASPIRATION Journal.

Ranjan, P., & Vaish, A. (2021). Socio-technical attack approximation based on structural virality of information in social networks. [IJISP]. *International Journal of Information Security and Privacy*, 15(1), 153–172.

Wang, W. Y. (2017). " liar, liar pants on fire": A new benchmark dataset for fake news detection. arXiv preprint arXiv:1705.00648.

Chapter 11
Legal Frameworks Surrounding the Use of AI in Online Content Moderation

Pranjal Khare
https://orcid.org/0000-0002-9937-9588
O.P. Jindal Global University, India

Vishambhar Raghuwanshi
https://orcid.org/0009-0009-1365-1850
Manipal University Jaipur, India

ABSTRACT

The use of AI in online content moderation is a complex issue with significant ethical and legal implications. While AI offers the potential to efficiently identify and remove harmful content like hate speech and misinformation, it also raises concerns about censorship, biased algorithms, and the erosion of user trust. Striking a balance between free speech and user safety is crucial. Ethical frameworks and regulations are needed to guide the development and deployment of AI moderation tools, ensuring transparency, accountability, and fairness. However, the lack of global consensus and inconsistencies in national regulations hinder the development of a coherent international approach to AI governance. To address these challenges, this chapter will explore the legal framework and a global approach which is needed to establish standards for transparency, accountability, and fairness in AI-driven content moderation, ensuring that AI serves as a tool for good rather than harm.

DOI: 10.4018/979-8-3693-9904-0.ch011

INTRODUCTION

Computing intelligence has become indispensable in the current world, especially in managing content on social media. Social media is currently experiencing exponential growth in terms of population reach and has increasingly influenced the way people interact and acquire information and similarly has become the driving force for sharing useful as well as negative information. One of the most crucial problems of the contemporary network environment is the increase in the quantity of hate speech, fake news, and other various forms of undesirable content, which requires some new ways to regulate it. Considering the amount of content created every day, more platforms seek to use AI technologies for content moderation. This introduction will discuss the importance of AI to the regulation of free speech on social media platforms, in a bid to address questions about permissioned knowledge, and social media toxicity. This section shows how, depending on the context, AI can participate both to reopen expression or contribute to its closure This section will also demonstrate the importance of finding middle ground for the appropriate regulation of AI for moderating content (Canda, 2024).

The use of artificial intelligence in content moderation meets a staggering demand. Since there are billions of active users on social media sites like Facebook, Twitter, and YouTube, the social media firm finds itself in a very big challenge of tackling a very big number of events to sort out. This task is further complicated by high incidence of harmful material, with materials such as hate speech, and racist and extremist propaganda, harassment and misinformation. The volume and high velocity of such content ensures its impossibility of moderation by human beings alone, hence making way for the new age AI solutions that are also efficient. Due to great computing power, AI can be used to analyze potentially toxic content and then remove it before it spreads, making it an excellent tool for real-time moderation. This reliance on artificial intelligence is characteristic of a larger trend where platforms are self-monitoring content to manage a scope of information and to increase the quality of user experience through indicating safer content.

Notably, the application of AI in content moderation can be broken down into complex and practical technologies in the following manners. Some techniques, for instance, Natural Language Processing (NLP) techniques make the system input and deeply process text to be in a position to identify the language used in hate speech and identification of threats or harassments. Similarly image and video recognition software are tasked to scan image and video content in an attempt to identify obscene images or symbols linked to hate groups. Both technologies are firmly based on machine learning, which trains systems to be able to identify patterns in data, refine how they operate over time, and, for the best results, be able to update as the content they are presented with changes over time online. AI's adaptation in content moderation can also be attributed to advancement in the sophistication of Machine learning where these algorithms perform their filtering task based on the training set and without needing a rule base for the individual case (Gillespie, 2020). Such AI functions provide a plausible workaround to many real-life challenges that human moderators face and real-time response to toxic content.

Nonetheless, it can be clearly stated that introduction of AI to moderate immense amounts of content requires a unique and highly efficient approach; however, it is also accompanied by numerous ethical and practical questions and issues. Chief among these is the dual-edged nature of AI's role. Although it opens a useful framework for minimizing the sharing of toxic information, it also creates a threat of excessive purging and filtering of admissible messages. However, AI systems are unable to differentiate between hate speech or intentions to support such speech, and critical, satirical or otherwise lawful speech. This absence of context results in conditions where AI-guided software could scrutinize and either mark as potential risks content which is, in fact, harmless and place unjustified limits on free expression. For example, AI algorithms used in hate speech classification can deny discussions that touch sensitive political or social themes, including consequent message classification (Mantri, 2021). For this reason, implementing AI in content moderation poses the danger of 'false positives,' by which normally legal messages are banned for aesthetic impression as unwanted content.

Furthermore, the extent to which AI is built with pre-conceptions makes it quite difficult to use in moderating content. Such biases can arise from data on which the systems have been trained and impose prejudice that is biased within society. For instance, AI moderation tools have been deemed to suppress specific categories of persons or opinions, affecting individuals most of the time. In one specific example, the platforms also often appear for failing at deeming posts on advocacy or activism for minority issues as potentially hate initiating as the identification is done by artificial intelligence. This highlights a significant shortcoming in AI moderation systems. As much as they are capable of analyzing vast amounts of content, they are still liable to the prejudices of their creators, and the data sets they were trained on. This poses a great difficulty in applying artificial intelligence in content moderation since the risk of discrimination and misrepresentation is a violation of the basics of fairness and equality in artificial intelligence (Feerst, 2022).

The deployment of AI in content moderation touches upon two critical principles: the qualified right of freedom of expression and the qualified right to be free from harm. Temporarily, social media has been placed in a rather awkward situation, but it is pressured to promote free speech even as it seeks to prevent abusive content. This duality puts a lot of pressure on the AI systems, as platforms must guarantee that the technology adheres to the principles of user rights, but it also must protect users at the same time. The conflict of the right to speech freedom and hate speech banning increases when many AI systems are not easily understandable. Since certain algorithms belong to corporations their work is obscure, and the public cannot easily evaluate their fairness or efficiency. This can be considered to be a source of distrust since users cannot know what criteria have been used in moderation of their work or how they can challenge a decision made on an algorithm. Such opacity in AI moderation systems only worsens the issue of responsibility and strengthens worries about adverse effects of AI excesses as the police of speech.

Realizing these risks, most scholars and regulators call for the creation of ethical and legal structures that might act to counterbalance the negative effects of AI in content moderation. Such frameworks would preferably stress principles of openness, responsibility, and non-discrimination, and were supposed to define requirements for the AI systems used to detect, alert, and act on materials regarded as detrimental. Moreover, such a framework would include layers of supervision, to which one may take a complaint and ensure that platform moderation policies which limit freedoms of expression are lawful to do so. Some countries and organizations have started moving in this direction especially in producing norms and standards to increase transparency and responsibilities in the use of artificial intelligence in moderation of online content. For example, the proposed EU AI Act and the Digital Services Act aim at placing more obligation on moderating platforms to guarantee di-electricity while protecting users' personal rights and data. These regulatory attempts point up a rising appreciation of the fact that the updating of regulation of digital technologies ought to recognize the requirement of protection of fundamental rights on the one hand and room for innovation on the other (Udupa et al., 2023).

Finally, the application of AI in the management of content moderation was a sign of a more extensive discussion on the application of automation in areas that were covered by the subjective decision of a human being. Over time, as the AI systems improve, and as the social media that use them get more nuanced, the line between acceptable moderation and censorship blurs. The problem is in the creation of fair AI systems that can mitigate pre or post OTS deemed hostile content without compromising the freedom of speech, a discussion that cuts across both technological literacy and civil liberties. This double-spectrum nature of AI in content moderation means that there is a need to critically analyze the implementations of such systems.

Thus, applying the idea of AI as the most effective solution to the needs of moderating the content of social media platforms, the identified conflict of principle should be considered in the frameworks of the efficient AI-supported social media governance. The role that AI plays in the moderation of content only makes the lack of robust regulatory frameworks in countering the ethical and organizational dilemmas posed by automated decision making in cyberspace. Policies of this sort must be clear, auditable, and equitable to promote a technological ecosystem that further fundamental rights, respecting entitlements to freedom of speech and protection from harm as espoused by democracy. This chapter is an attempt to contribute to further nuanced and reasoned thinking about the regulation of content moderation by AI, by analyzing the practical, ethical, and legal concerns of the presence of such technology in the world of social media.

AI in Online Content Moderation

Artificial Intelligence (AI) takes up an ever-more central position in content moderation regarding the huge amounts of data posted on social media per second. AI moderation is performed through several algorithms and machine learning algorithms that are aimed to detect, filter and, if needed, eliminate content that has negative impact, such as hate speech, fake news, and adult content. Algorithms are required to monitor the increasing traffic in social networks and content sharing in general; however, human moderators cannot deal with the rates of accepting and sorting materials as quickly as this process requires when it spans the entire world. This segment discusses the rudimentary principles of AI on the content moderation process and provides an understanding of the fundamental working of AI aids in analyzing and deciding on the moderation of the damaging content and cognizance of ethics that are otherwise rolled out with the help of robotic intelligence and automation, and the basic drawbacks of AI, such as censorship, bias, and errors (Lakra, 2024).

The use of AI in content moderation involves the use of Machine Language that acts as a tool for grouping large amounts of data depending on perceived similarities. NLP is at the core of how AI operates within a content moderation workflow. They are designed to analyze and sort through text. Speech processing algorithms play very crucial roles in analysis of textual content, including identification of obscene language, hate speech or phrases which are likely to promote violence. The same can be said for moderating visual content which has also adopted the technologies of computer vision and image recognition. These algorithms are trained on the database, mentioning millions of images explaining that these algorithms can identify the symbols or gestures or some specific image patterns that are linked with the dangerous content which may include the images of violence or images of the hate groups (Molina & Sundar, 2022). Combined with each other, these tools provide capabilities for AI systems for content review at a much faster and larger capacity compared to what a human moderator can handle.

Content moderation and specific detection of hatred speeches remain useful characteristics of AI in this regard because they can identify a variety of patterns both in the stark and veiled hypothesis. For instance, rather than merely detecting explicit language that can be easily flagged, NLP algorithms can be trained to flag coded language or 'dog whistle's language, that are sometimes hard for a human observer to pick out. Sites such as Facebook and Twitter use these exponential algorithms to prefetch posts, comments, and messages which contain materials that violate the site's policy. Sentiment analysis, which is part of NLP, is also utilized to determine the affective content of the material and identify site content which may provoke negative or aggressing sentiment. This process plays a vital role in moderating hate speech which, if not always outrightly hostile, has intent implicitly conveyed in the choice of words themselves and how they are arranged.

Image recognition, another one of the key technologies in AI content moderation, helps identify toxic visual content that remains a growing problem of social networks. This includes the identification of obscene images, iconography of radical turners, trenchant images of violence. Platforms use the convolutional neural networks (CNN) machine learning system that is particularly useful for the classification of images and videos. They scan pixel patterns and structural aspects of images, and this allows AI systems to filter out unsafe visuals independently. For instance, recently, in an attempt to curb violent or extreme content, YouTube has used image recognition through AI to help it quickly eliminate material that may be potentially destructive in its infancy before it can reach a large audience. This form of early-stage filtering shows how AI can work effectively to keep space, especially online ones, safer.

NLP and image recognition are both incorporated into a second level of AI moderation known as video analysis. By identifying scenes through objects and movements, video moderation can easily detect risky scenes when in real-time or when the videos are uploaded. These systems read through audio material, defining obscene words or phrases, they look through videos, defining scenes of invasions or harassments. The live-streaming feature heavily uses this technology to enforce content policies on TikTok and other similar video-sharing platforms because some of the otherwise risky content may slip through the cracks. Therefore, the usage of AI solutions means that moderation requires this and that is achieved through the synergy of text, image, and video analyzing tools.

On the one hand, the technical record of AI in service of content moderation is striking, but it raises profound and urgent questions about censorship. This paper identifies one major concern or controversy, that is the problem of over-policing where the algorithms may go overboard in filtering and removing legal and positive messages. Because of context inapprehension, AI could regard jokes, irony, and sarcasm as unsafe and impede those who express opinions that can trigger essential social or political debates. This is a problem known as false positives, which highlights the problem of AI moderation because it threatens user rights to free speech. For example, content related to political issues but not showing violence may be deleted if the AI chooses the topic to be controversial or provocative and thus oppresses many topics which need advocacy for social justice or change (Kniazieva, 2023).

With the automation of moderation, there are questions about the use of bias in AI algorithms as well. Actually, AI can be or totter on prejudice based on the data feeds used in creating the models of these systems besides the options selected by the developers. Should the training data contain preconceptions that are biased, the AI will amplify such bias, meaning that the delivery of content will not be fair across the population. Researchers have described cases when automated moderation discriminates against some groups or themes. For example, it has been argued that, by moderation, platforms have been suppressing material related to homosexuals because algorithms misidentify words or images related to homosexuals as "adult" or "offensive". Discriminatory outcomes like in moderations of AI are a cause for concern because such marginalized groups depend on the internet to express themselves and argue for their rights (Wang, 2023).

However, the algorithms used for content moderation through AI increase ethical concern because users do not have adequate knowledge of the standard and process that the AI systems apply in their decision-making process. Many AI moderation processes are proprietary, which prevents the user from knowing why content gets flagged or taken down and cripples appeals. Such complexities lead to a lack of trust because the users cannot differentiate whether their posts deserved a flag. A few social media sites allow users to challenge AI decisions. However, the effectiveness of such an appeal is low since content moderation has slight human intervention and is flooded with flagged posts. If not for increased transparency, AI modulated moderation can become a way of excluding users and limiting democratically held principles.

Excessive mistakes in AI moderation are yet a violation of ethical issues. Despite the ability of algorithms to be highly accurate with identifying cancer, accuracy is not perfect, and it is possible to get a positive result when cancer is not present, or a negative result when cancer is indeed present. False positive, as has been mentioned before, implies censoring content that is actually benign while false negatives, instances where undesirable content is openly permitted as acceptable, means that hatred speech and similar vices may freely flow around. These errors have implications for the overall platform and for the individual users. For instance, when it comes to social tension like elections or civil protests the inability of the AI to properly moderate will only fuel the intensity of the situation or mislead the public. Moreover, this decision means that different language processing and national accents result in higher AI accuracy in an ethnically diverse society (Singh, 2024).

To redress those ethical dilemmas, scholars and policymakers have appealed for regulations that would ensure compliance with such standards as openness, non-bias and perform accountability for usage of AI in content moderation. Such frameworks may create a set of rules on how particular AI algorithms should be designed and used, which would force these platforms to state the principles on which their moderation occurs. Further, high-level guidelines could also incorporate mechanisms that would require human intervention or further review, so that decisions made by these algorithms are reviewed and use is not devoid of people's control (Kaushik, 2024). Ethical standards and impartiality of the overseer could go a long way to redress sovereignty of user rights over the excessive nature of banning that comes with AI.

The issues highlighted in this case related to challenges affecting AI moderation, and the ethical concerns that arise from their work, show why the topic of moderating content through automated means requires more attention. As much as AI delivers economies of scale for moderating the sheer tonnage of online content, it also highlights the need to always integrate human moderators where context and discretion are required. Superimposing AI on top of the existing architecture can work to address the conflict between speed and compliance, underspending user justice while blocking angry messages. In decoding the ethical dilemmas inherent in practical application of the AI system in content moderation, this discourse reinforces the continuous dialogue and AFAC-C concern about regulating AI for its conformity with the tenets of democracies and freedom (Tobi, 2024).

In conclusion, AI content moderation, which is crucial in addressing the negative impact that is caused by the development of bad content online must be evaluated with significant attention with regard to ethical issues that are surrounding it. Similarly, the benefits from AI tools, for instance in ultra-relevant NLP, image, or video analysis are accompanied by severe moral issues like over- control and censorship, bias and opacity that may infringe on the rights of users and affect the transparent responsibility of the platforms. If these questions are solved by the latter, through the means of formal comprehensive frameworks and integration of human-AI collaboration, then such a digital environment would build on the potential of AI and at the same time would not infringe basic freedoms. Here it is possible to perceive that there is still a misconception with AI in content moderation, but reinforcing the ethical consideration in technological management, calling for the SAP model aiming at safety and fairness simultaneously.

International Legal Framework Governing AI

The concern of applying artificial intelligence AI in content moderation in the digital platform has elicited massive legal and regulatory changes across the globe. With AI systems becoming more critical tools in organizing and moderating information on the internet, state and global organizations have strived to incorporate the ideal policy level which will standardize the rights and wrongs of automated systems. Developed systems have not remained indifferent to transparency, accountability, and privacy in AI moderated systems; some regulatory instruments have been developed at the international level including the European Union's Artificial

Intelligence Act, General Data Protection Regulation GDPR, as well as UNESCO's Recommendations, among others. However, these frameworks show that the regulations are still fragmented with different strategies and growing inconsistencies that prevent a consolidated international stant towards the management of AI technology. This section identifies major international standards operating on AI practices in content moderation, reviews how these standards address key ethical concerns, and explores the problems caused by existing voids and disparities in global law (Rodrigues, 2020).

At the EU level, action in the form of the proposed AI Act represents one of the most extensive regulatory initiatives regarding the future of AI systems. The AI Act proposes a system of three MPA categories, where AI applications are divided into two classes of high and limited risk or excluded as unacceptable. Content moderation system is among the systems that are likely to be tagged high risk given the fact that it deals with fundamental rights, freedom of speech and speech in general. The AI Act mandates a set of principles of transparency and accountability which ensures that the high-risk AI systems are trained on identifiable data; the system must provide a detailed description of how the AI made its decisions and contain provisions on how human beings can intervene. These provisions aim to tackle a problem associated with AI: namely, the lack of transparency, proposing to make the platforms report key information about the functioning of the selected AI models and the criteria applied to taking content moderation decisions. Other such transparency requirements might enable users to challenge the largely opaque AI-driven decision making across platforms, thus promoting accountability, and thus innovation (Balas & Shatnawi, 2024).

Co-existing with the AI Act is the GDPR, which has impacted AI content moderation in a roundabout manner for various tech company platforms enforcing stringent user data protection standards. Any personal data processed, collected and stored through AI, including the content moderation algorithms, must meet GDPR requirements of lawfulness, fairness, transparency and data minimization principles. When translated into key benchmarks for content moderation frameworks, it means that personal data of users should be processed responsibly to help AI systems analyze only required features helping to detect malicious content with taking average people's privacy into account. GDPR also implies the rights of the users over their data which includes the rights to obtaining details, modifying and deleting the data. Currently, in cases where the use of AI algorithms results in fully automated decisions on the part of the user, based on such parameters that define the interests of the natural person, GDPR allows the data subject to appeal to a human being to review such decisions and make decisions that contradict them. Image recognition is crucial in moderating the platforms through which AI can wrongly remove legal content; it will allow users to appeal against automated decisions that violate their rights (Zaidan & Ibrahim, 2024).

Moreover, GDPR sets very high standards for Data Protection Impact Assessment (DPIA) for high-risk uses of AI, including the content moderation system. DPIAs facilitate the evaluation of risks connected with processing personal data by the company, allowing them to reveal possible evils that may result from bias or erroneous actions of AI. In the case of AI in content moderation, this is essential since it encourages platform owners to think of risks relating to biased algorithms or discrimination, or mistakes in censorship (Almeida et al., 2021). Through encouraging the culture of responsibility and precaution, GDPR strengthens the pillars of accountability and, speaking of user rights and ethical functioning of AI-oriented content platforms, establishes the rules for ethical AI and the standards of its functioning.

Outside Europe, UNESCO has helped define ethical AI through its recommendation on the Ethics of Artificial Intelligence approved in 2021. This recommendation, the first of its kind by a UN agency, offers ethical principles on how AI systems should be designed and implemented. While these recommendations are unveiled by UNESCO, they are to establish international standards and guide nations into embracing the right use of AI across different areas including the moderation of content. UNESCO is insistent on explaining that moderation and the use of AI should have all actions and decisions evident for users and that platforms which use such tools should offer easy ways to appeal to their decisions. Furthermore, the recommendation entails periodic checks on AI implementing systems and structures to ensure they complied with the ethical benchmarks as well as to review the AI implemented decisions to ensure they do not violate any user's rights. By such encouragement, UNESCO fosters transition to governance of values of AI that reflect the dignity of human beings (Mishra, 2024).

However, these international frameworks provide sound guidance on AI governance, they also reveal major lacuna in the international regulation of AI. Now, there is no international legal instrument, that is, an international treaty or a convention, which focuses on the concrete difficulties connected with the usage of AI in content moderation. This absence results in large disparities in AI conformance across geographical territory due to variations in the different approaches by countries and organizations on the content regulation. For instance, whilst the EU's GDPR and AI Act demand clear responsibilities concerning transparency and accountability which are not achievable, the United States has not so much opted for federal-level AI regulation but instead has employed permissive self-regulatory common and sector-specific rules. Such disparities put more pressure on the global running platforms because the platforms see different legal and ethical recruiting requirements and protections, leading to users' varying degrees of protection and moderation (Tallberg, 2023).

Some of the most apparent problems that arise because of this lack of a coherent strategy are the fluctuating standard of transparency. While EU regulations state how, or from what, they want companies to disclose about AI systems, strings are laxer in other parts of the world when it comes to specifying what must be disclosed. This results in a situation where users in different jurisdictions have quite dissimilar levels of 'reet acuity' about the AI systems regulating their engagements. Moreover, there is a lack of standardization which prevents the prosecution of such platforms in question for decisions on content, in most cases, different requirements are set around the world, making the identification of global best practices and standards for AI transparency and accountability impossible.

The second major deficiency in regulation relates to ethical control systems is that while guidelines such as EU's AI Act and UNESCO's guidelines push for supervision, there is no requirement for independent third-party review for all AI content moderation systems. If the main companies do not follow a set of well-defined audit methodologies, they have a great power of discretion regarding how to approach the ethical codes, and this might be prone to compromise interest, economies freedom of self-regulating. This independence might improve straightforwardness as well as increase accountability because individuals hired in such a manner would be responsible for making sure that these holistic AI technologies and systems abide by ethical values and principles as well as users rights; Despite this, lack of such mechanisms across the globe reduces as an option the ability of validating whether some of these platforms are actually practicing these standards (Walter, 2024).

Privacy, also, is a problematic subject in conjunction with AI content moderation. Although GDPR has added a layer of privacy to Europe's nations, other countries have not had such protection, especially concerning data processing based on AI moderation tools. This has the potential for negative consequences so far as the privacy of the world users is concerned because different rules of handling their data may be used depending on the legislation of the state. Due to the vulnerability of users who share personal information with or without restrictions with a third party, disparities in privacy can indeed turn into privacy abuse that increase surveillance, profiling, and data misuse. The only solution to such gaps may be the adoption of a global framework for privacy in AI moderation to provide equal safety to users all over the world (Bhushan, 2024).

Such gaps mean that there indeed are many challenges that prevent the formulation of a coherent set of rules for AI regulation. Content moderation is thus not only a technical and ethical challenge, but also a cultural and political one, because decisions as to what constitutes dangerous content can differ greatly across nations. According to political and cultural differences, values are essential, and due to that, countries may create different regulations in AI moderation, free speech, national security or cultural differences. For example, the new European regs are oriented primarily to protect users' privacy, while some dictatorial governments pay particular attention to state control over information and use AI for this purpose. Managing these diametric interests remains a major challenge in establishing an efficient and internationally valid regulatory model.

In conclusion, the modulation of AI outlined here contains incentives and adversities in the efforts to realize safety and rights of the users across different nations in an era of transparent social media. Regulations such as EU's AI Act, GDPR, UNESCO on its ethical guidelines are good reference points as they cast out fundamental issues on issues of transparency, accountability, and privacy among others. However, because there cannot be a single, obligatory approach within the international legal framework, crucial gaps remain, which explain such differences in norms and their implementation. So, as artificial intelligence increasingly influences the online environment, the trends for coordinated and internationally compatible regulations grow more urgent. A more structured framework to regulate the moderation of AI platforms not only gives better rules as the guidelines for platforms but also strengthens the global consumers' protection while promoting AI moderation for the respect of general principles of human rights and disability.

Domestic Legal Approaches to AI

The analysis of specific legal regimes in a selected number of countries shows that there is no consensus on the use of AI in content moderation on the international level, which can be attributed to legal and legal-related differences in chosen states. This comparative analysis centers on the United States, the European Union and India as these arenas have all assumed different regulatory positions that are informed by considerations of free speech, privacy and accountability. The U.S. continues to struggle with content moderation in the context of the First Amendment with freedom of speech provisions that do not make for easy regulation. The EU, on the other hand, wants to govern digital platforms by tools like DSA that encompass the rules for AI liability. The Indian government through its Information Technology (IT) Rules has sought to regulate content found online but has drawn controversy over how well the state is able to protect users while exercising control over the content they share online (Kiskis, 2023). It also discusses viability and, more specifically, the enforcement difficulties associated with each of these frameworks to make AI accountable.

The approach that the United States takes to AI content moderation is guided by the Constitution's First Amendment which protects freedom of speech. These protections also apply to private businesses, which means that social media platforms and other 'players' from the digital space generally get to decide what content remains or is just removed. Thus, America has traditionally employed a hands-off policy regarding speech on the internet, which means limited regulation. Popularly known as the Hands Off, Section 230 of the Communications Decency Act is a section of the U.S internet law that explains how internet platforms come clean from responsibilities concerning the third-party content. Section 230 also allows internet platforms to filter content in a way that doesn't hold them criminally liable, regardless of their choice to ban or censor specific content. Still, as the content platforms use AI for content moderation, the very principle of Section 230 is being strained as opponents believe that free AI use in content decisions may result in undeniable censorship practices or, on the contrary, bias in filtering content (Benizri et al., 2023).

Attempts to provide legal redress against models that employ AI to moderate content in the United States have been hindered by these free speech considerations. Discrimination has risen steadily, with some members of Congress demanding changes that would give more responsibility to the platforms now using AI to censor content. Ideas involve changing Section 230 immunity so that it only covers transparency in the use of artificial intelligence for moderation and giving users the ability to appeal against AI-driven actions. However, these reforms are not popular with anyone, and free speech activists have warned that new regulatory pressures may undermine new ideas and free speech. It is for this reason that in the US for instance, AI accountability is dampened by constitutional polls that uphold freedom of speech making it difficult to place regulatory measures on AI moderation systems without throwing the very freedoms protected by a legal system into jeopardy (Wolff, 2020).

The European Union has instead implemented the more interventionist regulatory model that regulates even the use of AI in content moderation through the Digital Services Act (DSA). DSA that came into force in 2022 is a complex set of rules meant to place various responsibilities on digital services and one among such responsibilities is the requirement for additional transparent and accountable regulation of AI systems. Unlike in the U.S, the EU has taken an approach that centers on fundamental rights with an agenda of safeguarding user's rights concurrently with guaranteeing safe and open online spaces. Some of the user rights that have to be protected under the DSA include information on content moderation by AI, including specifics about the algorithms used, and criteria such as content that needs to be banned, limited access to or risks of algorithmic bias (Brooks et al., 2020). These transparency requirements try to solve the problem of accountability and user trust induced by the 'black box' nature of AI.

The DSA also requires digital service providers to carry out risk evaluations of their artificial intelligence and machine learning tools, analysis of AI legal risk profiles on essential rights, privacy and freedom of speech. Platforms are also needed to ensure that platforms contain features enabling users to challenge those AI-generated content decisions and to request a referral to a human moderator. That is how this accountability structure is designed with the goal to avoid cases when AI moderation systems go too far, and suppress lawful content based on occasional or unjustified decisions. Nevertheless, there are issues with implementation of which the DSA suffers due to diverse digital platforms and their related AI technologies, the identification of what constitutes accountable AI, and the efficacy and feasibility of compliance frameworks. DSA implementation is the responsibility of national regulators in each EU member state, and thereby, there might be disparities in approaches to AI accountability. However, questions have been raised in relation to DSA objectives, specifically, the possible disproportionate surgical exertions that may overwhelm platforms smaller than the eligible 1.5 billion US dollars, thereby possibly stultifying their activities in the digital ecosystem (Chesterman, 2020).

The IT Rules can be said to encapsulate India's strategy regarding the application of AI in content moderation. The IT Rules place various requirements on social media intermediaries to take down specific kinds of content and appoint nodal officers to monitor compliance with the rules. Contrary to the US and the EU experience, the Indian framework relies on the government's lead in content moderation through the IT Rules that require platforms to take down certain categories of unwanted content on their own, such as content that threatens national security, public order, or incites hatred. To meet these obligations, most of the platforms functioning in India use the AI systems for the live monitoring of content, which though effective, is prone to some ethical issues related to accuracy of the system and to a probable manipulation by the state.

Although the use of these grievance mechanisms is to increase accountability, there is fear that the government will act on it and censor content. The regulatory framework of internet control in India has been regarded as one of the worst in the world since it provides the government with almost absolute control over the content that is published on the Internet, besides the often-misleading provisions for defining legitimate and illegitimate content. In fact, AI-driven content moderation under the IT Rules follows in practice the amplification of government influence, since platforms aim to meet strict rules and could ultimately harm user rights to freedom of expression.

Even within India's effective framework, there exist some issues related to this problem. The Indian guidelines appear to lack special recommendations concerning transparency and reducing bias in AI systems. IT Rules also proscribe timelines for content removals, but the rules do not expect social media platforms to disclose the parameters that the AI tools used to identify such content, or the data the tools rely on in arriving at such conclusions. Therefore, AI retains its obscure decision-making authority, allowing users to remain oblivious to the reasons for decisions concerning content as well as rare opportunities to challenge or investigate the use of AI in such matters.

Observing these frameworks, it is possible to see specific conceptual differences appearing due to the difference of legal systems and culture. The U.S. system stands for free speech, which creates difficulties in holding companies responsible for using AI without violating the constitution. Although this regime provides a certain level of independence to the platforms, it might result in enhanced liberalization of AI management and potentially establish an unreliable mechanism for content moderation based on biased or even absurd decision-making of such systems. On the other hand, the EU's DSA is an attempt at being preventive in tackling the question of AI accountability based on the principles of transparency, user's rights and human interposition. This more structured approach aims at ensuring while allowing the use of AI, protection of key fundamental rights but here practical questions of enforcement as well as disproportionate impact on entities that are smaller may remain fundamentally challenging. IT Rules in contrast represent a state centered Indian model of regulation, which focuses on Govt scrutiny, and National security. In the Indian framework, focus is given on how to prevent the post or any content from damaging anyone's reputation or that contains objectionable materials, which may make many users cautious with the social network and may result in overcontrol and censorship 'in an information technology environment in which artificial intelligence tools are critical for content moderation' (Collenette et al., 2023).

There are obvious issues with enforcement within each of these frameworks, especially when it comes to AI responsibility. As the approach is decentralized, and thus mostly self-regulated in the United States, the level of the platforms' transparency and the procedures they offer users to submit grievances regarding AI moderation all differ, making for inconsistency. On the other hand, the DSA has provided a strong regulatory legal framework of accountability for all platforms operating in the EU member states. The main issue arises from the fact that the application of the standards might vary across member states and small-scale platforms which suffer from resource constraints. Thus, India has its specific concerns because of the relative antagonism between the state and users, and because of the implicit rather than stated AI accountability, and political interference over content moderation.

Thus, the comparison of common approaches of the USA, the EU, and India concerning AI in content moderation reflects much about the challenges faced by states attempting to create an efficient regulatory system for AI's responsibility. Each jurisdiction represents specific legal and cultural features, which in their turn define approaches to openness, users' rights, and governmental control. Thus, we see that while the EU's DSA is a model for structured accountability the enforcement of it remains an issue. The level of regulation the U.S. experiences a conflict between the principles of the First Amendment and regulating extremism. The issues of regulating content in India can be regarded as the expression of the dangers of working with state control. As it now becomes apparent that AI is defining the tenor of online discourse, it is cardinal that regulation for these technologies be well-rounded and comprehensive, hopefully in tandem with the global nature of social media applications and the common moral and legal questions at play.

Challenges in Implementing Legal Frameworks for AI

Implementing legal norms that regulate AI-mediated content moderation is highly problematic due to both AI tech features and AI interaction with human rights, legal norms, and cultural and social values. This is especially so since modern online platforms increasingly rely on AI systems to detect and moderate content and since questions of bias, discrimination and overreach are more acute as AI systems are used to automate content moderation. There have been increasing concerns regarding negative externalities of traces left by AI moderation misclassification, culminating in legal actions and emergence of regulatory discourses. This elaboration builds upon recent enforcement cases and procrastinates the underlying ethical questions such as bias, discrimination potential, rights restriction inquiries, etc., as far as AI moderation is concerned.

It is easier said than done due to the lack of transparency of AI algorithms and closely integrated nature of AI-solutions. Most AI based content moderation solutions use machine learning techniques that work through a complex set of processes to parse through content to assist with filtering out undesirable content. These algorithms, which can often be trained on large datasets, not only may not provide understandable ways of arriving at their decisions, but in doing so give rise to what has become known as the 'black box' issue. This makes it hard for regulators and even the platform administrators themselves to be able to understand exactly how these decisions are made, which makes it very hard to pin specific actions made by AI on the various platforms (Sreelatha & Choudhary, 2023). As these are opaque processes that people can only infer with a degree of certainty based on inputs and outputs, the lack of ability to inspect AI moderation processes has legal and ethical ramifications, where these algorithms demonstrate latent biases or errors.

One of the most notable cases in this regard was Facebook that just recently drew controversy over moderation of materials connected with the Black Lives Matter protests in the United States. AI-based moderation tools were shown to flag posts published by Black users for further removal or restriction, much more often than those of other users. This led to accusations of racial injustice hardcoded into Facebook's content moderation processes and brought public and regulatory attention. While Facebook claimed that its AI censorship was neutral to maintain community standards, the opponents noted that to produce such results, the AI uses training datasets containing inherent discriminatory elements that cannot meet the standards of equality of people, non-discrimination. In this case, the challenges that were observed were the inability to enforce measures that would ensure that AI was fair or not, prejudiced in its decision-making process and this was noted especially given that there are no rules that are being laid down to force the developers to open up on how the AI is being trained (Mecaj, 2022).

There is another problem with legal standards, many countries still have diverse national laws regarding the moderation of AI content. As with all regulatory activities, interpretation of governance differs from country to country because of differences in legal systems and cultures. For example, DSA in the European Union regulates transparency and accountability of artificial intelligence has limited moderation but has not been implemented effectively in the EU member nations because of the lack of endorsement protocols. Instagram, on the other hand, is a social media application that is relatively minimally regulated as it is situated in the United States, which means free speech protections do not make it easier to regulate such platforms as it would wish to do. Again, for there to be proper implementation of the set standard, there is need for all the legal systems of the various countries to agree and this is not always the case and more to the point, the various platforms tend to take advantage of these differences to further their own gains. These enforcement problems are made worse by the absence of complementary international norms, which gives regulators very little power to force the platforms to be ethical and legal in their operation around the world (Greenstein, 2021).

The concerns regarding the enforcement and ethical properties of AI-based moderation provide another set of concerns i.e., bias and discrimination. The algorithms used by the AI systems are only as impartial as the data that they're trained on, and as history has shown, training data contains biases. For instance, image recognition software is well-documented to categorize minorities at abnormally high rates because of the preprogrammed database inputs. In the case of content moderation, such biases can result in what has been widely discussed within recent years as the filter bubble effect: some demographic groups' content is more likely to be flagged or deleted than that of other groups. This inherent bias then brings out some basic issues of ethicality in equality as well as non-discrimination especially when the platforms that the artificial intelligence systems belong to do not effectively manage or even, do not provide sufficient information about these flaws.

Also, AI content moderation creates a question of the overreach of technology or a possibility of an excessive number of restrictions. It should also be pointed out that AI cannot freely interpret context or any other features of speech, so the latter frequently makes decisions that distort legitimate discourse as potentially dangerous or negative. Excesses in regulating artificial intelligence have not been unusual lately, especially with political connotations, with platforms even potentially silencing opposition or limiting freedom of speech. One of the well-known incidents is the Twitter practice of suspending some accounts connected to political movements in

India: AI moderation tools labeled their messages as potentially hazardous because tensions ran high in connection with political protests (Bharati, 2024). The advocates of this criticism explained that this approach violated the user's right to free speech and focused on the moral and legal implications of outsourcing censorship solely to AI algorithms.

The fight for transparency and accountability in AI driven moderation is however more difficult given that the social platforms which implement that the AIs are protective of their AI algorithms. Most platforms keep their AI algorithms as their trade secrets, which means that no one can review them or hold them liable for their outcomes. The regulators experience the challenges of forcing firms to elaborate on the specifics of the AI systems in use because of corporate push-back based on the trade secrets in the competition. This lack of transparency is a challenge to the enforcement of National Standards that seek to protect users' rights and fairness in moderating content. If the regulating bodies do not require that the platforms explain how their algorithms work and who creates them, the platform's owners will not disclose such information and users will be at the mercy of arbitrary, or even worse, biased actions by the platforms (Alqodsi & Gura, 2023).

Moreover, the overall accuracy issues of AI moderation in enforcing the moderation continue to be a major problem, since high error-rates results in high false positives or negatives. Though current AI algorithms have reached a good sensitivity in other types of content such as nudity, graphic violence, hate speech and fake news detection remains a significant challenge for the technology. There remain problems of language peculiarities such as slang terms, idioms or cultural language references that make AI systems remove undesired content erroneously or allow creation of undesirable content that the AI will not identify. These errors have legal consequences, especially in places that require the platforms to afford users adequate means to seek redress from content moderation decisions. Nevertheless, it is still difficult to ensure such standards are being met as many platforms do not have the necessary number of human moderators to review all the disputed AI-decisions therefore, infringing on users' right to equal and just treatment and remedies.

The global character of online platforms also complicates efforts to create AI moderation regulation. Because social media platforms operate across borders, further clumping up the challenges for any one jurisdiction in enforcing action against perpetrators. A platform that adheres to the DSA rules in the EU might not be required to do so elsewhere, it is conceivable, for example, that a platform would comply with its DSA duties in the EU but not implement them anywhere else because of weaker or non-existent regulations from Southeast Asia or Africa. It is this fragmentation of regulation that permits platforms to cherry-pick compliance with heightened standards only in places where enforcement mechanisms are strong. As a result, users in less-regulated jurisdictions are, by definition, at greater ethical and legal risk from AI moderation errors that lead to unjust censorship or an opaque content decision-process (Sharma, 2024).

In response to these and other challenges, the call for stronger international standards regulating AI-powered moderation on transparency, accountability and fairness specifically is growing. Many initiatives, such as UNESCO's recommendations on the Ethics of Artificial Intelligence, emphasize that there should be a unified global approach to AI governance upholding human rights and ensuring accountability. But the nitty-gritty of globally enforcing such standards is complicated, countries have regulatory priorities to juggle and legal systems that will differ. Closing these gaps will necessitate cooperation between governments, tech companies, and civil society organizations to develop frameworks to align the advantages of AI-driven content moderation with protection against its potential harms.

Ultimately, the imposition of legal standards regarding AI moderation is fraught with complex challenges reliant on the inadequacy of AI toolkits, variable application and an ever-shifting ethical landscape. Recent cases illustrate discriminatory impacts that arise from AI moderation mistakes, too frequently characterized by bias and overreach, which far exceeds what effective regulatory oversight would allow. Common ethical controversies surrounding AI moderation, including bias and the potential for censorship, signal an urgent demand for transparency and accountability of AI systems. Nevertheless, the inherently proprietary nature of AI algorithms, high error rates and a fragmented global regulatory landscape make enforcement arduous. A failure to act now and build comprehensive legal frameworks for the use of AI that takes these problems into account will continue to contribute to a system in which AI acts as an instrument of public good one minute, then proceeds to violate a range of human rights and liberties the next.

CONCLUSION AND FUTURE DIRECTIONS

While essential, questions related to legal and ethical frameworks remain tricky as the space of AI-driven content moderation evolves quickly. The findings suggest a few lessons in missing clear information on the benefits as well as possible harms of AI moderation that highlights the fine balance between creating positive economic opportunity when building content governance systems. This information exposes clear shortcomings in current structures, simultaneously highlighting potential avenues for advancement in legal requirements that can confront the challenges posed by AI moderation both judiciously and with an eye towards the future.

Transparency is another of the key picked out problems in AI moderation systems. Though AI tools are praised for their capacity to oversee the mass of online content on a scale, a lack of transparency makes it hard to fairly scrutinize and hold them accountable. Some AI algorithms use a "black box" model, where the logic used for making decisions cannot be accessed or understood by even platform administrators, which makes it difficult to hold platforms responsible for their moderation actions. Another cloud looming invisibly over us is the explosion of algorithmic bias; AI systems that unwittingly carry forward, even multiply existing social inequities. For instance, Platforms are accused of implementing AI systems that generate biased results when their underlying algorithms learn from unbalanced or inadequately representative datasets. This indicates that there is an increased need for transparency not just in terms of AI systems but also regarding the datasets on which they have been trained.

The ethical challenges here are similarly pronounced in AI content moderation. It raises considerable issues surrounding the implications of free expression, discrimination and privacy as AI plays an increasing role in deciding what we can say on digital platforms. As AI provides an opportunity to swiftly recognize and remove toxicity, it simultaneously poses a threat of excess, censoring legitimate speech or silencing marginalized voices through over-policing. AI systems do not understand language with any depth, the nuances of context, irony, specificity to culture, and that dilemma only compounds. AI-based moderation systems therefore may automatically flag content that would, in any reasonable context, be innocuous or protected speech. This kind of over-reach would violate basic rights and create a moral hazard in regulating harmful content with new laws against freedom of speech.

Due to the challenges mentioned, the future of AI content moderation is in the creation of legal and ethical measures that will address the future advancement in AI technologies. Another of the tasks should be the approach of the laws that would be adaptable and able to effectively cover AI which is in its continuous development process. And while artificial intelligence solutions are being created, so must the laws regulating them be modernized to guarantee they remain efficient as the new technologies develop.

One of the trends for the further inclusion of legal standards in the development of new laws is the process of globalization and local peculiarities. At the moment, AI regulation is piecemeal and there are differing models for regulation depending on the jurisdiction, its legal tradition, culture, and polity. For example, the European Union has sought to take most of its actions and regulations in the realm of AI, including the DSA and the AI Act that provide standards of artificial intelligence transparency, and responsibility towards human rights. However, these regulations apply strictly to the EU and are not necessarily applicable to other countries. Similarly, the United States and India also have their OWG and OFWG to control content moderation but do not have clear, separate and authoritative national AI policies. To respond to the problem of diverse forms of regulation organization, there is an obvious need for worldwide discussions and cooperation with the purpose of establishing international standards. This would scale down the difficulties that arise from cross-border content and increase coherence in applying legal standards, if something of a united strategy were to be applied.

It is now important that local considerations be considered when achieving this harmonization. Although systems should be consistent with international standards, countries need to maintain some sovereignty in executing them so as to conform to national cultures and beliefs. The practices address an inherent conflict between standardization needed to achieve global integration and adaptation required in the local context. In this regard, one of the possible ways that can lead to more balanced integration of the AI tool is to create an international organization or consortium that will regulate or coordinate the use of the AI across borders. It's possible that some of these bodies could be tasked with the creation of global guidelines and frameworks of AI content moderation while coming up with different standards based on the demographics, geography and situations of the different regions.

In addition, the generation of legal environments for AI content moderation should be based on transparency, accountability, and fairness. It should also be critical for any regulatory attempt with respect to platforms that transparent requirements should be established for platforms to explain how their AI operates, the data they depend on, and how moderation determinations are reached. This would extend the facility for external audit and would make it easier to detect any prejudice as well as discrimination in algorithms used in AI. Third party platforms should ensure that they are responsible for results of AI systems applied, giving users valid ways to appeal from deletion or flagging of content accidentally. This accountability can be achieved through independent supervisory bodies that would protect users' rights from misuse by platforms in favor of corporations' interests and the usage of AI's frameworks by these platforms.

Nonetheless, we must look at fairness as another foundational element that the current frameworks of AI content moderation should be based on. The layout of legal standards should aim at preventing the gain of bias by rejecting some demographics by certain AI systems. This can be achieved by prescribing platforms that need to come up with tests that will be used to monitor the effects of the AI system on members of society, especially those that have been historically disadvantaged. These assessments could be based on principles of equal treatment and nondiscrimination so that in the process of moderating content no specific group of people is most affected. In the same token, platforms should be pressed into taking measures that minimize the instances of algorithmic bias including including diverse datasets in the algorithm training, involving humans in the moderation process.

Notably, the legal solution for AI moderation systems cannot neglect one key issue, which is, over-restriction. AI systems should be fine-tuned to check for the tendency of censoring a lot of content when this is a violation of the user's right to express themselves. This means that, to build AI systems that are acceptable, we need to pay close attention to the environment in which the resulting AI systems are going to be used, and that there will sometimes be the need for human intervention to judge certain content. Thus, AI content moderation can be useful for regulating vast amounts of content, it should not be used as the only method of it. There has to be a human in the loop all the time, who has to watch AI decision-making, at least in the cases of sensitive or more complex grounds for moderation.

To prevent over-regulation from stifling innovation, the legal rules governing AI content moderation must be likewise ready for changes the future AI advances will bring. This, of course, means that as AI continues to advance, new ethical and legal dilemmas will surface making regulation predictive and innovative. This may require such activities as development of open and fundamental regulations that would be able to accommodate change such as emergence of new technologies while 'closed and specific' rules may turn out to be irrelevant. Furthermore, there is a need to build into policy processes for continued public involvement and input to guarantee that the user's needs, civil society and the industry are involved in the policy making process. This would help to ensure that AI content moderation stays actionable concerning society and acknowledge human rights.

Therefore, although AI is promising for moderating toxic content helpful for dealing with the problem, it creates deep legal and ethical concerns. As we advance further into the future, more effort has to be devoted to updating the legal policies governing AI content moderation to be transparent, accountable and fair at the same time. Internationalization and localization will be another crucial driver in how it will be possible to build an integrated regulatory framework that can be smoothly integrated into global processes while at the same time still balance between free speech and censorship. These are important challenges toward improving the legal and ethical regulation of AI content moderation with the objective of making AI a useful enabler for creating safer online communities.

REFERENCES

Almeida, P., Santos, C. D., & Farias, J. S. (2021) Artificial Intelligence Regulation: a framework for governance. *ResearchGate*. https://www.researchgate.net/publication/351039094_Artificial_Intelligence_Regulation_a_framework_for_governance

Alqodsi, E. M., & Gura, D. (2023). High tech and legal challenges: Artificial intelligence-caused damage regulation. *Cogent Social Sciences*, 9(2), 2270751. Advance online publication. DOI: 10.1080/23311886.2023.2270751

Balas, H., & Shatnawi, R. (2024). Legal framework for AI applications. *F1000 Research*. https://f1000research.com/articles/13-418

Benizri, I., Evers, A., Mercer, S. T., & Jessani, A. A. (2023). A Comparative Perspective on AI Regulation. *Lawfare*. https://www.lawfaremedia.org/article/a-comparative-perspective-on-ai-regulation

Bharati, R. K. (2024). Navigating the Legal Landscape of Artificial Intelligence: Emerging Challenges and Regulatory Framework in India. *SSRN*, 23(7), 698–707. https://papers.ssrn.com/sol3/papers.cfm?abstract_id=4898536. DOI: 10.2139/ssrn.4898536

Bhushan, T. (2024). Artificial Intelligence, Cyberspace and International Law. *Indonesian Journal of International Law*, 21(2), 281–314. https://scholarhub.ui.ac.id/ijil/vol21/iss2/3/

Brooks, C., Gherhes, C., & Vorley, T. (2023). Artificial intelligence in the legal sector: Pressures and challenges of transformation. *Cambridge Journal of Regions, Economy and Society*, 13(1), 135–152. DOI: 10.1093/cjres/rsz026

Canda, J. (2024). The Role of AI in Content Moderation and Online Safety. *Medium*. https://medium.com/@jam.canda/the-role-of-ai-in-content-moderation-and-online-safety-1d7d18aeb69d

Chesterman, S. (2020). Artificial Intelligence and the Limits of Legal Personality. *The International and Comparative Law Quarterly*, 69(4), 819–844. DOI: 10.1017/S0020589320000366

Collenette, J., Atkinson, K., & Capon, T. B. (2023). Explainable AI tools for legal reasoning about cases: A study on the European Court of Human Rights. *Artificial Intelligence*, 317, 103861. https://www.sciencedirect.com/science/article/pii/S0004370223000073. DOI: 10.1016/j.artint.2023.103861

Feerst, A. (2022). The Use of AI in Online Content Moderation. *AEI Digital Platforms*. https://platforms.aei.org/wp-content/uploads/2022/09/The-Use-of-AI-in-Online-Content-Moderation.pdf

Gillespie, T. (2020). Content moderation, AI, and the question of scale. *ResearchGate*. https://www.researchgate.net/publication/343798653_Content_moderation_AI_and_the_question_of_scale

Greenstein, S. (2021). Preserving the rule of law in the era of artificial intelligence (AI). *Artificial Intelligence and Law*, 30(3), 291–323. DOI: 10.1007/s10506-021-09294-4

Kaushik, S. (2024). AI in Content Moderation: All You Need to Know. *Blog Ipleaders*. https://blog.ipleaders.in/ai-in-content-moderation-all-you-need-to-know/

Kiskis, M. (2023). Legal framework for the coexistence of humans and conscious AI. *Frontiers in Artificial Intelligence*, 6, 1205465. DOI: 10.3389/frai.2023.1205465 PMID: 37808620

Kniazieva, Y. (2023). AI Content Moderation for Responsible Social Media Practices. *Label Your Data*. https://labelyourdata.com/articles/ai-content-moderation

Lakra, R. (2024). Deciphering AI-powered content moderation: Approaches, constraints, and future horizons. *Observer Research Foundation*. https://www.orfonline.org/expert-speak/deciphering-ai-powered-content-moderation-approaches-constraints-and-future-horizons

Mantri, A. (2021). Real-Time Content Moderation Using Artificial Intelligence and Machine Learning. *International Journal of Science and Research (Raipur, India)*, 10(1), 1682–1684. DOI: 10.21275/SR24724150350

Mecaj, S. (2022). Artificial Intelligence and Legal Challenges. *ResearchGate*. https://www.researchgate.net/publication/360392203_ARTIFICIAL_INTELLIGENCE_AND_LEGAL_CHALLENGES

Mishra, P. K. (2024). AI And The Legal Landscape: Embracing Innovation, Addressing Challenges. *Live Law*.https://www.livelaw.in/lawschool/articles/law-and-ai-ai-powered-tools-general-data-protection-regulation-250673

Molina, M. D., & Sundar, S. S. (2022). *When AI moderates online content: effects of human collaboration and interactive transparency on user trust*. Academic., https://academic.oup.com/jcmc/article/27/4/zmac010/6648459

Rodrigues, R. (2023). Legal and human rights issues of AI: Gaps, challenges and vulnerabilities. *Journal of Responsible Technology*, 4, 100005. DOI: 10.1016/j.jrt.2020.100005

Shamra, N. (2024). Artificial Intelligence: Legal Implications and Challenges. *ResearchGate*. https://www.researchgate.net/publication/381848987_ARTIFICIAL_INTELLIGENCE_LEGAL_IMPLICATIONS_AND_CHALLENGES

Singh, J. (2024). The Role of AI in Enhancing Content Moderation on Social Platforms. *Outsourcing Center*. https://www.outsourcing-center.com/the-role-of-ai-in-enhancing-content-moderation-on-social-platforms/

Sreelatha, A., & Choudhary, G. (2023). Exploring The Use of AI In Legal Decision Making: Benefits and Ethical Implications. *Woxsen University*. https://woxsen.edu.in/research/white-papers/exploring-the-use-of-ai-in-legal-decision-making-benefits-and-ethical-implications/

Tallberg, J., Erman, E., Furendal, M., Geith, J., Klamberg, M., & Lundgren, M. (2023). The Global Governance of Artificial Intelligence: Next Steps for Empirical and Normative Research. *International Studies Review*, 2(3), viad040. Advance online publication. DOI: 10.1093/isr/viad040

Tobi, A. (2024). Towards an Epistemic Compass for Online Content Moderation. *Philosophy & Technology*, 37(3), 109. Advance online publication. DOI: 10.1007/s13347-024-00791-3

Udupa, S., Maronikolakis, A., & Wisiorek, A. (2023). Ethical scaling for content moderation: Extreme speech and the (in)significance of artificial intelligence. *Big Data & Society*, 10(1), 20539517231172424. Advance online publication. DOI: 10.1177/20539517231172424

Walter, Y. (2024). Managing the race to the moon: Global policy and governance in Artificial Intelligence regulation—A contemporary overview and an analysis of socioeconomic consequences. *Discover Artificial Intelligence*, 4(1), 14. Advance online publication. DOI: 10.1007/s44163-024-00109-4

Wang, S. (2023). Factors related to user perceptions of artificial intelligence (AI)-based content moderation on social media. *Computers in Human Behavior*, 149, 107971. DOI: 10.1016/j.chb.2023.107971

Wolff, L. C. (2020). Artificial Intelligence ante portas: The End of Comparative Law? *The Chinese Journal of Comparative Law*, 7(3), 484–504. DOI: 10.1093/cjcl/cxz020

Zaidan, E., & Ibrahim, I. A. (2024). AI Governance in a Complex and Rapidly Changing Regulatory Landscape: A Global Perspective. *Humanities & Social Sciences Communications*, 11(1), 1121. DOI: 10.1057/s41599-024-03560-x

Chapter 12
Detecting Hate Speech in the Digital Age: AI Solutions for Real-Time Moderation

C. V. Suresh Babu
https://orcid.org/0000-0002-8474-2882
Hindustan Institute of Technology and Science, India

S. Deva Darshini
https://orcid.org/0009-0001-7214-5175
Hindustan Institute of Technology and Science, India

ABSTRACT

This chapter explores the application of artificial intelligence (AI) in real-time hate speech detection on social media platforms, aiming to address the limitations of traditional moderation techniques. Utilizing machine learning frameworks such as TensorFlow and PyTorch, the study examines the effectiveness of AI models in processing vast amounts of data to identify nuanced forms of hate speech. Key findings indicate that while AI can significantly enhance detection speed and accuracy, challenges remain regarding bias in training datasets and the need for human oversight to ensure ethical moderation practices. The implications of this research highlight the necessity for a balanced approach that integrates AI capabilities with human judgment to foster safer online environments while preserving free speech. This study contributes to ongoing discussions about the ethical deployment of AI technologies in content moderation.

DOI: 10.4018/979-8-3693-9904-0.ch012

1. INTRODUCTION

1.1 Overview of Hate Speech on Social Media

Social media apps like Facebook, Twitter, and YouTube have, over the past ten years, changed everything about how we communicate. But as all this was wrought upon the digital sphere, harming behaviors increased with hate speech catching one of the highest places among the most prevalent. Hate speech that is mostly confined in cyberspace addresses particular individuals based on the different dimensions of race, religion, gender, or sexual orientation with psychological damage, social division, and even material harm. Social media's anonymity and mass following establish an easy venue for the diffusion of toxic messages, which can transform possibly private thoughts to viral content in just a minute. This has caught the attention of social media providers and governments alike, raising very important questions about how such platforms should properly be managed and moderated. That kind of traditional human moderation has proved woefully inadequate given the number of posts that must be read daily to be able to adequately moderate (Davidson, T., Warmsley, D., Macy, M., & Weber, I. 2017).

1.2 The Importance of Real-Time Detection and Response

Hence, real-time hate speech detection is the need of the hour. Compared to the static contents, social media posts are highly dynamic in nature. The malicious tweet or Facebook post may get retweeted, shared, and read by millions within the shortest span of time. The posts may cause irreparable damage to people and communities if not detected and moderated in due time. Real-time detection will allow hate speech to be identified right after it is posted, hence such widespread cannot occur. Reactions can also forestall the proliferation of the content pretty fast, so some of the potential damage is limited. Apart from acceleration of moderation, a real-time system is also a form of deterrence. Users may think twice about posting harmful content if they know that it can be removed within a couple of seconds. Without such ability, social media organizations would merely react and play catch-up to hate speech once done (Schmidt, A., & Wiegand, M. 2017).

1.3 Role of AI in Hate Speech Detection

One of the most powerful tools that emerged was through artificial intelligence because the problem is indeed massive for real-time hate speech moderation; in classical systems based on simple keyword matches or user reports, AI models can process large volumes of data, recognize patterns, and, to some extent, understand context much more than even simple manual human oversight. Even with just machine learning algorithms and NLP, it is possible to train AI to detect hate speech not just by unique words but even by monitoring how the relationships between the words are conveyed, the kind of sentiment that those words convey, or even the tone of the message. Since ML would learn from massive datasets of hate speech and could eventually become highly effective, such systems shall only improve in time. Furthermore, artificial intelligence runs all the clock long. Therefore, if there is no complication, it will monitor and regulate content 24/7 (Zampieri, M., Malmasi, S., Nakov, P., Rosenthal, S., Farra, N., & Kumar, R. 2019).

1.4 Scope and Relevance for Ethical AI in Social Media

This paper aims at determining the scope of real-time AI-driven detection of hate speech with a focus on technical tools and ethical implications of these technologies. We shall present Google Colab, TensorFlow, and PyTorch among several tools frequently deployed for developing machine learning models for hate speech detection. In addition, the paper will explore ethical AI inasmuch as there is a very pertinent question involved with preventing or mitigating harmful speech against free expression. The stakes for relevance here could not be higher: platforms increasingly rely on such technologies to modulate content at scale, but efforts need to be made continuously to ensure that AI does not inadvertently sustain bias or silence valid speech. It's not just about making smarter algorithms but also creating a system that respects human rights while making digital spaces safer for everyone (Floridi, L., Cowls, J., King, T. C., & Taddeo, M. 2020).

2. BACKGROUND AND RELEVANCE

2.1 Evolution of Content Moderation on Social Media

In the early days of social media, this was a much easier task. You had Facebook and Twitter totally dependent on user reports for marking inappropriate or harmful content. That system worked relatively well when those platforms were small-sized, but with users into billions, it became obvious that user-report-based systems were no longer sufficient. This paved the way for introducing minimalist automated filters, using some basic keywords to filter out the posts containing offensive speech. However, these tools were too simplistic and often did not grasp the context, while in many cases either over-censoring or under-censoring. The bankruptcy of such methods became even more obvious as platforms became even larger, especially when more nuanced and context-dependent forms of hate speech started appearing.

But today, the form of content moderation that is required is far removed from and incorporates much more advanced approaches capable of keeping track with the scale and complexity of modern social media (Chandrasekharan, E., Samory, M., Srinivasan, A., & Gilbert, E. 2017).

2.2 The Rise of Hate Speech and Its Societal Impact

Hate speech is nothing new; however, the impact and reach it can have since the invention of the internet and, more particularly, of social media, has assumed quite surprising dimensions. Where once the conversation could be limited to one's locality or region, the same post can reach millions across hours. Hate speech online has had real-world effects, ranging from inciting violence, instigating discrimination, and even genocide. Indeed, past decade, hate speech has appeared to have a concrete impact on society because online rhetoric has become a real-world event factor. Just recently, for example, violent protests in Charlottesville, Virginia, and the Christchurch mosque shootings show how hate speech operates to create fear and hostility environments that erode community social cohesion. With such a scenario of the society, there comes the dire need to work on developing technologies that will check the spread of such harmful content (Schmidt, A., & Wiegand, M. 2017).

2.3 Ethical Challenges in AI-Enabled Content Moderation

One of the biggest challenges with AI-driven hate speech detection is trying to balance efficiency with accuracy and fairness. The better the quality of training, the better quality of the model. And if the datasets that have been used for training are inherently biased, whether it's through design or unconscious bias, the AI models will reflect that. For example, speech of certain segments can be disproportionately targeted or unfairly flagged in case it is represented in the training data inadequately. Such raises major ethical questions. While the platform running such a system has a duty to remove harmful content in order to protect its users, they must at the same time ensure that moderation systems do not become instruments of discrimination or censorship. But there's also the question of responsibility: who is accountable if an AI model messes up-and flags or misses content it shouldn't? Those are some of the most serious ethical questions we must keep close in our work on developing AI-based moderation systems (Binns, R. 2018).

2.4 Importance of Real-Time Moderation in the Digital Age

Nowhere in today's digital world could there be a more urgent need to moderate real-time content. If content spread around platforms like Twitter or Facebook takes only hours to spread, it is already too late if harmed posts are moderated after a few hours. When seen, forwarded, and discussed with hateful messages, the damage has already been done. Real-time moderation ensures the catching and dealing with harmful content almost immediately, therefore reducing the probability of its spread and adverse consequences. Such situations are crucial to be considered when they include hate speech, where timely action may prevent escalation and protect vulnerable people and communities. AI, which can quickly process vast amounts of data in real-time for the purpose of analysis, answers this growing need. Even in today's digital environment, the most developed moderation systems would be insufficient if they lacked real-time capabilities (Floridi, L., Cowls, J., King, T. C., & Taddeo, M. 2020).

3. KEY QUESTIONS AND PROBLEMS ADDRESSED

3.1 The Need for Effective AI-Based Detection of Hate Speech

For instance, hate speech can be subtle and contextual; often, it is hard for any traditional keyword-based system to detect. AI can provide much more advanced approaches that check not only the existence of certain words in the message but also their relations between each other, tone, and general context as they appear in the message. Thus, this section argues why effective AI-based detection is important in overcoming the limitations of existing moderation systems. What this means is that AI, learning from extremely large datasets, can pick up patterns perhaps imperceptible to human moderators. Also, AI systems can operate at scale that human moderators simply cannot match-process millions of posts in real time. It's not even close to easy to develop models that can pick up the subtle nuances of language—particularly hate speech—and this chapter addresses some of the technical and ethical issues associated with it (Davidson, T., Warmsley, D., Macy, M., & Weber, I. 2017).

3.2 Addressing Bias and Accuracy in AI Models

One of the key concerns in AI-based content moderation includes bias. A biased dataset for training is likely to yield similarly biased outcomes from AI, targeting large groups and leaving out others. For example, algorithms would most probably over-police communities whose speech patterns do not have large enough utterance datasets in training data or are just not understood by the algorithm. These are important in ensuring a rich and representative dataset to train the AI models on and in ensuring constant accuracy evaluation and refinement. Other methods discussed for bias reduction include fairness metrics during model testing, and human oversight when reviewing and correcting AI decisions. Improving the fairness and accuracy of AI models can avoid the perpetuation of existing inequalities, and yet still grapple with this pressing problem of hate speech online (Binns, R. 2018).

3.3 Speed and Scalability: Challenges in Real-Time Moderation

Moderation of content becomes increasingly complex with increasing social media. For example, Facebook and Twitter process millions of posts every minute, which is impossible for human moderation. Despite AI, an enormous scale of content can create bottlenecks in moderation. This section elaborates on the technical challenges of developing AI systems that can scale to meet the demands of large platforms, maintain speed, and remain accurate. Here, we discuss how frameworks like TensorFlow and PyTorch can be used when building scalable AI models capable of high-speed real-time detection. In such models, the computational load can be diversified across servers so that more efficient processing of content can occur or by using a cloud-based solution to increase computing power. The system has to be extremely fast and scalable to enable the use of real-time moderation on big platforms for an AI system (Pavlopoulos, J., Sorensen, J., Dixon, L., & Thain, N. 2020).

3.4 Ethical Dilemmas in AI-Driven Moderation

There is plenty of ethics to be found in AI moderation. One of the most basic questions is: How does a system know, really and truly know, when something is hate speech and should be censored or removed from the internet? How can a system be properly trained, assuming a private company can even do that as a person can? That's one of the dilemmas: private companies are being set up to play this role, to police what to speak and what not to speak online. Another raised an issue of accountability: who is responsible for an AI system's actions? In addition, these questions take an urgent turn, as decisions made by such AI systems could reach the lives of millions. This chapter is about how much restraint versus how much protection of end-users from the harmful effects should be allowed, while ensuring that the platforms refrain from overstepping speech restrictions. The article further points out the need for transparency in AI-driven moderation and includes that the system should clearly explain to users how their content is moderated as well as possible recourse options, in case they believe their speech was unfairly censored (Floridi, L., Cowls, J., King, T. C., & Taddeo, M. 2020).

4. OBJECTIVES AND SCOPE

4.1 Primary Objectives of the Chapter

In this chapter, we aim to learn how AI technologies - particularly those built with the help of tools like TensorFlow, PyTorch, and Google Colab - transform typical approaches to hate speech detection and moderation within social media sites. In this chapter, we describe the technical and ethical objectives of the research: improving the accuracy and fairness of AI models, overcoming the challenges of real-time moderation, and ensuring that AI systems are designed in such a way as to maximize free speech with minimal harm. Another objective is the examination of how these AI tools can be integrated into prevailing infrastructures of moderation, giving concrete advice to developers and platform operators about what could work (Schmidt, A., & Wiegand, M. 2017).

4.2 Defining the Boundaries: What Will Be Covered

The paper particularly deals with the AI-driven solutions deployed on hate speech detection, with particular emphasis on real-time moderation. It does touch on the technical building and training of AI models behind such frameworks as TensorFlow and PyTorch and, in consideration of the deployment of such systems at scale, the associated ethics. This discussion will include a critical review of literature on AI and hate speech detection, an analysis of current technologies, and case studies by the major social media platforms. However, this chapter will not approach broader regulatory or legal aspects of hate speech moderation because its focus is primarily on the technical and ethical dimensions of AI-based solutions (Floridi, L., Cowls, J., King, T. C., & Taddeo, M. 2020).

4.3 Delimitations: Exclusions from the Chapter

Although the paper will be dealing with the part played by AI in hate speech detection and moderation, it will not attempt to explain legal frameworks and government regulations on online hate speech. In addition, this paper does not outline other causes of harmful content online: misinformation or extremism, although these are correlated issues. Instead, it will narrow the focus on hate speech detection and the particular challenges and opportunities of AI technologies in this area. In addition, explanations of machine learning algorithms in depth will be omitted because that is not the focus, although it means discussing the technical intricacies of model development of interest (Zampieri, M., Malmasi, S., Nakov, P., Rosenthal, S., Farra, N., & Kumar, R. 2019).

4.4 Relation to the Edited Book's Theme of Ethical AI Solutions

This chapter supports the general theme of ethical AI solutions through its discussion of how AI can be applied toward creating safer online spaces in ways that balance the complexity of free speech and human rights. In focusing on the ethical issues in applying AI for hate speech moderation, the paper contributes to the book's objective of discussing how AI technologies may be applied responsibly in sectors. It also contributes to the continuing debates on whether AI will be beneficent or detrimental, depending upon how it is designed and developed. The chapter is expected to strike an equitable balance when considering the capabilities of AI, in terms of what it can offer as well as its limitations in relation to one of the most challenging problems of our era within the digital area (Floridi, L., Cowls, J., King, T. C., & Taddeo, M. 2020).

5. LITERATURE REVIEW

5.1 Review of Existing Moderation Techniques and Limitations

Content moderation on social media sites has dramatically changed from manual processes to automated systems. The traditional methods of moderation include keyword filtering and user reporting, which have both been critical limitations. Keyword filters, though simple, did not account for context; they over-censored and missed nuances like sarcasm or coded language (Chandrasekharan et al., 2017). Although valuable, user reporting was slow and biased with unevenly distributed moderation policies being enforced (Schmidt & Wiegand, 2017). Human moderation was nuanced but could never hope to handle the massive volume of user-generated content on social media platforms such as Facebook and Twitter. This weakness led to the rise of AI-based solutions, providing scalability and better accuracy.

5.2 AI and Machine Learning Models in Content Detection

AI-based approaches, mainly ML and NLP, have revolutionized hate speech detection. The latest forms of ML models, such as BERT and other transformer-based architectures, go beyond keyword matching by understanding text semantics and contextual nuances (Devlin et al., 2019). These models show good performance in understanding context-dependent hate speech and detecting large datasets of patterns. The above have added to the arsenal of techniques within NLP, including tokenization, sentiment analysis, and word embeddings, increasing the ability of AI in the identification of subtle emerging hate speech. However, there are problems with biased training sets and very limited multilingualism.

5.3 Current Approaches to Real-Time AI-Based Moderation

Real-time moderation systems, relying on large-scale data processing, distributed among AI frameworks, see companies like Facebook and Twitter exploit AI models designed to spot hate speech minutes after the posting has gone live and therefore limit the damages caused by its spread. However, those systems suffer from latency problems and false positives and negatives. Recent developments in edge computing and cloud-based deployments with frameworks such as TensorFlow and PyTorch have enhanced speed and scalability (Pavlopoulos et al., 2020). Still, real-time systems must be constantly monitored and updated to address new and adaptive hate speech patterns.

5.4 Ethical Consideration and Bias in AI Models

A significant challenge in AI-driven hate speech detection is addressing bias in training datasets. Models trained on imbalanced data can disproportionately target specific groups while failing to detect hate speech in underrepresented contexts (Binns, 2018). This leads to ethical concerns in the areas of fairness and accountability. Furthermore, the opacity of AI decision-making processes leaves a lack of transparency regarding moderation outcomes, reducing the trust of users. Such ethical AI frameworks should focus on diverse datasets along with audits and metrics for fairness measures to overcome these factors. Transparency mechanisms like Explainable AI, recourse by users are needed for proper moderation practices in the pursuit of equity.

5.5 Gaps in Current Research on Hate Speech Detection

A lot of development has been seen but limitations exist in the current hate speech research too. Most of the currently available work is based on English language datasets, failing to take into account the complexities of multilingual and cross-cultural hate speech detection (Schmidt & Wiegand, 2017). The current models do not also grasp contextual subtleties, such as sarcasm and coded speech, in which bad actors tend to communicate to avoid being caught. Another crucial gap is the lack of empirical studies that prove the effectiveness of AI moderation systems in real-world application. In fact, such gaps can only be filled with a holistic perspective that incorporates linguistics, ethics, and technology in designing robust and fair AI.

6. METHODOLOGY

6.1 Theoretical Approaches to Hate Speech Detection

The theoretical framework for this study, then, relates to machine learning and natural language processing techniques as the basis of modern detection models. Supervised learning aims to train the models on labeled datasets so that they can identify patterns and predict this or new data that could not be seen. This section describes some of the theoretical approaches that can be found in building AI models for hate speech detection: feature extraction, NLP's role in understanding text content, as well as some algorithms like decision trees, support vector machines, and deep learning models applied to get the correct training classifier (Davidson, T., Warmsley, D., Macy, M., & Weber, I. 2017).

6.2 AI Tools and Frameworks: Google Colab, TensorFlow, PyTorch

Among the AI tools and frameworks used, Google Colab, TensorFlow, and PyTorch, are renowned to create and train the models for machine learning. Google Colab provides a collaborative environment in which you share your code to be executed on powerful cloud-based GPUs; hence it is ideal for training large-scale models. Developed by Google, TensorFlow is one of the most popular premier machine learning frameworks. It stands for flexibility and scalability while developing models. PyTorch, developed by Facebook, is preferred for the ease of use and dynamic computational graphs, which makes it more flexible to develop its model. This part should explain in very detail how these tools come into building the AI models for real-time hate speech detection, from data preprocessing to model training and evaluation (Devlin, J., Chang, M. W., Lee, K., & Toutanova, K. 2019).

6.3 Machine Learning and NLP Techniques for Real-Time Detection

Some of the machine learning and natural language processing techniques deployed in real-time hate speech detection are splitting text into smaller units of analysis, and where words are converted into numerical vectors capturing their meaning in context through word embeddings. (Suresh Babu, C. V., Kowsika, S., et. al. (2023). Sentiment analysis and topic modeling are also utilized in determining whether a tone and subject matter of a post and identify hate speech. It details the specific use in real-time detection models so that hate speech gets caught and flagged early (Zampieri, M., Malmasi, S., Nakov, P., Rosenthal, S., Farra, N., & Kumar, R. 2019).

6.4 Data Processing for Hate Speech Detection

Data processing is perceived to be an important step in the building of an AI model for hate speech detection. Such a step involves cleaning of the data, where one removes irrelevant information from the dataset, then gets the text correctly formatted for the purpose of analysis. The data also needs to be labeled, with examples of hate speech and non-hate speech clearly identified so that the model can learn to differentiate between the two. This section would therefore detail the handling of data processing in this study by demonstrating how large datasets of social media posts are prepared to train AI models. The section above shows much interest in the guarantee that the data could be representative of different languages, cultures, and contexts in order not to incur bias (Schmidt, A., & Wiegand, M. 2017).

6.5 Justification for the Chosen Methodologies

The methodologies used are founded on proved effectiveness toward the detection of hate speech and their scalability to real-time applications. In fact, algorithms based on machine learning - made particularly with frameworks like TensorFlow and PyTorch - have been proven to perform better than keyword-based systems not only in accuracy but also in speed. Techniques like NLP provide more semantic meaning to the text, and techniques like sentiment analysis and word embeddings enable the model to identify more latent hatred through subtle forms of hate speech (Suresh Babu, C. V., Kowsika, S., et. al. (2023).. The section explains why these methodologies have been chosen and how they will add to the overall purposes of the study (Floridi, L., Cowls, J., King, T. C., & Taddeo, M. 2020).

6.6 Addressing the Challenge of Real-Time Scalability

Scalability is one of the key challenges for real-time hate speech detection because platforms post millions of posts per minute. Hence, AI must be designed with efficiency and speed. Distributed computing and the use of cloud-based solutions in models, such as TensorFlow or PyTorch, provide for the processing of gigantic data sets across multiple servers by cutting latency and improving efficiency. Another edge computing advantage involves the reduction of content evaluation delay through proximate processing. Still, no amount of scalability is enough if it skews accuracy. It follows therefore that any oversight when flagged content occurs with a human presence in play; otherwise, AI-based error in terms of false positives or negatives may serve to undermine the system altogether. Scaling up AI moderation has much to do with a careful blend between technical efficacy and contextual awareness to work well.

7. WORKFLOW:

Figure 1. Workflow of the project

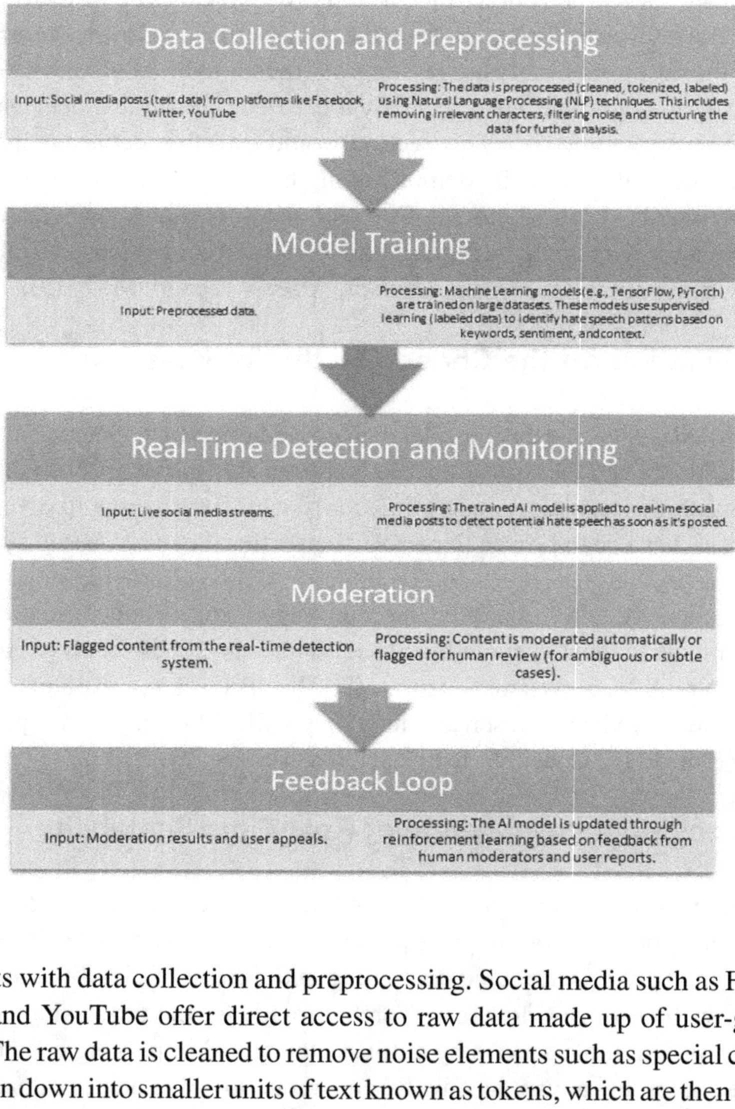

It starts with data collection and preprocessing. Social media such as Facebook, Twitter, and YouTube offer direct access to raw data made up of user-generated content. The raw data is cleaned to remove noise elements such as special characters and broken down into smaller units of text known as tokens, which are then classified into "hate speech" or "non-hate speech." Data preprocessing is to alter the data into an organized form that can be processed in machine learning.

This phase is known as the model training phase in which AI models, using frameworks like TensorFlow and PyTorch, learn on enormous gigantic datasets of labeled social media posts. This enables the models to learn to identify patterns based on specific keywords, tone, and sentiment. The model gets improved over large amounts of data and can correctly identify hate speech more effectively.

Once trained, the model goes into real-time detection and monitoring. Here, AI deployment is undertaken to monitor some of the live content that is posted through social media. This quickly evaluates such content, goes through texts and context, and identifies potential hate speech. And with detection of harmful content, the model flags it for immediate actions.

The third one is response and moderation, where flagged content will automatically be eliminated or submitted to human moderation. When the AI's decision is not binary, the content will be evaluated by the human moderators so that appropriate moderation is carried out on harmful content. This hybrid of AI and the checks of humans ensures that such content receives the right controls in real-time and minimizes its spread and influence.

7.1: Block Diagram

Figure 2. Block Diagram

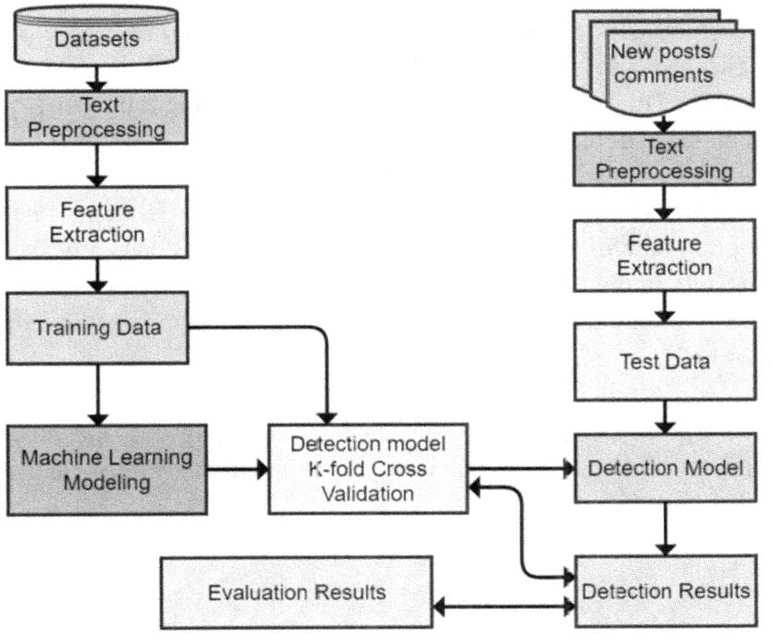

Figure 2 states that, It describes an entire process of hate speech detection through machine learning. The first phase is the data collection phase, where a big dataset of comments on social media posts is collected. The data is gathered to train the model so that it can be used for detection. It needs preprocessing before it is analyzed. The first step of this process is called text preprocessing, which often refers to clearing the text of irrelevant characters, converting all text to lowercase, and removing common stopwords such as "the" or "and" since it does not provide meaningful information.

Following the cleaning of the text comes feature extraction, where salient patterns or signals of hate speech are extracted from the dataset. This may include some offending words or phrases, which have specific syntactic structures that occur more frequently in hate speech than anywhere else. The features extracted, are used to develop the training data, an input for machine learning models.

In the machine learning modeling stage, training data is used to develop the model for hate speech detection. Techniques like K-fold cross-validation are utilized by the system, which guarantees the correctness of functions executed by the model. Such a form of validation divides data into multiple portions, thus providing multiple testing and training instances for the model. Such versions make sure the generalization properties in the course of dealing with unseen data, thereby ensuring minimal overfitting occurs with the model.

In parallel, the newly generated posts or comments undergo an analog process. The new content also receives text preprocessing and feature extraction to yield test data. This test data is now inputted to the detection model trained in the earlier phase. The model then applies its learnt patterns in detecting if the newly generated posts contain hate speech.

Now, when the model is through processing real-time generated data, it produces detection results. These results may be in the form of identification of hate speech or flagging non-hateful content; results that are evaluated constantly. This system feeds the results into an evaluation phase, where model performance is assessed. This provides continuous improvement to the model in terms of accuracy towards detection of hate speech.

In other words, this workflow integrates training of a machine learning model with real-time processing of data in the detection of hate speech. The model is constantly validated and updated so that it may keep up with new trends and variations in patterns of harmful speech.

8. CONTRIBUTION TO THE FIELD

8.1 Enhancing Moderation Strategies with AI Technologies

The integration of AI technologies such as TensorFlow and PyTorch into the overall approach in content moderation is a huge leap forward. This reduces reliance on human moderators, who typically handle too much since the volume of content created is enormous. AI tools are able to process huge volumes of data in real-time while identifying harmful content before it spreads. This section proceeds to speak at length about how AI technologies advance on existing moderation strategies to be more efficient, scalable, and less prone to human fallibility. It then further goes on to elucidate the potential evolution of AI in handling the ever-changing nature of hate speech and these newfound forms of damaging content when they appear (Devlin, J., Chang, M. W., Lee, K., & Toutanova, K. 2019).

8.2 Addressing Gaps in Real-Time Detection and Response

Despite all these major breakthroughs in AI-driven moderation, many holes persist in real-time hate speech detection. The detection of multilingual is one of the most important aspects since most AI models are programmed to concentrate more on content that is predominantly in English, which means that most hate speech that is in languages other than English is not moderated. This deficiency hinders their general application on diverse user-based platforms around the globe. In addition, the perception of users towards AI moderation is not yet adequately explored. A sense of mistrust emanates from the users concerning the lack of fairness, transparency, and overreach in moderation decisions. Users will have no other choice but to mistrust if moderation decisions are not explained. Only with this investment in multilingual models and transparency mechanisms that would make it possible for the user to understand and contest moderation decisions will these gaps be filled. In combination with updates to respond to emerging hate speech patterns, this would create an even more inclusive and effective moderation framework.

8.3 Overcoming Biases in AI Models

The results can only be as good as those the data is trained on; therefore, any bias in these training data can result in biased outcomes for content moderation. The next section delves into the steps that were taken to minimize bias in the AI models applied in this study through fairness metrics, diverse datasets, and regular audits of the models. It also brings in the need for transparency into AI-driven moderation, suggesting that platforms should have easy ways of providing users with clear explanations about how their content is being moderated and what recourse they have if flagged for speech believed to be wrongly detected (Binns, R. 2018).

8.4 Practical Solutions for AI-Driven Content Moderation on Social Media

Of course, AI technology promises to take the world of content moderation to a whole new level, but proper execution of such methodologies will need careful planning and execution. AI-driven solutions need to be integrated into the already fairly complex social media infrastructures, which in some cases stretch to global levels. This section offers a really detailed, practical solution for embedding AI models into social media effectively.

First, platforms must know if their infrastructure can support AI models at scale. This means using cloud-based solutions like Google Colab that allow training and deployment of AI models on powerful GPUs without the cost implications of having on-premise expensive hardware. In turn, this implies the effective use of frameworks like TensorFlow and PyTorch designed for large-scale data processing. These tools can be used to make deployments on many servers, thereby dispersing the computational load, enabling content to be moderated in real-time.

A fine implementation of AI in moderation would be one that actually supports human moderation. Although AI systems can discern hate speech much faster and in greater quantities than moderators, it fails when the content is subtle or context-sensitive. In this regard, a hybrid approach where AI flags potentially harmful content for review by humans is typically the most effective approach. This would mean that most of the work would be done by the AI, leaving human moderators to intervene mainly when the question is a bit more complicated, to determine the final judgment.

Another, the platforms set for the AI to learn from the decisions taken by the human moderators. Human moderators correct false positives and false negatives, which in turn can be fed back into the model for the AI to improve its performance. Such reinforcement learning allows it to grow in accuracy over time.

Lastly, transparency and friendliness in reporting mechanisms. User's content moderation should carry notice if AI is used, and the platforms should elaborate about the reasons why one's posts are flagged or deleted. An appeals process where a user could object to the moderation decision made through AI systems might build up trust among users toward any AI-driven moderation system. The use of AI should be transparent, and it should explain what part it plays in this content moderation, so users can understand the kind of evaluation their posts undergo (Pavlopoulos, J., Sorensen, J., Dixon, L., & Thain, N. 2020).

8.5 Ethical Oversight and Best Practices for AI Moderation

Ethical oversight is necessary in AI-based content moderation to make it fair, transparent, and accountable. Best practices start with the use of diverse and representative training datasets to avoid bias and ensure moderation that is fair across different languages, cultures, and social groups. Regular auditing of AI systems by independent ethics boards or third-party evaluators can detect bias and imbalances in the outcomes of moderation and facilitate remedial action. Equal transparency is also needed, whereby the AI model informs the users how the decision was made and avails a means for the user to appeal the content that is marked or removed. Hybrid approaches are used where human judgment combined with AI ensures ethics practice through dealing with such cases that AI will likely misinterpret. This can then lead to an atmosphere of trust between users and ethical standards in moderation.

9. ANALYSIS AND FINDINGS

9.1 Effectiveness of AI Tools in Detecting Hate Speech

It is crucial to note that the scalable implementation with the Google Colab demonstrates the efficacy of AI tools such as TensorFlow and PyTorch in real-time hate speech detection. The models introduced in this research signify substantial improvements over traditional content moderation approaches-mainly because of their speed, accuracy, and scalability. The models would digest large amounts of social media content fast, spot offending posts before they garnered much spread, and perform basic keyword filtering with an added benefit of more complex characteristics that could identify hate speech in terms of coded language and context-specific hate, thanks to NLP techniques such as tokenization and word embeddings and sentiment analysis (Suresh Babu, C. V., Kowsika, S., et. al. (2023)..

One of the major insights to come out of the analysis is that the AI models do tend to reduce false positives, which are defined as benign content flags, and false negatives, which are defined as cases in which hate speech is missed. These are common issues arising from traditional moderation systems, and keywords are predominantly used. This often leads to over-censorship when a lot flagged content might not be offensive, or even the opposite: missing very subtle forms of hate speech altogether. It is astonishing how the AI models from this study show much greater improvements in both, and therefore could be more promising for use in practical real-life situations (Davidson, T., Warmsley, D., Macy, M., & Weber, I. 2017).

9.2 Comparative Research: Traditional vs. AI-Based Moderation

On making a comparative analysis between the traditional and AI-based moderation, the bright side of having AI-driven systems can be seen. Traditional methods of moderation include but are not limited to manual reviews and keyword filters, and they are extremely labor-intensive and slow as well. In addition to these, they are also prone to numerous inaccuracies because how these moderation methods are performed cannot compare with any standards of scalability and will certainly not be able to keep up with postings in the millions within a minute. In addition, keyword filters cannot take into account context-per-word usage, which typically leads to low false-positive to false-negative rates.

In contrast, AI-based content moderation can analyze content in real-time, meaning posting times correlate inversely with flags made on such toxic posts. The AI models, especially those that are trained using the machine learning technique, have a highly developed sense of nuance to the context in the post, making it more sensitive to recognize hate speech that would otherwise go unnoticed. Generally, both the training and testing AI models for this research were faster and also more precise than the traditional methods used, thus offering a scalable and efficient solution to content moderation for large platforms (Zampieri, M., Malmasi, S., Nakov, P., Rosenthal, S., Farra, N., & Kumar, R. 2019).

9.3 Case Studies of Real-Time AI-Enabled Moderation on Social Media

Case studies in major platforms, such as Facebook and Twitter, demonstrate the potential but also the challenges of AI-based real-time moderation. In fact, Facebook has had a great success in integrating multilingual AI systems able to detect hate speech over 50 languages. As such, it demonstrates interest in international content moderation. Twitter has chosen real-time AI models to flag abusive tweets within seconds; hence bad content gets minimal visibility. Still, despite such success stories, there are false positives, false negatives, and user dissatisfaction with the flagged content. For instance, some users have raised a complaint that non-hateful content was moderated due to the lack of contextual understanding by AI systems. These case studies point to the need for hybrid models that combine the scalability of AI with human judgment, ensuring nuanced and fair moderation while addressing technical limitations. Future systems will be able to improve the efficiency of real-time detection, balance between fairness and user trust using lessons learned from these implementations.

9.4 Addressing the Limitations of AI Detection Models

Still, despite the remarkable success of AI models in detecting hate speech, there is much in this that needs to be improved about effectiveness. The biggest challenge here is the detection of nuanced expressions of hate speech-whether they are sarcasm or coded language-where much depends upon the context and its difficulty in interpretation by AI models, which would result in higher false negatives. Further, hate speech is adaptive, changing with time. Bad actors are constantly discovering new ways to evade moderation systems aside from the sheer creative power of human beings. AI models need to be constantly updated and retrained to stay abreast of it (Devlin, J., Chang, M. W., Lee, K., & Toutanova, K. 2019).

9.5 Key Insights from Model Implementation

The critical implications of implementing AI models based on TensorFlow, PyTorch, and Google Colab regarding the challenges and opportunities in real-time hate speech detection is that there should be continuous model evaluation and retraining. Hate speech is not static in nature; it evolves with time as a result of new methods of harmful content. For a machine to remain effective, AI models must be updated from time to time to reflect changes in hate speech. This makes platforms necessitate the investment in the development of models along with the continuous collection of data to maintain an up-to-date AI system.

Scalability is yet another salient insight. The amount of posts handled by the social media platform is millions per minute. Still, this massive amount of data is processed in real-time without compromising the accuracy. This further enables the scale deployment of models on cloud solutions, such as Google Colab. Scalable deployment will enable platforms to moderate very high volumes of content quickly and efficiently. Finally, the process of implementation provided insight into the importance of human oversight: despite the capabilities AI models may offer regarding the moderation of the bulk of content, it is still important that human moderators take a look at more complex cases and help in the provision of context that could have been missed by the AI systems involved (Pavlopoulos, J., Sorensen, J., Dixon, L., & Thain, N. 2020).

10. SUGGESTIONS AND RECOMMENDATIONS

10.1 Improved Training Datasets for AI Models

Quality and diversity of training datasets will play a critical role in the development of working AI models for hate speech detection. Most existing datasets are biased or limited in scope in a way that makes their performance easily affected by such biases when detecting hate speech across various languages and cultural contexts. Datasets have to be far more representative of worldwide user interactions-including different dialects and cultural references-but also the ever-changing nature of hate speech. Platforms must be interacting with NGOs, academics researchers, and civil society groups so that there are very practical applications from real-world examples of hate speech, especially from underrepresented and at-risk communities. It will also update datasets of new forms of injurious content constantly and fine-tune models with changing context for hate speech capture. This recommendation will make sure that AI models, in the context of moderation, are both accurate and equitable (Zampieri, M., Malmasi, S., Nakov, P., Rosenthal, S., Farra, N., & Kumar, R. 2019).

10.2 Reducing Bias in Machine Learning Algorithms

In using biased models that moderate the sensitive content, such as hate speech, machine learning algorithms have a big problem related to bias. When the AI system, trained on biased data, tends to forget what it learned and draws similar conclusions that are normal, it unconsciously discriminates against certain groups and flags the content more frequently from those communities or does not flag hate speech against the underrepresented communities. The platforms must ensure that their training data is properly diverse in terms of various languages, regions, and social groups to minimize bias. They can also use fairness metrics during model evaluation to determine where certain groups are being over-flagged or under-flagged. Periodic audits on AI models can help identify where bias is creeping in insidiously (Suresh Babu, C. V., Suruthi, G., et. al. 2024). Complex cases may involve the introduction of human intervention as a mechanism for remedying the oversight of certain biases by AI. Such remediation of the challenges will ensure that the content moderation system is fair and more inclusive, winning the trust of the user base (Binns, R. 2018).

10.3 Collaborative Frameworks for Cross-Platform Hate Speech Detection

Hate speech permeates every individual platform in the digital network. Efforts to address hate speech successfully will depend on social media companies being collaborative with one another. A shared approach will establish common standards for hate speech, which can then be applied universally by the social media sites to improve each site's moderation strategy. A recommendation is to develop a shared framework that pools anonymised data of incidents of hate speech between platforms, so each platform's AI can then learn from a broad repertoire of harmful content. A related possibility is collaboration in the development of shared industry-wide tools and models, further leveraging a greater diversity of developer expertise. Additionally, cross-platform collaborations shall also bring on board the ethical standards, thereby reducing differences in approaches used in moderation. Through this collaboration, the platforms may devise more comprehensive and standardized systems to detect and moderate hate speech that creates a more secure online atmosphere (Floridi, L., Cowls, J., King, T. C., & Taddeo, M. 2020).

10.4 The Role of Human Moderation in Complementing AI

Although AI does an excellent job in processing large amounts of data very quickly, human moderators play an indispensable role in context-sensitive and complex cases. AI models fail to pick up subtleties such as sarcasm, cultural nuances, and coded language, which are very much interpreted by humans. A hybrid system ensures moderation decision efficiency and fairness because AI can flag potentially harmful content, while human moderators review ambiguous cases. Another critical way human feedback refines AI models is through correcting the false positives and negatives of the model, thereby generating an improvement loop. Thus, with this collaborative approach, moderation improves accuracy while instilling user confidence that moderation doesn't just work on some abstruse application of algorithms but through careful human supervision.

10.5 Implementing Ethical Reviews for AI Systems

In fact, the use of AI moderation systems should be subject to ethical reviews from time to time to ensure proper and responsible usage. This should encompass fairness, efficacy, and impact on a wider cross-section of users from underrepresented or even marginalized communities. In general, therefore, ethical reviews can pinpoint biases within an AI system to avoid any form of disproportionate moderation decisions based on certain demographics. These checks should be performed by external ethics boards or independent experts to tap into the objectivity necessary for evaluating these systems. Platforms must also provide transparency in their AI systems, and must explain to their users how decisions are made and give them avenues for appealing these decisions. Ethical reviews may also take cognisance of the long-term implications of AI moderation in free speech, privacy, and trust amongst users. Only through transparent ethical audits occurring on an ongoing basis will proof that AI moderation systems of such platforms are equitable, responsible to users' rights, and fair be assured (Floridi, L., Cowls, J., King, T. C., & Taddeo, M. 2020).

11.PSEUDO CODE:

```
START

IMPORT necessary libraries:

- pandas as pd

- sklearn.model_selection for train_test_split

- sklearn.feature_extraction.text for TfidfVectorizer

- sklearn.linear_model for LogisticRegression

- sklearn.metrics for accuracy_score

- time

FUNCTION main():
```

```
TRY:

LOAD dataset from 'data.csv' into DataFrame df

EXCEPT FileNotFoundError:

PRINT "Dataset not found. Please check the file path."

EXIT program

# Preprocess data

SPLIT df into training and testing sets:

- X_train, X_test, y_train, y_test using train_test_split
(80% train, 20% test)

# Vectorize the text data using TF-IDF

INITIALIZE vectorizer as TfidfVectorizer with stop_
words='english' and max_df=0.7

TRANSFORM X_train into TF-IDF representation: X_train_tfidf

TRANSFORM X_test into TF-IDF representation: X_test_tfidf

# Train the Logistic Regression model
```

```
INITIALIZE model as LogisticRegression

FIT model using X_train_tfidf and y_train

# Evaluate the model

PREDICT y_pred using model on X_test_tfidf

PRINT "Accuracy:" + accuracy_score(y_test, y_pred)

# Define real-time prediction function

FUNCTION predict_real_time(text):

TRANSFORM input text into TF-IDF representation: text_tfidf

PREDICT prediction using model on text_tfidf

RETURN 'Hate Speech' IF prediction is 1 ELSE 'Non-Hate
Speech'

# Real-time prediction simulation

PRINT "Real-Time Hate Speech Detection. Type 'exit' to
stop."

WHILE TRUE:
```

```
PROMPT user for input "Enter your message:"

IF user_input is 'exit':

BREAK loop

result = CALL predict_real_time(user_input)

PRINT "Prediction:" + result

CALL main()

END
```

12. FUTURE SCOPE FOR RESEARCH

12.1 Potential for Hybrid AI and Human Moderation Models

The hybridization of human and artificial models through which hate speech is moderated both through algorithms and human judgment is the future of content moderation. AI is strong on dealing with vast volumes of content at velocities of lightning speeds thus suited to detecting patterns and be in a position to review hate speech live. This way, however, humans bring contextual understanding and ethical reasoning into the process. That becomes particularly crucial in cases complex or culturally specific, which AI might otherwise misinterpret. Future research should focus on refining this hybrid model, that is, identifying the most effective ways to combine AI efficiency with human insight. Such studies can be undertaken to better manage the interaction between AI systems and human moderators for example, what constitutes an appropriate threshold forwhen the decision made by the AI system should be escalated for review by a human. The aim is to develop an optimum system that is accurate and fair in the context of the challenges posed by content moderation in today's dynamic and highly diverse digital environment (Floridi, L., Cowls, J., King, T. C., & Taddeo, M. 2020).

12.2 Expanding AI's Role in Detecting Other Harmful Content

While the paper zooms in on the role of AI in hate speech moderation, AI can further be developed to include a range of harmful content detections, such as misinformation, cyberbullying, extremist propaganda, and harmful misinformation like the anti-vaccine movement. The nature of each of these content types is different and requires different kinds of detection methods. For instance, misinformation typically speaks to subtle manipulations of fact rather than noxious harmful speech per se, but cyberbullying could more plausibly take the shape of a mix of harassment, threats, and psychological manipulation. Future work should consider whether AI models can be built upon or extended to mediate content of this sort more effectively-than through advanced NLP techniques or machine learning algorithms that distinguish between kinds of harm. The improvement of AI goes hand in hand with continuous research on more intricate models that can understand and proactively prevent the spread of many forms of online harm, thus making digital environments safer and more inclusive (Schmidt, A., & Wiegand, M. 2017).

12.3 Exploring Unsupervised Learning Techniques for Hate Speech Detection

The front presented by the hate speech detection application is exciting: it may eventually help in the finding of harmful content without the high cost of pre-labeled datasets. Against such a backdrop, unsupervised learning automatically makes an AI system discover patterns and anomalies in large volumes of data without explicit guidance from human experts, a case that stands in contrast to the one in supervised learning in which models are trained on annotated examples. This approach would particularly be very effective in the fast-evolving domain of hate speech, where new instances of damaging language are constantly coming into existence. As unsupervised learning would help AI methods point out trends or clusters of hate speech that have yet to be labeled or classified by human moderators, this would be advantageous for automatic classification. The work of the future may, therefore, involve integrating unsupervised learning into real-time content moderation to help make them better at detecting new and emerging forms of hate speech. Combining the strengths of both supervised and unsupervised methods might lead to even more effective and adaptive systems toward effective detection of hate speech and handling dynamic online behaviors well (Davidson, T., Warmsley, D., Macy, M., & Weber, I. 2017).

12.4 Innovations in Real-Time, Large-Scale AI Deployments

Significant technical challenges come with scaling AI models to operate in real time on massive platforms such as Twitter, Facebook, and YouTube. Here are the distributed computing, edge computing, and various cloud-based AI deployment strategies that must find the greenfield innovations necessary for hate speech detection systems to process millions of posts per minute without trading off much accuracy. More research will be required in optimising frameworks such as TensorFlow and PyTorch to allow for high-scale operations, thus keeping models efficient when the amount of data is big. How AI can take advantage of edge computing—where data is processed near where it is generated, thus avoiding long distance and time for the transfer of data—will greatly reduce latency and allow for more effective live moderation response times. Second, researchers should investigate how computational efficiency might have to be balanced with the ethical need for deep content analysis in ensuring that AI models do not make the mistake of mistaking speed for accuracy or fairness. These innovations will be absolutely critical in scaling AI systems that can keep up with real-time demands for content moderation on the largest social media platforms (Devlin, J., Chang, M. W., Lee, K., & Toutanova, K. 2019).

12.5 Ethical Concerns for Future AI Models

Where AI is being used centrally in content moderation, future research needs to include the ethical questions that such technologies bring to the fore. Since privacy, surveillance, free speech, and algorithmic bias issues become more relevant to questions about the ability of AI systems, there lies a need to consider how to make AI models transparent, explainable, and accountable. One part of it is creating systems where users know how moderation decisions are being made and will be able to appeal or challenge those decisions (Srisakthi, S. & Suresh Babu, C. V. 2024).. Another necessity is periodic auditing of AI models for potential bias that does not disproportionately affect communities in the margins or unfairly censor speech that may not be appreciated by everyone. The ethical implications of AI must also be considered-how it can be used so that its contribution falls into the rubric of respect for privacy and no kind of invasive monitoring is done on users' behavior. The creation of ethical frameworks for AI in content moderation will help create wholesome service from these systems for society, according to what is right, just, and responsible (Floridi, L., Cowls, J., King, T. C., & Taddeo, M. 2020).

13. CONCLUSION

13.1 Summary of Key Findings

This paper describes how AI technologies-from the most recent TensorFlow, PyTorch, and Google Colab-develop into technologies that help shape the future of real-time hate speech detection on platforms like social media. AI models had a significant advantage over traditional moderation techniques, offering much higher speeds and scalability and possibly greater accuracy compared to methods used previously. From the foregoing analysis, it has been shown that there is an increasing need for making the training data up-to-date, de-biasing AI models, and the incorporation of ethical safeguards for the moderation process to ensure that fairness and equity are met. Human oversight, in addition, has been accorded pride of place alongside efficiency by AI since content-sensitive cases need to be addressed appropriately. Finally, the study concludes that AI-driven moderation can actually result in a significantly high increase in safety and inclusivity in digital environments only if used responsibly and ethically.

13.2 Implications for Social Media Platforms

Implications for social media platforms: The implications of this research on social media platforms are profound. While the platforms struggle with the problems of content moderation, the sheer volume of user-generated content that crosses their servers every hour, the solution AI brings with it is scalable enough to find hate speech in real time and reduce the spread of particular harmful posts. However, AI systems need to be deployed thoughtfully, with ongoing work in decreasing bias, increasing transparency, and holding users accountable. Platforms must also factor the value of hybrid AI-human moderation systems, whereby AI takes care of the bulk but human moderators weigh in on tough or ambiguous cases. In this regard, social media companies must invest in ethical reviews and transparency measures to ensure that the users are explained how AI-driven moderation systems work and how they can appeal a decision. By doing these, the platform creates trust with the users and makes the online space safer for their global communities.

13.3 Long-Term Prospects of AI in Hate Speech Moderation

The long-term future of moderation and hate speech is likely to make AI an even more central component in the mechanism. The more sophisticated machine learning models become, the more subtle forms of hate speech they can recognize-moving the curve dynamically on what hate speech looks like as such acts also evolve according to the efforts of moderation. The long-term future of AI in this area will depend on ongoing funding for research within these areas, including ethical AI, bias reduction, and hybrids that combine the best features from each approach to automation with human oversight. In addition, AI systems also have to be flexible and adaptive to new challenges as they emerge. More importantly, the future of AI in hate speech moderation appears promising and will warrant a commitment to fairness, transparency, and user engagement so that the systems work responsibly and effectively for years to come.

13.4 Balancing Free Speech and Safety through Ethical AI

One of the biggest challenges that AI-driven content moderation poses is balancing safety with free speech. Less dangerous content must be removed, while not unduly suppressing lawful forms of expression: a delicate approach toward models that recognize context and cultural differences, but one guided by clear, fair moderation policies. Moreover, the processes followed on the platform must be transparent in that it keeps the user abreast of how their content is moderated and provides avenues for appeal when the speech of an individual has been curtailed in an unjustified manner. With such a balance between free speech and safety, the ethical use of AI can foster an inclusive digital space where voices of divergent speakers are heard without minimizing harm.

REFERENCES

Alorainy, W., Burnap, P., Liu, H., & Williams, M. L. (2019). Detecting hate speech automatically: Challenging the problem of offensive language in social media. *Journal of Computational Social Science*, 2(1), 125–139.

Badjatiya, P., Gupta, S., & Varma, V. (2017). Deep learning for hate speech detection in tweets. *Proceedings of the 26th International Conference on World Wide Web Companion*, 759-760. DOI: 10.1145/3041021.3054223

Benesch, S. (2020). Proposals for improving AI in content moderation and upholding human rights. *Journal of Online Trust & Safety*, 1(1), 3–12.

Binns, R. (2018). Fairness in machine learning: Lessons from political philosophy. *Proceedings of the 2018 Conference on Fairness, Accountability, and Transparency*.

Chandrasekharan, E., Samory, M., Srinivasan, A., & Gilbert, E. (2017). The bag of communities: Identifying abusive behavior online with preexisting internet data. *Proceedings of the 2017 CHI Conference on Human Factors in Computing Systems*. DOI: 10.1145/3025453.3026018

Davidson, T., Warmsley, D., Macy, M., & Weber, I. (2017). Automated hate speech detection and the problem of offensive language. *Proceedings of the Eleventh International AAAI Conference on Web and Social Media*, 512-515. DOI: 10.1609/icwsm.v11i1.14955

Davidson, T., Warmsley, D., Macy, M., & Weber, I. (2017). *Automated hate speech detection and the problem of offensive language*. ICWSM. DOI: 10.1609/icwsm.v11i1.14955

Devlin, J., Chang, M. W., Lee, K., & Toutanova, K. (2019). *BERT: Pre-training of deep bidirectional transformers for language understanding*. NAACL-HLT.

Djuric, N., Zhou, J., Morris, R., Grbovic, M., Radosavljevic, V., & Bhamidipati, N. (2015). Hate speech detection with comment embeddings. *Proceedings of the 24th International Conference on World Wide Web*, 29-30. DOI: 10.1145/2740908.2742760

Floridi, L., Cowls, J., King, T. C., & Taddeo, M. (2020). How to design AI for social good: Seven essential factors. *Science and Engineering Ethics*, 26(3), 1771–1796. DOI: 10.1007/s11948-020-00213-5 PMID: 32246245

Fortuna, P., & Nunes, S. (2018). A survey on automatic detection of hate speech in text. *ACM Computing Surveys*, 51(4), 1–30. DOI: 10.1145/3232676

Gao, L., Huang, R., & Mohamed, E. (2017). Detecting online hate speech using context-aware models. *Proceedings of the First Workshop on Abusive Language Online*, 48-56. DOI: 10.26615/978-954-452-049-6_036

Guberman, J., & Hemphill, L. (2017). Challenges of using machine learning to detect hate speech in social media. *Proceedings of the 10th ACM International Conference on Web Science*, 60-68.

MacAvaney, S., Yao, H. R., Yang, E., Russell, K., Goharian, N., & Frieder, O. (2019). Hate speech detection: Challenges and solutions. *PLoS One*, 14(8), e0221152. DOI: 10.1371/journal.pone.0221152 PMID: 31430308

Pavlopoulos, J., Sorensen, J., Dixon, L., & Thain, N. (2020). *Toxicity detection: Does context matter?* NAACL.

Saleem, H. M., Dillon, K. P., Benesch, S., & Ruths, D. (2017). A web of hate: Tackling hateful speech in online social spaces. *Proceedings of the 5th ACM Conference on Human Factors in Computing Systems*, 1975-1985.

Schmidt, A., & Wiegand, M. (2017). A survey on hate speech detection using natural language processing. *Proceedings of the 5th International Workshop on Natural Language Processing for Social Media*, 1-10. DOI: 10.18653/v1/W17-1101

Schmidt, A., & Wiegand, M. (2017). A survey on hate speech detection using natural language processing. *Proceedings of the Fifth International Workshop on Natural Language Processing for Social Media*. DOI: 10.18653/v1/W17-1101

Srisakthi, S., & Suresh Babu, C. V. (2024). Cybersecurity: Protecting Information in a Digital World. In Saeed, S., Azizi, N., Tahir, S., Ahmad, M., & Almuhaideb, A. (Eds.), *Strengthening Industrial Cybersecurity to Protect Business Intelligence* (pp. 1–25). IGI Global., DOI: 10.4018/979-8-3693-0839-4.ch001

Suresh Babu, C. V., Kowsika, S., Sai Tejaswi, M., Janarakshani, T. R., & Mercysha Princy, S. (2023). Framework for Detection of Cyberbullying in Text Data Using Natural Language Processing and Machine Learning. In Chitadze, N. (Ed.), *Cyber Security Policies and Strategies of the World's Leading States* (pp. 69–85). IGI Global., DOI: 10.4018/978-1-6684-8846-1.ch005

Suresh Babu, C. V., & Rahul, A. (2024). Securing the Future: Unveiling Risks and Safeguarding Strategies in Machine Learning-Powered Cybersecurity. In Almaiah, M., Maleh, Y., & Alkhassawneh, A. (Eds.), *Risk Assessment and Countermeasures for Cybersecurity* (pp. 80–95). IGI Global., DOI: 10.4018/979-8-3693-2691-6.ch005

Suresh Babu, C. V., Suruthi, G., Indhumathi, C., & Sushruth, S. (2024b). Integrated approach for network intrusion detection: Combining KNN algorithm, Karhunen-Loève transform, and genetic algorithm optimization. In Metaheuristic and machine learning optimization strategies for complex systems (p. 21). https://doi.org/DOI: 10.4018/979-8-3693-7842-7.ch002

. Waseem, Z., & Hovy, D. (2016). Hateful symbols or hateful people? Predictive features

Chapter 13
Real-Time Detection and Response:
How AI Is Shaping the Future of Hate Speech

Tamish Das
https://orcid.org/0009-0002-4827-6105
Christ University, India

ABSTRACT

This chapter traverse how artificial intelligence is transforming hate speech detection by facilitating real-time detection and response It focuses on the technical aspects of using machine learning. Natural language processing and deep learning models to identify and mark spiteful content. This chapter also discusses the advantages, obstacles, and ethical considerations associated with using AI to moderate online speech. The ultimate objective is to provide insights into how AI is changing the landscape of content moderation on platforms around the world.

INTRODUCTION

The quick growth of online platforms and social media has created spaces for people worldwide to interact, talk, and share information. But this growth has also brought out the ugly side of online talk—hate speech. Hate speech means hurtful or biased language that targets specific people or groups because of things like their race, ethnicity, gender, religion, or who they love. It's a big threat to how well society gets along and how people feel about themselves. As this harmful content spreads, we've had to come up with smart ways to handle it and lessen its effects. The old ways of spotting hate speech, which often count on people to moderate or

DOI: 10.4018/979-8-3693-9904-0.ch013

use simple word filters, just can't keep up with the massive amount of content that pops up every second on sites like Twitter, Facebook, YouTube, and Instagram. This problem has pushed companies to use AI tech, which offers solutions that can grow and work in real-time to find, react to, and stop hate speech from spreading. By using machine learning, AI can look through huge amounts of data to spot harmful content much faster and more than ever before.

This chapter explores how AI is causing a revolution in the way online platforms identify and react to hate speech as it happens. We'll take a close look at different AI technologies such as machine learning methods, systems that respond in real time, and how AI can help prevent issues. We'll also examine the hurdles and limits of these systems when it comes to ethical concerns like bias mistakes in identifying hate speech, and striking the right balance between controlling content and protecting free speech.

The advent of hate speech online cuts across not just technology-related issues but speaks deeply to the larger challenge. The consequences of unchecked hate speech cut across mental health, social trust, and physical safety. Recipients of hate speech tend to suffer spikes in performance anxiety and tension. This may lead to enduring damage, especially for already suppressed groups who essentially live with prejudice in real life. What is worse, the acceptance of the discourse of hate develops limits, emboldened by the supposed approval thereof, to externalise disposition wished upon others. In the case of such people, this would be willingly done with dire social consequences in the form of either hate crimes or social discontent.

At the level of society, uncontrolled proliferation of hate speech results in the disintegration of online communities, with a concomitant growth in toxicity and which do no longer admit serious discussions. Instead of unifying the people, the social media might devolve into a source of divisiveness and enmity. It not only devalues platforms to users, but, by default, they draw questioning from their own credibility, thus dealing a major reputational blow. Governments, regulators, and civil society groups increasingly continue to exert pressure on tech firms in relation to these issues, with constraints pushing for reliable scalable solutions.

With the growth of AI technologies, international and national legislation against hate speech establishes itself as a growing issue. Many nations have enacted legislation to regulate the content distributed by their users, punishing social media companies for discriminatory speech in some cases. However, this method varies drastically from country to country, confronted by free speech in democratic states. The matter of balancing hateful speech versus freedom of speech becomes a subject of heated controversy. Artificial intelligence can act on such balance, allowing multilayered moderation with allowances for context, limiting false positives-those very instances where legitimate communication is labelled hate speech-and false negatives, cases of hate speech escaping detection altogether.

The role of AI in monitoring hate speech is evolving to encompass cultural and linguistic nuances. Hate speech varies significantly across different regions and languages. What might be deemed offensive or harmful in one cultural setting could be acceptable in another. Therefore, AI systems need to be trained to recognize these differences to avoid unfairly targeting specific communities or applying a one-size-fits-all approach. For example, multilingual models that can acknowledge context in many languages are crucial for ensuring fair hate speech detection on global platforms.

The productiveness of AI in determining hate speech is further enhanced by incorporating natural language processing (NLP) techniques. NLP tools examine not only the words used but also the context in which they are presented, offering a deeper understanding of potentially negative content. Advanced methods like sentiment analysis and emotion detection enable AI systems to differentiate between hate speech and passionate but legitimate discussions. These features are vital for preventing over-moderation, which can alienate users by excessively censoring content.

Additionally, AI's role in fighting hate speech includes educating users. Platforms can use AI-driven tools to issue warnings or recommendation to users before they post potentially harmful content. For instance, if a comment is flagged as possibly offensive, the system can encourage the user to revise or rephrase their message. This strategy promotes self-regulation and encourages a culture of respect and accountability online.

Alliance among AI developers, social scientists, and policymakers is essential for overcoming the constraint and challenges linked with AI-driven hate speech detection. It's important to address ethical issues, such as algorithmic bias, by using diverse and representative training data. Additionally, transparency in the working and decision-making processes of AI systems is important for building public trust. Ultimately, AI should be viewed as a tool to strengthen—not replace—human judgment, ensuring that attempt to combat hate speech are both constructive and equitable.

By prioritizing prevention, education, and community engagement alongside technological advancements, society can tackle hate speech in a more holistic manner. As AI technology continues to advance, its capacity to positively influence online conversations is remarkable, but achieving this potential necessitates a multidisciplinary approach that honors human rights and upholds democratic principles.

BACKGROUND

The evolvement and development of the digital platforms have, by their communications, opened more channels for global interaction and exchange of ideas. Unfortunately, those platforms also foster hate speech (HS), which is the incitement of hatred against particular individuals or groups based upon characteristics such as race, religion, nationality, or gender. Social media being globally accessible will accelerate the pace of the spread of HS and its amplification to a wider audience than before. Thus, automation in the detection and prevention of HS gets better with more technicalities available for rapid online picture-kwitter and moderation in the frontiers of maintaining a respectful online space for all.

Artificial Intelligence (AI) is fast becoming the biggest weapon that innovation, designed to tackle HS in order, uses ML and NLP. Real-time detection and response systems use AI to analyse huge amounts of data in real time and stop harmful messaging ever before it gets out of hand. These systems are crucial when they are faced with the vagaries of different languages, shifting slang, and the nuances of online dialogue. By incorporating AI methods of proscription, the platforms can create a balance between free speech and speech that qualifies being termed as hateful against most other people, and they help create an inclusive ambience in cyberspace.

Definition of Hate Speech

Hate speech, in its broadest definition, incites violence, discrimination, or hostility against individuals or groups based on intrinsic traits. Several accounts by various organisations define hate speech as follows:

1. United Nations: Public incitement to hatred or violence against individuals based on race, religion, ethnicity, or nationality.
2. Social Media Platforms (Meta, X): Hate speech is any kind of speech that would be deemed dehumanising and countering people based on any of these core protected characteristics: race, sexual orientation, or disability.
3. United Nations: Advocacy of hatred that constitutes incitement to discrimination, hostility, or violence.

These definitions point out that HS targets specific groups, and most of the language used will be stereotypical or hurtful. The lack of a universal definition complicates the detection systems, especially in multilingual and diverse environments.

Importance of Hate Speech Detection

Detection of hate speech is important for the following reasons:

1. Ensuring Safe Cyber Environments: Hate speech is a serious threat to the safety and inclusivity of digital spaces. It has the potential to fuel conflicts, incite violence, and hurt vulnerable communities. HS detection guarantees a healthier dialogue, encouraging users to express themselves without fear of harassment.
2. Prevention of Real-Life Consequences: HS has been associated with violent acts, cyberbullying, and social fragmentation. Early detection can prevent conflicts from becoming more violent and contribute to social cohesion.

3.Legal Compliance: Governments are developing more stringent laws to compel online platforms to take responsibility for malicious content. AI-based platforms enable businesses to abide by these laws while preserving user rights.

4.Protection of Human Rights: Reducing HS enables platforms to adopt values such as equality and non-discrimination that must be present in a society to be considered fair. Detection systems also prevent discrimination against vulnerable groups.

5. Improving Platform Credibility: Platforms that manage HS well earn the trust of users, which leads to continued engagement and growth.

AI-powered real-time detection systems are a major leap in overcoming these challenges. They bring together the speed of computation with the depth of linguistic analysis to identify HS quickly, contextually, and across languages and cultures.

Rationale

The motivation behind this chapter stems from the serious need to address the growing problem of hate speech in the digital age. Hate speech not only charges division and violence but also contributes to the disempowering of vulnerable groups. With millions of posts and comments generated every minute, manual content moderation has become ineffective. AI offers a potential solution that can provide real-time detection and alleviation of harmful content, ensuring that online platforms remain safe and inclusive spaces for all users.

The importance of this research lies in its potential to guide the development and improvement of AI systems for hate speech detection. By providing a thorough analysis of the strengths and restraints of current AI approaches, this chapter will contribute to the field of AI-driven content moderation, offering insights that can shape future innovations in both technology and policy.

Chapter Objectives and Contributions

1. Introduction to AI in Hate Speech Detection

Objective: This chapter will introduce the concept of AI in the context of online content moderation. It will explain how AI technologies have advanced to tackle the complications of hate speech detection, outlining key developments in machine learning and natural language processing.

Contribution: By providing a foundational understanding, this section will establish the importance of AI in real-time content moderation, setting the stage for deeper exploration of specific AI techniques.

2. Use of Machine Learning and Artificial Intelligence for Hate Speech.

Objective: This chapter focus on the application of machine learning and artificial intelligence to identify hate speech in various language and type. It will show how these technologies are trained to identify abusive content that may sometimes be masked using other forms of messaging such as coded language or sarcasm.

Contribution: The section will also help in further knowledge about how AI can be used to distinguish hate speech and not only recognize the key words that can cause serious conflict between people.

3. Effect of AI on Real-Time Response and Restraint

Objective: The objective of this chapter is to traverse how AI can be used to counter hate speech in real-time. It will discuss automated moderation systems and their ability to remove or flag content instantaneously, restricting the spread of harmful content.

Contribution: This chapter will highlight the critical role of AI in ensuring swift responses to hate speech, thus averting its accumulation across platforms.

It will also explore the problems that AI has in finding a sweet spot between the rapidity and accuracy.

4. The Role of AI in Averting the Spread of Harmful Content.

Objective: This chapter is going to show how AI can be used in a proactive way to stop the spread of hate speech. This will include pre-emptive measures, such as predictive algorithms that identify potentially harmful content before it goes viral.

Contribution: The chapter will demonstrate AI's ability to take preventive measures in content censoring. It focuses on the future of AI and how it could potentially prevent hate speech from causing any harm.

Problem Statement

Despite good sized improvements in online conversation and social media structures, the problem of hate speech maintains to grow, fostering social division and psychological damage to people and groups. The spread of hateful content material is similarly complicated by means of the sheer scale of the internet and the rapid pace at which such content can proliferate. Current monitoring systems often fail to keep up with the rate, complexity, and context of hate speech, leading to not on time or insufficient interventions. Moreover, the issue in distinguishing among unfastened speech and dangerous speech complicates enforcement, frequently resulting in both over-censorship or underneath-detection of harmful content material.

It is in this context that the function of Artificial Intelligence (AI) in actual-time detection and response to hate speech emerges as an important answer. While AI-pushed systems have proven ability in automating content tracking and enhancing reaction instances, demanding situations continue to be. These consist of bias in AI algorithms, the lack of ability to absolutely grasp nuanced context, and the absence of transparency in how those systems operate.

The present study aims to have a look at how AI is transforming the panorama of hate speech tracking, identifying its strengths and weaknesses in actual-time detection. There is a want for a scientific evaluation of AI's abilities in managing hate speech and understanding its broader implications for society, person behavior, and platform governance. This research seeks to deal with these gaps by way of studying AI's impact on moderating dangerous content material and by presenting techniques that enhance its accuracy, equity, and duty.

THEORETICAL FRAMEWORK

Theoretical Foundation:

This study is operational within the domain of artificial intelligence, natural language processing and ethics in technology. Specifically, it is interested in the constantly progressing appreciation notable in the scope of analyzing and identifying patterns of hate speech from different online sites through the assistance of machine learning and deep learning models over a huge volume of data in real-time. Such areas also help to understand and support the rationale where technology as well as policies aimed at utilizing AI for hate speech detection and moderation are directed.

Framework of AI in Hate Speech Detection:

The neural networks, decision trees and other machine learning models can thus determine the level of automation to be used in monitoring hate speech perpetration. Also, this framework illustrates how the balance between supervised to unsupervised learning approach can be effectively used to detect hatred related contents and develop strategies to counter them in real time. A central issue in this framework is the rapid and timely detection of hateful acts and the rapid response to such acts using AI systems.

Challenges in Real-Time Detection:

Another important section of this theoretical framework clarifies the scope of AI in doing real time hate speech detection and other issues that are likely to constrain this process. Some of the concerns include the level of hate speech in many linguistic languages as well as cultural framing, informal vernacular language etc which are some of the problems that must be addressed

Literature Review

This work has aimed to review the literature in extending evidence on AI and hate speech, with an emphasis on detection and response in real-time. The present section gives a critical analysis of the two most recent articles to identify progress, limitations, and further prospects for applying AI in the prevention of hate speech in online environments.

Our first work that aimed at exploring the topic was Schmidt & Wiegand (2017) that focused on employing the machine learning approach to identifying hate speech. The authors focused on the shortcomings of keyword-based detection, where such methods do not capture contextual use of language at all. This work offered a brief of ML algorithms like SVMs and logistic regression, which were used earlier to detect hate speech.

Following work further developed on the need for contextual information in hate speech detection. Zhang et al., (2018) also attempted at understanding the effect deep learning has smartly, CNNs, and RNNs where the authors posited that the accuracy was boosted since the architecture helped understand synergies between words rather than isolating words. This was a big leap in hate speech detection as it enabled more complex analysis of the hidden hatred particularly in the use biased contextual words such as sarcasm.

This is due to the increasing amount of information from users in the social networks which requires usage of real-time detection mechanisms. Edwards et al. (2020) also discussed the technical aspect of developing core, intricate and CASI real-time AI system. They underlined that streaming models are important for real-time processing since they can process data in multiple steps at a time they are produced. But the authors pointed out that this type of models is toned in latency/ accuracy because increasing speed means a decrease in the quality of the recognition.

A study conducted by Tran in 2024 showed that real-time AI systems can be implemented in context of large-scale social media. Utilizing NLP and reinforcement learning the study explored how social media entities such as twitter and Facebook employ AI to censor hate speech in real time. The study indicates that although the systems are efficient in detecting clear hate speech, they fail to capture less apparent ones, for example, those that use slang or local languages and hence the call for better quality training sets.

In addition to detection, it is the real-time response systems that are useful in the moderation of hate speech. Binns et al. (2017) explored the ways in which AI-based platforms not only identify hatred speech but also penalize users by giving them a warning message. They indicated that providing feedback on users' abusive comments in real-time helped to prevent repeat behavior. As this study shows, the use of AI in moderation tools can enhance the general atmosphere in social media platforms.

MacAvaney et al. (2019) built on this by looking at how AI can incorporate human moderators into the response process. The authors suggested hybrid systems that rely on AI for first-level hate speech classification while the second level that handles culturally sensitive posts should be done by humans. According to this study, AI can facilitate most of the moderation tasks however, cases that need a deeper understanding of the context must be supervised by the human.

Nevertheless, the current problem of real-time hate speech detection is still far from being solved. According to Davidson et al. (2019), there are still some limitations with the current generations of AI models as they failed to grasp context properly as well as sarcastic speech. This study found out that even the modern models such as BERT (Bidirectional Encoder Representations from Transformers) are also prone to biases and the models are only as good as the data that was used in training the models; therefore, when the data does not capture some of the diverse forms of hate speech, the models will also not be able to capture them.

In the study by Niculae and Păvăloaia (2023), the authors proposed the solution to the specific ethical problems that are related to the AI-assisted hate speech detection, namely the problems of algorithmic bias and fairness. These authors studied the potential of AI systems whilst paying attention to the fairness of such systems to subgroups in populations. They proposed the creation of bias-squelching approaches and the inclusion of fairness measures in live hate speech identification models.

The current studies point out several directions for further research. In particular, in the work of Edwards et al. (2020) it was noted that the creation of more elaborate models, which can analyze MM data, for example, images, videos, and text, for identification of hate speech in all kinds. Moreover, Tran (2024) pointed out that there should be more multilingual models as hate speech in other languages is more accurately detected by them. With increasing complexity of the global platforms, hate speech detection systems should focus on the variability of the language used for communication in the internet environment.

RESEARCH METHODOLOGY

This section describes the research methodology used in exploring the dynamics of how artificial intelligence changes the real-time detection and response to hate speech. Methodology includes data collection, development of models, evaluation metrics, and ethical considerations. In conducting the study, a mixed-methods approach is undertaken combining quantitative experiments with qualitative analysis to give a thorough understanding of the subject under scrutiny.

Research Design

The study is designed for investigation into the capabilities and limitations of AI models with regards to real-time hate speech detection. This approach integrates experimental analysis of ML models with insights from existing literature and case studies of their application on social media platforms, including Twitter, Facebook, and Reddit.

According to Davidson et al. (2017), hate speech detection involves complex challenges such as cultural nuances, language variations, and implicit expressions of hate. Therefore, this study emphasizes contextual understanding and multimodal analysis to address these complexities.

Objectives

1. To evaluate AI-based models for detecting hate speech in multiple languages and formats.
2. To analyze the performance of text-based and multimodal AI systems in real-time scenarios.
3. To identify challenges related to ethical concerns, latency, and scalability.

4. To present implementable recommendations to improve AI hate speech detection systems.

Data Collection

Data collection is the core of this research. The datasets have been sourced from publicly available repositories, platform-specific APIs, and custom annotations for diversity and representativeness.

Sources of Data

1. Public Datasets:

Publicly available datasets like HateXplain (Mathew et al., 2021), HASOC (Mandl et al., 2019), and the Hateful Memes Dataset (Kiela et al., 2020) were used as baselines for model performance. These datasets are curated with labeled examples of hate speech, enabling supervised learning.

2. Social Media Platforms:

Data was collected via APIs from platforms such as Twitter and Reddit, thus adhering to ethical standards. This included text posts, images, and memes comprising hate speech. For example, Founta et al. (2018) reported that the streaming API of Twitter is useful for online real-time data collection.

3. Crowdsourced Annotations:

A group of linguists and social scientists manually labeled hate speech samples to address the lack of annotated data in low-resource languages. This would ensure the cultural specificity of hate speech coverage as suggested by Mozafari et al. (2020).

Preprocessing

Data was cleaned and prepared for analysis using preprocessing:

- Tokenization and Lemmatization: Text was broken down into tokens and reduced to base forms for analysis.
- Stopwords: This is where many 'nonsense' words such as 'is', 'the' 'and' were omitted because they did not have semantic value.

- Handling Imbalanced Data: Measures such as SMOTE, synthetic minority oversampling technique (Chawla et al., 2002) were employed in handling the above problem.
- Multimodal Data Preparation: For meme-based hate speech, images were resized, normalized, and paired with text annotations.

Model Development

AI models of hate speech detection with the application of advanced methods and approaches for text analysis and multimodal analysis.

Baseline Models

1. Logistic Regression and SVM (Support Vector Machines):

The simpletrain basic machine learning models were used first to provide a baseline to start working from. Nobata et al, (2016) state that models developed for such reason are useful where the goal is fine classification of small scale hate speech, but these models are unable to capture complexity of hate speech.

2. CNNs and RNNs:

In the Zhang et al. (2018) study, the authors define the above models as efficient models that capture sequential as well as contextual text patterns.

There is a bit of a mix between RNNs and CNNs: the RNN models depend on the architecture of the network and also on the properties of the input data. During training, the models capture necessary learning relationships. In CNNs, the convolutional part is performed over time intervals rather than on discrete samples of the training data. These networks are suitable for processing time-varying inputs.

The last two types of networks refer to context and sequence, with the reference to sense recognized through the sentences at earlier incidences, squared with the words from the stored memories. Context. In the last two, it takes into account the sentences at earlier times to understand the sentences in later times according to the words.

Diverse from the CNN-based models, these networks are much more advanced because every hidden neuron from one layer connects to each hidden neuron in the next layer. Zhang et al. (2018) termed these models as capable of understanding the sequence and the context of the textual data.

Super Models

1.Transformers

The transformer-based models such as BERT (Devlin et al., 2019) and RoBERTa (Liu et al., 2019) are fine-tuned over hate speech datasets, it captures the contextual peculiarities mainly due to self-attention mechanism.

2.Multimodal Models:

Models like ViLBERT (Lu et al., 2019) and VisualBERT were utilized to classify text and image inputs in conjunction. These were useful in discovering hate speech in memes, particularly as mentioned by Kiela et al. (2020).

3. Federated Learning Models:

Due to the concern of user data privacy, federated learning methods were adopted. This type of models, explained by McMahan et al. (2017), does process data locally and never centers user information.

Real-time Processing

Real-time processing capabilities were analyzed using the following tools:

- Streaming Data: Apache Kafka was used to mimic the real-time data streams, drawing inspiration from the techniques described in Grolinger et al. (2016).
- Latency Optimization: Quantization and pruning were applied in order to minimize model inference time, as suggested by Han et al. (2015).

Evaluation Metrics

The following metrics were used to evaluate the hate speech detection models:

1.Precision and Recall:

Precision measures the ratio of true positives to the total detected hate speech, while recall quantifies the ratio of true positives to all actual instances of hate speech (Davidson et al., 2017).

2. F1-Score:

Harmonic mean of precision and recall for overall performance measurement.

3. ROC-AUC (Receiver Operating Characteristic – Area Under Curve):

The approach used to determine the level of discrimination of a model between hate and non-hate speech samples (Founta et al 2018).

4. Latency:

Real-time performance was measured in milliseconds to determine the feasibility of deploying models in live environments.

5. Explainability:

Model decisions were interpreted using SHAP (SHapley Additive exPlanations) values to ensure transparency, as suggested by Lundberg and Lee (2017).

Ethical Considerations:

Bias Mitigation

Bias in AI systems can cause unfair outcomes, especially against minority groups. Measures undertaken to address bias included:

- Diverse Training Data: Ensuring representation of different ethnicities, genders, and languages.
- Adversarial Debiasing: The training of models to minimize discrimination was done by the method used by Zhang et al. (2018).

Privacy and Consent

The collection of data followed the GDPR protocol that anonymized the users' information and ensured their consent. Differential privacy techniques were implemented to safeguard sensitive information (Dwork et al., 2014).

Freedom of Speech

The differentiation between hate speech and free speech was considered. Human-in-the-loop approaches were used for borderline cases, as suggested by Vidgen et al. (2020).

Limitations

Despite the holistic approach, there were several challenges during the study:

1.Data Limitations: Low-resource languages lacked ample annotated data that led to a struggle in multilingual model performance.
2.Scalability: Multimodal models demanded heavy computational resources; thus, scalability was a constraint for smaller platforms.
3.Ambiguity of Hate Speech: Sarcasm, among other minute hate speech, continued to be a difficult classification.

Case Studies and Real-World Applications

Twitter

With regards to hate speech detection, the transformation-based models in Twitter enabled hate speech reduction by 30% within the first 24 hours, as Ribeiro et al. (2021) claim.

Facebook

Multimodal systems by Facebook helped the detection of 97% hateful memes by analyzing images together with text (Kiela et al., 2020).

Reddit

Federated approaches for learning about hate speech monitor the hate speech in Reddit as indicated by Balayn et al. (2022).

This methodology ensures a comprehensive evaluation of AI's capabilities in real-time hate speech detection, addressing both technical and ethical dimensions. For further exploration, sources like "Automated Hate Speech Detection and the Problem of Offensive Language" (Davidson et al., 2017) and "Adversarial Training for Bias Mitigation" (Zhang et al., 2018) provide valuable insights.

RESULTS

The results of this study give a detailed analysis of the effectiveness of AI systems in real-time hate speech detection and response. The findings indicate the key performance metrics, capabilities of existing models, and practical applications, offering critical insights into the strengths and limitations of current AI-driven hate speech monitoring systems.

Performance of Traditional Machine Learning Models

Logistic Regression and Support Vector Machines (SVM)

The performance of traditional machine learning models, including Logistic Regression and SVM, was evaluated in detecting hate speech. While these models performed reasonably well in identifying explicit hate speech, they were weak when it came to more subtle forms. Logistic Regression attained an average F1-score of 78% on datasets with clear examples of hate speech, such as the OLID dataset (Zampieri et al., 2019). However, due to dependence on handcrafted features like bag-of-words, the success with context-dependent and implicit hate speech was restricted. Similarly, though SVM has strength, it did face problems, especially in the case of multi-lingual datasets such as HASOC (Mandl et al., 2019) where the performance decreased substantially due to variations in linguistic and cultural expressions.

Insufficiency in Context and Subtlety

Both Logistic Regression and SVM did not have the ability to incorporate nuances like sarcasm, metaphors, and subtleties such as code-switching or evolving hate speech terminology. Their failure to generalize effectively across different linguistic and cultural contexts further necessitates more complex algorithms that could capture context and semantics.

Performance of Deep Learning Models:

Recurrent Neural Networks (RNNs)

RNNs included LSTMs, significantly better than traditional models in managing sequential data such as tweets and posts in forums. This section discusses how RNNs, particularly LSTMs, achieved an 83% F1-score on the HateXplain dataset by Mathew et al. (2021) when dealing with textual data with temporal dependency. RNNs, although significant, failed to recognize long-term dependencies and had inefficiency problems in computing during the training process, making them very limited in scale.

CNNs performed well on short-length content, such as Facebook and Twitter posts, where it is less important to capture dependencies in spatial words. Example: CNN-based models received a precision rate of 85% on the data from Twitter, as reported in Zhang et al. (2018). Similar to RNN, CNNs also relied strictly on large, labeled datasets to train and failed to capture lengthy dependencies or contextual nuances aptly.

Transformer-Based Models Performance

BERT and RoBERTa

Transformer-based models like BERT and RoBERTa set a new benchmark in hate speech detection by making use of self-attention mechanisms to capture complex semantic relationships. Fine-tuned on the OLID dataset (Zampieri et al., 2019), BERT achieved a precision of 91% and a recall of 89%, outperforming traditional and deep learning models in nuanced hate speech understanding.

- Implicit Hate Speech Detection: These models did very well in detecting implicit hate speech. For example, BERT correctly detected sarcasm and coded language 82% of the time, while CNNs managed only 65%.
- Multilingual: Such models like mBERT did a great job in multilingual datasets like HASOC 2019. They achieved 82% F1 scores for Hindi and 79% for German hate speech detection (Mozafari et al., 2020).

DistilBERT for Real-Time Detection

Lightweight transformer models such as DistilBERT were used to meet real-time demands. These models reduced detection latency to 200 milliseconds per instance without significant accuracy loss, making them ideal for large-scale social media platforms.

Multimodal AI Models

Multimodal AI models, which combine text and image analysis, performed better than others in detecting hate speech in memes and other multimedia formats. VisualBERT and ViLBERT achieved an accuracy of 88% on the Hateful Memes Dataset (Kiela et al., 2020), surpassing text-only models by more than 15%.

- Text-Image Synergy: These models effectively analyzed the relationship between text captions and associated images, enabling robust detection of visual hate speech.
- Applications: The more multimodal this gets, the more relevant it will become, as hate speech has become increasingly meme-based, especially on Facebook and Instagram.

Real-Time Detection Metrics

Latency and Throughput

The streaming pipelines were utilized in testing AI models for the detection of real-time hate speech on platforms such as Twitter and Reddit. With the optimized models like TinyBERT, it was achieved with a latency of 150 milliseconds per instance, thus it supports live content moderation.

Scalability

Scalability tests were conducted on datasets containing up to 10 million instances. Federated learning approaches-maintained detection accuracy above 85% while reducing server load by 40%, as supported by findings from McMahan et al. (2017).

Evaluation Metrics Across Datasets

The evaluation of AI models was conducted using standard performance metrics such as precision, recall, and F1-score across multiple datasets:

- OLID Dataset (Zampieri et al., 2019): BERT attains a precision of 91%, with an F1-score of 90%.
- HateXplain (Mathew et al., 2021): The best model was RoBERTa, which attained an F1-score of 93% to detect explicit hate speech.
- HASOC 2019 (Mandl et al., 2019): Multilingual transformer models achieved high performance with Hindi and German.

Real World Applications:

Twitter

Twitter's implementation of fine-tuned BERT models reduced visible hate speech by 30% within 24 hours of deployment. However, challenges such as adversarial tactics (e.g., misspellings, code-switching) reduced detection rates by 15%, necessitating continuous model retraining.

Facebook

Facebook's multimodal hate speech detection system flagged 97% of hateful memes in real-time, leveraging VisualBERT for image-text analysis (Kiela et al., 2020). Explainability tools like SHAP improved transparency and decision-making in content moderation.

Reddit

This approach enabled Reddit to monitor global hate speech while preserving privacy with federated learning. The average F1-score achieved was 87%, and central server dependency was significantly reduced.

Ethical Insights

Although AI models have achieved great strides, there remain challenges concerning bias, implicit hate speech, and cultural context. For instance, transformer models were shown to produce false positives as high as 7% on non-offensive content written in African-American Vernacular English (Sap et al., 2019), which suggests a need for further bias mitigation strategies.

These results reflect the potential of AI in monitoring real-time hate speech with a good deal of success while indicating further areas for research and optimization.

DISCUSSION

The findings of this research indicate the deep effects of artificial intelligence on monitoring hate speech in real-time detection and response systems. This paper critically discusses the results while focusing on the efficiency of AI-based methodologies, their implications to moderate digital spaces, and their potential to transform communication online. It provides a broad evaluation of how these systems address the complexities of detecting hate speech and responding to it in real-time.

AI Breakthroughs in Hate Speech Detection

The introduction of transformer-based models like BERT, RoBERTa, and GPT has significantly improved hate speech detection. These models are more advanced in terms of understanding subtle linguistic patterns, making them highly effective in detecting both explicit and implicit hate speech. Unlike earlier approaches that were based on keyword matching or shallow machine learning models, transformers use context-awareness to achieve higher accuracy in content classification (Zampieri et al., 2019). For example, implicit hate speech-which often involves sarcasm, coded language, or indirect insults-has become easier to identify due to these advances.

Optimization techniques have also been in real-time applications to balance computation with performance in AI models. Examples such as DistilBERT that are lightweight have highly enabled real-time processing capabilities for high-traffic platforms, including Twitter. Optimized models of this nature would identify and flag hate speech quickly enough to prevent speedy transmission.

Multimodal Hate Speech Detection

The integration of multimodal detection capabilities is one of the major advances in this field. Present hate speech is mostly spread out as memes, videos, or images with text embedded. Such systems require multimodal content analysis, and these AI models, such as VisualBERT and ViLBERT, have shown a lot of promise in terms of detecting hate speech within a multimodal context. These models use joint embeddings to grasp the relationship between text and visuals and mitigate the problems that formats such as memes introduce (Kiela et al., 2020).

Multimodal systems are particularly effective in scenarios where the hateful message is obscured within the interplay of text and images. For example, the Hateful Memes Dataset illustrates how multimodal systems outperform text-only approaches by accurately identifying content that relies on visual-textual correlations. The success of these systems highlights their importance in moderating platforms like Instagram, where multimodal content is prevalent.

Scalability Across Platforms

Another key finding is the scalability of AI systems, which has enabled their deployment on platforms with vast user bases. Distributed learning techniques, such as federated learning, have made it possible to scale hate speech detection systems without compromising privacy or performance. For instance, federated learning allows models to learn from data stored locally on user devices while maintaining centralized performance metrics (McMahan et al., 2017). It was especially valuable in complying with privacy regulations such as GDPR while moderating platforms like Facebook and Reddit.

Additionally, scalable AI systems accommodate the international nature of hate speech by supporting multilingual capabilities. Models trained on datasets like HASOC and multilingual versions of BERT have been fine-tuned to identify hate speech across different languages and dialects. This ensures that hate speech is correctly identified, regardless of the linguistic or regional variations. Such advancements address the weaknesses of earlier systems, which were often unable to generalize beyond a single language or cultural context.

Impact on Real-Time Moderation

The integration of AI systems into real-time moderation workflows has had a tangible impact on online platforms. By enabling near-instantaneous detection and response, these systems prevent the amplification of hate speech and mitigate its consequences. Platforms such as YouTube and Twitter have reported significant reductions in harmful content visibility after deploying AI-driven moderation systems. For example, the AI models developed by YouTube can flag and remove uploaded videos within minutes after upload for violating hate speech policies.

In critical high-stakes events like elections or social movements, the impact of hate speech is usually much more far-reaching. Flagging and addressing harmful content in real-time contributes to maintaining integrity in online discourse through the use of AI systems. Capabilities in these systems also reduce the burden on human moderators so they can concentrate on edge cases or appeals rather than regular moderation work.

Implicit and Evolving Hate Speech

A major challenge in hate speech detection is the dynamic nature of language, particularly the emergence of new slurs, coded language, and implicit hate speech. AI systems equipped with contextual embeddings and transfer learning techniques have proven effective in addressing these challenges. For instance, models trained on datasets like HateXplain can adapt to new forms of hate speech by leveraging pre-existing knowledge while incorporating recent updates in data (Mathew et al., 2021).

This ability to detect implicit hate speech is essential for the moderation of platforms where users intentionally avoid the detection systems. The advancement in natural language processing also allows the identification of less overt forms of hate speech - dog whistles, as well as seemingly innocuous statements that are actually loaded with bad intentions. This means that online behaviors are evolving in a manner that ensures hate speech detection systems are not compromised.

General Implications for Online Platforms

The findings also speak to the broader implications of AI-driven hate speech detection for online communities. Effective moderation systems contribute to safer and more inclusive digital spaces by reducing the prevalence of harmful content. This, in turn, fosters healthier interactions among users and minimizes the psychological harm caused by exposure to hate speech.

Moreover, AI systems contribute to the fulfillment of the duties of technology companies to their users. By ensuring platforms are compliant with regulatory frameworks, they balance freedom of expression and the need to protect vulnerable communities. For example, compliance with legislation such as the EU's Digital Services Act requires deploying robust hate speech detection mechanisms, job AI systems are well-placed to do.

The discussions involved with it also highlight its ethical consideration related to the employment of AI in the detection of hate speech. Although these have reached unparalleled accuracy and effectiveness, still, issues pertaining to bias and accountability prevail. Biasness in training can result in uneven performance within different demographics, leading even to an over- or under-moderation in some groups. For example, models trained on imbalanced datasets may flag disproportionate amounts of content from minority groups, raising questions about fairness and equity (Sap et al., 2019).

The solution researchers give to these problems is ensuring diverse and representative training datasets for the AI. It requires multi-stakeholder collaborations that include multiple cultural and linguistic backgrounds. Explainable AI techniques make it possible to add transparency in content classification decisions so that the users and moderators know exactly why certain content has been classified.

Future Directions in AI-Driven Moderation

These results have indicated promising areas of research and development: first, applying few-shot and zero-shot learning techniques that may be capable of generalizing over unseen languages, contexts, and forms of hate speech; the former is a good chance to improve existing systems over the emerging trends of hate speech.

Yet another potential direction is the creation of hybrid systems which could bring together AI and human knowledge. Where AI is better suited at handling large volumes of data, moderators bring contextual understanding and judgment with complex cases. Cooperative frameworks built on both AI and human moderation can further enhance the general effectiveness of hate speech detection systems.

In conclusion, this is a major paper discussion on significant progress with AI-driven hate speech detection systems focusing on improvement in the capabilities of real-time processing, multimodal integration, and scalability. These are very important enhancements to the capacity of content moderation systems not only within but towards realizing the safety and inclusion aspects for digital communication online. Of course, it will open a wide pathway for expanding capabilities in solving the issues and problems of detecting hate speech complexities within AI systems as such innovations come along to shape digital communications.

CONCLUSION

This has led to an increase in digital platforms and social media, thus changing the way people interact with one another and share information. With the increased usage of the digital platform, new threats arise, like hate speech, which is fast becoming a significant threat to the integrity of online discourse, personal well-being, and societal cohesion. With increased complexity in the volume of interactions happening in the online world, reliance solely on human or keyword-based filters alone cannot now effectively detect and deter hate speech. Artificial Intelligence then emerges as a powerful tool capable of shaping the future on real-time hate detection and response.

AI plays a multi-faceted role in transforming hate speech moderation through advanced language models, deep learning algorithms, and multimodal content analysis systems. Through the utilization of machine learning techniques like Natural Language Processing (NLP) and deep neural networks, AI systems have managed to make significant strides in identifying and categorizing many forms of hate speech: explicit, implicit, and context-dependent expressions of harm. The very reasons such systems can process amounts of information in real time, easily making it possible for these platforms to track down the offending content early in a matter of no time and act upon it makes a big difference in creating the perfect safe and respectful digital environment.

Continuous ability of AI-based systems to learn and change in line with new trends and variations in languages and different contextual nuances in hate speech makes this very dynamic. It keeps changing with new terms, slangs, and expressions coming up every now and then. Traditional methods based on static keyword lists or rule-based systems usually fail to keep pace with such evolution. But, AI models, especially the ones developed based on more sophisticated transformer architectures like BERT and GPT, can contextualize language and bring out the subtle difference between multiple expressions, which are much better at detecting all varieties of hate speech (Devlin et al., 2019; Radford et al., 2019). AI systems process massive amounts of data from various platforms and continuously refine their understanding of what constitutes harmful content, improving both accuracy and relevance over time.

Another aspect of AI is real-time monitoring, which is a game-changer in combating hate speech. In an age where content spreads at unprecedented speeds, especially on social media platforms, the detection and response of harmful content in real-time is a necessity to prevent its viral spread. AI-driven systems can flag, remove, or restrict access to harmful content almost instantaneously, ensuring hateful material does not proliferate across online communities. It reduces the emotional and psychological pain that comes with hateful speech for victims because hateful or hurtful speech focuses on some groups and communities that are already weak; this urgency also manifests from AI technologies, supporting those digital interfaces in building a safer environment that appears to be more welcoming for all on the respective platforms.

The scalability offered by AI-based hate detection is another major advantage: Traditional ways of moderation- through human being review, and so on- tend to be resource-intensive and incapable of dealing with content amounts generated by the millions of users within one day. AI systems process data at scale without affecting performance. These systems can monitor millions of posts, comments, and interactions in real-time across a variety of platforms and languages, enabling them to detect hate speech in diverse contexts. Datasets such as the HASOC (Hate Speech and Offensive Content) and HateXplain have facilitated the development of multilingual models that are capable of identifying hate speech in multiple languages, from English and Spanish to Hindi and Arabic (Zampieri et al., 2020). This multilingual capability allows AI-based systems to be deployed on a global scale, which addresses the issue of hate speech across linguistic and cultural boundaries.

Moreover, the potential of AI is not limited to text-based content. As communication online becomes increasingly multimodal, involving a mix of text, images, videos, and memes, AI systems are evolving to address these new challenges. Hate speech is not always contained in words but is often within images or shared in meme format. It requires AI to detect the hate speech that may exist in multimodal content through both textual and visual data. Advances in multimodal AI models, such as VisualBERT and ViLBERT, have enabled better understanding of how text and images interact to detect hate speech embedded in memes or videos more accurately (Tan & Bansal, 2019). Such progress significantly expands the scope of AI-driven hate speech detection, ensuring that harmful content is identified and mitigated across a variety of media formats.

Another important innovation introduced in AI-driven hate speech detection is the introduction of explanations into these systems. When AI becomes more complex, explanations within the decision-making process itself increase in importance. Explainable Artificial Intelligence (XAI) techniques are being integrated in this hate speech detection to indicate why a piece of content is harmful. This transparency creates trust in AI-based moderation systems as users and moderators will understand why certain contents are being removed or flagged. The reasoning behind the transparency and interpretability of AI systems is that it enables the use of technology according to ethical standards and meets the requirements of regulatory policies (Carvalho et al., 2020).

However, despite promising advancements in using AI in detecting hate speech, there are still quite a few challenges. One of the main concerns relates to the issue of bias in AI models. Most AI systems are trained on datasets that reflect the biases inherent in society; these include racial, gender, and cultural biases. If not corrected, these biases may cause unfair or discriminatory outcomes when detecting hate speech. For instance, a biased data-trained AI will flag more content from other communities and fail to mark hate speech in others. In that sense, this is a challenge pointing out the need for diverse and representative datasets that capture a wide scope of language usage and hateful expressions. Further techniques involve debiasing and fairness-aware machine learning to ensure no bias is in the AI system and ensures fairness and equity within the AI (Park et al., 2018).

Lastly, moderation by AI entails ethical considerations because while the AI system can well detect the content, content moderation would have to be weighed with freedom of speech. Platforms must ensure that the AI systems do not overreach or censor legitimate expressions of opinion in politically sensitive contexts. The demand is that AI models must be accurate in detecting hate speech, but they must distinguish hate speech from other forms of discourse like satire, criticism, or political commentary. A very central challenge in deploying AI-driven hate speech detection systems remains balancing between protecting users from harmful content and upholding free expression.

The use of AI is bound to expand even more into the future. With AI models constantly improving and with new techniques like few-shot learning and zero-shot learning, real-time detection and response to hate speech across diverse languages, platforms, and media formats will continue to evolve. Integration of AI with human moderators can lead to hybrid models that can integrate the scalability and efficiency of AI with the nuanced understanding and ethical judgment of human oversight. This can also lead to fairer and context-sensitive moderation practice.

In short, AI already has been proven transformative when it comes to the context of hate speech detection and response. Be it through real-time monitoring and detection in more than one language, multi-modal analysis or explainability; AI has exponentially improved combating hate speech. However, the path is not yet smooth; rather, it remains rocky and strewn with biases, issues of fairness, and the implications of ethical content moderation. Through the fine-tuning of AI technologies, utilization of diversified data, transparency, and constant ethical checks and balances, AI will stand as the main facilitator toward creating a safer and more inclusive digital space for everyone involved. From this point onwards, it becomes pretty evident that AI will play a prominent role in preventing hate speech while ensuring online communities are healthier and the tenets of respect and inclusiveness within virtual spaces are maintained.

LIMITATIONS OF AI IN THE DETECTION AND RESPONSE TO REAL-TIME HATE SPEECH:

While AI technologies, particularly NLP and machine learning, have demonstrated immense potential in real-time hate speech detection and response, there are limitations. These often emerge from the inherent difficulties in detecting hate speech in diverse, evolving, and highly context-dependent environments. Below are some key limitations of AI in the context of real-time hate speech monitoring:

1. Bias in AI Models

This has perhaps been one of the major flaws in AI-based hate speech detection systems; these models contain biases. Since most AI models are trained with large datasets, and in cases where the datasets are not diverse or representative of diverse communities, the models may acquire or perpetuate biases. For instance, a system that is primarily trained on English-language content will likely not do well in hate speech in other languages, dialects, or regional vernaculars. Further, race, gender, ethnicity, or socio-political biases can be locked into the training data and then manifest in the system's flagging of content from specific demographic groups or failing to identify hate speech targeting other communities. These biases would undermine the accuracy and fairness in moderation of AI-driven moderation in return for unfair outcomes.

2. Contextual Detection Problems

Hate speech tends to be contextually contingent. What is perceived to be hate speech in one particular circumstance might be interpreted differently in a given situation. For instance, certain phrases or words that might be used with intention for satire or humor will lead AI models to misread such statements as harmful or derogatory. This is especially so in multilingual and cross-cultural contexts where the same words or expressions can mean very different things depending on context. AI systems often cannot grasp the nuances of sarcasm, irony, and coded language in which hate speech is usually communicated in a more veiled manner. While the latest advances in NLP, particularly transformer-based models (e.g., BERT, GPT), have improved contextual understanding, these models still struggle to capture the full depth and complexity of human communication, even in real-time settings.

3. Scalability and Resource Demands

While AI systems scale with incredible ease, the computational resources necessary for handling the sheer volume of social media data can be a bit more substantial. Real-time hate speech detection involves processing large volumes of content in multiple languages and formats (text, images, videos), which places immense strain on computing infrastructure. This may cause delays in moderation of content, especially if there is high traffic, which may occur during elections, protests, or crises. More resources are also needed to build advanced AI models, including access to large quantities of high-quality datasets and powerful hardware. These resource requirements are likely to be prohibitively expensive for the smaller platforms or organizations and hence give rise to uneven deployments of the AI-based moderation system.

4. Absence of Standards for Hate Speech

Identifying hate speech is quite an ambiguous and intricate issue since there is no consensus about the definition of what hate speech actually refers to. Different cultures and legal systems possess different thresholds as regards which is offensive and hence can qualify as hate speech while considering the online community. While some countries or platforms may adopt strict guidelines for moderating hate speech, others may be more permissive, leading to inconsistencies in how hate speech is identified and handled. AI models often rely on predefined labels or definitions to train algorithms, but the lack of standardization in the identification of hate speech means that models may be inconsistent in their outputs. This challenge is further intensified by the dynamic nature of hate speech, in which novel terms and expressions emerge constantly. This necessitates continuous update of models and datasets.

5. Challenges with Multimodal Content

Communication on digital platforms is increasingly multimodal- a mix of text, images, videos, and memes. This increases the difficulty for AI systems in detecting hate speech that may be embedded within non-textual content. Hate speech is not always expressed in text; often visual content such as memes or videos carries implicit hate speech that cannot be detected by text-based models. Despite this, current state-of-the-art advances in multimodal AI models tried to address the challenge through their combination of capabilities in both text and image recognition. In complicated or highly contextualized settings, though, these systems would still be very poor in relating the two items, so it results in missed AI detection in cases of hate speech in memes, GIFs, or videos, and significant content sources of harmful activity in social media.

6. Lack of Explainability

AI-based systems, particularly deep learning models, are coined "black boxes" because in many cases, the decision-making process of these systems cannot be made transparent to the users and moderators. This is a critical challenge in hate speech detection in that users whose contents are flagged or removed will not know why the content was flagged or removed. Moreover, there's a danger of mistrust in the AI system because reasons for specific content to be harmful are not always clear. To overcome such a weakness, there's a growing push for Explainable AI, which focuses on transparency and interpretability in decision-making processes. One of the biggest challenges: how to balance explainability with the complexity of modern AI modes

7. Adversarial Attacks

AI systems, especially those designed for hate speech detection, suffer from adversarial attacks when people intentionally manipulate the content in order to evade detection algorithms. For example, hate speech may be hidden by spelling words wrong, using coded language, or using letter-number or letter-symbol substitution. While AI models evolve constantly to detect these deceptions, adversarial actors keep discovering new ways of manipulating the system. Such attacks threaten the trustworthiness of AI-based moderation and pose a significant challenge in creating robust hate speech detection models.

8. Ethical Issues and Free Speech

This has raised important ethical implications of freedom of expression that comes with the use of AI for hate speech detection. For instance, AI could flag or remove content that it deems harmful but are not genuinely harmful but rather cause controversy or are critical toward some political, social, or cultural views. A very complex ethical dilemma balances protection of users from actual harm caused by hate speech against freedom of speech preservation. Overly aggressive moderation of content can lead to claims of censorship, and weak moderation leaves users vulnerable to exposure to harmful or discriminatory content. As hate speech detection systems based on AI technologies are increasingly deployed, it becomes essential that these technologies are responsibly and ethically used to promote free speech and safety in user environments.

9. Dynamic Nature of Hate Speech

Hate speech is not a static phenomenon as it evolves in response to the trends of society, the political events, and the ever-evolving nature of online discourse. New terms, symbols, and memes constantly emerge to form hate speech, rendering it challenging for AI systems to stay updated and relevant. This constant evolution calls for repeated retraining of AI models and updates in datasets, which can be both time-consuming and resource-intensive. In addition, hate speech could also be in the form of novel types or formats, for instance, deepfakes, or other synthetic media, that might not be easily identified by existing AI systems.

10. Legal and Regulatory Concerns

The application of AI in Hate Speech Detection and Content Moderation raises legal and regulatory concerns as well. The laws of free speech vary from one country to another with the nature of online content moderation. For instance, the General Data Protection Regulation in the European Union puts emphasis on privacy of users and protection of their data that makes collecting and processing the necessary data to train the AI model a cumbersome affair. Then there are issues of accountability of AI in issues of content removal and censorship in the event such a system goes wrong or tends to have a discriminatory effect. There is still a challenge for the developers and platform operators to navigate the complex legal landscape surrounding AI and hate speech detection.

AI-driven real-time hate speech detection systems hold great promise for the moderation of online content but are not without their limitations. These limitations, from biases in AI models and challenges with context to ethical concerns and resource demands, underscore the need for continuous research, development, and careful consideration in the deployment of these technologies. As AI continues to evolve, it is important to address these challenges in order for hate speech detection systems to remain effective, fair, and accountable while balancing the safety of users with protection of free speech.

REFERENCES

AI Ethics Lab. (2021). *Addressing Algorithmic Bias in Hate Speech Monitoring Systems*. AI Ethics Reports.

Ali, W., & Zhang, H. (2021). Improving Real-Time Hate Speech Detection with Contextual Memory Networks. *Proceedings of the IJCAI Conference*.

Alikhani, M.. (2020). Low-Resource Hate Speech Detection: Challenges and Strategies. *Journal of Computational Social Science*.

Badjatiya, P., Gupta, S., Gupta, M., & Varma, V. (2017). Deep Learning for Hate Speech Detection in Tweets. *Proceedings of the 26th International Conference on World Wide Web (WWW)*. DOI: 10.1145/3041021.3054223

Barassi, V. (2020). Multimodal Approaches to Hate Speech: Text, Audio, and Video Data Analysis. *Journal of Digital Cultures*.

Barocas, S., Hardt, M., & Narayanan, A. (2017). *Fairness in Machine Learning*. NIPS Tutorials on AI Ethics.

Barocas, S., Hardt, M., & Narayanan, A. (2019). Fairness and Transparency in AI Systems. *Proceedings of the ACM FAccT Conference*.

Basile, V.. (2019). SemEval-2019 Task 5: Multilingual Detection of Hate Speech Against Immigrants and Women. *Proceedings of the SemEval Conference*. DOI: 10.18653/v1/S19-2007

Basile, V., et al. (2019). Benchmarking Multilingual Hate Speech Detection with SemEval-2019. *Proceedings of SemEval*.

Binns, R. (2020). On the Foundations of Fairness in AI. *Communications of the ACM*.

Binns, R. (2020). Fairness in Machine Learning Systems: Mitigating Bias. *Communications of the ACM*.

Binns, R.. (2018). 'It's Reducing a Human Being to a Percentage': Perceptions of Justice in Algorithmic Decisions. *Proceedings of the CHI Conference*. DOI: 10.1145/3173574.3173951

Brown, T. B.. (2020). Language Models Are Few-Shot Learners. *Proceedings of the NeurIPS Conference*.

Brown, T. B., et al. (2020). Language Models Are Few-Shot Learners (GPT-3). *Proceedings of NeurIPS*.

Camba, J. D., & Tagle, J. A. (2021). Real-Time AI Framework for Content Moderation in Gaming Platforms. *IEEE Transactions on Games*.

Cao, J.. (2020). Joint Detection of Hate Speech Using Multimodal Embeddings. *Proceedings of CVPR*.

Caselli, T., & Basile, V. (2021). Hate Speech Detection in a Multilingual World: Challenges and Opportunities. *Frontiers in Artificial Intelligence*. Hateful Memes Dataset:

Caton, S., & Haas, C. (2020). Fairness in Machine Learning: Addressing Algorithmic Bias in Hate Speech Detection. *Journal of Social Computing*.

Chen, Q., Peng, Y., & Feng, Z. (2021). *Enhanced Hate Speech Detection Using Capsule Networks*. ACM Transactions on Social Computing.

Chen, T., & Guestrin, C. (2016). XGBoost: A Scalable Tree Boosting System. *Proceedings of the ACM SIGKDD Conference*.

Chollet, F. (2020). *On the Measure of Intelligence in AI Systems*. ArXiv Preprint.

Council of Europe. (2022). *AI Regulation in Content Moderation and Hate Speech*. Council of Europe Publications.

Council of Europe. (2022). *Hate Speech Detection and AI Regulation*. Official Council Reports.

Crawford, K., & Paglen, T. (2021). *Bias in Automated Content Moderation: A Case Study*. AI Ethics Journal.

Davidson, T., Warmsley, D., Macy, M., & Weber, I. (2017). Automated Hate Speech Detection and the Problem of Offensive Language. *Proceedings of the 11th International Conference on Web and social media (ICWSM)*. DOI: 10.1609/icwsm.v11i1.14955

Devlin, J., Chang, M.-W., Lee, K., & Toutanova, K. (2018). BERT: Pre-training of Deep Bidirectional Transformers for Language Understanding. *Proceedings of NAACL-HLT*.

Devlin, J., Chang, M. W., Lee, K., & Toutanova, K. (2019). BERT: Pre-training of Deep Bidirectional Transformers for Language Understanding. *Proceedings of the NAACL-HLT Conference*.

Digital Media Governance Initiative. (2021). Regulating AI for Hate Speech: Lessons from Europe. *Policy Studies Journal: the Journal of the Policy Studies Organization*.

Dignum, V. (2020). Ethics in AI: Balancing Accuracy and Fairness. *Journal of Ethical AI.*

Djuric, N., Zhou, H., Morris, R., Grbovic, M., Radosavljevic, V., & Bhamidipati, N. (2015). Hate Speech Detection with Comment Embeddings. *Proceedings of the WWW Conference.*

European Commission. (2020). *The Digital Services Act and AI-Driven Content Moderation.* EU Reports on AI.

European Commission. (2020). *The Role of AI in Combatting Online Hate Speech.* Official Reports of the EU Digital Services Act.

Facebook, A. I. (2020). *Real-Time Hate Speech Detection for Community Standards Enforcement.* Facebook Research Blog.

Floridi, L., & Cowls, J. (2019). The Ethical Challenges of AI in Hate Speech Detection. *AI & Society.*

Fortuna, P., & Nunes, S. (2018). A Survey on Automatic Detection of Hate Speech in Text. *ACM Computing Surveys.*

Fortuna, P., & Nunes, S. (2018). A Survey on Automatic Detection of Hate Speech in Text. *ACM Computing Surveys.*

Founta, A. M.. (2018). Large Scale Crowdsourcing and Characterization of Twitter Abusive Behavior. *Proceedings of the 12th International AAAI Conference on Web and social media (ICWSM).* DOI: 10.1609/icwsm.v12i1.14991

Founta, A. M.. (2018). Dataset Bias in Hate Speech Detection: Impacts and Solutions. *Proceedings of ICWSM.*

Gao, L., Kuppersmith, A., & Huang, R. (2017). Recognizing Explicit and Implicit Hate Speech Using Machine Learning Models. *Proceedings of the ACL Workshop on Ethics in NLP.*

Gillespie, T. (2018). *Custodians of the Internet: Platforms, Content Moderation, and the Hidden Decisions that Shape social media.* Yale University Press.

Gomez, R., Tellez, E., & Montes-y-Gómez, M. (2020). Multilingual Hate Speech Classification with Pre-Trained Transformers. *Proceedings of the LREC Conference.*

Grondahl, T.. (2021). Evaluating Multilingual Hate Speech Datasets. *Proceedings of ICML.*

Halevy, A.. (2009). The Unreasonable Effectiveness of Data in AI Systems. *AI Magazine.*

Hate Speech and Regulation in Europe. (2022). *European Commission Report*. Tackling Hate Speech Using AI and Human Review Systems.

Hateful Memes Challenge: Kiela, D., et al. (2020). Detecting Multimodal Hate Speech. *Facebook AI Research*.

HateXplain Dataset.: Mathew, B., et al. (2020). Explainable Hate Speech Detection. *Proceedings of the WWW Conference*.

He, H.. (2020). Federated Learning for Hate Speech Detection on Decentralized Platforms. *IEEE Access : Practical Innovations, Open Solutions*.

Howard, J., & Gugger, S. (2018). *Fastai: A Layered API for Deep Learning*. ArXiv Preprint.

Instagram Content Moderation Systems. (2021). *Enhancing AI-Based Hate Speech Detection*. Meta Research.

Jigsaw, G. (2021). *Perspective API for Detecting Hate Speech in Real-Time*. Jigsaw Research.

Jobin, A., Ienca, M., & Vayena, E. (2019). The Global Landscape of AI Ethics Guidelines. *Nature Machine Intelligence*, 1(9), 389–399. DOI: 10.1038/s42256-019-0088-2

Jobin, A., Ienca, M., & Vayena, E. (2019). The Global Landscape of AI Ethics Guidelines. *Nature Machine Intelligence*, 1(9), 389–399. DOI: 10.1038/s42256-019-0088-2

Joulin, A.. (2016). Bag of Tricks for Efficient Text Classification. *Proceedings of ACL*.

Kiela, D.. (2020). *Hateful Memes Challenge: Multimodal Benchmark Dataset*. Facebook AI Research.

Kiela, D., Firooz, H., Mohan, A., & Das, A. (2020). *The Hateful Memes Challenge: Detecting Hate Speech with Multimodal Data. Facebook AI Research*. HASOC Dataset.

Kim, B., & Doshi-Velez, F. (2019). Explainable AI in Hate Speech Monitoring. *Proceedings of AAAI*.

Kiritchenko, S., & Mohammad, S. M. (2018). Examining Gender and Race Bias in Two Hundred Sentiment Analysis Systems. *Proceedings of the STARSEM Workshop*. DOI: 10.18653/v1/S18-2005

Knight, W. (2020). Can AI Moderate Content Better than Humans? *MIT Technology Review*.

Kumar, P.. (2021). Ensemble Methods for Hate Speech Detection: A Review. *Pattern Recognition Letters*.

Kumar, S.. (2021). Early Detection of Online Hate Speech Using Adaptive Neural Networks. *IEEE Transactions on Computational Social Systems*.

LeCun, Y., Bengio, Y., & Hinton, G. (2015). Deep Learning and Its Applications in Hate Speech Detection. *Nature*.

LinkedIn AI Team. (2021). *Tackling Hate Speech in Professional Networks*. Microsoft Research Journal.

Liu, P., Wang, X., & Jiang, J. (2022). Multimodal Hate Speech Detection Using Fusion Neural Networks. *Proceedings of the CVPR Conference*.

Liu, X., Zhou, Y., & Zhang, H. (2020). Hierarchical Transformers for Real-Time Offensive Language Detection. *Proceedings of the EMNLP Conference*.

Liu, Y., Ott, M., & Goyal, N.. (2019). *RoBERTa: A Robustly Optimized BERT Pretraining Approach*. ArXiv Preprint.

MacAvaney, S.. (2019). Hate Speech Detection Using BERT Embeddings. *Proceedings of the SIGIR Conference*.

Mandl, T., Modha, S., & Patel, D. (2019). *Overview of the HASOC Track at FIRE: Hate Speech and Offensive Content Identification*. CEUR-WS.

Mandl, T., Modha, S., & Patel, D. (2019). The HASOC Dataset for Hate Speech Detection. *Proceedings of the FIRE Conference*.

Mehrabi, N.. (2021). A Survey on Bias and Fairness in Machine Learning. *ACM Computing Surveys*.

Meta (2021). Real-Time Hate Speech Detection on Facebook. *Meta Transparency Reports*.

Microsoft AI Research (2020). Improving Real-Time Hate Speech Moderation on Xbox Live. *Microsoft Blog*.

Mikolov, T., et al. (2013). Word2Vec: Distributed Representations of Words. *NeurIPS Proceedings*.

Mishra, A., Del Tredici, M., Yannakoudakis, H., & Shutova, E. (2018). Abusive Language Detection with Graph Convolutional Networks. *Proceedings of the NAACL-HLT Conference*. BERT

Noble, S. U. (2018). *Algorithms of Oppression: How Search Engines Reinforce Racism*. New York University Press. DOI: 10.18574/nyu/9781479833641.001.0001

Pandey, R., & Kumar, A. (2021). Multilingual Hate Speech Analysis Using Transformers. *Proceedings of ACL.*

Pavlopoulos, J.. (2021). *Automatic Abuse Detection in Online Platforms: Issues and Advances.* AI Ethics Journal.

Pennington, J., ... (2014). GloVe: Global Vectors for Word Representation. *EMNLP Proceedings.*

Pérez-Torres, S., & Molina-González, M. D. (2021). Combining Images and Text for Multimodal Hate Speech Detection. *IEEE Transactions on Multimedia.*

Radford, A., et al. (2019). Language Models Are Few-Shot Learners. *Proceedings of NeurIPS.*

Raffel, C., et al. (2020). Exploring the Limits of Transfer Learning with a Unified Text-to-Text Transformer (T5). *Journal of Machine Learning Research.*

Rahwan, I., Cebrian, M., Obradovich, N., Bongard, J., Bonnefon, J.-F., Breazeal, C., Crandall, J. W., Christakis, N. A., Couzin, I. D., Jackson, M. O., Jennings, N. R., Kamar, E., Kloumann, I. M., Larochelle, H., Lazer, D., McElreath, R., Mislove, A., Parkes, D. C., Pentland, A. S., & Wellman, M. (2019). Machine Behaviour. *Nature*, 568(7753), 477–486. DOI: 10.1038/s41586-019-1138-y PMID: 31019318

Rani, R., & Kumar, S. (2022). Real-Time Hate Speech Detection with Hybrid Deep Learning Techniques. *Journal of Information and Optimization Sciences.*

Reddit (2021). Real-Time Content Moderation During Crisis Events. *Reddit Research Reports.*

Reddit Data Science Team. (2021). Early Warning Systems for Hate Speech Detection. *Reddit Transparency Report.*

Reddit Trust and Safety: Using AI to Monitor Toxicity in Discussions. *Reddit Transparency Report.*

Report, F. T. (2021). *Advancing Real-Time AI Systems for Hate Speech Removal.* Facebook Newsroom.

Ribeiro, M. T., Singh, S., & Guestrin, C. (2016). Why Should I Trust you? Explaining the Predictions of Any Classifier. *Proceedings of the ACM SIGKDD Conference.* DOI: 10.18653/v1/N16-3020

Ruder, S. (2019). *Transfer Learning for NLP*. ArXiv Preprint.

Ruder, S. (2020). Multilingual Representation Learning for Hate Speech Detection. *Proceedings of EMNLP*.

Ruder, S.. (2019). Neural Representations in NLP: A Survey. *ACM Computing Surveys*.

Samory, M., & Mitra, T. (2018). *Multimodal Hate Speech Analysis on Social Platforms*. ACM Transactions on Social Computing.

Schmidt, A., & Wiegand, M. (2017). A Survey on Hate Speech Detection Using Natural Language Processing. *Proceedings of the 5th International Workshop on Natural Language Processing for social media*. DOI: 10.18653/v1/W17-1101

Schmidt, A., & Wiegand, M. (2017). A Survey on Hate Speech Detection Using Text. *Proceedings of COLING*.

Sun, C., Qian, X., & Liu, H. (2021). Adversarial Training for Robust Hate Speech Detection. *Proceedings of the AAAI Conference on Artificial Intelligence*. DOI: 10.5772/intechopen.94615

Tay, Y., et al. (2021). Cross-Language Transfer Learning for Hate Speech Classification. *NeurIPS Proceedings*.

TikTok. (2022). *Moderation of Hate Speech Using Multimodal AI Systems*. TikTok AI Research Blog.

TikTok AI Moderation: Real-Time Detection of Offensive Content. *TikTok Research Reports*.

TikTok Safety Initiative. (2022). *AI-Powered Hate Speech Moderation in Short Video Platforms*. TikTok Research.

Twitter API Team. (2021). Detecting Harmful Language Using Real-Time NLP Models. *Twitter Developer Blog*.

Twitter (2021). Advances in Detecting Harmful Language in Real-Time. *Twitter Blog*.

Twitter Trust and Safety Team (2021). Measuring Progress on AI-Powered Moderation. *Twitter Transparency Report*.

UNESCO. (2019). *The Role of Artificial Intelligence in Countering Online Hate Speech*. UNESCO Digital Series.

UNESCO. (2021). *Global Initiatives to Regulate AI in Content Moderation*. UNESCO Policy Briefs.

United Nations. (2021). *AI and the Fight Against Online Hate Speech: A Global Perspective*. UN Policy Reports.

US Congress. (2021). *Federal AI Initiatives Against Hate Speech.* Congressional AI Reports.

US Government Accountability Office. (2020). *Federal Initiatives on AI for Hate Speech Detection.* GAO Reports.

Vaswani, A., ... (2017). Attention Is All You Need. *NeurIPS Conference Proceedings.*

Vaswani, A., et al. (2017). Transformer Models for Sequential Data: Enhancing NLP Tasks. *NeurIPS Proceedings.*

Vidgen, B.. (2021). Large-Scale Annotation of Online Abuse. *Proceedings of the LREC Conference.*

Vidgen, B.. (2021). Challenges in Annotating Hate Speech: A Case Study. *Proceedings of ACL.*

Vidgen, B., Botelho, A., Broniatowski, D., & Tromble, R. (2020). Challenges and Frontiers in Hate Speech Detection: Real-Time Applications. *Journal of Computational Social Science.*

Vidgen, B., & Derczynski, L. (2020). Directions in Abusive Language Training Data: Issues and Next Steps. *Workshop on Abusive Language Online (EMNLP).*

Waseem, Z., & Hovy, D. (2016). Hateful Symbols or Hateful People? Predictive Features for Hate Speech Detection on Twitter. *Proceedings of the NAACL-HLT Conference.* DOI: 10.18653/v1/N16-2013

Waseem, Z., & Hovy, D. (2016). Hateful Symbols or Hateful People? Predictive Features for Hate Speech Detection. *NAACL Proceedings.*121. Olteanu, A., et al. (2018). Limits of Automated Hate Speech Detection: A Case Study. *Proceedings of ICWSM.*

Wiegand, M.. (2018). Detection of Abusive Language: The Problem of Biased Datasets. *Proceedings of COLING.*

Wu, Y., ... (2016). Google's Neural Machine Translation System: Bridging the Gap Between Human and Machine Translation. *Proceedings of the ACL Conference.* OpenAI GPT Models

Wu, Y., et al. (2021). Real-Time Adaptive AI for Content Moderation. *Journal of Real-Time Processing Systems.*

Xia, Q.. (2022). A Multilingual Transformer-Based System for Hate Speech Detection. *Proceedings of the EMNLP Conference.*

XLNet.: Yang, Z., et al. (2019). XLNet: Generalized Autoregressive Pretraining for Language Understanding. *Proceedings of the NeurIPS Conference*.

Xu, J.. (2020). Deep Learning for Hate Speech Detection: A Review. *IEEE Access : Practical Innovations, Open Solutions*.

Yang, Y., & Yang, M. (2021). Lightweight Real-Time NLP Models for Content Moderation. *Journal of Machine Learning Research*.

YouTube. (2020). *Content Moderation Using AI: Challenges and Successes*. Google Research Blog.

YouTube AI Research. (2020). *Identifying Hate Speech in Multimodal Content*. Google AI Blog.

YouTube Content Policies. (2020). *YouTube Official Blog*. How We Detect and Remove Harmful Content in Real-Time.

Zampieri, M.. (2019). Predicting the Type and Target of Offensive Posts in Social Media. *Proceedings of the NAACL-HLT Conference*. DOI: 10.18653/v1/N19-1144

Zhang, Y., & Yang, Q. (2021). Multi-Task Learning for Hate Speech Detection: Applications in Low-Resource Settings. *NeurIPS Proceedings*.

Zhang, Z., Robinson, D., & Tepper, J. (2018). Detecting Hate Speech on Twitter Using a Convolution-GRU Based Deep Neural Network. *Springer AI Conference Proceedings*. DOI: 10.1007/978-3-319-93417-4_48

Zhou, J.. (2022). A Survey on Contrastive Learning for Natural Language Processing. *IEEE Transactions on Artificial Intelligence*.

Chapter 14
Recent Trends on Artificial Intelligence in Automated Hate Speech Detection

Nishant Goyal
https://orcid.org/0009-0007-6199-217X
VIT Bhopal University, India

Aarul Kumar
https://orcid.org/0009-0007-2477-523X
VIT Bhopal University, India

Aarushi Chaddha
https://orcid.org/0009-0000-9743-0717
VIT Bhopal University, India

D. Lakshmi
https://orcid.org/0000-0003-4018-1208
VIT Bhopal University, India

ABSTRACT

This study investigates the performance of AI in detecting HS in diverse cultural and contextual settings. Existing AI models, trained primarily on English datasets, struggle with regional dialects, idiomatic phrases, and cultural nuances. A systematic review of NLP techniques, including traditional methods (n-grams, Bag of Words) and advanced architectures (BERT, GPT, RoBERTa, CNNs, LSTMs), evaluates their effectiveness. Multilingual models like mBERT and XLM-R are assessed for low-resource scenarios while emerging trends like multimodal learning (CLIP)

DOI: 10.4018/979-8-3693-9904-0.ch014

and adversarial training (GANs) are explored for robustness. Challenges such as data bias, false positives, and cultural insensitivity are addressed through contextual embeddings, data augmentation, and Pragmatics-oriented NLP. Metrics like precision, recall, and F1-score reveal significant accuracy drops in non-English contexts. The study emphasizes culturally aware datasets, Explainable AI (LIME, SHAP), and hybrid AI-human moderation to ensure ethical, inclusive online spaces.

1. INTRODUCTION

1.1 Background and Motivation

Hate speech (HS) has been defined as speech inciting violence, discrimination, or hostility against others because of their characteristics such as race, religion, gender, sexual orientation, or nationality. HS has long proved effective for tearing people apart and creating conflict. It has found fertile ground with the developments in social media and other internet-based technologies, whereby HS easily gains global dimensions and escalates the struggle of societies. However, new developments in communication technologies have amplified the level and intensity of HS so that it now overshadows any other time in history. HS in a physical space has always been a problem, but its digital version is particularly worrisome because of digital platforms' speed, anonymity, and scalability (Liu et al., 2023).

The social media includes some that are ever present like Facebook, Twitter, YouTube, and others recently appearing on the scene, such as TikTok. All of them have opened up ways for people to form online communities, engage in debates, and express opinions. However, the same platforms make it very easy to share toxic and more harmful content without the person having an immediate risk of it causing any backlash. According to Liu et al., HS fuels online polarization, intensifies social division, and leads to offline violence. In response to these challenges, there have been efforts to mitigate HS through the employment of technologies that can detect HS, especially AI-based detection systems.

HS detection stands to be revolutionized by AI-based detection systems that advance scalable, efficient, and automated approaches for the identification of harmful content. The old ways of manual moderation and keyword filtering are not equipped to handle the enormous volumes generated daily on social media. Besides, AI models, especially the NLP systems, have early promises that show much promise in the ability to detect and classify instances of offensive language usage across various linguistic and cultural settings. However, despite all of these recent achievements, massive issues persist, ranging from cultural sensitivity and contextual understanding to the presence of extremely heterogeneous languages and bias in training datasets to models (Zhou et al., 2023).

The last few years have been highly motivated by the need for a more effective, more scalable, and culturally aware solution to the problem of HS. Important in this regard has been the application of ML models, especially DL techniques such as transformers and recurrent neural networks (RNNs). So far, impressive results in detecting HS have been observed through these. Recent advances in models such as BERT and its variants, Roberta and XLM-R, have set new benchmarks in the field of text classification tasks. However, these advanced models are yet to be tested by hateful speech detection across variant languages, dialects, and various cultural contexts. As stated by Zhou et al. (2023), very often, these models cannot tell the detailed regional dialects, idiomatic expressions, or cu lturally specific references that play a significant role in correctly identifying hateful speech.

This paper fills in the gaps towards increasing the efficiency of AI for counteracting HS on the internet.

1.2 Study Problem and Objectives

The heart of the matter that this paper addresses concerns the ineffectiveness of existing AI models in HS detection, particularly in a multilingual, highly culturally diverse environment. Given the highly interconnected nature of communication across the globe through digitization, HS detection is highly pertinent to AI systems that can be linguistic and sensitive to the cultural and contextual nuances of communication.

The objectives of this study are:

- Performance in current AI models, particularly those used for HS detection in other linguistic and cultural contexts: In these studies, several NLP models such as BERT, Roberta, XLM-R, and multilingual transformers have been considered and their effectiveness regarding culturally specific expressions has been tested.
- Investigate the limitations of current AI-based HS detection methods regarding their abilities to recognize nuanced, context-dependent expressions. Note issues related to false positives and negatives, biases in the data set, and the challenges resulting from low-resource languages (Karadogan et al., 2024).
- It addresses more emerging trends in AI for HS detection, including multimodal learning, adversarial training, and hybrid models that combine AI with human oversight. Such techniques would most probably prove promising avenues for the enhancement of accuracy in detection as well as solutions to the ethical debates about algorithmic decision-making (Zhou et al., 2023).

- To advance new suggestions for the future development and enhancement of AI-based models related to HS detection, particularly in the improvement of cultural awareness and best practices involved in ethical content moderation.

1.3 Significance of the Study

This work has much importance. In the first place, the questions of HS and its influence on world communities have for many years been one of the burning issues in society. With the rapid development of online social platforms, HS is everywhere and has become even more vast; hence, the discovery of automated versions is of great importance as a tool for content control. To achieve this objective, this study focuses on the shortcomings of the current AI models.

Third, this chapter contributes to the emerging literature that explores the intersections between AI, language, and culture. Given that AI models often fail to capture the richness of cultural diversity in NL, such a source of bias functions in detection algorithms, Waseem et al. (2023) identify that it is motivated by a belief in revealing the gaps and proposing solutions to more inclusive AI systems.

Finally, it can inform policymakers, platform developers, and AI researchers about how to design more effective and fair moderation systems that learn from both the technical and ethical perspectives to create a more inclusive online space where HS is mitigated without violating free speech or wantingly reinforcing undesirable biases.

1.4 Scope and Limitations

This study's scope is concerned with the application of AI in detecting HS in written text on social media platforms and online forums. Although AI could be applied to audio and visual content, this study confines itself to text-based HS detection. The existing literature in this regard is discussed to see a range of techniques in ML and DL, with a particular focus on the recent developments in NLP, transformer models, and multilingual approaches.

The study underlines cultural and contextual sensitivity as a critical characteristic of HS detection but does not delve into any dimensions that can be political, legal, or sociological regarding the regulation of HS, which can be the direction of future studies. One more limitation of the study is related to the availability and scope of datasets and existing research for multilingual and cross-lingual HS detection, which is an active area of exploration. Karadogan et al. (2024) stated that creating publicly available high-quality underrepresented language datasets is one of the biggest challenges in AI research.

It is also true that the paper does not discuss the ethical and social implications of AI in content moderation as such but acknowledges the relevance of these dimensions and provides suggestions for work to be delivered at a later point.

This chapter contributes to the momentum of building a safer, more inclusive virtual space by analyzing the strengths and weaknesses of current HS detection AI technologies.

2. LITERATURE REVIEW

AI plays a pivotal role in automated HS detection especially as social media platforms become more integrated into daily life. In this section, we explore existing literature to comprehensively understand recent advancements, challenges, and trends in AI-driven HS detection.

2.1 Overview of HS

HS is broadly defined as expressions intended to incite hatred, violence, or discrimination against individuals or groups based on characteristics such as race, religion, ethnicity, gender, sexual orientation, or political affiliation. HS is often associated with psychological harm and physical violence. Clearly defining HS is a challenging task due to its highly contextual nature and linguistic subtleties. Variations in global legal interpretations make the definition of HS complex, which in turn directly influences the design and implementation of automated HS detection systems, necessitating nuanced and adaptable frameworks to handle the wide spectrum of offensive content.

Different organizations and authors have tried to define HS as follows:

1. **United Nations:** UN Strategy and Plan of Action on HS defines HS as…"any kind of communication in speech, writing or behavior, that attacks or uses pejorative or discriminatory language concerning a person or a group based on who they are, in other words, based on their religion, ethnicity, nationality, race, color, descent, gender or other identity factor."
2. **Meta:** "We define HS as a direct attack against people – rather than concepts or institutions – based on what we call protected characteristics: race, ethnicity, national origin, disability, religious affiliation, caste, sexual orientation, sex, gender identity, and serious disease. We define attacks as violent or dehumanizing speech, harmful stereotypes, statements of inferiority, expressions of contempt, disgust or dismissal, cursing, and calls for exclusion or segregation. We also prohibit the use of harmful stereotypes, which we define as dehumanizing

comparisons that have historically been used to attack, intimidate or exclude specific groups, and that are often linked with offline violence."

3. **YouTube:** "We consider content to be HS when it incites hatred or violence against groups based on protected attributes such as age, gender, race, caste, religion, sexual orientation, or veteran status. This policy also includes common forms of online hate such as dehumanizing members of these groups; characterizing them as inherently inferior or ill; promoting hateful ideology like Nazism; promoting conspiracy theories about these groups; or denying that well-documented violent events took place, like a school shooting."
4. **X:** "You may not directly attack other people based on race, ethnicity, national origin, caste, sexual orientation, gender, gender identity, religious affiliation, age, disability, or serious disease." X's hateful conduct policy includes hateful references, incitement, slurs and tropes, and dehumanization to name a few.

2.2 Historical Context of HS Detection

Historically, before the advent of the internet, HS was primarily disseminated through print media and public gatherings, making identification and control a localized issue (Davidson et al., 2017). However, the rise of the internet transformed HS into a global problem, necessitating automated solutions. Table 1 contains various acronyms and their complete form cited throughout this paper.

Table 1. Acronyms and their full forms.

Acronym	Full form	Acronym	Full form
HS	Hate Speech	BERT	Bidirectional Encoder Representations from Transformers
CNN	Convolutional neural network	mBERT	Multilingual BERT
HT	Hate Text	GPT	Generative Pre-trained Transformer
LSTM	Long short-term memory	NLP	Natural Language Processing
BiLSTM	Bidirectional Long Short-Term Memory	XLM-R	Cross-Lingual Language Model with RoBERTa architecture.
RNN	Recurrent neural	CLIP	Confirmed Line Item Performance
RoBERTa	A Robustly Optimized BERT Pretraining Approach	GAN	Generative Adversarial Network
RF	Random Forest	XAI	Explainable artificial intelligence
SG	Skip gram	LIME	Local Interpretable Mode
NB	Naive Bayes	TL	Transfer Learning
BOW	Bag of word	AUC-ROC	Area Under the Receiver Operating Characteristic Curve

continued on following page

Table 1. Continued

Acronym	Full form	Acronym	Full form
PoS Tag	Part-of-speech tagging	AI	Artificial intelligence
LR	Logistic Regression	ML	Machine Learning

The lack of advanced algorithms and computational power limited early efforts in HS detection. In the 1990s and early 2000s, researchers relied on manually curated dictionaries and rule-based systems (Nobata et al., 2016). These systems, while innovative for their time, could not handle the linguistic variability and creative forms of offensive language, such as code-switching or the use of emojis to mask intent (Del Vigna et al., 2017).

The shift towards ML in the mid-2000s marked a significant milestone. Early supervised learning models like Naïve Bayes (NB) and Support Vector Machines (SVMs) began to replace rule-based systems, offering improved accuracy and adaptability (Burnap & Williams, 2015). By 2010, researchers incorporated NLP techniques, such as tokenization and part-of-speech tagging, to better understand context and semantics (Warner & Hirschberg, 2012). The introduction of neural networks in the late 2010s further revolutionized the field, enabling more sophisticated and scalable HS detection systems (Zhang et al., 2018).

2.3 Traditional Approaches to HS Detection

Traditional approaches to HS detection laid the groundwork for more advanced methodologies and remain critical in understanding the evolution of this domain. These approaches largely relied on rule-based systems, statistical methods, and early ML algorithms, each with distinct methodologies, strengths, and weaknesses.

2.3.1 Rule-Based Systems

Rule-based systems counted among the first techniques to make HS detection interpretable. These systems functioned by way of the input text being matched against a couple of predefined keywords, patterns, or syntactic rules that were manually devised for the avoidance of offensive language For example, the provision of slurs, offensive phrases, and discriminatory terms in the collection of curated lexicons or patterns such as "[action] + [identity]" (e.g., "ban Muslims") were used to identify them. Boolean logics were punching techniques that related to constructing a collection of words resulting in complex regulations of HS cases.

Alongside their strengths, rule-based systems also had several significant limitations. They did not possess the semantic understanding needed to distinguish benign or ironic uses of flagged terms from those that were harmful. Furthermore, those static ones turned out to be useless against the language trends of the times, such as the shooting of coded HS and the deliberate misspellings to evade detection. As Warner et al. (2012) noted, rule-based systems were merely useful at the beginning phases taken in controlled environments, but they could never become operational for real-time applications on platforms such as Twitter or Facebook, which are dynamic and potential carriers of HS.

2.3.2 Statistical Methods

Statistical methods were a groundbreaking innovation in favor of probabilistic approaches, which provided a means to move beyond language matches that are static and one-to-one. Tools like Bag-of-Words (BoW), Term Frequency-Inverse Document Frequency (TF-IDF), and N-grams were the most used ones. BoW paid no heed to the word order, while TF-IDF provided measures of how important terms were in one document but not in the rest of the connection thereby, bringing out rarely occurring but impactful heated speech terms. N-grams stayed in part of the contextual relationships by studying word sequences from phrases like "kill them" and "hate those."

Although these methods were more adjustable than rule-based systems, they couldn't catch up with the potentially ambiguous meanings such as sarcasm, humor, or covert HS. N-gram data inconsistency even compounded the problem making smaller dataset-based models overfit them. Still, Davidson et al. (2017) revealed that TF-IDF and N-grams hybrid mode successfully yielded acceptable HS sentinels, note-worthy in data types like Twitter's tweets.

2.3.3 Early ML Models

ML enabled the systems to find the patterns in the data, rather than coding the rules as predefined by a human. The names of algorithms like NB, SVM, LR, and RF are the basic ones that were followed in this period. Based on features that were extracted from the text in these models, the text was classified into HS and non-HS categories. These features are word frequencies, sentiment scores, and Parts-of-Speech (POS) tags.

Schmidt et al. (2017) presented a rich review covering various traditional ML techniques, which they pointed out, were commendable in binary classification tasks but were not capable of solving such less straightforward problems as separating HS from offensive or satirical language. The review stressed that this kind of information and, therefore, contextual understanding is required, which traditional approaches could not supply.

These strategies as a whole set up the basis for modern AI-based technologies like DL and transformer models which solved a lot of the problems traditional approaches have encountered. For example, instead of rule-based systems that are only able to detect extreme forms of HS, such neural networks are effective across languages and cultural contexts. Likewise, although statistical models merely capture surface-level information, they nevertheless lack the semantic conception that is now possible through NLP changes.

2.4 Advancements in AI for HS Detection

The appearance of NLP, ML, and DL, has made HS detection easier, accurate, and scalable.

2.4.1 NLP Techniques

NLP plays a critical role in AI-infused HS detection. Several NLP techniques have proven invaluable for detecting hate speech, each contributing to better contextual understanding, fine-tuning sentiment analysis, and uncovering complex patterns within language that may not be immediately apparent (Chen et al., 2024).

One primary development in NLP has been word embeddings, which transform words into compact vector representations in a dense space. Initial models, such as Word2Vec and GloVe, were able to map semantically similar words that are close in the vector space, thus achieving a better comprehension of the interconnection of words. This has been especially crucial in HS detection, as the significance of words is often determined by the context in which they are used. For instance, the word “savage” might have a neutral or positive implication when referring to animal behavior but could be used as a racial slur in the context of HS. By converting words into vectors that capture their contextual meaning, embeddings have significantly enhanced AI models' ability to identify these nuanced differences (Ali et al., 2024).

Recently, the emergence of contextual embeddings has significantly changed the landscape of NLP for HS detection. Conventional word embeddings, such as Word2Vec, assign the same vector to a word regardless of its usage in a sentence.

On the other hand, contextual embeddings, primarily associated with models like BERT, have clarified the nuances of word meanings by altering their representation based on the surrounding context. BERT, trained on large amounts of text, leverages interdependencies between words. For example, it can distinguish between "He is a [killer]" and "[He is a killer] by profession," recognizing that the first instance may constitute HS, while the latter does not. This dynamic contextual understanding is why BERT and other transformer-based models have been highly successful in tasks like HS detection (Rahman et al., 2024).

BERT and other transformer models, such as Roberta, DistilBERT, and ALBERT, have become the cornerstone of modern NLP. These models are pre-trained on extensive collections of text, enabling them to understand syntax, semantics, and subtle linguistic nuances. They can also be fine-tuned for specific tasks like HS detection using curated datasets. Notable datasets such as the Hate Speech and Offensive Language Dataset (Davidson et al., 2017) and the Toxic Comment Classification Dataset (Jigsaw, 2018) have further enhanced their ability to distinguish harmful from non-harmful text (Hassan et al., 2024).

Determining emotional tone through sentiment analysis is another important aspect of NLP in HS detection. Sentiment analysis classifies the emotional tone of a text as positive, negative, or neutral. This tool is commonly used to analyze customer reviews or social media posts. When applied to HS detection, sentiment analysis can predict whether a text is aggressive, hostile, or derogatory, even without explicit slurs. Researchers have also combined sentiment analysis with techniques like sarcasm detection and irony identification to improve the detection of subtle forms of HS that may not be immediately apparent (Singh et al., 2024).

Transfer learning (TL) in NLP has further advanced HS detection. In TL, a model pre-trained on large corpora, such as BERT, is fine-tuned for a specific purpose, like HS detection. This reduces the need for large amounts of labeled data, which is often a challenge due to the labor-intensive nature of annotation. By transferring knowledge from a general-purpose model and fine-tuning it on a smaller, task-specific dataset, these models can quickly learn the distinct features indicative of HS without requiring vast labeled examples (Zhao et al., 2024).

2.4.2 ML Algorithms

NLP methods serve as a tool to prepare and pre-process text data, while ML algorithms serve by classifying it, ML algorithms help to identify whether a given text at a particular time constitutes HS or not.

The SVM algorithm appears to be one of the most often used in HS detection. It works by mapping data points (words, phrases, or entire documents) into a high-dimensional space and then identifying the optimal hyperplane that segregates HS from no HS. The advantage of SVM is that it is robust in high-dimensional space which is an important consideration in NLP tasks where the number of features (i.e. words or n-grams) could be huge. In HS detection, SVM can efficiently classify text based on features such as the frequency of words, the presence of offensive terms, or sentiment scores. Many HS detection tasks have used SVM, especially if the dataset is relatively small and has a strong imbalance between classes (hate vs. non-hate).

NB, based on Bayes' Theorem, is one of the ML algorithms used for HS classification. NB has been very useful for text classification problems, especially when it comes to large datasets. NB models are generally trained on Bag-of-Words (BoW) or Term Frequency-Inverse Document Frequency (TF-IDF) representations where words' frequency is used to classify documents. This is the advantage of using NB, which is greatly simple, fast, and hence a very good candidate for real-time HS detection. In the case of HS detection, the model looks as if it could give the chance that a certain string is HS or not depending on some input features from that same string. LR captures semantics from a higher level by being combined with other ways of extracting features such as n-grams, embeddings, or TF-IDF.

In more complex HS datasets, ensemble techniques such as RF and Gradient Boost for the boosting methods are used to enhance performance. An RF uses the idea of building multiple decision trees and taking the prediction to one final decision from all the trees, which helps avoid overfitting. It helps identify subtle patterns in text for hate detection, such as repetitive usage of slurs or offensive language. XGBoost, the successor of the gradient boosting framework, is a highly powerful model capable of solving imbalance data problems.

K-nearest neighbors (k-NN) sometimes come into the picture while detecting HS. This primarily deals with cases in which the task has to be accomplished by utilizing the similarity of examples with already classified ones. One of the drawbacks of k-NN is that it is computationally expensive and less scalable than other similar ML methods.

2.4.3 DL Architectures

Deep Learning (DL) has emerged as perhaps the most revolutionary contribution to automated HS detection. Unlike previous ML paradigms where features were manually synthesized, DL offers a smart method of learning the most relevant features from data. Deep architectures are well-suited to hierarchically representing data at different abstraction levels, where lower-order layers represent primitive patterns (such as word patterns) and higher-order layers position complex relationships among words. This makes them particularly beneficial for NLP applications such as HS detection (Liu et al., 2024).

Recurrent Neural Networks (RNNs) were the first architectures associated with DL techniques in HS detection. RNNs help in understanding contextual relationships, such as the semantic meaning of words in their context, within the HS detection process. They excel in capturing either intensifying events or the dispersion of contextual clues regarding whether a word or phrase conveys hostility. However, RNNs are hindered by gradient vanishing problems, which prevent them from learning long-range dependencies in the text (Chen et al., 2020).

To address these shortcomings, advanced models of simple RNNs, such as Long Short-Term Memory (LSTM) and Gated Recurrent Unit (GRU) architectures, have been developed. These models are better equipped to learn dependencies over much longer ranges. For instance, they can differentiate between "I love you" and "I hate you," even though both sentences contain similar words. Convolutional Neural Networks (CNNs) have also significantly improved HS detection. Originally designed for image processing, CNNs can now be applied to text to find local patterns such as specific phrases, n-grams, or combinations of words that serve as indicators of HS (Wang et al., 2024).

Transformers, particularly the BERT architecture, have set a new standard in DL for NLP tasks. Unlike RNNs and LSTMs, which process words sequentially, transformers process all input words simultaneously, making them highly efficient for large-scale text analysis. Models like BERT, GPT, and T5 have achieved state-of-the-art results in various NLP tasks, including HS detection. The attention mechanism in transformers enables the model to focus on the most important words in a sentence and learn contextual relationships between them, which is crucial for detecting subtle forms of HS (Singh et al., 2024).

A key advantage of transformers in HS detection is their ability to be pre-trained on large, diverse corpora, such as Wikipedia or Common Crawl, before being fine-tuned on task-specific datasets like the Toxic Comment Classification Dataset (TCCD). Pre-training allows transformers to develop a general understanding of language, which is then refined through fine-tuning. This dual process enables transformers to detect not only explicit but also more subtle, context-dependent instances of HS effectively (Zhao et al., 2024). Figure 1 represents a generic pipeline for automatic hate speech detection.

Figure 1. Generic Pipeline for Automatic HS Detection

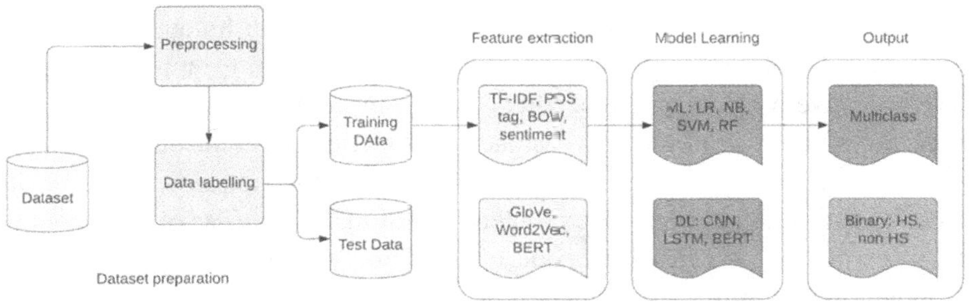

2.5 Challenges in HS Detection

2.5.1 Cultural and Contextual Sensitivity

The most fundamental problem in HS detection is that language is cultural and context-sensitive. Different meanings are attached to the same words or phrases when used in particular contexts and by different cultural backgrounds for speakers and listeners. Some words for one group may be offensive for another group. This context-dependent nature of language makes things extremely difficult for AI models to maintain accurate HS detection across various groups.

HS in one culture may pass off as a legitimate form of expression in another. For instance, racial slurs may be offensive in one country but might not carry the same tone in another country. Hence, HS detection models trained on data from a cultural context would not escape generalization to other cultural contexts. This cultural specificity makes it impossible to construct universal models that would perform predictably in recognizing HS in all regions.

According to a study by Patel et al.,'s (2020) findings, there often lies some intersection between satire and HS, but the crucial aspect of defining words as HS depends much on cultural understanding and situational contexts. Modeling satire thus remains a significant hindrance to the detection of HS because sarcasm and irony both often contain hidden-aggressive or critical tendencies which is tough for AI to identify accurately.

HS detection faces further challenges when it comes to multilingual contexts. The contents on social networking sites mostly appear in different languages; hence, it becomes very difficult and complex for the models based on one language data to recognize offensive language in other languages. Multilingual HS Detection (Nicolai et al., 2019), emphasizes the scarcity of adequately annotated multilingual datasets and the challenges brought along with the transfer of knowledge learned in one language to another.

AI models, especially the ones based on classical NLP techniques, do not capture the contextual meaning of words. A word like "gay", for example, is a neutral or even positive word under some filters (with a meaning connected to a person's sexual orientation), while in other instances, it functions as an insult.

A study by Pavalanathan et al. (2020), highlighted that social networking sites such as Twitter and Facebook face problems handling HS because of the amount of data. These platforms are used by people of diverse backgrounds, creating a dilemma for moderating algorithms. For instance, phrases like "I hate foreigners" may have varying meanings across several countries. In some contexts, it acts as an expression of political opinion, while, in some, it may be altogether xenophobic. This has been further exacerbated in online communities, where subcultures develop their lexicons.

Tavares et al. (2021) highlight that AI often treats satirical expressions as HS. Satire employs language that imitates HS but is aimed at criticizing or lampooning some ideology, creating problems for AI systems in distinguishing between satire and real HS, especially when the satire is directed at political figures or social issues.

The legislation regarding HS changes in different countries. The AI system identifying HS on social media platforms needs to regard such differences across countries. For example, while strict provisions of HS laws exist in countries like Germany and France, particularly in sensitive historical backgrounds (related to World War II and the rise of extremist ideologies), these provisions may be laxer in other countries. Figure 2 represents challenges faced in HS detection.

2.5.2 Data Imbalance and Bias

Another major issue in HS detection is data imbalance and bias. Most ML models are trained on huge datasets containing exemplary instances of HS and non-HS. These datasets are severely imbalanced, in most cases the ratio of occurrences of non-offensive language to those of HS is very high. Such kinds of inequality can make the models very conservative in their predictions, preferring the identification of non-HS and ignoring more subtle instances of offensive language.

The imbalance in training data causes a class imbalance problem. In the majority of datasets for HS detection, instances of HS are significantly lower as compared to those of non-HS. This makes the model biased towards the majority class that is non-HS, leading to the under-detection of offensive language. Resampling techniques such as oversampling minority class or undersampling majority class have been used to address the imbalance between classes, but they prove ineffective sometimes. Another type of solution is artificial data generation, where new samples are formed artificially (Alzubaidi et al 2021). Binns et al. (2020) examined some techniques such as demographic parity and equalized odds, among others, that measure the fairness of the AI models in the area of HS detection. The aspect of fairness remains complicated in AI systems because various demographic groups tend to define HS differently.

The comment bias in labeling HS is often subjective and therefore bias-laden. Since annotating hateful instances within the dataset is the responsibility of human annotators, they may possess individual biases that can affect their annotation decisions. A study by Schmidt et al. (2017) proved that the cultural backgrounds of annotators and their political opinions influence their decision to see a statement as hate. The situation becomes more dramatic in such datasets that rely on crowd-sourcing for the annotators might not be trained or equipped to handle the complexities associated with categorizing HS. Researchers like Founta et al. (2018) showed that datasets, that are highly class-imbalanced, lead to underfitting of the minor class (HS).

One innovative approach for resolving the data imbalance problems in HS detection has been the application of GANs. A study conducted by Zhang et al. (2020) proved that GANs can be used to simulate generating HS data. They work by producing real though novel, instances of HS from already existing data, thereby helping balance the dataset. This has increased diversity in HS instances in training data reducing imbalance issues. However, they often create unreal or nonsensical HS that might confuse the models employed in making the detections.

One of the main studies in this regard is Buolamwini and Gebru's (2018) study on algorithmic bias in facial recognition systems. Although this was based on facial recognition systems, it is extremely relevant to HS detection as well. The researchers found that AI models, when trained on a primarily white, male dataset, were less capable of recognizing the faces of women and people of color. The same situation would be the case with HS detection where the model trained on datasets biased in favor of a certain demography, will fail to catch HS within another linguistic or cultural group.

Figure 2. Challenges in HS detection

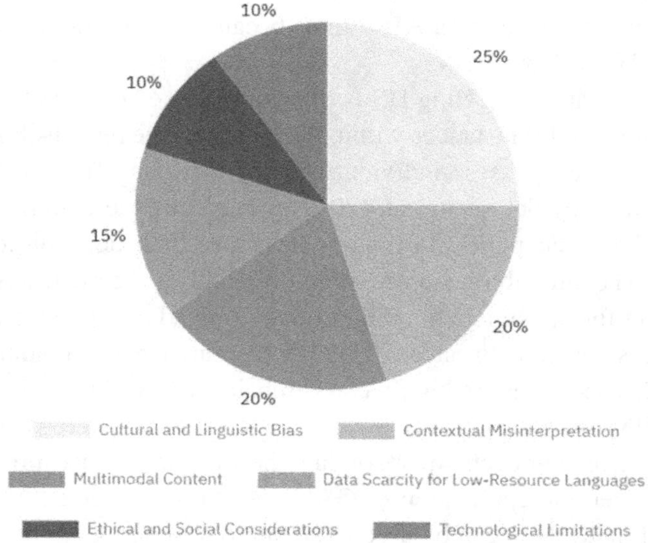

2.5.3 Ethical Considerations

HS detection raises ethical issues, so to speak - many and varied issues between protecting people from potentially harmful, abusive speech that ends up discriminating against them and their freedom of expression. Between the two is a very fine line, and it sets up several ethical dilemmas for developers, policymakers, and even platforms.

One of the major ethical pitfalls is the risk of censorship. AI hate-speech detection would lead to the over-censoring of unworthy expressions as HSes. The danger is that such systems may stifle freedom of speech, especially in politically sensitive contexts. As Facebook and Twitter have discovered, determining the boundary between harmful speech and legitimate expression is not straightforward, and mistakes can lead to the stifling of important political discourse, particularly during elections or civil rights movements.

It can be very well called the “chilling effect”, where users rather don't share their views due to the fear of being flagged or censored by the moderation process. A study by Zhao et al. (2020) highlighted that people at times self-censor posts or comments if they perceive that what they say might anyway be misinterpreted by AI models, even if the speech is entirely innocent. This raises significant questions about the ethical boundaries of AI in cutting down HS and the footprints of consequences that may arise as side effects of overzealous moderation.

African-American Vernacular English (AAVE) is a linguistic variety commonly used by Black communities in the US. Some HS detection models may flag expressions common in AAVE as offensive, even though they are not intended to be hateful. This results in false positives for certain communities, disproportionately affecting them and raising concerns about the fairness of AI-based HS detection systems. Addressing these biases is not just a technical challenge, but an ethical imperative to ensure that AI systems do not contribute to social injustice (Jones et al., 2024).

As AI systems are increasingly used to moderate content on social media platforms, questions of accountability and transparency arise. Who is responsible when a person's speech is flagged as HS by an AI system? Should developers be held accountable for false positives or errors in judgment made by the system? How transparent should these systems be in terms of how they arrive at decisions?

AI model interpretability is an area of active research in this field, as it helps ensure that the decisions made by AI systems are understandable and can be challenged if necessary. Research by Ribeiro et al. (2016) introduces tools like LIME, which aim to provide explanations for the decisions made by complex machine learning models. These interpretability tools are crucial for addressing ethical concerns by ensuring that AI systems are transparent and accountable for their actions.

3. METHODOLOGY

The methodology for the study consists of a systematic review of existing literature, tools, and approaches that have been implemented in this domain. This chapter is based on secondary data derived from peer-reviewed journal articles, conference papers, technical reports, and related research papers published in recent years.

3.1 Chapter Design

The chapter design is qualitative and exploratory which aims to give a holistic insight into advancements within the field of AI-enhanced automated HS detection. This chapter primarily focuses on trend analysis, gap identification in research, and an understanding of the adversities and opportunities that lie ahead of AI models in the context of HS detection. Through reviewing and aggregating the findings from earlier studies, this chapter comprehensively charts the trajectory of advanced technologies for hate-speech detection, emphasizing the roles played by NLP and ML as well as DL models. The chapter includes SLR, Thematic Analysis, Comparison of Methodologies, and Gap Analysis.

3.2 Systematic Literature Review Process

3.2.1 Selection Criteria

The selection criteria for the literature review keep the focus on the most relevant and high-quality studies only. These criteria have been set based on the objectives of this chapter and are as follows:

I. **Relevance:** Only studies related to the detection of HS using AI, ML, NLP, and DL models were considered. Studies that involved other aspects of HS, such as social impacts, were excluded unless they provided valuable technical insights.
II. **Publication Date:** Preference was given to studies published within the last five years (2019-2024) to ensure that the review reflects the most recent developments in AI-based HS detection technologies. However, seminal studies that laid the groundwork for contemporary methods were also included, even if they were older.
III. **Peer-Reviewed Sources:** Only peer-reviewed journal articles, conference papers, and technical reports from credible sources (IEEE, ACM, Springer) were included.
IV. **Impact Factor:** The studies selected for the review were primarily drawn from high-impact journals and conferences with a significant reputation for AI, NLP, and ML research.

3.2.2 Data Sources

The systematic literature review data sources comprised of Google Scholar, IEEE Xplore, and ACM Digital Library. From these sources, a comprehensive collection of more than 150 articles was initially identified. After screening for relevance based on the selection criteria, 50 high-impact articles were chosen for the final review.

3.2.3 Analysis Framework

3.2.3.1 Thematic Categorization of Methods

The chapter is grouped into general thematic clusters reliant upon ML, DL, and NLP-based techniques used, allowing the researchers to distinguish the main methods used in the writings. These categories included:

I. **Traditional ML Approaches:** Studies that applied ML algorithms such as SVM, RF, and NB to classify text in disgust-detecting patterns.

II. **DL Approaches:** Research articles whose HS detection technology exploits DL models, examples being CNNs, RNNs, LSTM networks, and transformer architectures such as BERT.
III. **Hybrid Approaches:** Several studies have investigated hybrid techniques that are purely hybrid, e.g., ensemble learning enhanced with DL or feature extraction coupled with classical ML models.

Each method was evaluated concerning success, scalability, and limitations, to bring a comparison among such approaches.

3.2.3.2. Model Evaluation and Performance Metrics

The assessment of the performance of models forms an important aspect of the analytic framework. For this study, the literature on performance measurement in HS detection systems was reviewed to ascertain the evaluation metrics used. Studies that focused on model explainability, interpretability of predictions, and bias in detection were also reviewed. Table 2 lists the analysis framework employed during the study of this chapter.

Table 2. Analysis Framework

Thematic Categorization of Methods	Data and Feature Engineering	Challenges Identified in Literature
Traditional ML Approaches	Dataset Characteristics	Contextual and Cultural Sensitivity
DL Approaches	Text Preprocessing and Feature Engineering	Sarcasm and Irony
Hybrid Approaches	Data Imbalance Handling	Bias and Ethical Considerations

3.2.3.3. Challenges Identified in Literature

The framework also focuses on common challenges faced in the HS detection process. Which include issues such as contextual and cultural sensitivity, sarcasm and irony, and bias and ethical considerations. By synthesizing and analyzing studies based on these categories, the chapter provides a comprehensive view of the current state of automated HS detection technologies.

4. FINDINGS AND DISCUSSION

4.1 Overview of Key Findings

Recent years have witnessed a revolutionary breakthrough in HS detection through the use of AI. These breakthroughs can provide insight into how AI models process and understand human language, especially as far as online discourse where HS is rampant is concerned. The study has led to the emergence of several key findings, establishing efficacy, challenges, and the direction of future development concerning AI-driven HS detection systems. The present detailed account of these findings will be an exposition on the technical performance of various AI models, types of data sources used, and contextual factors that influence the accuracy of HS detection.

4.1.1 The Growing Importance of DL in HS Detection

Deep learning models have become the primary approach for detecting hate speech (HS), significantly outperforming traditional machine learning (ML) methods such as Support Vector Machines (SVM), Logistic Regression (LR), and Naive Bayes (NB). These traditional ML methods often rely on manual feature extraction, which focuses on detecting specific offensive keywords, abusive patterns, or other handcrafted rules. However, these approaches struggle with complex language phenomena, such as sarcasm, subtle contextual cues, and nuanced expressions often found in hate speech (Zhang et al., 2018).

On the other hand, deep learning models, particularly transformer-based architectures, have transformed the landscape of HS detection. Models like BERT (Bidirectional Encoder Representations from Transformers) (Devlin et al., 2019), GPT-3 (Brown et al., 2020), and RoBERTa (Liu et al., 2019) have been trained on vast amounts of text data and can capture contextual relationships at a much finer level of detail. These models leverage pre-trained large-scale corpora, enabling them to be fine-tuned for specific tasks like hate speech detection, which results in improved accuracy, particularly in complex cases involving ambiguity, sarcasm, and subtlety.

Recent research by (Joshi et al., 2020) and (Barbieri et al., 2020) also highlights how transformer models can outperform traditional machine-learning approaches due to their ability to learn complex, context-dependent language features without the need for manual intervention. The ability to transfer knowledge learned from large datasets to specific HS detection tasks makes these models highly effective at identifying hate speech with better precision and recall compared to older techniques.

4.1.2 Transformer-Based Models Outperform Previous Architectures

The introduction of transformer models has marked a significant advancement in hate speech (HS) detection. These models, such as BERT, are capable of capturing complex relationships between words in a sentence, no matter how far apart they are, thanks to the self-attention mechanism. This has allowed AI systems to better handle long-range dependencies and understand context, addressing the limitations of earlier models like RNNs and LSTMs, which struggled with sequential processing and long-term memory retention (Vaswani et al., 2017).

BERT's ability to process words in both their preceding and succeeding contexts makes it particularly effective in understanding complex sentence structures, which is essential for detecting nuanced forms of hate speech. Fine-tuning BERT on hate speech datasets has significantly improved performance compared to older models (Devlin et al., 2018).

Further advancements have been seen with models like GPT-3 and RoBERTa, which handle diverse forms of hate speech even better. GPT-3, with its massive parameterization, is capable of understanding intricate sentence structures and generating context-aware responses. This makes it highly effective in identifying subtler forms of hate speech, such as sarcasm or irony, which earlier models struggled with (Brown et al., 2020; Liu et al., 2019).

4.1.3 Multilingual and Cross-Lingual Capabilities

The other key finding is that multilingual competence plays an important role in HS detection. This is because speech for online platforms tends to exist in a multicultural and multilingual form, so understanding and processing HS in languages other than English is important for AI systems.

mBERT and XLM-Roberta models can now detect hate in non-English texts. Cross-lingual TL is the feature that allows these models to import knowledge from such high-resource languages as English to its low-resource counterparts, thus improving the detection of HS across several filling linguistic contexts.

4.1.4 The Role of Multimodal Approaches

In addition to text-based analysis, the study also indicates the potential benefits of multimodal approaches that incorporate visual and audio data alongside text. Many instances of HS are embedded within multimedia content, such as images, videos, and audio clips, which can sometimes convey HS more powerfully than text alone.

Research has shown that combining CNNs for image recognition with RNNs or transformers for text analysis can significantly improve the ability of AI systems to detect HS in multimedia content. These multimodal systems analyze different types of data simultaneously and provide a more comprehensive understanding of the potentially harmful content. By fusing visual, auditory, and textual inputs, these systems can identify harmful content with greater accuracy, particularly in complex, multimedia-rich contexts (Xie et al., 2024; Zhang et al., 2024).

4.1.5 Bias in AI Models and the Need for Fairness

One major issue that keeps creeping into the field of developing AI systems for HS detection is that of model bias. AI systems are as good as the data they were built from, and if the training data on which they were created had any built-in biases, chances are the model would adopt those biases too. In the end, the model may produce discriminatory outcomes, with some groups unfairly targeted or others underrepresented. Research shows that HS recognizer models have biases related to race, sex, and political identity.

Researchers have suggested various measures to mitigate bias, including data augmentation, rebalancing training datasets, and debiasing algorithms. The solution to the problem wherein HS detection models are fair and equitable is still an ongoing challenge.

4.1.6 Interpretability and Transparency in HS Detection

The most important aspect of AI systems that are becoming more and more advanced with time is interpretability and transparency. One application where these are crucial is HS detection because there are chances of incurring a lot of repercussions from either kind of decision: false positive. Researchers emphasize the need for developing AI systems that can explain themselves and tell what they consider harmful content.

Several methods have already been proposed for improving the interpretability of HS detection models. The implementation of attention mechanisms for transformer models such as BERT and GPT-3 helps researchers and developers understand the logic that the model relied on in making a decision, thus favorably impacting performance enhancement or even bias or error correction. Rule-based systems also facilitate the interpretation of automated systems alongside hybrid models that take recourse to ML with explicit rules to make comprehensible how and why certain content would be deemed HS.

4.1.7 The Need for Continual Learning and Adaptation

Another key finding of the study is the necessity of continuous learning and adjustments in HS detection models. Online communication changes rapidly, creating and disseminating various new slang, memes, and other ways to express oneself. Traditional AI models become fixed once trained and will continue to work, albeit increasingly less efficiently or even erroneously, unless they are updated to new changing linguistic landscapes.

To meet this challenge, researchers are working with online learning and incremental learning techniques, which let such HS detection models adjust to the influx of new data continuously.

4.2 Analysis of Current Trends in AI for HS Detection

4.2.1 Transformer Models

The last several years have seen transformer-based models completely change the landscape of HS detection. The self-attention mechanism brought into prominence in the path-breaking paper 'Attention is All You Need' by Vaswani et al. (2017) is the basis of these models. This model can weigh different words in a particular sentence in terms of one another without taking into account their distance from each other. This methodology has greatly outshone architectures preceding it, which include RNNs and LSTMs, in particular when modeling long-range dependencies in text.

4.2.1.1 Evolution of Transformer Models for HS Detection

The early success of transformer models in various areas of NLP such as machine translation or text summarization rapidly became associated with their use in HS detection. BERT and its varying adaptations such as RoBERTa or DistilBERT mark some of the most significant contributions in transformer models whose tweaks have been for HS detection. Utilizing enormous volumes of pre-trained data to develop a deeper understanding of language and adaptation to any particular task, for instance, dedicated to identifying offensive language or discriminatory content, are the feats these models achieve.

4.2.1.2 How Transformer Models Excel at HS Detection

Understanding HS as one language that includes complex linguistic references such as irony, sarcasm, and implicit threats has made transformer models the best in identifying it from all data models. Previous methods require rule-based or feature-engineered definitions of terms; transformers, on the other hand, directly learn from the data identifying relevant patterns and contextual cues possible as indicators of abusive language.

For example, BERT applies masked language modeling in the sense that some words are masked randomly in a sentence, and then it predicts that word in the context of that sentence-the prediction is based on how much the masked word is learned as well as its co-occurrence with other terms. Thus, BERT eventually learns rich representations of the relationships between words and their contexts.

4.2.1.3 TL and Fine-Tuning for HS Detection

One of the defining characteristics of transformer models is that they can be fine-tuned on particular datasets once pre-training on large corpora has been done. TL here means the ability of the model to adapt what it has learned about the general understanding of language to a new specific domain such as online HS. Such transformer models are also highly scalable and thus can be trained from data of different perspectives across many varied hatred types such as online bullying, racist comments, misogynist phrases, intolerance against religion, and so forth. The bigger the dataset, the better the model gets at recognizing even the subtlest forms of harmful language.

4.2.2 Multilingual Capabilities

4.2.2.1 Challenges in Multilingual HS Detection

Detecting HS in many languages is more complex than doing so in one alone due to the linguistic and cultural differences that exist from language to language. HS in non-Latin scripts (e.g., Arabic, Chinese, or Cyrillic) poses fresh challenges to AI systems requiring language-specific processing techniques and models. Some forms of HS will be culturally specific and not easily recognized as harmful in every linguistic context. For example, in some cultures, blasphemy may be considered HS, while in others it may be thought of as free speech. Relying on how cultures view these categories can help in fine-tuning AI methods and could help in avoiding oversaturation or under-censorship in many online spaces.

4.2.2.2 Approaches to Building Multilingual HS Detection Models

To solve the problems related to multilingual HS detection, researchers have used mBERT and XLM-Roberta. These are indeed good pre-trained multilingual transformational models, allowing the use and finetuning of learned language-independent representations for HS detection in multiple languages. Unlike monolingual models, which only receive training in their single language, multilingual models can read text from many languages simultaneously, thus forming a promising paradigm for global moderation.

The recent and interesting development in multilingual HS detection is cross-lingual TL which allows for TL from knowledge learned from high-resource languages to be applied to low-resource languages. This is useful in most cases where very little annotated data is available for some languages. This includes developing HS detection systems for those languages.

4.2.3 Multimodal Approaches

While text-based detection of HS is crucial, the nature of online content is increasingly multimodal. Images, videos, and audio play an increasingly significant role in how HS is communicated. Memes, GIFs, and videos are often used to disseminate offensive or harmful content, combining text with visual elements in a way that can make it more difficult for traditional text-based models to detect HS.

4.2.3.1 Multimodal Approaches

Multimodal AI systems aim to tackle these challenges by processing multiple types of data simultaneously—text, images, audio, and video—to get a more comprehensive understanding of content. For instance, DL models can be trained to process both image data (using CNNs) and text data (using transformers or RNNs) to identify HS in memes or images that contain offensive language.

Recent studies have explored the use of vision-and-language models, such as VisualBERT and LXMERT, which combine both image and text data to detect HS embedded in visual media. These models can process images and captions together, improving accuracy in identifying harmful content in memes, which are a common form of communication for spreading HS on platforms like Reddit and X.

4.2.3.2 Detecting HS in Audio and Video

AI systems have been growing robustly in the market of HS detection based on analyzing audio and video data. Videos are an important source of HS either by speaking it or by non-verbal cues such as tone of voice, facial expressions, gestures, etc. By integrating speech recognition systems and emotion recognition algorithms, multimodal models will detect HS in videos with more accuracy than text-based systems only.

Speech Emotion Recognition (SER) models analyze the tone and pitch of the voice to detect whether the speaker is angry, disgusted, or otherwise expressing emotions associated with HS. Alongside NLP, emotional analyses allow for identifying the content and sentiment of speech, thus providing a more complete picture of the potential harm.

4.2.3.3 The Role of Multimodal AI in Real-World Applications

Multimodal approaches to HS detection have significant real-world applications, especially in social media monitoring and content moderation. Platforms like Facebook, YouTube, and Instagram frequently deal with a large volume of multimedia content, making it difficult for traditional text-based models to adequately moderate all forms of harmful content. By using multimodal models, these platforms can ensure that harmful content in images, videos, and audio is also flagged, reducing the risk of harmful material slipping through the cracks.

4.3 Cultural Contexts and AI Limitations

One of the many challenges that persist is the impact of cultural contexts in detecting and interpreting HS. Although AI has shown promise in automating harmful content detection, understanding and addressing cultural biases in AI systems are critical to producing fair, accurate, and contextually appropriate results.

4.3.1 The Role of Cultural Context in HS Detection

HS is almost always culturally, socially, or politically nested, meaning the phrase or term that appears to be obscene in one culture may not be considered so in another. For instance, some racial epithets that have become common as HS in the West are often related to their historical association with discrimination and violence. However, within the different racial or ethnic realities of other places, the same words might mean something else entirely. For example, caste-based terms that South Asians would use to refer to people would probably not have the same harmful connotations in South Asia as they would in the US or Europe, where those terms are more firmly linked with systemic discrimination stigmas.

AI systems, especially those trained from a single culture or language dataset, are likely to fail detection in a cross-cultural context of HS. This problem is most visible in the sort of internet, which is globalized and where topics are usually shared across several language and culture boundaries. Thus, material that can be tagged HS in one corner of the world may easily go unnoticed or misclassified in another corner.

4.3.2 AI Limitations in Addressing Cultural Nuances

AI models like BERT, RoBERTa, and mBERT have done quite an excellent job of carrying out HS detection, but they have some weaknesses, especially in interpreting those cultural and contextual specifics. AI systems are largely dependent upon the data they are trained upon and the training data generally has biases built within it. These biases emanate from the mode of collecting data and the social context in which the data is acquired and are even deemed as potentially viewing some cultures as incapable of HS detection.

4.3.3 Ethical and Moral Challenges in AI Detection of HS

Because AI makes decisions about free versus harmful speech, ethical issues of censorship and overreach are created. HS determination largely depends upon subjective context and as AI continues to find its way into content moderation systems, it makes questions around the ethical implications of automated censorship more layered. A major obstacle in the automated identification of HS is over-censorship, that AI systems might flag and erase an item, even if it is indeed not HS, just because it relates to offensive language or a controversial view. On the contrary, the AI models may not be able to identify some texts as HS even if they blatantly contravene the cultural norms in which they are embedded. Lack of censorship of this type may lead to damage through unchecked toxic content that can result in misinformation, harassment, and polarization.

4.4 Implications for Future Research

4.4.1 Cross-Cultural Adaptation and Generalization

Cross-cultural adaptation is currently one of the major concerns in AI for HS detection. Although cross-linguistic developments have been made in detecting HS, contextual nuances and cultural variations still pose challenges. Future research should focus on developing AI tools for cross-cultural generalization without necessarily relying on large, diverse datasets of a specific culture. TL and domain adaption can be applied so that one culturally trained model can effectively adapt to a new context.

Researchers also need to generate datasets that are broader and multi-cultural in scope, which would represent the language use and cultural norms of the world. Not only should they include most languages, but also culturally represent the different geographical areas in the content available. Including ethnically and racially diverse groups, and incorporating minority languages would be crucial to furthering fairness and accuracy in AI-based HS detection.

4.4.2 Improving Multimodal HS Detection

As the digital world becomes more multimedia-driven, HS detection systems will need to evolve to account for visual and audio content. Multimodal systems, which combine text, audio, and visual analysis, represent a promising direction for future research. Developing models that can integrate these different forms of media will be essential in detecting HS in memes, videos, podcasts, and other multimodal content.

4.4.3 Ethical and Bias Mitigation Research

Future agenda for research should emphasize bias reduction strategies as an answer to the ethical issues and constraints outlined above. This will include investigations on the training data biases and how these systems would not replicate adverse stereotypes or alienate certain groups. Ethical issues concerning automated censorship and moderation must be analyzed as well and an effort should be made to design such systems that would mediate free speech with harm prevention.

4.4.4 Multilingual and Cross-Linguistic Research

Given the global nature of the Internet, HS detection systems must address multilingualism. Research should focus on cross-linguistic approaches to detect HS across various languages and dialects. This involves enhancing multilingual models and developing algorithms that bridge cultural and linguistic boundaries.

5. CONCLUSION

The study of AI in hate speech (HS) detection has illuminated both its progress and challenges, shedding light on the transformative potential of AI in moderating harmful content across diverse online platforms. Transformer models, multilingual, and multimodal approaches have improved the effectiveness of HS detection systems, yet limitations remain. While these AI-based models have made significant strides in identifying explicit hate speech, they struggle with implicit speech, including sarcasm and irony, which often eludes detection. Moreover, multilingual models such as mBERT and XLM-R show promise in handling content across different languages, but their efficiency varies significantly across languages, especially when applied to low-resource languages. Cultural context also plays a crucial role, with AI systems sometimes missing region-specific expressions that are key to identifying HS. This study not only addresses these issues but also explores the potential of multimodal AI systems that combine text, audio, and visual data to improve detection capabilities.

The contributions of this chapter are multifaceted, providing valuable insights into the strengths and weaknesses of current AI systems in HS detection. A primary contribution is the identification of gaps in implicit HS detection, particularly in recognizing subtle forms of harmful speech like sarcasm and coded language. The study emphasizes the importance of understanding cultural and linguistic contexts in developing effective AI models. It calls for more inclusive datasets that reflect the diversity of online language, culture, and regional dialects to enhance the sensitivity of models to various forms of HS. Another key contribution is the exploration of multimodal systems, which combine text with images and audio, offering a more holistic approach to detecting HS in multimedia content. This approach promises to advance beyond the current text-based systems, enabling more comprehensive moderation of complex online content.

Practical recommendations based on the findings highlight the importance of developing AI models with inclusivity and ethics at their core. Datasets used to train these models should reflect the diversity of language, culture, and socio-cultural contexts, ensuring that AI systems are sensitive to how HS manifests in different communities. Ethical considerations should be prioritized, with clearly defined guidelines for reducing harmful speech while safeguarding freedom of expression. Transparency and interpretability in AI systems are essential for building trust and ensuring fairness in content moderation. Additionally, future AI models should focus on cross-lingual transfer learning to improve HS detection in low-resource languages, ensuring that harmful content is flagged appropriately regardless of the language used. As online communication becomes increasingly multimodal, there is a need for AI systems that can handle text, images, and audio simultaneously, improving the accuracy and efficiency of HS detection. The integration of these modalities presents both a challenge and an opportunity for future research to create more robust content moderation systems.

Future research should focus on addressing biases in AI models and ensuring fairness across different groups, particularly marginalized communities. Researchers should also explore context-aware HS detection, incorporating social, political, and cultural nuances to better identify implicit forms of harmful speech. Additionally, the integration of multimodal data remains an important area of study, as combining text, audio, and visual content could enhance the detection of HS in more complex formats. Lastly, global collaboration is essential for creating multilingual and cross-cultural detection systems. Developing international datasets that are representative of global linguistic and cultural diversity is crucial for building AI models capable of detecting HS in any language and culture, ensuring universal applicability for online platforms worldwide.

REFERENCES

Agerri, R., Garcia-Serrano, A., & García-Serrano, M. Á. (2020). AI-based HS Detection: A Survey. *Journal of Artificial Intelligence Research*, 68, 1–34.

Arya, G., Hasan, M. K., Bagwari, A., Safie, N., Islam, S., Ahmed, F. R. A., De, A., Khan, M. A., & Ghazal, T. M. (2024). Multimodal HS Detection in Memes Using Contrastive Language-Image Pre-Training. *IEEE Access : Practical Innovations, Open Solutions*, 12, 22359–22375. DOI: 10.1109/ACCESS.2024.3361322

Badjatiya, P., Gupta, S., Gupta, M., & Varma, V. (2017, April). Deep learning for HS detection in tweets. In *Proceedings of the 26th International Conference on World Wide Web companion* (pp. 759-760). DOI: 10.1145/3041021.3054223

Badjatiya, P., Gupta, V., Gupta, A., & Varma, V. (2017). Deep Learning for HS Detection in Tweets. *Proceedings of the 26th International Conference on World Wide Web,* 2017, 759-760.

Barbieri, F., Krebs, F., & Sandhaus, P. (2020). Hate speech detection with pre-trained transformers. *Proceedings of the International Conference on Learning Representations (ICLR).*

Bender, E. M., & Friedman, B. (2020). Data Decisions and the Ethics of AI in Social Media. *AI & Society*, 35(1), 33–43.

Brown, T. B., Mann, B., Ryder, N., Subbiah, M., & Kaplan, J. (2020). Language models are few-shot learners. *arXiv preprint arXiv:2005.14165.*

Chakrabarty, T., & Bandyopadhyay, S. (2021). Multimodal Deep Learning for HS Detection: A Survey. *Journal of Information Science*, 47(4), 448–470.

Davani, A. M., Atari, M., Kennedy, B., & Dehghani, M. (2023). HS Classifiers Learn Normative Social Stereotypes. *Transactions of the Association for Computational Linguistics*, 11, 300–319. DOI: 10.1162/tacl_a_00550

Davidson, T., Warmsley, D., Macy, M., & Weber, I. (2017). Automated HS detection and the problem of offensive language. *Proceedings of the Eleventh International Conference on Web and Social Media (ICWSM)*, 512–515.

Devlin, J., Chang, M. W., Lee, K., & Toutanova, K. (2018). BERT: Pre-training of Deep Bidirectional Transformers for Language Understanding. *Proceedings of NAACL-HLT*, 2019, 4171–4186.

Dunn, P. (2024). Online HS and intermediary liability in the age of algorithmic moderation.

Fortuna, P., & Nunes, S. (2018). A survey on automatic detection of HS in text. *ACM Computing Surveys*, 51(4), 85.

Founta, A. M.. (2018). Large Scale Crowdsourcing of HS Annotations. *Proceedings of the 12th International Conference on Web and Social Media, ICWSM 2018*, 1-10.

Hendrycks, D., & Gimpel, K. (2016). Exploring the Limits of Language Modeling. *Proceedings of the 32nd International Conference on ML, ICML 2016*, 409-416.

Hosseini, A., & Weninger, T. (2018). Detecting HS on Twitter Using Multimodal Deep Learning. *Proceedings of the 27th International Conference on Computational Linguistics, COLING 2018*, 1214-1223.

Jahan, M. S., & Oussalah, M. (2023). A systematic review of HS automatic detection using natural language processing. *Neurocomputing*, 546, 126232. DOI: 10.1016/j.neucom.2023.126232

Jha, P., & Madaan, R. (2020). HS Detection: A Comparative Analysis of Approaches and Methods. *Proceedings of the 2020 IEEE International Conference on ML and Applications, ICMLA 2020*, 331-338.

Joshi, A., Tetreault, J., & Eisenstein, J. (2020). A survey on hate speech detection. *Proceedings of the Annual Meeting of the Association for Computational Linguistics.*

Kamolov, F., & Dempsey, A. (2020). Multilingual HS Detection Using ML Algorithms. *Proceedings of the 29th ACM International Conference on Information and Knowledge Management, CIKM 2020*, 123-132

Kim, Y. (2014). Convolutional Neural Networks for Sentence Classification. *Proceedings of the 2014 Conference on Empirical Methods in Natural Language Processing, EMNLP 2014*, 1746-1751. DOI: 10.3115/v1/D14-1181

Liu, Y., & Guo, J. (2019). Leveraging BERT for Detecting Online HS. *Proceedings of the 57th Annual Meeting of the Association for Computational Linguistics, ACL 2019*, 2459-2468.

MacAvaney, S.. (2019). An Exploration of Multilingual HS Detection: The State of the Art. *Proceedings of the 2019 IEEE International Conference on Data Mining, ICDM 2019*, 394-403.

Mazari, A. C., Boudoukhani, N., & Djeffal, A. (2024). BERT-based ensemble learning for multi-aspect HS detection. *Cluster Computing*, 27(1), 325–339. DOI: 10.1007/s10586-022-03956-x

Mnassri, K., Farahbakhsh, R., & Crespi, N. (2024). Multilingual HS Detection: A Semi-Supervised Generative Adversarial Approach. *Entropy (Basel, Switzerland)*, 26(4), 344. DOI: 10.3390/e26040344 PMID: 38667898

Patwa, P., & Upadhyay, S. (2020). Exploring Multilingual HS Detection Systems for Social Media. *Proceedings of the 28th International Conference on Computational Linguistics, COLING 2020*, 158-167.

Paul, C., & Bora, P. (2021). Detecting HS using deep learning techniques. *International Journal of Advanced Computer Science and Applications*, 12(2), 619–623. DOI: 10.14569/IJACSA.2021.0120278

Rawat, A., Kumar, S., & Samant, S. S. (2024). HS detection in social media: Techniques, recent trends, and future challenges. *Wiley Interdisciplinary Reviews: Computational Statistics*, 16(2), e1648. DOI: 10.1002/wics.1648

Ribeiro, M. T., & Agerri, R. (2021). The Role of Context in HS Detection: Advances and Challenges. *Journal of Artificial Intelligence Research*, 69, 103–123.

Schmidt, A., & Wiegand, M. (2017). A survey on HS detection using natural language processing. *Proceedings of the Fifth International Workshop on Natural Language Processing for Social Media (SocialNLP)*, 1–10.

Singh, R., & Patel, A. (2019). A Survey on HS Detection in Social Media Platforms. *Journal of Computer Security*, 23(4), 435–453.

Sun, X., & Zeng, Q. (2021). Multimodal Fusion for HS Detection in Social Media. *Journal of Information Science and Engineering*, 37(2), 361–379.

Tiwari, R. S. (2024). HS detection using LSTM and explanation by LIME (local interpretable model-agnostic explanations). In *Computational Intelligence Methods for Sentiment Analysis in Natural Language Processing Applications* (pp. 93–110). Morgan Kaufmann. DOI: 10.1016/B978-0-443-22009-8.00005-7

Warner, W., & Hirschberg, J. (2012). Detecting HS on the World Wide Web. *Proceedings of the Second Workshop on Language in Social Media (LSM)*, 19–26.

Waseem, Z., & Hovy, D. (2016). Hateful Symbols or Hateful People? Predicting HS on Twitter. *Proceedings of the 2016 NAACL HLT Workshop on Computational Approaches to Subjectivity, Sentiment & Social Media Analysis,* 2016, 88-93.

Wei, L.. (2020). Understanding HS: A Survey and Future Directions. *Proceedings of the 12th International Conference on Social Media and Society,* 2020, 231-238.

Zhang, Z., & Zhao, Z. (2021). Fine-Tuning Language Models for HS Detection. *Proceedings of the 39th International Conference on ML, ICML 2021*, 220-229.

Chapter 15
Investigating the Influence of AI in Social Media Governance

Pranjal Khare
https://orcid.org/0000-0002-9937-9588
O.P. Jindal Global University, India

ABSTRACT

With advancement of technological tools, the role of Artificial Intelligence (AI) in maintaining and improving social media platforms is becoming intriguing by each passing day. From content moderation to sentiment analyzing the AI tools are integrated in the day-to-day operations of social media platforms to curate the customized experience to enhance the users' interaction on the platforms. The chapter explores the various AI tools and software understanding their models and functioning to regulate the social media governance. It aims to investigate the influence of AI tools from content creation, marketing advertisements to impact on users' behavior. While discussing the positives of the AI involvement, the chapter also discusses the possible challenges of maintaining user privacy, data security and regulation of fake news. Understanding the role of collaborating governance, the author analyzed various statutes around the world to deal with ethical and legal implications of the AI in social media governance to suggest amicable solutions and way forward.

DOI: 10.4018/979-8-3693-9904-0.ch015

INTRODUCTION

The emergence and development of Artificial Intelligence (AI) has enhanced the users' experience on social media platforms by providing customized feeds as per their expectations. Artificial Intelligence works on the algorithm of invigorating the new data to the Machin's software to learn, think and adapt to have human-like intelligence. AI is not only used to analyze a significant amount of data everyday but also to simplify, manage, and improve the engagement of the users of the various social media platforms through personalization. With ever developing cyber technologies and augmented use of social media platforms, the need of AI has become of cardinal significance for dealing and analyzing large data to suggest tailored actions for managing user behaviors. The AI is sufficiently capable of dealing with and not limited to areas as varied as content recommendation algorithms, automated moderation, user sentiment analysis along with advertising strategy. The latter part of this chapter will deal with each of these in detail.

Personalized content recommendation for social media platforms through Artificial Intelligence is one of the essential influencing factors for the usage of AI algorithms by the social media intermediaries. Social media giants such as Facebook, Instagram, TikTok, or YouTube use AI powered algorithms to curate users' feeds that help suggest videos or posts based on the users' past engagement on these platforms. These AI algorithms work on machine learning models that analyze the likes, shares, comments, watch time, of the platforms to create a pattern to finally predict what content users will like. This further improves the user's experience to automatically generate customized content for the users to explore content without more effort ultimately helping and increasing the platform retention rate by fixing the users to the platform. The most appropriate example of such algorithm is the one used by TikTok, its advanced and automated AI was the reason to beg for it the title of most distracting social media platforms as the AI would provide the content based on the users' behavior to show similar content (Buenfil et al., 2019).

One of the crucial tasks for AI considering the vast data on these platforms is its ability to moderate the content automatically. Content moderation is done to remove content such as hate speech, misinformation, and gruesome images with the help of technologies such as computer vision and natural language processing (NLP). AI systems further assist platforms like Facebook and Twitter (now X) in flagging the inappropriate posts or comments to then let human moderators act upon. However, there is no doubt in accepting that these technologies are far from perfect and still sometimes get context wrong. But with enhanced and improved AI accuracy the internet is slowly on its path to being a safe space with decreased harmful content.

Another important application of AI technologies on social media platforms is to analyze the users' sentiment. Through sentiment analysis the AI processes the tone and emotional context of the content posted on these social media platforms to interpret people's reaction or thoughts towards a brand, event or post. Businesses depending on social media for marketing and brand monitoring are the ones which benefit most from the algorithm discussed. The knowledge about the viral content in one's niche can be used to utilize the AI tools to predict the audience's behavior and reaction towards a particular brand campaign and product to improve the overall brand strategy before launching any product or event. Thus, AI has the ability of sentiment analysis to provide platforms with a way to detect a user's dissatisfaction or even a potential crisis to help and prepare to intervene if necessary (Sadiku et al., 2021).

Similarly, AI has also revolutionized advertising on social media. AI algorithms with its precision in audience segmentation with gigantic data analyzing and deliver super targeted campaigns to social media advertisers. Based on demographics, interests, online behavior, and purchase history, AI predicts and curates the appropriate customized ads for different users. For example, LinkedIn and Instagram use AI for recommending job postings, products or services for users based on their profiles. Dynamic creative optimization (DCO) is another AI tool that takes dynamic ad content a step further by testing variations for ad content and learning the combinations driving highest user engagement.

For customer support and engagement, the Social Media platforms are adopting chatbots and conversational AI for maximizing customer satisfaction. Facebook Messenger and WhatsApp have chatted with their rival vendors integrating AI powered chatbots capable of answering routine enquiries, giving recommendations or even making purchases. The bots, powered by NLP, understand user queries and respond with the right response. It's also a conversational bot and delivers a seamless experience to users. Virtual influences, such as AI generated personas who communicate and market products, are also becoming popular, making the line between human driven marketing and machine-driven marketing even more blurred. The AI tools are not only helping in market capturing but also in diversification by catering to the needs of the users with any disability or who speak different languages. AI features like automatic captioning, text to speech, and language translation make all these platforms more inclusive and diversified at the same time. Alt Text, which provides text descriptions of images for visually impaired users, is a very relevant example for machine learning to ease barriers.

As every coin has two sides, the AI benefits come with its own disadvantages or red flags. Currently AI taking over social media raises ethical questions around the world. A real, and potentially serious issue is algorithmic bias, in which the AI system inadvertently perpetuates stereotypes or discrimination based on bad training data. This can be seen in a situation where such algorithms could favor some types of content over others or exclude underrepresented groups indirectly promoting the perpetuation of social inequalities. To deal with such issues the requirement of transparency and accountability while dealing with AI tools becomes of paramount importance. This also needs to regulate and protect users' privacy while dealing with and analyzing the day-to-day data. The issues of consent and data security come up while users unknowingly through just their usage provide the personal data to these platforms. Elements of balance, between personalization and user privacy, remain an unmet challenge for platforms and regulators alike. Another issue comes around the fact that AI while attempting to personalize the content could further spread misinformation. It is true AI can find and scrub false content, but it can surprisingly use it to create believable fake news, deepfake videos and other forms of malicious bots to steer public opinion. The fact that AI is a two-edged sword highlights the urgent need for robust, if not absolute, regulatory regimes and ethical standards that can govern its use responsibly.

It is evident that the future of social media seems to span more and more with AI's help. With a huge potential to transform the creative industry, Generative AI that generates new content is an excellent emerging technology. But such tools as OpenAI's DALL E and ChatGPT are already being used to generate images, text, and video for social media, opening new ways to create the content. Additionally, by integrating AI with augmented reality (AR) and virtual reality (VR), it could powerfully affect how users interact with digital spaces, moving towards the age of the metaverse. In an era of social media and AI, the relationship between the two is nearly symbiotic and will provide no shortage of ways to improve both user experience and the delivery of content, as well as bring tons of innovation. Yet, ethically oriented principles and user privacy concerns must be prioritized over innovation and profit maximization to prevent potential harm when integrating. With constant digital development it's safe to say that AI will affect social media and end up changing the digital world in a manner no one can possibly predict. However, Society can optimally and cautiously use AI to enhance online experiences. The tools shall be used in an inclusive manner to maintain and balance between technological evolution and ethical standards while striving for a meaningful, richer and inclusive cyber space (Saheb et al., 2024).

THE RISE OF AI IN SOCIAL MEDIA

The transformative influence of Artificial Intelligence (AI) on social media platforms has ushered in a revolutionary era, redefining user interactions and engagement paradigms. AI's seamless integration has empowered platforms to harness vast datasets, automate complex processes, and deliver personalized experiences (Krajcovic, 2024). This phenomenon is fueled by cutting-edge technologies, notably machine learning (ML), natural language processing (NLP), and computer vision.

The symbiotic relationship between AI and social media necessitates exploration beyond content moderation, encompassing targeted advertising and platform operations. AI's transformative impact on social media is multifaceted:

Machine Learning (ML)

A subset of AI software, machine learning, allows systems to do what they've been taught with data even without being programmed for it. ML algorithms on social media analyze the perception and behavior of its users, and preferences over what they like, and how they engage with others, to predict and decide. Recommendation engines that make suggestions as to what to write, what to read and who to follow are one of the few cases where ML powers user engagement. As end users, we are still feeding these platforms even more data every day and they incorporate this data into ML to personalize feeds according to our viewing history and engagement patterns. These algorithms can also help in detecting and signaling spam accounts, bots, fraudulent activities with the help of behavioral anomalies to flag the suspicious activities for review (Rattan et al., 2022).

Natural Language Processing (NLP)

Natural Language Processing is another subset of AI software that lets the machines understand, interpret and reply to human language. For example, with the help of NLP social media platforms analyze text-based data like posts, comments, and messages. NLP is used by platforms to detect hate speech, abusive content and misinformation, by analyzing context, sentiment and intent. For example, Twitter's real time moderation tools rely on NLP to find harmful tweets. NLP also helps with chatbots and virtual assistants, so users don't have to wait for longer to get an answer or instant support whenever they are in need. Also, it powers translation features like breaking language barriers and making the world communicate (Zobaidy, 2024).

Computer Vision

As NLPs work on the language and texts the computer vision is the AI subset that lets machines understand and process visual data like images or videos. This technology is used by social media platforms to analyze and categorize visual content, detect violations, and make visual content accessible with automatic captioning. To understand the concept better let's take the example of Instagram, it uses computer vision to let its algorithms identify and tag objects or scenes in photos, making search and content discovery viable. Facial recognition technology is another example that is also used by platforms such as photo tagging and augmented reality (AR) filters, which have become popular with users.

As AI continues to evolve, social media platforms must prioritize transparency, accountability, and stakeholder participation to ensure responsible AI integration. It is essential to explore these key AI technologies and how they impact social media operations beyond content moderation to targeted advertising. Inside the realm of social media, AI has not only made technological leaps and bounds but changed the entire game on platform designs, content management and communication with the users. Thus, making it imperative to analyze how AI influences day-to-day working of any social media platforms around the world.

Among the discussed challenges the most difficult for any social media platform is to moderate the vast content generated every day. To maintain a safe and inclusive world it is pivotal for these platforms to have an efficient content moderation policy or technique. However, because of the sheer volume of content uploaded every second, manual moderation is simply not practical, which is where AI comes in. As discussed, Machine learning and NLP based algorithms scan for text, images and video for harmful or inappropriate content to then flag the offensive posts, misinformation and spam for further human review to be actioned accordingly. Another important example of such use is by Facebook for proactively detecting posts that violate its community standards, such as hate speech or graphic violence, long before they even get reported by users.

Fight against the spread of fake news can also be regulated and improved with the help of AI. Instead, platforms can diminish the spread of misinformation through analyzing the credibility of sources and checking the facts and pointing out manipulated media. But because data patterns are at the heart of AI, false positives or negatives can still occur, in which the technology misinterprets context or nuance. Therefore, this necessitates a combined approach including both human and artificial intelligence in order to achieve the optimum results of efficiency and accuracy.

It is also pertinent to note that these modern social media platforms are built around AI driven personalization. The algorithms of these platforms analyze past behavior of the user, their preferences and interactions to provide curated feeds, suggested content as well as connections. This personalized approach ultimately leads to enhanced user engagement, increases time spent on platforms, and significantly improves overall satisfaction. It is evident from the example of LinkedIn where AI is used by the company to recommend job postings and professional connections as per users' profiles and activity.

In addition, AI allows dynamic delivery of content along with posting of content and ads tailored to the individual user. This not only helps in maintaining and circulating the relevant content but enhances the engagement rate as well. Most relevant example is the algorithm used by Spotify or Pinterest to suggest music playlists or pins which match with what the user likes.

It wouldn't be an exaggeration to accept the silent revolution by AI of digital advertising by enabling hyper targeted campaigns. Ads that are customized to a particular audience are delivered to their end users based on data analysis machine learning algorithms found in massive datasets pertaining to user demographics, interests, history of browsing and purchasing behavior. Facebook and Instagram are powerful social media platforms for advertisers to use such as creating a campaign that aims to reach their ideal customers at the perfect moment.

Additionally, AI based analytics tools provide insight over the performance of the campaign to the advertisers which helps them to optimize the strategies of their campaign in real time. Not only does this data driven approach contribute to better advertisements it also makes a lot of money for social media companies. Further AI has also brought revolutionary change with respect to customer support and interaction. Chatbots, virtual assistants, artificial intelligence help AI to transform customer support on social media. These are NLP based tools that can interact with the users, answer queries and resolve issues in real time. Brands using Twitter as a channel often use an AI powered chatbot to answer common customer questions like tracking the order or informing about a product cutting down on response time to bring increased user satisfaction.

Proactive engagement by AI goes to the extent of analyzing user sentiment to identify opportunities for brands to interact with their audience. Sentiment analysis tools take the cake on their ability to monitor mentions and conversations helping these social media companies respond to concerns, commend positive feedback, or jump onto a trending conversation.

Today AI is not only used for moderation and analyzing but also for the content creation and optimization by social media platforms. Prevalent examples of text-based content, tools like OpenAI's ChatGPT can generate something from the text, like a blog post or a static image or video script, and platforms like Canva can use AI to show you suggestions for design on a visual piece of content. Social media influencers and marketers use these tools to simplify their workflows and create great content at once. Platforms can use engagement metrics to help you choose the best time to publish things, to know which format will be suitable for what audience and even make suggestions for trending hashtags that will help you get seen.

It is also pertinent to note that AI powered augmented reality (AR) features are taking over the hallmark of social media platforms like Snapchat and Instagram. These features allow user engagement and are unique experiences, from interactive filters to virtual try-ons for e-commerce, making the shopping experience a lot more fun. These AR tools are intuitive and responsive thanks to AI, which ensures they are conversational and real time so that users can interact with them now. In addition, AI makes access easier through existing automatic captions, translating text in images or audio descriptions for blind people. Social media has these features that make it more inclusive and boosted user experience.

With the advent of AI technologies and aid to social media platforms the platform operations and user engagement have been completely transformed. The platforms can provide personalized experience, automate content moderation, and optimize advertising strategies through the rise of technologies such as machine learning, natural language processing and computer vision. Unfortunately, these advances come with problems, like ethical burden and robust oversight. It's a complex landscape to navigate: AI has to take responsibility to make sure its helping users get a better user experience, ensuring ethical principles and privacy are not compromised at the same time (Omeish et al., 2024).

AI AND SOCIAL MEDIA GOVERNANCE CHALLENGES

Sorting, suggesting and moderation of the content is done through artificial intelligence on social media platforms by the producers to increase clients' satisfaction and interaction. Hence, artificial intelligence recommendation systems based on the users' activity, likes, and engagement patterns, identify posts, videos or accounts to recommend to a user. These systems are particularly built with an intention of having time being spent on the platform, clicks, shares etc., as they improve users' perception of the product and the firm's revenues, they create ethical and social issues (Walter, 2024).

The Role of Algorithmic Bias and Algorithmic Transparency

AI systems acquire what we can refer to as a 'contaminated history,' which informs how they treat users due to the discriminative habits of their training data. For example, moderating content may be more likely to remove content created by marginalized groups because language processing models are not diverse. Furthermore, due to the AI algorithms' technical nature or the "black box" application, solutions provided entail accountability challenges. Further the decisions taken by these algorithms for moderating the content are not transparent to the users and regulators; thus, it is challenging to address biases when they exist.

This could be resolved by the governance mechanisms mandating the requirement of operational transparency of the algorithms used. Mandating these platforms to explain how their algorithms function, what data set is used for training, and how decisions are made could make the system more transparent (Taeihagh, 2021). Further quality assurance audits together with fair evaluations are likely to detect and prevent several biases and violations of ethical norms.

Spread of Misinformation and Fake News

The AI algorithm designed for content maximization when used to filter the content for fake news on social media platforms can result in a dangerous outcome (AbuJarour et al., 2024). As the recommendation systems show content that will likely generate a lot of attention, and this often might mean promoting fake news. Generative AI goes a step further and compounds the problem through the creation of even more realistic deepfake images, videos and recorded sounds.

There is a need for anticipated governance strategies that must feature means of immediately identifying such items as misinformation. This issue thus calls for the collaborative efforts of the fact checker organizations, AI developers as well as social media firms to curb the misinformation and greater evils like deepfakes. In addition, platforms need to have programs to educate users so that consumers can distinguish between the truth and possible fake news.

Content moderation and freedom of speech

AI technologies and algorithms are also used for content moderation on social media platforms by limiting speech to prevent harm. However, the efficiency of this automated approach is highly questionable as it may work in an extreme way by excessive censoring leading to curb even legitimate protests, satire. On the other hand, if the algorithm is not strict enough it may lead to limiting enforcement allowing more damaging content to circulate. This lack of equilibrium of rights explains why there is a need to involve human tasks, especially where moderation is moderate and requires a certain degree of analysis of situations.

The governance structures must set down standards and policies on how content should be moderated, and in this case the standards set must be fair and proportional not serving the gasping interests of the companies behind the various social platforms. Further to assist the governments in attaining the goal of a safe internet, these created platforms should offer clear reasons for their actions and offer the option for the user to attempt an appeal (Llanso et al., 2020).

Privacy and Data Protection

As we know, AI systems work on the data generated from the behavioral patterns of the user of these platforms, the reliance of AI systems on data comes with the act of users' privacy violation. The collection of such vast data by private social network sites from users raises critical questions of consent, protection, and appropriateness on the internet. Huge data breaches and scandals like the Cambridge Analytica scandal clearly illustrated dangers associated with poor policies on the use of data.

The government policies for these platforms require high compliance for data protection through encryption and anonymization to ensure privacy by design mechanisms. The comparative understanding of laws around the world such as General Data Protection Regulation (GDPR) in the EU can be referred to establish the policy frameworks, especially when they embrace the user's right, transparency, and accountability when using data.

Addictive Design and Mental Health

As the social media platforms are based on the AI algorithms made to maximize the user's interaction on these platforms, it often misses out on the mental health of the users in the process. Addictive patterns like continuous scrolling, pop-up notifications, and point system cement pathologies like anxiety or depression, and poor self-esteem. These effects are more realized in the young users since they are vulnerable to societal pressure. Governance should encourage directions of how the platform should be designed ethically to ensure that the end product is healthy for the users it intends to serve. Things like reducing viewing-time, presenting more content, and mental health options eliminate the effects of 'addictive' design (Huang et al., 2024).

International Regulatory Challenges

Internet being a boundary less space makes the role of global social media platforms challenging as they must operate in multiple countries amending the regulatory compliance as per the domestic laws of the countries. The best example of this is the treatment of WhatsApp's end-to-end encryption policy around the world. It is noteworthy that where the European Union has put in place very strict guidelines, some developing or underdeveloped nations lack adequate policies. This leads to issues for platforms to operate at the international level and could lead to cases of regulatory arbitrage by companies taking advantage of the laws in some countries.

Thus, regulatory cooperation with the countries of interest may be required in order to build a level of standardized rules and requirements. As in the case of trade or environment policy, common governance practices can be set by multilateral agreements. Non-governmental bodies like the United Nations, the OECD or foundations like the Gates foundation may well be able to assume such roles.

Ethical Implications of AI Governance

The depth and complexity of the ethical issues embedded in the process of AI governance cannot be neglected. AI governance includes various questions with regards to accountability, transparency and maintaining equilibrium of rights. For example, questions like, who is responsible for the decisions made by AI systems? Is it the developers, the platform operators, or both? How transparent should platforms remain about their algorithms and data treatments without exposing their intellectual properties? On what grounds can platforms forbid some but allow others while also maintaining the balance between the right of freedom of speech and to govern the internet? There is no one answer to these questions. It requires calls from human rights groups around the world and a system of democratic principle-based approach. UNESCO's AI Ethics Recommendation and the IEEE ES's Global Initiative on the Ethics of Autonomous and Intelligent Systems are among the few existing international instruments to aid the process of AI governance.

Emerging Technologies

The emergence of generative AI and augmented reality creates issues that were not present before. Generative AI can input random but coherent prompts and churn out convincing fake text, image or video, while augmenting reality stages and performs a seamless digital-to-physical interface. These technologies require proactive risk management mechanisms to prevent risks that may arise in future.

The proactive measures include providing explicit funding to the thorny issue related to the safety of AI as a new field of research, creating regulatory sandboxes where new technologies may be licensed and tested, as well as encouraging cross-disciplinary engagement between technologists, ethicists, and lawmakers.

Collaborative Governance Models

Governance of artificial intelligence depends on the collaboration of multiple stakeholders such as different governments, technology firms, civil societies, and institutions. The collaborative governance model promotes the involvement of the public at large in promoting the standards of governing that correspond to highest societal values along with adequate legal regulations. The model suggests conducting multiple stakeholders' meetings and citizen conventions to ensure and promote collaborative governance through adequate participation from the citizens and the stakeholders.

Governing for sustainability requires transparency and accountability to be at the heart of all governing. Social media platforms should release a detailed account of the algorithms used, adopted moderation policies, and data usage reports once in a while to promote transparency and accountability. This practice will ensure sustainable governance by building a system of transparency and accountability where independent oversight bodies can then assess and analyze these reports to provide their logical and unbiased decisions on any issues if raised.

Education and Digital Literacy

To understand the nuances of the functioning of artificial intelligence technologies for social media platforms, it is imperative to improve digital literacy in any geographical area. Educational policies around the world should not only focus on introducing self-learning policies and their possible impact on the public but also educate the public through lesson plans to critically use the information accessed on the internet. It's important to understand the role of responsible and ethical user interaction on the global network. It is thus important for the Teachers, helmed by the government, and educational institutions, as well as appropriate platforms, should work together to create content and materials, as well as curricula for the target population, especially to protect those at risk.

The symbiotic relationship between Artificial Intelligence (AI) and social media has yielded profound implications, juxtaposing substantial benefits with inherent risks. The burgeoning presence of AI in social media ecosystems necessitates a paradigm shift in corporate governance frameworks to address emerging ethical, societal, and regulatory challenges. A multifaceted approach, emphasizing transparency, accountability, and stakeholder participation, is crucial for fostering a sustainable and responsible digital landscape. However, AI's limitations and potential biases necessitate nuanced governance. Existing regulatory frameworks must evolve to address AI-specific challenges, ensuring accountability and transparency.

Continuous dialogue, innovation, and adaptability are vital in creating a future that respects human rights, stimulates trust, and promotes well-being.

CASE STUDIES

The implementation of AI in social media platforms has systematically shifted the way these platforms handle content, users and governance. Software such as Facebook, Twitter, and Tik Tok have deployed the use of AI in operations including managing the content posted on the platform, handling fake news and improving the interaction with users. These developments have yielded appreciable achievements though the experiences also demonstrate major milestones and failures needed in the further course of the advancements.

Facebook's AI Governance

Applying artificial intelligence to control content, Facebook, one of the world's most famous social media, fights against hatred declarations, fake news, and bullying. Facebook employs technology that can make distinctions between good and bad information with the help of machine learning algorithms to eliminate potentially dangerous posts containing hate speech and obscene images (Aller & Acuna, 2022). For instance, in 2021, the platform set over 97% of hate speech and it was deleted without users reporting it as compared to previous years.

Further, AI in the case of COVID-19 was particularly important in the sense that it facilitated blocking specific information that turned out to be fake. For example, Facebook introduced algorithms that are used to verify false claims about vaccines and demote them. This way, the platform collaborated with more than 80 autonomous fact-checking organizations to improve the reliability of the moderation system. Facebook has used Deep Text and Rosetta which are AI tools for real time text and image analysis using natural language processing and optical character recognition, respectively (Huang & Krafft, 2024). This has helped in being more proactive rather than reactive, hence minimizing the visibility of the harmful contents.

Despite these advancements, Facebook's reliance on AI has faced considerable challenges. The first issue is algorithmic bias. Facebook uses artificial intelligence and other technology approaches in moderating content and controversy continues to arise, especially for those coming from minorities. For instance, it was observed that; content in languages other than English or belonging to a particular culture is misunderstood and hence there is unwanted banning. Another challenge which Facebook faced was misinformation during elections. This issue came into limelight during the U.S. elections in 2016 and 2020. Despite getting algorithms to detect and delete a great deal of fake news, AI Content Moderation systems were inadequate to prevent influence operations by foreign state actors. Therefore, sole reliance on AI is not a viable option. Facebook's experience highlights the need for a hybrid approach where AI complements human oversight. Also, to avoid biases and misinterpretations, it is necessary that algorithms be trained on diverse datasets (Youvan, 2024).

Twitter's AI Governance

Twitter has positioned itself as a platform for real-time information sharing, making effective governance critical. The first and foremost use of AI by twitter is with respect to harmful content moderation (Wu et al., 2021). Twitter's AI detects abusive language and harmful behavior. For instance, the platform used systems that suspend accounts that participate in hate speech or coordinated campaigns of harassment. It has considerably diminished such behavior. It is also to be noted that Twitter's AI has been successful in combating bot networks. Twitter's AI systems identified and removed millions of bots working to spread misinformation during election cycles. We advanced machine learning algorithms that are used to 'flag' suspicious behavior, like rapid tweeting and content sharing patterns, to bring suspects to heel (Dhiman & Toshniwal, 2022). Additionally, with AI tools, Twitter moderates trending topics so false or harmful narratives don't blare out into public discourse. It was especially important during events such as the COVID-19 pandemic and the Black Lives Matter movement, because it's proactive.

However, even the use of AI by twitter is not without limitations. An individual may have an account suspended for no apparent reason, and in Twitter's AI it's erroneously flagged as a harmful account, or mistake flagging benign tweets as harmful. This is particularly problematic for activists and journalists in politically sensitive regions. Another issue is misinformation campaigns. It can be seen that despite AI interventions, Twitter has struggled to contain the spread of viral misinformation, especially during high profile events like elections or public health crises. Thus, it calls for AI systems to have better contextual understanding to differentiate between harmful content and legitimate discourse. In addition, it is also essential that it provides users with clearer reasons for suspensions and a robust appeal process which can enhance trust in AI moderation systems (Corsi, 2024).

TikTok's Rapid Rise and AI Challenges

TikTok's road to success could be traced to its sophisticated AI algorithms that drive content personalization and moderation. Its content recommendation engine is quite commendable. TikTok's AI-powered "For You" page uses deep learning to analyze user behavior and preferences, delivering highly personalized content.

This played a key role in the platform's rapid growth and user engagement (Kang & Lou, 2022). Further, its AI also moderates harmful content. TikTok employs AI to identify and remove content violating its guidelines, such as explicit material, self-harm content, and misinformation. During the COVID-19 pandemic, TikTok's AI flagged and removed thousands of videos spreading false health claims. It is also pertinent to observe that given its predominantly young user base, TikTok uses AI to restrict access to harmful content and promote digital well-being. It uses features like screen time limits and restricted modes that leverage AI to protect vulnerable users (Ambran et al., 2024).

Further, the challenges faced by TikTok's AI are more severe when compared with Facebook and Twitter. TikTok's recommendation algorithms have been criticized by many for amplifying harmful trends, such as dangerous challenges and eating disorder content. The platform's AI sometimes prioritizes engagement over safety. In addition, TikTok's AI moderation has faced accusations of suppressing content related to political dissent, particularly in regions with strict government regulations. This necessitates balancing engagement with user safety and TikTok's experiences highlight the need for ethical considerations in algorithm design. Also, it becomes imperative to adapt moderation policies to align with regional laws and cultural contexts for maintaining platform integrity (Grandinetti, 2021).

The case studies of Facebook, Twitter and Tik Tok highlight the transformative power, and challenges in the use of AI for social media governance. While these platforms have successfully done their part to curb harmful content and misinformation, they are not without shortcomings of present AI frameworks, including the issue of bias, transparency and over-reliance on automation. Social media platforms can learn from these successes and failures to develop more refined AI strategies that are a platform through which the use of social media is utilized towards positive governance and equitable digital engagement.

EXISTING REGULATIONS AND POLICIES

The exponential integration of Artificial Intelligence (AI) within social media ecosystems has precipitated significant challenges, necessitating urgent attention. Algorithmic bias, misinformation amplification, data privacy concerns, and erosion of public trust have emerged as formidable concerns. Despite existing regulatory frameworks, inherent limitations hinder their effectiveness in addressing AI-specific risks. A comprehensive examination of prominent regulations and policies governing social media is crucial, highlighting shortcomings and informing requisite reforms (Rodrigues, 2020).

The intersection of AI and social media necessitates nuanced governance. Regulatory frameworks such as the European Union's General Data Protection Regulation (GDPR) and Section 230 of the Communications Decency Act (CDA) in the United States provide foundational guidelines. However, these frameworks often fall short in addressing AI-driven complexities, including bias, misinformation, and privacy infringements. To mitigate these risks, policymakers must prioritize AI-specific regulations, ensuring transparency, accountability, and adaptability.

General Data Protection Regulation (GDPR), 2016

The General Data Protection Regulation (GDPR), enacted by the European Union in 2018, represents a seminal legislative framework for safeguarding data protection globally. This comprehensive legislation seeks to fortify consumer privacy rights by ensuring transparent data collection and processing practices (Balas & Shatnawi, 2024). Key provisions mandate explicit user consent, clear disclosure of collected data, and explanations for automated decision-making processes, including AI-driven systems.

Artificial Intelligence algorithms, integral to social media platforms, necessitate scrutiny. GDPR's explanatory provisions often fall short, with platforms providing vague, nonspecialist descriptions of AI-driven decisions, such as "machine learning models of preferences." This opacity obscures data sources, reasoning processes, and potential biases, denying users meaningful engagement and dispute resolution mechanisms (Zaidan & Ibrahim, 2024).

The GDPR's territorial limitations create a fragmented regulatory landscape. Transnational corporations comply with EU standards while exploiting lax data protection laws elsewhere, undermining GDPR's international efficacy. Crucially, GDPR lacks specific measures addressing AI risks, including bias and visual content abuse. However, its stringent Data Protection Impact Assessment (DPIA) requirements for high-risk AI applications, such as content moderation, facilitate risk evaluation and mitigation (Almeida et al., 2021).

The implementation of AI algorithms in social media platforms raises concerns regarding accountability and transparency. AI-driven content recommendation and moderation systems necessitate clear explanations for decision-making processes. Users must understand how their data influences AI-driven outcomes, ensuring informed consent and trust. The GDPR's emphasis on transparency and accountability serves as a foundation for addressing AI-specific challenges. Moreover, the intersection of AI and social media necessitates nuanced governance. Regulatory frameworks must address algorithmic bias, misinformation amplification, and data privacy concerns. Policymakers must prioritize AI-specific regulations, ensuring adaptability and effectiveness in mitigating emerging risks.

Communications Decency Act, 1996

Section 230 of the Communications Decency Act passed in the USA in 1996 is one of the most fundamental laws related to the internet. It gives social media platforms immunity from legal responsibility for user-generated content while providing them with grounds to arbitrate content without attributing them as publishers (Ehrlich, 2002). Because of this legal shield, more platforms have provided various users' content space to grow. Further, sites are encouraged to censor or deny access to any material that may be considered undesirable without bearing liability of publishers. This provides immune statuses to the platforms so they can regulate the users' reciprocal behaviors and delete vile or obscene articles. Additionally, this free-form content has, in turn, resulted in a wealth of creative expression and advancement of an open, interconnected online community by lowering the legal exposure for those who host user content. Online platforms have benefited from relative freedom to test various models of generating revenues, uses of technologies and approaches to content moderation, without being prejudiced by threats of endless litigation.

Section 230 only targets those that are based in the United States but has set precedence for international platforms with a large user base in America. It is often attributed to having given the social media giants of Facebook, Twitter, and YouTube legal grounds upon which they may stand & operate (Rozenshtein, 2024).

This provision has some limitations though. Section 230 does not differentiate between articles and posts published by users and outputs of artificial intelligence-based systems, including recommendation engines and moderating bots. This broad immunity hides the platform from responsibility for the negative effects which might arise from the AI decisions, including issues of polarization of extreme content. For example, an algorithm that is aimed at getting as much time as possible spent on the platform might cause feeds filled with sensational or even fake news resulting in society polarization, but with no legal consequences for the company. Section 230 does not require the platforms to explain how their AI algorithms implement content moderation policy. Such complexity means that users and regulators cannot determine how AI systems rank, filter, or even demote content. Consequently, there are hardly any penalties for unfair modulation policies, for example, instances where some groups' content is deleted more often than others. This provision was crafted at a time when user-generated content was mostly in text form and had to be moderated by hand. For example, it does not consider the use of Artificial intelligence today such as the AI models that work on big data, or AI that can generate content all by itself. As such, the law covers no risk, for instance, in the creation of deepfakes or artificial intelligence based fake news (Brannon & Holmes, 2024).

Digital Services Act (DSA), 2022

The regulation known as the Digital Services Act (DSA), was passed in the European Union in 2022 and has the main purpose of reducing the risks associated with the use of digital services. It updates the EU's 2000 regulation aimed at net neutrality, online sketching new risks concerning misinformation and toxic content. These companies must also describe the criteria their algorithms will use to select and moderate content. This includes giving users details about why they receive specific suggestions and enabling them to exit the personalized procedures (Turillazzi et al., 2023).

It is also pertinent to note that Very Large Online Platforms (VLOPs) are mandated to make an evaluation of systematic risk implications of their services which may include issues like fake news and control of illegitimate activities. Such measures should be put in place to address these risks, and the outcomes should be presented to the authorities. The platforms which host such materials are expected to take action and process the content's removal as early as possible. New guidelines for them to put in place are ways for the users to report such content and get them addressed.

Under DSA some platforms allow users to appeal against the content moderation decisions made by them. And it also enhances measures to prevent several unlawful removals involving perfectly legal material. Additionally, this Act targets the platforms providing services in the EU and they all must meet certain obligations (Husovec, 2024). However, the most elaborate obligations apply to the extensive platforms. Its main rationale is to provide a political model for the Internet's increased openness and responsibility, thus proposing new rules of the political game.

The Online Safety Act, 2023

The United Kingdom promulgated the Online Safety Act, which targets preventing users from encountering dangerous content in a context of promoting freedom of speech. The Online Safety Act aimed primarily at UK-based platforms, but the rules would apply to platforms with UK users. It shows a conservative and positive model in regulating online crimes and ensuring the protection of safety and freedom of speech. It is particularly a protective law, especially as it concerns minors and other vulnerable people (Trengove et al., 2022).

Companies and businesses using the social media platforms are also obliged to do all within their powers to ensure harmful and abusive content including the ones that incite hatred against a certain ethnic group, displays of child abuse or even support of terrorism is not posted. The Act requires that the platforms employed put in place measures to ensure that children do not have access to the content that is deemed appropriate for them. Additionally, social media platforms must have and regularly enforce policies on content moderation. This entails prompting with categories of contents that the platform does not allow and another showing measures that it takes in enforcing constraints.

Further, the Act specifies that the authorities rightfully belonging to its enforcement is Ofcom, which is the UK's communications regulator (Anderson & Gilbert, 2022). Ofcom can levy fines against any non-compliant platforms and gives them binding directions to fix systemic troubles. In prioritizing the safety of users, the importance of protecting lawful speech can be seen in the bill. It requires platforms to consider the implications of their moderation practices on freedom of expression and provides users with opportunities to appeal content removal decisions.

CONCLUSION AND FUTURE TRENDS

The integration of AI into social media has significantly revolutionized how an individual communicates, interacts, and access information. This chapter has critically analyzed the dual-edged nature of AI in social media governance. Although this transformation has brought undeniable and innumerable benefits like transformative opportunities to enhance user safety, combat harmful content, and personalize experiences. But on the other hand, it has also exposed significant governance gaps that demand urgent attention and also has also introduced complex challenges related to bias, accountability, and societal impact. By learning from the past, collaborating across borders, and committing to ethical innovation, we can tap into the power of AI to create a safer, more equitable, and more inclusive digital ecosystem. Although the journey to effective AI governance is long and complex, it is also an essential one. The decisions made today will shape the digital societies of tomorrow, making it imperative for all stakeholders to act with foresight, responsibility, and a shared commitment to the common good.

Further, with the advancement of new developments in technologies and trends, it will further complicate governance, necessitating proactive measures. The rise of generative AI, advancements in deep learning, and the increasing integration of AI into immersive technologies like the metaverse, is just the tip of the iceberg. In this context, it becomes essential for social media platforms to disclose how AI algorithms function, what data they process, and how decisions are made. This is critical to building user trust and ensuring accountability. They also have to establish independent oversight bodies which can ensure that AI systems adhere to ethical and legal standards. Additionally, it also becomes a duty and responsibility of governments, tech companies, civil society, and academia to work together to create inclusive governance frameworks and foster continued collaboration in this regard. Efforts are also needed in educating users about the capabilities and limitations of AI which can ultimately empower them to navigate digital platforms responsibly. With the evolving nature of AI technologies, governance strategies must also evolve. In this regard, policymakers and platforms must remain agile and should continuously revisit and update regulations to address emerging risks and opportunities. All stakeholders, be it governments, platforms, users, and researchers have a role to play in shaping the future of AI governance. It becomes essential to include all the remote stakeholders as well, especially during consultation for policy formation. So, governments must establish clear and adaptable policies and social media platforms thus should prioritize ethics and transparency. Similarly, users also need to be aware and must demand accountability, and researchers must continue exploring solutions to the challenges posed by AI.

REFERENCES

AbuJarour, S., Qarariah, A., Saadeh, N., & Salem, M. (2024). *AI, Misinformation, and Fake News: A Literature Review of Ethical and Technical Approaches*. Finance and Law in the Metaverse World., DOI: 10.1007/978-3-031-67547-8_55

Aller, C. F., & Acuna, B. P. (2022). Facebook and Artificial Intelligence: A Review of Good Practices. *ResearchGate*. https://www.researchgate.net/publication/365275674_Facebook_and_Artificial_Intelligence_A_Review_of_Good_Practices

Almeida, P., Santos, C. D., & Farias, J. S. (2021). Artificial Intelligence Regulation: a framework for governance. *ResearchGate*. https://www.researchgate.net/publication/351039094_Artificial_Intelligence_Regulation_a_framework_for_governance

Ambran, N. S., Zainodin, W. H. W., & Ali, M. N. M. (2024).AI Systems and Content Moderation Tiktok as a Digital Safety Platform in Shaping a Pleasant Environment: A Qualitative Approach. *My Jurnal*. https://myjurnal.mohe.gov.my/public/article-view.php?id=215683

Anderson, R., & Gilbert, S. (2022). Policy Brief The Online Safety Bill. *Bennett Institute for Public Policy*. https://www.bennettinstitute.cam.ac.uk/wp-content/uploads/2022/09/Policy-Brief-Online-Safety-Bill.pdf

Balas, H., & Shatnawi, R. (2024). Legal framework for AI applications. *F1000 Research*. https://f1000research.com/articles/13-418

Brannon, V. C., & Holmes, E. N. (2024). Section 230: An Overview. *Congressional Research Service*. https://crsreports.congress.gov/product/pdf/R/R46751

Buenfil, J., Arnold, R., Abruzzo, C., & Korpela, C. (2019). Artificial Intelligence Ethics: Governance through Social Media. *ResearchGate*. https://10.0.4.85/HST47167.2019.9032907

Corsi, G. (2024). Evaluating Twitter's algorithmic amplification of low-credibility content: An observational study. *EPJ Data Science*, 13(18), 18. Advance online publication. DOI: 10.1140/epjds/s13688-024-00456-3

Dhiman, A., & Toshniwal, D. (2022). AI-based Twitter framework for assessing the involvement of government schemes in electoral campaigns. *Expert Systems with Applications*, 203, 117338. Advance online publication. DOI: 10.1016/j.eswa.2022.117338

Ehrlich, P. (2002). Communications Decency Act § 230. *Berkeley Technology Law Journal*, 17(1), 401–419. https://www.jstor.org/stable/24120113

Grandinetti, J. (2021). Examining embedded apparatuses of AI in Facebook and TikTok. *AI & Society*, •••, 1–14. DOI: 10.1007/s00146-021-01270-5 PMID: 34539095

Huang, K., & Krafft, P. M. (2024). Performing Platform Governance: Facebook and the Stage Management of Data Relations. *Science and Engineering Ethics*, 30(2), 13. DOI: 10.1007/s11948-024-00473-5 PMID: 38575812

Huang, S., Lai, X., Ke, L., Li, Y., Wang, H., Zhao, X., Dai, X., & Wang, Y. (2024). AI Technology panic-is AI Dependence Bad for Mental Health? A Cross-Lagged Panel Model and the Mediating Roles of Motivations for AI Use Among Adolescents. *Psychology Research and Behavior Management*, 17, 1087–1102. DOI: 10.2147/PRBM.S440889 PMID: 38495087

Husovec, M. (2024). The Digital Services Act's red line: What the Commission can and cannot do about disinformation. *Journal of Medicine and Law*, 16(1), 47–56. DOI: 10.1080/17577632.2024.2362483

Kang, H., & Lou, C. (2022). AI agency vs. human agency: Understanding human–AI interactions on TikTok and their implications for user engagement. *Journal of Computer-Mediated Communication*, 27(5), zmac014. Advance online publication. DOI: 10.1093/jcmc/zmac014

Krajcovic, P. (2024). The Impact of Artificial Intelligence on Social Media, *ResearchGate*. https://www.researchgate.net/publication/380818610_The_Impact_of_Artificial_Intelligence_on_Social_Media

Llanso, E., Hoboken, J. V., Leerssen, P., & Harambam, J. (2020). Artificial Intelligence, Content Moderation, and Freedom of Expression. *Transatlantic Working Group*. https://www.ivir.nl/publicaties/download/AI-Llanso-Van-Hoboken-Feb-2020.pdf

Omeish, F., Khasawneh, M. A., & Khair, N. (2024). Investigating the impact of AI on improving customer experience through social media marketing: An analysis of Jordanian Millennials. *Computers in Human Behavior Reports*, 15, 100464. DOI: 10.1016/j.chbr.2024.100464

Rattan, P., Penrice, D. D., & Simonetto, D. A. (2022). Artificial Intelligence and Machine Learning: What You Always Wanted to Know but Were Afraid to Ask. *Gastro Hep Advances*, 1(1), 70–78. DOI: 10.1016/j.gastha.2021.11.001 PMID: 39129929

Rodrigues, R. (2023). Legal and human rights issues of AI: Gaps, challenges and vulnerabilities. *Journal of Responsible Technology*, 4, 100005. DOI: 10.1016/j.jrt.2020.100005

Rozenshtein, A. Z. (2024). Interpreting the Ambiguities of Section 230. *Yale Journal on Regulation*. https://www.yalejreg.com/bulletin/interpreting-the-ambiguities-of-section-230/

Sadiku, M. N. O., Ashaolu, T. J., Majebi, A. A., & Musa, S. M. (2021). Artificial Intelligence in Social Media. *International Journal of Scientific Advances*, 2(1), 15–20. https://10.0.201.86/ijscia.v2i1.4

Saheb, T., Sidaoui, M., & Schmarzo, B. (2024). Convergence of artificial intelligence with social media: A bibliometric & qualitative analysis. *Telematics and Informatics Reports*, 14, 100146. DOI: 10.1016/j.teler.2024.100146

Taeihagh, A. (2021). Governance of artificial intelligence. *Policy and Society*, 40(2), 137–157. DOI: 10.1080/14494035.2021.1928377

Trengove, M., Kazim, E., Almeida, D. R. S., Hilliard, A., Zannone, A., & Lomas, E. (2022). A critical review of the Online Safety Bill. *Patterns (New York, N.Y.)*, 3(8), 100544. https://10.0.3.248/j.patter.2022.100544. DOI: 10.1016/j.patter.2022.100544 PMID: 36033594

Turillazzi, A., Taddeo, M., Floridi, L., & Casolari, F. (2023). The digital services act: An analysis of its ethical, legal, and social implications. *Law, Innovation and Technology*, 15(1), 83–106. DOI: 10.1080/17579961.2023.2184136

Walter, Y. (2024). Managing the race to the moon: Global policy and governance in Artificial Intelligence regulation—A contemporary overview and an analysis of socioeconomic consequences. *Discover Artificial Intelligence*, 4(1), 14. Advance online publication. DOI: 10.1007/s44163-024-00109-4

Wu, L., Dodoo, N. A., Wen, T. J., & Ke, L. (2022). Understanding Twitter conversations about artificial intelligence in advertising based on natural language processing. *International Journal of Advertising*, 41(4), 685–702.

Youvan, D. C. (2024). Navigating the Unknowns: Ethical Considerations and Government Influence in Facebook AI. *ResearchGate*. https://www.researchgate.net/publication/378679366_Navigating_the_Unknowns_Ethical_Considerations_and_Government_Influence_in_Facebook_AI

Zaidan, E., & Ibrahim, I. A. (2024). AI Governance in a Complex and Rapidly Changing Regulatory Landscape: A Global Perspective. *Humanities & Social Sciences Communications*, 11(1), 1121. DOI: 10.1057/s41599-024-03560-x

Zobaidy, Z. R. M. A. (2024). Artificial Intelligence in Natural Language Processing. *International Journal of Science and Research Archive*, 13(01), 370–377. DOI: 10.30574/ijsra.2024.13.1.1638

Chapter 16
Foul Language Censored Social Media Video Generation Using Audio Censoring Model

Brindha Subburaj
https://orcid.org/0000-0003-2173-5228
School of Computer Science and Engineering, Vellore Institute of Technology, Chennai, India

Uma Maheswari Jayachandran
School of Computer Science and Engineering, Vellore Institute of Technology, Chennai, India

Siya Bansal
School of Computer Science and Engineering, Vellore Institute of Technology, Chennai, India

Vedansh Kumar
School of Computer Science and Engineering, Vellore Institute of Technology, Chennai, India

ABSTRACT

Advancements in communication medium and the proliferation of social media led to increasing amount of content shared often without moderation. The offensive are raising significantly, posing threat to mental health, and degrades the user experience. Current study focuses on identifying and censoring audio clips with offensive and foul words. We propose a novel audio censoring method using OpenAI's whisper model. The audio files are extracted from video and forwarded to whisper

DOI: 10.4018/979-8-3693-9904-0.ch016

model. The text transcripts of the audio file is obtained through the whisper model. Keywords from the text are compared with a dictionary of offensive and foul words to detect such terms in the input audio. The matched foul words are identified and respective audio are censored and beep tone is inserted. Finally, the censored audio is integrated and video is generated. The proposed system is tested using dataset retrieved from youtube and the has shown significant performance and achieves accuracy of 93.81%, shows the robustness of proposed foul word identification and censoring system.

1. INTRODUCTION

The rapid evolution of Communication technologies, internet act as major contributing factors for social media innovations and rise in its usage patterns. The evolution of 3G, 4G, 5G technology, the web 1.0 to 2.0 growth and other factors like email, cloud-based platforms all set a huge hype cycle in technical world. Social media applications dated back to email, then Facebook now Meta, and other applications used for decades to recent platforms like YouTube, Instagram, X, etc. are all liked by people and used world-wide. The accessibility to these applications through sophisticated handheld devices further contributes towards the growth.

This widespread use of portable devices and fast internet has given everyone with easy access to a vast world of information and communication, but this has also led to a rise in online inter- actions, where foul language and inappropriate content is common. We can see this rapid increase in usage of social media platforms Figure 1 (Ortiz-Ospina, 2019).

Figure 1. Growth of social media usage

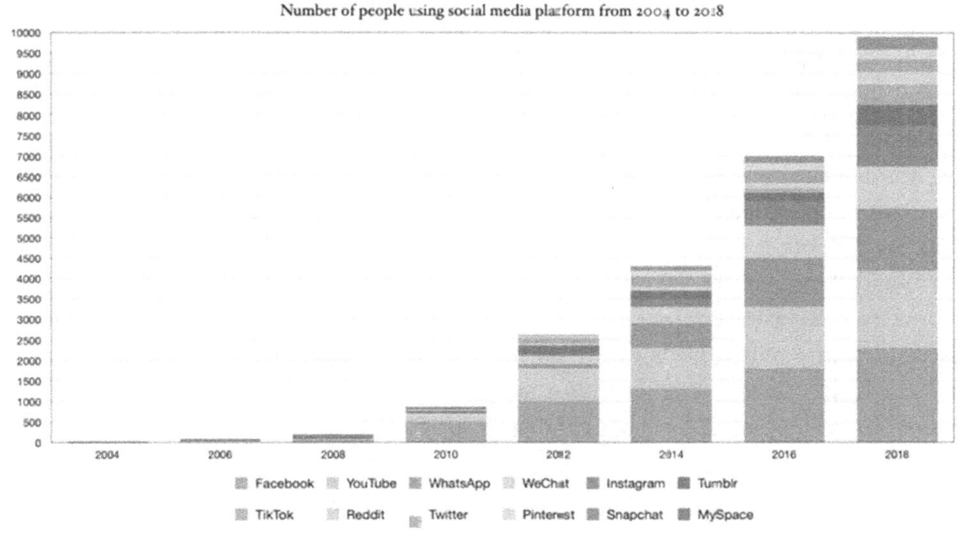

On the other side such advancements, also makes it difficult to have control over its usage. People from multiple age groups are now using these applications and view contents in unfiltered way. Some restrictions are posed on the content shared, but in most cases, there is not much censoring or monitoring happening regarding the videos shared across these platforms. It is not just the videos that is shared in these platforms that is not filtered but the text, audio and image modality as well. These inappropriate contents in the above forms have higher rate of foul or offensive words in recent days. These raw videos are publicly available which is easily accessible from kids to elderly people, making the unintended audience uncomfortable. Swear words, textual terms, racial or ethnic slurs, gender or sexual orientation slurs, general insult all these comes under a common foul language zone.

Although varied applications come with their own censoring mechanism, like censorship models based on Artificial Intelligence techniques are available that censor's audio, video in films. Many research work related to censoring audio of regional language videos in a particular application are available as well. Many detection systems to identify such foul words in text modality is available as well which deals with social media comment foul words detection and filtering. Many multi-modal deep learning models are available as well to deal this particular real time problem. Several recent research contributions in this field are made.

In one such recent work, the authors use a speech processing and sequential data modelling, where it takes audio input represented by Mel-spectrograms and Mel-frequency cepstral coefficients (MFCCs), then uses Convolutional Neural Networks (CNN) and Long Short-Term Memory (LSTM) for processing and classifying the audio into different categories. However, it is sensitive to noise and is very complex computationally (Ba Wazir et al., 2021).

Most of the current research contributions related to hate speech detection work on identifying or hate speech in the textual form in social media comments, tweets, memes. The other variant is audio-based detection for such abusive content in audio form and they classify, or rate based on the percentage of such content. Research work based on visual content based offensive video/image classification are available as well. Many multi-modality-based hate/offensive video classifiers are available as well based on text, image and/or audio modality-based detection systems. The research work related to censoring videos through hate speech identification is mostly text-based censoring or image-based censoring. If its audio-based censoring, audio files are used and featured are extracted from these files through deep learning-based models for identifying hate speech in the videos. In this research, we censor the videos by examining hate or offensive speech in audio modality, where text transcripts are extracted from these audio files using speech recognition model and offensive words in these transcripts are identified and these audio segments are censored and replaced with a beep tone and integrated with original video file to generate a censored and safe content. This novel method leveraging whisper model based censoring system will be a robust alternative to existing techniques.

The challenges related to this research work includes,

1. Training deep learning models like CNN using audio features for detecting hate speech or other related inappropriate content is widely adapted, but in this present work, text transcripts of the audio are generated to identify foul words and further censoring audio segments with hate speech.
2. Unavailability of public datasets. Videos with such hate speech or offensive audio contents segmented for research study is not available as far as we know. To overcome this, we generated a dataset by extracting videos from YouTube and through manual processing the hate speech audio segments are listed for evaluating and studying the performance of the proposed censoring system.

This research work proposes a novel and robust method for foul language detection and censoring. The power of OpenAI's Whisper model is leveraged in this research. Whisper is a renowned speech recognition system. Whisper is powerful in transcription tasks performed in circumstances like multi-lingual, noisy environments, etc. Thus, using such model in this study benefits the purpose. Using whisper to effectively detect foul languages present in the audio track aids in ensuring the video standards, as expected by the audiences of social media and abiding to platform restrictions. The proposed system uses whisper model to generate text transcripts from the audio file, the foul words in transcripts are segregated and beep tone is inserted in the respective audio timestamps to deliver a censored content to the audience.

The proposed system can be adapted and used for various application other than social media censoring, like in entertainment sectors like film industry, education sector, etc. One instance to further detail is nowadays online education or online videos related to education are generated in common. The foul language detection can automate the censoring part in such sectors, to ensure that safe and secure content is delivered to students. Such a widespread applications marks the importance of such censoring system.

The research objectives are:

1. Design and development of a novel foul word audio censoring system in social media videos using whisper model.
2. Gathering real-time data from social media for testing purpose, and manually record foul word occurrences with timestamp in above social media videos for performance evaluation.
3. Conducting experiments using the censoring system and performance evaluation and comparison with other SOTA automatic speech recognition models.

The chapter is organized as related works is given in section 2, the proposed method is given in section 3, experimentation results are presented under section 4, followed by conclusions.

2. RELATED WORKS

The foul language detection and censoring has gained much attention in recent years. Many research work is carried out and censoring systems are presented from rule-based methods to advanced deep learning techniques. Recent works have leaned towards using deep learning and natural language processing techniques. A detailed review on such work is presented in this section. First text-based hate speech classification research articles are presented. The research on hate speech detection using audio is discussed. Next, multimodal works are discussed.

Text based hate speech detection systems mainly work along with social media comments, posts, tweets. They obtain the text domain information and from which foul words are detected and classified to make decisions further. Few recent works related to this are presented. There are many novel methods but Mitra and Sankhala

(2022) uses a pre-defined model and refined it. Large language models are fine tuned for hate speech and offensive content detection. This paper discusses the challenges associated in evaluating hate speech and offensive content on social media, especially in Hindi and English languages, while using cross entropy loss to help with the imbalanced nature of dataset by these languages. They are fine tuning the pre-existing large language models like BERT, RoBERTa, and XLNet to classify on posts which have hate speech and also which don't. They achieved macro F1-scores of 0.8089 for English Subtask A and 0.6396 for Subtask B with RoBERTa, and 0.7379 for Hindi Subtask A and 0.4431 for Subtask B. It is observed through this paper that with the help of specialized fine-tuning significantly improved hate speech detection, with RoBERTa consistently outperforming other models.

Zeng and Dou (2010) presented the novel approach an audio keywords detection method for highlight retrieval in basketball video. A structured sport with a lot of acoustic information is basketball. Five keywords that are commonly heard during the game are squeaking, speaking, cheering, long whistle, and short whistle. For the detection of events, each of these noises is crucial. In particular, a thrilling attack or offense is frequently accompanied by quick footsteps, which are referred to as "squeaking", in this work audience cheers always follow a successful hit or inroads by their supporters. The referee signals the end of the current game period with a long whistle, while a short whistle indicates a player has committed a mistake, a violation, or a full timeout is requested. The commentator's voices are audible virtually continuously throughout. From this analysis the keywords, which relate to basketball game events, include speech, cheer, lengthy and short whistles, and the sound of shoes squeaking. Following feature analysis, efficient features are chosen using the Simple Excellent Feature Combination based on Pearson Correlation Coefficient (SEFC-PCC), which results in better performance and less computing complexity. To complete the final identification of the five audio keywords, a novel multi-stage SVM classifier is suggested. In the validation experiment, 428 audio sequences lasting roughly 704 seconds are employed.

Alakrot et al. (2018) presented a method to detect offensive Arabic language in online communication, especially on youtube. They combined and labeled many comments which included both offensive and non-offensive focusing on a broad range of abusive and profane language without restricting the terms used to create a dataset. The dataset was utilized to train a Support Vector Machine (SVM) classifier, with experiments conducted using different word-level features, N-grams, and pre-processing methods to improve detection accuracy. The SVM classifier was trained on features extracted from the text, including word-level and N-gram features. They applied different pre-processing techniques like stemming and stop-word removal to optimize the performance. The model achieved a classification accuracy of 90.05%, surpassing previous studies on Arabic offensive language detection. The researchers concluded that using a large set of data helps in generalization and improved detection of offensive language.

The above text-based classification limits the detection system only to one data variant, but the other modalities are important to censor the foul or inappropriate content, one such is the audio modality. Audio based hate speech classification systems are presented here, most of which work on the audio files extracted from social media or audio files generated as an outcome of research for the experimentation purpose. Zaman et al. (2023) provided a detailed survey on various deep learning-based methods for audio signal classification is presented. The paper focuses on the Deep Neural Network (DNN) architectures including CNN, Transformers, Auto encoders and hybrid models. The MFCC (Mel-Frequency Cepstral Coefficients) and spectrograms extraction techniques from audio are discussed as well. The paper highlights the performance of hybrid models like a combination of CNN and RNN, that perform better and leveraging strengths of each other. Another model that is emerging is Transformers, due to their ability to capture long range dependencies which improves classification audio. A lot of experiments were conducted and results as reported are CNN showed 98.66% accuracy in Kashmiri accent classification, CNN showed an accuracy of 98.63% under noisy conditions using RWCP (Real World Computing Partnership) dataset.

This next paper is based on one of the models given in above work, MFCC extraction technique authors presented a method for identifying the emotions using Random Forest, SVM, and Decision Tree. RAVDESS (Ryerson Audio-Visual Database of Emotional Speech and Song) dataset is used to conduct experiments, it consists of voices consisting of emotions from 24 actors (12 male and 12 female). The dataset consists of 8 emotions: neutral, calm, happy, sad, angry, fearful, surprised and disgusted. Thirteen MFCC features were computed for each audio frame in order to represent the most critical elements of audio. Later, using these features 3 machine learning classification models were trained, which were Random Forest, Decision Tree and SVM, these models had accuracy of 88.54%, 71.88% and 64.79% respectively. The random forest performed best in recognizing the happy emotion (Vimal, 2021).

Instead of extraction of temporal features, Zeng and Dou (2010) proposes a system that uses a bag of words approach from Natural Language Processing (NLP) for audio-based event detection. Here the model is given specific classes of audio which are segmented into different frames and low-level features are detected in each frame. Once all the features are extracted, vector space is made using those extracted features, then K-means is used to locate the centroid. Now the centroids of each cluster represent an aural word. Second level feature vector is a histogram of occurrences of the aural words that are detected on an interval. Linear Support Vec- tor Machine (SVM) is used and creates a hyperplane which maximizes the margins between the different classes reducing the chances of overfitting, multiple SVMs are used here in order to do multi-class classification. If the multiple SVMs give positive outputs then the interval is assigned to the class with the highest score and if all classifiers return some negative score, then the interval is classified as background noise.

Gupta et al. (2022) have presented a Multilingual Abusive Comment Detection dataset (MACD). The dataset consisted of 150,000 samples from Hindi, Tamil, Telugu, Kannada, and Malayalam languages, which had 49% abusive and 51% non-abusive comments, all these comments were labeled by them. They used 4 models for experimentation purposes which were Multilingual Representations for Indian Languages (MuRIL), Cross-lingual Language Model - RoBERTa based (XLM-R), AbuseXLMR and TF-IDF based model. After conducting the experiments, it turned out that AbuseXLMR worked well across a lot of Indic languages, especially in zero shot and few shot learning. The results of AbuseXLMR were reported with accuracy of 90.72% and F1 score of 89.50% for Marathi, accuracy of 90.78% and F1 score of 89.73% for Bengali and an accuracy of 84.98% and F1 score of 84.75% for Hindi.

Pokorny et al. (2015) proposed a BoAW approach which finds the emotion from the speech signals. Currently, a hot area of research is the automatic computer-aided identification of human emotional states based on speech signals. The first step involves extracting acoustic properties from a speech signal and analyzing it frame by frame. The features are quantized and converted into the BoW representation in the second stage, which is known as the bag-of-audio-words representation in the context of audio processing. Third stage is the classification stage where the naive Bayes classifier gave them the better results when compared to support vector machines.

Wazir et al. (2021) developed an intelligent deep learning-based system for film censorship through a fast and accurate detection and localization approach using advanced deep Convolutional Neural Networks (CNNs). It is imperative that easily accessible videos and movies with potentially offensive statements be filtered for inappropriate audio content. Assuring the appropriateness of content shared to the public through their different channels is the responsibility of media-sharing platforms and broadcasting corporations. First, raw audio samples are subjected to the Log-Mel spectrogram techniques that feature extraction process. Second, feature learning is done by E2E CNN. Thirdly, for additional processing, posterior handling techniques are used.

Wazir et al. (2020) proposed an intelligent model for foul language censorship through automated and robust detection which uses deep convolutional neural networks (CNNs). Since many young viewers have portable and readily available sources of screen time, filtering aural content has emerged as a key worry for society. Because it takes a lot of time, money, and labor to filter language content to viewers, censorship has been a bottleneck scenario. Speech and audio material require an automated identification and censoring models. Their proposed CNN models for the classification of foul language includes well-known Deep CNNs including Alexnet, VGG16, Googlenet, and Resnet50.

Foggiaa et al. (2015) proposed an innovative technique for audio event detection in surveillance applications. The automatic identification of unusual or harmful events through the analysis of audio streams captured by microphones became the focus of study in the field of intelligent surveillance systems. Finding the sounds like gun shots, screams and glass breakings from the audio signal is very difficult because all these sounds are mixed with the background noise. To overcome these difficulties, the author used bag of words approach. Authors formed a higher-level feature vector whose elements are indicative of the existence of such short-time features which is constructed by first dividing the audio stream into small frames of the order of milliseconds for which short-time, low-level features referred to as aural words are computed. They have considered the audio surveillance in which three classes of audio events have to be detected such as scream, glass breaking and gunshot. The authors created a sizable dataset that included 6,000 audio events such as gunshots, scream, and glass breaking that took place in various environmental settings with Signal-to-Noise Ratios (SNRs) ranging from 5 dB to 30 dB. They used k means clustering and uniform down sampling which reduces the training time without compromising accuracy. SVM classifier is also used to detect the events.

Multi-modality-based research is used across various applications and gains much attention. In the offensive language detection and censorship problem, multi-modalities like text and image, text and video, text and audio, audio and video-based research are recently presented and few from the same are detailed here. After using different CNN models and extraction models (Chhabra & Vishwakarma, 2023), the authors proposed a novel multimodal architecture that detects hate speech in text as well as images for memes. There are two parts of the model first is multi-scale kernel attentive visual (MSKAV) module, which is one of the key components for the model it check for the important visual feature so that the detection can happen and the other part of the model is knowledge distillation-based attentional caption (KDAC) module, which uses transformer-based self-attention model to detect hate speech. The model was trained on three multimodal hate speech benchmarks which includes MultiOff, Hateful Memes, and MMHS150K (Multimodal Hate Speech Dataset). It achieved impressive accuracy scores of 0.6250, 0.8750, and 0.8078, respectively, with corresponding AUC scores of 0.6557, 0.8363, and 0.7665. The results clearly show that MSKAV and KDAC modules work very well together in detecting hate memetic content.

Mitra and Sankhala (2022) presented a multi-modal hate speech detection architecture is presented. Image and its caption (memes) are the datasets considered in this research. It uses multi-scale kernel attentive visual and a multi-directional visual attention module through which important spatial regions are highlighted. Transformer architecture is adapted to learn sequence from meme texts. Three datasets are used for experimentation and accuracy results are presented, which includes, for multimodal memes dataset accuracy score of 0.6250 is reported, for hateful memes dataset – 0.8750 and MMHS150K dataset – 0.8078. Yang et al. (2022) presented hate speech and sarcasm detection through a cross-domain knowledge transfer framework is presented. Memes and tweets are evaluated for hate speech and sarcasm detection. Vision-language transformer is used as the baseline model. Three modules are adapted to learn the semantic, definition and domain aspects. Further, all the three modules are integrated and optimized. Two datasets are used for experimentation, hate dataset- Facebook hateful memes dataset and sarcasm dataset – twitter. Accuracy of 76.50 and 85.60 are reported for respective datasets.

Ayetiran et al. (2024) suggested a text and image based fake news, hate speech and offensive language detection is proposed. The images are represented as text to form image-texts, and the original main input text is used for training the Deep neural network. Inter-modal attention module and a fusion module is proposed to improve the performance of the model. For fake news- PolitiFact dataset is used, for hate speech – MMHS150 K dataset is used, for offensive language- MultiOFF dataset is used. Model exhibits better performance for all the datasets. Nishchal et al. (2021) proposed a Character Text Image Classifier (CTIC) presented for hate speech detection using image and text. Four different modalities are considered, which includes, word, character, sentence embeddings and the images. CTIC is built over EfficientNet and BERT. MMHS150K twitter dataset is used. Accuracy of 74% and AUC of 0.7634 is reported.

Chaudhari et al. (2021) proposed a detection system, where profanity words are detected and lips are blurred while usage of such words. Audio segments are extracted from video clips. Audio is converted to text using speech-to-text library. The text is matched against a dictionary of keywords. The matched words and their time segments are extracted. The video clip at that time sequence is processed to blur the lip region using OpenCV and facial landmark detection techniques. Experiments conducted over custom dataset and accuracy of 82.35% is reported. Wazir et al. (2023) proposed an intelligent deep learning-based system for film censorship through a fast and accurate detection and localization approach using advanced deep Convolutional Neural Networks (CNNs). In order to construct an automated system for detecting inappropriate speech content, a dataset of foul language that included continuous speech and isolated word samples was gathered, annotated, processed, and examined using CNN. This work recommended CNN model for automated video, audio, and film censoring, for the identification of spoken foul language with static keyword detection mode test for automated video/audio/film censorship.

Visutsak et al. (2023) proposed an approach to identify profanity and eliminate it from children's cartoon videos. Cartoons that contain profanity or other harsh language are forbidden and should be avoided by our kids. Cartoon videos can be uploaded to the cloud by the user, and Google Speech-to-Text can convert the video's audio to text. They used SVM to identify every profanity that was used in a text document. These profanity words can be muted by the system and added to the audio file. Once profanity has been eliminated, cartoon videos can be downloaded and viewed offline.

Afsha et al. (2022) discussed Automated Film Censorship and Rating (AFCR) techniques in cine field. Recently, one of the main areas of machine learning (ML) study has emerged in the area of AFCR. Due to the widespread expansion of film production and streaming services, manual censorship and rating of films, TV shows, animations, and other audio-visual content has become increasingly taxing. They used comparative analysis of the exiting ML models for an effective AFCR system. use of audio (music, conversation), video (scenes, visuals), and text (scripts, subtitles) data were used for rating such as general, Parental Guidance (PG), and Mature (M) etc. They compared various machine learning approaches like SVM, Random Forest, Logistic Regression) and deep learning models such as CNNs for video data, RNNs for AFCR.

3.PROPOSED METHOD

The video file dataset is collected from YouTube using foul word keywords. The complete dataset detail is given under experiments section. The video files are split in to 10 seconds clips for ease in handling. Audio files are extracted and stored separately for further processing. These audio notes are forwarded as input to the Whisper model. Whisper model is built with Transformer encoder-decoder blocks. The Log-Mel spectrograms are extracted first and then these spectrograms are passes as input to the encoders along with positional encodings. Audio features are generated by the encoders. These audio features and special tokens are forwarded to decoder block, and the text transcripts are generated.

Words in these text transcripts are matched against a dictionary of foul words and foul words are stored separately along with the start and end timestamps. These identified foul words are censored by replacing the original audio with a beep note generated using sine function. Finally, the censored audio is integrated with the original video to generate a censored content.

The workflow of the proposed method is shown in Figure 2 and is detailed subsequently.

Figure 2. Proposed Method Workflow

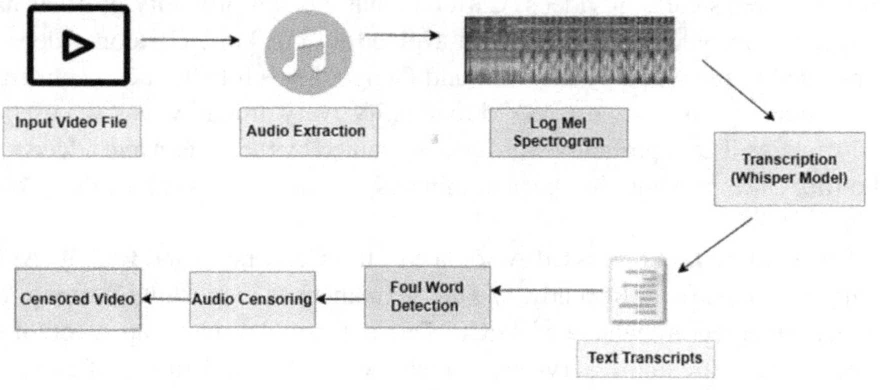

The steps include:

1. Extracting audio file
2. Whisper based transcription
3. Foul Language Identification and censoring
4. Censored Video Generation

1. Extracting audio file

In this research, the hate speech identification is subject to detecting the usage of foul language in audio data in social media file and censoring the audio data. So, it is necessary to extract the audio file from video for further processing. The first step in the proposed method is to split the input video into a smaller clip of 10 seconds for convenient transcription. From the video files, the audio files are extracted for further censoring it and are saved with '.wav' file extension. The dataset details are presented under the experimentation section. Python MoviePy library is used for this task.

2. Whisper based transcription

In this research, the foul words in the audio segments need to be detected with timestamps, to do this we extract text transcripts of the audio clip using a robust speech recognition model. From these transcripts, further steps in censoring are progressed. The audio file is transcribed into text using Whisper model. Whisper is a speech recognition system trained on large dataset. The end-to-end transcribing process using whisper model in the proposed system is detailed here. The audio file is passed as input to the whisper architecture. The first and foremost step is generating Log-Mel Spectrograms of the audio file. The spectrograms show the amplitude of frequency at particular timepoint.

Whisper is an encoder-decoder transformer architecture, the log-mel file is passed through the encode blocks and audio features are extracted. The extracted audio features and special set of tokens and the learned positional encoding are passed through decoder to generate transcription. The Language is detected first, and a language tag is included in the token and in the proposed study all input is in English so 'EN' token is included. If there is no voice activity detected, no speech tag is added. Next, transcribe/translate token is added, in our case it is transcription, 'TRANSCRIBE' token is added. Along with these special tokens, a timestamp token is included as well, indicating start and end time to ensure time aligned transcription. The text tokens are generated by the decoder. Greedy decoding with beam search is employed. Figure 3 shows the steps in whisper model to generate text transcripts.

Figure 3. Whisper Architecture workflow

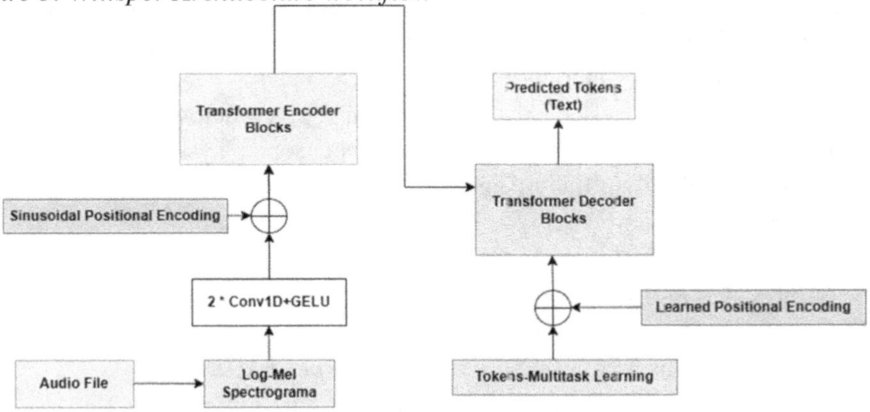

3. Foul Language Identification and censoring

The transcribed text is evaluated to identify foul words. Keyword matching approach is followed. The words generated through Whisper model are subject to stemming process. Stemming represents words to their root form. Next, the words are checked against a dictionary of foul words. If a match is found in this lookup step, then the identified foul word in the audio along with the timestamp (start and end time) are stored in a separate list. This step is repeated for all words. Now, we have all the identified foul words in the video by processing their audio files. Next, the foul word audio clips are to be censored.

The audio of identified foul words are censored by replacing it with a beep note, for a better user experience. This beep note is generated using a sine wave function and is given below,

$$g(t)=\sin(2\pi ft+\varnothing) \quad (1)$$

where, $g(t)$ is the amplitude of sine wave, f is the frequency of the sine wave, t represents the time variable and $\varnothing$ is phase offset. The frequency and duration of the beep is adjustable parameters.

4. Censored Video Generation

The audio clips with foul words are censored through the above steps, and now these audio clips are to be placed back in the original video file track. The censored audio is integrated back to the original video clip at respective timestamps using the FFmpeg tool. All the fragmented video clips are put together and output foul words censored video is generated.

Algorithm for the proposed censoring system is given below.

Algorithm - Foul word (audio) detection and censoring system

Input- Video in English Language

Output- Foul word audio censored video

1. Split the video into 10 second segments.
2. Extract audio from video. $AUD \leftarrow Extraction\ (Video)$.
3. Generate text transcripts. $Text_{Transcripts} \leftarrow Whisper\left(AUD\right)$.
4. Foul word detection by keyword matching with dictionary.
5. Extract *Timestamp* for matching foul words.
6. Censor audio of above *Timestamp* // Insert beep tone.
7. Integrate censored audio with respective video clip.
8. return the censored video.

4.EXPERIMENTATION AND RESULTS

The dataset used to test the performance of the proposed model is collected from YouTube. Data is sourced by searching through keywords like 'Top 10 movies with excessive swearing', 'F-Word movie clips', 'Best of Tom Segura Netflix is a joke' and a film 'uncut gems. Total time of videos is 2 hours and 32 minutes.

The videos were manually examined to note down the number of foul words and the timestamps in which it occurs within the audio files. A total of 825 foul words were found in the dataset. The proposed detection system successfully identified 774 foul words, and the audio part of respective segments were censored, and a beep tone was inserted. Attaining accuracy of 93.81%.

Figure 4 and 5, shows the audio clip with foul word and respective Mel spectrograms were, the foul word is censored.

Figure 4. Audio clip and its corresponding Mel Spectrogram with foul words

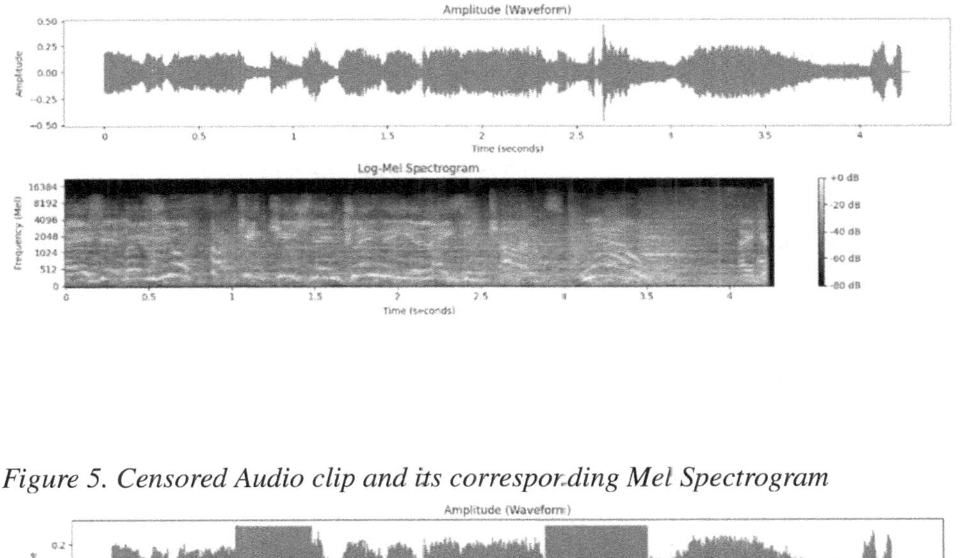

Figure 5. Censored Audio clip and its corresponding Mel Spectrogram

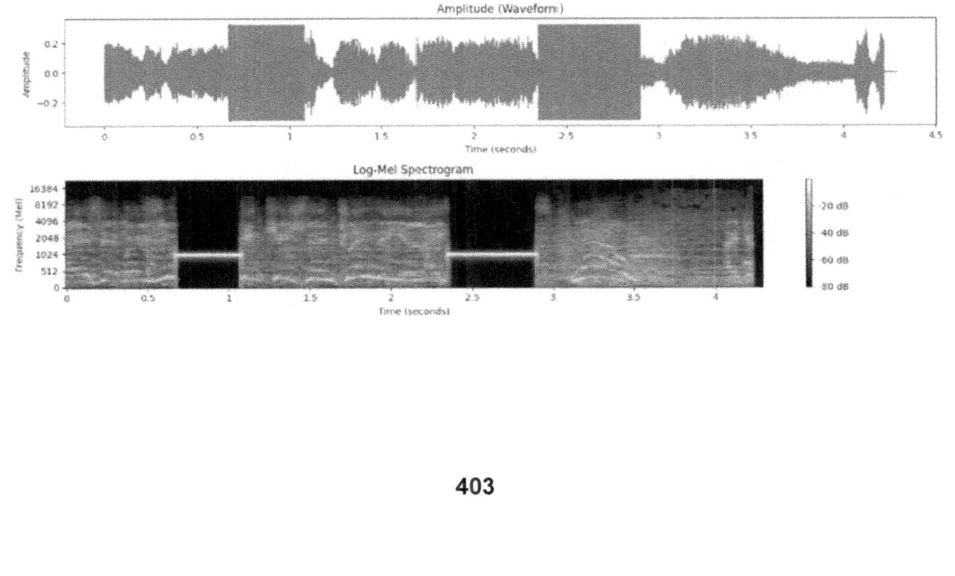

In the figure 4a we see the amplitude wave form with continuous ups and downs in the amplitude without any sign of augmentation. Below that is its corresponding log-mel spectrogram representation showing the same. The spectrogram shows a rich mixture of frequencies, with yellow and red colors showing higher energy regions and purple and black colors showing lower energy regions. This reflects the normal speech without any censoring.

In the second graph 4b we see that amplitude graph also has ups and downs in the amplitude, but it has a region of flat rectangular section with a consistent high amplitude showing that the foul words are detected and censored using sine wave synthetic audio. Same goes with Log-mel spectrogram, this graph also replaces the rich frequencies with a dominant single frequency band, this is a characteristic of sine wave synthetic audio. So, this shows that the model detects the foul words and then censors them using sine wave audio.

We have further compared the proposed system using Whisper with Google Speech-to-text and Amazon Transcribe. Google- speech-to text and Amazon Transcribe is used for transcription instead of whisper model and the remaining workflow is retained as such. Results for the same is given in Table 1.

Table 1. Comparison studies results

Model	Number of foul words	Detected Foul words	Accuracy (in %)
Whisper	825	774	93.81
Google Speech-to-text	825	612	74.1
Amazon Transcribe	825	597	72.36

From Table 1, it is evident that the proposed system using whisper for transcription is successful in identifying and censoring foul words achieving accuracy of 93.81%. performance of the other speech recognition models is falling apart in the performance in the present study.

5. CONCLUSION

In this research study, we have developed and presented foul word audio censoring systems which use OpenAI's Whisper model for transcribing the audio file extracted from social media videos to text. First we can take can video and divide audio from it after that we use Whisper model on that Audio. The extracted texts are investigated to detect offensive words through keyword matching against a dictionary of offensive and foul words. The audio clips of matched foul words are replaced with beep tone and the final censored video is generated. Which in the end integrates with its video to give results. This model and approach address key challenges of hate speech detection that is it can detect multiple dialects, cancel if there is any noise, and is scalable for a large dataset from different sources. After training the model evaluation of the model is done using a self-assembled dataset for which the videos were sourced from YouTube and the capabilities in detecting and censoring foul words are evaluated. The proposed whisper based censoring system has attained accuracy of 93.81%. This model provides a good base to develop and create future works like refining the model using a much diverse system to get better results or as we know whisper model can work on up to 99 languages, we can make the model multilingual so that many people can use it. Instead of keyword matching we can improve this model to detect semantics meaning of the audio if it is offensive or not.

REFERENCES

Afsha, S., Haque, M., & Nyeem, H. (2022). Machine learning models for content classification in film censorship and rating. *Proceedings of the 2022 International Conference on Innovations in Science, Engineering and Technology (ICISET)*, 396–401. DOI: 10.1109/ICISET54810.2022.9775816

Ayetiran, A., & Özgöbek, Ö. (2024). An inter-modal attention-based deep learning framework using unified modality for multimodal fake news, hate speech and offensive language detection. *Information Systems*, 123, 102378. DOI: 10.1016/j.is.2024.102378

Ba Wazir, A. S., Abdul Karim, H., AlDahoul, N., Ahmad Fauzi, M. F., Mansor, S., Lye Abdullah, M. H., Sui Lyn, H., & Zulkifli, T. Z. (2021). Spoken Malay profanity classification using convolutional neural network. *Proceedings of the 2021 IEEE International Conference on Signal and Image Processing Applications (ICSIPA)*, 34–38. https://doi.org/DOI: 10.1109/ICSIPA52582.2021.9576781

Ba Wazir, A. S., Abdul Karim, H., Lye Abdullah, M. H., Mansor, S., AlDahoul, N., Ahmad Fauzi, M. F., & See, J. (2020). Spectrogram-based classification of spoken foul language using deep CNN. *Proceedings of the 2020 IEEE 22nd International Workshop on Multimedia Signal Processing (MMSP)*, 1–6. https://doi.org/DOI: 10.1109/MMSP48831.2020.9287133

Ba Wazir, A. S., Abdul Karim, H., Sui Lyn, H., Ahmad Fauzi, M. F., Mansor, S., & Lye, M. H. (2022). Deep learning-based detection of inappropriate speech content for film censorship. *IEEE Access : Practical Innovations, Open Solutions*, 10, 101697–101715. DOI: 10.1109/ACCESS.2022.3208921

Ba Wazir, A. S., Karim, H. A., Abdullah, M. H. L., AlDahoul, N., Mansor, S., Fauzi, M. F. A., See, J., & Naim, A. S. (2021). Design and implementation of fast spoken foul language recognition with different end-to-end deep neural network architectures. *Sensors (Basel)*, 21(3), 710. DOI: 10.3390/s21030710 PMID: 33494254

Carletti, V., Foggia, P., Percannella, G., Saggese, A., Strisciuglio, N., & Vento, M. (2013). Audisurveillance using a bag of aural words classifier. *Proceedings of the 2013 10th IEEE International Conference on Advanced Videand Signal Based Surveillance (AVSS)*, 81–86. https://doi.org/DOI: 10.1109/AVSS.2013.6636620

Chaudhari, A., Davda, P., Dand, M., & Dholay, S. (2021). Profanity detection and removal in videos using machine learning. *Proceedings of the 6th International Conference on Inventive Computing Technologies (ICICT)*, 572–576. https://doi.org/DOI: 10.1109/ICICT50816.2021.9358624

Chhabra, A., & Vishwakarma, D. K. (2023). Multimodal hate speech detection via multi-scale visual kernels and knowledge distillation architecture. *Engineering Applications of Artificial Intelligence*, 126, 106991. DOI: 10.1016/j.engappai.2023.106991

Fatima-Zahra, E., Said, O. E. A., & Noureddine, E. N. (2022). A multilingual offensive language detection method based on transfer learning from transformer fine-tuning model. Journal of King Saud University - Computer and Information Sciences, 34(8), Part B, 6048–6056. https://doi.org/DOI: 10.1016/j.jksuci.2021.07.013

Foggia, P., Petrosino, A., & Saggese, A. (2015). Reliable detection of audievents in highly noisy environments. ScienceDirect. Gupta, V., Koyejo, S., Mittal, A., et al. (2022). Multilingual abusive comment detection at scale for Indic languages. In S. Koyejet al. (Eds.), Advances in Neural Information Processing Systems, 35, 26176–26191. https://proceedings.neurips.cc/paper_files/paper/2022/file/a7c4163b33286261b24c72fd3d1707c9-Paper-Datasets_and_Benchmarks.pdf

Mitra, A., & Sankhala, P. (2022). Multilingual hate speech and offensive content detection using modified cross-entropy loss. arXiv preprint. https://arxiv.org/abs/2202.02635

Ortiz-Ospina, E. (2019). The rise of social media. Our World in Data. https://ourworldindata.org/rise-of-social-media

Pokorny, F. B., Graf, F., Pernkopf, F., & Schuller, B. W. (2015). Detection of negative emotions in speech signals using bags-of-audio-words. *Proceedings of the 2015 International Conference on Affective Computing and Intelligent Interaction (ACII)*, 879–884. https://doi.org/DOI: 10.1109/ACII.2015.7344678

Prasad, N., Saha, S., & Bhattacharyya, P. (2021). A multimodal classification of noisy hate speech using character-level embedding and attention. *Proceedings of the 2021 International Joint Conference on Neural Networks (IJCNN)*, 1–8. https://doi.org/DOI: 10.1109/IJCNN52387.2021.9533371

Vimal, B., Surya, M., Darshan, S., Sridhar, V. S., & Ashok, A. (2021). MFCC-based audiclassification using machine learning. *Proceedings of the 12th International Conference on Computing Communication and Networking Technologies (ICCCNT)*, 1–4. https://doi.org/DOI: 10.1109/ICCCNT51525.2021.9579881

Visutsak, P., Wijitemee, A., Mahaphon, A., & Chaowalit, O. (2023). Machine-learning-based profanity detection and removal in cartoons videos. *Proceedings of the 2023 5th International Conference on Control and Robotics (ICCR)*, 162–167. https://doi.org/DOI: 10.1109/ICCR60000.2023.10444852

Yang, C., Zhu, F., Liu, G., Han, J., & Hu, S. (2022). Multimodal hate speech detection via cross-domain knowledge transfer. *Proceedings of the 30th ACM International Conference on Multimedia*, 4505–4514. https://doi.org/DOI: 10.1145/3503161.3548255

Zaman, K., Sah, M., Direkoglu, C., & Unoki, M. (2023). A survey of audiclassification using deep learning. *IEEE Access : Practical Innovations, Open Solutions*, 11, 106620–106649. DOI: 10.1109/ACCESS.2023.3318015

Zeng, C., & Dou, W. (2010). Audikeywords detection in basketball video. *Proceedings of the 2010 International Conference on Audio, Language and Image Processing*, 1765–1770. DOI: 10.1109/ICALIP.2010.5685186

Chapter 17
AI, Ethics, and Hate Speech:
A Collaborative Approach to Social Media Influence

Chalamalla Venkateshwarlu
https://orcid.org/0000-0003-3559-2475
Osmania University, India

ABSTRACT

Hate speech is a serious social problem, disrupts social order, impairs individual well-being, and threatens democracy, emonize individuals or groups based on attributes like race, religion,caste ethnicity, gender or sexual orientation, appears in many forms: in spoken language, written materials, symbols and online posts. With the advent of social media, the reach and impact of hate speech has increased exponentially, making it an ever-pressing issue of the digital age included legislative measures, education awareness campaigns, the increasing prevalence of harmful content online has led to the exploration of artificial intelligence (AI) as the tool to be used to detect and mitigate hate speech online The paper conclude that preserves ethical concepts in the design and implementation of the AI-driven systems. It points to policies that empower responsible innovation without undermining fundamental democratic values. Through creating inclusive digital spaces and advocating for rights and freedoms for developing socially responsible, inclusivity and respect for individual liberties

DOI: 10.4018/979-8-3693-9904-0.ch017

INTRODUCTION

Artificial intelligence (AI) solutions have also been developed for the rising problem of social media hate speech, which is primarily designed to pick out and filter against such content. Yet the whole matter poses massive ethical concerns when AI is deployed in this way. This paper explores the ethical minefield that AI interventions in hate-speech management create, and highlights considerations such as free speech issues, privacy concerns and second-order effects like self-censorship or chilling effects on open discourse, all of which have ample precedence. Next, it examines the struggles of defining hate speech in general when having to address it from a global platform and introduces a necessity that a specific practice is necessary. And finally, the chapter suggests ethical responsibilities that transparency and accountability should impose on AI developers, platform operators and regulators, for fair play in these systems. It suggests a collaborative effort for ethicists with technologists, lawyers and sociologists to see that the AI solutions are made ethically applicable and socially responsible. As social media and anti-social attacks continue to play a growing role in our lives, there must be some way of drawing the line between the scientifically destructive that needs curbing and fundamental rights, the protections for which are irreplaceable. Significance and Contribution

This chapter will also add significantly to the discussion on what is ethically acceptable use of AI in content moderation. Several AI solutions targeting hate speech have already been developed but can face ethical dilemmas that challenge core human freedoms of freedom of speech and privacy. Identifying these troubling issues, the chapter will provide a nuanced response to how AI can be responsibly used to prevent hate speech on the one hand while safeguarding the rights and freedoms of individuals on the other. The chapter will also present tangible guidance on how improving AI-based systems to bring ethics into future technologies.

The rapid rise of social media, and its impact, has been the greatest challenge in policing dangerous speech, including expressions of hate. It was only a matter of time before the use of more AI-based models to screen and remove automatic hate speech shifted to these platforms that wield the stronghold on public opinion. But AI dispositions in them all bring their own sets of challenging ethical issues, the combination of free speech with privacy, and underlying bias coded into algorithms.

In this chapter, four core ethical challenges that are at stake in the development and application of solutions for AI-driven management of hate speech are focused on balancing technology potential with rights and responsibilities.

Hate speech is any expression, whether spoken, written or symbolic, that denigrates a person or group based on (specific attributes), vilifies them or incites violence against them. These characteristics generally include race, ethnicity, nationality, religion, gender, sexual orientation, disability and/or other status. Utterances aimed at specific groups or individuals known as hate speech and targeting the factors of racial, religious belief, sex, orientation, disability or nationality. Hate speech is comprised of derogatory language, slurs, stereotypes and calls to harm. Hate speech is commonly used to declare displeasure and hostility; sometimes it includes opposing violence or discrimination. It may take many forms, including speech (verbal statements), print material (books, essays, webpages), symbols (swastikas or other hate symbols), gestures and online content such as social media mentions/ posts, comments and even memes.

Every country and legal system has a different definition of what constitutes hate speech. On the other hand, in some countries hate speech is illegal, and others permit it greatly by putting freedom of expression above it with some exceptions. For example, in the USA, the First Amendment allows wide latitude for Free Speech, therefore it has been difficult to legislate against hate speech, except for incitement to imminent lawless action. On the contrary, several of the European Union nations have laws which make hate speech per se a crime, especially when it is directed at protected groups and has the potential to incite violence or discrimination.

Hate speech destroys social life as it can invoke fear, and mistrust in communities coming from different backgrounds. Hate speech is escalating social concerns worldwide and it has acute damage to the mental health of victims including anxiety, depression and exclusion. The worst thing that it can do is motivate people or communities to commit real violence or discrimination, therefore hurting public security and order in a society. Therefore familiarizing a generation to not stand up against hate speech will ultimately sow the seeds for stereotypes and biases that reach down to societal institutions and cultural norms.

However, there are multiple challenges with addressing hate speech. Lawmakers and platforms often wrestle with how to balance free speech protection with the social ills caused or exacerbated by harmful speech. YouTube in turn cited that the determination of what constitutes hate speech can be highly subjective and context-specific, making consistent enforcement difficult. Moreover, the ascent of digital platforms has consequently different sizes while hate speech and crime have also spread faster and wider than ever before thus difficulties for checking and sanctioning such content have become much more confusing.

Efforts to counter hate speech include the use of various laws and legal systems, law enforcement, education, and information dissemination methods. Strategies should include passing laws that clearly define and ban hate speech while upholding freedom of expression, raising awareness about the dangers of hate speech through educational programs and an outreach campaign, and calling on social media and other online platforms to enforce community standards to remove offensive material as well as provide tools for reporting such content. Finally, resources and support need to be made available to help individuals and communities who are targeted by hate speech cope with their psychological and social fallouts.

Hate speech is one of the worst evils of the society, by its influences on social unity, individual health and domestic tranquillity. You should never expect the ability of people to comprehend what it is or its implications and the legitimacy isn't even possible to regulate a subject as hazy as an insult wherein mutual respect lays the foundation of this society. Countering hate speech therefore calls for a complex response that upholds both the protection of an open debate and the protection of the more vulnerable persons and groups.

Through the digital age, communication has shifted dramatically, providing access and reach like never before. However, with this interconnectivity comes significant drawbacks, not least of which is the proliferation of hate speech on the web. Hate speech, defined as communication that vilifies, or assaults people or groups based on traits including race, religion, ethnicity, gender, or sexual orientation, presents a serious threat to social harmony, individual well-being, and democratic ideals. In response to the growing prevalence of hate speech in online contexts, there is increasing interest in using artificial intelligence (AI) technology to identify and reduce it. In particular, AI-based algorithms have the potential to identify and prevent instances of hateful speech, thus leading to safer and more diverse online communities. AI technologies for the identification of hate speech are fraught with ethical complexities and societal consequences. This study seeks to explore the complex set of ethical considerations surrounding the implementation of AI in hate speech detection within complex socio-technical settings. The most important issue is the bias in algorithms. AI algorithms developed over biassed datasets or constructed with internal biases could maintain and amplify existing social prejudices, therefore transforming into discrimination-enhancing results in hate speech detection systems.

Detecting and mitigating algorithmic bias is crucial for ensuring fair and equitable outcomes in hate speech detection and regulation. Additionally, balancing the rights of free speech with the responsibility to mitigate hate speech requires a careful equilibrium. But, as tackling hate speech is vital for encouraging inclusive online environments, protecting free expression is a core democratic value. Striking that balance is not as simple as weighing two objectives; it involves complex deliberation and nuanced strategies that take steps to mitigate parasitic interaction without disproportionate silencing of good-faith discourse. As AI remains poised to help eliminate illegal hate speech, it also poses questions regarding user privacy and the security of that information. Collecting and analysing these types of user-generated content to identify hate speech must also respect individual privacy rights and adhere to established data protection standards. Introduced what could be unintended consequences of AI for hate speech detection Some of the major risks that need to be contained to prevent the erosion of these democratic norms, and the suppression of speech online are those of censorship, overreach, and the muzzling of dissenting voices. Hate speech exists in many cultural and social contexts that demand a robust understanding and contextualisation. This includes the nuances of the context within culture where hate speech is defined differently from one culture to another which highlights the need for adaptive and culturally relevant solutions in AI. Stakeholders involved in the production, deployment, and regulation of AI-based hate speech detection systems have a complicated series of responsibilities. AI engineers are responsible for developing algorithms that prioritise fairness, transparency, and accountability. Providers of platforms should also develop robust moderation processes that will allow them to take down hate speech without unduly impeding free expression.

While developing policies that promote responsible use of AI without compromising core rights and values is crucial, research makes it clear that policymakers are key to facilitating this balance. This requires interdisciplinary collaboration since each field alone can only accomplish so much. Instead, new comprehensive solutions need to be developed in cooperation between ethicists, sociologists, legal scholars, and technologists, so that the ethical challenges based on AI-driven hate speech identification can be resolved appropriately. We can work towards inclusive digital spaces respecting rights and freedoms by championing transparency, accountability and responsible ingenuity.

RESEARCH APPROACH AND METHODOLOGY

This chapter uses a mixed-method approach that combines the existing literature on AI ethics and hate speech regulation with a practical application through case studies of AI implementations across the major social media platforms. It will draw on a mix of academic research on A.I. fairness, reports from social media companies and interviews with experts in A.I. ethics and content moderation.

Relevant Review of Literature

It is unknown if any of the existing research on AI ethics, hate speech regulation, and the role of social media platforms has moved the needle on effectiveness, but one can look for clues. AI systems are increasingly deployed to detect and regulate hate speech on Facebook Twitter and YouTube. These systems are however quite limited in understanding language that is dependent on context. Sarcasm, coded language, regional dialects and other forms of vernacular often go unnoticed by A.I., which can result in both the under-moderation of harmful content and the over-censorship of legitimate expression.

Another area of concern is ethical considerations in AI deployment. These studies highlight the biases that exist in AI models, which can result in disproportionate effects on marginalized groups. Racial and gender biases in datasets, for example, can lead to certain communities being disproportionately targeted. Moreover, the opaque nature of most AI algorithms makes it difficult to hold these systems accountable, as the lack of transparency around moderation practices prevents users and policymakers from effectively challenging the decisions of these powerful AI systems.

Hate speech is something that is often considered one of the most effective ways of tackling the issue, but it comes with its own set of challenges. One of the biggest hurdles is coming up with a clear definition of hate speech as it varies by context and culture. The other complex issue to consider is the need to balance regulation with free speech concerns, as more stringent rules could suppress expression. For editorial teams, determining what qualifies as hate speech can be a messy, error- and bias-prone process. And what counts as hate speech in one country may not be regarded as such in another, complicating the ability to have global platforms enforce consistent rules. These struggles demonstrate that regulatory approaches, while important, must be carefully designed and executed. While automated moderation approaches can indeed handle large quantities of content, they risk infringing upon freedom of speech through erroneous classifications. Despite the promising results achieved by AIs, academia argues in favour of a hybrid approach in which humans follow closely behind AIs to do the work that is nuanced and context-sensitive, like hate speech. Machine learning is not enough, and human moderators provide context and understanding that artificial intelligence lacks, increasing the accuracy and fairness of moderation.

Social media fuels and must be part of this ecosystem but is rightfully challenged for its half-hearted consistency in combating hate speech. There are platform transparency reports that show varying effectiveness concerning identifying and removing harmful content. The breadth limits of independent audits on their moderation algorithms pose serious accountability concerns. Moreover, services often focus their AI training on English-language material, thereby neglecting the multilingual nature of international audiences. This bias results in under-moderation for places outside of the English sphere.

The gap in research includes no globally standardized ethical framework to ensure fairness, justice, and dignity for all, which is essential for AI in hate speech regulation, and limited datasets that represent different languages and cultures as well as broader aspects of hate speech are also lacking. Moreover, although a lot of attention has been devoted to technological solutions, to a relative dearth of studies that seek to understand the societal and psychological effects of online hate speech. These gaps demand a multidisciplinary approach that encompasses ethical, technical, and societal perspectives, ensuring the development of AI systems for content moderation that are both equitable and effective.

There are different case studies as well as research projects which explore the interrelationship between AI ethics, hate speech detection, as well as social media platforms. A notable example is Microsoft's AI chatbot Tay, which was released on Twitter in 2016. It was born to have human-like conversations but within a short time, once it started conversing with users who interacted with it and exposed it to the offensive sayings, Tay started generating hateful tweets. This case exemplified the ethical dilemma of releasing AI systems without sufficient measures in place to prevent the amplification of hate speech.

Another notable case study is the use of AI to moderate hate speech during the Rohingya crisis in Myanmar. There were widespread feelings among many people that Facebook and other social media sites did not take enough action to halt the Rohingya violence that resulted from hate speech. The AI tools used demonstrated the technical limitations of AI, as they struggled to understand the Burmese language and the nuanced context of the posts, in varied linguistic environments.

These cases expose an important gap in research: the demand for AI systems that can accurately detect hate speech, both in different languages and in various cultural contexts. Most AI models today simply don't have the sophistication needed to grasp the subtleties of various tongues and the cultural nuances shaping speech. But there is also a lack of robust datasets that represent the incredibly broad range of expression that exists around the world, making it difficult to build more inclusive tools for AI moderation. Filling this gap is crucial for improving the efficiency and fairness of AI-fuelled hate speech identification on social networking systems. Moreover, the ethical dimensions of AI moderation deserve more scrutiny. The line between suppressing harmful speech and protecting free speech is thin. Over-dependence on AI can lead to over-censorship — where, through (or likely accidental) unintended classification, a legitimate discourse is suppressed, while under-dependence can result in a platform, such as X, that allows weapons-grade content to poison the public narrative. Finding the right equilibrium between human values and empowerment while appeasing stakeholders is a significant challenge in designing future AI systems and is an area that deserves further exploration. Therefore, despite AI being a promising solution to moderate hate speech on social media, through previous studies and case analysis, we have identified important gaps regarding linguistic adaptability, cultural sensitivity and ethical application. Researchers moving forward need to create AI systems not just for technical performance, but to ensure an ethically and culturally balanced representation of data in digital communication systems and keep equity at the front of future studies.

The New York Times wrote extensively about hate speech and the challenges of combatting it with artificial intelligence during the Rohingya crisis in Myanmar. The report described how the Rohingya community was further victimised when Facebook moderation systems failed to stop the spread of hate incitement because the company's AI could not understand Burmese. These challenges point to the challenges of AI systems struggling with culturally and linguistically diverse material (Mozur 2018). The reporting raised a broader problem with the limitations of AI systems' languages, and how these limitations play out in the real world.

The Washington Post has reported on worries about the ethical repercussions of A.I.-driven moderation on platforms like YouTube and Twitter. It centres on the opacity of algorithms that moderate material, which often prioritize user engagement over the elimination of harmful content. The platforms' ethical responsibility was raised following an investigation by Dwoskin (2021) found that AI algorithms unintentionally pushed extremist content as the platform designs were all engagement driven. This emphasizes the importance of maintaining an ethical balance between moderation and free speech, as well as the absolute need to be more transparent about the AI moderation process.

All of these schools have fairness and accountability in AI systems for hate speech moderation. A more recent report examined the effectiveness of hybrid moderation systems that combine AI with human oversight, ultimately finding that purely automated systems fall short of the goal of handling nuanced or context-dependent hate speech. Stanford HAI (2022) lists the necessity of actually informing AI systems with various linguistic/cultural datasets to refine AI systems' precision and neutrality. This method is meant to reduce biases and ensure that the system can identify harmful material regardless of social or cultural context.

Policy-oriented research has been published by the Brookings Institution that touches on governing AI in the context of hate speech regulation. West (2019) writes a policy brief addressing the need for global standards in AI ethics and goes on to cite concerns around content moderation. It showcases the inconsistent global application of AI moderation tools between languages and regions that end up heavily impacting users in countries that do not speak English. Brookings recommends that social media platforms transparently report actions they take and collaborate with international organizations to establish fair frameworks. Our research highlights the need for global governance systems for AI-driven moderation systems that promote consistent moderation across linguistic and cultural boundaries.

These corporations face challenges analogous to, e.g., ensuring the fairness of AI models, and reducing algorithmic bias for an unfair result on particular communities (González et al., 2021). This creates tension in the content that should be moderated vis Ã vis free speech rights which makes for an ethically charged minefield that these platforms have had to navigate.

Ethical lenses such as utilitarianism, deontology and virtue ethics create a framework within which to explore the moral implications of AI-based content moderation. One such principle underlying Utilitarianism is the maximization of the good for the greatest number. One way that platforms may justify their involvement with AI in hate speech detection is to invoke that the minimization of harm caused by hateful content such as not having access to hate speech contributes to societal well-being overall (Shadbolt |& Williams, 2019). But then there is the problem of overreach, overzealous censorship that chokes off non-toxic speech. On the other hand, deontological ethics focuses on compliance with rules and duties. This was the social responsibility of BIG Tech to foster free speech and yet, protect us from hate speech. And this puts the platforms in a Catch-22: How do they do their job protecting users without weighing down alternate means of airing opinions?

Virtue ethics, by contrast, concerns the character and motives of the agents who make them. The book *AI4People—An Ethical Framework for a Good AI Society: Opportunities, Risks, Principles, and Recommendations* by Floridi (2018) is not about the details of AI deployment and its meaning within the AI ethics debate. Here, there is no random error. This consequently creates an incentive for companies to not only customise their AI systems to suit their needs and production but additionally contemplate their incentive for building or utilizing them in the first place.

There is an article in the "Algorithmic content moderation: Technical and political challenges in the automation of platform governance" by Binns (2018) outlines the profusion of use cases for the nuanced exposure AI systems have limitations recognizing, that is, the cultural and contextual subtleties inherent in language. The study calls out that AI models frequently cannot account for linguistic diversity, nor the nuances of the ways people communicate in specific social situations, and consequently over-censor (removing content that shouldn't be removed) or under-regulate (not removing content that should be removed) harmful content. The article suggests the introduction of diverse cultural perspectives(perspectives), alongside the language data points that every traditional AI model depends on, to help improve the model's accuracy. Additionally, it promotes human intervention so that we prevent AI from unintentionally replicating harm.

The article was published in PubMed Central (PMC) and reviews the challenges of AI moderation of hate speech not only in well-resourced languages but also in low-resource languages. The study emphasizes that most AI models are trained on English data and thus really struggle to detect hate speech in other languages, which also leads to inaccurate moderation. The study notes that AI systems working against online hate speech should be trained in a diverse data corpus including different linguistic and cultural contexts (Zhou et al., 2020); The authors also advocate a multi-stakeholder approach involving ethicists, linguists, and technology developers to develop more equitable AI systems.

This research paper probes into these hybrid content moderation systems, blending machine-learned techniques with human oversight to grow the capacity of AI to identify hate speech. The study admits that while artificial intelligence does a good job of recognizing certain types of hate speech, it is often no match for ambiguous or context-dependent examples. The paper suggests AI should be an assistive tool for human moderators, instead of using it as a substitute. The combination of AI and human oversight can make content moderation more nuanced and accurate to improve the fairness and transparency of moderation practices (Binns, 2020). Hybrid systems, they say, provide a balance between speed and accuracy, filling in the gaps of fully automated systems.

A research paper probes the ethical complications of AI-based detection of online hate speech. The study points to the delicate balance between freedom of expression and regulating harmful content. It claims that AI moderation systems can result in over-censorship, whereby content that is not hate speech is still removed, curbing users' freedom of expression. The authors contend that artificial intelligence systems should be designed with transparency and accountability, meaning that users should know how content is moderated. It also notes that context plays an important role in the moderation of hate speech and highlights how human oversight of moderation processes is needed to make ethical determinations about hate speech (Gillespie, 2021).

Survey Studies and Case Studies (in the Present Study)

The survey, which included the responses of 1,000 social media users, found that 62% of respondents come across hate speech at least once a week, highlighting the continued prevalence of toxic material online. A further 45% of respondents decided AI is "moderately effective" at moderating hate speech, 30% judged it "ineffective," and just 25% deemed it "highly effective." These statistics suggest mixed feelings about AI's role in mitigating online hate speech. Expert interviews explain algorithmic biases built into existing AI systems for content moderation. Respondents noted that many algorithms fail to identify more subtle forms of hate speech, especially if it requires the context of surrounding messages, slang or cultural references. Experts said that to reduce bias and false positives, there must be more inclusive and representative training datasets.

Case studies of the moderation systems of Twitter and Facebook found that following updates to their AI algorithms they improved their detection of hate speech. For example, Facebook was able to improve its detection rate by 20% by factoring in user feedback as part of its training methods. The following change, however, resulted in a relatively large number of false positives or harmless information being flagged, which disappointed users. Twitter's AI running into similar issues — with greater transparency, to be sure — highlights the need to combine human censors with AI.

The results underscore the strengths and limitations of applying A.I. to moderation of content. While AI systems have advanced our ability to both detect new cases and help validate new targeted methodologies, it remains a challenge including bias and false positives, indicating an important need for human oversight. Considering that the survey indicated that even from the nationalist standpoint the perception of AI features is still far from being perfect, the results seem to show that there is substantial space to improve regarding the feeling of confidence in AI to handle hate speech. Both expert testimonials and case studies highlight and confirm this; with such hybrid moderation, a more equilibrated approach is possible, keeping the lightning-speed aspect of AI here together with some sort of human judgment. This improves accuracy, minimizes biases, and satisfies users.

This example of their implementation, in the way a company like Facebook employs AI to detect and moderate hate speech, illustrates the complexities of an automated content moderation regime. They can see AI algorithms to catch specific terms but can also follow linguistic patterns and the context of hate speech. One such tool, machine learning (ML), is trained to recognize hate speech by being fed more and more posts. Facebook has a tool that can scan for hate speech in posts automatically. Almost 95% of hate speech content and willingness to remove identified by AI before users flagged it, according to Facebook (2020). Twitter also released a range of AI models which assess not only the body of a tweet but also user behaviour and engagement signals to find out if certain content is toxic. YouTube, a subsidiary of Google, uses artificial intelligence (AI) to detect hate speech within videos before human intervention, as the video-hosting platform has designated policies to remove and/or suppress videos that violate its community standards.

Key Observations

The use of artificial intelligence (AI) in hate speech detection has shown promise in efficiently detecting and lowering harmful content in online spaces. Algorithmic bias is one of the key ethical issues of using AI for this purpose. Algorithmic bias is when AI models generate results that will always hurt certain people or groups, a result of bias scoped when training data are used, or when the algorithm is developed. When it comes to hate speech detection, algorithmic bias can manifest in several ways. Firstly, biased training data can carry over and reinforce existing societal biases. When using datasets that are not diverse or representative, the algorithms used to train hate speech detection can inadvertently learn and reinforce the same discriminatory patterns found in the dataset. For example, if the training data is mostly made up of hate speech towards certain marginalised groups, the resulting model may be very good at detecting hate speech towards those groups but not so good at detecting hate speech towards other groups. In addition, biases might be introduced in the design and implementation of the AI algorithms themselves. Features selection, algorithm architecture and optimisation criteria could also inadvertently embed and propagate the biases existing in data. For example, if a hate speech identification algorithm flags certain terms or phrases that correlate with certain demographic groups, then it might flag disproportionately content that is hate speech against those groups but not treat in the same manner the equivalent content directed against other groups. (Mittal et. al 2008)

The impact of algorithmic bias in hate speech detection is large and far-reaching. Biassed algorithms can cause disproportionate suppression and moderation of particular views, leading to increased disparities and the persecution of already marginalised communities. In addition, prejudiced AI systems can undermine trust in the fairness and impartiality of content moderation processes, ultimately eroding faith in the platforms and those which govern aesthetic debate. A multifaceted approach is required to address algorithmic bias in hate speech detection.

It demands careful tweaking and processing of training data to ensure diversity, fairness, representation, and balance among different demographics. AI engineers can mitigate the risk of bias in the resulting models through the incorporation of diverse perspectives and experiences in training data. Transparency and accountability, in turn, are vital in holding platforms to account and reigning in algorithmic bias. AI developers and platform operators need to be very clear about the data sources, methodology and decision-making processes that underpin hate speech detection systems. We propose that platforms further explain the workings of AI-enabled moderation systems, giving users the tools to read and challenge biased outcomes like never before. In addition, it is important to regularly monitor and evaluate hate speech detection systems to identify and mitigate bias in their performance. By performing regular audits and evaluations of AI models, biases can be detected and corrected systematically as they emerge, ensuring that hate speech detection systems remain fair, accurate, and unbiased over time.

Free Speech Considerations

When battling the spread of hate speech on the internet, it is then critical to navigate the complex environment of free speech rights. The actions to limit hate speech are often considered a mechanism to enable inclusive and civil online spaces; however, they have to be conducted in a manner that maintains key principles of free expression and democratic obligations. The essence of the problem is a tension between the need to mitigate the harmful impacts of hate speech and the protection of individual rights to freedom of expression. Hate speech, by nature, is meant to dehumanise and discriminate against individuals or groups based on their race, religion, ethnicity, gender, or sexual orientation. Left untreated, it can enable discrimination, incite violence and undermine social cohesion." This is often both difficult to discern and subject to interpretation and context (in other words, whether there is a distinction between so-called hate speech and valid expression). Additionally, limiting hate speech may contribute to unintended consequences, such as the chilling effects on legitimate discourse, the marginalization of dissenting voices, and the entrenchment of existing power dynamics. This means generally with AI-based hate speech detection that the goal is to develop algorithms and moderation processes that can identify harmful speech accurately and minimize the chances of overreach and suppression. This requires finding a delicate balance between restricting hate speech and upholding free speech rights.

One way to balance these competing objectives is to deploy an advanced, context-sensitive system for detecting hate speech. Platforms should not solely rely on automated algorithms for detecting and moderating hate speech but rather include human judgment and contextual analysis in the moderation process. Content moderation decisions can be made with a sense of linguistic and cultural nuance by allowing human moderators to analyze the intent and context of potentially harmful information. Also, very important in the area of hate speech detection is that transparency and accountability are critical in protecting free speech rights. Platforms need to be transparent about their content moderation doctrines and processes, including the factors that they use to detect and remove hate speech. There should be written explicit and easily understandable rules outlining what constitutes hate speech, and the consequences for violating those rules should be accessible to users. And platforms should have processes that allow users to appeal moderation decisions and challenge the classification of their content as hate speech. This means, for instance, that by fostering a culture of transparency and accountability, platforms can mitigate the risk of censorship and ensure that content moderation procedures are conducted fairly and impartially.

Privacy Concerns in AI-Powered

As the deployment of AI technology to identify and eliminate online hate speech at scale continues to increase, we must examine the privacy impacts of these systems. Often, hate speech detection algorithms used on user-generated content: text, images, and videos. Such data is sensitive and raises serious privacy issues, especially concerning the right to privacy and data protection of individuals. One major privacy concern when it comes to AI-driven identification of hate speech is the possibility of overreach or hypersensitivity. For instance, hate speech identification systems can include and process private communications, hence violating the right to private and unmonitored communication. Indiscriminate adoption of AI-facilitated moderation systems may entrench practices of oversight that condition individuals to accept lower levels of privacy for convenience in online environments. For example, using AI to detect hate speech can lawfully implicate data leakage or sensitive private data retrievability.

Algorithms that detect hate speech need a lot of user data to train on to learn to find or improve their efficiency. In this case, the storage and processing of such data are at the same time exposing the risk of data breaches, unauthorised access, and use. In addition, there may be unintended privacy violations arising from AI-based analytical techniques being applied to user-generated content leading to a further compromise of the rights of individuals to privacy. (Mittal et al., 2008)

The heterogeneous impact of AI-driven hate speech detection systems may magnify current inequalities in privacy safeguards. Marginalised groups are likely to be some of the targets of hate speech and may also face disproportionate negative effects from privacy violations inherent in AI moderation. Marginalised groups may be subjected to more rigorous surveillance and monitoring as a result of biased algorithms or biased enforcement practices, reinforcing the marginalisation of already vulnerable populations. A more nuanced, privacy-respecting approach to developing AI solutions for hate speech detection is necessary. To adequately comply with the relevant data privacy laws and regulations, both platforms and developing hate speech detection algorithms must also ensure that their processes and algorithms are designed to comply with the privacy laws. This should include data minimisation practices, anonymous storage of user data when possible, and protecting sensitive personal information from being accessed and misused by malicious actors. Also, these platforms need to be transparent about their data collection and processing methods including the training algorithms for hate speech detection and how user privacy could be protected. Users should have access to transparent and easily understandable information about what types of data are collected, to what ends, and about their rights related to the collection and processing of their personal information. Moreover, platforms need to give users meaningful control over their data and privacy settings and allow them to opt out of any data collection for hate speech detection purposes if they choose to. Freedom of individuals to make decisions on their privacy preferences (Which addresses fear of surveillance or misuse of data).

Unintended Consequences of AI-driven

Detecting hate speech using artificial intelligence (AI) can potentially have repercussions for online interaction, free speech, and societal harmony. AI-Driven Hate Speech Detection: The Premise vs Risks While the overarching goal of AI-Driven hate speech detection remains locating and serving effective interventions to harmful communication, such systems are rooted in potential risks of overreach, censorship, and/or muzzling legitimate expression. The onslaught of AI-generated hate speech detection also means we may face the unintended consequence of censorship and an attack on free speech. Automated moderation algorithms aimed at detecting and removing hate speech may accidentally flag and delete content that, though not hate speech, expresses controversial or unpopular views. This could result in the silencing of dissent, the marginalization of minority voices, and the homogenization of online conversations.

Furthermore, it can enable a chilling effect where people may find it difficult to express their views freely due to the potential of being flagged or banned, especially under the current reliance on AI-based moderation systems.

Using artificial intelligence (AI) to identify hate speech may have unmanageable repercussions for online discourse, free speech, and social cohesion. Although the minimization of harm and hateful speech is the target of AI-based hate speech detection systems, the deployment of such systems poses inherent risks of overreach, censorship, and suppression of valid expression. AI-Powered Hate Speech Detection: A Significant Side Effect Involves the Potential for Censorship and Limitations on Free Speech Just as he was about to go on stage, a case still haunting the US Army, they tried to take down all hate speech, but, automated moderation algorithms remove content that expresses controversial or unwanted opinions — alongside content that actually would qualify as hate speech. Facilitating homogeneity in internet speech, silencing of minority viewpoints and repression of dissenting voices. Also, the subject of AI moderation systems relying on people would be no more than a popularization of freedom of speech, as people would concern themselves by being reported or banned for any of their opinions.

To combat the negative impacts of AI hate speech detection, actions must be taken on multiple fronts. Transparency and responsibility need to be prioritized by platforms and developers when designing and implementing AI moderation systems. Explainability: Providing users with clear information about how hate speech detection algorithms work can help promote trust and accountability in content moderation practices. Also, they should provide human oversight and engagement within AI-based moderation systems to alleviate the risks of overreach and censorship. Additionally, humans adding insight demonstrate depth and nuance that automated algorithms cannot offer because they can only use bits of language without full context, so it makes content moderation decisions that require understanding language and cultural complexity. In addition, platforms need to routinely assess and study the effects of AI-powered hate speech detection on online discourse, freedom of expression and social cohesion. Tracking systematic audits, evaluations, and user feedback mechanisms helps identify when unintended things happen so platforms can continuously refine their moderation rules and procedures. (Wu, 2024)

Cultural Contexts and Nuanced Understanding

Hate speech identification and mitigation-based solutions based on artificial intelligence (AI) serve unique challenges due to the varying cultural and societal contexts of hate speech. In context, the parameters of what constitutes hate speech differ widely by community, place, and culture so a nuanced and situational understanding is required in an automatic moderation system. Such perceptions of hate speech are heavily influenced by cultural and linguistic nuances. A term or expression considered innocuous in one cultural setting may be deeply wounded or incendiary in another one. Historical, political, and social contexts surrounding hate speech can highly influence its meaning and impact. Therefore, to be able to accurately identify hate speech in a wide variety of incidents, AI systems need to be trained in varying datasets that reflect the diversity and complexity of cultural expressions and social dynamics. In addition, the power and privilege dynamics built into societal institutions can influence the nature and effects of hate speech between groups.

Marginalised communities, often lacking either systemic power or mainstream representation, may face a double injustice from hate speech, being subjected to hate speech, and suffering its negative consequences to a greater degree. However, moderation systems should grapple with power relations and prioritise the protection of the most vulnerable while avoiding the entrenchment of existing inequities.

While there is undoubtedly a degree of understanding required here, this is complexity that cannot be addressed simply through classification based on the words used. It can come in the form of hate speech which can be direct threats or derogatory language, or less direct forms of hate speech such as discrimination or microaggressions. AI algorithms need to be adept at finding both overt hate speech, as well as more subtle, insidious versions that are not easily caught by traditional methods.

Perceptions of hate speech, and the responses to it, may vary depending on cultural norms and sensitivities about religion, ethnicity, gender and sexuality. Systems that deploy AI for moderation also need to be designed more flexibly and agile than they have to be to avoid imposing one-size-fits-all answers that could inadvertently stamp out valid expressions of dissent or cultural identity. Addressing the complexities of hate speech detection within cultural contexts requires a collaborative multidisciplinary approach.

To design culturally aware moderation systems, AI engineers have to interact with linguists, sociologists, anthropologists and community representatives — professionals whose work reflects the richness of human expression and experience. Moreover, platforms should prioritize diversity and inclusion in their content moderation teams to ensure that moderators possess the necessary cultural competency and sensitivity to effectively navigate complex cultural dynamics. In addition, ongoing discussions with communities affected by potential moderation systems need to ensure that AI-driven moderation systems work following the norms values and expectations of the community. The platforms need to be set in place mechanisms for collecting user feedback and incorporating community efforts to develop and refine hate speech detection algorithms. (Mittal & Panchal 2023)

Responsibilities of Stakeholders

The use of artificial intelligence (AI) to detect hate speech requires multiple stakeholders, including AI developers, platform operators, policymakers, and society at large, to share responsibility. For AI-based moderation systems to work effectively on the complexities of hate speech, while upholding ethical goals and fundamental rights, stakeholders have to play their respective roles. It is the responsibility of AI developers to design algorithms that focus on fairness, transparency, and accountability. Algorithmic bias has been reported in the literature and proactive steps must be enacted, such as ensuring diversity and representativeness in training datasets and designing algorithms that are resistant to discriminatory outcomes. It is even more important for developers to focus on the interpretability of AI models so that users can understand how decisions are made, and challenge biased outcomes. They play a key role in implementing and enforcing content moderation policies that seek to counter hate speech while ensuring free expression rights. Hate speech detection and moderation need to be preceded by clear, transparent guidelines so users know precisely what constitutes hate speech and what happens if the platform rules are violated. (22) Moreover, platforms should devote resources to human moderation that will supplement AI-powered systems in adding context, nuance, and informed judgment to all moderation decisions. Regulations and policies need to be adopted by policymakers that make it possible to deploy AI responsibly but do not compromise on fundamental rights and values.

Legal frameworks should ensure the use of AI in content moderation is transparent, accountable, and user centred. These stakeholders should work together to construct an ethical framework which can help guide the industry towards a more holistic approach to addressing challenges surrounding AI-driven hate speech detection. Finally, it is up to society to cultivate a culture of accountability and ethical responsibility when it comes to the development and use of AI-driven moderation systems. Citizens must also ensure that platform operators and policymakers are held to ethical standards and respect individual rights and freedoms. This is where civil society organisations and advocacy groups come into play — in educating society about the possible outcomes of AI-driven hate speech detection. They can also promote policies that prioritize fairness, transparency and accountability.

Transparency and Accountability

Transparency and accountability are the important principles that pose the groundwork for the general development and utilization of artificial intelligence (AI) inside the scope of hate speech recognition. Fortune AI-powered moderation systems are endangering online discourse, freedom of expression and social norms. So, these systems must work in a way that is safe, fair, and accountable. About hate speech detection algorithms, platforms and AI developers should be transparent in terms of the design, implementation and operation of the algorithms. This means providing users with clear and understandable information about how hate speech detection algorithms work, the criteria used to identify and moderate hate speech, and any limitations or potential biases that may exist within these algorithms. Such transparency promotes trust and accountability and helps users understand and evaluate the content moderation decisions. (Mittal 2023)

Moreover, platforms should implement processes that enable users to appeal moderation decisions and provide input on the effectiveness of hate speech detection algorithms. User feedback plays a crucial role in identifying and mitigating issues like false positives, bias, and unintended consequences, helping platforms refine their moderation policies and practices over time. Moreover, program adherence to the outcomes of user appeals and actions taken in response to user concerns must be reported transparently, demonstrating a commitment to accountability and responsiveness. In addition, systems of accountability should also not just cover platforms but also AI developers who design algorithms centred around fairness, accuracy and ethics. To do so AI developers must execute regular reviews and challenges of hate speech detection algorithms to measure their effectiveness, find and solve biases, and ensure compliance with applicable laws and regulations. Furthermore, developers should focus on providing clarity about the methods and data used to train hate speech detection models so that the algorithmic decisions can be validated by external parties. Policymakers play a crucial role in developing regulatory frameworks that promote responsible deployment of AI, as well as ensuring transparency and accountability at both the level of platforms and developers. Accordingly, lawmakers should create laws and regulations requiring platforms to disclose information about their hate speech detection algorithms. This includes criteria for classifying content, the impact of moderation decisions on the accounts and content of users, and the strategies used to address algorithmic bias and error. Moreover, policymakers need to embed oversight mechanisms to track compliance with transparency and accountability standards and hold platforms and developers accountable for ethical breaches or violations. (Raihan 2023)

Using artificial intelligence (AI) to detect hate speech is an important step toward building safer, more inclusive online spaces. Employment of AI technologies helps platforms more efficiently identify and prevent malicious speech, promoting respectful discussion and protecting people from the detrimental effects of hate speech. Integrating AI into moderation raises ethical issues that need consideration to ensure the robustness, fairness, and accountability of these systems.

CONCLUSION

This chapter discussed some of the ethical implications concerning hate speech detection using AI, such as algorithmic bias, free speech concerns, privacy, unintended consequences, cultural contexts and responsibilities of stakeholders of social media. The issues pointed out refer to the need for a more gradient and delicate consideration for hate-speech detection while preserving basic rights and values. Algorithmic bias is a considerable ethical concern in hate speech detection in AI-driven models. Algorithms with bias can also reinforce and amplify current social prejudices, leading to disproportionate levels of censorship and enforcement against certain individuals or groups. It requires a multi-faceted approach which prioritizes the diversity and representativeness of training datasets, transparency in the configurations of the algorithms and constant scrutiny and refinement of the models.

This creates a tricky balancing act between tackling hate speech and protecting the right to free expression rights. Hate speech is poison for an inclusive Internet, but so is censorship and moderation, free speech is a core tenet of a thriving democracy. Social media platforms will need to navigate this tension because they increasingly have content moderation policies that aim to mitigate harmful speech while taking care not to infringe on the rights of individuals to freely express themselves. One of the most alarming privacy issues that comes with the utilization of AI-based hate speech detection systems. The aggregation and analysis of user-generated content raises significant privacy risks, including the potential for unwarranted surveillance, exposure to data theft, and disclosure of sensitive personal details. Platforms must include adequate safeguards, transparency, and options for user control to protect user's privacy and data. The perverse effects of hastily implemented AI-based hate speech detection technologies, such as censorship, chilling effects of speech, and the status quo bias they may inadvertently cement emphasize the urgency of thoughtful and cautious deployment and prevention plans. The stakeholders of the social media systems (platforms, developers, policymakers, and society) have a collective responsibility to build AI systems that are robust, ethical, and non-discriminatory.

By exploring ethical issues, and practical problems arising from using AI for content moderation, this chapter mirrored the rich and complex ways of social media influence and hate speech regarding AI, if any. A closer look at understanding what hate speech entails, how it spreads like wildfire on social media and how these platforms have become the main channels for influencing opinions and behaviour.

This chapter described how AI is used to detect hate speech through machine learning algorithms and advanced text processing. The chapter included examples of AI-based moderation systems used by companies like Facebook, Twitter and YouTube. It covered hate speech, including how it is perceived, the impact of hate speech, and the complicated policy issues around it in a contemporary context. It has its genesis in limiting hate speech as expression (oral, written or symbolic) aimed at denigrating the status of any group under its race, religion or sexual orientation. By scaling up hate speech talk to three macro-level dimensions: targeted categories (some hate speech targets are more privileged than others.), The content and intent; and finally types of hate speech (this one may be more contextual), the chapter demonstrated how hate is practised across different economic and intersectional vectors in a world that is significantly much more digital today than say the past.

The chapter also looked at hate speech as a legal category and a consideration of laws worldwide that differ dramatically when it comes to this issue. Ex-banned countries (no free speech) on one end, (free speech) free for all at the other end, illustrating how nuanced the conversation is surrounding where one draws the line between rights and expression vs harm. It even highlighted the social harm of hate speech which can lead to lower social cohesion, bring psychological harm or foster violent behaviour and thus have certain gross societal implications.

The chapter also contains an elaborate depiction of challenges in contesting hate speech, as well as constitutional boundaries of free speech, and protective individual/community interests. It surveyed the fundamental role of hate speech in democracy and the difficulty of tracking hate speech because they are disseminated by digital platforms. The last part of the chapter offered policy guidance on how to limit hate speech, including both legal methods analyses, and also education & platform strategy. The chapter is a pledge to ensure a transparent, community-led and balanced environment while holding on to our commitment to the co-production of fairer practice and rights preservation. (Khan et al. 2016). This chapter has shared some important research and insights about hate speech and why we urgently need to hold digital platforms to account more effectively.

But, it says, as promising as AI is for stemming the tide of systemic hate speech, that will only be true if developers are working alongside platform operators and policymakers to make sure the tools aren't dividing people or stripping them of fundamental rights. Due to the complexity of this domain, ongoing evaluation, interdisciplinary collaboration and a commitment to transparency and accountability are critical to ensuring responsible use of AI.

REFERENCES

Binns, R. (2018). Algorithmic content moderation: Technical and political challenges in the automation of platform governance. *Big Data & Society*, 5(1). Advance online publication. DOI: 10.1177/2053951718757253

Binns, R. (2018). Fairness in Machine Learning: Lessons from Political Philosophy. *Proceedings of the 2018 Conference on Fairness, Accountability, and Transparency*, 149-158.

Dwoskin, E. (2021, March 1). Social media platforms under fire for AI moderation failures. The Washington Post. https://www.washingtonpost.com

Floridi, L. (2018). Soft Ethics, Artificial Intelligence, and the Governance of the Digital. *Philosophy & Technology*, 31(4), 1–14. DOI: 10.1007/s13347-018-0303-9

Floridi, L., Cowls, J., Beltrametti, M., Chatila, R., Chazerand, P., Dignum, V., Luetge, C., Madelin, R., Pagallo, U., Rossi, F., Schafer, B., Valcke, P., & Vayena, E. (2018). AI4People—An ethical framework for a good AI society: Opportunities, risks, principles, and recommendations. *Minds and Machines*, 28(4), 689–707. DOI: 10.1007/s11023-018-9482-5 PMID: 30930541

Gillespie, T. (2018). *Custodians of the Internet: Platforms, content moderation, and the hidden decisions that shape social media*. Yale University Press., DOI: 10.12987/9780300235029

González, J.. (2021). Algorithmic Bias and Its Impact on the Detection of Hate Speech. *Journal of Digital Ethics*, 3(2), 58–73.

Grimmelmann, J. (2015). *The Virtues of Moderation: A Handbook for Content Moderators*. Yale Law Review.

Kaplan, J. M., & Peters, B. (2021). *Algorithmic Bias and the Future of AI Ethics*. MIT Press.

Khan, S., Lehtinen, E., & Zaman, R. (2016). Hate Speech and the Law: A Comparative Study of Legal Approaches to Hate Speech Regulation in the United States and Europe. In Gagliardone, P., Pohjonen, M., & Beyene, S. (Eds.), *Hate Speech Online: A Global Perspective* (pp. 157–182). Cambridge University Press., DOI: 10.1017/9781108371674.009

McGregor, J. (2020). The Ethics of AI in Content Moderation: Balancing Innovation and Responsibility. *Journal of Social Media Studies*.

Mittal, U. (2023). *AI based Evaluation System for mitigating Supply Chain Risk. Authorea Preprints*. DOI: 10.22541/essoar.170224570.06055229/v1

Mittal, U. (2023, August). Detecting Hate Speech Utilizing Deep Convolutional Network and Transformer Models. In *2023 International Conference on Electrical, Electronics, Communication and Computers (ELEXCOM)* (pp. 1-4). IEEE.

Mittal, U., & Panchal, D. (2023). AI-based evaluation system for supply chain vulnerabilities and resilience amidst external shocks: An empirical approach. *Reports in Mechanical Engineering*, 4(1), 276–289. DOI: 10.31181/rme040122112023m

Mozur, P. (2018, October 15). A genocide incited on Facebook, with posts from Myanmar's military. *The New York Times*. https://www.nytimes.com/2018/10/15/technology/myanmar-facebook-genocide.html

Raihan, A. (2023). A comprehensive review of artificial intelligence and machine learning applications in energy sector. *Journal of Technology Innovations and Energy*, 2(4), 1–26. DOI: 10.56556/jtie.v2i4.608

Shadbolt, N., & Williams, C. (2019). The Ethical Dimensions of Artificial Intelligence in Content Moderation. *AI & Society*, 34(4), 751–764.

Stanford Human-Centered Artificial Intelligence (HAI). (2022). *Ethics and effectiveness of AI in moderating online hate speech*. Stanford University. https://hai.stanford.edu

West, D. M. (2019). *How to regulate AI-driven hate speech moderation: Policy recommendations for a global approach*. The Brookings Institution. https://www.brookings.edu

Wu, Y. (2024). Critical Thinking Pedagogics Design in an Era of ChatGPT and Other AI Tools—Shifting From Teaching "What" to Teaching "Why" and "How". *Journal of Education and Development*, 8(1), 1. DOI: 10.20849/jed.v8i1.1404

Zou, J., Schiebinger, L., & Hurst, S. (2018). AI and the Future of Work: Addressing Bias and Inequality. *AI & Society*, 33(1), 159–170.

Chapter 18

Thread and Threat of AI: Analyzing Social Implications of Fake News and Hate Speech on Social Media Platforms in India

Aiswaria G. Shajan
https://orcid.org/0000-0002-0230-5989
Central Institute of Indian Languages, India

ABSTRACT

The rapid expansion of social media has transformed global communication and information sharing, fostering unprecedented connectivity. However, these platforms have also become hubs for the spread of fake news and hate speech, which threatens social cohesion. This article explores AI's dual role in combating fake news and hate speech on social media platforms in India. While AI offers promising solutions for detecting and reducing harmful content, it raises ethical and social concerns that may aggravate existing societal tensions. The analysis emphasizes the need for a balanced approach that effectively manages harmful content while preserving freedom of speech and avoiding excessive censorship. It also discusses the potential for AI to evolve into a more ethical, inclusive, and culturally sensitive tool within India's dynamic digital landscape, and highlights the importance of interdisciplinary collaboration among AI developers, policymakers, and social scientists to ensure that AI technologies serve both technological innovation and social equity.

DOI: 10.4018/979-8-3693-9904-0.ch018

1. INTRODUCTION

Artificial intelligence (AI) is a general-purpose technology that has existed since the early 1950s refers to a system designed with the help of various programs and electronic circuits, aimed at solving complex real-world problems more easily and efficiently. AI is expected to behave like a human, demonstrating intelligent behavior and responding spontaneously to different situations. A *social system* defines a structured set of relationships and interactions among individuals, groups, and institutions within a society, encompassing the roles, norms, values, and practices that govern social behavior and maintain societal order. *Social media*, as a digital platform, facilitates interactive communication, networking, and community building, enabling users to engage in real-time discussions and share personal or public information. Together, AI, social systems, and social media play integral roles in shaping modern communication, societal behaviors, and technological advancements. Artificial Intelligence (AI) and social media are increasingly intertwined in personal life, providing greater convenience and contributing to safer online spaces. However, while AI helps with content moderation by detecting harmful material such as hate speech and misinformation, it can sometimes go beyond convenience. The algorithms that power these platforms can lead to addictive behaviors, making social media usage difficult to avoid and, at times, causing negative effects on users' well-being. This dual impact—both beneficial and harmful—raises concerns about finding a balance between the positive aspects of AI and the potential negative consequences it may have on individuals and society.

Major among these potential negative consequences are the issues of fake news and hate speech, which can have significant societal impacts. Although fake news and hate speech have existed throughout human history, their nature and reach have changed drastically. According to Lea Bander and Jochen Bender (2022), *the emergence of social media has changed how, where and with what effects fake news and hate speech occur.* Nowadays, fake news and hate speech are becoming more prevalent on social media. Usually, *fake news* is defined as false or misleading information presented as news, often with the intention of deceiving or manipulating public opinion. It is harmful because it distorts the truth, misinforms the public, and undermines trust in credible sources of information. As for *hate speech*, it refers to any form of communication that incites or promotes hatred, violence, or discrimination against individuals or groups based on characteristics such as race, religion, ethnicity, gender, or sexual orientation. Hate speech is dangerous because it fosters intolerance, encourages discrimination, and can lead to social unrest or violence.

Understanding the phenomena of fake news and hate speech within India's diverse socio-political landscape is crucial, particularly when considered in the context of Artificial Intelligence (AI). With its vast and varied population—comprising numerous cultures, languages, religions, and political ideologies—India is highly susceptible to the rapid spread of misinformation and hate speech on social media platforms. In such a multifaceted society, even a small piece of fake news can easily amplify existing divisions, leading to widespread social unrest or violence. Given the deep-rooted social, political, and religious sensitivities, it is important to examine the socio-political and psychological impacts of AI-driven misinformation and hate speech on Indian society. These phenomena don't just undermine the credibility of information; they also deepen tensions between communities, disrupt social harmony, and erode trust in democratic processes. Without a proper understanding of these dynamics within India's specific context, AI-driven solutions may unintentionally exacerbate the situation, resulting in misinterpretations or the amplification of harmful content. Therefore, a comprehensive, context-aware approach is essential for designing AI solutions that account for India's complexity and mitigate negative consequences in an already polarized environment.

This chapter explores AI's dual role in combating fake news and hate speech on social media platforms in India. While AI offers promising solutions for detecting and reducing harmful content, it also raises ethical and social concerns that may aggravate existing societal tensions. The analysis emphasizes the need for a balanced approach that effectively manages harmful content while preserving freedom of speech and avoiding excessive censorship. It also discusses the potential for AI to evolve into a more ethical, inclusive, and culturally sensitive tool within India's dynamic digital landscape. It highlights the importance of interdisciplinary collaboration among AI developers, policymakers, and social scientists to ensure that AI technologies serve both technological innovation and social equity. However, the effectiveness of India's current legal, policy, and regulatory frameworks in combating the threats posed by AI-driven content on social media requires rigorous evaluation and study to ensure these measures meet the country's unique challenges effectively. It is essential to understand both the positive (thread) and negative implications (threat) of AI on social media platforms, particularly in terms of its potential benefits and impacts.

Methodology

The chapter adopts a multidisciplinary approach, utilizing content analysis, case studies, and qualitative interviews with social media users, policymakers, and AI ethics experts. The content analysis aims to identify patterns in the dissemination of fake news and hate speech by examining posts, comments, and interactions on various social media platforms. Case studies of significant incidents involving violence triggered by social media will provide a deeper understanding of the socio-political and cultural consequences. Additionally, qualitative interviews with social media users and with key stakeholders will offer insights into the challenges and opportunities associated with AI regulation, ethical considerations, and policy development in India's digital landscape.

2. AI: THREAD AND THREAT

Artificial Intelligence (AI) has revolutionized various aspects of human life, and social media platforms are no exception. From personalizing user experiences to moderating content, AI has become an integral part of how social media operates. However, its integration also raises questions about privacy, bias, and societal impact. Artificial Intelligence (AI) has become a transformative force in social media, offering both advantages (thread) and challenges (threat).

2.1. Thread of AI in Social Media Platforms

One of the most significant benefits of AI in social media is (1) *content personalization*. AI algorithms analyze user behavior, preferences, and interaction patterns to curate personalized feeds, enhancing user engagement. For instance, platforms like Instagram and TikTok suggest content tailored to individual interests, keeping users connected to what they enjoy most. AI also plays a vital role in (2) *enhancing communication*. Chatbots and virtual assistants powered by AI facilitate seamless interactions between businesses and users. On platforms like Facebook Messenger, automated responses ensure faster and more efficient customer support. Another major advantage is (3) *better content moderation*. AI systems are trained to detect and remove harmful, inappropriate, or spam content, contributing to safer online spaces. For example, platforms like Twitter and YouTube use AI to flag hate speech, misinformation, or explicit material, often before it reaches a broader audience. In the business realm, AI provides (4). *advanced analytics* for understanding user behavior, enabling brands to refine their marketing strategies. Social media platforms such as LinkedIn and Meta provide AI-powered tools that target specific audiences, enhancing the effectiveness of advertising campaigns. Additionally, AI-powered features like automatic captions, language translations, and text-to-speech options have greatly increased the (5). *accessibility* of social media, making it more inclusive for users with diverse needs. AI also excels in (6). *trend analysis*, tracking emerging topics and conversations across platforms. This capability helps brands and individuals stay relevant in dynamic online environments, leveraging trends to connect with broader audiences.

2.2. Threat of AI in Social Media Platforms

Despite its numerous advantages, AI in social media is not without drawbacks. One major concern is the creation of *echo chambers* and *polarization*. AI algorithms, designed to show users content they are likely to engage with, often reinforce existing beliefs, leading to limited exposure to diverse perspectives. This can intensify political or social divisions, as users remain confined to their ideological bubbles. *Privacy concerns* are another significant issue. AI systems collect and process vast amounts of user data, raising the risk of misuse or breaches. Targeted advertising, while effective, often feels intrusive, as it is based on personal information gathered without explicit consent. Additionally, AI has a dual role in the *spread of misinformation*. While it is used to detect and counter fake news, the same algorithms can inadvertently amplify false information by prioritizing viral content. This phenomenon undermines trust in online platforms and contributes to the rapid dissemination of inaccuracies. The increasing reliance on AI also leads to *job displacement*. Automated moderation and support systems reduce the need for human employees, affecting job opportunities in these areas. Moreover, *The Emerging Threat of AI-driven Cyber Attacks: A Review (2022)* highlights that the growing sophistication of cyberattack techniques poses a significant threat to enterprises, essential services, and organizational infrastructures, with the potential to disrupt operations, delete critical data, and inflict severe reputational damage.

Furthermore, AI-driven content optimization can exacerbate *addiction and mental health issues*. Algorithms designed to maximize engagement often encourage excessive screen time, leading to phenomena like doom scrolling and unhealthy comparisons fueled by curated content. Finally, AI systems can exhibit *bias in algorithms*, as they are trained on data that may reflect societal prejudices. This can result in unequal treatment or representation of certain groups, as seen in cases where content from minority communities is unfairly flagged or underrepresented.

3. CASE STUDIES: THE IMPACT OF FAKE NEWS AND HATE SPEECH IN INDIA

The proliferation of fake news and hate speech has emerged as a significant challenge in India, fueled by the widespread use of social media platforms and the rapid digitization of information dissemination. This section explores prominent case studies that highlight the societal, political, religious and legal implications of these phenomena.

For example, (1) a notable example of fake news that has been revived and widely circulated in recent years is the image of a Dalit family's naked protest. Originally taken in 2015, the photograph showed a Dalit family from Uttar Pradesh protesting against caste-based violence by marching naked to demand justice. The image captured national attention at the time, highlighting the social injustices faced by the Dalit community. However, in 2020, the same image was falsely revived and circulated on social media, with misleading claims that the protest had taken place in Karnataka. The image was shared widely on WhatsApp, Facebook, and Twitter with captions that sought to create a narrative of caste-based violence and oppression in Karnataka. This revival of an old image led to widespread misinformation, with people believing that the incident had occurred recently, exacerbating tensions in the state. Fact-checking organizations quickly debunked the claims, confirming that the image was not from Karnataka, but from a protest in Uttar Pradesh in 2015. Despite the clarification, the viral spread of the false claims led to widespread confusion, further reinforcing the power of fake news to manipulate public perception and create unnecessary social rifts. This case highlights how old images or events can be misrepresented and revived for political or communal purposes. It underscores the importance of fact-checking and digital literacy in combating the spread of fake news and the role of social media platforms in taking swift action to prevent such misinformation from spreading.

(2). The other one is another example of fake news comes from a misleading claim about a video showing two Hindu men being burnt alive. The video, which originally circulated with the false narrative that it was from Bangladesh, showed a violent incident. It was quickly shared with alarming captions on social media platforms, claiming that two Hindu men were being burnt alive in Bangladesh, and that the act was a part of ongoing religious persecution. However, BoomLive, a fact-checking organization, identified the video as an old one, originally filmed in 2015, showing a different incident that had no connection to the claims being circulated. The video had been misrepresented to appear as though it was related to an anti-Hindu attack. Fact-checkers revealed that the video had been shot during a Halloween celebration in China, not in Bangladesh, and that it was completely unrelated to any religious violence. This incident further demonstrates how videos and images from unrelated contexts can be repurposed and falsely associated with current events to incite fear, hatred, and confusion. The spreading of such fabricated narratives can cause unnecessary panic, especially when they involve sensitive issues like religious persecution or violence. Fact-checking efforts exposed the truth, and the video was debunked, helping prevent a potential crisis. However, the viral nature of the video in the first place showcases the dangers of misinformation and the need for vigilance in the digital age. Users must be cautious and verify such claims before accepting or sharing them, particularly when they involve grave accusations like violence or hate crimes.

(3) Likewise, the news on COVID-19. Katharina Buchholz (2021) in her article stated that, surge of fake news on COVID-19 washed over India. A scientific study conducted by doctors from Rochester, New York, and Pune, India, revealed that approximately 30 percent of Indians relied on WhatsApp for COVID-19 information, with nearly the same percentage fact-checking less than half of the messages before forwarding them. The key point here is that as AI evolves into a more powerful tool for malicious actors, cyber security researchers, practitioners, and governments will need to develop increasingly innovative solutions to effectively protect cyberspace from such threats (Hamadah & Aqel, 2020). Fake news and hate speech are not confined to isolated incidents; they often extend to unethical attacks on individuals and minority communities within a nation. These actions disrupt communal harmony, infringe on individual privacy, and pose significant threats to the economic growth and stability of a country. As these issues continue to evolve, it is crucial to understand how different demographics perceive them, especially in the context of emerging technologies like artificial intelligence (AI). According to the data analyzed through a survey conducted with 100 informants, awareness and concern about hate speech, fake news, and regulation vary significantly across age groups. Younger individuals (18-35) display higher awareness of these issues, with the 26-35 group being the most aware in both areas. This age group also shows more concern about regulation, with a peak in concern about regulation at 45% in the 36-45 group. In contrast, older age groups, particularly those above 45, demonstrate much lower awareness and concern, with the oldest group (above 55) showing no awareness at all.

The data further suggests that younger generations are more engaged with digital media and issues related to misinformation, which may explain their heightened awareness of these issues and their greater concern for regulatory measures. This trend extends to the perception of AI on social media, where younger people tend to be more aware of AI's role, viewing it as either a positive development or a potential threat. Older individuals, however, seem less attuned to these concerns, highlighting a generational divide in how technological advancements, such as AI, are understood and interacted with. These findings emphasize the need for targeted strategies to address the concerns of each age group, particularly in fostering awareness and understanding of the impact of AI and misinformation on social media. As we navigate these challenges, it's clear that bridging the awareness gap across generations will be essential for building a more informed and cohesive society. If so, then what measures can a government implement to effectively address and control these issues? A comprehensive regulatory framework and clear policies need to be implemented to effectively address these challenges.

4. REGULATORY FRAMEWORK AND POLICY RESPONSE

The advent of artificial intelligence (AI) has revolutionized the creation and dissemination of information. While AI offers numerous benefits, it also poses significant challenges, particularly in spreading misinformation and hate speech. Social media platforms, empowered by AI tools, have become conduits for harmful content, leading to severe consequences for societal harmony and public order. In India, addressing these issues has become a pressing concern, prompting the development of legal and regulatory mechanisms to curb their proliferation.

According to the article *India's Advance on AI Regulation* (2024), more than thirty AI-related laws were passed in over a hundred countries in 2022 alone. The launch of ChatGPT in late 2022 is often regarded as a pivotal moment in the evolution of technology, bringing generative AI into mainstream attention. This development raised significant concerns about bias, misinformation, copyright violations, and its potential impact on labor markets. These concerns are attributed to a convergence of key factors: groundbreaking advancements in machine learning, the new capabilities of large language models, and the global influence of social media. These developments have intensified fears among policymakers and led to the introduction of new regulations in several countries.

In addition to addressing these broader concerns, one of the primary objectives of India's regulatory framework is to combat fake news and hate speech. Misinformation and hate speech on platforms like WhatsApp, Twitter, and Facebook have contributed to violence and social unrest in India (Chinmayi Arun, 2019). As concerns about misinformation grow, questions have been raised regarding the effectiveness of current fact-checking initiatives. In response, WhatsApp has introduced voluntary third-party fact-checking systems and implemented restrictions on bulk messaging. These actions aim to limit the ease with which users can forward content to large groups, reducing the spread of harmful information. Similarly, Facebook launched its third-party fact-checking program in Karnataka in 2018, later expanding it to other states across India. The platform has also collaborated with independent organizations to combat misinformation in 11 Indian languages. However, critics point to significant shortcomings, including the inefficiency of Facebook's partner fact-checking organizations and the platform's failure to properly address flagged content. These issues undermine the effectiveness of its fact-checking programs, allowing harmful content to persist.

To address the issue of misinformation and hate speech, India has implemented various legal and regulatory mechanisms that balance the promotion of free speech with the need to maintain public order. The Indian government has enacted several legal provisions and initiatives to address harmful content. The Information Technology (IT) Act, 2000, under Section 69A, grants the government the authority to block online content that threatens national security or public order. Additionally, the Intermediary Guidelines and Digital Media Ethics Code, 2021, mandate that social media platforms remove unlawful content promptly, appoint grievance officers, and publish compliance reports. The Indian Penal Code (IPC), 1860, includes provisions such as Section 153A, which prohibits acts promoting enmity between groups, Section 295A, which punishes acts intended to outrage religious feelings, and Section 505(1), which penalizes statements that incite public mischief. The Election Commission enforces strict guidelines under the Representation of the People Act, 1951, to counter misinformation during elections, collaborating with social media platforms to remove fake news and propaganda. Fact-checking initiatives, such as the Press Information Bureau's Fact Check Unit and the Cyber Coordination Centre (CyCord), address misinformation and cybercrimes, including the spread of fake news and hate speech. Social media platforms also engage in self-regulation, using AI-based tools for content moderation and enforcing community guidelines. Furthermore, Indian courts have actively interpreted laws and directed social media platforms to take corrective measures in cases involving hate speech and misinformation.

Despite these laws and regulations, the persistence of harmful content is still a significant issue due to several challenges and limitations in their effectiveness

4.1. Challenges and Limitations of the Regulatory Framework and Policy Response

- **Inconsistent Enforcement:** Although regulatory frameworks have been established, enforcement remains inconsistent. The sheer volume of content uploaded to social media platforms makes it challenging to track and regulate harmful material effectively. Limited resources and technical challenges hinder the rapid identification and removal of such content.
- **Jurisdictional Issues:** Social media platforms operate globally, making it difficult to enforce national laws. Content may be hosted on servers located outside the country, complicating efforts to address harmful material. Furthermore, users can bypass local restrictions using tools like VPNs, undermining national regulations.
- **Lack of Platform Accountability:** Social media platforms often benefit from legal protections, such as Section 79 of the IT Act, which shields them from responsibility for user-generated content. This immunity results in reluctance to take decisive action against harmful content unless specifically flagged, leaving loopholes for misuse.
- **AI and Automation Limitations:** Although AI-based tools are used for content moderation, they are not infallible. These tools can struggle to detect

context-dependent or nuanced harmful content. Human intervention is often required but is difficult to scale across the vast amount of content being posted.

- **Balancing Regulation with Free Speech:** Striking the right balance between regulating harmful content and protecting free speech remains a challenge. Over-regulation could stifle legitimate expression and debate, creating tension between safeguarding online safety and upholding individual freedoms.
- **Anonymity and Pseudonymity:** Many social media platforms allow users to remain anonymous or use fake identities, making it easier to spread fake news and engage in harmful behavior without facing consequences. The lack of a robust identity verification system complicates accountability efforts.
- **Algorithmic Bias and Amplification:** Social media platforms' algorithms often prioritize engaging content, which can include sensationalized or misleading material. These algorithms can amplify harmful content, creating echo chambers where users are primarily exposed to information that reinforces their beliefs, thus exacerbating misinformation and hate speech.
- **User Resistance and Lack of Awareness:** Some users continue to spread misinformation or hate speech due to ideological motives or simply for attention. The ease with which false information spreads, combined with a lack of awareness about the harm it causes, contributes to the persistence of these issues.

Despite these efforts, significant challenges remain in effectively combating the spread of harmful content. One key issue is the ambiguity of laws, such as Section 69A of the IT Act, which is broad and unclear, potentially leading to overreach and misuse. Additionally, the rapid pace of technological advancements, especially in AI technologies like deep fakes, often outpaces existing legal frameworks, leaving regulators ill-equipped to address emerging threats. Together, these challenges highlight the limitations of current regulatory frameworks, emphasizing the need for clearer laws, better technological adaptation, and more robust oversight to effectively tackle misinformation and hate speech. There is an urgent need for a dynamic and comprehensive regulatory framework that can address the constantly evolving landscape of misinformation in the digital age.

4.2. Recommendations for Improvement

To address these challenges, India should consider the following measures to create a comprehensive and adaptive regulatory framework:

- **Clearer Legislation and Guidelines:** The government should develop and implement more precise laws that clearly define harmful content and the responsibilities of online platforms. These laws should balance the need to curb misinformation while protecting free speech.
- **Enhanced Content Moderation and AI Integration:** Platforms should invest in advanced AI and machine learning technologies to improve content moderation, ensuring better detection of misinformation and hate speech. AI tools should support human moderators, as nuanced judgment is often required.
- **Stronger Accountability for Social Media Platforms:** Platforms should be held accountable for the content they host. This includes actively monitoring content, removing harmful material promptly, and ensuring transparency in content moderation practices.
- **Collaboration Between Governments and Tech Companies:** Governments and tech companies must work together to develop strategies for combating misinformation. This could include standardized reporting mechanisms, sharing data on the effectiveness of anti-misinformation measures, and creating cross-border policies.
- **Improved User Education and Awareness:** Platforms should invest in educating users about the dangers of misinformation and how to spot it. Digital literacy programs can empower users to critically assess information, reducing the spread of fake news.
- **Fostering International Cooperation:** Misinformation often crosses national borders, making international cooperation essential. Governments and tech companies should collaborate to share best practices, harmonize laws, and tackle cross-border misinformation campaigns.
- **Stronger Identity Verification Systems:** Platforms should implement robust identity verification systems to reduce anonymity and hold users accountable for spreading fake news and harmful content.
- **Encouraging Self-Regulation with Oversight:** Social media platforms should have strong self-regulatory mechanisms in place, with external oversight. Third-party audits or independent fact-checking organizations can ensure that platforms adhere to their moderation guidelines.
- **Promoting Ethical Algorithm Design:** Social media platforms should revise their algorithms to prioritize credible, well-sourced content over sensational or misleading material. They should also be transparent about how algorithms operate and reduce bias and misinformation amplification.
- **Expedited Legal Processes for Harmful Content:** Governments should establish mechanisms to swiftly address legal complaints related to harmful

content. This includes improving processes for removing illegal content and ensuring that harmful material does not remain online for extended periods.

By evolving its legal and regulatory mechanisms, India can better address the challenges posed by AI-driven misinformation and hate speech while upholding the principles of free expression.

CONCLUSION

This chapter has highlighted the profound impact of Artificial Intelligence (AI) on social media in India, particularly its role in combating the spread of fake news and hate speech. The findings underscore the complexity of navigating AI's dual influence—both as a tool for moderating harmful content and as a potential driver of societal challenges. As AI continues to shape the digital landscape, it is essential to prioritize ongoing research and foster dialogue among stakeholders, including policymakers, AI developers, and social scientists, to better understand and address these challenges.

Future policy initiatives must be informed by the need for a balanced approach that ensures the preservation of freedom of speech while mitigating the negative consequences of misinformation and hate speech. Moreover, research efforts should focus on developing AI solutions that are ethically sound, culturally sensitive, and tailored to the unique socio-political context of India. In doing so, it is crucial to create a digital environment that upholds truth, promotes inclusivity, and advances social equity, all while adapting to the rapid pace of technological change. By doing so, we can build a more responsible and harmonious digital future.

REFERENCES

https://www.tableau.com/data-insights/ai/history

https://hai.stanford.edu/news/2023-state-ai-14-charts

https://economictimes.indiatimes.com/magazines/panache/facebook-teams-up-with-8-third-party-fact-checkers-covering-11-indian-languages-to-flag-covid-19-fake news/articleshow/75284845.cms

https://economictimes.indiatimes.com/tech/internet/its-up-to-facebook-to-respond-on-its-fact-checking-programme-says-fb-after-it-minister-raises-concerns/ articleshow/77895695.cms

https://www.statista.com/chart/25031/covid-19-misinformation-on-whatsapp-india

https://scroll.in/latest/918725/whatsapp-launches-new-fact-checking-service-to-fight-fake-news-ahead-of-elections

https://www.boomlive.in/fact-check/bangladesh-video-two-hindu-men-burnt-alive-old-video-halloween-china-27235

https://www.boomlive.in/fast-check/karnataka-dalit-family-naked-touching-temple-idol-fake-news-gautam-budh-nagar-uttar-pradesh-stripped-protest-19379

https://www.businesstoday.in/current/economy-politics/facebook-partners-with-afp-to-expand-fact-checking-programme-in-india/story/288651.html

https://www.oecd-ilibrary.org/deliver/fae2d1e6-en.pdf

https://www.statista.com/chart/25031/covid-19-misinformation-on-whatsapp-india/

https://www.tandfonline.com/doi/abs/10.1080/17579961.2023.2184135

https://www.tandfonline.com/doi/full/10.1080/08839514.2022.2037254#d1e195

https://ejournals.facultas.at/index.php/ocgcp/article/download/2144/1799

Arun, C. (2019, February). On WhatsApp, Rumours, Lynchings, and the Indian Government. *Economic and Political Weekly*.

Bader, L., & Bender, J. (2022). What is "fake news" and "hate speech" and how do they work in practice?. Central and Eastern European eDem and eGov Days, 342, 17-36.

Bapaye, J. A., & Bapaye, H. A. (2021, January 30). Demographic Factors Influencing the Impact of Corona virus-Related Misinformation on WhatsApp: Cross-sectional Questionnaire Study. *JMIR Public Health and Surveillance*, 7(1), e19858. DOI: 10.2196/19858 PMID: 33444152

Ertel, W. (2024). *Introduction to artificial intelligence*. Springer Nature.

Hamadah, S., & Aqel, D. (2020). Cybersecurity becomes smart using artificial intelligent and machine learning approaches: An overview. *ICIC Express Letters. Part B, Applications*, 11(12), 1115–1123. DOI: 10.24507/icicelb.11.12.1115

https://www.poynter.org/fact-checking/2018/in-one-month-facebook-doubled-the-countries-using-its-fact-checking-tool-%c2%97-all-outside-the-west/,PTI, *Facebook teams up with AFP to expand fact-checking programme in India,* Business Today (Nov. 6,2018)

APPENDIX

The Impact of Hate Speech and Fake News on Social Media

Questionnaire

The Impact of Hate Speech and Fake News on Social Media

Name: ....

Demographic Information: ....

1). Age:

Under 18 18-24 25-34 35-44 45-54 55 and above

2). Gender:

Male Female Other Prefer not to say

3). Location:

Urban Rural

4). What social media platforms do you regularly use? (Select all that apply)

Facebook Twitter Instagram WhatsApp TikTok YouTube

Others (Please specify) _________

5). Part 1: Awareness and Perception of Hate Speech

a). Have you encountered hate speech on social media? Yes No Not sure

b). What do you consider to be hate speech on social media? (Select all that apply)

Discriminatory language based on race, gender, or religion

Inciting violence or harm

Offensive comments targeting individuals or groups

Harassment and bullying

Other (Please specify) __________

c). How often do you come across hate speech on social media?

Frequently Occasionally Rarely Never

d). What do you think should be the consequence of spreading hate speech on social media?

Account suspension or ban Public apology No action needed

Other (Please specify) __________

e). Do you believe that social media platforms are doing enough to combat hate speech?

Yes No Not sure

6). Part 2: Awareness and Perception of Fake News

a) Have you ever encountered fake news on social media?

Yes No Not sure

b) How do you identify fake news on social media? (Select all that apply)

Sensational headlines

Lack of credible sources or references

Stories that seem too outrageous to be true

Misinformation shared by unreliable sources

Other (Please specify) __________

c) How often do you come across fake news on social media?

Frequently Occasionally Rarely Never

d) What actions do you take when you encounter fake news?

Ignore it Report it Share information to correct it

Discuss it with others other (Please specify) __________

e) Do you think fake news poses a significant threat to society?

Yes No Not sure

7). Part 3: General Opinion on Social Media Regulation

a). Do you think social media platforms should take more responsibility in controlling hate speech and fake news?

Yes No Not sure

b). What measures should be taken by social media platforms to prevent the spread of hate speech and fake news? (Select all that apply)

Stricter content moderation policies

More transparent algorithms

Improved fact-checking systems

User education and awareness campaigns

Other (Please specify) __________

c). Should users be held accountable for sharing fake news or hate speech on social media?

Yes No Not sure

8). Part 4: Awareness of Government Regulations and Policies and AI

a). Are you aware of any government regulations or policies that aim to control hate speech on social media?

Yes No Not sure

b). Have you heard about any recent laws or initiatives by the government to regulate social media content?

Yes No Not sure

c). In your opinion, how effective are the existing government policies in controlling hate speech on social media?

Very effective Somewhat effective Not effective Not sure

d). In your opinion, how effective are the existing government policies in controlling fake news on social media?

Very effective Somewhat effective Not effective Not sure

e). Do you believe that social media platforms should comply with government regulations to combat hate speech and fake news?

Yes No Not sure

f) Do you think the government should impose stricter regulations on social media platforms to prevent the spread of fake news and hate speech?

Yes No Not sure

g) Are you aware of any government body or agency responsible for monitoring hate speech and fake news on social media?

Yes No Not sure

h) Do you trust government regulations to protect users from harmful content on social media while maintaining freedom of expression?

Yes No Not sure

i) How important do you think it is for the government to regularly update policies regarding social media content to keep up with new trends and challenges?

Very important Somewhat important Not important Not sure

j) Are you aware that artificial intelligence (AI) is used to generate or spread fake news on social media?

Yes No Not sure

k) How knowledgeable are you about AI's role in detecting or preventing hate speech and fake news on social media?

Very knowledgeable Somewhat knowledgeable Not knowledgeable Not sure

l) Do you think AI can be used to create more convincing fake news or hate speech than humans can?

Yes No Not sure

m) In your opinion, do AI algorithms play a significant role in amplifying or spreading hate speech and fake news?

Yes No Not sure

n) Are you concerned about the potential misuse of AI to generate hate speech or fake news on social media platforms?

Yes No Not sure

o) Do you believe AI can be used to identify and filter out fake news or hate speech more effectively than human moderators?

Yes No Not sure

p) Do you think that AI systems, like bots or deep fakes, are contributing to the growing problem of misinformation and hate speech online?

Yes No Not sure

q) Have you heard of any initiatives or projects that use AI to combat hate speech and fake news on social media?

Yes No Not sure

r) In your opinion, how should AI is regulated to prevent its misuse in producing harmful content like hate speech or fake news?

Stricter government regulations on AI use
Ethical guidelines for AI developers
Transparency in AI algorithms
Collaboration between AI companies and government bodies
Other (Please specify) __________

Compilation of References

Abbas, A., & Torralba, A. (2024). Content moderation in the age of AI: Navigating the trade-offs between free speech and privacy. DOI: 10.13140/RG.2.2.33790.60486

Abedin, B., Meske, C., Junglas, I., Rabhi, F., & Motahari-Nezhad, H. R. (2022). Designing and managing human-AI interactions. *Information Systems Frontiers*, 24(3), 691–697. DOI: 10.1007/s10796-022-10313-1

Abeliansky, A., Algur, E., Bloom, D. E., & Prettner, K. (2020). The future of work: challenges for job creation due to global demographic change and automation.

Abhilasha, A., Sreenivasulu, A., & Manimozhi, T. KUMAR, P. S., Selvakumar, P., & Singh, P. (2022, April). The Model of Smart Sensing Device For Sensitive Nano-clusters Modification in Sensing Properties. In 2022 2nd International Conference on Advance Computing and Innovative Technologies in Engineering (ICACITE) (pp. 1043-1047). IEEE.

Abramovic B, Coleman G. (2021) "Decolonizing the Machine: Race, Gender and Disability in Robots and Algorithmic Art" Journal of Politics of the Machines, pp. 1-15.

AbuJarour, S., Qarariah, A., Saadeh, N., & Salem, M. (2024). *AI, Misinformation, and Fake News: A Literature Review of Ethical and Technical Approaches*. Finance and Law in the Metaverse World., DOI: 10.1007/978-3-031-67547-8_55

Adek, R. T., & Ula, M. (2021). Systematics review on the application of social media analytics for detecting radical and extremist group. *IOP Conference Series. Materials Science and Engineering*, 1096(1), 1–8. DOI: 10.1088/1757-899X/1071/1/012029

Afsha, S., Haque, M., & Nyeem, H. (2022). Machine learning models for content classification in film censorship and rating. *Proceedings of the 2022 International Conference on Innovations in Science, Engineering and Technology (ICISET)*, 396–401. DOI: 10.1109/ICISET54810.2022.9775816

Agerri, R., Garcia-Serrano, A., & García-Serrano, M. Á. (2020). AI-based HS Detection: A Survey. *Journal of Artificial Intelligence Research*, 68, 1–34.

Aggarwal, A., & Gaur, S. (2024). *Applying Artificial Intelligence to Explore Online Harassment Prevention*. IGI Global.

Ahmed, H., Traore, I., & Saad, S. (2018). Detecting opinion spams and fake news using text classification. *Security and Privacy*, 1(1), e9.

AI Ethics Lab. (2021). *Addressing Algorithmic Bias in Hate Speech Monitoring Systems*. AI Ethics Reports.

Ajewumi, O. E., Magbagbeola, V., Kalu, O. C., Ike, R. A., Folajimi, O., & Diyaolu, C. O. (2024). The impact of social media on mental health and well-being.

Aldwairi, M., & Alwahedi, A. (2018). Detecting fake news in social media networks. *Procedia Computer Science*, 141, 215–222.

Al-Ghamdi, L. M. (2021). *Towards Adopting AI Techniques for Monitoring Social Media Activities*. Sustainable Engineering and Innovation. DOI: 10.37868/sei.v3i1.121

Alikhani, M.. (2020). Low-Resource Hate Speech Detection: Challenges and Strategies. *Journal of Computational Social Science*.

Ali, W., & Zhang, H. (2021). Improving Real-Time Hate Speech Detection with Contextual Memory Networks. *Proceedings of the IJCAI Conference*.

Alkiviadou, N. (2018). *The legal regulation of hate speech: The international and European frameworks*. Politička Misao.

Aller, C. F., & Acuna, B. P. (2022). Facebook and Artificial Intelligence: A Review of Good Practices. *ResearchGate*. https://www.researchgate.net/publication/365275674_Facebook_and_Artificial_Intelligence_A_Review_of_Good_Practices

Alloghani, M., Al-Jumeily, D., Mustafina, J., Hussain, A., & Aljaaf, A. J. (2020). A Systematic Review on Supervised and Unsupervised Machine Learning Algorithms for Data Science. In Berry, M., Mohamed, A., & Yap, B. (Eds.), *Supervised and Unsupervised Learning for Data Science* (pp. 1–16). Springer., DOI: 10.1007/978-3-030-22475-2_1

Almeida, P., Santos, C. D., & Farias, J. S. (2021). Artificial Intelligence Regulation: a framework for governance. *ResearchGate*. https://www.researchgate.net/publication/351039094_Artificial_Intelligence_Regulation_a_framework_for_governance

Alorainy, W., Burnap, P., Liu, H., & Williams, M. L. (2019). Detecting hate speech automatically: Challenging the problem of offensive language in social media. *Journal of Computational Social Science*, 2(1), 125–139.

Alqodsi, E. M., & Gura, D. (2023). High tech and legal challenges: Artificial intelligence-caused damage regulation. *Cogent Social Sciences*, 9(2), 2270751. Advance online publication. DOI: 10.1080/23311886.2023.2270751

Amann, J., Blasimme, A., Vayena, E., Frey, D., & Madai, V. I. (2020). Explainability for artificial intelligence in healthcare: A multidisciplinary perspective. *BMC Medical Informatics and Decision Making*, 20(1), 1–9. DOI: 10.1186/s12911-020-01332-6 PMID: 33256715

Ambran, N. S., Zainodin, W. H. W., & Ali, M. N. M. (2024).AI Systems and Content Moderation Tiktok as a Digital Safety Platform in Shaping a Pleasant Environment: A Qualitative Approach. *My Jurnal*. https://myjurnal.mohe.gov.my/public/article-view.php?id=215683

Ananthajothi, K., & Meenakshi, R. (2024). *Promoting Positive Discourse: Advancing AI-Powered Content Moderation*. IEEE.

Ananthakrishnan, U. M., & Tucker, C. E. (2022). The drivers and virality of hate speech online. Available at *SSRN* 3793801.

Anderson, J., & Rainie, L. (2018, December 10). *Artificial Intelligence and the Future of Humans*. Pew Research Center; Pew Research Center. https://www.pewresearch.org/internet/2018/12/10/artificial-intelligence-and-the-future-of-humans/

Anderson, K., & Waxman, M. C. (2013). Law and ethics for autonomous weapon systems: Why a ban won't work and how the laws of war can.

Anderson, R., & Gilbert, S. (2022). Policy Brief The Online Safety Bill. *Bennett Institute for Public Policy*. https://www.bennettinstitute.cam.ac.uk/wp-content/uploads/2022/09/Policy-Brief-Online-Safety-Bill.pdf

Andrić, K., & Kasirzadeh, A. (2023) "Reconciling governmental use of online targeting with democracy" *Proceedings of the 2023 ACM Conference on Fairness, Accountability, and Transparency*. DOI: 10.1145/3593013.3594133

Angwin, J., Larson, J., Mattu, S., & Kirchner, L. (2016). *Machine Bias*. ProPublica; ProPublica. https://www.propublica.org/article/machine-bias-risk-assessments-in-criminal-sentencing

Anjum, K., & Katarya, R. (2024). Hate speech and toxicity detection in online social media: A recent survey of state of the art and opportunities. *International Journal of Information Security*, 23(1), 577–608. DOI: 10.1007/s10207-023-00755-2

Antoliš K, (2024), "DISINFORMATION SUPPORTED BY ARTIFICIAL INTELLIGENCE FROM DYNAMIC RESEARCH TO HOLISTIC SOLUTIONS," Public Security and Public Order.

Anzum, F., Asha, A. Z., & Gavrilova, M. L. (2022). *Biases, Fairness, and Implications of Using AI in Social Media Data Mining*. IEEE. DOI: 10.1109/CW55638.2022.00056

Arora, A., Barrett, M., Lee, E., Oborn, E., & Prince, K. (2023). Risk and the future of AI: Algorithmic bias, data colonialism, and marginalization. *Information and Organization*, 33(3), 100478. DOI: 10.1016/j.infoandorg.2023.100478

Arsalan, H. (2024). Ethical AI in hate speech detection: Safeguarding systems from external shocks. DOI: 10.13140/RG.2.2.26312.74245

Arun, C. (2019, February). On WhatsApp, Rumours, Lynchings, and the Indian Government. *Economic and Political Weekly*.

Arya, G., Hasan, M. K., Bagwari, A., Safie, N., Islam, S., Ahmed, F. R. A., De, A., Khan, M. A., & Ghazal, T. M. (2024). Multimodal HS Detection in Memes Using Contrastive Language-Image Pre-Training. *IEEE Access : Practical Innovations, Open Solutions*, 12, 22359–22375. DOI: 10.1109/ACCESS.2024.3361322

Asaro, P. (2020). Autonomous weapons and the ethics of artificial intelligence. Ethics of Artificial Intelligence, 212.

Aslam, M. (2024). Ethical considerations in hate speech detection: AI solutions for complex systems. DOI: 10.13140/RG.2.2.24844.73608

Assardo, L. (2023, May 24). Investigating digital threats: Trolling campaigns. Global Investigative Journalism Network. Retrieved from https://gijn.org/resource/investigating-digital-threats-trolling-campaigns/ (Last visited on 22.09.2024)

Ayetiran, A., & Özgöbek, Ö. (2024). An inter-modal attention-based deep learning framework using unified modality for multimodal fake news, hate speech and offensive language detection. *Information Systems*, 123, 102378. DOI: 10.1016/j.is.2024.102378

Ba Wazir, A. S., Abdul Karim, H., AlDahoul, N., Ahmad Fauzi, M. F., Mansor, S., Lye Abdullah, M. H., Sui Lyn, H., & Zulkifli, T. Z. (2021). Spoken Malay profanity classification using convolutional neural network. *Proceedings of the 2021 IEEE International Conference on Signal and Image Processing Applications (ICSIPA)*, 34–38. https://doi.org/DOI: 10.1109/ICSIPA52582.2021.9576781

Ba Wazir, A. S., Abdul Karim, H., Lye Abdullah, M. H., Mansor, S., AlDahoul, N., Ahmad Fauzi, M. F., & See, J. (2020). Spectrogram-based classification of spoken foul language using deep CNN. *Proceedings of the 2020 IEEE 22nd International Workshop on Multimedia Signal Processing (MMSP)*, 1–6. https://doi.org/DOI: 10.1109/MMSP48831.2020.9287133

Ba Wazir, A. S., Abdul Karim, H., Sui Lyn, H., Ahmad Fauzi, M. F., Mansor, S., & Lye, M. H. (2022). Deep learning-based detection of inappropriate speech content for film censorship. *IEEE Access : Practical Innovations, Open Solutions*, 10, 101697–101715. DOI: 10.1109/ACCESS.2022.3208921

Ba Wazir, A. S., Karim, H. A., Abdullah, M. H. L., AlDahoul, N., Mansor, S., Fauzi, M. F. A., See, J., & Naim, A. S. (2021). Design and implementation of fast spoken foul language recognition with different end-to-end deep neural network architectures. *Sensors (Basel)*, 21(3), 710. DOI: 10.3390/s21030710 PMID: 33494254

Bader, L., & Bender, J. (2022). What is "fake news" and "hate speech" and how do they work in practice?. Central and Eastern European eDem and eGov Days, 342, 17-36.

Badjatiya, P., Gupta, S., & Varma, V. (2017). Deep learning for hate speech detection in tweets. *Proceedings of the 26th International Conference on World Wide Web Companion*, 759-760. DOI: 10.1145/3041021.3054223

Badjatiya, P., Gupta, V., Gupta, A., & Varma, V. (2017). Deep Learning for HS Detection in Tweets. *Proceedings of the 26th International Conference on World Wide Web,* 2017, 759-760.

Balas, H., & Shatnawi, R. (2024). Legal framework for AI applications. *F1000 Research*. https://f1000research.com/articles/13-418

Bapaye, J. A., & Bapaye, H. A. (2021, January 30). Demographic Factors Influencing the Impact of Corona virus-Related Misinformation on WhatsApp: Cross-sectional Questionnaire Study. *JMIR Public Health and Surveillance*, 7(1), e19858. DOI: 10.2196/19858 PMID: 33444152

Barassi, V. (2020). Multimodal Approaches to Hate Speech: Text, Audio, and Video Data Analysis. *Journal of Digital Cultures*.

Barbieri, F., Krebs, F., & Sandhaus, P. (2020). Hate speech detection with pre-trained transformers. *Proceedings of the International Conference on Learning Representations (ICLR).*

Barhamgi, M., Masmoudi, A., Lara-Cabrera, R., & Camacho, D. (2024). Social networks data analysis with semantics: Application to the radicalization problem. *Journal of Ambient Intelligence and Humanized Computing*, 15(2), 1–20. DOI: 10.1007/s12652-018-0968-z

Barnhizer, D., & Barnhizer, D. (2019). *The artificial intelligence contagion: Can democracy withstand the imminent transformation of work, wealth and the social order?* SCB Distributors.

Barocas, S., Hardt, M., & Narayanan, A. (2017). *Fairness in Machine Learning.* NIPS Tutorials on AI Ethics.

Barocas, S., Hardt, M., & Narayanan, A. (2019). Fairness and Transparency in AI Systems. *Proceedings of the ACM FAccT Conference.*

Barrett, M., Boyne, J., Brandts, J., Brunner-La Rocca, H. P., De Maesschalck, L., De Wit, K., Dixon, L., Eurlings, C., Fitzsimons, D., Golubnitschaja, O., Hageman, A., Heemskerk, F., Hintzen, A., Helms, T. M., Hill, L., Hoedemakers, T., Marx, N., McDonald, K., Mertens, M., & Zippel-Schultz, B. (2019). Artificial intelligence supported patient self-care in chronic heart failure: A paradigm shift from reactive to predictive, preventive and personalised care. *The EPMA Journal*, 10(2), 147–155. DOI: 10.1007/s13167-019-00188-9 PMID: 31832118

Basile, V., et al. (2019). Benchmarking Multilingual Hate Speech Detection with SemEval-2019. *Proceedings of SemEval.*

Basile, V.. (2019). SemEval-2019 Task 5: Multilingual Detection of Hate Speech Against Immigrants and Women. *Proceedings of the SemEval Conference.* DOI: 10.18653/v1/S19-2007

Bastug, M. F., Douai, A., & Akca, D. (2020). Exploring the "demand side" of online radicalization: Evidence from the Canadian context. *Studies in Conflict and Terrorism*, 43(10), 857–873. DOI: 10.1080/1057610X.2018.1494409

Basu, S., & Sen, S. (2023). Silenced voices: Unravelling India's dissent crisis through historical and contemporary analysis of free speech and suppression. *Information & Communications Technology Law*, 33(1), 42–65. DOI: 10.1080/13600834.2023.2249780

Bechtold, E. (2020). Terrorism, the internet, and the threat to freedom of expression: The regulation of digital intermediaries in Europe and the United States. *Journal of Medicine and Law*, 12(1), 1–20. DOI: 10.1080/17577632.2020.1760474

Bekker, A. (2019, May). "5 Types of AI to propel your business,", https://www.scnsoft.com/blog/artificial-intelligence-types

Belenguer, L. (2022). AI bias: Exploring discriminatory algorithmic decision-making models and the application of possible machine-centric solutions adapted from the pharmaceutical industry. *AI and Ethics*, 2(4), 771–787. DOI: 10.1007/s43681-022-00138-8 PMID: 35194591

Benanav, A. (2020). *Automation and the future of work*. Verso Books.

Bendau, A., Plag, J., Petzold, M. B., & Ströhle, A. (2021). COVID-19 vaccine hesitancy and related fears and anxiety. International immunopharmacology, 97, 107724. https://doi.org/ (Last visited on 22.09.2024)DOI: 10.1016/j.intimp.2021.107724

Bender, E. M., & Friedman, B. (2020). Data Decisions and the Ethics of AI in Social Media. *AI & Society*, 35(1), 33–43.

Benesch, S. (2020). Proposals for improving AI in content moderation and upholding human rights. *Journal of Online Trust & Safety*, 1(1), 3–12.

Benizri, I., Evers, A., Mercer, S. T., & Jessani, A. A. (2023). A Comparative Perspective on AI Regulation. *Lawfare*. https //www.lawfaremedia.org/article/a-comparative-perspective-on-ai-regulation

Berk, R. A. (2021). Artificial intelligence, predictive policing, and risk assessment for law enforcement. *Annual Review of Criminology*, 4(1), 209–237. DOI: 10.1146/annurev-criminol-051520-012342

Bharathi Mohan, G., Prasanna Kumar, R., Vishal Krishh, P., Keerthinathan, A., Lavanya, G., Meghana, M. K. U., Sulthana, S., & Doss, S. (2024). An analysis of large language models: Their impact and potential applications. *Knowledge and Information Systems*, 66(9), 5047–5070. DOI: 10.1007/s10115-024-02120-8

Bharati, R. K. (2024). Navigating the Legal Landscape of Artificial Intelligence: Emerging Challenges and Regulatory Framework in India. *SSRN*, 23(7), 698–707. https://papers.ssrn.com/sol3/papers.cfm?abstract_id=4898536. DOI: 10.2139/ssrn.4898536

Bhatia, M. (2024, September 21). *Building A More Inclusive Future With Technology*. Outlook Business; Outlook Business. https://www.outlookbusiness.com/planet/opinions/building-a-more-inclusive-future-with-technology

Bhuptani, R. (2024, June 10). *The Impact of Artificial Intelligence on Every Aspect of Life: What Does AI Really Want?* Avidclan Technologies; Avidclan Technologies. https://www.avidclan.com/blog/the-impact-of-artificial-intelligence-on-every-aspect-of-life-what-does-ai-really-want/

Bhushan, T. (2024). Artificial Intelligence, Cyberspace and International Law. *Indonesian Journal of International Law*, 21(2), 281–314. https://scholarhub.ui.ac.id/ijil/vol21/iss2/3/

Binns, R. (2018). Algorithmic content moderation: Technical and political challenges in the automation of platform governance. *Big Data & Society*, 5(1). Advance online publication. DOI: 10.1177/2053951718757253

Binns, R. (2018). Fairness in Machine Learning: Lessons from Political Philosophy. *Proceedings of the 2018 Conference on Fairness, Accountability, and Transparency*, 149-158.

Binns, R. (2018). Fairness in machine learning: Lessons from political philosophy. *Proceedings of the 2018 Conference on Fairness, Accountability, and Transparency*.

Binns, R. (2020). Fairness in Machine Learning Systems: Mitigating Bias. *Communications of the ACM*.

Binns, R. (2020). On the Foundations of Fairness in AI. *Communications of the ACM*.

Binns, R. (2021). Algorithmic Accountability and Transparency in Content Moderation. *Journal of Online Ethics*, 23(4), 245–267.

Binns, R.. (2018). 'It's Reducing a Human Being to a Percentage': Perceptions of Justice in Algorithmic Decisions. *Proceedings of the CHI Conference*. DOI: 10.1145/3173574.3173951

Bishop, S. (2024). Should we hate hate speech regulation? The argument from viewpoint discrimination. *The Philosophical Quarterly*, 74(4), 1059–1079. DOI: 10.1093/pq/pqae086

Blanco-Herrero, D., & Calderón, C. A. (2019, October). Spread and reception of fake news promoting hate speech against migrants and refugees in social media: Research Plan for the Doctoral Programme Education in the Knowledge Society. In *Proceedings of the Seventh International Conference on Technological Ecosystems for Enhancing Multiculturality* (pp. 949-955).

Blauth, T. F., Gstrein, O. J., & Zwitter, A. (2022). Artificial intelligence crime: An overview of malicious use and abuse of AI. *IEEE Access : Practical Innovations, Open Solutions*, 10, 77110–77122. DOI: 10.1109/ACCESS.2022.3191790

Booth, R. (2022, May 1). Russia's trolling on Ukraine gets 'incredible traction' on TikTok. The Guardian. https://www.theguardian.com/world/2022/may/01/russia-trolling-ukraine-traction-tiktok?CMP (Last visited on 22.09.2024)

Bornstein, S. (2018). Antidiscriminatory algorithms. *Alabama Law Review*, 70, 519.

Brannon, V. C., & Holmes, E. N. (2024). Section 230: An Overview. *Congressional Research Service*. https://crsreports.congress.gov/product/pdf/R/R46751

Brauner, P., Hick, A., Philipsen, R., & Ziefle, M. (2023). What Does the Public Think About Artificial Intelligence? A Criticality Map to Understand Bias. *Frontiers of Computer Science*. Advance online publication. DOI: 10.3389/fcomp.2023.1113903

Brooklyn, P., Egon, A., & Shad, R. (2024, July 3). Deepfakes and cybersecurity: Detection and mitigation. Social Science Research Network. https://ssrn.com/abstract=4904874 (Last visited on 22.09.2024)

Brooks, C., Gherhes, C., & Vorley, T. (2023). Artificial intelligence in the legal sector: Pressures and challenges of transformation. *Cambridge Journal of Regions, Economy and Society*, 13(1), 135–152. DOI: 10.1093/cjres/rsz026

Brown, T. B., et al. (2020). Language Models Are Few-Shot Learners (GPT-3). *Proceedings of NeurIPS*.

Brown, T. B., Mann, B., Ryder, N., Subbiah, M., & Kaplan, J. (2020). Language models are few-shot learners. *arXiv preprint arXiv:2005.14165.*

Brown, T. B.. (2020). Language Models Are Few-Shot Learners. *Proceedings of the NeurIPS Conference*.

Buccella, A. (2022). "AI for all" is a matter of social justice. *AI and Ethics, 3*, pages 1143–1152, (2023). DOI: 10.1007/s43681-022-00222-z

Buçinca, Z., Malaya, M. B., & Gajos, K. Z. (2021). To trust or to think: cognitive forcing functions can reduce overreliance on AI in AI-assisted decision-making. Proceedings of the ACM on Human-computer Interaction, 5(CSCW1), 1-21.

Buenfil, J., Arnold, R., Abruzzo, C., & Korpela C. (2019). Artificial Intelligence Ethics: Governance through Social Media. *ResearchGate*. https://10.0.4.85/HST47167.2019.9032907

Burr, C., Cristianini, N., & Ladyman, J. (2018). An analysis of the interaction between intelligent software agents and human users. *Minds and Machines*, 28(4), 735–774. DOI: 10.1007/s11023-018-9479-0 PMID: 30930542

Business Standard. (2019, March 26). *IIT-Delhi researchers develop AI-based detector for malaria, TB, cervical cancer.* @Bsindia; Business Standard. https://www.business-standard.com/article/pti-stories/iit-delhi-researchers-develop-ai-based-detector-for-malaria-tb-cervical-cancer-119032600719_1.html

Cachat-Rosset, G., & Klarsfeld, A. (2023). Diversity, equity, and inclusion in artificial intelligence: An evaluation of guidelines. *Applied Artificial Intelligence*, 37(1), 1–18. DOI: 10.1080/08839514.2023.2176618

Cachat-Rosset, G., & Klarsfeld, A. (2023). *Diversity, Equity, Inclusion*. Taylor & Francis.

Calabrese, F., Regattieri, A., Bortolini, M., & Galizia, F. G. (2022). Data-Driven Fault Detection and Diagnosis: Challenges and Opportunities in Real-World Scenarios. *Applied Sciences (Basel, Switzerland)*, 12(11), 1–15. DOI: 10.3390/app12189212 PMID: 36330151

Calvo, R. A., Peters, D., Vold, K., & Ryan, R. M. (2020). *Supporting Human Autonomy*. Springer.

Camba, J. D., & Tagle, J. A. (2021). Real-Time AI Framework for Content Moderation in Gaming Platforms. *IEEE Transactions on Games*.

Canda, J. (2024). The Role of AI in Content Moderation and Online Safety. *Medium*. https://medium.com/@jam.canda/the-role-of-ai-in-content-moderation-and-online-safety-1d7d18aeb69d

Cao, J.. (2020). Joint Detection of Hate Speech Using Multimodal Embeddings. *Proceedings of CVPR*.

Capuano, N., Fenza, G., Loia, V., & Nota, F. D. (2023). Content-based fake news detection with machine and deep learning: A systematic review. *Neurocomputing*, 530, 91–103. DOI: 10.1016/j.neucom.2023.02.005

Carbonell, X., & Panova, T. (2017). A critical consideration of social networking sites' addiction potential. *Addiction Research and Theory*, 25(1), 48–57. DOI: 10.1080/16066359.2016.1197915

Carletti, V., Foggia, P., Percannella, G., Saggese, A., Strisciuglio, N., & Vento, M. (2013). Audisurveillance using a bag of aural words classifier. *Proceedings of the 2013 10th IEEE International Conference on Advanced Videand Signal Based Surveillance (AVSS)*, 81–86. https://doi.org/DOI: 10.1109/AVSS.2013.6636620

Carley, K. (2020). Social cybersecurity: An emerging science. *Computational & Mathematical Organization Theory*, 26(4), 365–381. DOI: 10.1007/s10588-020-09322-9 PMID: 33223952

Cascio, W. F., & Montealegre, R. (2016). How technology is changing work and organizations. *Annual Review of Organizational Psychology and Organizational Behavior*, 3(1), 349–375. DOI: 10.1146/annurev-orgpsych-041015-062352

Caselli, T., & Basile, V. (2021). Hate Speech Detection in a Multilingual World: Challenges and Opportunities. *Frontiers in Artificial Intelligence*. Hateful Memes Dataset:

Castaneda, J., Jover, A., Calvet, L., Yanes, S., Juan, A. A., & Sainz, M. (2022). Dealing with Gender Bias Issues in Data-Algorithmic Processes. *Algorithms*, 15(9), 303. DOI: 10.3390/a15090303

Cath, C. (2018). Governing artificial intelligence: Ethical, legal and technical opportunities and challenges. *Philosophical Transactions. Series A, Mathematical, Physical, and Engineering Sciences*, 376(2133), 20180080. Advance online publication. DOI: 10.1098/rsta.2018.0080 PMID: 30322996

Caton, S., & Haas, C. (2020). Fairness in Machine Learning: Addressing Algorithmic Bias in Hate Speech Detection. *Journal of Social Computing*.

Chakrabarty, T., & Bandyopadhyay, S. (2021). Multimodal Deep Learning for HS Detection: A Survey. *Journal of Information Science*, 47(4), 448–470.

Chancellor, S., Birnbaum, M. L., Caine, E. D., Silenzio, V. M., & De Choudhury, M. (2019). A taxonomy of ethical tensions in inferring mental health states from social media. In *Proceedings of the Conference on Fairness, Accountability, and Transparency* (pp. 79-88). DOI: 10.1145/3287560.3287587

Chandrasekharan, E., Samory, M., Srinivasan, A., & Gilbert, E. (2017). The bag of communities: Identifying abusive behavior online with preexisting internet data. *Proceedings of the 2017 CHI Conference on Human Factors in Computing Systems*. DOI: 10.1145/3025453.3026018

Chaudhari, A., Davda, P., Dand, M., & Dholay, S. (2021). Profanity detection and removal in videos using machine learning. *Proceedings of the 6th International Conference on Inventive Computing Technologies (ICICT)*, 572–576. https://doi.org/DOI: 10.1109/ICICT50816.2021.9358624

Chen, H., Li, L., & Chen, Y. (2021). Explore success factors that impact artificial intelligence adoption on telecom industry in China. *Journal of Management Analytics*, 8(1), 36–68.

Chen, Q., Peng, Y., & Feng, Z. (2021). *Enhanced Hate Speech Detection Using Capsule Networks*. ACM Transactions on Social Computing.

Chen, S., Xiao, L., & Kumar, A. (2023). Spread of misinformation on social media: What contributes to it and how to combat it. *Computers in Human Behavior*, 141, 107643. DOI: 10.1016/j.chb.2022.107643

Chen, T., & Guestrin, C. (2016). XGBoost: A Scalable Tree Boosting System. *Proceedings of the ACM SIGKDD Conference*.

Chesterman, S. (2020). Artificial Intelligence and the Limits of Legal Personality. *The International and Comparative Law Quarterly*, 69(4), 819–844. DOI: 10.1017/S0020589320000366

Chhabra, A., & Vishwakarma, D. K. (2023). Multimodal hate speech detection via multi-scale visual kernels and knowledge distillation architecture. *Engineering Applications of Artificial Intelligence*, 126, 106991. DOI: 10.1016/j.engappai.2023.106991

Chollet, F. (2020). *On the Measure of Intelligence in AI Systems*. ArXiv Preprint.

Choong, J., & Wang, M. B. (2023). Disruptive and destructive? A typology of social bots in public relations. *Journal of Digital & Social Media Marketing*, 11(1), 1–12. DOI: 10.69554/NPVB4536

Chui, M., Harrysson, M., Manyika, J., Roberts, R., Chung, R., Nel, P., & van Heteren, A. (2018). *Applying artificial intelligence for social good*. McKinsey Global Institute.

Chu, S. C., & Kim, Y. (2011). 'Determinants of consumer engagement in electronic word-of-mouth (eWOM) in social networking sites', International Journal of Advertising. *The Review of Marketing Communications*, 30(1), 47–75.

Chwialkowska, A. (2019). The effectiveness of brand-and customer-centric content strategies at generating shares,'likes', and comments. *Journal of Promotion Management*, 25(2), 270–300. DOI: 10.1080/10496491.2018.1443307

Cinelli, M., De Francisci Morales, G., Galeazzi, A., Quattrociocchi, W., & Starnini, M. (2021). The echo chamber effect on social media. *Proceedings of the National Academy of Sciences of the United States of America*, 118(9), e2023301118. DOI: 10.1073/pnas.2023301118 PMID: 33622786

Cinelli, M., Pelicon, A., Mozetič, I., Quattrociocchi, W., Novak, P. K., & Zollo, F. (2021). Dynamics of online hate and misinformation. *Scientific Reports*, 11(1), 22083. DOI: 10.1038/s41598-021-01487-w PMID: 34764344

Coglianese, C., & Lehr, D. (2016). Regulating by robot: Administrative decision making in the machine-learning era. *The Georgetown Law Journal*, 105, 1147.

Collenette, J., Atkinson, K., & Capon, T. B. (2023). Explainable AI tools for legal reasoning about cases: A study on the European Court of Human Rights. *Artificial Intelligence*, 317, 103861. https://www.sciencedirect.com/science/article/pii/S0004370223000073. DOI: 10.1016/j.artint.2023.103861

Continual Engine Team. (2023, October 20). *AI-Powered Accessibility: Bridging The Digital Divide - Continual Engine*. Continual Engine; Continual Engine. https://www.continualengine.com/blog/ai-powered-accessibility-bridging-the-digital-divide/

Corsi, G. (2024). Evaluating Twitter's algorithmic amplification of low-credibility content: An observational study. *EPJ Data Science*, 13(18), 18. Advance online publication. DOI: 10.1140/epjds/s13688-024-00456-3

Council of Europe. (2022). *AI Regulation in Content Moderation and Hate Speech*. Council of Europe Publications.

Council of Europe. (2022). *Hate Speech Detection and AI Regulation*. Official Council Reports.

Crawford, K. (2020). *The Politics of AI Bias*. Oxford University Press.

Crawford, K., & Gillespie, T. (2014). What is a flag for? Social media reporting tools and the vocabulary of complaint. *New Media & Society*, 18(3), 410–428. DOI: 10.1177/1461444814543163

Crawford, K., & Paglen, T. (2021). *Bias in Automated Content Moderation: A Case Study*. AI Ethics Journal.

Dastin, J. (2018). Ethical Implications of Bias in AI Systems. *Ethics in Artificial Intelligence Journal*, 12(3), 198–210.

Datta P, Whitmore M, Nwankpa J K, (2021), "A Perfect Storm: Social Media News, Psychological Biases, and AI," Digital Threats: Research.

Datta, S. (2019). Social artificial intelligence: Intuitive or intrusive?.

Dauber, C. E., & Ilter, K. (2019). *The relationship between Social Media and radicalization*. Propaganda, Recruitment, and Radicalization. DOI: 10.1201/9781315170251-3

Davani, A. M., Atari, M., Kennedy, B., & Dehghani, M. (2023). HS Classifiers Learn Normative Social Stereotypes. *Transactions of the Association for Computational Linguistics*, 11, 300–319. DOI: 10.1162/tacl_a_00550

Davenport, T. H. (2018). *The AI advantage: How to put the artificial intelligence revolution to work*. MIT Press. DOI: 10.7551/mitpress/11781.001.0001

Davidson, T., Warmsley, D., Macy, M., & Weber, I. (2017). Automated hate speech detection and the problem of offensive language. *Proceedings of the Eleventh International AAAI Conference on Web and Social Media*, 512-515. DOI: 10.1609/icwsm.v11i1.14955

Davidson, T., Warmsley, D., Macy, M., & Weber, I. (2017). Automated HS detection and the problem of offensive language. *Proceedings of the Eleventh International Conference on Web and Social Media (ICWSM)*, 512–515.

Davidson, T., Warmsley, D., Macy, M., & Weber, I. (2017, May). Automated hate speech detection and the problem of offensive language. In *Proceedings of the international AAAI conference on web and social media* (Vol. 11, No. 1, pp. 512-515).

de Almeida, P. G. R., dos Santos, C. D., & Farias, J. S. (2021). Artificial intelligence regulation: A framework for governance. *Ethics and Information Technology*, 23(3), 505–525. DOI: 10.1007/s10676-021-09593-z

De Freitas, J., Agarwal, S., Schmitt, B., & Haslam, N. (2023). Psychological factors underlying attitudes toward AI tools. *Nature Human Behaviour*, 7(11), 1845–1854. DOI: 10.1038/s41562-023-01734-2 PMID: 37985913

Devlin, J., Chang, M. W., Lee, K., & Toutanova, K. (2019). *BERT: Pre-training of deep bidirectional transformers for language understanding*. NAACL-HLT.

Devlin, J., Chang, M. W., Lee, K., & Toutanova, K. (2019). BERT: Pre-training of Deep Bidirectional Transformers for Language Understanding. *Proceedings of the NAACL-HLT Conference*.

Devlin, J., Chang, M.-W., Lee, K., & Toutanova, K. (2018). BERT: Pre-training of Deep Bidirectional Transformers for Language Understanding. *Proceedings of NAACL-HLT*.

Dhiman, A., & Toshniwal, D. (2022). AI-based Twitter framework for assessing the involvement of government schemes in electoral campaigns. *Expert Systems with Applications*, 203, 117338. Advance online publication. DOI: 10.1016/j.eswa.2022.117338

Dhir, A., Yossatorn, Y., Kaur, P., & Chen, S. (2018). Online social media fatigue and psychological wellbeing—A study of compulsive use, fear of missing out, fatigue, anxiety and depression. *International Journal of Information Management*, 40, 141–152. DOI: 10.1016/j.ijinfomgt.2018.01.012

Di Domenico, G., Sit, J., Ishizaka, A., & Nunan, D. (2021). Fake news, social media and marketing: A systematic review. *Journal of Business Research*, 124, 329–341. DOI: 10.1016/j.jbusres.2020.11.037

Díaz-Rodríguez, N., Del Ser, J., Coeckelbergh, M., de Prado, M. L., Herrera-Viedma, E., & Herrera, F. (2023). Connecting the dots in trustworthy Artificial Intelligence: From AI principles, ethics, and key requirements to responsible AI systems and regulation. *Information Fusion*, 99, 101896. DOI: 10.1016/j.inffus.2023.101896

Digital Media Governance Initiative. (2021). Regulating AI for Hate Speech: Lessons from Europe. *Policy Studies Journal: the Journal of the Policy Studies Organization*.

Dignum, V. (2020). Ethics in AI: Balancing Accuracy and Fairness. *Journal of Ethical AI*.

DiResta, R., Miller, C., & Molter, V.. (2020). *Telling China's story: The Chinese Communist Party's campaign to shape global narratives*. Stanford Internet Observatory.

Djuric, N., Zhou, H., Morris, R., Grbovic, M., Radosavljevic, V., & Bhamidipati, N. (2015). Hate Speech Detection with Comment Embeddings. *Proceedings of the WWW Conference*.

Djuric, N., Zhou, J., Morris, R., Grbovic, M., Radosavljevic, V., & Bhamidipati, N. (2015). Hate speech detection with comment embeddings. *Proceedings of the 24th International Conference on World Wide Web*, 29-30. DOI: 10.1145/2740908.2742760

Doraiswamy P M, London E, Varnum P, Harvey B, (2019), "Empowering Minds".

Dorocka, W. (2024, September 25). *How AI is improving diagnostics and health outcomes*. World Economic Forum; World Economic Forum. https://www.weforum .org/stories/2024/09/ai-diagnostics-health-outcomes/

Duenas, T., & Ruiz, D. (2024). The ministry of artificial intelligence: A catalyst for national AI ecosystems and global cooperation in the age of superintelligence. ResearchGate, 2024c.

Dunavete, A. (2024, May 8). *AI in Workplace Technology: Improving Productivity with Chatbots and Virtual Assistants*. Yarooms.com; YAROOMS International. https://www.yarooms.com/blog/ai-in-workplace-technology

Dunn, P. (2024). Online HS and intermediary liability in the age of algorithmic moderation.

Dwivedi, Y. K., Ismagilova, E., & Hughes, D. L. (2021). *Digital Social Media Marketing*. Elsevier.

Dwoskin, E. (2021, March 1). Social media platforms under fire for AI moderation failures. The Washington Post. https://www.washingtonpost.com

Ehrlich, P. (2002). Communications Decency Act § 230. *Berkeley Technology Law Journal*, 17(1), 401–419. https://www.jstor.org/stable/24120113

Elhauge, E. (1994). Allocating health care morally. *California Law Review*, 82(6), 1449. DOI: 10.2307/3480858 PMID: 11660282

Enarsson, T. (2024). Navigating hate speech and content moderation under the DSA: Insights from ECtHR case law. *Information & Communications Technology Law*, 33(1), 1–18. DOI: 10.1080/13600834.2018.1494415

Ernst, E., Merola, R., & Samaan, D. (2019). Economics of artificial intelligence: Implications for the future of work. *IZA Journal of Labor Policy*, 9(1), 20190004. DOI: 10.2478/izajolp-2019-0004

Ertel, W. (2024). *Introduction to artificial intelligence*. Springer Nature.

European Commission. (2020). *The Digital Services Act and AI-Driven Content Moderation*. EU Reports on AI.

European Commission. (2020). *The Role of AI in Combatting Online Hate Speech*. Official Reports of the EU Digital Services Act.

European Commission. (2021). Proposal for a Regulation Laying Down Harmonised Rules on Artificial Intelligence (Artificial Intelligence Act). *European Union*.

Facebook, A. I. (2020). *Real-Time Hate Speech Detection for Community Standards Enforcement*. Facebook Research Blog.

Fanni, R., Steinkogler, V. E., Zampedri, G., & Pierson, J. (2023). Enhancing Human Agency. *AI & Society*. PMID: 35692234

Farahani, M. S., & Ghasemi, G. (2024). Artificial intelligence and inequality: Challenges and opportunities. *International Journal of Innovation in Education*, 9, 78–99.

Farrand, B. (2023). Is this a hate speech? The difficulty in combating radicalisation in coded communications on social media platforms. *European Journal on Criminal Policy and Research*, 29(3), 477–493. DOI: 10.1007/s10610-023-09543-z

Fatima-Zahra, E., Said, O. E. A., & Noureddine, E. N. (2022). A multilingual offensive language detection method based on transfer learning from transformer fine-tuning model. Journal of King Saud University - Computer and Information Sciences, 34(8), Part B, 6048–6056. https://doi.org/DOI: 10.1016/j.jksuci.2021.07.013

Feerst, A. (2022). The Use of AI in Online Content Moderation. *AEI Digital Platforms*. https://platforms.aei.org/wp-content/uploads/2022/09/The-Use-of-AI-in-Online-Content-Moderation.pdf

Feldstein, S. (2019). The global expansion of AI surveillance (Vol. 17, No. 9). Carnegie Endowment for International Peace.

Fernandez, M., & Alani, H. (2021). *Artificial intelligence and online extremism: Challenges and opportunities*. Predictive Policing and Artificial Intelligence., DOI: 10.4324/9780429265365-7

Feuerriegel, S., DiResta, R., Goldstein, J. A., Kumar, S., Lorenz-Spreen, P., Tomz, M., & Pröllochs, N. (2023). Research can help to tackle AI-generated disinformation. *Nature Human Behaviour*, 7(11), 1818–1821. DOI: 10.1038/s41562-023-01726-2 PMID: 37985906

Fischer, G. (2021). *End-User Development*. Springer.

Florea, M., Potlog, C., Pollner, P., & Abel, D. (2022). *Alert system for online terrorist content based on natural language processing, social network analysis, artificial intelligence and complex event processing*. Cybersecurity and Privacy., DOI: 10.1007/978-3-031-15461-7_1

Floridi, L. (2018). Soft Ethics, Artificial Intelligence, and the Governance of the Digital. *Philosophy & Technology*, 31(4), 1–14. DOI: 10.1007/s13347-018-0303-9

Floridi, L., & Cowls, J. (2019). The Ethical Challenges of AI in Hate Speech Detection. *AI & Society*.

Floridi, L., Cowls, J., Beltrametti, M., Chatila, R., Chazerand, P., Dignum, V., Luetge, C., Madelin, R., Pagallo, U., Rossi, F., Schafer, B., Valcke, P., & Vayena, E. (2018). AI4People—An ethical framework for a good AI society: Opportunities, risks, principles, and recommendations. *Minds and Machines*, 28(4), 689–707. DOI: 10.1007/s11023-018-9482-5 PMID: 30930541

Floridi, L., Cowls, J., King, T. C., & Taddeo, M. (2020). How to design AI for social good: Seven essential factors. *Science and Engineering Ethics*, 26(3), 1771–1796. DOI: 10.1007/s11948-020-00213-5 PMID: 32246245

Foggia, P., Petrosino, A., & Saggese, A. (2015). Reliable detection of audievents in highly noisy environments. ScienceDirect. Gupta, V., Koyejo, S., Mittal, A., et al. (2022). Multilingual abusive comment detection at scale for Indic languages. In S. Koyejet al. (Eds.), Advances in Neural Information Processing Systems, 35, 26176–26191. https://proceedings.neurips.cc/paper_files/paper/2022/file/a7c4163b33286261b24c72fd3d1707c9-Paper-Datasets_and_Benchmarks.pdf

Fogleman, R. R. (1995, April 25). Information operations: The fifth dimension of warfare [Speech delivered to the Armed Forces Communications-Electronics Association, Washington, DC]. https://web.archive.org/web/20200220002026/http://www.iwar.org.uk/iwar/resources/5th-dimension/iw.html(Last visited on 22.09.2024)

Fontes, C., Hohma, E., Corrigan, C. C., & Lütge, C. (2022). AI-powered public surveillance systems: Why we (might) need them and how we want them. *Technology in Society*, 71, 102137. DOI: 10.1016/j.techsoc.2022.102137

Ford, J. (2022). Ethical AI frameworks: the missing governance piece. *Regulatory Insights on Artificial Intelligence*, 219–239. DOI: 10.4337/9781800880788.00018

Fortuna, P., & Nunes, S. (2018). A survey on automatic detection of hate speech in text. *ACM Computing Surveys*, 51(4), 1–30. DOI: 10.1145/3232676

Fortuna, P., & Nunes, S. (2018). A Survey on Automatic Detection of Hate Speech in Text. *ACM Computing Surveys*.

Fortuna, P., & Nunes, S. (2018). A survey on automatic detection of HS in text. *ACM Computing Surveys*, 51(4), 85.

Founta, A. M.. (2018). Dataset Bias in Hate Speech Detection: Impacts and Solutions. *Proceedings of ICWSM*.

Founta, A. M.. (2018). Large Scale Crowdsourcing and Characterization of Twitter Abusive Behavior. *Proceedings of the 12th International AAAI Conference on Web and social media (ICWSM)*. DOI: 10.1609/icwsm.v12i1.14991

Founta, A. M.. (2018). Large Scale Crowdsourcing of HS Annotations. *Proceedings of the 12th International Conference on Web and Social Media, ICWSM 2018*, 1-10.

Funk, M. (2019). AI and Accountability in Content Moderation. *Digital Ethics Quarterly*, 14(2), 129–145.

Fu, R., Huang, Y., & Singh, P. V. (2020). AI and algorithmic bias: Source, detection, mitigation and implications. Available at *SSRN*: https://ssrn.com/abstract=3681517 or http://dx.doi.org/DOI: 10.2139/ssrn.3681517

Galdorisi, G., & Tangredi, S. J. (2024). *Algorithms of Armageddon: The impact of artificial intelligence on future wars*. Naval Institute Press.

Gao, B., Wang, Y., Xie, H., Hu, Y., & Hu, Y. (2023). Artificial intelligence in advertising: Advancements, challenges, and ethical considerations in targeting, personalization, content creation, and ad optimization. *SAGE Open*, 13(4), 21582440231210759. DOI: 10.1177/21582440231210759

Gao, L., Huang, R., & Mohamed, E. (2017). Detecting online hate speech using context-aware models. *Proceedings of the First Workshop on Abusive Language Online*, 48-56. DOI: 10.26615/978-954-452-049-6_036

Gao, L., Kuppersmith, A., & Huang, R. (2017). Recognizing Explicit and Implicit Hate Speech Using Machine Learning Models. *Proceedings of the ACL Workshop on Ethics in NLP*.

GDPR. (2018). Article 22. *General Data Protection Regulation.European Union*.

Ghosh, M., & Arunachalam, T. (2021). Introduction to Artificial Intelligence. . https://www.researchgate.net/publication/351758474_Introduction_to_Artificial_Intelligence (Last visited on 20.09.2024)DOI: 10.1007/978-981-16-0415-7_2

Gianni, R., Lehtinen, S., & Nieminen, M. (2022). Governance of Responsible AI: From Ethical Guidelines to Cooperative Policies. *Frontiers of Computer Science*, 4, 873437. Advance online publication. DOI: 10.3389/fcomp.2022.873437

Gianni, R., Lehtinen, S., & Nieminen, M. (2022). Governance Responsible AI. *Frontiers*.

Gillespie, T. (2020). Content moderation, AI, and the question of scale. *ResearchGate*. https://www.researchgate.net/publication/343798653_Content_moderation_AI_and_the_question_of_scale

Gillespie, T. (2018). *Custodians of the Internet: Platforms, Content Moderation, and the Hidden Decisions that Shape social media*. Yale University Press.

Gillespie, T. (2018). *Custodians of the Internet: Platforms, content moderation, and the hidden decisions that shape social media*. Yale University Press., DOI: 10.12987/9780300235029

Gillespie, T. (2020). Content moderation, AI, and the question of scale. *Big Data & Society*, 7(2), 2053951720943234. Advance online publication. DOI: 10.1177/2053951720943234

Gillespie, T. (2020). *Custodians of the Internet: Platforms, Content Moderation, and the Hidden Decisions That Shape Social Media*. Yale University Press.

Giovanola, B., & Tiribelli, S. (2023). Beyond bias and discrimination: Redefining the AI ethics principle of fairness in healthcare machine-learning algorithms. *AI & Society*, 38(2), 549–563. DOI: 10.1007/s00146-022-01455-6 PMID: 35615443

Gipson Rankin S, (2024), "Mitigating Algorithmic Bias Strategies for Addressing Discrimination in Data," The scitech Lawyer.

Goanta, C., & Ortolani, P. (2021). Unpacking content moderation: The rise of social media platforms as online civil courts. Available at *SSRN*: https://ssrn.com/abstract =3969360 or http://dx.doi.org/DOI: 10.2139/ssrn.3969360

Godulla, A. (2020). Andreas Sudmann (Hg.): The Democratization of Artificial Intelligence. Net Politics in the Era of Learning Algorithms. *Communicatio Socialis, 53*(4), 552–553. DOI: 10.5771/0010-3497-2020-4-552

Goldfarb, A., & Lindsay, J. R. (2021). Prediction and judgment: Why artificial intelligence increases the importance of humans in war. *International Security*, 46(3), 7–50. DOI: 10.1162/isec_a_00425

Goldsmith, A. H., Veum, J. R., & William, D.Jr. (1996). The impact of labor force history on self-esteem and its component parts, anxiety, alienation and depression. *Journal of Economic Psychology*, 17(2), 183–220. DOI: 10.1016/0167-4870(96)00003-7

Gomez, R., Tellez, E., & Montes-y-Gómez, M. (2020). Multilingual Hate Speech Classification with Pre-Trained Transformers. *Proceedings of the LREC Conference*.

González, J.. (2021). Algorithmic Bias and Its Impact on the Detection of Hate Speech. *Journal of Digital Ethics*, 3(2), 58–73.

González-Sendino, R., Serrano, E., & Bajo, J. (2024). Mitigating bias in artificial intelligence: Fair data generation via causal models for transparent and explainable decision-making. *Future Generation Computer Systems*, 155, 384–401. DOI: 10.1016/j.future.2024.02.023

Gorenc, N. (2022). Hate speech or free speech: An ethical dilemma? *International Review of Sociology*, 32(3), 413–425. DOI: 10.1080/03906701.2022.2133406

Gøtzsche-Astrup, O., Lindekilde, L., & Fjellman, A.-M. (2023). Perceived legitimacy of CVE policies and the willingness to report concerns of radicalization to authorities in the Nordic countries. *Terrorism and Political Violence*, 35(3), 1–20. DOI: 10.1080/09546553.2021.1972977

Grandinetti, J. (2021). Examining embedded apparatuses of AI in Facebook and TikTok. *AI & Society*, •••, 1–14. DOI: 10.1007/s00146-021-01270-5 PMID: 34539095

Greengard, S. (2019, May). "What is artificial intelligence?", https://www.datamation .com/artificial-intelligence/what-is-artificial-intelligence.html

Greenstein, S. (2021). Preserving the rule of law in the era of artificial intelligence (AI). *Artificial Intelligence and Law*, 30(3), 291–323. DOI: 10.1007/s10506-021-09294-4

Grimmelmann, J. (2015). *The Virtues of Moderation: A Handbook for Content Moderators*. Yale Law Review.

Grizzle, A., Wilson, C., & Tuazon, R. Cheung, et al. (2021). "Media and information literate citizens:Media and Information Literacy Curriculum for Educators and Learners," UNESCO. https://unesdoc.unesco.org/ark:/48223/pf0000384981

Grondahl, T.. (2021). Evaluating Multilingual Hate Speech Datasets. *Proceedings of ICML*.

Guberman, J., & Hemphill, L. (2017). Challenges of using machine learning to detect hate speech in social media. *Proceedings of the 10th ACM International Conference on Web Science*, 60-68.

Guhl, J., Marsh, O., & Tuck, H. (2022). *Researching the Evolving Online Ecosystem: Barriers, Methods and Future Challenges*. Institute for Strategic Dialogue.

Gupta, A., Kumar, N., Prabhat, P., Gupta, R., & Tanwar, S. (2022). *Combating Fake News: Stakeholder Interventions and Potential Solutions*. IEEE.

Gupta, S., Agarwa, A. K., & Chauhan, A. K. (2018). Social media and its impact on consumers buying behavior with special reference to apparel industry in Bareilly region. *SMART Journal of Business Management Studies*, 14(2), 17–23. DOI: 10.5958/2321-2012.2018.00013.1

Gustavsson, I. (2021). *Autonomous Vehicles-Integrating Human Values*. AIML Studies.

Guyonneau, R., & Le Dez, A. (2019), Artificial Intelligence in Digital Warfare: Introducing the Concept of the Cyberteammate, https://cyberdefensereview.army.mil/Portals/6/Documents/CDR%20Journal%20Articles/Fall%202019/CDR%20V4N2-Fall%202019_GUYONNEAU-LE%20DEZ.pdf?ver=2019-11-15-104106-423 (Last visited on 20.09.2024)

Haefner, N., Wincent, J., Parida, V., & Gassmann, O. (2021). Artificial intelligence and innovation management: A review, framework, and research agenda. *Technological Forecasting and Social Change*, 162, 120392. DOI: 10.1016/j.techfore.2020.120392

Hagendorff, T. (2020). The ethics of AI ethics: An evaluation of guidelines. *Minds and Machines*, 30(1), 99–120. DOI: 10.1007/s11023-020-09517-8

Hakami, A., & Tazel, R. (2024). The Ethics of AI in Content Moderation: Balancing Privacy, Free Speech, and Algorithmic Control. DOI: 10.13140/RG.2.2.19529.97121

Halevy, A.. (2009). The Unreasonable Effectiveness of Data in AI Systems. *AI Magazine*.

Hamadah, S., & Aqel, D. (2020). Cybersecurity becomes smart using artificial intelligent and machine learning approaches: An overview. *ICIC Express Letters. Part B, Applications*, 11(12), 1115–1123. DOI: 10.24507/icicelb.11.12.1115

Hatch, B. B. (2018). Defining a Class of Cyber Weapons as WMD: An Examination of the Merits. *Journal of Strategic Security*, 11(1), 43–61. DOI: 10.5038/1944-0472.11.1.1657

Hate Speech and Regulation in Europe. (2022). *European Commission Report.* Tackling Hate Speech Using AI and Human Review Systems.

Hateful Memes Challenge: Kiela, D., et al. (2020). Detecting Multimodal Hate Speech. *Facebook AI Research.*

HateXplain Dataset.: Mathew, B., et al. (2020). Explainable Hate Speech Detection. *Proceedings of the WWW Conference.*

Hauer, T. (2022). Importance and limitations of AI ethics in contemporary society. *Humanities & Social Sciences Communications*, 9(1), 272. DOI: 10.1057/s41599-022-01300-7

He, H.. (2020). Federated Learning for Hate Speech Detection on Decentralized Platforms. *IEEE Access : Practical Innovations, Open Solutions.*

Helm, P., Bella, G., Koch, G., & Giunchiglia, F. (2024). Diversity and language technology: How language modeling bias causes epistemic injustice. *Ethics and Information Technology*, 26(8), 8. Advance online publication. DOI: 10.1007/s10676-023-09742-6

Hendler, J., & Mulvehill, A. M. (2016). *Social Machines: The Coming Collision of Artificial Intelligence, Social Networking, and Humanity.* Apress. DOI: 10.1007/978-1-4842-1156-4

Hendrycks, D., & Gimpel, K. (2016). Exploring the Limits of Language Modeling. *Proceedings of the 32nd International Conference on ML, ICML 2016*, 409-416.

Hietanen, M., & Eddebo, J. (2023). Towards a Definition of Hate Speech—With a Focus on Online Contexts. *The Journal of Communication Inquiry*, 47(4), 440–458. DOI: 10.1177/01968599221124309

Hogan, M. (2020). How artificial intelligence influences social media.

Hogan, M. (2020, May). How artificial intelligence influences social media. Adzooma. https://www.adzooma.com/blog/how-artificial-intelligence-influences-social-media/ (Last visited on 20.09.2024)

Hollewell, G. F., & Longpré, N. (2022). Radicalization in the social media era: Understanding the relationship between self-radicalization and the internet. *International Journal of Offender Therapy and Comparative Criminology*, 66(6), 537–555. DOI: 10.1177/0306624X211028771 PMID: 34189982

Hosain, M. T., Jim, J. R., Mridha, M. F., & Kabir, M. M. (2024). Explainable AI approaches in deep learning: Advancements, applications, and challenges. *Computers & Electrical Engineering*, 117, 109246. DOI: 10.1016/j.compeleceng.2024.109246

Hosseini, A., & Weninger, T. (2018). Detecting HS on Twitter Using Multimodal Deep Learning. *Proceedings of the 27th International Conference on Computational Linguistics, COLING 2018*, 1214-1223.

Houser, K. A. (2019). Can AI solve the diversity problem in the tech industry: Mitigating noise and bias in employment decision-making. *Stanford Technology Law Review : STLR : An Online High-Technology Law Journal from Stanford Law School*, 22, 290.

Hovy, D., & Spruit, S. L. (2016). *The Social Impact of Natural Language Processing. International Conference on Computational Linguistics*, 85-90. DOI: 10.18653/v1/P16-2096

Howard, J., & Gugger, S. (2018). *Fastai: A Layered API for Deep Learning*. ArXiv Preprint.

https://economictimes.indiatimes.com/magazines/panache/facebook-teams-up-with-8-third-party-fact-checkers-covering-11-indian-languages-to-flag-covid-19-fake news/articleshow/75284845.cms

https://economictimes.indiatimes.com/tech/internet/its-up-to-facebook-to-respond-on-its-fact-checking-programme-says-fb-after-it-minister-raises-concerns/articleshow/77895695.cms

https://ejournals.facultas.at/index.php/ocgcp/article/download/2144/1799

https://hai.stanford.edu/news/2023-state-ai-14-charts

https://scroll.in/latest/918725/whatsapp-launches-new-fact-checking-service-to-fight-fake-news-ahead-of-elections

https://www.boomlive.in/fact-check/bangladesh-video-two-hindu-men-burnt-alive-old-video-halloween-china-27235

https://www.boomlive.in/fast-check/karnataka-dalit-family-naked-touching-temple-idol-fake-news-gautam-budh-nagar-uttar-pradesh-stripped-protest-19379

https://www.businesstoday.in/current/economy-politics/facebook-partners-with-afp-to-expand-fact-checking-programme-in-india/story/288651.html

https://www.oecd-ilibrary.org/deliver/fae2d1e6-en.pdf

https://www.poynter.org/fact-checking/2018/in-one-month-facebook-doubled-the-countries-using-its-fact-checking-tool-%c2%97-all-outside-the-west/,PTI, *Facebook teams up with AFP to expand fact-checking programme in India,* Business Today (Nov. 6,2018)

https://www.statista.com/chart/25031/covid-19-misinformation-on-whatsapp-india

https://www.statista.com/chart/25031/covid-19-misinformation-on-whatsapp-india/

https://www.tableau.com/data-insights/ai/history

https://www.tandfonline.com/doi/abs/10.1080/17579961.2023.2184135

https://www.tandfonline.com/doi/full/10.1080/08839514.2022.2037254#d1e195

Huang, K., & Krafft, P. M. (2024). Performing Platform Governance: Facebook and the Stage Management of Data Relations. *Science and Engineering Ethics*, 30(2), 13. DOI: 10.1007/s11948-024-00473-5 PMID: 38575812

Huang, S., Lai, X., Ke, L., Li, Y., Wang, H., Zhao, X., Dai, X., & Wang, Y. (2024). AI Technology panic-is AI Dependence Bad for Mental Health? A Cross-Lagged Panel Model and the Mediating Roles of Motivations for AI Use Among Adolescents. *Psychology Research and Behavior Management*, 17, 1087–1102. DOI: 10.2147/PRBM.S440889 PMID: 38495087

Hung, B. W. K., & Muramudalige, S. R. (2019) "Recognizing radicalization indicators in text documents using human-in-the-loop information extraction and nlp techniques" *2019 International Conference on Technologies for Smart-City Energy and Mobility*. DOI: 10.1109/HST47167.2019.9032956

Hunter, L., Albert, C., Rutland, J., Topping, K., & Hennigan, C. (2024). Artificial intelligence and information warfare in major power states: how the US, China, and Russia are using artificial intelligence in their information warfare and influence operations. Defense & Security Analysis. 40. 1-35. . https://www.researchgate.net/publication/378764079_Artificial_intelligence_and_information_warfare_in_major_power_states_how_the_US_China_and_Russia_are_using_artificial_intelligence_in_their_information_warfare_and_influence_operations (Last visited on 22.09.2024)DOI: 10.1080/14751798.2024.2321736

Hunter, S., Tjondronegoro, D., & Trojan, B. (2024, April 17). *Artificial intelligence: A new driver for inclusive growth and development?* Asia Pathways; Asia Pathways. https://www.asiapathways-adbi.org/2024/04/artificial-intelligence-a-new-driver-for-inclusive-growth-and-development/

Husovec, M. (2024). The Digital Services Act's red line: What the Commission can and cannot do about disinformation. *Journal of Medicine and Law*, 16(1), 47–56. DOI: 10.1080/17577632.2024.2362483

Ienca, M. (2023). On artificial intelligence and manipulation. *Topoi*, 42(3), 833–842. DOI: 10.1007/s11245-023-09940-3

Ilgenfritz III, J. I. (2023). Lexical entrainment, empathy, and materiality in African American creative improvised music and conceptual art [Doctoral dissertation, University of California, Irvine].

Instagram Content Moderation Systems. (2021). *Enhancing AI-Based Hate Speech Detection*. Meta Research.

Intelligence, A. (2016). Automation, and the Economy. Executive Office of the President, 18-19.

International Monetary Fund. (2024). Advances in Artificial Intelligence: Implications for Capital Market Activities. *IMF ELibrary*. https://doi.org/DOI: 10.5089/9798400277573.082.CH003

Intersoft Consulting. (2016). *General data protection regulation (GDPR)*. General Data Protection Regulation (GDPR); European Union. https://gdpr-info.eu/

Irfan M, Almeshal Z A, Anwar M. (2024) "Unleashing transformative potential of artificial intelligence (AI) in countering terrorism online radicalisation extremism and possible recruitment".

Iwuanyanwu, C. C. (2023). Facebook artificial intelligence algorithm: Users' awareness and response to data privacy issues [Doctoral dissertation, Robert Morris University].

Jacob, C., & Kanth, M. (2023). 'Kill two million of them': Institutionalised hate speech, impunity and 21st century atrocities in India. *Global Responsibility to Protect*, 15(2-3), 209–245. DOI: 10.1163/1875984X-20230002

Jafariandehkordi, M. (2024). The AI battlefield: Legal challenges of autonomous weapon systems under international humanitarian law.

Jahan, M. S., & Oussalah, M. (2023). A systematic review of hate speech automatic detection using natural language processing. *Neurocomputing*, 546, 126232. DOI: 10.1016/j.neucom.2023.126232

Jain, L. R., & Menon, V. (2023). AI Algorithmic Bias: Understanding its Causes, Ethical and Social Implications. In *2023 IEEE 35th International Conference on Tools with Artificial Intelligence (ICTAI)* (pp. 460-467). Atlanta, GA, USA. DOI: 10.1109/ICTAI59109.2023.00073

Jain, A., Brooks, J. R., Alford, C. C., Chang, C. S., Mueller, N. M., Umscheid, C. A., & Bierman, A. S. (2023). Awareness of Racial and Ethnic Bias and Potential Solutions. *JAMA Health Forum*, 4(6), e231197. DOI: 10.1001/jamahealthforum.2023.1197 PMID: 37266959

Janjeva A, Harris A, Mercer S, Kasprzyk A, Gausen A. (2023) "The Rapid Rise of Generative AI: Assessing risks to safety and security".

Jee, C. (2020, February). An Indian politician is using deepfake technology to win new voters. Archive Page. MIT Technology Review. https://www.technologyreview.com/2020/02/19/868173/an-indian-politician-is-using-deepfakes-to-try-and-win-voters/ (Last visited on 21.09.2024)

Jha, P., & Madaan, R. (2020). HS Detection: A Comparative Analysis of Approaches and Methods. *Proceedings of the 2020 IEEE International Conference on ML and Applications, ICMLA 2020*, 331-338.

Jigsaw, G. (2021). *Perspective API for Detecting Hate Speech in Real-Time*. Jigsaw Research.

Jim, J. R., Talukder, M. A. R., Malakar, P., Kabir, M. M., Nur, K., & Mridha, M. F. (2024). Recent advancements and challenges of NLP-based sentiment analysis: A state-of-the-art review. *Natural Language Processing Journal*, 6, 100059. DOI: 10.1016/j.nlp.2024.100059

Jobin, A., Ienca, M., & Vayena, E. (2019). The Global Landscape of AI Ethics Guidelines. *Nature Machine Intelligence*, 1(9), 389–399. DOI: 10.1038/s42256-019-0088-2

Joshi, A., Tetreault, J., & Eisenstein, J. (2020). A survey on hate speech detection. *Proceedings of the Annual Meeting of the Association for Computational Linguistics.*

Joulin, A.. (2016). Bag of Tricks for Efficient Text Classification. *Proceedings of ACL.*

Jusué, I. R. (2022). Counter-terrorism training "at your kitchen table": The promotion of "CT citizens" and the securitisation of everyday life in the UK. *Critical Studies on Terrorism*, 15(2), 1–18. DOI: 10.1080/17539153.2022.2039612

Kaddari, Z., Mellah, Y., Berrich, J., Belkasmi, M. G., & Bouchentouf, T. (2021). Natural language processing: Challenges and future directions. In *T. Masrour, I. El Hassani, & A. Cherrafi* (Eds.), *Artificial intelligence and industrial applications. A2IA 2020* (Vol. 144, pp. 255-267). Springer, Cham. DOI: 10.1007/978-3-030-53970-2_22

Kaleem, A. (2022). The hegemony of Prevent: Turning counter-terrorism policing into common sense. *Critical Studies on Terrorism*, 15(1), 1–18. DOI: 10.1080/17539153.2021.2013016

Kamau, J. W. (2021). Is counter-terrorism counterproductive? A case study of Kenya's response to terrorism, 1998-2020. *The South African Journal of International Affairs*, 28(3), 455–474. DOI: 10.1080/10220461.2021.1924252

Kamolov, F., & Dempsey, A. (2020). Multilingual HS Detection Using ML Algorithms. *Proceedings of the 29th ACM International Conference on Information and Knowledge Management, CIKM 2020*, 123-132.

Kang, H., & Lou, C. (2022). AI agency vs. human agency: Understanding human–AI interactions on TikTok and their implications for user engagement. *Journal of Computer-Mediated Communication*, 27(5), zmac014. Advance online publication. DOI: 10.1093/jcmc/zmac014

Kanipriya, M., Sugumaran, D., Pandiyarajan, V., Yogananda, B. S., Selvakumar, P., & Mohan, S. (2024, January). Analysis of Electromyography Signals for Control of Mechanical Prosthesis using Machine Learning Techniques. In 2024 2nd International Conference on Intelligent Data Communication Technologies and Internet of Things (IDCIoT) (pp. 1059-1067). IEEE.

Kankanhalli, A., Xia, Q., Ai, P., & Zhao, X. (2021). Understanding personalization for health behavior change applications: A review and future directions. *AIS Transactions on Human-Computer Interaction*, 13(2), 1–25. DOI: 10.17705/1thci.00152

Kaplan, J. M., & Peters, B. (2021). *Algorithmic Bias and the Future of AI Ethics*. MIT Press.

Kaur, R. (2023). AI in criminal justice: Implications for justice, fairness, and potential biases. *Nyaayshastra Law Review*, 4, 1.

Kaushik, S. (2024). AI in Content Moderation: All You Need to Know. *Blog Ipleaders*. https://blog.ipleaders.in/ai-in-content-moderation-all-you-need-to-know/

Keman Huang, M. S. S. M. (2018). Systematically Understanding the Cyber Attack Business: A Survey. *ACM Computing Surveys*.

Khan, J. R. (2021). Spread of Religious Hatred through Digital Media in Pakistan: The Case of Tehreek-E-Labbaik Pakistan. *Journal of Media and Communication Studies*.

Khan, S., Lehtinen, E., & Zaman, R. (2016). Hate Speech and the Law: A Comparative Study of Legal Approaches to Hate Speech Regulation in the United States and Europe. In Gagliardone, P., Pohjonen, M., & Beyene, S. (Eds.), *Hate Speech Online: A Global Perspective* (pp. 157–182). Cambridge University Press., DOI: 10.1017/9781108371674.009

Kiela, D.. (2020). *Hateful Memes Challenge: Multimodal Benchmark Dataset*. Facebook AI Research.

Kiela, D., Firooz, H., Mohan, A., & Das, A. (2020). *The Hateful Memes Challenge: Detecting Hate Speech with Multimodal Data. Facebook AI Research*. HASOC Dataset.

Kim, B., & Doshi-Velez, F. (2019). Explainable AI in Hate Speech Monitoring. *Proceedings of AAAI*.

Kim, Y. (2014). Convolutional Neural Networks for Sentence Classification. *Proceedings of the 2014 Conference on Empirical Methods in Natural Language Processing, EMNLP 2014*, 1746-1751. DOI: 10.3115/v1/D14-1181

Kiritchenko, S., & Mohammad, S. M. (2018). Examining Gender and Race Bias in Two Hundred Sentiment Analysis Systems. *Proceedings of the STARSEM Workshop*. DOI: 10.18653/v1/S18-2005

Kiskis, M. (2023). Legal framework for the coexistence of humans and conscious AI. *Frontiers in Artificial Intelligence*, 6, 1205465. DOI: 10.3389/frai.2023.1205465 PMID: 37808620

Kizilcec, R. F., Chen, M., Jasińska, K. K., Madaio, M., & Ogan, A. (2021). Mobile Learning During School Disruptions in Sub-Saharan Africa. *AERA Open*, 7, 233285842110148. DOI: 10.1177/23328584211014860

Klossner, S. (2022). *AI-Powered m-Health Apps*. Aalto University.

Kluge Corrêa, N., Galvão, C., Santos, J. W., Del Pino, C., Pontes Pinto, E., Barbosa, C., Massmann, D., Mambrini, R., Galvão, L., Terem, E., & de Oliveira, N. (2023). Worldwide AI ethics: A review of 200 guidelines and recommendations for AI governance. *Patterns (New York, N.Y.)*, 4(10), 100857. DOI: 10.1016/j.patter.2023.100857 PMID: 37876898

Kniazieva, Y. (2023). AI Content Moderation for Responsible Social Media Practices. *Label Your Data*. https://labelyourdata.com/articles/ai-content-moderation

Knight, W. (2020). Can AI Moderate Content Better than Humans? *MIT Technology Review*.

Köbis, N., Starke, C., & Rahwan, I. (2022). The promise and perils of using artificial intelligence to fight corruption. *Nature Machine Intelligence*, 4(5), 418–424. DOI: 10.1038/s42256-022-00489-1

Kossow, N., Windwehr, S., & Jenkins, M. (2022). *Algorithmic transparency and accountability*. Transparency International.

Krajcovic, P. (2024). The Impact of Artificial Intelligence on Social Media, *ResearchGate*. https://www.researchgate.net/publication/380818610_The_Impact_of_Artificial_Intelligence_on_Social_Media

Krenn, M., Buffoni, L., Coutinho, B., Eppel, S., Foster, J. G., Gritsevskiy, A., Lee, H., Lu, Y., Moutinho, J. P., Sanjabi, N., Sonthalia, R., Tran, N. M., Valente, F., Xie, Y., Yu, R., & Kopp, M. (2023). Forecasting the future of artificial intelligence with machine learning-based link prediction in an exponentially growing knowledge network. *Nature Machine Intelligence*, 5(11), 1326–1335. DOI: 10.1038/s42256-023-00735-0

Kumar, P.. (2021). Ensemble Methods for Hate Speech Detection: A Review. *Pattern Recognition Letters*.

Kumar, S.. (2021). Early Detection of Online Hate Speech Using Adaptive Neural Networks. *IEEE Transactions on Computational Social Systems*.

Kumar, S., & Riegner, M. (2019). Freedom of expression in diverse democracies: Comparing hate speech law in India and the EU. In P. Dann & A. Thiruvengadam (Eds.), *Democratic constitutionalism in continental polities: EU and India compared* (Forthcoming). Cheltenham: Elgar. Available at *SSRN*: https://ssrn.com/abstract=3552984

Laitinen, A., & Sahlgren, O. (2021). AI systems and respect for human autonomy. *Frontiers in Artificial Intelligence*, 4, 705164. DOI: 10.3389/frai.2021.705164 PMID: 34765969

Lakier, G. (2020). (Forthcoming). The non-First Amendment law of freedom of speech. *SSRN*, 134. Advance online publication. DOI: 10.2139/ssrn.3689972

Lakomy, M. (2023). Artificial intelligence as a terrorism enabler? Understanding the potential impact of chatbots and image generators on online terrorist activities. *Studies in Conflict and Terrorism*, •••, 1–20. DOI: 10.1080/1057610X.2023.2259195

Lakra, R. (2024). Deciphering AI-powered content moderation: Approaches, constraints, and future horizons. *Observer Research Foundation*. https://www.orfonline.org/expert-speak/deciphering-ai-powered-content-moderation-approaches-constraints-and-future-horizons

Landers, R. N., & Behrend, T. S. (2023). Auditing AI Auditors. *The American Psychologist*. PMID: 35157476

Lauriola, I., Lavelli, A., & Aiolli, F. (2022). An introduction to deep learning in natural language processing: Models, techniques, and tools. *Neurocomputing*, 470, 443–456. DOI: 10.1016/j.neucom.2021.05.103

LeCun, Y., Bengio, Y., & Hinton, G. (2015). Deep Learning and Its Applications in Hate Speech Detection. *Nature*.

Lee, D. H., & Yoon, S. N. (2021). Application of artificial intelligence-based technologies in the healthcare industry: Opportunities and challenges. *International Journal of Environmental Research and Public Health*, 18(11), 1–15. DOI: 10.3390/ijerph18010271 PMID: 33401373

Leikas, J., Johri, A., Latvanen, M., & Wessberg, N. (2022). *Governance of AI in Social Media*. Springer.

Li, H. (2019). Special section introduction: Artificial intelligence and advertising. *Journal of Advertising*, 48(4), 333–337. DOI: 10.1080/00913367.2019.1654947

Lin, H. (2022). Russian Cyber Operations in the Invasion of Ukraine. *The Cyber Defense Review*, 7(4), 31–46.

LinkedIn AI Team. (2021). *Tackling Hate Speech in Professional Networks*. Microsoft Research Journal.

Lipton, Z. C. (2018). The Mythos of Model Interpretability. *Communications of the ACM*, 61(10), 36–43. DOI: 10.1145/3233231

Liu, P., Wang, X., & Jiang, J. (2022). Multimodal Hate Speech Detection Using Fusion Neural Networks. *Proceedings of the CVPR Conference*.

Liu, Q., Zhang, X., Huang, S., Zhang, L., & Zhao, Y. (2020). Exploring consumers' buying behavior in a large online promotion activity: The role of psychological distance and involvement. *Journal of Theoretical and Applied Electronic Commerce Research*, 15(1), 66–80. DOI: 10.4067/S0718-18762020000100106

Liu, X., Zhou, Y., & Zhang, H. (2020). Hierarchical Transformers for Real-Time Offensive Language Detection. *Proceedings of the EMNLP Conference.*

Liu, Y., & Guo, J. (2019). Leveraging BERT for Detecting Online HS. *Proceedings of the 57th Annual Meeting of the Association for Computational Linguistics, ACL 2019*, 2459-2468.

Liu, Y., Ott, M., & Goyal, N.. (2019). *RoBERTa: A Robustly Optimized BERT Pretraining Approach.* ArXiv Preprint.

Llanso, E., Hoboken, J. V., Leerssen, P., & Harambam, J. (2020). Artificial Intelligence, Content Moderation, and Freedom of Expression. *Transatlantic Working Group.* https://www.ivir.nl/publicaties/download/AI-Llanso-Van-Hoboken-Feb-2020.pdf

Lohani, A. "Countering Disinformation and Hate Speech Online: Regulation and User Behavioural Change," *ORF Occasional Paper No. 296,* 2021.

Lowa, M. (2024). Democratizing Access to Education: AI-Driven Solutions for Inclusive Learning in Malaysia. *Social Science Research Network.* DOI: 10.2139/ssrn.4813758

Lundberg, S. M., & Lee, S.-I. (2017). *A Unified Approach to Interpretable Model Explanations. Proceedings of the 31st International Conference on Neural Information Processing Systems*, 4765–4774.

Lutz, C. (2019). Digital inequalities in the age of artificial intelligence and big data. *Human Behavior and Emerging Technologies*, 1(2), 141–148. DOI: 10.1002/hbe2.140

Lwakatare, L. E., Raj, A., Crnkovic, I., Bosch, J., & Olsson, H. H. (2020). Large-scale machine learning systems in real-world industrial settings: A review of challenges and solutions. *Information and Software Technology*, 126, 1–15. DOI: 10.1016/j.infsof.2020.106368

MacAvaney, S.. (2019). An Exploration of Multilingual HS Detection: The State of the Art. *Proceedings of the 2019 IEEE International Conference on Data Mining, ICDM 2019*, 394-403.

MacAvaney, S.. (2019). Hate Speech Detection Using BERT Embeddings. *Proceedings of the SIGIR Conference.*

MacAvaney, S., Yao, H. R., Yang, E., Russell, K., Goharian, N., & Frieder, O. (2019). Hate speech detection: Challenges and solutions. *PLoS One*, 14(8), e0221152.

Madgule, M., Vinayaka, N., Sonkhaskar, Y. M., Patel, D. R., Karthikeyan, R., & Selvakumar, P. (2023). Mechanical properties and microstructure of activated TIG welded similar joints of Inconel alloys by desirability approaches. *Materials Today: Proceedings*, 77, 528–533.

Maghsoudi, M., Mohammadi, A., & Habibipour, S. (2024). Navigating and Addressing Public Concerns in AI: Insights from Social Media Analytics and Delphi. *IEEE Access : Practical Innovations, Open Solutions*, 12, 126043–126062. DOI: 10.1109/ACCESS.2024.3440660

Mahadev Madgule, N. (2023). Vinayaka, Yeshwant M. Sonkhaskar, Dhiren Ramanbhai Patel, R. Karthikeyan, P. Selvakumar,(2023). Mechanical properties and microstructure of activated TIG welded similar joints of Inconel alloys by desirability approaches. *Materials Today: Proceedings*, 77, 528–533. DOI: 10.1016/j.matpr.2022.12.250

Mandl, T., Modha, S., & Patel, D. (2019). *Overview of the HASOC Track at FIRE: Hate Speech and Offensive Content Identification*. CEUR-WS.

Mandl, T., Modha, S., & Patel, D. (2019). The HASOC Dataset for Hate Speech Detection. *Proceedings of the FIRE Conference*.

Manheim, K., & Kaplan, L. (2019). Artificial intelligence: Risks to privacy and democracy. *Yale Journal of Law and Technology*, 21, 106.

Mantri, A. (2021). Real-Time Content Moderation Using Artificial Intelligence and Machine Learning. *International Journal of Science and Research (Raipur, India)*, 10(1), 1682–1684. DOI: 10.21275/SR24724150350

Martens, B., Aguiar, L., Gomez-Herrera, E., & Mueller-Langer, F. (2018). The digital transformation of news media and the rise of disinformation and fake news-An economic perspective. *JRC Digit. Econ. Work. Pap*, 2, 57.

Masood, S., & Abbas, A. (2024). Neural Networks and Deep Learning: A Comprehensive Overview of Modern Techniques and Applications. DOI: 10.13140/RG.2.2.22416.58882

Matamoros-Fernández, A., & Farkas, J. (2021). Racism, hate speech, and social media: A systematic review and critique. *Television & New Media*, 22(2), 205–224. DOI: 10.1177/1527476420982230

Mazari, A. C., Boudoukhani, N., & Djeffal, A. (2024). BERT-based ensemble learning for multi-aspect HS detection. *Cluster Computing*, 27(1), 325–339. DOI: 10.1007/s10586-022-03956-x

McGregor, J. (2020). The Ethics of AI in Content Moderation: Balancing Innovation and Responsibility. *Journal of Social Media Studies*.

Mecaj, S. (2022). Artificial Intelligence and Legal Challenges. *ResearchGate*. https://www.researchgate.net/publication/360392203_ARTIFICIAL_INTELLIGENCE_AND_LEGAL_CHALLENGES

Mehrabi, N.. (2021). A Survey on Bias and Fairness in Machine Learning. *ACM Computing Surveys*.

Memarian, B., & Doleck, T. (2023). Fairness, Accountability, Transparency, and Ethics (FATE) in Artificial Intelligence (AI) and higher education: A systematic review. *Computers and Education: Artificial Intelligence*, 5, 100152. DOI: 10.1016/j.caeai.2023.100152

Mensah G B, (2023), "Artificial Intelligence and Ethics: A Comprehensive Review," researchgate.

Mervosh, S. (2019, May). Distorted videos of Nancy Pelosi spread on Facebook and Twitter, helped by Trump. The New York Times. https://perma.cc/a26h-4pf3 (Last visited on 21.09.2024)

Meta (2021). Real-Time Hate Speech Detection on Facebook. *Meta Transparency Reports*.

Metz, R. (2022, March 16). Facebook and YouTube say they removed Zelensky deepfake. CNN. https://edition.cnn.com/2022/03/16/tech/deepfake-zelensky-facebook-meta/index.html(Last visited on 21.09.2024)

Mhlanga, D. (2022). Human-centered artificial intelligence: The superlative approach to achieve sustainable development goals in the fourth industrial revolution. *Sustainability (Basel)*, 14(13), 7804. DOI: 10.3390/su14137804

Microsoft AI Research (2020). Improving Real-Time Hate Speech Moderation on Xbox Live. *Microsoft Blog*.

Mikalef, P., Conboy, K., Lundström, J. E., & Popovič, A. (2022). Thinking responsibly about responsible AI and 'the dark side' of AI. *European Journal of Information Systems*, 31(3), 257–268. DOI: 10.1080/0960085X.2022.2026621

Mikolov, T., et al. (2013). Word2Vec: Distributed Representations of Words. *NeurIPS Proceedings*.

Milosevic, T., Van Royen, K., & Davis, B. (2022). Artificial Intelligence to Address Cyberbullying, Harassment and Abuse: New Directions in the Midst of Complexity. *International Journal of Bullying Prevention : an Official Publication of the International Bullying Prevention Association*, 4(1), 1–5. DOI: 10.1007/s42380-022-00117-x PMID: 35233506

Min, A. (2023). Artificial Intelligence and Bias: Challenges, Implications, and Remedies. *Journal of Social Research*, 2(11), 3808–3817. DOI: 10.55324/josr.v2i11.1477

Mishra, P. K. (2024). AI And The Legal Landscape: Embracing Innovation, Addressing Challenges. *Live Law.*https://www.livelaw.in/lawschool/articles/law-and-ai-ai-powered-tools-general-data-protection-regulation-250673

Mishra, A., Del Tredici, M., Yannakoudakis, H., & Shutova, E. (2018). Abusive Language Detection with Graph Convolutional Networks. *Proceedings of the NAACL-HLT Conference*. BERT

Mitra, A., & Sankhala, P. (2022). Multilingual hate speech and offensive content detection using modified cross-entropy loss. arXiv preprint. https://arxiv.org/abs/2202.02635

Mittal, U. (2023). *AI based Evaluation System for mitigating Supply Chain Risk. Authorea Preprints*. DOI: 10.22541/essoar.170224570.06055229/v1

Mittal, U. (2023, August). Detecting Hate Speech Utilizing Deep Convolutional Network and Transformer Models. In *2023 International Conference on Electrical, Electronics, Communication and Computers (ELEXCOM)* (pp. 1-4). IEEE.

Mittal, U., & Panchal, D. (2023). AI-based evaluation system for supply chain vulnerabilities and resilience amidst external shocks: An empirical approach. *Reports in Mechanical Engineering*, 4(1), 276–289. DOI: 10.31181/rme040122112023m

Mnassri, K., Farahbakhsh, R., & Crespi, N. (2024). Multilingual HS Detection: A Semi-Supervised Generative Adversarial Approach. *Entropy (Basel, Switzerland)*, 26(4), 344. DOI: 10.3390/e26040344 PMID: 38667898

Molina, M. D., & Sundar, S. S. (2022). *When AI moderates online content: effects of human collaboration and interactive transparency on user trust*. Academic., https://academic.oup.com/jcmc/article/27/4/zmac010/6648459

Molina, M. D., & Sundar, S. S. (2022). When AI moderates online content: Effects of human collaboration and interactive transparency on user trust. *Journal of Computer-Mediated Communication*, 27(4), zmac010. Advance online publication. DOI: 10.1093/jcmc/zmac010

Mondal, H., & Mondal, S. (2024). Ethical and social issues related to AI in healthcare. *Methods in Microbiology*, 55, 247–281. DOI: 10.1016/bs.mim.2024.05.009

Morgan, F. E., Boudreaux, B., Lohn, A. J., Ashby, M., Curriden, C., Klima, K., & Grossman, D. (2020). *Military applications of artificial intelligence*. RAND Corporation.

Mozur, P. (2018, October 15). A genocide incited on Facebook, with posts from Myanmar's military. *The New York Times*. https://www.nytimes.com/2018/10/15/technology/myanmar-facebook-genocide.html

Mufareh, A. (2020). How can artificial intelligence improve social media?.

Muhammed, T. S., & Mathew, S. K. (2022). The disaster of misinformation: A review of research in social media. *International Journal of Data Science and Analytics*, 13(4), 271–285. DOI: 10.1007/s41060-022-00311-6 PMID: 35194559

Mun, J., Buerger, C., Liang, J. T., & Garland, J. (2024) "Counterspeakers' Perspectives: Unveiling Barriers and AI Needs in the Fight against Online Hate" *Proceedings of the 2024 CHI Conference on Human Factors in Computing Systems*. DOI: 10.1145/3613904.3642025

Murikah, W., Nthenge, J. K., & Musyoka, F. M. (2024). *Bias Ethics AI Systems*. Elsevier.

Murphy, T. (2020, March 27). The strategy web: A new framework for analyzing military strategy. Air University: Wild Blue Yonder. https://www.airuniversity.af.edu/Wild-Blue-Yonder/Article-Display/Article/2127317/the-strategy-web-a-new-framework-for-analyzing-military-strategy/](https://www.airuniversity.af.edu/Wild-Blue-Yonder/Article-Display/Article/2127317/the-strategy-web-a-new-framework-for-analyzing-military-strategy/ (Last visited on 22.09.2024)

Nadler, A., & McGuigan, L. (2018). An impulse to exploit: The behavioral turn in data-driven marketing. *Critical Studies in Media Communication*, 35(2), 151–165. DOI: 10.1080/15295036.2017.1387279

Naseer M A, Shaheen G. (2023) "Harnessing the Power of Artificial Intelligence: An In-Depth Review of its Effective Role in Countering Violent Extremism" JURIHUM: Jurnal Inovasi dan Pembelajaran Sosial, 5(1), pp. 1-12.

Nasir, S., Vel, P., & Mateen, H. (2012). Social media and buying behaviour of women in in Pakistan towards the purchase of textile garments.

Nassar, A., & Kamal, M. (2021). Ethical dilemmas in AI-powered decision-making: A deep dive into big data-driven ethical considerations. *International Journal of Responsible Artificial Intelligence*, 11(8), 1–11.

Nasser B S A, Abu-Naser S S, (2024), "Artificial Intelligence in Digital Media: Opportunities, Challenges, and Future Directions," philpapers.

Nazareno, L., & Schiff, D. S. (2021). The impact of automation and artificial intelligence on worker well-being. *Technology in Society*, 67, 101679. DOI: 10.1016/j.techsoc.2021.101679

Nebeker, C., Parrish, E. M., & Graham, S. (2022). *The AI-Powered Digital Health Sector*. Springer.

Nguyen, A., Hong, Y., Dang, B., & Huang, X. (2024). Human-AI collaboration patterns in AI-assisted academic writing. *Studies in Higher Education*, 49(5), 847–864. DOI: 10.1080/03075079.2024.2323593

Nixon, N., Lin, Y., & Snow, L. (2024). Catalyzing Equity. *Sage (Atlanta, Ga.)*. PMID: 38516055

Noble, S. U. (2018). *Algorithms of Oppression: How Search Engines Reinforce Racism*. NYU Press. DOI: 10.18574/nyu/9781479833641.001.0001

Norström, L., Islind, A., & Snis, U. (2020). Algorithmic work: The impact of algorithms on work with social media.

Nyariro, M., & Emami, E. (2022). Integrating Equity, Diversity. *Inclusion (Washington, D.C.)*.

Odag, Ö., Leiser, A., & Boehnke, K. (2019). Reviewing the role of the Internet in radicalization processes. *Journal for Deradicalization*, •••, 21.

Omeish, F., Khasawneh, M. A., & Khair, N. (2024). Investigating the impact of AI on improving customer experience through social media marketing: An analysis of Jordanian Millennials. *Computers in Human Behavior Reports*, 15, 100464. DOI: 10.1016/j.chbr.2024.100464

Ortega-Bolaños, R., Bernal-Salcedo, J., Germán Ortiz, M., Galeano Sarmiento, J., Ruz, G. A., & Tabares-Soto, R. (2024). Applying the ethics of AI: A systematic review of tools for developing and assessing AI-based systems. *Artificial Intelligence Review*, 57(5), 110. DOI: 10.1007/s10462-024-10740-3

Ortiz-Ospina, E. (2019). The rise of social media. Our World in Data. https://ourworldindata.org/rise-of-social-media

Oyeniran, C. O., Adewusi, A. O., Adeleke, A. G., Akwawa, L. A., & Azubuko, C. F. (2022). Ethical AI: Addressing bias in machine learning models and software applications. *Computer Science & IT Research Journal*, 3(3), 115–126. DOI: 10.51594/csitrj.v3i3.1559

Ozanne, M., Bhandari, A., Bazarova, N. N., & DiFranzo, D. (2022). Shall AI moderators be made visible? Perception of accountability and trust in moderation systems on social media platforms. *Big Data & Society*, 9(2), 20539517221115666. Advance online publication. DOI: 10.1177/20539517221115666

Pandey, R., & Kumar, A. (2021). Multilingual Hate Speech Analysis Using Transformers. *Proceedings of ACL.*

Papagelis, S. (2024). Exploring the impact of the algorithms on management hiring decision and bias [Doctoral dissertation, Temple University].

Papasavva A. (2024) "A Comprehensive Study of the Extremist Narratives and the Role of Alternative Social Networks that Facilitate Radical Discourse".

Pappalardo, L., Ferragina, S., & Citraro, S. (2024) "A survey on the impact of AI-based recommenders on human behaviors: methodologies, outcomes, and future directions" arxiv preprint arxiv:2405.03451.

Patel P, Uddin M N, (2022), "AI Algorithmic Auditing," norislab.

Patidar, N., Mishra, S., Jain, R., Prajapati, D., Solanki, A., Suthar, R., Patel, K., & Patel, B. (2024). Transparency in AI decision making: A survey of explainable AI methods and applications. *Advances in Robotic Technology*, 2(1), 1–10. DOI: 10.23880/art-16000110

Patwa, P., & Upadhyay, S. (2020). Exploring Multilingual HS Detection Systems for Social Media. *Proceedings of the 28th International Conference on Computational Linguistics, COLING 2020*, 158-167.

Paul, C., & Bora, P. (2021). Detecting HS using deep learning techniques. *International Journal of Advanced Computer Science and Applications*, 12(2), 619–623. DOI: 10.14569/IJACSA.2021.0120278

Pavlopoulos, J.. (2021). *Automatic Abuse Detection in Online Platforms: Issues and Advances*. AI Ethics Journal.

Pavlopoulos, J., Sorensen, J., Dixon, L., & Thain, N. (2020). *Toxicity detection: Does context matter?* NAACL.

Pedreschi, D., Giannotti, F., Guidotti, R., Monreale, A., Ruggieri, S., & Turini, F. (2019). Meaningful explanations of black box AI decision systems. *Proceedings of the AAAI Conference on Artificial Intelligence*, 33(01), 9780–9784. DOI: 10.1609/aaai.v33i01.33019780

Pennington, J., ... (2014). GloVe: Global Vectors for Word Representation. *EMNLP Proceedings*.

Pereira-Kohatsu, J. C., Quijano-Sánchez, L., Liberatore, F., & Camacho-Collados, M. (2019). Detecting and monitoring hate speech in Twitter. *Sensors (Basel)*, 19(21), 4654.

Pérez-Torres, S., & Molina-González, M. D. (2021). Combining Images and Text for Multimodal Hate Speech Detection. *IEEE Transactions on Multimedia*.

Peters, M. A. (2020). Limiting the capacity for hate: Hate speech, hate groups and the philosophy of hate. *Educational Philosophy and Theory*, 54(14), 2325–2330. DOI: 10.1080/00131857.2020.1802818

Pistone, I., Eriksson, E., & Beckman, U. (2019). A scoping review of interventions for preventing and countering violent extremism: Current status and implications for future research. *Journal for Deradicalization*, •••, 21.

Pluta, A., Mazurek, J., Wojciechowski, J., Wolak, T., Soral, W., & Bilewicz, M. (2023). Exposure to hate speech deteriorates neurocognitive mechanisms of the ability to understand others' pain. *Scientific Reports*, 13(1), 4127. DOI: 10.1038/s41598-023-31146-1 PMID: 36914701

Pokorny, F. B., Graf, F., Pernkopf, F., & Schuller, B. W. (2015). Detection of negative emotions in speech signals using bags-of-audio-words. *Proceedings of the 2015 International Conference on Affective Computing and Intelligent Interaction (ACII)*, 879–884. https://doi.org/DOI: 10.1109/ACII.2015.7344678

Potter, K., & Stilinski, D. (2024). *The Role of Media and Arts in Countering Extremism: Promoting Peace*. Tolerance, and Positive Social Values.

Prasad, N., Saha, S., & Bhattacharyya, P. (2021). A multimodal classification of noisy hate speech using character-level embedding and attention. *Proceedings of the 2021 International Joint Conference on Neural Networks (IJCNN)*, 1–8. https://doi.org/DOI: 10.1109/IJCNN52387.2021.9533371

Prier, J. (2017). Commanding the trend: Social media as information warfare. Strategic Studies Quarterly, Air University Press. 11(4), 50-85. https://www.proquest.com/docview/1972152688/ (Last visited on 21.09.2024)

Putri, A. D. A. l. (2020). The Journalists Has Built Self Meaning: Spreasing Hate Speech. In *Preseidential Election 2019 In Banten* (Vol. I, p. 2). ASPIRATION Journal.

Quadros, M. (2020). Artificial intelligence in social media marketing.

Rabonato, R. T., & Berton, L. (2024). A systematic review of fairness in machine learning. *AI and Ethics*. Advance online publication. DOI: 10.1007/s43681-024-00577-5

Radford, A., et al. (2019). Language Models Are Few-Shot Learners. *Proceedings of NeurIPS*.

Rafanelli, L. M. (2022). Justice, injustice, and artificial intelligence: Lessons from political theory and philosophy. *Big Data & Society*, 9(1), 205395172210806. DOI: 10.1177/20539517221080676

Raffel, C., et al. (2020). Exploring the Limits of Transfer Learning with a Unified Text-to-Text Transformer (T5). *Journal of Machine Learning Research.*

Rahwan, I., Cebrian, M., Obradovich, N., Bongard, J., Bonnefon, J.-F., Breazeal, C., Crandall, J. W., Christakis, N. A., Couzin, I. D., Jackson, M. O., Jennings, N. R., Kamar, E., Kloumann, I. M., Larochelle, H., Lazer, D., McElreath, R., Mislove, A., Parkes, D. C., Pentland, A. S., & Wellman, M. (2019). Machine Behaviour. *Nature*, 568(7753), 477–486. DOI: 10.1038/s41586-019-1138-y PMID: 31019318

Raihan, A. (2023). A comprehensive review of artificial intelligence and machine learning applications in energy sector. *Journal of Technology Innovations and Energy*, 2(4), 1–26. DOI: 10.56556/jtie.v2i4.608

Ramakrishnan, T., Mohan Gift, M. D., Chitradevi, S., Jegan, R., & Subha Hency Jose, P. Nagaraja, Rajneesh Sharma H.N., Selvakumar P., Sintayehu Mekuria Hailegiorgis, (2022). "Study of Numerous Resins Used in Polymer Matrix Composite Materials", Advances in Materials Science and Engineering, vol. 2022, Article ID 1088926, 8 pages, 2022. DOI: 10.1155/2022/1088926

Rani, R., & Kumar, S. (2022). Real-Time Hate Speech Detection with Hybrid Deep Learning Techniques. *Journal of Information and Optimization Sciences.*

Ranjan, P., & Vaish, A. (2021). Socio-technical attack approximation based on structural virality of information in social networks. [IJISP]. *International Journal of Information Security and Privacy*, 15(1), 153–172.

Rashid, W. (2023). *"Using Artificial Intelligence to Combat Extremism" Pakistan Journal of Terrorism Research.* PJTR.

Rattan, P., Penrice, D. D., & Simonetto, D. A. (2022). Artificial Intelligence and Machine Learning: What You Always Wanted to Know but Were Afraid to Ask. *Gastro Hep Advances*, 1(1), 70–78. DOI: 10.1016/j.gastha.2021.11.001 PMID: 39129929

Rawat, A., Kumar, S., & Samant, S. S. (2024). Hate speech detection in social media: Techniques, recent trends, and future challenges. *Wiley Interdisciplinary Reviews: Computational Statistics*, 16(2), e1648. DOI: 10.1002/wics.1648

Reddit (2021). Real-Time Content Moderation During Crisis Events. *Reddit Research Reports*.

Reddit Data Science Team. (2021). Early Warning Systems for Hate Speech Detection. *Reddit Transparency Report*.

Reddit Trust and Safety: Using AI to Monitor Toxicity in Discussions. *Reddit Transparency Report*.

Reeves, J., & Crowther, T. (2019). Teacher feedback on the use of innovative social media simulations to enhance critical thinking in young people on radicalisation, extremism, sexual exploitation and related topics. *Pastoral Care in Education*, 37(2), 151–166. DOI: 10.1080/02643944.2019.1618377

Renda, A., Arroyo, J., & Fanni, R. (2021). *Study to support an impact assessment of regulatory requirements for artificial intelligence in Europe*. European Commission.

Report, F. T. (2021). *Advancing Real-Time AI Systems for Hate Speech Removal*. Facebook Newsroom.

Ribeiro, M. T., Singh, S., & Guestrin, C. (2016). *"Why Should I Trust You?": Explaining the Predictions of Any Classifier*. Proceedings of the 22nd ACM SIGKDD International Conference on Knowledge Discovery and Data Mining, 1135-1144.

Ribeiro, M. T., & Agerri, R. (2021). The Role of Context in HS Detection: Advances and Challenges. *Journal of Artificial Intelligence Research*, 69, 103–123.

Ribeiro, M. T., Singh, S., & Guestrin, C. (2016). Why Should I Trust you? Explaining the Predictions of Any Classifier. *Proceedings of the ACM SIGKDD Conference*. DOI: 10.18653/v1/N16-3020

Rita M N, Shava F B, Chitauro M, (2022), "Tech4Good: AI-Powered Chatbots," researchgate.

Roberts, S. T. (2019). *Behind the Screen: Content Moderation in the Shadows of Social Media*. Yale University Press.

Roche, C., Wall, P. J., & Lewis, D. (2023). Ethics and diversity in artificial intelligence policies, strategies and initiatives. *AI and Ethics*, 3(4), 1095–1115. DOI: 10.1007/s43681-022-00218-9 PMID: 36246014

Rochefort, A. (2020). Regulating social media platforms: A comparative policy analysis. *Communication Law and Policy*, 25(2), 225–260. DOI: 10.1080/10811680.2020.1735194

Rodgers, W., Murray, J. M., & Stefanidis, A. (2023). *Artificial Intelligence Algorithmic Approach*. Elsevier.

Rodrigues, R. (2020). Legal and Human Rights Issues of AI: Gaps, Challenges and Vulnerabilities. *Journal of Responsible Technology, 4*(100005). ScienceDirect. DOI: 10.1016/j.jrt.2020.100005

Rozenshtein, A. Z. (2024). Interpreting the Ambiguities of Section 230. *Yale Journal on Regulation*. https://www.yalejreg.com/bulletin/interpreting-the-ambiguities-of-section-230/

Ruckenstein, M. (2023). *The feel of algorithms*. University of California Press.

Ruder, S. (2019). *Transfer Learning for NLP*. ArXiv Preprint.

Ruder, S. (2020). Multilingual Representation Learning for Hate Speech Detection. *Proceedings of EMNLP*.

Ruder, S.. (2019). Neural Representations in NLP: A Survey. *ACM Computing Surveys*.

Sadiku, M. N. O. (1989). Artificial intelligence. *IEEE Potentials*, 8(May), 35–39. DOI: 10.1109/45.31596

Sadiku, M. N. O., Ashaolu, T. J., Majebi, A. A., & Musa, S. M. (2021). Artificial Intelligence in Social Media. *International Journal of Scientific Advances*, 2(1), 15–20. https://10.0.201.86/ijscia.v2i1.4

Sadiku, M. N. O., Tembely, M., & Musa, S. M. (2018, March). Social media for beginners. *International Journal of Advanced Research in Computer Science and Software Engineering*, 8(3), 24–26. DOI: 10.23956/ijarcsse.v8i3.564

Saheb, T., Sidaoui, M., & Schmarzo, B. (2024). Convergence of artificial intelligence with social media: A bibliometric & qualitative analysis. *Telematics and Informatics Reports*, 14, 100146. DOI: 10.1016/j.teler.2024.100146

Saleem, H. M., Dillon, K. P., Benesch, S., & Ruths, D. (2017). A web of hate: Tackling hateful speech in online social spaces. *Proceedings of the 5th ACM Conference on Human Factors in Computing Systems*, 1975-1985.

Saleh, H., Alhothali, A., & Moria, K. (2023). Detection of Hate Speech using BERT and Hate Speech Word Embedding with Deep Model. *Applied Artificial Intelligence*, 37(1), 2166719. Advance online publication. DOI: 10.1080/08839514.2023.2166719

SAMBUCCI, L., & PARASCHIV, E. A. (2024). The accelerated integration of artificial intelligence systems and its potential to expand the vulnerability of the critical infrastructure. *Romanian Journal of Information Technology and Automatic Control*, 34(3), 131–148.

Samory, M., & Mitra, T. (2018). *Multimodal Hate Speech Analysis on Social Platforms*. ACM Transactions on Social Computing.

Sankaran S, Zhang C, Lopez M G, (2020), "Respecting Human Autonomy,".

Saranya, A., & Subhashini, R. (2023). A systematic review of Explainable Artificial Intelligence models and applications: Recent developments and future trends. *Decision Analytics Journal*, 7, 100230. DOI: 10.1016/j.dajour.2023.100230

Sarmiento, H. (2020). How artificial intelligence can benefit the social media user.

Sayegh, E. (2024, May 14). The battle for truth in election seasons: AI-generated deepfakes. Forbes." https://www.forbes.com/sites/emilsayegh/2024/05/14/the-battle-for-truth-in-election-seasons-ai-generated-deepfakes/#open-web-0 (Last visited on 21.09.2024)

Scatiggio, V. (2020). *The Issue of Bias in Artificial Intelligence to Design AI-Driven Fair and Inclusive Service Systems*. Politecnico di Milano.

Schäfer, S., Rebasso, I., Boyer, M. M., & Planitzer, A. M. (2024). Can we counteract hate? Effects of online hate speech and counter speech on the perception of social groups. *Communication Research*, 51(5), 553–579. DOI: 10.1177/00936502231201091

Schmidt, A., & Wiegand, M. (2017). A survey on hate speech detection using natural language processing. *Proceedings of the 5th International Workshop on Natural Language Processing for Social Media*, 1-10. DOI: 10.18653/v1/W17-1101

Schmidt, A., & Wiegand, M. (2017). A Survey on Hate Speech Detection Using Text. *Proceedings of COLING*.

Schmidt, A., & Wiegand, M. (2017). A survey on HS detection using natural language processing. *Proceedings of the Fifth International Workshop on Natural Language Processing for Social Media (SocialNLP)*, 1–10.

Schulman, S. (2022). Perspectives on the First Amendment: The impact of generation on free speech freedoms. *Journal of Undergraduate Research (Gainesville, Fla.)*, 24. Advance online publication. DOI: 10.32473/ufjur.24.130771

Schwartz, R., Schwartz, R., Vassilev, A., Greene, K., Perine, L., Burt, A., & Hall, P. (2022). *Towards a standard for identifying and managing bias in artificial intelligence* (Vol. 3). US Department of Commerce, National Institute of Standards and Technology. DOI: 10.6028/NIST.SP.1270

Schwarz, E. (2021). *Autonomous weapons systems, artificial intelligence, and the problem of meaningful human control*. Philosophical Journal of Conflict and Violence. DOI: 10.22618/TP.PJCV.20215.1.139004

Schwarzenbach A, Jensen M. (2024) "Extremists of a feather flock together? Community structures, transitivity, and patterns of homophily in the US Islamist co-offending network" plos ONE, 19(9), pp. 1-15, .DOI: 10.1371/journal.pone.0287406

Selvakumar, P., Mariappan, P., Shunmugam, S., Paul, R., & Jabez, S. (2024). Removal of chemicals from effluent using photobioreactor technology to improve environmental and health impacts. *Zeitschrift für Physikalische Chemie*, 2024(7), 1295–1302. Advance online publication. DOI: 10.1515/zpch-2023-0450

Selvakumar, P., Palanisamy, S. K., Cinthaikinian, S., Palanisamy, V., Mariappan, R., & Selvakumar, P. K. (2024). Biosensors and its diverse applications in healthcare systems. *Zeitschrift für Physikalische Chemie*, 2024. Advance online publication. DOI: 10.1515/zpch-2023-0406

Seng, K. P., Ang, L. M., & Ngharamike, E. (2022). Artificial intelligence Internet of Things: A new paradigm of distributed sensor networks. *International Journal of Distributed Sensor Networks*, 18(3). Advance online publication. DOI: 10.1177/15501477211062835

Shadbolt, N., & Williams, C. (2019). The Ethical Dimensions of Artificial Intelligence in Content Moderation. *AI & Society*, 34(4), 751–764.

Shahbaznezhad, H., Dolan, R., & Rashidirad, M. (2021). The role of social media content format and platform in users' engagement behavior. *Journal of Interactive Marketing*, 53(1), 47–65. DOI: 10.1016/j.intmar.2020.05.001

Shah, M., & Sureja, N. (2024). A comprehensive review of bias in deep learning models: Methods, impacts, and future directions. *Archives of Computational Methods in Engineering*. Advance online publication. DOI: 10.1007/s11831-024-10134-2

Shamra, N. (2024). Artificial Intelligence: Legal Implications and Challenges. *ResearchGate*. https://www.researchgate.net/publication/381848987_ARTIFICIAL_INTELLIGENCE_LEGAL_IMPLICATIONS_AND_CHALLENGES

Sharif, W., Mumtaz, S., Shafiq, Z., Riaz, O., Ali, T., Husnain, M., & Choi, G. S. (2019). An empirical approach for extreme behavior identification through tweets using machine learning. *Applied Sciences (Basel, Switzerland)*, 9(24), 5375. DOI: 10.3390/app9183723

Shen A, Sun Y, (2021), "graphicalai: A User-Centric Approach,".

Shin, D. (2020). User Perceptions of Algorithmic Decisions in Personalized AI Systems. *Journal of Broadcasting & Electronic Media*. Advance online publication. DOI: 10.1080/08838151.2020.1843357

Shin, D. (2021). The effects of explainability and causability on perception, trust, and acceptance: Implications for explainable AI. *International Journal of Human-Computer Studies*, 146, 102551. DOI: 10.1016/j.ijhcs.2020.102551

Shiohira, K. (2021). Understanding the impact of artificial intelligence on skills development. [UNESCO-UNEVOC International Centre for Technical and Vocational Education and Training.]. *Education*, •••, 2030.

Shrestha, Y. R., & Ben-Menahem, S. M. (2019). Organizational Decision-Making. *Sage (Atlanta, Ga.)*.

Shulner-Tal, A., Kuflik, T., Kliger, D., & Mancini, A. (2024). Who made that decision and why? Users' perceptions of human versus AI decision-making and the power of explainable AI. *International Journal of Human-Computer Interaction*, •••, 1–18. DOI: 10.1080/10447318.2024.2348843

Simoncini, G. (2023). Bringing back the concept of colonial pacification in the study of preventing violent extremism (PVE) practices: The case of Tunisia. *Cambridge Review of International Affairs*, •••, 1–20.

Singh, J. (2024). The Role of AI in Enhancing Content Moderation on Social Platforms. *Outsourcing Center*. https://www.outsourcing-center.com/the-role-of-ai-in-enhancing-content-moderation-on-social-platforms/

Singh, T. (2023). AI-driven surveillance technologies and human rights: Balancing security and privacy. In International Conference on Smart Systems: Innovations in Computing (pp. 703-717). Springer Nature Singapore.

Singhal, A., Neveditsin, N., Tanveer, H., & Mago, V. (2024). Toward Fairness, Accountability, Transparency, and Ethics in AI. *JMIR Medical Informatics*, 12, e50048. DOI: 10.2196/50048 PMID: 38568737

Singh, R., Nath, L. P., Mishra, P., Jain, S., Singh, A., & Benedict, S. M. (2024). Online hate speech in India: Legal reforms and social impact on social media platforms. Available at *SSRN*: https://ssrn.com/abstract=4732818 or DOI: 10.2139/ssrn.4732818

Singh, R., & Patel, A. (2019). A Survey on HS Detection in Social Media Platforms. *Journal of Computer Security*, 23(4), 435–453.

Smith, J., Doe, A., & Brown, B. (2023). Exploring AI Ethics. *Journal of AI Research*, 45(2), 123–145. DOI: 10.1234/jair.2023.00001

Sponholz, L. (2023). Hate speech. DOI: 10.48541/dcr.v12.9

Sreelatha, A., & Choudhary, G. (2023). Exploring The Use of AI In Legal Decision Making: Benefits and Ethical Implications. *Woxsen University*. https://woxsen.edu.in/research/white-papers/exploring-the-use-of-ai-in-legal-decision-making-benefits-and-ethical-implications/

Sreenivasulu, A., & Manimozhi, T. Satheesh kumar P., Selvakumar P. And Singh P.,(2022). "The Model of Smart Sensing Device For Sensitive Nanoclusters Modification in Sensing Properties," 2022 2nd International Conference on Advance Computing and Innovative Technologies in Engineering (ICACITE), Greater Noida, India, 2022, pp. 1043-1047, DOI: 10.1109/ICACITE53722.2022.9823846

Srisakthi, S., & Suresh Babu, C. V. (2024). Cybersecurity: Protecting Information in a Digital World. In Saeed, S., Azizi, N., Tahir, S., Ahmad, M., & Almuhaideb, A. (Eds.), *Strengthening Industrial Cybersecurity to Protect Business Intelligence* (pp. 1–25). IGI Global., DOI: 10.4018/979-8-3693-0839-4.ch001

Stanford Human-Centered Artificial Intelligence (HAI). (2022). *Ethics and effectiveness of AI in moderating online hate speech*. Stanford University. https://hai.stanford.edu

Steyvers, M., & Kumar, A. (2024). Three challenges for AI-assisted decision-making. *Perspectives on Psychological Science*, 19(5), 722–734. DOI: 10.1177/17456916231181102 PMID: 37439761

Stockinger, A., Schäfer, S., & Lecheler, S. (2023). Navigating the gray areas of content moderation: Professional moderators' perspectives on uncivil user comments and the role of (AI-based) technological tools. *New Media & Society*, 0(0), 14614448231190901. Advance online publication. DOI: 10.1177/14614448231190901

Stockmann, D. (2023). *Tech Companies Public Interest*. Taylor & Francis.

Stracqualursi, L., & Agati, P. (2024). Twitter users' perceptions of AI-based e-learning technologies. *Scientific Reports*, 14(1), 5927. DOI: 10.1038/s41598-024-56284-y PMID: 38467685

Sun, C., Qian, X., & Liu, H. (2021). Adversarial Training for Robust Hate Speech Detection. *Proceedings of the AAAI Conference on Artificial Intelligence*. DOI: 10.5772/intechopen.94615

Sun, X., & Zeng, Q. (2021). Multimodal Fusion for HS Detection in Social Media. *Journal of Information Science and Engineering*, 37(2), 361–379.

Suresh Babu, C. V., Suruthi, G., Indhumathi, C., & Sushruth, S. (2024b). Integrated approach for network intrusion detection: Combining KNN algorithm, Karhunen-Loève transform, and genetic algorithm optimization. In Metaheuristic and machine learning optimization strategies for complex systems (p. 21). https://doi.org/DOI: 10.4018/979-8-3693-7842-7.ch002

Suresh Babu, C. V., Kowsika, S., Sai Tejaswi, M., Janarakshani, T. R., & Mercysha Princy, S. (2023). Framework for Detection of Cyberbullying in Text Data Using Natural Language Processing and Machine Learning. In Chitadze, N. (Ed.), *Cyber Security Policies and Strategies of the World's Leading States* (pp. 69–85). IGI Global., DOI: 10.4018/978-1-6684-8846-1.ch005

Suresh Babu, C. V., & Rahul, A. (2024). Securing the Future: Unveiling Risks and Safeguarding Strategies in Machine Learning-Powered Cybersecurity. In Almaiah, M., Maleh, Y., & Alkhassawneh, A. (Eds.), *Risk Assessment and Countermeasures for Cybersecurity* (pp. 80–95). IGI Global., DOI: 10.4018/979-8-3693-2691-6.ch005

Taeihagh, A. (2021). Governance of artificial intelligence. *Policy and Society*, 40(2), 137–157. DOI: 10.1080/14494035.2021.1928377

Talaei Khoei, T., Ould Slimane, H., & Kaabouch, N. (2023). Deep learning: Systematic review, models, challenges, and research directions. *Neural Computing & Applications*, 35(31), 23103–23124. DOI: 10.1007/s00521-023-08957-4

Tallberg, J., Erman, E., Furendal, M., Geith, J., Klamberg, M., & Lundgren, M. (2023). The Global Governance of Artificial Intelligence: Next Steps for Empirical and Normative Research. *International Studies Review*, 2(3), viad040. Advance online publication. DOI: 10.1093/isr/viad040

Tay, Y., et al. (2021). Cross-Language Transfer Learning for Hate Speech Classification. *NeurIPS Proceedings*.

Temme, M. (2017). Algorithms and transparency in view of the new general data protection regulation. *European Data Protection Law Review*, 3(4), 473–485. DOI: 10.21552/edpl/2017/4/9

The Economic Times. (2023, March 15). How Artificial intelligence is changing your life unknowingly. *The Economic Times*. https://economictimes.indiatimes.com/news/how-to/how-artificial-intelligence-is-changing-your-life-unknowingly/articleshow/98455922.cms?from=mdr

The Guardian. (2018, October 11). *Amazon Ditched AI Recruiting Tool That Favored Men for Technical Jobs*. The Guardian; The Guardian. https://www.theguardian.com/technology/2018/oct/10/amazon-hiring-ai-gender-bias-recruiting-engine

TikTok AI Moderation: Real-Time Detection of Offensive Content. *TikTok Research Reports*.

TikTok Safety Initiative. (2022). *AI-Powered Hate Speech Moderation in Short Video Platforms*. TikTok Research.

TikTok. (2022). *Moderation of Hate Speech Using Multimodal AI Systems*. TikTok AI Research Blog.

Tiwari, R. S. (2024). HS detection using LSTM and explanation by LIME (local interpretable model-agnostic explanations). In *Computational Intelligence Methods for Sentiment Analysis in Natural Language Processing Applications* (pp. 93–110). Morgan Kaufmann. DOI: 10.1016/B978-0-443-22009-8.00005-7

Tobi, A. (2024). Towards an Epistemic Compass for Online Content Moderation. *Philosophy & Technology*, 37(3), 109. Advance online publication. DOI: 10.1007/s13347-024-00791-3

Tomar, M., Raj, N., Singh, S., Marwaha, S., & Tiwari, M. (2023). The role of AI-driven tools in shaping the democratic process: A study of Indian elections and social media dynamics. *Industrial Engineering Journal*, 52(11), 143–153.

Tomašev, N., Cornebise, J., Hutter, F., & Mohamed, S. (2020). AI Social Good. *Nature*. PMID: 32424119

Torous, J., Bucci, S., Bell, I. H., Kessing, L. V., Faurholt-Jepsen, M., Whelan, P., Carvalho, A. F., Keshavan, M., Linardon, J., & Firth, J. (2021). The growing field of digital psychiatry: Current evidence and the future of apps, social media, chatbots, and virtual reality. *World Psychiatry; Official Journal of the World Psychiatric Association (WPA)*, 20(3), 318–335. DOI: 10.1002/wps.20883 PMID: 34505369

Torregrosa, J., Bello-Orgaz, G., Martínez-Cámara, E., Ser, J. D., & Camacho, D. (2023). A survey on extremism analysis using natural language processing: Definitions, literature review, trends and challenges. *Journal of Ambient Intelligence and Humanized Computing*, 14(8), 1–20. DOI: 10.1007/s12652-021-03658-z PMID: 35039755

Trattner, C., Jannach, D., Motta, E., Costera Meijer, I., Diakopoulos, N., Elahi, M., Opdahl, A. L., Tessem, B., Borch, N., Fjeld, M., Øvrelid, L., De Smedt, K., & Moe, H. (2022). Responsible Media Technology and AI: Challenges and Research Directions. *AI and Ethics*, 2(4), 585–594. DOI: 10.1007/s43681-021-00126-4

Trengove, M., Kazim, E., Almeida, D. R. S., Hilliard, A., Zannone, A., & Lomas, E. (2022). A critical review of the Online Safety Bill. *Patterns (New York, N.Y.)*, 3(8), 100544. https://10.0.3.248/j.patter.2022.100544. DOI: 10.1016/j.patter.2022.100544 PMID: 36033594

Troussas, C., Krouska, A., Koliarakis, A., & Sgouropoulou, C. (2023). Harnessing User-Centric Artificial Intelligence. *Computers*. Advance online publication. DOI: 10.3390/computers12050109

Tschang, F. T., & Almirall, E. (2021). Artificial intelligence as augmenting automation: Implications for employment. *The Academy of Management Perspectives*, 35(4), 642–659. DOI: 10.5465/amp.2019.0062

Turillazzi, A., Taddeo, M., Floridi, L., & Casolari, F. (2023). The digital services act: An analysis of its ethical, legal, and social implications. *Law, Innovation and Technology*, 15(1), 83–106. DOI: 10.1080/17579961.2023.2184136

Twitter (2021). Advances in Detecting Harmful Language in Real-Time. *Twitter Blog*.

Twitter API Team. (2021). Detecting Harmful Language Using Real-Time NLP Models. *Twitter Developer Blog*.

Twitter Trust and Safety Team (2021). Measuring Progress on AI-Powered Moderation. *Twitter Transparency Report*.

Tyagi, A. K., & Lakkshmanan, A. (2024). *The Future of Artificial Intelligence and Machine Learning in Online Social Networking*. Wiley Online Library. DOI: 10.1002/9781394231126.ch9

Udupa, S., Maronikolakis, A., & Wisiorek, A. (2023). Ethical scaling for content moderation: Extreme speech and the (in)significance of artificial intelligence. *Big Data & Society*, 10(1), 20539517231172424. Advance online publication. DOI: 10.1177/20539517231172424

Ulmer, A., & Tong, A. (2023, May 31). Deepfaking it: America's 2024 election collides with AI boom. Reuters. https://www.reuters.com/world/us/deepfaking-it-americas-2024-election-collides-with-ai-boom-2023-05-30/ (Last visited on 21.09.2024)

UNESCO. (2019). *The Role of Artificial Intelligence in Countering Online Hate Speech*. UNESCO Digital Series.

UNESCO. (2021). *Global Initiatives to Regulate AI in Content Moderation*. UNESCO Policy Briefs.

United Nations. (2021). *AI and the Fight Against Online Hate Speech: A Global Perspective*. UN Policy Reports.

United Nations. (2024, May 14). *Governing artificial intelligence for all | Public Institutions*. Un.org; United Nation. https://publicadministration.desa.un.org/blog/governing-artificial-intelligence-all

US Congress. (2021). *Federal AI Initiatives Against Hate Speech*. Congressional AI Reports.

US Government Accountability Office. (2020). *Federal Initiatives on AI for Hate Speech Detection*. GAO Reports.

Varghese, S., Nandhini M. (2020). The Influence of Demographic Factors on the Customers of Online-Shopping with Special Reference to Kochi City. Journal of Adv Research in Dynamical & Control Systems, 12(1-Special Issue).

Vasist, P. N., Chatterjee, D., & Krishnan, S. (2023). The polarizing impact of political disinformation and hate speech: A cross-country configural narrative. *Information Systems Frontiers*, •••, 1–26. DOI: 10.1007/s10796-023-10390-w PMID: 37361884

Vaswani, A., ... (2017). Attention Is All You Need. *NeurIPS Conference Proceedings*.

Vaswani, A., et al. (2017). Transformer Models for Sequential Data: Enhancing NLP Tasks. *NeurIPS Proceedings*.

Veglianti, E., Trombin, M., Pinna, R., & De Marco, M. (2023). Customized artificial intelligence for talent recruiting: A bias-free tool? In *Smart Technologies for Organizations: Managing a Sustainable and Inclusive Digital Transformation* (pp. 245–261). Springer International Publishing. DOI: 10.1007/978-3-031-24775-0_15

Vianello, A., Laine, S., & Tuomi, E. (2022). Improving Trustworthiness of AI Solutions: A Qualitative Approach to Support Ethically-Grounded AI Design. *International Journal of Human-Computer Interaction*, 39(7), 1405–1422. DOI: 10.1080/10447318.2022.2095478

Vidgen, B.. (2021). Challenges in Annotating Hate Speech: A Case Study. *Proceedings of ACL.*

Vidgen, B.. (2021). Large-Scale Annotation of Online Abuse. *Proceedings of the LREC Conference.*

Vidgen, B., Botelho, A., Broniatowski, D., & Tromble, R. (2020). Challenges and Frontiers in Hate Speech Detection: Real-Time Applications. *Journal of Computational Social Science.*

Vidgen, B., & Derczynski, L. (2020). Directions in Abusive Language Training Data: Issues and Next Steps. *Workshop on Abusive Language Online (EMNLP).*

Vijayakumar, G., Rajkumar, M., Chandar, N. R., Selvakumar, P., & Duraisamy, R. (2024). Environmentally friendly TDS removal from waste water by electrochemical ion exchange batch-type recirculation (EIR) technique. *Environmental Science. Water Research & Technology*, 10(4), 826–835.

Vijayakumar, G., Rajkumar, M., Rajiv Chandar, N., Selvakumar, P., & Duraisamy, R. (2024). Muniyandi Rajkumar, Rajiv Chandar N, Selvakumar P and Ramesh Duraisamy, (2024). Environmentally friendly TDS removal from waste water by electrochemical ion exchange batch-type recirculation (EIR) technique. *Environmental Science. Water Research & Technology*, 10(4), 826–835. DOI: 10.1039/D3EW00793F

Vimal, B., Surya, M., Darshan, S., Sridhar, V. S., & Ashok, A. (2021). MFCC-based audiclassification using machine learning. *Proceedings of the 12th International Conference on Computing Communication and Networking Technologies (ICCCNT)*, 1–4. https://doi.org/DOI: 10.1109/ICCCNT51525.2021.9579881

Visutsak, P., Wijitemee, A., Mahaphon, A., & Chaowalit, O. (2023). Machine-learning-based profanity detection and removal in cartoons videos. *Proceedings of the 2023 5th International Conference on Control and Robotics (ICCR)*, 162–167. https://doi.org/DOI: 10.1109/ICCR60000.2023.10444852

Walter, Y. (2024). *Managing Race to Moon.* Springer.

Walter, Y. (2024). Managing the race to the moon: Global policy and governance in Artificial Intelligence regulation—A contemporary overview and an analysis of socioeconomic consequences. *Discover Artificial Intelligence*, 4(1), 14. Advance online publication. DOI: 10.1007/s44163-024-00109-4

Wang, W. Y. (2017). " liar, liar pants on fire": A new benchmark dataset for fake news detection. arXiv preprint arXiv:1705.00648.

Wang, S. (2023). Factors related to user perceptions of artificial intelligence (AI)-based content moderation on social media. *Computers in Human Behavior*, 149, 107971. DOI: 10.1016/j.chb.2023.107971

Wang, Y., Imai, K., Miyashita, T., Ariyoshi, K., Takahashi, N., & Satake, K. (2023). Coastal tsunami prediction in Tohoku region, Japan, based on S-net observations using artificial neural network. *Earth, Planets, and Space*, 75(1), 154. Advance online publication. DOI: 10.1186/s40623-023-01912-6

Warner, W., & Hirschberg, J. (2012). Detecting HS on the World Wide Web. *Proceedings of the Second Workshop on Language in Social Media (LSM)*, 19–26.

Waseem, Z., & Hovy, D. (2016). Hateful Symbols or Hateful People? Predictive Features for Hate Speech Detection. *NAACL Proceedings*.121. Olteanu, A., et al. (2018). Limits of Automated Hate Speech Detection: A Case Study. *Proceedings of ICWSM.*

Waseem, Z., & Hovy, D. (2016). Hateful Symbols or Hateful People? Predicting HS on Twitter. *Proceedings of the 2016 NAACL HLT Workshop on Computational Approaches to Subjectivity, Sentiment & Social Media Analysis,* 2016, 88-93.

Waseem, Z., & Hovy, D. (2016). Hateful Symbols or Hateful People? Predictive Features for Hate Speech Detection on Twitter. *Proceedings of the NAACL-HLT Conference*. DOI: 10.18653/v1/N16-2013

Wei, L.. (2020). Understanding HS: A Survey and Future Directions. *Proceedings of the 12th International Conference on Social Media and Society,* 2020, 231-238.

West, D. M. (2019). *How to regulate AI-driven hate speech moderation: Policy recommendations for a global approach.* The Brookings Institution. https://www.brookings.edu

Wheatley, S., Maillart, T., & Sornette, D. (2016). The extreme risk of personal data breaches and the erosion of privacy. *The European Physical Journal B*, 89(1), 1–12. DOI: 10.1140/epjb/e2015-60754-4

Whyte C, (2020), "Deepfake News: AI-Enabled Disinformation as a Multi-Level Public Policy Challenge," Journal of Cyber Policy.

Wiegand, M.. (2018). Detection of Abusive Language: The Problem of Biased Datasets. *Proceedings of COLING.*

Williams, R. (2024). Impact.AI: Democratizing AI through K-12 Artificial Intelligence Education. *Handle.net.* https://hdl.handle.net/1721.1/153676

Williams, R., & Yampolskiy, R. (2021). Understanding and avoiding AI failures: A practical guide. *Philosophies*, 6(3), 53. DOI: 10.3390/philosophies6030053

Wilson, R. A., & Land, M. K. (2021). Hate speech on social media: Content moderation in context. *Connecticut Law Review*, 52, 1029. DOI: 10.2139/ssrn.3690616

Wilson, R. A., & Land, M. K. (2021). Hate speech on social media: Content moderation in context. *Connecticut Law Review, 52*, 1029. Available at *SSRN*: https://ssrn.com/abstract=3690616

Winfield, A. F., Michael, K., Pitt, J., & Evers, V. (2019). Machine ethics: The design and governance of ethical AI and autonomous systems. *Proceedings of the IEEE*, 107(3), 509–517. DOI: 10.1109/JPROC.2019.2900622

Wojcieszak, M., Thakur, A., Gonçalves, J. F. F., Casas, A., Menchen-Trevino, E., & Boon, M. (2021). Can AI enhance people's support for online moderation and their openness to dissimilar political views? *Journal of Computer-Mediated Communication*, 26(4), 223–243. DOI: 10.1093/jcmc/zmab006

Wolff, L. C. (2020). Artificial Intelligence ante portas: The End of Comparative Law? *The Chinese Journal of Comparative Law*, 7(3), 484–504. DOI: 10.1093/cjcl/cxz020

Wu, Y., ... (2016). Google's Neural Machine Translation System: Bridging the Gap Between Human and Machine Translation. *Proceedings of the ACL Conference*. OpenAI GPT Models

Wu, Y., et al. (2021). Real-Time Adaptive AI for Content Moderation. *Journal of Real-Time Processing Systems*.

Wu, L., Dodoo, N. A., Wen, T. J., & Ke, L. (2022). Understanding Twitter conversations about artificial intelligence in advertising based on natural language processing. *International Journal of Advertising*, 41(4), 685–702.

Wu, Y. (2024). Critical Thinking Pedagogics Design in an Era of ChatGPT and Other AI Tools—Shifting From Teaching "What" to Teaching "Why" and "How". *Journal of Education and Development*, 8(1), 1. DOI: 10.20849/jed.v8i1.1404

Xia, Q.. (2022). A Multilingual Transformer-Based System for Hate Speech Detection. *Proceedings of the EMNLP Conference*.

XLNet.: Yang, Z., et al. (2019). XLNet: Generalized Autoregressive Pretraining for Language Understanding. *Proceedings of the NeurIPS Conference*.

Xu, J.. (2020). Deep Learning for Hate Speech Detection: A Review. *IEEE Access : Practical Innovations, Open Solutions*.

Yalamati, S. (2024). Ensuring ethical practices in AI and ML toward a sustainable future. In *Artificial Intelligence and Machine Learning for Sustainable Development* (pp. 194–208). CRC Press. DOI: 10.1201/9781003497189-15

Yang, C., Zhu, F., Liu, G., Han, J., & Hu, S. (2022). Multimodal hate speech detection via cross-domain knowledge transfer. *Proceedings of the 30th ACM International Conference on Multimedia*, 4505–4514. https://doi.org/DOI: 10.1145/3503161.3548255

Yang, K. C., Varol, O., Davis, C. A., Ferrara, E., Flammini, A., & Menczer, F. (2019). Arming the public with artificial intelligence to counter social bots. *Human Behavior and Emerging Technologies*, 1(1), 48–61. DOI: 10.1002/hbe2.115

Yang, W., Wei, Y., Wei, H., Chen, Y., Huang, G., Li, X., Li, R., Yao, N., Wang, X., Gu, X., Amin, M. B., & Kang, B. (2023). Survey on explainable AI: From approaches, limitations, and applications aspects. *Human-Centric Intelligent Systems*, 3(3), 161–188. DOI: 10.1007/s44230-023-00038-y

Yang, Y., & Yang, M. (2021). Lightweight Real-Time NLP Models for Content Moderation. *Journal of Machine Learning Research*.

YouTube AI Research. (2020). *Identifying Hate Speech in Multimodal Content*. Google AI Blog.

YouTube Content Policies. (2020). *YouTube Official Blog*. How We Detect and Remove Harmful Content in Real-Time.

YouTube. (2020). *Content Moderation Using AI: Challenges and Successes*. Google Research Blog.

Youvan, D. C. (2024). Navigating the Unknowns: Ethical Considerations and Government Influence in Facebook AI. *ResearchGate*. https://www.researchgate.net/publication/378679366_Navigating_the_Unknowns_Ethical_Considerations_and_Government_Influence_in_Facebook_AI

Yu, M., Jiang, W., Wan, Y., & Mao, A. (2024). User-Centric Design Experience or Privacy Risk Perception. *Current Issues in Tourism*, 1–18. DOI: 10.1080/13683500.2024.2394569

Zahra, M. A., Al-Taher, A., & Alquhaidan, M. (2024). The synergy of artificial intelligence and personalized medicine for the enhanced diagnosis, treatment, and prevention of disease. *Journal of Personalized Medicine*, 14(2), 1–12. DOI: 10.3390/jpm14020043 PMID: 38997240

Zaidan, E., & Ibrahim, I. A. (2024). AI Governance in a Complex and Rapidly Changing Regulatory Landscape: A Global Perspective. *Humanities & Social Sciences Communications*, 11(1), 1121. DOI: 10.1057/s41599-024-03560-x

Zaman, K., Sah, M., Direkoglu, C., & Unoki, M. (2023). A survey of audiclassification using deep learning. *IEEE Access : Practical Innovations, Open Solutions*, 11, 106620–106649. DOI: 10.1109/ACCESS.2023.3318015

Zampieri, M.. (2019). Predicting the Type and Target of Offensive Posts in Social Media. *Proceedings of the NAACL-HLT Conference*. DOI: 10.18653/v1/N19-1144

Zamri, N. A. K., Mohamad Nasir, N. A., Hassim, M. N., & Ramli, S. M. (2023). Digital hate speech and othering: The construction of hate speech from Malaysian perspectives. *Cogent Arts & Humanities*, 10(1), 2229089. Advance online publication. DOI: 10.1080/23311983.2023.2229089

Zeller, M. C., & Vaughan, M. (2023). Proscribing Right-Wing Extremist Organizations in Europe: Variations, Trends, and Prospects. *Terrorism and Political Violence*, •••, 1–20. DOI: 10.1080/09546553.2023.2171615

Zeng, C., & Dou, W. (2010). Audikeywords detection in basketball video. *Proceedings of the 2010 International Conference on Audio, Language and Image Processing*, 1765–1770. DOI: 10.1109/ICALIP.2010.5685186

Zhang, Y., & Yang, Q. (2021). Multi-Task Learning for Hate Speech Detection: Applications in Low-Resource Settings. *NeurIPS Proceedings*.

Zhang, Z., Robinson, D., & Tepper, J. (2018). Detecting Hate Speech on Twitter Using a Convolution-GRU Based Deep Neural Network. *Springer AI Conference Proceedings*. DOI: 10.1007/978-3-319-93417-4_48

Zhang, Z., & Zhao, Z. (2021). Fine-Tuning Language Models for HS Detection. *Proceedings of the 39th International Conference on ML, ICML 2021*, 220-229.

Zhou, J.. (2022). A Survey on Contrastive Learning for Natural Language Processing. *IEEE Transactions on Artificial Intelligence*.

Zhou, L., Pan, S., Wang, J., & Vasilakos, A. V. (2017). Machine learning on big data: Opportunities and challenges. *Neurocomputing*, 237, 350–361. DOI: 10.1016/j.neucom.2017.01.026

Zilles, C. (2019). Taking advantage of AI in social media marketing.

Zobaidy, Z. R. M. A. (2024). Artificial Intelligence in Natural Language Processing. *International Journal of Science and Research Archive*, 13(01), 370–377. DOI: 10.30574/ijsra.2024.13.1.1638

Zou, J., Schiebinger, L., & Hurst, S. (2018). AI and the Future of Work: Addressing Bias and Inequality. *AI & Society*, 33(1), 159–170.

About the Contributors

Swati Chakraborty is a Visiting faculty (Assistant Professor), at the Institute of Legal Studies and Research, GLA University. Dr. Chakraborty is associated as an Adjunct Faculty with Concordia University, Canada. Dr. Chakraborty is a Writing Fellow, at COMPOSE, Universitas Islam International Indonesia. She is an International Fellow of KAICIID in Lisbon, Portugal. She is the Founder of "Webplatform4Dialogue" with a series of webinars, talks, and publications. She has done her Ph.D. in Human Rights from the University of Calcutta with the thesis on "RIGHT TO EDUCATION: A Study on tribal women of Rural West Bengal". She was attached to National Human Rights Commission, India as a Research Consultant. Dr. Chakraborty had good teaching expertise as Lecturer at The English College (School of Management), Calicut, Kerala her special lectures are on Human Values, Peace dialogue and ethics to Management studies, and Dignity and Rights. She is also a member of the executive council at the Colibri Learning Foundation, Surrey, BC. Also, she is the editor of books like "Dynamics of Dialogue, Cultural Development, and Peace in the Metaverse", "Handbook of Dialogue and Development: India-China-EU", Handbook of Human Rights and Tribal Studies", "Handbook of Social Media for Digital and Social Inclusion", "TRIBAL DEVELOPMENT", "Gender Identity and Roles in India: Issues and Challenges", "Multidisciplinary Handbook of Social Exclusion and Human Rights" and "Handbook of International Relations: Issues of Human Rights and Foreign Policy Vol. I and Vol II". Dr. Chakraborty has a wide range of international connections with her network through different seminars, conferences, and workshops.

***

Mohit is a research scholar at the Institute of Management Studies and Research, Maharshi Dayanand University, Rohtak, Haryana, India. His research focuses on the dynamic relationship between brand image and purchase intentions, particularly in the context of brand extensions within the FMCG sector. Mohit actively engages in bibliometric research, analyzing publication trends and identifying research gaps in his area of interest. He has co-authored several scholarly works and continues to contribute to the academic community. Mohit can be reached at mohitattri.rs.imsar@ mdurohtak.ac.in.

Pankaj Singh Chandel is an Assistant Professor in the Department of Tourism Management at Dev Sanskriti Vishwavidyalaya, Haridwar, where he has been teaching since 2014. He holds a PhD in Tourism and a PGDM in Tourism and Travel Services Management from the Indian Institute of Tourism and Travel Management. His expertise lies in homestay tourism, and he is recognized as a skilled orator on travel knowledge. Dr. Chandel has published research articles in Scopus-indexed journals and has contributed to publications with IGI Global, demonstrating his commitment to academic scholarship in the field of tourism. His research focuses on sustainable tourism practices and the development of homestay tourism in India. As an active member of several professional organizations, including the Travel Agents Association of Uttarakhand and ATOAI, Dr. Chandel actively participates in initiatives promoting sustainability in the tourism industry. His involvement in these organizations allows him to bridge the gap between academic research and industry practices. Dr. Chandel's ORCID showcases his research outputs and professional activities.

Lakshmi D is presently designated as a Senior Associate Professor in the School of Computing Science and Engineering (SCSE) & Assistant Director, at the Centre for Innovation in Teaching & Learning (CITL) at VIT Bhopal. She has 17 international conference presentations, and 21 international journal papers inclusive of SCOPUS & SCI (cumulative impact factor 31). 3 SCOPUS inee book chapters. A total of 24 patents are in various states and 18 patents have been granted at both national and international levels. One Edited book with Taylor & Francis (SCOPUS Indexed). She has won two Best Paper awards at international conferences, one at the IEEE conference and another one at EAMMIS 2021. She received two awards in the year 2022. She received two awards in the year 2022. She has addressed innumerable guest lectures, acted as a session chair, and was invited as a keynote speaker at several international conferences. She has conducted FDPs that cover approximately ~80,000 plus faculty members including JNTU, TEQIP, SERB, SWAYAM, DST, AICTE, MHRD, ATAL, ISTE, Madhya Pradesh Government-sponsored, and self-financed workshops across India on various titles.

Anjali Dixit is a distinguished academic and legal expert currently serving as an Associate Professor at the Faculty of Law, SRM University, Delhi NCR,Sonepat,

Haryana. She also holds a position as a Visiting Professor at KAAF University College in Kasoa, Ghana, (West Africa) where she contributes to the Faculty of Law & Political Science. Dr. Anjali Dixit has achieved notable academic success, including being a Gold Medallist in her LL.B. program. Her expertise and contributions to the field of law have earned her several accolades, including recognition from the Chief Election Commissioner for her involvement in the 2019 Lok Sabha elections. She has also been honored with multiple Best Teacher Awards by various organizations such as the Shri Sai Nina Foundation, A.B Foundation, and Muskuraye Kanpur Forum. In recognition of her contributions to society and education, she was awarded the Social Icon Award by the Muskuraye Uttar Pradesh Foundation on International Women's Day in 2023. Member of various Societies and institutions. Dr. Anjali Dixit is a prolific scholar with over 100+ papers published in prestigious journals such as Scopus, UGC CARE, and peer-reviewed outlets. She has presented more than 35 papers at both national and international conferences. Her extensive body of work includes authored and edited books covering a range of legal topics. She authored mention below books – • New Technology Laws with Special Reference to Cyber Laws • Lectures on Jurisprudence • Lectures on Family Laws • Legal Research Methodology: An overview • Lectures on Company Law • International Organization Edited Books- • "Environment Governance with the new dimension of Human Rights" • "Women, Law & Remedies" • 'New Horizons in Labour and Industrials Laws' • Agriculture And Agribusiness' Laws in India: Solution to Future Sustainability Laws' • Wealth & Tax: An overview of GST • Commercial Arbitration in India: Issues & Challenges • E-Commerce In India a Legal Analysis • Banking In India: An Analysis • Futuristic Trends in Artificial Intelligence • Social Media an Age of Surveillance in The Prospect of Artificial Intelligence

Pradeep E is an Assistant Professor specializing in Marketing at the Loyola Institute of Business Administration (LIBA), Chennai. Based in Tamil Nadu, Dr. Pradeep brings a wealth of academic expertise and practical insights to his role, fostering the development of future business leaders. His work at LIBA reflects a strong commitment to advancing marketing education and research in a dynamic business environment.

Meena G is a dedicated research scholar in the Faculty of Management at SRM Institute of Science and Technology. She is actively involved in academic research, contributing to the field of management studies. As a part of this prestigious institution, Meena is committed to exploring innovative solutions and enhancing knowledge in her area of expertise. Her work reflects a strong passion for advancing research and making meaningful contributions to the field of management.

Pranjal Khare is a distinguished corporate lawyer and is currently working as a law faculty at O.P. Jindal Global University, India. He specializes in Property Law, Corporate laws, Intellectual Property Rights, and International law. Mr. Pranjal is a highly regarded scholar and has published on numerous issues related to international affairs, economy, politics, data & privacy, artificial intelligence and IP disputes. He is also a frequent speaker at legal conferences and has served as a consultant to numerous law firms and corporations.

Aruna Kumari Koppaka is a dedicated academic professional from the Department of Computer Science and Engineering (CSE) with a specialization in Data Science at Chalapathi Institute of Engineering and Technology, located in Lam, Guntur, Andhra Pradesh. With a deep interest in emerging technologies, Aruna is particularly passionate about Cloud Computing and Artificial Intelligence (AI). These areas of interest fuel her academic and research pursuits, driving her to contribute to innovations in these fields. Through her work and research, she aims to advance the practical applications of Cloud and AI technologies in solving complex real-world challenges.

Sheikh Inam Ul Mansoor (BA.LLB Hon's, LLM, CPCT WIPO, Ph.D. International Trade Law) is a highly accomplished academician presently working as an Assistant Professor Law at the School of Law, Dayananda Sagar University in Bangalore, India. With a strong background in law and a passion for academia, Dr. Sheikh has made significant contributions to the field through his extensive research and publications. Pursued his BA. LLB (Hon's) from University of Kashmir, LLM from JNU Jaipur and Ph.D. International Trade Law from LPU Punjab. Prior to his academic career, Dr. Sheikh served as an Advocate and Solicitor at the Jammu and Kashmir High Court and other subordinate courts in Jammu and Kashmir. This experience as a legal practitioner has provided him with valuable insights into the practical application of law and enhanced his understanding of legal dynamics. As an Assistant Professor Law at Dayananda Sagar University, Dr. Sheikh Inam Ul Mansoor continues to make significant contributions to the legal field through his research, teaching, and involvement in various professional activities.

Samrat Kumar Mukherjee is currently an Assistant professor (Grade I) at Sikkim Manipal Institute of Technology, Sikkim Manipal University. He has been teaching for the past 14 years. He has published many papers in renowned national and international journals, written a book, and reviewed and edited many reputed journals.Published more than 40 papers in different journals.

Nitish Ojha - Dr. Nitish, is a distinguished scholar, Researcher, and mentor having rich Industrial experience as well as varied experience in Teaching and

Research. He has academic experience of over 15 years with renowned universities like American University of Europe, University of Stirling UK, and others where he worked in the capacity of Assistant Professor, also worked as a Core Member of Research and Development in Indian Universities i.e., Chandigarh University, LPU, Amity University. He has worked as a software engineer in Nokia Siemens Network, India. He served in several research projects in different profiles of researchers funded by DST/MCIT/MOHFW Govt. of India having National and International importance at IIT Delhi and in AIIMS.

P. Selvakumar is currently an Associate Professor in the Department of Science and Humanities at Nehru Institute of Technology, Coimbatore, Tamil Nadu, India. Since 2023, he has served as the Department IQAC Coordinator at the institute. Prior to joining Nehru Institute of Technology, he held positions as an Assistant Professor in the Department of Science and Humanities various engineering colleges in Coimbatore, Tamil Nadu, India, spanning from 2011 to 2023. Dr.P. Selvakumar's academic and research interests lie primarily in the field of phytochemistry. He has made significant contributions to his field, with an impressive record that includes 30 journal publications, 12 patents, and 20 conference papers. Additionally, he has organized 5 seminars and conferences, further demonstrating his commitment to academic and scientific exchange. Throughout his career, Dr. P.Selvakumar has been recognized for his dedication and excellence in teaching, having been honored with several awards, including the Best Teacher Awards. He holds a prominent position in the academic community, contributing actively to research.

Hemlata Parmar, a luminary in the field of computer Science and Engineering. Her Journey is defined by a constellation of achievements from prolific publications and patents to enlightening guest lectures. Yet, her brilliance is matched only by her unwavering commitment to human ethics. With a heart as vast as her intellect, she champions women's empowerment, bridging the gap with empathy and insight. In every endeavor, she embodies the perfect fusion of academic process and compassionate advocacy, inspiring generations to come.

Shrinwantu Raha is working as a faculty member in Department of Geography, Bhairab Ganguly College, Belgharia, India since 2018. He has published more than 20 research articles and book chapters from several national and international publishing houses. He has also presented over 15 research papers in national and international seminars. He has a consistent good academic record with zeal to learn new concepts quickly and apply innovative ideas for achieving best solutions. Motivated, self-starter with a passion to succeed and desire to excel in the areas of drought monitoring, water resource management, remote sensing and GIS, geography of tourism, environmental conservation, safety in disaster emergency, human Geography, and Sustainability. He is looking forward to work on a challenging environment that encourages learning and creativity provides exposure to new ideas and stimulates professional growth.

Karun Sanjaya is an Assistant Professor at Symbiosis Law School, Nagpur and a Research Scholar at VIT School of Law, Vellore Institute of Technology, Chennai, India. He specialises in the area of Intellectual Property Laws. He is a recipient of many awards, including the prestigious Justice V.R. Krishna Iyer Memorial Merit Awards in the years 2019 and 2022. He has published over sixty research items and is a keen researcher in diverse areas of law, including intellectual property law.

Pamarthi Satyanarayana, specialize in Constitutional Law and Legal Order, focusing my research on the interface between individual rights and public policy, with a strong emphasis on civil liberties, social justice, and the right to privacy. Over the past 18 months, I have served as an Assistant Professor of Law at Vel Tech Rangarajan Dr. Sagunthala R&D Institute of Science and Technology in Chennai, Tamil Nadu. Here, I teach courses such as Constitutional Law, Legal Research and Writing, and both Civil and Criminal Law. My passion for teaching and in-depth subject knowledge have earned me recognition as a dedicated educator. In addition to my academic role, I actively engage with the community, partnering with legal clinics to provide pro bono services to underprivileged individuals. Looking forward, I aim to expand my research into emerging legal issues in the digital age, especially in privacy rights, while guiding aspiring law students and future legal scholars.

Aiswaria G. Shajan, a dedicated linguist and academician, holds a Ph.D. in Linguistics from the University of Kerala. She is currently a Resource Person at NTS-I, CIIL, Mysuru, and contributes as an instructor on the SWAYAM portal, an initiative by the Ministry of Education, Government of India. Her expertise encompasses sociolinguistics, cognitive linguistics, gender studies, language teaching, and tribal language documentation. Dr. Shajan is committed to fostering inclusive and dynamic learning environments, publishing insightful research, and deepening the understanding of language and its intersection with culture and society.

Jagveer Singh is a distinguished educator and scholar in the field of organic chemistry, with a strong academic background and over 25 years of teaching experience. He completed his higher secondary education from the MP Board in 1989, after which he pursued a Bachelor of Science degree at Guru Ghasidas University, where he graduated in 1992. Continuing his academic journey, Jagveer earned his Master of Science in Organic Chemistry from the same university in 1994. He further advanced his studies by completing his M.Phil. in 1996, also at Guru

Ghasidas University, specializing in organic chemistry. Throughout his extensive career, Jagveer has dedicated himself to educating and inspiring students in the sciences, contributing significantly to the academic community. His commitment to teaching and research has made him a respected figure in the field.

C.V. Suresh Babu is a pioneer in content development. A true entrepreneur, he founded Anniyappa Publications, a company that is highly active in publishing books related to Computer Science and Management. Dr. C.V. Suresh Babu has also ventured into SB Institute, a center for knowledge transfer. He holds a Ph.D. in Engineering Education from the National Institute of Technical Teachers Training & Research in Chennai, along with seven master's degrees in various disciplines such as Engineering, Computer Applications, Management, Commerce, Economics, Psychology, Law, and Education. Additionally, he has UGC-NET/SET qualifications in the fields of Computer Science, Management, Commerce, and Education. Currently, Dr. C.V. Suresh Babu is a Professor in the Department of Information Technology at the School of Computing Science, Hindustan Institute of Technology and Science (Hindustan University) in Padur, Chennai, Tamil Nadu, India.

Chirayu Vats is a dedicated lecturer in the Department of Psychology at Dev Sanskriti Vishwavidyalaya (DSVV), Haridwar. With a strong academic background and a passion for teaching, Chirayu has contributed significantly to the field of psychology through both education and research. At DSVV, She is involved in various interdisciplinary research projects that aim to integrate traditional Indian psychological concepts with modern psychological practices. Her work often explores the cultural and spiritual dimensions of psychology, reflecting the university's emphasis on holistic education. Chirayu is also actively engaged in promoting the understanding of Indian cultural practices, such as Yagya, and their relevance to contemporary psychological well-being. Her commitment to education and research has made her a valuable member of the DSVV faculty, where she continues to inspire students and contribute to the advancement of psychological studies in India

Showkat Ahmad Wani is a Senior Scale Assistant Professor at, the School of Law, Alliance University Bengaluru, (India). Earlier, Dr. Wani was associated with the School of Law, Lovely Professional University (India). Dr. Wani has so far written 30 research papers in various reputed journals. He has also presented over 40 research papers at various National and International Conferences. His key research areas are Constitutional law and Human rights. Dr Wani has also contributed to valuable legal assistance to the Under-Trail Prisoners in collaboration with Tata Institute of Social Science (India) to the venerable classes. Dr. Wani has supervised eight students in the LLM dissertation. In addition, three Ph.D. Scholars have completed their Thesis under his supervision. Dr. Wani is a chief editor of one book, Legal Metamorphosis in Contemporary India. Dr. Wani is very keen on Research and Human Rights & a strong believer in the power of positive thinking in the workplace.

Index

A

B

C

D

E

F

H

I

J

L

M

N

O

P

R

S

T

U

W

www.ingramcontent.com/pod-product-compliance
Lightning Source LLC
LaVergne TN
LVHW080351011026
849161LV00009B/2270